Lecture Notes in Computer Science 12727

More information about this subseries at http://www.springer.com/series/7410

Kazue Sako · Nils Ole Tippenhauer (Eds.)

Applied Cryptography and Network Security

19th International Conference, ACNS 2021
Kamakura, Japan, June 21–24, 2021
Proceedings, Part II

 Springer

Editors
Kazue Sako
Waseda University
Tokyo, Japan

Nils Ole Tippenhauer ⓘ
CISPA Helmholtz Center
for Information Security
Saarbrücken, Germany

ISSN 0302-9743   ISSN 1611-3349 (electronic)
Lecture Notes in Computer Science
ISBN 978-3-030-78374-7   ISBN 978-3-030-78375-4 (eBook)
https://doi.org/10.1007/978-3-030-78375-4

LNCS Sublibrary: SL4 – Security and Cryptology

This Springer imprint is published by the registered company Springer Nature Switzerland AG
The registered company address is: Gewerbestrasse 11, 6330 Cham, Switzerland

Preface

We are pleased to present the proceedings of the 19th International Conference on Applied Cryptography and Network Security (ACNS 2021).

ACNS 2021 was planned to be held in Kamakura, Japan. Due to the ongoing COVID-19 crisis, we decided to have a virtual conference again to ensure the safety of all participants. The organization was in the capable hands of Chunhua Su (University of Aizu, Japan) and Kazumasa Omote (University of Tsukuba, Japan) as general co-chairs, and Ryoma Ito (NICT, Japan) as local organizing chair. We are deeply indebted to them for their tireless work to ensure the success of the conference even in such complex conditions.

For the second time, ACNS had two rounds of submission cycles, with deadlines in September 2020 and January 2021, respectively. We received a total of 186 submissions from authors in 43 countries. This year's Program Committee (PC) consisted of 69 members with diverse backgrounds (among them, 27% female experts) and broad research interests. The review process was double-blind and rigorous, and papers were evaluated on the basis of research significance, novelty, and technical quality. 539 reviews were submitted in total, with at least 3 reviews for most papers.

Some papers submitted in the first round received a decision of major revision. The revised version of those papers were further evaluated in the second round and most of them were accepted. After the review process concluded, a total of 37 papers were accepted to be presented at the conference and included in the proceedings, representing an acceptance rate of around 20%.

Among those papers, 27 were co-authored and presented by full-time students. From this subset, we awarded the Best Student Paper Award to Angèle Bossuat (IRISA, France) for the paper "Unlinkable and Invisible γ-Sanitizable Signatures" (co-authored with Xavier Bultel). The reviewers particularly appreciated its clear and convincing motivation and explanation of the intuition behind the approach, and the strong properties achieved by the proposed sanitizable signature scheme. The monetary prize of 1,000 euro was generously sponsored by Springer.

We had a rich program including eight satellite workshops in parallel with the main event, providing a forum to address specific topics at the forefront of cybersecurity research. The papers presented at those workshops were published in separate proceedings.

This year we had three outstanding keynote talks: "Privacy-Preserving Authentication: Concepts, Applications, and New Advances" by Prof. Anja Lehmann (Hasso Plattner Institute, Germany), "Digital Being" presented by Nat Sakimura (OpenID Foundation, Japan), and "Cryptography and the Changing Landscape of Payment Fraud" by Prof. Ross Anderson (University of Cambridge and University of Edinburgh, UK). To them, our heartfelt gratitude for their outstanding presentations.

In this very unusual year, the conference was made possible by the untiring efforts of many individuals and organizations. We are grateful to all the authors for their submissions. We sincerely appreciate the outstanding work of all the PC members and the external reviewers, who selected the papers after reading, commenting, and debating them. Finally, we thank all the people who volunteered their time and energy to put together the conference, speakers and session chairs, and everyone who contributed to the success of the conference.

Last, but certainly not least, we are very grateful to Mitsubishi Electric for sponsoring the conference, and Springer for their help in assembling these proceedings.

June 2021   Kazue Sako
                                                      Nils Ole Tippenhauer

Organization

General Co-chairs

Chunhua Su   University of Aizu, Japan
Kazumasa Omote   University of Tsukuba, Japan

Program Co-chairs

Kazue Sako   Waseda University, Japan
Nils Ole Tippenhauer   CISPA, Germany

Publicity Chair

Keita Emura   NICT, Japan

Workshop Chair

Jianying Zhou   Singapore University of Technology and Design, Singapore

Poster Chair

Masaki Shimaoka   University of Tsukuba/SECOM, Japan

Local Organizing Chair

Ryoma Ito   NICT, Japan

Program Committee

Mitsuaki Akiyama	NTT, Japan
Cristina Alcaraz	UMA, Spain
Giuseppe Ateniese	Stevens Institute of Technology, USA
Man Ho Au	The University of Hong Kong, Hong Kong
Lejla Batina	Radboud University, the Netherlands
Alex Biryukov	University of Luxembourg, Luxembourg
Ferdinand Brasser	TU Darmstadt, Germany
Christopher Brzuska	Aalto University, Finland
Alvaro Cardenas	The University of Texas at Dallas, USA
Sudipta Chattopadhyay	SUTD, Singapore
Liqun Chen	University of Surrey, UK
Xiaofeng Chen	Xidian University, China

Reihaneh Safavi-Naini	University of Calgary, Canada
Kazue Sako	Waseda University, Japan
Steve Schneider	University of Surrey, UK
Sooel Son	Korea Advanced Institute of Science and Technology, South Korea
Hung-Min Sun	National Tsing Hua University, Taiwan
Willy Susilo	University of Wollongong, Australia
Pawel Szalachowski	Google, USA
Qiang Tang	University of Sydney, Australia
Vanessa Teague	Thinking Cybersecurity, Australia
Nils Ole Tippenhauer	CISPA Helmholtz Center for Information Security, Germany
A. Selcuk Uluagac	Florida International University, USA
Edgar Weippl	University of Vienna, Austria
Christian Wressnegger	Karlsruhe Institute of Technology, Germany
Kehuan Zhang	The Chinese University of Hong Kong, Hong Kong

Additional Reviewers

Akand, Mamun
Amjad, Ghous
Anada, Hiroaki
Anagnostopoulos, Marios
Banik, Subhadeep
Blazy, Olivier
Booth, Roland
Braeken, An
Briongos, Samira
Bultel, Xavier
Buser, Maxime
Chen, Long
Chen, Xihui
Chen, Yi
Chengjun Lin
Co, Kenneth
Cui, Tingting
Dekker, F. W.
Diao, Wenrui
Diugan, Raluca
Duong, Dung Hoang
Dutta, Sabyasachi
El Hirch, Solane
Eliyan, Lubna
Ersoy, Oguzhan
Feng, Hanwen
Fentham, Daniel
Ferreira Torres, Christof

Florez, Johana
Gan, Qingqing
Gardham, Daniel
Genise, Nicholas
Gerault, David
Ghesmati, Simin
Ghosh, Koustabh
Gontier, Arthur
Grassi, Lorenzo
Guo, Kaiwen
Gálvez, Rafa
Hameed, Muhammad Zaid
Han, Jinguang
Hashimoto, Keitaro
Hirano, Takato
Homoliak, Ivan
Hoshino, Fumitaka
Hou, Zhenduo
Hsu, Chingfang
Hu, Kexin
Huguenin-Dumittan, Loïs
Hülsing, Andreas
Ichikawa, Atsunori
Isobe, Takanori
Isshiki, Toshiyuki
Jangid, Mohit
Jiang, Shaoquan
Jiang, Yuting

Judmayer, Aljosha
Kannwischer, Matthias J.
Kasra, Shabnam
Kim, Joongyum
Laing, Thalia May
Larangeira, Mario
Leurent, Gaëtan
Li, Jiguo
Li, Tianyu
Li, Xinyu
Li, Yanan
Libert, Benoît
Liu, Jia
Lopez, Christian
Lu, Xingye
Lu, Yuan
Ma, Jinhua
Mahawaga Arachchige,
  Pathum Chamikara
Marotzke, Adrian
Mazumdar, Subhra
McMurtry, Eleanor
Mirza, Shujaat
Miteloudi, Konstantina
Moreau, Solène
Niederhagen, Ruben
Ning, Jianting
Nishide, Takashi
Orsini, Emmanuela
Pan, Jiaxin
Pan, Jing
Pang, Bo
Papamartzivanos, Dimitrios
Park, Sunnyeo
Pasquini, Dario
Pereira, Vitor
Pilgun, Aleksandr
Prabel, Lucas
Qiu, Tian
Rabbani, Md Masoom
Ramírez-Cruz, Yunior
Reijsbergen, Daniel
Rivera, Esteban
Roenne, Peter
Sato, Masaya
Schindler, Philipp

Schuldt, Jacob
Schwabe, Peter
Shen, Jun
Shirase, Masaaki
Sideri, Maria
Smith, Zach
Song, Ling
Song, Yongcheng
Song, Zirui
Stifter, Nicholas
Sun, Siwei
Suzuki, Koutarou
Tang, Di
Tengana, Lizzy
Terner, Ben
Tiepelt, Marcel
Tikhomirov, Sergei
Tomita, Toui
Tsohou, Aggeliki
van Bruggen, Christian
van Tetering, Daphne
Vaudenay, Serge
Vitto, Giuseppe
Vliegen, Jo
Wang, Jianfeng
Wang, Qingju
Wang, Yongqi
Weiqiang Wen
Wi, Seongil
Wu, Jiaojiao
Xu, Yanhong
Xue, Haiyang
Yamakawa, Takashi
Yan, Hailun
Yang, Guomin
Yang, Rupeng
Yang, S. J.
Yang, Wenjie
Yin, Qilei
Yoneyama, Kazuki
Yuan, Xingliang
Zeilberger, Hadas
Zhang, Peng
Zhang, Xiaoyu
Zhang, Yuexin
Zhang, Zeyu

Contents – Part II

System Security

Cryptography and Its Applications

Contents – Part I

Embedded System Security

Lattice Cryptography

Analysis of Applied Systems

Breaking and Fixing Third-Party Payment Service for Mobile Apps

Shangcheng Shi, Xianbo Wang, and Wing Cheong Lau[✉]

The Chinese University of Hong Kong, Hong Kong, China
{ss016,xianbo,wclau}@ie.cuhk.edu.hk

Abstract. Riding on the widespread user adoption of mobile payment, a growing number of mobile apps have integrated the service from third-party payment service providers or so-called Cashiers. Despite its prevalence and critical nature, no existing standard can guide the secure deployment of mobile payment. Thus, the protocol designs and implementations from different Cashiers are diverse. Given the complicated multi-party interactions in mobile payment, either the Cashiers or the apps may not fully consider various threat models, which enlarges the attack surface and causes the exploits with severe consequences, ranging from financial loss to privacy violations. In this paper, we perform an in-depth security analysis of real-world third-party payment services for mobile apps. Specifically, we examine the mobile payment systems from five top-tier Cashiers that serve over one billion users globally. Leveraging insecure protocol designs and practical implementation flaws, *e.g.*, vulnerable backend SDKs for mobile apps, we have discovered six types of exploits. These exploits enable the attacker to violate user privacy and shop for free in the victim apps, affecting millions of users. Finally, we propose the fixings to defend against these exploits. We have shared our findings with the affected Cashiers and got their positive responses.

Keywords: Mobile security · Mobile payment · Protocol analysis

1 Introduction

Mobile payment service is becoming globally popular in recent years, whose overall transaction value reaches $1.18 trillion in 2019 [4]. This service enables end-users to pay for the order in a mobile app through third-party Cashiers without presenting other physical tokens, *e.g.*, a credit card or cash. Driven by the boom of mobile payment, an increasing number of mobile apps, including both native apps and mobile web apps, have integrated the services from the Cashiers. Meanwhile, the Cashiers provide different solutions for these two types of mobile apps, namely in-app payment and web app payment (WAP). To ease the deployment of mobile payment[1], the Cashiers release Software Development Kits (SDKs) for both frontend mobile apps and backend app servers and publish

---

[1] For the rest of the paper, we use mobile payment to denote the third-party payment services for mobile apps, if not specified otherwise.

© Springer Nature Switzerland AG 2021
K. Sako and N. O. Tippenhauer (Eds.): ACNS 2021, LNCS 12727, pp. 3–26, 2021.
https://doi.org/10.1007/978-3-030-78375-4_1

their technical documents online. Some Cashiers also offer demo app accounts or separate sandbox environments to the developers for testing.

In spite of the broad adoption, it is noteworthy that there is no unified standard for the mobile payment service like other well-defined protocols, *e.g.*, OAuth [5,13], such that the protocol designs and implementations from the Cashiers are heterogeneous. Therefore, each Cashier defines different protocol flows and credentials to secure payment-related messages. Considering the sophisticated multi-party authentication and authorization process in mobile payment, average app developers are prone to misinterpret the protocol and deploy the insecure service. Moreover, the mobile payment protocols from the Cashiers are usually not fool-proofing by design. In other words, the attacker can exploit the flawed implementations directly to harm the apps and their end-users.

The literature [3,25] has discovered several vulnerabilities in practical mobile payment systems in recent years, which all bring about serious security threats, including both privacy violations and financial loss. For example, [25] finds that some developers customize the server-side logic, *e.g.*, signing payment order, in the frontend, and thus expose the credentials in their mobile apps. On the other hand, some app servers fail to verify the digital signature within the instant payment notifications from the Cashiers. Nevertheless, all the existing works focus on specific implementation flaws, while little effort has been spared to study the designs of mobile payment protocols from the Cashiers, especially their differences, underlying security implications, and the consequent drawback.

To bridge the gap, we conduct a comprehensive security analysis of mobile payment services from five mainstream third-party Cashiers in this paper. These Cashiers provide online payment services for websites, mobile apps, as well as Point-of-Sale terminals, serving over *one billion users and tens of millions of merchants* worldwide. To be specific, we investigate and compare the mobile payment systems from these Cashiers. Consequently, we discover six types of exploits that are caused by additional implementation flaws from either the Cashiers or their (merchant) apps, *e.g.*, vulnerable backend SDKs. These exploits enable the attacker to cheat the app to shop for free or violate user privacy, which affect millions of users. Based on the lessons learned, we propose the fixings on current practices to secure the apps and their end-users. We summarize our contributions as follows.

- We study and examine the mobile payment systems from five top-tier Cashiers.
- Combining the insecure protocol designs and other implementation flaws, we find six types of exploits with serious security consequences.
- We conclude the best practice and propose the fixings to mitigate the discovered exploits.

The rest of the paper is organized as follows. Section 2 gives the background of mobile payment, while Sect. 3 introduces the cryptographic primitives. We present practical mobile payment systems in Sect. 4 and discuss the potential

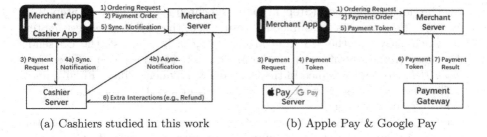

(a) Cashiers studied in this work (b) Apple Pay & Google Pay

Fig. 1. Workflow of existing mobile payment services

exploits in Sect. 5. Section 6 proposes the fixings to mitigate these exploits. We review the related work in Sect. 7 and conclude the paper in Sect. 8.

2 Mobile Payment System Overview

An e-payment system consists of three entities, including the third-party payment service provider, *i.e.*, Cashier, the Merchant, and the User (or User-Agent).

In the mobile payment systems under study, the Cashier and Merchant are represented by their backend servers, namely Cashier Server (*CS*) and Merchant Server (*MS*). Meanwhile, the User-Agent becomes the frontend mobile apps, namely Cashier App (*CA*) and Merchant App (*MA*). Besides, unlike the native apps, *e.g.*, Android apps, within the in-app payment, the *MA* in WAP is accessed through the web browser in the smartphone. We use the notations in the parentheses to denote these four related parties if not specified otherwise.

The goal of the mobile payment service is to convince the Merchant that the user has paid the order (in the Merchant App) with his balance in the Cashier.

2.1 Workflow of Mobile Payment System

As there is no unified standard for mobile payment, the systems from the Cashiers differ. After reviewing the official technical documents, we get its general workflow depicted in Fig. 1a. It is noteworthy that some Cashiers customize their payment protocols, which will be discussed in detail in Sect. 4.

In short, the workflow in Fig. 1a consists of the following three phases:

1. **Ordering & Payment Phase.**
   In Step 1, the end-user makes an ordering and chooses a third-party Cashier to check out in the *MA*. Then, the *CA* processes the payment order from the *MS* in Step 2 and presents the payment details for user consent. Once the user authorizes the payment, the *CA* will send the payment request to its server in Step 3, which completes the first phase.
2. **Settlement Phase.**
   In this phase, the Cashier acknowledges the Merchant about the payment result. Specifically, the *CS* will send two payment notifications, namely, the

synchronous notification (Step 4a) and asynchronous notification (Step 4b). Notably, the former is the immediate response to the payment request in Step 3, which arrives at the *MS* from *MA* via Step 5. In contrast, the *CS* sends the asynchronous notification to the *MS* directly based on a parameter, *i.e.*, *backURL*, that pre-specified in the Ordering & Payment Phase. Finally, after validating the notifications, the Merchant can update the order status.

3. **Management Phase.**
   The studied Cashiers also provide other management interfaces. Thus, the Merchant can invoke them to refund paid orders or obtain its transaction record, namely, Step 6 in Fig. 1a. Given their critical nature, the Cashiers set different authentication requirements on the Merchant (*i.e.*, *MS*) to secure these interfaces. We will discuss more details in Sect. 4.4.

The Cashiers under study have a dual role and also act as the Payment Gateway, which can operate on the cash accounts of end-users. Thus, these Cashiers can complete the transaction by themselves and return the payment result to the Merchants directly, leaving space for the attacker to cheat the Merchants by forging payment notifications (Sect. 5.3). In contrast, Apple Pay and Google Pay need to work with a separate Payment Gateway. Consequently, the Merchants in Apple Pay and Google Pay need to actively submit the payment token, in the form of a random string, to the Payment Gateway to complete the transaction, *i.e.*, Step 6 and 7 in Fig. 1b. Due to the same reason, the management interfaces are not available in Apple Pay and Google Pay.

2.2 Threat Model

In our threat model, the target of the attacker includes:

- Tricking victim users into paying for the attacker by substituting with his payment order (*i.e.*, Step 2 in Fig. 1a) in the Ordering & Payment Phase
- Shopping for free in the victim Merchant App by crafting fake payment notifications (*i.e.*, Step 4 in Fig. 1a) for deception in the Settlement Phase
- Impersonating the Merchant for privileged operations like refunding by forging requests to the *CS* (*i.e.*, Step 6 in Fig. 1a) in the Management Phase
- Violating the privacy of end-users by misusing the services from the Cashiers

We consider two types of attackers in this paper:

- **App Attacker**: This type of attackers can decompile the frontend apps of the Cashier or Merchant for analysis, repackage *MA*s, and lure the victims into using them. Meanwhile, they can send requests to either the *CS* or *MS*.
- **Malicious Merchant**: The Merchants are not trusted in our threat model. These malicious ones may misuse the services from Cashiers to violate user privacy or harm another Merchant (App).

3   Cryptographic Primitives

Most of the messages in the mobile payment systems are protected cryptographically. We introduce the related credentials and other necessary details here.

Table 1. Summary of payment credentials

Cashier	Credential type	Usage	Merchants share the same cashier's public key?
Cashier1(a)	Secret key	HMAC	N/A
	RSA key	Digital signature	✓
Cashier1(b)	RSA key	Digital signature	✓
	RSA' key	Digital signature	✕
Cashier1(c)	Secret key	HMAC	N/A
	RSA Key	Digital signature	✓
	RSA' key	Digital signature	✕
Cashier2	Secret key	HMAC	N/A
	Client cert	SSL client authentication	N/A
Cashier3	Secret key	HMAC	N/A
	PFX cert	Digital signature	✓
Cashier4	Secret key	HMAC	N/A
Cashier5	RSA key	Digital signature	✓
	Encryption key	Symmetric encryption	N/A

†*Cashier1* provides three sets of payment services, *i.e.*, *Cashier1*(a), *Cashier1*(b), and *Cashier1*(c)

3.1 Payment Credentials

Table 1 summarizes various credentials defined by the Cashiers, including:

Secret Key Some Cashiers use the hash-based message authentication code (HMAC) to secure protocol messages. Thus, both the *MS* and *CS* will use the identical secret key as the salt of a hash function, *e.g.*, MD5, to generate the HMAC of payment messages.

Signing Key Most Cashiers, except *Cashier2*, support the digital signature. Then, both the Cashier and Merchant need to hold a separate pair of asymmetric keys and share their public keys. In runtime, either party signs the request with its own private key and validates the response with the other party's public key.

Since *Cashier1* adopts two cryptographic hash functions in generating the digital signature, it also defines two types of signing keys, namely, RSA key and RSA' Key. On the other hand, the private key of the Merchant in *Cashier3* is issued by the Cashier and packaged in a PFX certificate. Last but not least, as shown in Table 1, *the Cashier's public key tends to be shared among the Merchants*. The only exception is the RSA' key in *Cashier1*.

Client Certificate [23] *Cashier2* issues this credential to its Merchants for extra authentication on SSL. Then, the Merchant, namely, *MS*, must present it when invoking money-related management interfaces, *e.g.*, refund.

Encryption Key For confidentiality, *Cashier5* shares this type of key with its Merchants to support symmetric encryption. Then, all the protocol messages in *Cashier5* are encrypted with the same key by either the *MS* or *CS*. In contrast, the other Cashiers under study do not encrypt their payment messages.

3.2 Other Details

1. *Cashier1* and *Cashier3* support both HMAC and digital signature. However, *only one method will be used in one payment session*, which is specified by the Merchant in the payment order, *i.e.*, Step 2 in Fig. 1a.

2. All the Cashiers take the same method to organize the payment-related parameters, which are converted into *key* = *value* format, alphabetically sorted, and linked using & symbol, before signing or computing the HMAC.

Unfortunately, ***this customized method introduces ambiguity in parsing payment messages***. Figure 2 gives a concrete example. To be specific, by mixing up the *key* with *value*, the attacker may manipulate the value of *order_num* to introduce a new parameter, *i.e.*, *status*, in the re-formulated message. It is also feasible to hide a parameter from the original message, *e.g.*, *trade_amount*, by merging it into another parameter value, *i.e.*, *subject*.

```
{"order_num":"5&status=1", "trade_amount":100, "subject":"test"}
// parameters in a payment-related message
order_num=5&status=1&subject=test&trade_amount=100
// constructed string before signing / calculating HMAC
{"order_num":5, "status":1, "subject":"test&trade_amount=100"}
// another possible parsing output
```

Fig. 2. Ambiguity in parsing payment-related messages

4   Demystifying Practical Mobile Payment Systems

The Cashiers under study tend to customize their systems. In this section, we introduce the current practices and discuss their underlying security implications.

4.1   Our Approach

We take both static and dynamic approaches to study practical mobile payment systems. Specifically, we manually examine the SDKs from the Cashiers at first. These SDKs are provided to the Merchants for integrating the payment services in their frontend mobile apps, *i.e.*, *MA*s, and backend servers, *i.e.*, *MS*s. We also analyze the mobile apps of the Cashiers, *i.e.*, *CA*s, with reverse engineering.

As to the dynamic testing, we use these official SDKs to set up dummy Merchants. Notably, the studied Cashiers all provide the demo (Merchant) accounts or separate sandbox environment. Thus, we configure the related payment credentials (Sect. 3.1) to deploy our Merchant Server. Then, we can monitor and modify the related protocol messages during the mobile payment process.

4.2   Ordering and Payment Phase

Figure 3 details the workflow of mobile payment, where the dashed part represents customized operations by Cashiers. Table 2 summarizes their protocol differences in the Ordering & Payment Phase, and we explain the related concepts here.

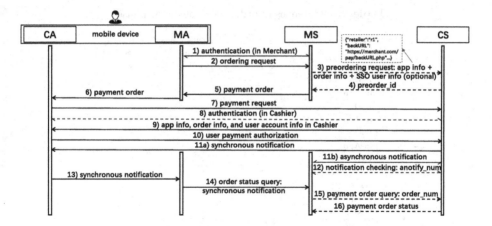

Fig. 3. Detailed workflow of mobile payment services

Preordering. This operation maps to Step 3 and Step 4 in Fig. 3, which happens between the two servers before the generation of payment order in Step 5. Specifically, the preordering request in Step 3 contains app information and order information. The former includes the app identifier, *i.e.*, *retailer*, and *back-URL* that specifies the address in the *MS* for receiving asynchronous notification in Step 11b. Besides, the response from the Cashier in Step 4 only includes an opaque parameter, *preorder_id*, which is a random ID for the payment order.

As shown in Table 2, not all the Cashiers support preordering in their payment protocols. Once the preordering is not enabled, the app information and order information mentioned above will be included in the payment order in Step 5 instead, which also becomes visible to the user-controlled smartphone.

SSO Involvement. Other than payment, some Cashiers offer the Single Sign-On (SSO) service to mobile apps. As such, the user can log into the *MA* with his account in the Cashier, *i.e.*, Step 1 in Fig. 3, without creating a new one in the Merchant. Thus, these two user accounts/identities, in the Cashier and Merchant, are automatically associated. In other words, through the same Cashier, the user can perform both login and payment in the *MA*. Consequently, the *MS* may involve the related SSO user information in payment, *e.g.*, Step 3 in Fig. 3.

Then, from the payment order in Step 6, *CA* can infer the user identity who makes the ordering in Step 2 based on the associated SSO user information. By comparing it with the current user identity, the Cashier can check whether the payment order has been replaced. *Cashier2* conducts the checking above, while *Cashier1* does not. However, as indicated in Table 2, the related SSO user information is optional in the in-app payment service of *Cashier2*. In contrast, the (mobile) web apps in *Cashier2* are only accessible through the built-in browser in its *CA*, where the Cashier can enforce the SSO process and its involvement.

Table 2. Differences in ordering & payment phase

Cashier	Type	Preordering	SSO involvement	Client-side verification	Identity federation
Cashier1 (a)	In-App	×	×	×	×
	WAP	×	?	×	×
Cashier1 (b)	In-App	×	×	×	×
	WAP	×	×	×	×
Cashier1 (c)	In-App	×	×	×	×
	WAP	×	×	×	×
Cashier2	In-App	✓	?	✓	×
	WAP	✓	✓	✓	×
Cashier3	In-App	✓	N/A	×	×
	WAP	×	N/A	×	×
Cashier4	In-App	×	×	✓	×
	WAP	×	×	×	×
Cashier5	In-App	✓	N/A	×	×
	WAP	×	N/A	×	✓

* ? means optional operations.

In summary, involving SSO in mobile payment is not a general defense due to the following reasons: (1) Some Cashiers do not provide SSO service. (2) It is hard to enforce the paying users to always log into the *MA* via the same Cashier.

Client-Side Verification. Once receiving the payment order, *i.e.*, Step 6 in Fig. 3, some Cashiers check the integrity of *MA*. For in-app payment, *Cashier2* and *Cashier4* compare its package signature with the pre-configured value by the developers. In WAP, only *Cashier2* checks the HTTP referer header against the whitelist. Nevertheless, most Cashiers do not perform a proper verification of their *MA*s. Specifically, these Cashiers only check the digital signature or HMAC within the received payment order. As a result, the attacker may repackage a *MA* (in Sect. 2.2) and trick victim users into paying for his order in it.

On the other hand, Cashiers may not always implement the client-side verification properly and securely. As we will present in Sect. 5.1, the practical verification can be flawed and bypassed under some conditions.

Identity Federation. The mobile payment system involves two user identities in the Cashier and Merchant. For a better user experience, *Cashier5* deploys the identity federation mechanism in its WAP service. To be specific, this Cashier requires the Merchant to include its user identifier in the payment order, *i.e.*, Step 6 in Fig. 3. Thus, the Cashier can establish the mapping of the two user identities and bind them together after one payment. Then, in the next payment, the user can use his Merchant account to skip the authentication in *Cashier5*, *i.e.*, Step 8 in Fig. 3, which is opposite to the SSO service mentioned above. As such, *Cashier5* will return all the user account details directly in Step 9, which includes the balance in the user's Cashier account and card binding information.

In short, *Cashier5* makes two assumptions when deploying the identity federation mechanism: (1) It is the same user that initiates new payment sessions after he paid to the Merchant once. (2) The Cashier user is the same one in the Merchant so that these two identities can be associated.

Table 3. Differences in settlement phase

Cashier	Notification checking	Backward order query	Protected sync. notification
Cashier1 (a)	✓	×	✓
Cashier1 (b)	×	×	✓
Cashier1 (c)	✓	×	✓
Cashier2	×	✓	×
Cashier3	×	?	✓
Cashier4	×	?	✓
Cashier5	×	×	✓

* ? means suggested options.

However, as we will discuss in Sect. 5.2, these two assumptions can be broken under some scenarios. Consequently, the attacker can misuse this function and steal the account information of the victim users from the Cashier.

4.3   Settlement Phase

In this phase, the Cashier confirms to the Merchant the payment result with two types of notifications (in Sect. 2.1). Given the crucial nature of these notifications, the Cashiers design different mechanisms to ensure their authenticity.

Notification Checking. Some Cashiers use HMAC to secure the messages (Sect. 3.1). Since the related secret key is shared between the Merchant and Cashier, the property of non-repudiation is missing. Thus, the attacker can forge payment notifications to the *MS* to shop for free once the secret key is leaked [25].

To make up for this limitation, *Cashier1* designs the notification checking mechanism. Specifically, the asynchronous notification, *i.e.*, Step 11b in Fig. 3, contains a parameter, *anotify_num* (short for asynchronous notification number). By sending it back to the Cashier, the Merchant can validate the received notification, which helps to defend the potential exploit of notification forgery.

However, such protection is not implemented by the other Cashiers using HMAC, *e.g.*, *Cashier2*. Worse still, the notification checking mechanism does not apply to the synchronous notification in *Cashier1*, leaving space for the attacker to cheat the Merchants. We will give more details in Sect. 5.3.

Backward Order Query. As the network delay is unpredictable during payment, the Merchant may not receive the two notifications in a fixed order. In other words, the synchronous notification, *i.e.*, Step 11a in Fig. 3, may reach the *MS* before the asynchronous one, although it goes through the smartphone first.

In this situation, some Cashiers require the Merchant, *i.e.*, *MS*, to actively query the Cashier about the order status with *order_num* in Step 15. The underlying reason is that the asynchronous notification is sent from the Cashier directly and thus more trustable.

Besides, as indicated in Table 3, the synchronous notification in *Cashier2* is not protected cryptographically. Thus, *Cashier2* enforces the backward order query, while *Cashier3* and *Cashier4* only suggest this operation.

Table 4. Management services from Cashiers

Extra requirements	Refunding	Money transferring	Transaction record
Cashier1(a)	×	Merchant's login_id	×
Cashier1(b)	×	×	×
Cashier1(c)	×	N/A	IP whitelist
Cashier2	Client cert	Client cert	×
Cashier3	×	N/A	×
Cashier4	×	×	IP whitelist
Cashier5	×	N/A	IP whitelist

* N/A means the related service does not exist in the Cashier.

4.4 Management Phase

The studied Cashiers provide management interfaces. Therefore, the *MS* can request the *CS* to refund the paid order, transfer money into the user account, or download its transaction record. Since these interfaces involve critical money transactions or user privacy, some Cashiers set other authentication requirements to their Merchants besides checking the digital signature or HMAC. As presented in Table 4, these additional requirements differ among the interfaces, even in the same Cashier. For example, the Merchant can obtain the transaction record from *Cashier4* only if it uses a pre-registered IP address, which is unnecessary in the money transferring interface, although it is more sensitive than the former.

Unfortunately, the attacker can escape some of these extra security checks. For example, the Merchant's *login_id*, namely, the email or phone number used to login *Cashier1*, is always visible to the end-user from the synchronous notification, *i.e.*, Step 11a in Fig. 3. Meanwhile, as we will present in Sect. 5.5, the Merchant, *i.e.*, *MS*, can leak its client certificate (in Sect. 3.1) inadvertently due to the insecure SDK from *Cashier2*. Worse still, exploiting these vulnerable backend SDKs, the attacker may even unauthorizedly access the management interfaces with zero knowledge of payment credentials (in Sect. 5.6).

5   Exploiting Mobile Payment System

In this section, we talk about the potential exploits on mobile payment. These exploits leverage both the insecure protocol designs discussed in Sect. 4 and flawed implementations by either the Cashier or Merchant. All of them bring about serious consequences, ranging from financial loss to privacy violations.

5.1 Order Replacement

As identified by [25], many *MAs* use HTTP to interact with their servers, despite the warnings by the Cashiers. Then, by intercepting the network traffic, the attacker can replace the payment order, *i.e.*, Step 5 in Fig. 3, so that the victim users will be tricked into paying for his order. Although involving SSO in payment mitigates the exploit, this solution is not general, as discussed in Sect. 4.2.

Meanwhile, most of the Cashiers fail to validate the MAs (in Table 2), so that this exploit is also feasible for the repackaged MA (Sect. 2.2), which replaces the payment order to the CA, $i.e.$, Step 6 in Fig. 3, instead. Besides, we decompile the mobile apps of $Cashier2$ and $Cashier4$ to study how they validate the MA. Beyond our expectations, we find the verification by $Cashier2$'s mobile app to be flawed in its in-app payment service and can be bypassed under some conditions. More details about the related exploit can be found in Appendix A.

5.2 Identity Federation Misuse

The identity federation mechanism (Sect. 4.2) enables the user to skip the authentication by $Cashier5$, $i.e.$, Step 8 in Fig. 3. However, the attacker can break the assumptions behind the mechanism and misuse it to violate user privacy.

First of all, the Malicious Merchant (in Sect. 2.2) may generate the payment order without involving the end-user and send it to the Cashier, $i.e.$, Step 7 in Fig. 3. Then, the attacker can get the response from $Cashier5$, $i.e.$, Step 9, which contains the desired user privacy. It is noteworthy that the attacker can apply this trick to keep tracking the victim's Cashier account.

Even if the Merchant is trusted, the App Attacker can conduct the Order Replacement (in Sect. 5.1) and lure the victim user into paying for the attacker for once. As such, the victim's Cashier account is associated with the attacker's Merchant account. Thus, the attacker can persistently track the victim's Cashier account information by creating new orders. Notably, according to our empirical testing, $Cashier5$ allows one user account to be associated with multiple accounts in the same Merchant, such that the exploit can be launched silently.

5.3 Payment Notification Forgery

This type of exploit enables the attacker to craft fake payment notifications to deceive the Merchant, $i.e.$, MS, and shop for free. Due to the preordering (in Sect. 4.2) or symmetric encryption (in Sect. 3.1), $backURL$, namely, the address for the MS to receive asynchronous notification (Step 11b in Fig. 3), may be invisible to the attacker to send the forged notifications. Nevertheless, many official backend SDKs from the Cashiers define the handler for synchronous notification, $e.g.$, "frontURL.php" in Fig. 5, such that the $backURL$ can be inferred from its location, $i.e.$, Step 14 in Fig. 3. For example, the attacker can infer the URL endpoint, "https://www.example.com/payment/backURL.php", from "https://www.example.com/payment/frontURL.php". In summary, this type of exploits can be classified into three subtypes. We will illustrate them here.

Order-to-Notification Forgery. Yang $et\ al.$ [25] show that the leaked secret key in the MA enables the attacker to forge payment notifications with valid HMAC for deception. Despite this known exploit, we find the attacker may cheat the Merchants with zero knowledge of their secret key. In short, the attacker leverages the shared secret key in HMAC and the ambiguity in parsing payment

```
https://merchant.com/pay/demo.php?
order_num=abc%26status%3Dsuccess&trade_amount=10
// crafted request to the demo script in the Merchant Server
order_num=abc%26status%3Dsuccess&...&trade_amount=10&HMAC=x
// responded payment order from the Merchant Server
https://merchant.com/pay/backURL.php?
order_num=abc&status=success&...&trade_amount=10&HMAC=x
// replaying the re-formulated payment order as the payment notification
to the Merchant Server
// %26 and %3D stand for & and = in URL encoding.
```

(a) Order-to-Notification Forgery

```
https://cashier.com/pay?
backURL=https%3A%2F%2Fattacker.com&order_num=abc%26r
etailer%3Dr2%26sa%3D&retailer=r1&...&signature=x
// crafted payment request to the Cashier Server by the attacker
https://attacker.com?order_num=abc%26retailer%3Dr2%26sa%
3D&retailer=r1&...&status=success&signature=x
// signed payment notification to the attacker
http://merchant.com/pay/backURL.php?order_num=abc&retailer
=r2&sa=%26retailer%3Dr1&...&status=success&signature=x
// replaying the re-formulated notification to the victim Merchant
```

(b) Cross-Merchant Notification Forgery

Fig. 4. Order-to-Notification Forgery

messages, e.g., Fig. 2, in the discovered exploit. Specifically, he can manipulate the payment order from the Merchant, i.e., Step 5 in Fig. 3. Then, he may reformulate this payment order to be a fake payment notification.

Notably, for mobile web apps, the Cashiers always include a demo script in their backend SDKs, e.g., "demo.php" in Fig. 5. This script accepts external requests and returns the payment order to the sender. As shown in Fig. 4, the request parameters appear in the responded payment order such that the attacker can manipulate their values to forge payment notifications. Specifically, the attacker can craft the value of order_num and introduce a new parameter status in the re-formulated message. In other words, the attacker takes the Merchant, i.e., MS, as the oracle to get the desired message with a legitimate HMAC, which is then replayed as the notification.

Meanwhile, the existing protection mechanisms in the Settlement Phase, discussed in Sect. 4.3, are not comprehensive. For example, the backward order query occurs under certain conditions. Besides, the notification checking mechanism in Cashier1 only applies to the asynchronous notification. Then, the attacker may escape such a checking by sending the synchronous notification only to cheat the Merchant. Therefore, the attacker can always construct an appropriate scenario to bypass the protections from the Cashiers.

Remark: **We have done the Proof-of-Concept (PoC) tests with the SDKs from Cashier1, Cashier3, and Cashier4. As Cashier2 adopts preordering, its payment order only contains the preorder_id, making this exploit infeasible. Besides, we collect and examine 100 mobile web apps that use third-party payment services. The result shows 5 of these apps keep the demo script in their servers and are vulnerable.**

Cross-merchant Notification Forgery. The notification forgery is also feasible when the digital signature is used. In this exploit, the attacker leverages the shared public key of the Cashier among the Merchants (in Table 1).

To be specific, the attacker may control another Merchant, e.g., official demo (Merchant) accounts, to get signed notifications from the Cashier for free, which share the same trade_amount and order_num with the target order. Then, he can inject them into the payment session of the victim Merchant. Once this Merchant Server overlooks the app identifier within the notification, e.g., retailer in Fig. 4b, it will be cheated and enable the attacker to shop for free. For interesting readers, the detailed workflow and explanation are given in Appendix B.

Besides, we find one of the studied Cashiers allows special characters, *e.g.*, &
and =, in the payment request, *i.e.*, Step 7 in Fig. 3. Exploiting the parsing ambiguity mentioned in Sect. 3.2, the attacker can manipulate his payment request
to overwrite the benign app identifier in the forged notification. Figure 4b gives
an example, where the original app identifier, *i.e.*, *retailer*, is taken over by a
non-existent parameter *sa* injected by the attacker. *Thus, all the Merchants in
this Cashier will be affected, even if they verify payment notifications properly.*

**Remark: For ethical considerations, we cannot attack real Merchants
to quantify the impact of this exploit. However, we have identified an
open-source framework for Merchant Servers to be vulnerable. This
framework integrates the services from the studied Cashiers and has
over 100,000 downloads. Towards this end, we set up our dummy
Merchant with this framework and complete a PoC test on it.**

**On the other hand, we have notified the aforementioned vulnerable
Cashier about our finding. This Cashier has acknowledged the potential security threat and fixed the issue in its backend server rapidly
after our responsible disclosure.**

Null Key Exploit. *Cashier3* serves over 100 million users globally. Despite
the prevalence of *Cashier3*, we have identified a *zero-day vulnerability* in its
SDK in PHP, enabling the attacker to forge payment notifications to deceive the
Merchant, *i.e.*, *MS*, with no knowledge of payment credentials.

In *Cashier3*, the Merchants can choose either digital signature or HMAC to
secure the messages (Sect. 3.2), including the payment notifications. Besides, the
digital signature is the de facto protection method.

```
1  static function validate($params) {
2      // 11 indicates the usage of HMAC
3      if($params['signMethod']=='11') {
4          $isSuccess = AcpService::validateBySecureKey(
               $params, getSDKConfig()->secureKey);}
5      ...
6      return $isSuccess;}
7
8  static function getSDKConfig() {
9      $this->secureKey =  array_key_exists("secureKey",
           $sdk_array)?$sdk_array["secureKey"]: null;
10     ...}
11
12 static function validateBySecureKey($params, $secureKey) {
13     ...
14     $key = hash('sha256', $secureKey);
15     ...}
```

Listing 1.1. Vulnerable code in *Cashier3*'s backend SDK

Fig. 5. Structure of an official backend SDK

Listing.1.1 presents the snippet of the vulnerable code, where the function "validate()" checks the signature or HMAC within the received payment notifications. Notably, this function dynamically extracts the "signMethod" field from the notification on line 3 to determine the protection method. Therefore, by controlling the "signMethod", the attacker can send an HMAC-protected notification to the Merchant that adopts the digital signature. Then, the server will read the "secureKey" from the local configuration on line 4. Since the "secureKey" is not set by default, the SDK will return null on line 9. Nevertheless, "validateBySecureKey()" fails to check if the "secureKey" is null or not and instead passes it to the hash function on line 14, which expects two string-type variables as input [16]. Then, due to the automatic type conversion in PHP, the "secureKey" will be converted to an empty string if it is null. As a result, the attacker can forge payment notifications using the null key to pass the checking.

Remark: **Due to strong typing, this exploit does not apply to the SDKs in Java or C#, where the null key will trigger Null Pointer Exception in both cases. Nevertheless, PHP is still the most prevalent programming language used for web application development [11], while the script with the vulnerability has not been modified for over two years. Thus, there should still be many vulnerable Merchant Servers in the wild. We have completed a PoC test for this exploit and reported our finding to *Cashier3*. The Cashier confirms the vulnerability and immediately updates its SDK.**

5.4   Payment Notification Misuse

The payment notifications in *Cashier1* are over-informative and leak user privacy. To be specific, these notifications contain the *login_id*s of both the Merchant and user, whose value is an email address or phone number. In other words, the Cashier provides personally identifiable information (PII) of its users to the Merchants without permission, while the latter may not be trusted (in Sect. 2.2). Worse still, *Cashier1* maintains a social network, where each user is searchable based on his *login_id*. As such, the Malicious Merchant can misuse this private data to get the victim's identity in *Cashier1* and get more user privacy.

Table 5. Summary of official backend SDKs

Inaccessibility	Credential files			Control scripts			Log files		
	PHP	Java	C#	PHP	Java	C#	PHP	Java	C#
Cashier1 (a)	×	✓	✓	N/A	N/A	N/A	×	✓	×
Cashier1 (b)	✓	✓	✓	×	×	×	×	✓	✓
Cashier1 (c)	×	✓	×	N/A	N/A	N/A	×	✓	×
Cashier2	×	✓	×	×	N/A	×	×	✓	×
Cashier3	×	✓	✓	×	×	×	✓	✓	✓
Cashier4	×	✓	✓	N/A	N/A	N/A	×	✓	✓
Cashier5	×	✓	✓	×	✓	×	✓	✓	✓

Meanwhile, the SDKs from the Cashiers log the payment notifications in static files, *e.g.*, "log.txt" in Fig. 5. Nonetheless, some SDKs do not restrict the access to log files by default, as indicated in Table 5. Once the Merchant fails to set proper access control on these files, the attacker can infer their locations from the addresses of the payment notification handlers, *e.g.*, "backURL.php" and "frontURL.php" in Fig. 5, and crawl them. Then, the attacker can recover the transaction records based on the log files, which also include the *login_ids*.

Remark: **We examine 100 top-ranked Android apps that use third-party payment services. Specifically, we extract their *backURLs* pointing to their backend servers to apply the approach above. However, we do not directly download the exposed log files but use the HTTP HEAD method to check their existence and metadata, *e.g.*, file size. The result shows that 8 of the tested servers (8%) expose their logs to the wild, where the maximum file size exceeds 500 MB. Remarkably, these vulnerable apps have over 6.5 million downloads on average.**

5.5   Merchant Impersonation Attack

Some Merchant Apps embed payment credentials [25]. For Android apps, their installation packages are public online, *e.g.*, APKPure [1], so that the attacker can use the existing tool like Apktool [20] to recover the included credentials.

On the other hand, we find that the Merchant Servers can be another leaking source of payment credentials. Figure 5 presents the structure of an SDK, where "payment_config.php" stores the local configuration and sets the client certificate (Sect. 3.1) to a static file, *i.e.*, "client_cert.pem". Although some Cashiers like *Cashier2* suggest changing the filename and blocking the access to these files, some Merchants fail to do so. Thus, based on the SDK structure (*e.g.*, Fig. 5) and payment notification handler address (*e.g.*, Step 14 in Fig. 3), the attacker can guess the location of payment credential files in the *MS*. For example, he may infer "https://www.example.com/payment/credential/client_cert.php" from "https://www.example.com/payment/frontURL.php". Most Cashiers make the same mistake (in Table 5), while some other SDKs lay payment credentials in inaccessible scripts or directories and are thus secure in normal cases.

With the leaked payment credentials, the attacker can impersonate the Merchants to access the management interfaces from the Cashiers. Even though some Cashiers use other factors to strengthen the authentication on the Merchants, the attacker may still bypass them, as discussed in Sect. 4.4.

Remark: **We analyze the 100 most popular Android apps supporting the mobile payment function. The result turns out that 11 of these apps (11%) embed payment credentials. Moreover, we use the HTTP HEAD method to probe the backend servers behind another set of 100 apps, where 7 of their servers (7%) use the flawed SDKs and do not restrict access to the stored payment credential files. Notably, the average downloads of these vulnerable apps exceed 3.1 million.**

5.6   Hidden Control Scripts

Some backend SDKs from the Cashiers include the control scripts for demo usage, *e.g.*, "refunding.php" and "transaction_record.php" in Fig. 5. Notably, these scripts accept the external request and accordingly use the stored payment credentials, *e.g.*, "client_cert.pem", to generate a separate request to the Cashier.

Despite their critical nature, most of these official SDKs do not set access control on the control scripts, as indicated in Table 5. Using the approach for stealing credentials or logs, the attacker may uncover the URL endpoints of these control scripts. Then, he can craft requests to these scripts and take them as the backdoor to access the management services without knowing any payment credentials, deactivating all the protections by the Cashiers (in Sect. 4.4).

Remark: **We test the backend servers behind 100 top-ranked Android apps. According to the result, six of these Merchant Apps (6%) are vulnerable, which have 3.96 million downloads on average.**

6   Suggested Fixings to Mobile Payment

In this section, we talk about the fixings to mitigate the exploits in Sect. 5.

6.1   Modifications on Protocol Design

Figure 6 depicts the revised workflow for mobile payment. In short, we have made three main changes, which are elaborated as follows.

One-Time Ticket Mechanism. The current mobile payment system is susceptible to flawed implementations by the Merchants, *i.e.*, unencrypted HTTP network interactions, in most cases, which lead to the Order Replacement Attack (Sect. 5.1). Therefore, we introduce the one-time ticket mechanism to fix the issue, which corresponds to Step 2 to 5 in Fig. 6.

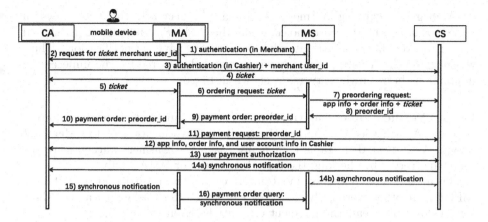

Fig. 6. Revised workflow of mobile payment service

Specifically, we move the authentication in the Cashier ahead to Step 3. At the beginning of each payment, the *MA* needs to apply for a one-time ticket in Step 2 with the user identifier of the payer in the Merchant as input. Then, the Cashier can establish a temporary binding of the two involved user identities (in the Merchant and Cashier) and encode it into the *ticket*, which is returned to the Merchant through Step 4 and Step 5. Afterward, the Merchant is required to include the received *ticket* in the preordering request in Step 7, while the Cashier will associate it with the generated *preorder_id* before Step 8.

From the payment order in Step 10, the Cashier can then get the identity of the user who makes the ordering in Step 6. Thus, by comparing it with the current user identity in the *CA*, the Cashier manages to check whether the current payment session is corrupted or not. As long as the *MA* (in the victim's smartphone) is benign, the attacker cannot bind his account in the Merchant to the victim's identity in the Cashier in the first stage, making the Order Replacement Attack unfeasible. Notably, this assumption holds once the Cashier authenticates the *MA* properly, which will be discussed later. Besides, in contrast to the existing identity federation mechanism in Sect. 4.2, the proposed scheme is not persistent and always launched by the end-user through the *MA* in Step 2 so that the attacker cannot misuse it to violate user privacy (Sect. 5.2).

Adoption of Secure Payment Key. The existing mechanisms in the Settlement Phase (Sect. 4.3) are designed to make up for the imperfection of the payment credentials. For example, when the secret key is adopted, the non-repudiation property is missing in HMAC so that *Cashier1* designs the notification checking mechanism as remediation at the cost of extra network interactions between the servers. Since the Cashier's public key tends to be shared among the Merchants (in Table 1), the same issue remains in the digital signature, where the Cashiers count on the Merchants to validate the payment notifications properly. However, as presented in Sect. 5.3, the existing protection mechanisms are not comprehensive, while the verifications from the Merchants can be flawed.

Among the existing payment credentials in Sect. 3.1, the RSA' keys in *Cashier1* are the most secure choice, where the Cashier's public key is not shared among the Merchants and the attacker cannot forge payment notifications. Thus, we suggest using this type of key, which also helps to reduce the unnecessary interactions between the servers, as shown in Fig. 6.

Proper Verification of the Merchant The root cause of the Merchant Impersonation Attack (Section. 5.5) is the insufficient verification of the Merchant Server. As indicated in Table 4, in many cases, the Cashiers authenticate the Merchant Server by checking the digital signature or HMAC only.

Then, the related management interfaces suffer a single point of failure (SPOF). In other words, the attacker can cheat the Cashier to access these services once he steals the payment credentials. Even though the Cashiers use other factors to strengthen the authentication on their Merchants, most of them can be bypassed (Sect. 4.4). Given the importance of these management services, the Cashier should set more strict authentication requirements, *e.g.*, IP whitelist, to the Merchants. Then, *the attacker cannot consume the leaked payment credentials*.

Similarly, the proper verification of the *MA* is also necessary. Otherwise, the attacker may repackage malicious apps to harm the victim users (in Sect. 5.1).

6.2   Other Operational Issues

Some operational or software issues contribute to the exploits in Sect. 5, so we propose the following fixings.

Removing Redundant Information. The Cashiers should review their systems to avoid leaking redundant information in the protocol messages. Otherwise, the attacker may steal related information, enabling other exploits, and causing privacy violations. For example, in *Cashier1*, the payment notifications contain the privacy of both the Merchant and end-users, *i.e.*, *login_id*. Notably, this private data acts as the identity proof of the Merchant and is required in the money transferring interface (in Table 4). Thus, the attacker can obtain its value to exploit the stolen payment credentials, *i.e.*, Merchant Impersonation in Sect. 5.5. Meanwhile, the attacker may also recover the *login_ids* of end-users from the exposed logs from the Merchants (Sect. 5.4) to find their identities.

Providing Secure SDKs to Merchants. The backend SDKs from the Cashiers also give rise to the exploits in Sect. 5. As indicated in Table 5, these SDKs usually miss the access control on the critical credential and log files. Some of the SDKs also include the control scripts but do not forbid public access to them by default. Then, the attacker can uncover their locations in the Merchant Server to conduct the exploits. Thus, Cashiers *must* remove these control scripts from their SDKs and set strict access control on the sensitive credentials and logs.

Meanwhile, the official SDKs can be vulnerable by themselves (Sect. 5.3). However, fingerprinting the backend SDK in the Merchant Servers remains an open question, so that it is tricky for the Cashiers to recall the vulnerable SDKs once they are distributed to the Merchants. According to previous experiences, e.g., [14], the Cashiers can only alert their Merchants passively.

On the other hand, the frontend SDKs can also be problematic. Specifically, two of the Cashiers under study include the payment credential in their demo projects. Although these codes are claimed for illustration only, many Merchants directly reuse them, which enables the exploit in Sect. 5.5. In short, the Cashiers *must* provide secure SDKs to their Merchants. After all, the Merchants are usually not knowledgeable, while it is unreliable to count on their security awareness to deploy secure mobile payment service.

Using JWT to Secure the Messages. As mentioned in Sect. 3.2, all the Cashiers adopt the same customized approach to process the payment-related messages. However, this approach introduces ambiguity in parsing. Consequently, the attacker can take either the Merchant or Cashier as the oracle to get the desired message for payment notification forgery (Sect. 5.3).

To prevent these exploits, we suggest the Cashiers use the existing mature solution to secure the messages in payment. Toward this end, the JSON Web Token (JWT) can be a good option, which is an Internet standard and has detailed documents [7] to follow. Notably, this technique has been widely applied in the Single Sign-On (SSO) services that involve similar multi-party interactions.

Fixing the Value of backURL. The Cashiers use two types of payment notifications to confirm the payment result to the Merchants (Sect. 2.1). Since the asynchronous notification is directly sent to the Merchant, i.e., *MS*, it is more trustable. Notably, in each session, the Merchant needs to specify the address in its server, namely, backURL, for the Cashier to send the asynchronous notification. Thus, by controlling this variable, the attacker can use the demo account to forge cryptographically-correct notifications and use them to cheat other Merchants (Sect. 5.3). Compared to a similar concept, i.e., redirect_url in OAuth [5] for SSO service, it is strange that all the Cashiers allow the dynamic setting of backURL, while the other is defined as a constant. In *Cashier1*, the backURL is even set to be optional. Then, the Cashier will not send the asynchronous notification if the Merchant ignores the parameter. Given the critical role of the asynchronous notification, we suggest fixing the value of backURL.

7   Related Work

Motivated by the prevalent adoption of e-payment services in web and mobile applications, its security analysis has aroused increasing attention during the past decade. Wang et al. [21] manually study the third-party payment services for web applications and construct several practical attacks. Combining symbolic execution and taint analysis, Sun *et al.* [19] propose an automated approach and detect 12 logic flaws in 22 PHP modules for payment service. As the defense, Xing *et al.* [24] develop InteGuard to detect exploit attempts toward the payment service, which protects the vulnerable integration of payment services by the websites. Notably, all the studies mentioned above only work on web applications, while we focus on the third-party payment service for mobile applications.

Meanwhile, some other works concentrate on the security of digital wallets or banking apps. Haupert *et al.* [6] evaluate the security of N26, a pan-European banking app, and present several exploits against it. Reaves *et al.* [17] study 7 Android apps for branchless banks in developing countries and detect 28 significant vulnerabilities. Kumar *et al.* [10] use a principled methodology to analyze the unpublished payment protocol for digital wallet apps in India and get 11 CVEs. Kaur *et al.* [9] propose security recommendations for digital wallet apps and assess three leading e-wallet Android apps in Canada. Following these works, Chen *et al.* [2] conduct a large-scale empirical study on 693 banking apps across over 80 countries and collect 2,157 security weaknesses from them. However, compared to the third-party payment service for mobile apps under our study, most of the digital wallets or banking apps only work for Point-of-Sale (PoS) terminals and peer-to-peer money transfers.

As to the third-party payment service for mobile apps, [8] is the first work to study its security schemes. Following this work, Liu *et al.* [12] make a comprehensive survey on mainstream service providers, *i.e.*, Cashiers, and their mobile payment security technology framework. Wang *et al.* [22] summarize the security services desired in mobile payment systems. Mulliner *et al.* [15] study the OS-provided in-app billing service within 85 first-tier Android apps and find 60% of them are vulnerable. Reynaud *et al.* [18] present the FreeMarket attack to automatically identify and exploit the insecure in-app billing coding practices in Android. Ye *et al.* [26] find several non-trivial hidden assumptions and bugs in the payment SDKs from PayPal and Visa Checkout. Chen *et al.* [3] use a suite of NLP techniques to analyze the documents from fourth-party payment syndicators and identify 5 logic flaws. Nevertheless, this work [3] trusts the payment systems from the Cashiers and supposes them to be secure, which has instead been proven wrong.

The most relevant work to ours is [25], where Yang *et al.* analyze the third-party payment services integrated by Android apps and discover four types of exploits. Although this work formulates a set of security rules for mobile payment, most of them are specific to certain implementation flaws by the Merchants and thus incomplete. For example, [25] asks the Merchant Servers to verify the signature in received payment notifications from the Cashiers. Nonetheless, we find that the attacker may still deceive the Merchants with cryptographically-correct notifications or even without any knowledge of payment credentials (Sect. 5.3). Similarly, the previous work [25] requires the Merchants not to embed their payment credentials in the frontend apps as one of the rules, while the credentials can still be leaked from their backend servers (in Sect. 5.5).

In comparison, we spare more effort on understanding the various system designs by the Cashiers and their underlying security implications (in Sect. 4) so that we manage to construct more novel attack scenarios (in Sect. 5). Besides, Yang *et al.* [25] do not propose comprehensive defenses against the discovered exploits. For instance, they count on the security awareness of end-users to detect the Order Replacement Attack (Sect. 5.1), which is not a reliable solution as the human is the weakest link in cybersecurity. On the contrary, we propose the fixings based on the current practice, which are also fault-tolerant to the flawed implementations by the Merchants, *e.g.*, credential leaks (in Sect. 6.1).

8   Conclusion

In this paper, we perform a security analysis of real-world third-party payment services for mobile apps from five top-tier Cashiers, which serve more than one billion end-users over the world. We conduct a comprehensive study of their payment systems and discover six types of exploits, including a zero-day vulnerability in the official backend SDK. All of these exploits bring about severe security consequences, ranging from financial loss to privacy violation of the Merchants and their users. Moreover, we summarize the best practice and propose the fixings to mitigate these exploits. We have reported our findings to the affected Cashiers and got their positive feedback.

Acknowledgements. This research is supported in part by the CUHK Project Impact Enhancement Fund (Project# 3133292), the CUHK Direct Grant #4055155, and the CUHK MobiTeC R&D Fund.

A   More Details on Order Replacement

Figure 7 shows a snippet of the log during the verification process within *Cashier2*'s Android app, which consists of two steps:

1. *getAppInfo*: the *CA* extracts the app identifier, *i.e.*, *retailer*, from the received payment order and requests for the related app information from its backend server.
2. *verifyAppInfo*: the *CA* compares the package name and signature of the *MA* against the received app information.

Notably, *getAppInfo* will only occur for once because the *CA* will locally store the mapping between *retailer* and the related app information. Nevertheless, we find that the *CA* in *Cashier2* suffers a software bug in *getAppInfo*. Consequently, this bug will enable the repackaged *MA* to bypass the checking from the Cashier in the first payment attempt, even if it does not have a benign signature.

Remark: **This exploit can be persistent once the repackaged *MA* injects the order from a new Merchant, with an unknown *retailer*, in each payment. We have done the Proof-of-Concept (PoC) experiment, reported the issue to *Cashier2*, and got its confirmation.**

```
retailer: ***930ea5d5a258f4f        // app identifier in the payment order
appName: Cashier2 SDK Demo          // app name from the Cashier2's server
server sig: ak187ed67e05c2***   // package signature from Cashier2's server
pkd: com.source***                  // package name from Cashier2's server
gen sig: ak187ed67e05c2***      // package signature generated locally
```

Fig. 7. Running log from *Cashier2*'s app

B   More Details on Cross-merchant Notification Forgery

Figure 8 details the Cross-Merchant Notification Forgery mentioned in Sect. 5.3, which works as follows.

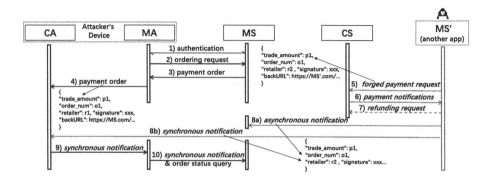

Fig. 8. Cross-merchant notification forgery

1–4 The attacker purchases products in the victim Merchant, namely, *MA*, until Step 4. Then, the attacker suspends the payment session and identifies necessary information, namely *order_num*, *trade_amount*, and *backURL*, from the payment order.

5. Using the payment credentials from another app, *i.e.*, **MS'**, the attacker forges a payment request with the same *order_num* and *trade_amount*. Besides, the *backURL* is set to the host controlled by the attacker.

6. After paying for the forged order in **MS'**, the attacker receives the signed payment notifications from the Cashier, which contain the app identifier of the **MS'**, *order_num*, and *trade_amount*.

7. The attacker refunds the order to get the money back.

8. The attacker resumes the payment session in the *MA* and injects the forged synchronous notification (from Step 6) into the *CA*. Meanwhile, he sends the asynchronous one to the *MS* according to the *backURL* in Step 4.

9. The *CA* propagates the forged notification to the *MA*.

10. The *MA* sends the forged notification back to the *MS* and queries the payment status of the related order.

Finally, the victim Merchant verifies the digital signatures in the forged notifications and extracts the *order_num* and *trade_amount*. Then, it compares their values with the local record (generated before Step 3) and passes the checking due to the setting in Step 5. Nonetheless, the *MS* overlooks the app identifier, *i.e.*, *retailer*, inside the received payment notifications, trusts the settlement of order payment, and delivers the products to the attacker.

References

1. Apkpure: Apkpure (2019). https://apkpure.com/
2. Chen, S., et al.: An empirical assessment of security risks of global android banking apps. In: ICSE 2020 (2020)
3. Chen, Y., et al.: Devils in the guidance: predicting logic vulnerabilities in payment syndication services through automated documentation analysis. In: USENIX 2019 (2019)
4. Fortune Business Insights: Mobile payment market size, share & industry analysis (2020). https://www.fortunebusinessinsights.com/industry-reports/mobile-payment-market-100336
5. Hardt, D.: The OAuth 2.0 authorization framework (2012)
6. Haupert, V., Maier, D., Müller, T.: Paying the price for disruption: how a fintech allowed account takeover. In: ROOTS 2017 (2017)
7. Jones, M., et al.: JSON web token (JWT) (2012)
8. Kadhiwal, S., Zulfiquar, A.U.S.: Analysis of mobile payment security measures and different standards. Comput. Fraud Secur. **2007**(6), 12–16 (2007)
9. Kaur, R., Li, Y., Iqbal, J., Gonzalez, H., Stakhanova, N.: A security assessment of HCE-NFC enabled e-wallet banking android apps. In: COMPSAC 2018, vol. 02 (2018)
10. Kumar, R., Kishore, S., Lu, H., Prakash, A.: Security analysis of unified payments interface and payment apps in India. In: USENIX Security 2020 (2020)
11. Li, X., Xue, Y.: A survey on server-side approaches to securing web applications. ACM Comput. Surv. **46**(4), 1–29 (2014)
12. Liu, W., Wang, X., Peng, W.: State of the art: secure mobile payment. IEEE Access **8**, 13898–13914 (2020)
13. Lodderstedt, T., McGloin, M., Hunt, P.: OAuth 2.0 threat model and security considerations (2013)
14. MITRE: CVE-2018-13439 (2018). https://www.cvedetails.com/cve/CVE-2018-13439/
15. Mulliner, C., Robertson, W., Kirda, E.: VirtualSwindle: an automated attack against in-app billing on android. In: ASIA CCS 2014 (2014)
16. PHP: API document of hash function in PHP (2020). https://www.php.net/manual/en/function.hash.php
17. Reaves, B., Scaife, N., Bates, A., Traynor, P., Butler, K.R.: Mo(bile) money, mo(bile) problems: analysis of branchless banking applications in the developing world. In: USENIX Security 2015 (2015)
18. Reynaud, D., Song, D., Magrino, T.R., Wu, E., Shin, E.C.: FreeMarket: shopping for free in android applications. In: NDSS 2012 (2012)

19. Sun, F., Xu, L., Su, Z.: Detecting logic vulnerabilities in e-commerce applications. In: NDSS 2014 (2014)
20. Tumbleson, C.: Apktool (2020). https://ibotpeaches.github.io/Apktool/
21. Wang, R., Chen, S., Wang, X.F., Qadeer, S.: How to shop for free online security analysis of cashier-as-a-service based web stores. In: S&P 2011 (2011)
22. Wang, Y., Hahn, C., Sutrave, K.: Mobile payment security, threats, and challenges. In: MobiSecServ 2016 (2016)
23. Wikipedia: Client Certificate (2020). https://en.wikipedia.org/wiki/Client_certificate
24. Xing, L., Chen, Y., Wang, X., Chen, S.: InteGuard: toward automatic protection of third-party web service integrations. In: NDSS 2013 (2013)
25. Yang, W., et al.: Show me the money! finding flawed implementations of third-party in-app payment in android apps. In: NDSS 2017 (2017)
26. Ye, Q., Bai, G., Dong, N., Dong, J.S.: Inferring implicit assumptions and correct usage of mobile payment protocols. In: Lin, X., Ghorbani, A., Ren, K., Zhu, S., Zhang, A. (eds.) SecureComm 2017. LNICST, vol. 238, pp. 469–488. Springer, Cham (2018). https://doi.org/10.1007/978-3-319-78813-5_24

DSS: Discrepancy-Aware Seed Selection Method for ICS Protocol Fuzzing

Shuangpeng Bai[1,2], Hui Wen[1,2(⊠)], Dongliang Fang[1,2], Yue Sun[1,2], Puzhuo Liu[1,2], and Limin Sun[1,2]

[1] School of Cyber Security, University of Chinese Academy of Sciences, Beijing 100049, China
{baishuangpeng,wenhui,fangdongliang,sunyue0205,liupuzhuo, sunlimin}@iie.ac.cn
[2] Beijing Key Laboratory of IOT Information Security Technology, Institute of Information Engineering, Chinese Academy of Sciences, Beijing 100093, China

Abstract. Industrial Control System (ICS), as the core of the critical infrastructure, its vulnerabilities threaten physical world security. Mutation-based black-box fuzzing is a popular method for vulnerability discovery in ICS, and the diversification of seeds is crucial to its performance. However, the ICS devices are dedicated devices whose programs are challenging to get, protocols are unknown, and execution traces are hard to obtain in real-time. These restrictions impede seed selection, thereby reducing the efficiency of fuzzing. Therefore, it has become our primary goal to select a high-quality seed set containing as few seeds as possible with extensive triggered traces.

In this paper, we present a novel automatic seed selection method called DSS, selecting high-quality seeds for improving fuzzing efficiency. The method is based on the observation that dissimilar response messages are generated by different device execution processes in most cases, which helps us build the connection of messages discrepancy and execution traces discrepancy to guide DSS. Expressly, we point out that dissimilar messages are effective indicators of different execution paths. Therefore, choosing ICS messages with high discrepancy as seeds can bring more initial execution traces and fewer seeds with the same semantic, which are essential to black-box fuzzing. Our experiments show that the quantity of seeds selected by DSS is significantly less than the traditional method when achieving the same trace coverage.

Keywords: ICS protocol · Fuzzing · Seed selection

1 Introduction

Industrial Control System (ICS) is a system that combines software and hardware, and is widely used in critical infrastructure, such as critical manufacturing, energy, and other fields. If the security risks are not adequately handled, it will pose a severe threat to the real world. ICS protocol is a set of special rules used for the interaction between industrial software in supervisory control layer

© Springer Nature Switzerland AG 2021
K. Sako and N. O. Tippenhauer (Eds.): ACNS 2021, LNCS 12727, pp. 27–48, 2021.
https://doi.org/10.1007/978-3-030-78375-4_2

and industrial devices in control layer. It works on monitoring remote physical devices' status and controlling remote physical devices. ICS protocols include open protocols and proprietary protocols. The former includes IEC 61850 and Modbus, etc.; the latter includes S7comm and FINS, etc. The ICS protocol has high control authority over the device, but the limited security protection puts the industrial device at risk. In recent years, the frequency and severity of attacks on industrial control systems have increased [18]. For example, national power grids of Venezuela [19] and Ukraine [2] were attacked causing widespread power outages, and the Stuxnet virus [11] attacked Iran's nuclear facilities. These events have shown how essential is the security of ICS devices to the real world. Therefore, ensuring the correct implementation of the protocols in the device is of great significance for protecting critical infrastructure.

Many traditional vulnerability discovery methods (such as static analysis and fuzzing) have achieved good results. However, ICS device security analysis has some restricted conditions, including industrial device programs are challenging to get, protocols are unknown, and execution traces are hard to obtain in real-time. Due to limited conditions, most traditional methods fail, except for black-box fuzzing. However, as a pointless method, black-box fuzzing needs information as a guide to test enough code traces in a limited time.

Rebert [16] points out that the quality of seeds is one of the decisive factors for the effect of mutation-based fuzzing. While more seeds can trigger more internal execution processes of the device, the resulting high cost of computing resources is disproportionate to improved effectiveness. Considering this contradiction, we define high-quality seeds as seeds with small quantities and extensive triggered traces. Accordingly, it is our goal to select high-quality seeds from messages with unknown semantics.

To achieve this goal, we propose DSS, a method to select high-quality seeds for fuzzing proprietary ICS protocols. DSS reduces redundant test cases by excluding seeds with repeated meanings, thereby improving the efficiency of black-box fuzzing. We find that similar messages correspond to similar program execution paths. Conversely, messages with large differences correspond to different program execution paths. Based on this observation, DSS select dissimilar messages as high-quality seeds, which contains different triggered traces.

The experiment shows that our method can select high-quality seeds from ICS messages with repeated meanings. Moreover, when the same amount of execution paths is reached, the quantity of seeds provided by our method is significantly less than the random method, and the proportion is only 0.7% in the optimal situation.

Contributions. In summary, we make the following main contributions.

- We point out that dissimilar messages are effective indicators of different execution paths. This observation provides information to reduce duplicate seeds, thereby reducing similar test cases.

- We propose a seed selection method by analyzing the discrepancy between messages. A small number of seeds with different characteristics are obtained, which can be used as a fuzzing corpus.
- We evaluate the effect of seed selection on Modbus and S7comm protocols. The seeds selected by our method is significantly less than the traditional method.

Roadmap. The remainder of this paper is organized as follows. In Sect. 2, we provide background on the industrial control system, ICS protocol, and related work. Then we propose our approach based on messages discrepancy in Sect. 3. We evaluate our method and verified its effectiveness in Sect. 4. Finally, we introduce how to apply our method to security analysis in Sect. 5.

2 Background

2.1 Industrial Control System

A typical industrial control system includes two parts: industrial software in supervisory control layer and industrial devices in control layer, as shown in Fig. 1. The industrial software sends a network request to the industrial device to control it and requires the industrial device to return information, such as start-stop status, current I/O value. The industrial device executes the instructions sent by the industrial software, converts the request message into a series of operations, and sends the response message back through the network.

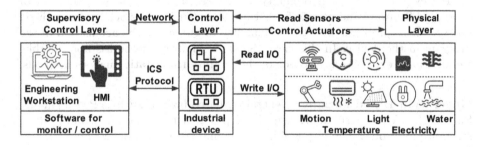

Fig. 1. Industrial control system framework.

The ICS protocol is used for the communication between industrial software and industrial devices, and it specifies the mapping of messages to functions. Apart from the standard protocol defined functions, many industrial manufacturers have expanded their products' functions, which exceed the established scope of the original protocol. Specifically, though some public and standard protocols such as Modbus and IEC 61850 are widely used, many proprietary protocols are proposed for customized features (such as controlling the start and stop, connection management, file transfer, firmware update). As a result of being defined by various manufacturers separately, these implementations lack the support of well-tested underlying libraries. Furthermore, some manufacturers firmly believe that their products are only used in a network-isolated environment. Therefore, security issues are not considered well in implementation, and the implementation has not undergone adequate safety testing. The intellectualization of industrial control systems requires breaking the isolation of the network. It is possible to expose the communication interface of the industrial device, which brings opportunities to the attacker.

2.2 Obstacles in ICS Protocol Vulnerability Discovery

Industrial device is a kind of dedicated device, so that the vulnerability discovery of ICS devices often faces the following situations: some internal programs of the devices are challenging to get, protocols are unknown, and execution traces are hard to obtain in real-time. These restricted conditions cause traditional software vulnerability discovery methods to fail for industrial devices.

Static Binary Analysis Methods. First, static binary analysis methods, such as static symbolic execution and static taint analysis, analyze binary programs to find vulnerabilities. Some firmware are hard to obtain through official channels, although some ICS manufacturers provide device firmware (such as Schneider). Some even need to be read from flash using JTAG, which is also challenging for industrial device. Second, the firmware needs to be decompressed to get the binary program. Some tools can analyze standard file systems, such as binwalk [7]. However, the extracting difficulty has increased because of the emergence of encrypted firmware and private format firmware (such as the Schneider Modicon series). These problems lead to the inability to guarantee the acquisition of the program in the device. In this case, the static analysis method is not suitable. Besides, path explosion is also one of the limitations of static analysis methods.

Generation-Based Fuzzing. Generation-based fuzzers, such as Peach [4], and Sulley [1], need expert knowledge about protocol information, including field structure division, range of possible values, and data dependence among fields. Some works use automated or manual methods to analyze traffic and reverse the protocol, such as PULSAR [5], which uses the Markov model representing the state machine of the protocol. However, these approaches may introduce new problems. If the protocol reverse is not comprehensive enough, the template's expression ability will be limited, and some input space will be missed. If there is a misunderstanding in the reverse engineering result, it will lead to error accumulation, resulting in many invalid mutations. Comprehensive and accurate protocol reverse requires manual analysis, which leads to the high cost.

Gray-Box Fuzzing. A gray-box fuzzer obtains the program execution paths triggered by the current input in real-time, thereby guiding the mutation with high efficiency. However, because it is difficult to obtain the industrial device program's execution paths in real-time, gray-box fuzzing methods, such as AFL [20], cannot be used directly unless the firmware image is emulated correctly. Some works emulate the firmware of embedded devices, such as Firmadyne [3]. Furthermore, some works combine emulation and fuzzing, such as FirmAFL [22], BaseSAFE [15] and Frankenstein [17]. However, these works are mainly focused on Linux and some specific RTOS systems, but not ICS devices. Emulating some system-independent tasks functions rather than the whole system is simpler and enough for fuzzing. The emulation needs function addresses to hook system functions. But for VxWorks, the commonly used ICS operating system, it is difficult to automatically get system function addresses because of the mixing of task code and kernel code. Therefore, the correct emulation of the ICS device requires manual analysis of the function address.

Some works use path coverage information to guide a gray-box fuzzing, focusing on ICS protocol code libraries. Polar [13] based on static code analysis and dynamic taint analysis technique, locates the function code processing statements and some security-sensitive points. And then use the knowledge of these key locations to guide the fuzzing of the ICS protocol code libraries. Peach* [14] identifies valuable data covering the new code area based on the path information collected during the fuzzing and then constructs a puzzle corpus to optimize the input generation process based on cracked packet pieces. The above methods are based on the execution path coverage for fuzzing. These methods apply to ICS protocol libraries, but not to black-box devices. As a result, coverage-guided gray-box fuzzing is not yet applicable.

Black-Box Fuzzing. Original black-box fuzzer generates test cases by mutating existing messages. Due to its wide application range and low cost, this method is often used in ICS scenarios. Because pointless mutation generates a high percentage of invalid test cases, it is necessary to analyze existing information to improve efficiency.

Some emerging black-box fuzzers for the ICS protocol generate test cases based on learning existing messages. SeqFuzzer [21] extracts format information of the EtherCAT protocol based on deep learning and generates EtherCAT test cases. GANFuzz [8] uses Generative Adversarial Network (GAN) to train a generative model on Modbus protocol data, learn protocol syntax and generate Modbus test cases. The above methods use machine learning to analyze traffic, learn protocol knowledge, and automatically generate test cases. These methods are suitable for black-box fuzzing, but these methods' versatility needs to be evaluated when applied to proprietary protocols. In addition, the above methods have potential problems. When the data distribution is unbalanced, some information hidden in the less frequent messages can be easily missed, although it may represent some essential special functions.

Also, Kim [9] put forward a fuzzing tool for Modbus protocol. It updates the seeds pool during the test in two conditions. The first is that the number of the changed bytes in requests is not equal to that of responses. The second is that response time has a significant change. However, this condition is not applicable in some situations. For example, when reading two registers and eight registers in Modbus, the request has only a one-byte difference in value, but the response changes more. The two messages are considered to have passed different program areas in the method, but they have the same function and execution process.

Table 1. Comparison of vulnerability discovery methods for ICS device

Method	Requirement	Challenge
Static binary analysis	Acquisition of firmware/program	① ②
Generation-based fuzzing	Expert knowledge about ICS protocol	③
Gray-box fuzzing	Acquisition of firmware/program, emulation	① ④
Black-box fuzzing	Messages between software and device	⑤

① Non-public firmware or program. ② Path explosion. ③ High cost of comprehensive and accurate protocol reverse. ④ Difficulty of emulation for ICS device. ⑤ Low efficiency without guidance.

In Table 1 we summarize the vulnerability discovery methods, their requirements when applied to ICS device, and the main challenges.

2.3 Seed Selection for Improving Fuzzing Efficiency

Black-box fuzzer is suitable for ICS test scenarios but lacks information guidance, resulting in low efficiency. Rebert [16] studied the influencing factors of the effect of mutation-based fuzzing, in which the quality of seeds is one of the decisive factors. While more seeds can trigger more internal execution processes of the device, the resulting high cost of computing resources is disproportionate to improved effectiveness. Moreover, compared with traditional software testing, since network-based testing is slow, there are higher requirements for fuzzing efficiency. To ensure that, black-box fuzzers need a small number of seeds that retain high execution path coverage.

Seeds selection in gray-box fuzzers such as AFL tools generates the seed set using software instrumentation technique to obtain the execution traces and use the greedy algorithm to select the optimal set. Since the program is inside the industrial device, it is challenging to obtain instrumentation information except for emulating firmware. Considering that the industrial device emulation is still difficult, but the network traffics are easy to get, it is feasible to select seeds by analyzing the relationship of message and execution trace.

3   Approach

In this section, we describe our observation and method. In Sect. 3.1, we elaborate our observation on the relationship between ICS messages and execution paths. In Sect. 3.2, we propose calculation methods to measure the difference between messages. In Sect. 3.3, we design a seed selection method based on the comparison of message discrepancy.

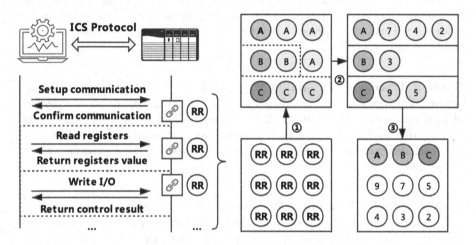

Fig. 2. Discrepancy-aware seed selection method.

In order to facilitate subsequent explanations, the combination of a response message and its request message is named an **RR** (request-response). ①*Selecting Typical RRs.* Choose typical RRs and distribute the others to the most similar typical RR. In the Fig. 2, different letters mean different types. A darker circle represents a typical RR, and the other lighter circles of the same color series are similar RRs of the typical RR. ②*Scoring all RRs.* For each typical RR, score its similar RRs by comprehensively considering the discrepancy between requests and the discrepancy between responses in the same type. In the Fig. 2, the number in the circle means the score of the RR. The larger the number, the lower the similarity within the same type. ③*Sort RRs.* Sort RRs in descending order of score and take out RRs one by one from the list until the expected number is reached.

3.1   Technique Foundation

Key Observation. Our key observation is that dissimilar response messages are generated by different device execution processes in most cases. Our strategy is choosing dissimilar response messages for a greater probability of triggering non-repetitive execution traces based on this observation. It should be noted that dissimilar response messages are not a sufficient condition for different execution traces. Dissimilar messages may also trigger the same execution process.

In more detail, we divide the situation into the following four categories according to whether the response messages in the ICS protocol are similar and whether the traces corresponding to the messages are the same.

Same Trace with Similar Response. This type includes reading values multiple times, such as reading I/O or time. Except for a small number of changes, the response messages of the same function remain similar. Selecting dissimilar responses can exclude responses with the same function and ensure that the seed set size is small.

Different Trace with Dissimilar Response. This type includes establishing a connection, reading time, reading I/O value, writing I/O value, etc. Different functions correspond to dissimilar responses, which means that this type of response is bound to its function. Selecting dissimilar responses can select messages with different functions, ensuring that more original input execution paths are covered.

Same Trace with Dissimilar Response. This type includes the function of reading a large amount of data at one time, such as reading the value of multiple consecutive addresses or downloading programs from the device. Because the data part in protocol is easy to change and the structure part is relatively stable. Taking Modbus as an example, when the request messages contain different reading bytes, industrial devices will give back responses with different lengths. The similarity of these responses is low, but the execution traces are basically the same. However, in this case, request messages with the same function are similar. Moreover, the dissimilar response is often caused by long messages, which are rare because industrial devices need to ensure real-time performance, and most of the packets are small in length.

Different Trace with Similar Response. This type includes some controlling commands and writing operations. Although the functions are different, the response messages only contain similar and simple confirmation information. In this case, only choosing dissimilar response messages may result in missing response with different functions. However, if there are discernible differences between the request messages of different functions, we can get different execution paths by selecting dissimilar requests. Otherwise, some functions may be ignored, in the rare case where the request message and the received message are both very similar to other messages, but the function is unique.

Statistical Results. We have counted the average execution path differences corresponding to response messages with different similarities. In the S7comm protocol, the top 20% most dissimilar response messages have an average execution path difference of 58.18%, and the top 20% most similar response messages have an average execution path difference of 29.28%. In the Modbus protocol, the top 20% most dissimilar response messages have an average execution path difference of 69.23%, and the top 20% most similar response messages have an average execution path difference of 33.80%.

3.2   Calculation of Discrepancy

In this part, we propose a normalized discrepancy calculation formula between messages based on text distance. Levenshtein distance [12] refers to the minimum number of editing operations (replacing, inserting, and deleting a character) required to convert two strings from one to the other. The hamming distance [6] refers to the number of different bytes at the same position in two equal-length strings.

First, we propose a general discrepancy calculation method based on text distance.

$$discrepancy = distance(str_1, str_2) \qquad (1)$$

Second, $discrepancy_{lev}$ and $discrepancy_{ham}$ are designed based on levenshtein distance and hamming distance. The range of $discrepancy_{lev}$ is between 0 and the maximum length of two strings. Hamming distance requires two strings to be equal in length so that the longer string needs to be curtailed to the same length as the other before calculating. The range of $discrepancy_{ham}$ is between 0 and the minimum length of two strings.

$$discrepancy_{lev} = distance_{lev}(str_1, str_2) \qquad (2)$$

$$discrepancy_{ham} = distance_{ham}(str_1, str_2) \qquad (3)$$

Third, due to the considerable value of the distance between long messages, our method normalizes the distance to eliminate the influence of long messages. The discrepancy ranges from 0 to 1.

$$discrepancy_{lev} = \frac{distance_{lev}(str_1, str_2)}{len(str_1) + len(str_2) + 1} \qquad (4)$$

$$discrepancy_{ham} = \frac{distance_{ham}(str_1, str_2)}{min(len(str_1), len(str_2))} \qquad (5)$$

3.3   Seed Selection Method Based on Discrepancy Comparison

We propose a seed selection method based on discrepancy comparison.

Preprocessing. The preprocessing process generates RRs from existing network traffic by completing the following steps. ①Divide traffic into different streams according to IP address and port. ②Remove duplicate request messages and their response. ③If there are a huge number of messages with basically repeated content, these are heartbeat packets used to confirm the survival status of the device in the ICS protocol. These packets are deleted and will not be analyzed later. ④By binding the request message with its response, a series of RRs are obtained for subsequent selection.

Selecting Typical RRs. Our method calculates and compares discrepancy between response messages and constructs a typical-set containing RRs which have typical responses. Each typical RR in the typical-set has a similar-list containing RRs similar to this typical RR. Similar-list will be used to score RRs later.

Algorithm 1: Constructing typical RR set

Input: Total_set containing all RRs, Discrepancy threshold
Output: Typical_set containing typical RRs
1 initialize p = first element of total_set;
2 initialize typical_set = empty set;
3 add p to typical_set;
4 p = Next(p);
5 **while** *p is not the last element of total_set* **do**
6   initialize q = first element of typical_set;
7   initialize t = False;
8   **while** *q is not the last element of typical_set* **do**
9   d = discrepancy of q.response_message and p.response_message;
10   **if** *d < discrepancy threshold* **then**
11   add p to similar_list of q;
12   **else**
13   t = True;
14   break;
15   q = Next(q);
16   **if** *t is True* **then**
17   add p to typical_set;
18   initialize similar_list of p = empty list;
19   p = Next(p);
20 return typical_set;

In Algorithm 1, add the first RR to the typical-set and traverse the remaining elements. During the traversal, for each element p, calculate the minimum difference between it and all typical-set elements. The difference is calculated by using Eq. 4 in Sect. 3.2. If the difference is greater than the threshold parameter, p is added to the typical-set, and the similar-list of p is initialized to empty.

Otherwise, find the element q in the typical-set that makes the difference smaller than the threshold, and add p to the similar-list of q.

Calculating the Optimal Threshold. In selecting typical RRs, input parameters include a discrepancy threshold used to control the minimum discrepancy of typical RRs' response messages. The minimum discrepancy determines the number of typical RRs. An excessively high threshold will divide RRs with different functions into the same typical RR, causing some omissions of functions. On the contrary, a too low threshold will divide RRs with the same function into different typical RRs, causing repeated selection of the same function.

A smaller threshold will get more typical RRs. ①Use random annealing method to find the threshold that makes the number of RRs approach 100. ②As the threshold decreases by 0.01 each time, Algorithm 1 is called repeatedly, and the number of typical RRs is recorded until the number of typical RRs reaches 300. ③Calculate the proportion of the increase in the number of typical RRs caused by each threshold reduction, and the optimal threshold is the one with the largest increase ratio.

Scoring All RRs. For each typical RR, calculate its minimum difference with other typical RRs as its score. For RRs in similar-lists, our method scores them in Algorithm 2, considering both requesting and responding information.

Algorithm 2: Scoring RRs in similar-lists

Input: Typical_set containing typical RRs, Similar_list of each typical RR
Output: Scores of each RR in similar-lists

```
1  initialize t = first element of typical_set;
2  while t is not the last element of typical_set do
3  │   initialize similar_list = similar_list of t;
4  │   initialize p = first element of similar_list;
5  │   while p is not the last element of similar_list do
6  │   │   initialize other_l = similar_list_t without p;
7  │   │   p.score_response = min response discrepancy of p and RRs in other_l;
8  │   │   p.score_request = min request discrepancy of p and RRs in other_l;
9  │   └   p = Next(p);
10 │   response_l = similar_list sorted in descending order of score_response;
11 │   request_l = similar_list sorted in descending order of score_request;
12 │   p = first element of similar_list;
13 │   while p is not the last element of similar_list do
14 │   │   if response_l.index(p) < request_l.index(p) then
15 │   │   │   p.score = p.score_response;
16 │   │   else
17 │   │   └   p.score = p.score_request;
18 └   t = Next(t);
```

For each RR, in Algorithm 2, calculate the minimum discrepancy between the RR and the others in the same similar list. The discrepancy includes the discrepancy between request messages and between response messages. And then, sort the similarity list in descending order to generate request-list/response-list by the minimum discrepancy of request/response messages. Finally, the score is equal to the minimum discrepancy of the request messages if the RR index in the request-list is smaller than the index in the response-list. Otherwise, the minimum discrepancy of the response messages is used as the score. If any of the RR's request or response message is unique, the RR will get a high score through the above steps. Otherwise, our method considers the RR has a low possibility to trigger new execution traces.

Sort RRs. The higher the score of RR is, the more likely it is to be unique. Sort typical RRs in descending order by scores, and do the same for RRs in similar-lists so that RRs with different execution paths are placed first. Concatenate two sorted lists, with typical RRs first, and then our method can take out RRs one by one from the list until the expected number is reached. Choosing more messages can get higher coverage before reaching full coverage. In actual use, the selected number depends on the estimated computing resources and allowable time consumption.

4   Evaluation

4.1   Experiment Setup

Analysis Target. Since the device's program cannot be directly used for analysis, we choose common industrial protocol code libraries for analysis. The public library used here is only to evaluate the effectiveness of our method and does not limit the scope of the application of our method. The ICS protocol library used for the experiment has the requirements, including the library implements a server program, and the server can normally work under instrumentation. For the Modbus protocol, our analysis is based on the unit-test-server provided by the libmodbus library. And for the S7comm protocol, we use the server in the snap7 library.

Legitimate Messages Acquisition. The messages need to match the server software. Otherwise, the requests may look legitimate, but the server cannot parse and respond them correctly. For example, in the Modbus protocol, the used I/O addresses need to be defined in the server; otherwise, an error will be notified. Therefore, many packets that can be correctly parsed by the mentioned software are needed for experiments. To emulate these packets in an industrial control system, we obtain notwork traffic by expanding the original input. ①Perform byte-by-byte mutation on the original industrial control data packet to generate legitimate and illegitimate data packets. ②Send these packets to the server and record the response. ③Mark packets which are parsed as legitimate by Wireshark. Use these marked packets as subsequent candidates, and discard those illegitimate data packets. The basis for the above operation is that if the device response to our request with a non-abnormal response, it means that the device has correctly executed the request, which also means that the request is legitimate.

Besides, some ICS protocols need to maintain communication status. For example, the S7comm protocol requires "Setup communication" before reading and writing, and the Modbus protocol defines a serial number. For this kind of protocol, we need to send predecessor messages before sending a mutated message to ensure the test case can be parsed correctly. The status may be defined in some protocols but not mandatory to implement in code. For example, the server provided by libmodbus does not handle the serial number; that is, the test case can be sent directly without considering its predecessor data.

For the unit-test-client and unit-test-server provided by the libmodbus library, the experiment mutates the original traffic to expand the execution space. The number of edges before the expansion is 133, and after the expansion is 185, an increase of 38.1%. For the snap7 library, the number of edges changes from 199 to 734, an increase of 268.8%. Table 2 provides a comparison between the original message function and the expanded function. It is worth noting that because the original input "Start upload" function was not implemented in the server, the request for this function returned an error, which was detected by Wireshark and filtered out.

Table 2. Summary of functions under testing

Modbus		S7comm	
Function	Change	Function	Change
Read Coils	Unchanged	Setup communication	Unchanged
Read Discrete Inputs	Unchanged	CPU → Read SZL	Unchanged
Read Holding Registers	Unchanged	Start upload	Disappear
Read Input Registers	Emerge	Read Var	Unchanged
Write Single Coil	Unchanged	CPU → Message service	Emerge
Write Single Register	Unchanged	Write Var	Emerge
Write Multiple Coils	Unchanged	Time → Read clock	Emerge
Write Multiple Registers	Unchanged	PLC Stop	Emerge
Report Slave ID	Emerge	Block → List blocks	Emerge
Mask Write Register	Unchanged	Security → PLC password	Emerge
Read Write Register	Unchanged		

Binary Instrumentation. The execution path triggered by the network request needs to be obtained to evaluate the seed selection method's effectiveness. The instrumentation of ICS protocol libraries is only for the experiment. When faced with real industrial control devices, it is too challenging to achieve.

First, we limit the recorded address to the code segment of the target program. This limitation is to prevent instrumentation of the code of system library functions. These functions will generate many execution paths with low relevance to ICS protocols, and their security has been extensively studied. If these system library functions are not precluded, irrelevant information will be introduced, which will confuse subsequent analysis.

Second, the industrial control server often has multiple threads working simultaneously, including accepting network requests, running industrial control functions, and sending data packets. Therefore, we instrument all threads and record them separately. For each thread, the execution path is obtained by sequentially recording the basic block's first address.

Third, due to protection measures such as ASLR, the addresses obtained by the instrumentation are random and cannot be directly compared. In order to align these instrumentation results, we process each execution as follows: Take the first address of the first basic block of the first thread as the base address, and record the offset of each address executed to the base address.

Finally, every two consecutive basic blocks' addresses are combined as an **edge**, and all edges executed this time are added to a set. This set represents the code execution path of this message. Remove edges that can be triggered in all messages, which are not related to the function.

Evaluation Setting. As mentioned earlier, each path is transformed into a set, with internal elements as edges. To measure the quality of the selected seeds, we propose edge **coverage** as a measurement standard, which refers to the proportion of edges provided by the selected seeds. The higher the coverage, the more representative the seeds we choose; the lower the coverage, the more functions we have missed.

Besides, we compare the effectiveness of the methods by comparing the number of seeds required between different methods to achieve the same coverage. Use the ratio of the quantity required by Method A to the quantity of Method B as the measurement standard when reaching the same coverage. If the ratio exceeds 1, the performance of method A is better than method B. On the contrary, it shows that the B method is better. When the ratio is close to 1, the performance of the two methods is similar.

4.2 Message Similarity and Trace Similarity

We use the following steps to verify whether dissimilar messages indicate different execution paths. ①Select dissimilar messages by Algorithm 1 and use $discrepancy_{lev}$ as the discrepancy. Giving RR sequences in different orders and random thresholds, many message combinations, whose internal messages are dissimilar to each other, can be obtained. Calculate the number of non-repeated edges corresponding to each combination; the higher the number, the less similar the execution path. ②Randomly select messages and count the number of corresponding edges. Random sampling is performed with different selection numbers, respectively. ③Compare the corresponding edge coverage of dissimilar messages and random messages.

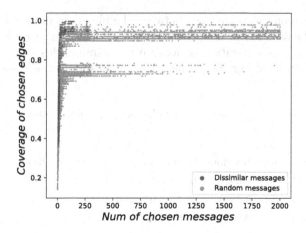

Fig. 3. Coverage of dissimilar messages and random messages in Modbus.

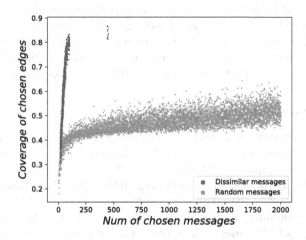

Fig. 4. Coverage of dissimilar messages and random messages in S7comm. (Color figure online)

As shown in Fig. 3 and Fig. 4, dissimilar message combinations correspond to a higher number of edges, meaning divergent execution path combinations are selected. More specifically, because the Modbus protocol is relatively simple, a combination of 250 dissimilar messages is sufficient to correspond to 95% of the execution path. At the same number of messages, random combinations that close to the same execution path just account for a small proportion. When the coverage is the same, the points corresponding to dissimilar packets are clustered on the figure's left edge, which means that fewer packets are needed. In the S7comm protocol, the effect is more significant. When the number of elements of the combination is about 100, the edge coverage of dissimilar packets has reached 80%, while the highest coverage of random packets is less than 50%. Besides, it can be drawn from the figure that it is difficult to obtain high coverage for random messages unless using a vast number of messages.

There is an apparent separation between the blue dots in each figure, and a small part of the dots are in the position where the number of packets is higher than most dots. This separation is because the minimal degree of discrepancy discrimination brings a significant increase in the number of messages in the combination.

Table 3. Average coverage in dissimilar messages and random messages

Modbus				S7comm			
Range	Dissimilar	Random	↑ratio	Range	Dissimilar	Random	↑ratio
0–100	0.81	0.69	16.6%	0–100	0.49	0.36	34.7%
100–200	0.96	0.79	20.4%	100–200	0.80	0.42	89.7%
200+	0.96	0.83	15.6%	200+	0.83	0.45	84.6%

As shown in the Table 3, in each range, the average edge coverage of dissimilar messages is more than that of random messages. Furthermore, due to the slow rise of the *Random method*'s effect, it must choose a disproportionate number of messages to achieve the same effect. In summary, this experiment shows that dissimilar messages are effective indicators of different execution paths.

4.3 Comparing with Traditional Method

A seed selection experiment is performed from the data packets obtained during the experiment preparation process in 4.1. Evaluate the performance of seed selection methods compared with *Random method*.

Seed selection methods include *Hamming method* (based on $discrepancy_{ham}$) and *Levenshtein method* (based on $discrepancy_{lev}$). The *Random method* counts the average, maximum, and minimum values of edge coverage of randomly selected message for 100 times each number. The experiment evaluated the effectiveness of the seed selection method on Modbus and S7comm protocols. The edge coverage here refers to the proportion of edges triggered by the selected seed to the edges triggered by all to-be-selected messages.

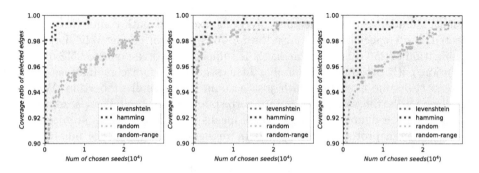

Fig. 5. Edge coverage in Modbus.

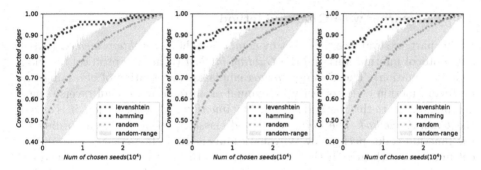

Fig. 6. Edge coverage in S7comm.

Figure 5 and Fig. 6 show that when the number of seeds is the same, the method based on discrepancy comparison can get more edges than the *Random method*, no matter which distance algorithm is based on. Each small picture represents an independent experiment based on different data, showing that the effect is robust.

Table 4. Compare with traditional method in Modbus

	Levenshtein	Hamming	Random
Coverage-0.75	**48**(41,58)	67(27,145)	64(38,94)
Coverage-0.80	**49**(42,59)	107(29,147)	143(81,215)
Coverage-0.85	**49**(42,59)	111(40,147)	314(209,390)
Coverage-0.90	**49**(42,59)	113(44,150)	648(336,838)
Coverage-0.95	**61**(42,96)	201(158,227)	3722(870,5720)

Table 5. Compare with traditional method in S7comm

	Levenshtein	Hamming	Random
Coverage-0.75	**66**(62,70)	197(193,200)	8676(8242,9055)
Coverage-0.80	**146**(64,306)	773(202,1848)	10781(10259,11187)
Coverage-0.85	**797**(188,1940)	2273(1364,2733)	13619(12982,14142)
Coverage-0.90	**3193**(1760,5658)	5188(3548,6043)	17433(17100,17655)
Coverage-0.95	**9039**(8371,9899)	14272(9029,20051)	22371(22238,22485)

The experiment also evaluates the number of seeds required by different methods when the same coverage is reached. Among them, the smaller the number, the better the seed selection performance. As Shown in Table 4 and Table 5, in both Modbus and S7comm protocol experiments, the order of the effects of methods is *Levenshtein method* > *Hamming method* ≫ *Random method*. Specifically, when achieving the same effect, the *Levenshtein method* provides about 60 seeds, which is only 0.76% to 1.64% of the traditional method.

4.4 Comparing with Guiding Method

In this part, we evaluate the effect by comparing the *Levenshtein method* (without protocol information) and the *Guiding method* (using the protocol function code information). The *Guiding method* emulates the situation of obtaining the protocol function code correctly by manual or automatic protocol reverse engineering. Owing to this method is guided by function code information, it is called the *Guiding method*. The *Guiding method* classifies the messages according to the function code specified by Wireshark and then selects messages from different functions each time. It should be noted that this method is only designed for comparison with our method and cannot be directly applied to real situations. As proprietary protocols cannot be parsed in Wireshark, obtaining information about function codes in the real world requires much extra work.

In the Modbus experiment, both *Levenshtein method* and *Guiding method* are significantly better than the *Random method*, and the *Guiding method* is slightly better than *Levenshtein method*. This small gap shows that our method adaptively learns the function code information of Modbus. As shown in Fig. 7, the effect of the *Guiding method* is very significant, indicating that for the Modbus protocol, function code information can distinguish functions well. Under the same function code, there are relatively few different traces. The average number of trace types for each function code is 3.4, so that the information provided by the function code is sufficient for efficient seed selection. The function-code-based *Guiding method* can quickly achieve complete coverage of the original edges.

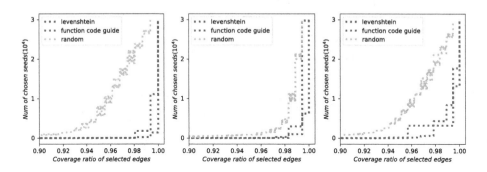

Fig. 7. Comparison of *Levenshtein method* and *Guiding method* in Modbus.

In the S7comm experiment, as shown in Fig. 8, the *Levenshtein method* and *Guiding method* have similar effects when coverage less than 0.7, which significantly better than the *Random method*. But when the coverage is higher, the *Guiding method*'s effect begins to deteriorate until it is close to the *Random method*. However, our method is still significantly better than those methods. This is because the S7comm protocol is more complicated so that the function code provides insufficient information. There are relatively more different traces under the same function code, and the average trace type number of each function code is

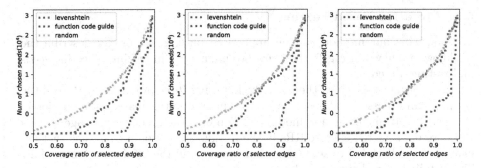

Fig. 8. Comparison of *Levenshtein method* and *Guiding method* in S7comm.

30.8. This leads to the fact that *only using function code information is not enough to select seeds with high coverage.* The experiment also shows that our method can learn more complex protocol information than function codes. Therefore, it is also effective for more complex protocols and has universality for ICS protocols.

5 Discussion

In the previous sections, we propose the seed selection method DSS and evaluated it. In this part, we will introduce how DSS is applied to security analysis. It has been verified that DSS can provide high-quality seeds for mutation-based fuzz testing. Besides, the core algorithm of DSS can also be applied to other proprietary protocol security analysis because of its ability to extract messages with different meanings. We will introduce three application scenarios, including the main application: mutation-based fuzzing, and two other scenarios: test case reduction and protocol reverse engineering.

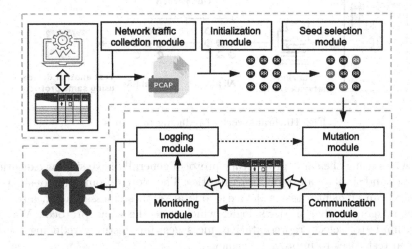

Fig. 9. Framework of fuzzing prototype using seed selection method

5.1   Mutation-Based Fuzzing

To show how our method can be applied to fuzzing, we briefly describe the workflow, as shown in Fig. 9, there are two main steps in fuzzing: selecting seeds and testing a seed.

In selecting seeds stage, there are the following three processes. ①Record the IP, port, and message information of each interaction in real work scenarios in the Network traffic collection module. ②Combine each request message and its response message to generate RRs in the Initialization module. ③Using method elaborated in Sect. 3.3 to select high-quality seeds in the Seed selection module. The detailed steps have been elaborated in Sect. 3.

In testing a seed stage, there are the following four processes. ①Mutate the seed to generate test cases in Mutation module. ②Establish a connection with the industrial device in the Communication module so that the fuzzer can interact with the device. ③Monitor the ICS device's status to determine whether it is working correctly in the Monitoring module. ④Record messages and events during the fuzzing in the Logging module. Since this fuzzer is based on a small number of seeds with high coverage, it will explore more program execution paths in a shorter time, and then efficiently discover vulnerabilities.

5.2   Reduction of Test Cases

Our method can also be used in another security testing process: reduce test cases, shown in Fig. 10. ①Fuzz an ICS device that using a proprietary protocol and record all the messages in this process as test cases. ②Transform these request and response messages to RRs and use the method proposed in Sect. 3.3 to select test cases with different meanings. ③Use these chosen test cases to test other devices using the same proprietary protocol.

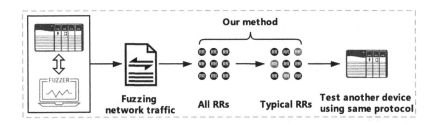

Fig. 10. Framework of reducing test cases

Devices using the same proprietary protocol generally have similar execution processes and similar causes of vulnerabilities. Therefore, if some previously used messages can efficiently test a device's code area, these messages can also efficiently trigger another device's logic, which uses the same protocol. We use Algorithm 1 to select representative messages for testing, reducing many repeated test cases to improve efficiency.

5.3   Protocol Reverse Engineering

There is a step in protocol reverse engineering called message type identification [10], which aims at dividing the message into different categories for next step, analyzing each category's specific protocol format. Our method also has the ability to classify messages, as shown in Fig. 11. The following will introduce how it assists in protocol reverse engineering. ①Convert the messages to RRs. ②Use Algorithm 1 to process all RRs to get the typical-set and the similar-list of each typical RR. ③The classification is completed by treating the packets in the same similar-list as the same type.

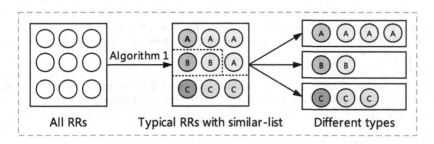

Fig. 11. Application in message type identification for protocol reverse engineering

6   Conclusion

We introduce DSS, a discrepancy-aware seeds selection method for ICS protocol fuzzing. DSS compares ICS messages to determine whether they trigger the same execution path, thereby selecting a high-quality seed set containing a small number of seeds but obtaining high edge coverage. The DSS is suitable for black-box industrial devices and proprietary protocol scenarios, where many methods cannot be applied.

When achieving the same trace coverage, the seeds selected by the *Levenshtein method* is significantly less than the traditional *Random method*, and the proportion is only 0.7% in the optimal situation. Fuzzing based on the high-quality seeds selected by the *Levenshtein method* can test core code traces in a limited time.

Acknowledgement. This paper is supported by the science and technology project of State Grid Corporation of China: "Research on 5G Electric Power security protection system and key technology verification" (Grant No. 5700-202058379A-0-0-00).

References

1. Amini, P., Portnoy, A.: Sulley fuzzing framework (2010)
2. Case, D.U.: Analysis of the cyber attack on the Ukrainian power grid. Electricity Information Sharing and Analysis Center (E-ISAC) 388 (2016)

3. Chen, D.D., Woo, M., Brumley, D., Egele, M.: Towards automated dynamic analysis for linux-based embedded firmware. In: NDSS, vol. 16, pp. 1–16 (2016)
4. Eddington, M.: Peach fuzzing platform. Peach Fuzzer **34** (2011)
5. Gascon, H., Wressnegger, C., Yamaguchi, F., Arp, D., Rieck, K.: PULSAR: stateful black-box fuzzing of proprietary network protocols. In: Thuraisingham, B., Wang, X.F., Yegneswaran, V. (eds.) SecureComm 2015. LNICST, vol. 164, pp. 330–347. Springer, Cham (2015). https://doi.org/10.1007/978-3-319-28865-9_18
6. Hamming, R.W.: Error detecting and error correcting codes. Bell Syst. Techn. J. **29**(2), 147–160 (1950)
7. Heffner, C.: Binwalk: firmware analysis tool (2010). https://code.google.com/p/binwalk/. Visited 03 Mar 2013
8. Hu, Z., Shi, J., Huang, Y., Xiong, J., Bu, X.: GANfuzz: a GAN-based industrial network protocol fuzzing framework. In: Proceedings of the 15th ACM International Conference on Computing Frontiers, pp. 138–145 (2018)
9. Kim, S., Cho, J., Lee, C., Shon, T.: Smart seed selection-based effective black box fuzzing for IIoT protocol. J. Supercomput. **76**, 1–15 (2020)
10. Kleber, S., Maile, L., Kargl, F.: Survey of protocol reverse engineering algorithms: decomposition of tools for static traffic analysis. IEEE Commun. Surv. Tutorials **21**(1), 526–561 (2019). https://doi.org/10.1109/COMST.2018.2867544
11. Langner, R.: Stuxnet: dissecting a cyberwarfare weapon. IEEE Secur. Priv. **9**(3), 49–51 (2011)
12. Levenshtein, V.I.: Binary codes capable of correcting deletions, insertions, and reversals. Soviet Physics Doklady **10**, 707–710 (1966)
13. Luo, Z., Zuo, F., Jiang, Y., Gao, J., Jiao, X., Sun, J.: Polar: function code aware fuzz testing of ICS protocol. ACM Trans. Embed. Comput. Syst. (TECS) **18**(5s), 1–22 (2019)
14. Luo, Z., Zuo, F., Shen, Y., Jiao, X., Chang, W., Jiang, Y.: ICS protocol fuzzing: coverage guided packet crack and generation. In: 2020 57th ACM/IEEE Design Automation Conference (DAC), pp. 1–6. IEEE (2020)
15. Maier, D., Seidel, L., Park, S.: BaseSAFE: baseband sanitized fuzzing through emulation. In: Proceedings of the 13th ACM Conference on Security and Privacy in Wireless and Mobile Networks, pp. 122–132 (2020)
16. Rebert, A., et al.: Optimizing seed selection for fuzzing. In: 23rd USENIX Security Symposium (USENIX Security 14), pp. 861–875 (2014)
17. Ruge, J., Classen, J., Gringoli, F., Hollick, M.: Frankenstein: advanced wireless fuzzing to exploit new Bluetooth escalation targets. In: 29th USENIX Security Symposium (USENIX Security 20), pp. 19–36 (2020)
18. Slowik, J.: Evolution of ICS attacks and the prospects for future disruptive events. Threat Intelligence Centre Dragos Inc. (2019)
19. Vaz, R., et al.: Venezuela's power grid disabled by cyber attack. Green Left Weekly (1213) 15 (2019)
20. Zalewski, M.: American fuzzy lop (2014)
21. Zhao, H., Li, Z., Wei, H., Shi, J., Huang, Y.: SeqFuzzer: an industrial protocol fuzzing framework from a deep learning perspective. In: 2019 12th IEEE Conference on Software Testing, Validation and Verification (ICST), pp. 59–67. IEEE (2019)
22. Zheng, Y., Davanian, A., Yin, H., Song, C., Zhu, H., Sun, L.: FIRM-AFL: high-throughput greybox fuzzing of IoT firmware via augmented process emulation. In: 28th USENIX Security Symposium (USENIX Security 19), pp. 1099–1114 (2019)

Threat for the Secure Remote Password Protocol and a Leak in Apple's Cryptographic Library

Andy Russon[1,2（✉）]

[1] Orange, Applied Crypto Group, Cesson-Sévigné, France
`andy.russon@orange.com`
[2] Univ. Rennes, CNRS, IRMAR - UMR 6625, 35000 Rennes, France

Abstract. The Secure Remote Password protocol is a password-based authenticated key-exchange between two parties. One advantage is to prevent offline dictionary attacks from an adversary eavesdropping the communication. We present how such an attack is feasible if the modular exponentiation at the heart of the protocol is vulnerable and leaks some data related to the password.

In the case of a fixed exponent, adding randomness during the execution is a classical protection mechanism, and such a mechanism is present in Apple's cryptographic library to randomize the exponent. Despite being intended to protect against complex side-channel attacks, we show that its usage makes the implementation vulnerable to simple side-channels such as power analysis.

This leakage observed in the library is mild but is useful for the attack we propose on the Secure Remote Password protocol.

Keywords: Apple · Dictionary attack · Euclidean splitting · Exponentiation · Secure Remote Password

1 Introduction

The Secure Remote Password (SRP) protocol [21,24] allows two parties to securely establish a session key. It belongs to the class of augmented Password-based Authenticated Key-Exchange (PAKE), attributing an asymmetric role to the two parties. One is a client and knows a secret password, and the other is a server that only stores a verifier of the password. The advantages over a Diffie-Hellman key-exchange protocol are that its design ensures mutual authentication of the parties and protection against a Man in the Middle that eavesdrops or even interferes with the communication between the client and the server.

Calculations in the SRP protocol require several modular exponentiations in a finite field defined by a large prime. The exponents are secret, and one of them is specifically derived from the password. The knowledge of this value is sufficient to impersonate a client. An open question is whether partial knowledge of it could be enough.

© Springer Nature Switzerland AG 2021
K. Sako and N. O. Tippenhauer (Eds.): ACNS 2021, LNCS 12727, pp. 49–75, 2021.
https://doi.org/10.1007/978-3-030-78375-4_3

Recently, it has been shown that implementations of a similar PAKE protocol can lead to a timing difference related to the password [4,22]. The authors used this leak as a distinguisher to filter passwords in a dictionary that do not correspond. While it is not a secret exponent that is derived from the password, a similar approach could be applied to the SRP protocol if the exponentiation algorithm is vulnerable to side-channels.

Many methods have been proposed to attack implementations of exponentiation algorithms. One category of those is passive attacks, consisting of observing the executions [15], either remotely by measuring the time taken for the calculation, or with physical access using probes to capture power consumption or electromagnetic emanations. Targets of these attacks are mainly algorithms whose behavior is dependent on the secret exponent, revealing the whole exponent or partial knowledge of it. These attacks remain relevant as recent research shows [1,2,14].

To protect against these side-channel attacks, several methods have been designed over the years. Timing attacks and simple power analysis can be avoided using algorithms with regular behavior to assure a constant-time flow of operations independent of the secret exponent. One example is the Montgomery ladder algorithm [17] that processes each bit of the exponent with the same operations. In the case of a fixed exponent, such as the SRP protocol, the exponentiation is vulnerable to more complex attacks that require the capture of many traces of execution [16]. Mechanisms relying on randomization were introduced as a protection against those attacks. One of the most known is exponent blinding by adding a random multiple of the order of the base element [9]. Another one central to this paper consists of splitting the exponent randomly in several shares [7].

However, these countermeasures do not necessarily protect from all attacks. For instance, the blinding of the exponent on NIST elliptic curves might not mask the exponent entirely due to the particular nature of the sparse order of the curves [10,20]. Concerning the exponent splitting, it was shown a correlation between the shares in the additive version of the splitting [18], and a template attack was applied on the Euclidean version of the splitting [12].

It is of interest to look at the choices made to achieve security of exponentiation algorithms in widely used cryptographic libraries, in particular for use with the SRP protocol. The source code of Apple's cryptographic library is made available to allow for "verification of its security characteristics and correct functioning".[1] This library implements the low-level implementations of primitives that can be used by developers through high-level APIs for security operation for operating systems iOS and macOS, in particular through the CommonCrypto interface for cryptographic operations or the Security Framework. Several protection mechanisms are implemented in the modular exponentiation used in the SRP protocol, including the Euclidean splitting technique, and analysis has shown the presence of a variation in its execution.

---

[1] https://developer.apple.com/security/ (bottom of the page).

In this paper, we introduce an attack on the SRP protocol when the underlying exponentiation algorithm is vulnerable to side-channels. This allows running an offline dictionary attack with two variants. The first where the attacker only observes the communication and the vulnerable exponentiation, while the other assumes an attacker that interferes as a Man in the Middle similar to the Dragonblood attack on the Dragonfly handshake [22]. We also present a vulnerability in the modular exponentiation of Apple's cryptographic library. We found that randomization of the exponent with the Euclidean splitting technique of [7] has been added in the most recent version of the library.[2] We show that it leads to a small leakage that can be measured with simple side-channels. While it is mild, it becomes much more significant from many measurements with a fixed exponent, making it possible to approximate the exponent by placing it in a smaller range. This is useful for the attack on SRP, in particular for the first variant. Although not present in the core of the paper, we found the same vulnerability in the exponentiation algorithm used with elliptic curves in the library.

The paper is organized as follows. We start in Sect. 2 with a general description of the SRP protocol. We introduce in Sect. 3 our attack on the protocol in the situation where the client uses a vulnerable exponentiation algorithm, even in the case of a small leak. Section 4 describes the modular exponentiation in Apple's cryptographic library and the leakage we found due to the Euclidean splitting of the exponent that leads to an approximation of the secret exponent. In Sect. 5, we present a simulation of a power trace of the modular exponentiation, and experiments to illustrate the effectiveness of the attack on SRP using the leak from Apple's library. We present countermeasures to avoid the leak with the Euclidean splitting in Sect. 6, and a conclusion in Sect. 7.

Responsible Disclosure. The vulnerability has been disclosed to Apple Product Security following their procedure. A security update has been made available in iOS 14.5 and macOS 11.3.

2   The Secure Remote Password Protocol

The Secure Remote Password (SRP) was introduced in [25] and is described as SRP-3 in RFC 2945 [24], and SRP-6 for use in TLS authentication is described in RFC 5054 [21]. The difference between the two versions is minor and addresses vulnerabilities that are not relevant to the paper, and we will describe the protocol using versions SRP-6 and SRP-6a. It is a password-based protocol whose main goal is to establish a key agreement between two parties in a client/server model. The password is known only from the client, while the server stores a *verifier*. They authenticate themselves by sending ephemeral data similar to a Diffie-Hellman exchange. As a result of successful authentication, the two parties share a cryptographically strong secret.

---

[2] No version number is indicated, but copyright notice and last file update refer to late 2019.

The protocol is designed such that the password cannot be derived from the communication between the parties. Therefore, an eavesdropper is unable to run an offline dictionary attack, making the protocol secure against weak passwords (e.g., a 4 or 6-digit passcode). Furthermore, if the server is compromised, the leaked data is insufficient to impersonate the client if the password is strong enough.

The protocol is described below and summarized in Fig. 1.

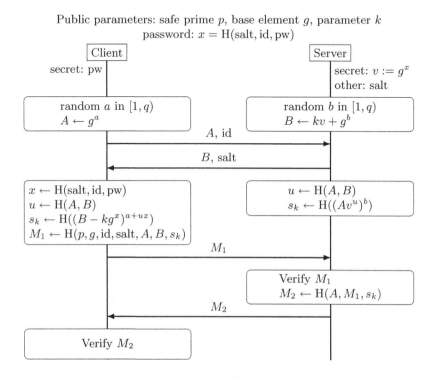

Fig. 1. Secure Remote Password (SRP) protocol, version SRP-6(a).

2.1 Description

Initialization. All calculations are performed in a finite field defined by a large prime p, and a base element g that generates a large multiplicative subgroup of order q. In particular, it is recommended that p is a safe prime (i.e., $p = 2q + 1$ with q a prime) for maximal security. Such parameters are defined in [21] to be used with the protocol for TLS authentication.

Before any authentication, a password **pw** and a salt must be chosen by the client, and a secret exponent x is derived as follows:

$$x = \mathrm{H}(\text{salt} \mid \mathrm{H}(\text{id} \mid \text{“:”} \mid \text{pw})),$$

where H is a secure hash function and | is a concatenation. For simplicity, we will omit the specific construction of the input of the hash function and specify only the values that influence the output. The client computes $v := g^x \bmod p$, and the server stores the verifier v and the salt. The client does not need to store the value x. The matter of how the server gets the verifier and the salt depends on the application that uses the protocol and is not a part of the description.

Start of Authentication. The first phase consists of the client that sends their identity and a public value $A := g^a \bmod p$ where a is an ephemeral exponent randomly generated. From the client's identity, the server retrieves the corresponding verifier and salt, then sends the salt and a public value $B := kv + g^b$ where b is an ephemeral exponent randomly generated, and k a public parameter of the protocol ($k = 3$ in SRP-6, while it is deterministically generated from the other parameters in the SRP-6a variant).

Challenge Processing and Key Agreement. The two parties can compute a value u derived from the public outputs A and B. Then we have the following equality:

$$(B - kg^x)^{a+ux} \bmod p = (Av^u)^b \bmod p.$$

Using the salt to calculate x, the client can compute the expression on the left, and the server the one on the right. From this shared secret, a session key s_k is derived. A final step is necessary to prove to each other that their keys are identical. Both client and server exchange a value that each can verify. In case of a disagreement, the authentication is aborted.

2.2   Security

To impersonate a client, it is necessary to learn the exponent x for the challenge processing phase and construct a shared secret with the server. This value is neither exchanged nor stored, and cannot be derived from the public outputs exchanged. In the case the server is compromised, an attacker learns $v := g^x \bmod p$ and x can be recovered only by dictionary attack if the password is weak (the attacker finds candidates x' for x until $g^{x'} \bmod p$ is equal to v), or by solving a discrete logarithm problem. The latter is a hard problem if the group parameters are secure (the record as of the writing of this paper is a discrete logarithm in a 795-bit finite field [3]). This is equivalent to a breach of database password hashes and is not in the security scope of the SRP protocol.

On the client's side, the value x is reconstructed when the client enters the password, using the salt sent by the server, and needs to compute the exponentiation $g^x \bmod p$. Therefore, this operation is susceptible to be done several times and is the main topic of the paper.

3   Attack on the SRP Protocol

In this section, we present the attack on the SRP protocol. The goal is to run an offline dictionary attack against weak passwords using partial knowledge of the secret exponent obtained from a vulnerable exponentiation. While everything is described using the SRP protocol, we point out that the attack could be adapted for similar protocols involving an exponentiation related to a password.

3.1   Attack Model

The target of the attack is the client's side implementation of the protocol on the part relevant to the exponentiation with the secret exponent x derived from the password. The attack consists of three main steps:

1. Obtention of the salt and client's identity (once for each salt);
2. Observe through side-channels the vulnerable implementation (might be necessary to repeat this step depending on the vulnerability);
3. Run a dictionary attack using the side-channel leakage.

The first step is necessary since those values are the other entries outside of the password for the exponent derivation. The second allows the attacker to collect data related to the exponent x that is leaked by the implementation.

When those conditions are met, the attacker creates a distinguisher of the secret exponent from the side-channel leakage. Then, from the salt and the client's identity previously obtained, a dictionary attack can be performed as summarized in Algorithm 1. The distinguisher acts as an indicator to filter out wrong passwords. Indeed this value is derived from the correct exponent, so the correct password will satisfy the verification against the distinguisher. However, it does not mean the correct password has been found, and unless great precision, many other passwords will pass the test. The performance of filtering out wrong passwords depends heavily on the precision given by the distinguisher.

Algorithm 1. Password filtering given a distinguisher.

Require: salt, id, dictionary, distinguisher
Ensure: list of password candidates
1: list ← {}
2: **for** pw' **in** dictionary **do**
3:     $x' \leftarrow H(\text{salt}, \text{id}, \text{pw'})$
4:     **if** check$(x', \text{distinguisher})$ **then**
5:         list ← list ∪ {pw'}
6: **return** list

3.2 Passive Attacker

In this version, the attacker only observes the execution on the client's side. From the observation of one or several executions, a single distinguisher is created. The password filtering is limited when the leak is identical in each execution. The main problem being one cannot improve the distinguisher precision with more observations. Nonetheless, it is more interesting with a vulnerability that leaks more data at each execution, as is the case in Apple's cryptographic library.

One possibility to make this attack more effective is to compare the list of password candidates of two users. If the number of password candidates in each list is low enough, only a few wrong passwords will appear on both lists. Then, a common password can be found in the intersection of the two lists.

3.3 Active Attacker

The previous attacker is limited to one distinguisher and its precision. In the Dragonblood attack [22], it was noticed that the modification of a MAC address allowed the acquisition of fresh measurements from an identical password, i.e., a new distinguisher. The same idea can be applied in the SRP protocol using the salt which influences the output of the hash function. An alteration of this value with a Man in the Middle attack results in a new exponent derived from the same password. A distinct distinguisher can be created from the side-channel leakage, and the password filtering of Algorithm 1 can be used to reduce even further the number of candidates iteratively.

This variant implies that the session key computed by the client is incorrect, and this could be detected with many attempts. To prevent detection on the server's side, an alternative would be an attacker that poses as the server and sends directly the chosen value for the salt. It would still imply failed authentication for the client.

Another possibility would be a service or product that changes the salt value for an identical password.

3.4 Practical Considerations

Obtention of the Client's Identity and Salt. The client's identity (email address, username, identification number, etc.) can be easily guessed when the target is identified. As for the salt, it is exposed to an eavesdropper when the communications are sent in plaintext.

However, the communication could be encrypted using a certificate-based TLS, preventing the exposure of the salt. A bypass of this added security is possible if the attacker initializes an authentication with the server by posing as the client. The attacker would receive an ephemeral public output B and the salt that corresponds to the client. An accessible example is the ProtonMail service that uses SRP for authentication since version 3.6 [19]. The data of the SRP protocol are exchanged in JSON format and can be extracted using a web browser inspector. Then it is easy to get the salt of any user by attempting an authentication.

Another layer of security could be present in the application that uses SRP, such as a second factor of authentication before the start of the SRP protocol. This would make it more difficult to pose as a client and retrieve the salt. We give details in Sect. 3.5 of the case of the Apple iCloud Keychain recovery service.

Side-Channel Observation. A leakage that can be observed at distance such as timing attacks is difficult to obtain in this protocol: calculations involving the secret exponent are only a part of the whole process, so timing analysis could be hard or impossible to exploit. Other means of attacks require physical access to the client's device, whether it is a smartphone or a personal computer. This is a limit to the application of the attack since the observation follows the entering of a password.

However, the authors of [11] have shown how a side-channel attack can be mounted using a magnetic probe near a device, or a power probe on the phone's USB charger in a discreet manner. In particular, their experiments were on an Apple iPhone.

Man in the Middle. The main problem for the second variant of the attack is that certificate-based TLS communication between client and server may harden the possibility to modify transmitted values such as the salt. So the Man in the Middle attacker would require to impersonate the server. A salt modification implies a failed authentication, and the client might take this as a mistyped password. Since it only needs to be done a few times, the attacker can space out the attack over time to pass unnoticed.

There are other possible leads to make the second variant possible such as a fault injection in the salt or the user's identity on the client device. Those solutions come with their difficulties; the one of importance here is that the effect must be controlled so the modified salt (or user's identity) must be predictable by the attacker.

Distinguishers and Efficiency of Dictionary Attack. To estimate the efficiency of the dictionary attack, we illustrate with the distinguisher that the paper focuses on: the exponentiation leaks data revealing that the exponent lies in a small interval of width w. The smaller this value is, the more effective the filtering.

The explanation lies in the construction of the exponent in the SRP protocol where it is the integer representation of the output of a cryptographic hash function. Let ℓ the maximum bit length possible of a hash function (e.g., $\ell = 256$ for SHA-256), then their outputs are expected to be evenly distributed so the exponent can be any integer in the interval $[0, 2^\ell - 1]$. Under the same salt and user's identity, running through all passwords in a dictionary will result in exponents uniformly distributed, so around $w/2^\ell$ of the exponents are expected to satisfy the distinguisher. If D is the dictionary size, then the number of password candidates is close to

$$D \cdot \frac{w}{2^\ell}.$$

In the context of the paper, this distinguisher is made possible by a leak explained in Sect. 4.1, and present in Apple's cryptographic library. The width w of the interval is related to the number of measurements of the exponentiation. That makes the first variant of the attack interesting in practice since the only lever to reduce the number of password candidates is to refine the distinguisher.

However, the use of several distinguishers in the second variant makes the filtering very effective. Indeed, a modification of the salt implies a fresh exponent and distinguisher that are independent of the original values thanks to the hash function. Then the list of password candidates can be reduced significantly by each distinguisher of width w_i:

$$D \cdot \prod_i \frac{w_i}{2^\ell}.$$

In particular, the case where two users share the same password is equivalent to the possession of two distinguishers of widths w_1 and w_2.

If the distinguisher is the bit length n of the exponent, then the exponent lies in an interval of width $w = 2^{n-1}$. Thus, around $1/2^{\ell-n+1}$ of the passwords correspond, and in the worst case, it means half the passwords are expected to be filtered out. A few dozens bit length distinguishers are generally enough depending on the dictionary size. We refer to the Dragonblood paper [22] for this particular case. While not related to the bit length of an exponent, the leak also follows a geometric distribution.

Remark 1. The reliability of the distinguisher is important. For instance, it is not guaranteed that the exponent lies in the subinterval obtained with the analysis of the leak in the modular exponentiation in Apple's cryptographic library, which could filter out the correct password.

3.5 iCloud Keychain Recovery

The iCloud ecosystem is the heart of Apple's online services and can be shared across devices from one account, and the SRP protocol is used in several places. One of the services is iCloud Keychain Recovery that allows users to escrow their keychain with Apple (that contains sensitive data such as passwords or credit cards). This service has a supplementary layer of protection through the SRP protocol (with the 2048-bit group of RFC 5054, SHA-256 as the hash function, and 64 bytes salts) using a separate password from the iCloud account: for each device, iCloud stores a backup of the keychain as a record protected with the device's password (the default when the iCloud account has a second factor of authentication activated). Thus, the keychain is secured if the iCloud account is compromised, and the content stays inaccessible from Apple. More details on the iCloud Keychain services are given in the Apple Platform Security guide.[3]

Our investigation has shown the following HTTP requests when a user signs out and back into iCloud on their device:

1. A request `get_records` is transmitted, and the server answers with a list of records associated with the iCloud account;
2. A request `srp_init` initiates the first phase of the SRP protocol containing the client's ephemeral value to access a record, and the server answers with the corresponding data: `DSID` (unique identifier of the iCloud account used as identity in SRP), the server's ephemeral value, and the salt;
3. A request `recover` for the second phase with the client's proof, and the servers replies with its proof and the record;
4. The client sends a request `enroll` with a new record protected with the same password, but with a different salt.

We have seen two situations where the recovered record is either the old one corresponding to the device or one corresponding to another enrolled device. The first case is interesting for the variant of the attack that uses several distinguishers.

Though, the realization of the attack requires the obtention of the salt and identifier. Monitoring the encrypted communications between the target's device and Apple's servers could overcome this issue, but our attempts by setting up a proxy server failed on a MacBook Pro. An alternative would be to run the `srp_init` request, but a password-based token is necessary on 2FA protected iCloud accounts (which has become mandatory for new accounts and cannot be deactivated). This token is acquired after successful authentication on the iCloud account.

In the case an attacker has already compromised an iCloud account and can bypass the second factor of authentication once, then the device can be enrolled as a trusted device. By doing so, it might happen the keychain will be synchronized directly with the other enrolled devices if the keychain option is checked in system preferences. This synchronization does not use SRP, so that makes our attack useless if the goal is to retrieve a keychain, but it could still be used to recover the target's device password.

The attack to recover a weak password on an Apple device can be realized under the following assumptions:

- Compromise the iCloud password of the targeted user;
- Bypass the second factor of authentication at least once;
- Force the user to disconnect their iCloud account on their device several times;
- Observe the side-channel leakage when the user reconnects during the execution of the SRP protocol in iCloud Keychain recovery.

Every time a new leak and salt are obtained, the dictionary attack can be performed as given in Algorithm 1.

---

[3] https://support.apple.com/guide/security/welcome/web.

4 Modular Exponentiation in Apple's Library

This section presents the modular exponentiation in Apple's cryptographic library and the leakage from the exponent randomization with the Euclidean splitting technique.

4.1 Exponent Randomization

Let x an exponent of n bits whose binary representation is

$$x = \sum_{i=0}^{n-1} x_i 2^i.$$

This value is randomized by choosing a random integer m of λ bits and compute the Euclidean division of x by m. The quotient is $a = \lfloor x/m \rfloor$ and the remainder is $b = x \bmod m$, then the exponentiation g^x is rewritten as

$$g^x = (g^a)^m g^b,$$

with three exponentiations.

This technique is called the Euclidean splitting and was introduced in [7] as an alternative to other exponent blinding methods. The authors proposed to compute simultaneously the exponentiation with the quotient a and the remainder b with Strauss-Shamir double exponentiation [8, Algorithm 9.23] for efficiency. In the case of Apple, it is computed as three successive individual exponentiations.

Quotient Bit Length Variation. A variation regarding the quotient bit length and related to the exponent was found: when divided by an integer of a fixed bit length, then the quotient bit length has two possible values. The probability that each of them is produced depends on the position of the exponent in the interval $[2^{n-1}, 2^n)$.

The definition and theorem below give the details on the partitioning of the interval and the associated probabilities.

Definition 1. *Let n, λ and β three non-negative integers with $\lambda \leq n$ and $\beta \in [0, 2^{\lambda-1})$. We note*

$$I(n, \lambda, \beta) = [2^{n-\lambda}(2^{\lambda-1} + \beta), \quad 2^{n-\lambda}(2^{\lambda-1} + \beta + 1)),$$

a subinterval of $[2^{n-1}, 2^n)$ of width $2^{n-\lambda}$.

Theorem 1. *Let d the bit length of the quotient of the Euclidean division of an integer x by an integer m chosen uniformly at random in $[2^{\lambda-1}, 2^\lambda)$. Then d is either $n - \lambda$ or $n - \lambda + 1$ and we have*

$$\Pr[d = n - \lambda + 1 \mid x \in I(n, \lambda, \beta)] = \frac{\beta + 1}{2^{\lambda-1}}. \tag{1}$$

Proof. Suppose $x \in I(n, \lambda, \beta)$ and let $x = am + b$ the Euclidean division of x by an integer m of λ bits. The lower and upper bounds on the quotient a are

$$\frac{2^{n-1} - b}{2^\lambda} \leq a = \frac{x - b}{m} < \frac{2^n - b}{2^{\lambda-1}},$$

and since $b < 2^\lambda$ and a is an integer, we have $a \geq 2^{n-\lambda-1}$. Overall, only the bit length $n - \lambda$ and $n - \lambda + 1$ are possible.

Now, if $m \leq 2^{\lambda-1} + \beta$, then we have

$$a = \frac{x - b}{m} \geq \frac{2^{n-\lambda}(2^{\lambda-1} + \beta) - b}{m} \geq 2^{n-\lambda} - \frac{b}{m},$$

and since $b < m$ and a is an integer, we have $a \geq 2^{n-\lambda}$ so the bit length of a is $n - \lambda + 1$. In this case there are $\beta + 1$ possible values for m out of $2^{\lambda-1}$, hence the probability.

The other case is when $m > 2^{\lambda-1} + \beta$, then we have

$$a < \frac{2^{n-\lambda}(2^{\lambda-1} + \beta + 1) - b}{m} \leq 2^{n-\lambda},$$

and the bit length of a is $n - \lambda$.   □

The consequence is that if m is randomly generated at uniform and its bit length is λ, then the probability that the quotient bit length is $n - \lambda + 1$ depends on which interval $I(n, \lambda, \beta)$ contains the exponent x. It is represented in Fig. 2 for $\lambda = 4$ as an illustration, to make the staircase apparent, and $\lambda = 32$ the use case in Apple's library, where the intervals are too small and close to a linear correlation between an exponent and the probability.

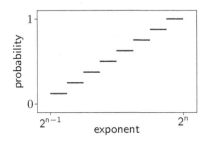
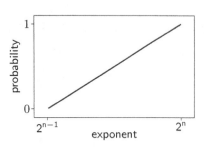

Fig. 2. Correlation between an exponent of n bits, and the probability that the bit length of the quotient of the Euclidean division with a λ-bit divisor is $(n - \lambda + 1)$ (left: $\lambda = 4$, right: $\lambda = 32$).

Exponent Approximation. An oracle that reveals $d = \lceil \log_2(x/m) \rceil$ for a fixed unknown integer x and N random integers m of an identical bit length λ follows a binomial distribution of parameters N and probability $(\beta + 1)/2^{\lambda-1}$ according to Theorem 1. This oracle acts as binomial trials to construct a confidence interval on the unknown probability when only the number of repeated experiments N and the number of successes n_{obs} that d takes the value $n - \lambda + 1$ are known. Since this probability is a characteristic of the interval $I(n, \lambda, \beta)$, then an approximation of x is deduced.

The steps are straightforward. A binomial proportion confidence interval $[p_1, p_2]$ on the probability is made observing the number of outcomes n_{obs} of successes (quotient bit length observed is $d = n - \lambda + 1$) out of N outcomes. Then, β can be estimated too by

$$p_1 2^{\lambda-1} - 1 \leq \beta \leq p_2 2^{\lambda-1} - 1,$$

and since β is an integer, let $\beta_{min} = \lceil p_1 2^{\lambda-1} - 1 \rceil$ and $\beta_{max} = \lfloor p_2 2^{\lambda-1} - 1 \rfloor$. Finally, the approximation on x is made by the concatenation of the contiguous intervals $I(n, \lambda, \beta_{min})$ to $I(n, \lambda, \beta_{max})$:

$$[2^{n-\lambda}(2^{\lambda-1} + \beta_{min}), \quad 2^{n-\lambda}(2^{\lambda-1} + \beta_{max} + 1)).$$

This interval is likely to contain the secret exponent x depending on the confidence level.

This approximation makes it possible to construct a distinguisher for the attack on the SRP protocol.

4.2 Exponentiation Algorithm

There are several exponentiation algorithms in the library. The blinded modular exponentiation is implemented in the function `ccdh_power_blinded`[4]. The overall process consists of three individual successive exponentiations, with other blinding techniques, and is summarized in Algorithm 2 with a random divisor of $\lambda = 32$ bits.

The exponentiation algorithm used from line 5 to line 7 is a 2-bit windowing method presented in Algorithm 3 called *square-square-multiply-always*. The number of iterations is dependent on the input bit length: if the input bit length is d, there are $\lceil d/2 \rceil$ iterations of the loop. This can be revealed by side-channels by counting the number of patterns on power consumption or electromagnetic trace (see Sect. 5.1). The divisor bit length is fixed and known in advance, but those of the quotient and the remainder are variable.

---

[4] In the file `ccdh/src/ccdh_power_blinded.c`.

Algorithm 2. Blinded modular exponentiation in Apple's CoreCrypto library

Require: x, g, p
Ensure: $g^x \bmod p$

   Modulus, exponent, and base blinding
1: $p^\star \leftarrow$ **blinding**(p) ▷ $p^\star = p \cdot$ random
2: $g^\star \leftarrow$ **blinding**(g) ▷ $g^\star = g + p \cdot$ random
3: $m \leftarrow$ random integer in $[2^{31}, 2^{32})$
4: $a \leftarrow \lfloor x/m \rfloor, b \leftarrow x \bmod m$

   Exponentiation
5: $t_1 \leftarrow g^{\star a} \bmod p^\star$
6: $t_2 \leftarrow t_1{}^m \bmod p^\star$
7: $t_3 \leftarrow g^{\star b} \bmod p^\star$
8: **return** $(t_2 \cdot t_3) \bmod p$ ▷ $(g + p \cdot \text{random})^{am+b} \bmod p = g^x \bmod p$

Algorithm 3. Square-square-multiply always exponentiation.

Require: $g, a = (a_{d-1}, \ldots, a_0)_2$ with $a_{d-1} = 1$
Ensure: g^a

1: **for** $i = 0$ to 3 **do**
2:     tab$[i] \leftarrow g^i$
3: $r \leftarrow 1$
4: **for** $i = \lceil d/2 \rceil - 1$ **down to** 0 **do**
5:     $r \leftarrow r^2$
6:     $r \leftarrow r^2$
7:     $r \leftarrow r \cdot$ tab$[2a_{2i+1} + a_{2i}]$
8: **return** r

For a fixed exponent of bit length n, we have seen that there are two possible bit lengths d for the quotient and can be used to make an approximation on the exponent. Both can happen using different values for m, but it is not always possible to distinguish them with the *square-square-multiply-always*. If $n - \lambda$ is odd, then

$$\left\lceil \frac{n - \lambda}{2} \right\rceil = \left\lceil \frac{n - \lambda + 1}{2} \right\rceil = \frac{n - \lambda + 1}{2}, \tag{2}$$

so the quotient bit length is not leaked, but n can still be deduced from the formula. On the contrary, if $n - \lambda$ is even, then

$$\left\lceil \frac{n - \lambda + 1}{2} \right\rceil = \left\lceil \frac{n - \lambda}{2} \right\rceil + 1, \tag{3}$$

so the algorithm runs with a different number of iterations for each of the possible quotient bit lengths, and the bit length n of the exponent x can also be deduced. Though, it requires several observations of exponentiations to be sure if we are situated in one or the other case. As a consequence, one measure is not sufficient to know exactly the bit length n, but the remark below can make it possible in the SRP protocol.

Remark 2. On the client's side in the SRP protocol, the exponentiation involving the exponent derived from the password is computed in the call of the function in line 4 of Fig. 3 using the blinded exponentiation. But we noticed it is also computed with a different algorithm in line 1, but the result stored in the variable v is never used thereafter (only to be cleared from memory). This algorithm is Montgomery ladder [17] and starts the process at the most significant bit, leaking the bit length of x. Therefore, the bit length can be known from one measure.

```
1   cczp_power(ccsrp_ctx_zp(srp), v, ccsrp_ctx_gp_g(srp), x);
2
3   /* Client Side S = (B - k*(g^x)) ^ (a + ux) */
4   ccsrp_generate_client_S(srp, S, k, x, u, B);
```

Fig. 3. Dummy exponentiation $g^x \bmod p$ on the client side in the SRP protocol in Apple's cryptographic library.

5 Experimental Results

In this section, we present the captures of power consumption of the modular exponentiation to observe the leak from Apple's library, and experiments to illustrate the effectiveness of the attack on SRP with this leak.

5.1 Power Trace Capture

This part has been made in collaboration with Cyril Delétré, a member of the author's team.

The variation of the quotient bit length can be revealed by side-channel by counting the number of patterns on power consumption or electromagnetic trace. We have selected the Raspberry Pi Zero SoC as it offers a good compromise between computing performances, hardware complexity, and power supply configuration. First, to get a constant computing capacity and minimize the noise on the power line the CPU frequency has been fixed to 700 MHz and the HDMI/TV output has been turned off (this allowed cleaner traces). Starting with a fresh Raspberry Pi OS setup we have built and installed the CoreCrypto library from the sources. Then we have written in C language a program that toggles a GPIO line on the SoC before and after the function from CoreCrypto has been called. This way the oscilloscope can:

- Measure the power consumption with a first probe connected to a resistor (3.3 Ω in our case) in series on the 5 V power line;
- Trigger the start of the computing on a second probe connected to the GPIO line (Figs. 4 and 5).

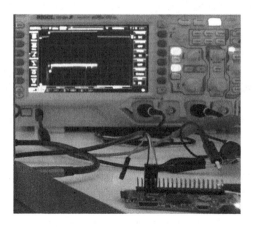

Fig. 4. Measurement of power consumption on a Raspberry Pi Zero.

Finally, we have automated the batch of measurements with a script written in Python 3 that:

- Launches the calculation on the Raspberry Pi Zero using the UART serial console (less disturbance compared to a USB or SSH/telnet console);
- Downloads after each run the data from the oscilloscope using its TCP remote console.

We chose the 2048-bit group of RFC 5054 [21] for the experiment, and the exponent

$$x = \texttt{d3afa905fededc64bc907b809da3dcb} \\ \texttt{484763c25c3b4728bb081a97cf9f0a5} \tag{4}$$

in hexadecimal format. For each execution, the pseudo-random number generator of CoreCrypto used in the function `ccdh_power_blinded` was initialized with a random seed and was repeated 10000 times.

We give two sample traces in Fig. 6 where we see that the major part of each trace corresponds to the exponentiation with the quotient (a vertical line indicates the beginning of the individual exponentiations), and a zoom on the end of this part in Fig. 7 reveals that it is shorter on the first trace than the second one by one pattern of *square-square-multiply*.

It is interesting to note that we do not necessarily need to count the patterns *square-square-multiply* every time since the approximation only needs to distinguish between the two cases. However, it is important to do it at least once to find the bit length of the exponent. In this example, we found that there are respectively 108 and 109 loop iterations on the quotient exponentiation. According to Eq. (3), we deduce that the exponent is a 248-bit integer which is consistent with the given value in Eq. (4).

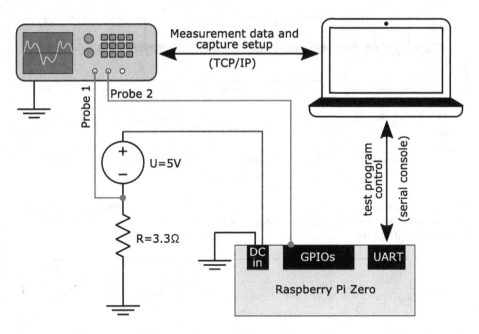

Fig. 5. Configuration of the experimental setup of the oscilloscope and Raspberry Pi Zero.

We remark that this can still be found even when the patterns are hard to distinguish if the noise is too high, as long as the beginnings of the individual exponentiations are exposed. Indeed, using the fact that the random divisor is always a 32-bit integer, then there are always 16 iterations of the loop. Therefore, the number of iterations with the exponentiation with the quotient can be deduced from the length between the two first dashed lines (taking into account the square and multiply of the precomputation).

We can find easily the start of the exponentiations in the captures thanks to the presence of a valley that corresponds to the first loop of the *square-square-multiply-always* algorithm. Because the exponentiation is initialized with the value $p - 1$, the second squaring is 1^2 followed by a multiplication by 1. Both operations manipulate very low Hamming weight values, and this has a significant impact on power consumption.

We used this to classify the traces in the two expected groups using the position of the valley corresponding to the first loop of the exponentiation with the random divisor. Many traces had major disruptions, but this method proved to work well enough for 9356 traces, with 6099 corresponding to the "109" group. Then the observed frequency was 0.6519 which is close to the probability we tried to estimate around 0.6538 for the exponent x.

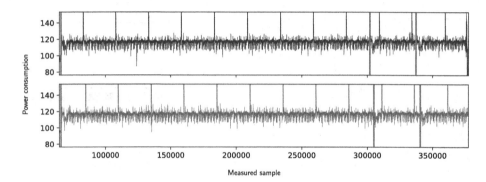

Fig. 6. Two power trace captures of an exponentiation blinded with the Euclidean splitting with an identical exponent (vertical lines represent the start of each of the three exponentiations).

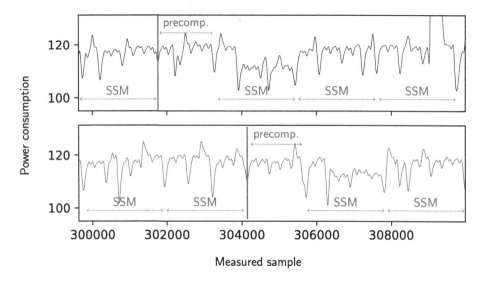

Fig. 7. Zoom on the end of the exponentiation with the quotient, and the start of the one with the random divisor. The second trace has one more pattern of *square-square-multiply* (SSM).

5.2   Dictionary Attack on SRP

The case of several bit length distinguishers known to the attacker has been well established in [4,22], so we focus on the distinguisher given by the Euclidean splitting of the exponent as implemented in Apple's library.

We ran the experiment with the following parameters for the SRP protocol:

- SHA-256 as the hash function (exponents are in the interval $[0, 2^{256})$);
- 2048-bit group of RFC 5054;
- Salt of 16 bytes;
- 6-digit password.

Given a random password and salt, the secret exponent x was derived according to the SRP protocol (using "id" as the client's identity). We simulated the leak for $N = 1000$ exponentiations following the description of the modular exponentiation in Apple's library, then an approximation was made in the form $[x_{min}, x_{max}]$ using the Wilson score interval [23] and a confidence level of 95%, as described in Sect. 4.1. It has the advantage over a normal approximation to be more suited for a small sample size N or when the probability to estimate is close to 0 or 1. All guessed passwords whose derived exponent fell in the interval were kept as candidates.

We repeated the experiment for 10000 different passwords and collected the exponent values, the number of password candidates found, and if the password was correctly included amongst the candidates. The results are given in Fig. 8.

An approximation on the exponents of odd bit length cannot be made as we have seen in Sect. 4.2, so the number of password candidates for those is way higher and does not appear (except for exponents of odd bit length less than 251 represented by the isolated dots on the left).

As a result, there were only 6846 cases with less than 32000 password candidates, and the correct password was included in the list for 95.5% of them, which is consistent with the confidence level.

We see that the number of candidates is way lower for exponents near a power of 2. This is a consequence of the Wilson score interval that gives a better approximation when the probabilities are near 0 or 1. Therefore there is a concave curve between each power of 2 for exponents of even bit length.

The best result was a password with a corresponding exponent around $2^{243.17}$ and was successfully included amongst a list of 8 candidates.

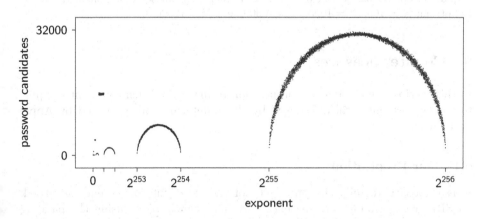

Fig. 8. Number of password candidates with $N = 1000$ measures as a function of the secret exponent x.

In a second experiment, we looked at the effects of the number N of measures on the number of password candidates. We kept the same settings as the previous with the two following changes:

- Exponents have bit length $n = 256$;
- The number of measures N ranged from 10^2 to 10^5.

The results are given in Fig. 9, where we can see that when the sample size is increased by a factor of 10, the number of password candidates is decreased by a factor around $\sqrt{10}$ due to the binomial approximation.

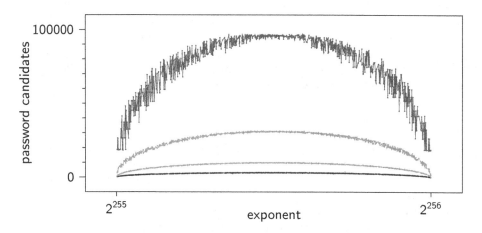

Fig. 9. Number of password candidates as a function of the secret exponent (from top to bottom: $N = 100$, $N = 1000$, $N = 10000$, and $N = 100000$).

6   Countermeasures

In this section, we present our proposition to make the Euclidean splitting protected against our attack, followed by the countermeasure proposed by Apple developers.

6.1   Our Proposition

It is necessary to hide the bit length of the exponent to prevent the attack on SRP using a bit length distinguisher. This can be done using the padding proposed in [5] where x is padded with the group order q so the result of the exponentiation is unchanged. Combined with an exponentiation algorithm with a regular behavior, nothing on the exponent is leaked from simple side-channels.

However, in the context of SRP, the group order can be much higher than the exponents, so the above technique adds a large cost to the execution. We present an alternative using a precomputed value. If the exponent x can have a maximum bit length ℓ, then it can be replaced by

$$x_{\text{pad}} = x + 2^{\ell}.$$

Let $y := g^{-2^{\ell}} \bmod p$ a precomputed value, then $g^x \bmod p$ can be calculated as follows:

$$g^{x_{\text{pad}}} \cdot y \bmod p.$$

The extra cost is moderate since it adds one multiplication, and the exponentiation involves an exponent with one bit longer than the largest exponent possible.

The Euclidean splitting can be used, but it is necessary to take care of the quotient bit length. We suppose the exponent has been replaced by the padded value x_{pad} with one of the two techniques above, and the Euclidean splitting technique is applied with a random divisor m of λ bits:

$$a = \lfloor x_{\text{pad}}/m \rfloor, \quad b = x_{\text{pad}} \bmod m.$$

From the padding technique we know the bit length n of x_{pad} in advance, so the two possible quotient bit lengths are $n - \lambda$ and $n - \lambda + 1$. We can replace the quotient a by

$$a_{\text{pad}} = a + 2^{n-\lambda+1}$$

to hide the bit length, and use the precomputed value $z := g^{\lambda-n-1}$ to compute $g^{x_{\text{pad}}} \bmod p$ as:

$$(g^{a_{\text{pad}}} \cdot z)^m \cdot g^b \bmod p.$$

Again, the extra cost is moderate since it adds one multiplication and only 1 or 2 bits on one exponent.

Remark 3. In the case where the exponentiation algorithm is the 2-bit windowing method of Algorithm 3 used in Apple's library, the quotient bit length can be directly hidden with a padding on x only. With exponents less than 2^{ℓ} for ℓ even, the padded value $x_{\text{pad}} = x + 2^{\ell}$ is an integer of odd bit length $\ell + 1$. In Sect. 4.2 we saw that the number of iterations of the loop with the quotient as an exponent is always the same in this situation (when λ is even).

6.2 Apple's Proposition

The solution retained by Apple is to replace the exponentiation by the Montgomery ladder algorithm [17] given in Fig. 10, while still using the Euclidean splitting.

The algorithm works even if the leading bits of the exponent are set to 0. However, this case would imply a multiplication by 1 and a squaring of 1 which is easy to detect on a power trace as we proved in Sect. 5.1. To avoid this pitfall, the modular arithmetic has been replaced with the Montgomery representation so the unity does not have a low Hamming weight representation. This is done by the function cczp_to_ws before the loop in Fig. 10.

When used for iCloud Keychain, we have confirmed that the loop bounds are fixed with 225, 32, and 32 loop iterations respectively for the exponentiations with the quotient, random divisor, and remainder.

```
1   ccn_set(n, r1, s);
2   ccn_seti(n, r, 1);
3   cczp_to_ws(ws, zp, r, r);
4
5   cc_unit ebit = 0;
6   for (int bit = (int)ebitlen - 1; bit >= 0; --bit) {
7       ebit ^= ccn_bit(e, bit);
8       ccn_cond_swap(n, ebit, r, r1);
9       cczp_mul_ws(ws, zp, r1, r, r1);
10      cczp_sqr_ws(ws, zp, r, r);
11      ebit = ccn_bit(e, bit);
12  }
13
14  // Might have to swap again.
15  ccn_cond_swap(n, ebit, r, r1);
```

Fig. 10. Excerpt of the Montgomery ladder for modular exponentiation in the updated version of CoreCrypto.

7   Conclusion

We showed an attack on the SRP protocol when the modular exponentiation is vulnerable to side-channels, so an attacker can perform a dictionary attack to find a weak password. Then, we presented a leak we found in Apple's cryptographic library that comes from the presence of a protection mechanism that randomizes exponents through Euclidean divisions. We analyzed it and showed that a passive attacker can approximate the secret exponent from several measures, and run an offline dictionary attack on SRP. It is not negligible from a few thousand observations of the exponentiation and can produce a list of hundreds of candidates from a dictionary containing millions of passwords.

Our findings were shared with Apple in responsible disclosure and the vulnerability was patched in iOS 14.5 and macOS 11.3.

Like other works, this paper highlights that insecure exponentiations are still deployed in cryptographic libraries and that a small leak can be enough to diminish the security of a protocol such as SRP.

Acknowledgments. The author would like to thanks the anonymous reviewers for their comments, Apple Product Security for their collaboration, and finally his colleague Cyril Delétré who provided the power trace captures.

A   SRP Requests and Responses in iCloud Keychain Recovery

In this appendix, we present the HTTP request srp_init in the context described in Sect. 3.5.

The captures were made on a secondary device using Wireshark[5] and Frida[6] to export the TLS session keys for decryption.

```
1  POST /escrowproxy/api/srp_init HTTP/1.1
2  Host: p49-escrowproxy.icloud.com:443
3  (...)
4  Authorization: Basic Y29 (...) BFVA==
5  (...)
6
7  <?xml version="1.0" encoding="UTF-8"?>
8  <!DOCTYPE plist PUBLIC "-//Apple//DTD PLIST 1.0//EN" "http://www.apple.com/
      DTDs/PropertyList-1.0.dtd">
9  <plist version="1.0">
10 <dict>
11   <key>blob</key>
12     <string>pIC8heH+SbC1HjnugsfBBc (...) +2+CM8q8hItheOscqwA==</string>
13   <key>command</key>
14     <string>SRP_INIT</string>
15   <key>label</key>
16     <string>com.apple.icdp.record.et3n (...) 8HqM</string>
17   (...)
18 </dict>
19 </plist>
```

Fig. 11. Client's side of the initialization phase of the SRP protocol in iCloud Keychain recovery.

In Fig. 11, the ephemeral value A is base64 encoded and corresponds to 256 bytes, consistent with the 2048-bit group. The server's answer is given in Fig. 12, and contains the salt and ephemeral value B at the end of the data in the base64 string respBlob, each preceded by their length in bytes: 64 and 256.

```
1  <?xml version="1.0" encoding="UTF-8" standalone="yes"?>
2  <!DOCTYPE plist PUBLIC "-//Apple//DTD PLIST 1.0//EN" "http://www.apple.com/
      DTDs/PropertyList-1.0.dtd">
3  <plist version="1.0">
4  <dict>
5    <key>status</key>
6      <string>0</string>
7    <key>message</key>
8      <string>Success</string>
9    <key>version</key>
10     <integer>1</integer>
11   <key>dsid</key>
12     <string>28 (...)</string>
13   <key>ClubTypeID</key>
14     <integer>0</integer>
15   <key>respBlob</key>
16     <string>AAABiAAAAKQAAAAAPbZQrX (...) jsxg48nknPybRNHkTM=</string>
17 </dict>
18 </plist>
```

Fig. 12. Server's side of the initialization phase of the SRP protocol in iCloud Keychain recovery.

---

[5] https://www.wireshark.org.
[6] https://frida.re.

We confirmed on the first device that the SRP protocol is executed to retrieve the same record and salt after signing in and out. The new record created for the first device is the one that is used on the secondary device when the experiment is repeated.

B   Elliptic Curve and SPAKE2+

In this appendix, we present briefly the implementation of the exponentiation (scalar multiplication) with elliptic curves where the Euclidean splitting technique is also used. We first present the differences of the algorithm implementation, and the consequence on the password-based authenticated key-exchange protocol SPAKE2+, which can be attacked similarly as with SRP.

B.1   Elliptic Curve Scalar Multiplication

The elliptic curves named `secp192r1`, `secp224r1`, `secp256r1`, `secp384r1`, and `secp521r1` share the same exponentiation algorithm that is implemented in the function `ccec_mult`.[7]

The whole exponentiation is given with generic group notations in Algorithm 4. It is randomized with the Euclidean splitting, but we note differences with the previous case of modular exponentiation:

- A padding to hide the bit length of the exponent x with the group order is applied [5];
- A padding is applied on the remainder of the Euclidean division, so the bit length of the remainder is hidden;
- The individual exponentiations are executed with the Montgomery ladder algorithm that leaks the bit length of the exponents.

With a padding on the remainder, the only variation in the execution of the `ccec_mult` function is the exponentiation with the quotient. As a consequence, the timing execution of the whole exponentiation leaks the bit length of the quotient. An approximation of the secret exponent can be done with timing analysis if the auxiliary processing before and after the call of the function can be controlled.

This issue has been addressed in the updated version of the library. The Montgomery ladder algorithm has been tweaked to make it work when leading bits are set to 0 using characteristics of the algorithm and the point addition formulas from co-Z arithmetic [13].

---

[7] In the file `ccec/src/ccec_mult.c`.

Algorithm 4. Blinded elliptic curve scalar multiplication with NIST elliptic curves in Apple's cryptographic library

---

Require: x, g of order q
Ensure: g^x

1: $x_1 \leftarrow x + q - 2^{32}$
2: $x_2 \leftarrow x + 2q - 2^{32}$
3: **if** $\lceil \log_2(x_1) \rceil = \lceil \log_2(q) \rceil + 1$ **then**
4: $\quad x_{\text{pad}} \leftarrow x_1$
5: **else**
6: $\quad x_{\text{pad}} \leftarrow x_2$
7: $m \leftarrow$ random integer in $[2^{31}, 2^{32})$
8: $a = \lfloor x_{\text{pad}}/m \rfloor$, $b \leftarrow x_{\text{pad}} \bmod m$
9: $t_1 \leftarrow g^a$
10: $t_2 \leftarrow t_1{}^m$
11: $t_3 \leftarrow g^{b+2^{32}}$
12: **return** $t_2 \cdot t_3$ $\triangleright\ g^{am} \cdot g^{b+2^{32}} = g^x$

B.2 SPAKE2+

The SPAKE2+ protocol [6] is another PAKE protocol similar to the SRP protocol and shares properties such as protection against an eavesdropper or a Man in the Middle. In Apple's library, it is solely used with elliptic curves.

The attack on SRP can be adapted to work with this protocol, and there are a few differences. The first is that two exponents are derived from the password, and, according to the source code of the library, the client computes two distinct exponentiations with these values. Since the exponentiation is vulnerable, it gives two distinguishers to run an offline dictionary attack. In the situation of the first variant, where the attacker is only an observer, this makes the filtering more effective.

References

1. Aldaya, A.C., García, C.P., Brumley, B.B.: From A to Z: projective coordinates leakage in the wild. IACR Trans. Cryptogr. Hardw. Embed. Syst. **2020**(3), 428–453 (2020). https://doi.org/10.13154/tches.v2020.i3.428-453
2. Aranha, D.F., Novaes, F.R., Takahashi, A., Tibouchi, M., Yarom, Y.: LadderLeak: breaking ECDSA with less than one bit of nonce leakage. In: Ligatti, J., Ou, X., Katz, J., Vigna, G. (eds.) 2020 ACM SIGSAC, CCS 2020, pp. 225–242. ACM (2020). https://doi.org/10.1145/3372297.3417268
3. Boudot, F., Gaudry, P., Guillevic, A., Heninger, N., Thomé, E., Zimmermann, P.: Comparing the difficulty of factorization and discrete logarithm: a 240-digit experiment. In: Micciancio, D., Ristenpart, T. (eds.) CRYPTO 2020. LNCS, vol. 12171, pp. 62–91. Springer, Cham (2020). https://doi.org/10.1007/978-3-030-56880-1_3
4. Braga, D.D.A., Fouque, P., Sabt, M.: Dragonblood is still leaking: practical cache-based side-channel in the wild. In: ACSAC 2020, pp. 291–303. ACM (2020). https://doi.org/10.1145/3427228.3427295

5. Brumley, B.B., Tuveri, N.: Remote timing attacks are still practical. In: Atluri, V., Diaz, C. (eds.) ESORICS 2011. LNCS, vol. 6879, pp. 355–371. Springer, Heidelberg (2011). https://doi.org/10.1007/978-3-642-23822-2_20
6. Cash, D., Kiltz, E., Shoup, V.: The twin Diffie–Hellman problem and applications. J. Cryptol. **22**(4), 470–504 (2009). https://doi.org/10.1007/s00145-009-9041-6
7. Ciet, M., Joye, M.: (Virtually) free randomization techniques for elliptic curve cryptography. In: Qing, S., Gollmann, D., Zhou, J. (eds.) ICICS 2003. LNCS, vol. 2836, pp. 348–359. Springer, Heidelberg (2003). https://doi.org/10.1007/978-3-540-39927-8_32
8. Cohen, H., et al. (eds.): Handbook of Elliptic and Hyperelliptic Curve Cryptography. Chapman and Hall/CRC (2005). https://doi.org/10.1201/9781420034981
9. Coron, J-S.: Resistance Against Differential Power Analysis For Elliptic Curve Cryptosystems. In: Koç, Ç.K., Paar, C. (eds.) CHES 1999. LNCS, vol. 1717, pp. 292–302. Springer, Heidelberg (1999). https://doi.org/10.1007/3-540-48059-5_25
10. Feix, B., Roussellet, M., Venelli, A.: Side-channel analysis on blinded regular scalar multiplications. In: Meier, W., Mukhopadhyay, D. (eds.) INDOCRYPT 2014. LNCS, vol. 8885, pp. 3–20. Springer, Cham (2014). https://doi.org/10.1007/978-3-319-13039-2_1
11. Genkin, D., Pachmanov, L., Pipman, I., Tromer, E., Yarom, Y.: ECDSA key extraction from mobile devices via nonintrusive physical side channels. In: Weippl, E.R., Katzenbeisser, S., Kruegel, C., Myers, A.C., Halevi, S. (eds.) ACM SIGSAC 2016, pp. 1626–1638. ACM (2016). https://doi.org/10.1145/2976749.2978353
12. Goudarzi, D., Rivain, M., Vergnaud, D.: Lattice attacks against elliptic-curve signatures with blinded scalar multiplication. In: Avanzi, R., Heys, H. (eds.) SAC 2016. LNCS, vol. 10532, pp. 120–139. Springer, Cham (2017). https://doi.org/10.1007/978-3-319-69453-5_7
13. Goundar, R.R., Joye, M., Miyaji, A., Rivain, M., Venelli, A.: Scalar multiplication on Weierstraß elliptic curves from co-Z arithmetic. J. Cryptogr. Eng. **1**(2), 161–176 (2011). https://doi.org/10.1007/s13389-011-0012-0
14. Jancar, J., Sedlacek, V., Svenda, P., Sýs, M.: Minerva: the curse of ECDSA nonces. Systematic analysis of lattice attacks on noisy leakage of bit-length of ECDSA nonces. IACR Trans. Cryptogr. Hardw. Embed. Syst. **2020**(4), 281–308 (2020). https://doi.org/10.13154/tches.v2020.i4.281-308
15. Kocher, P.C.: Timing attacks on implementations of Diffie-Hellman, RSA, DSS, and other systems. In: Koblitz, N. (ed.) CRYPTO 1996. LNCS, vol. 1109, pp. 104–113. Springer, Heidelberg (1996). https://doi.org/10.1007/3-540-68697-5_9
16. Kocher, P., Jaffe, J., Jun, B.: Differential power analysis. In: Wiener, M. (ed.) CRYPTO 1999. LNCS, vol. 1666, pp. 388–397. Springer, Heidelberg (1999). https://doi.org/10.1007/3-540-48405-1_25
17. Montgomery, P.L.: Speeding the pollard and elliptic curve methods of factorization. Math. Comput. **48**, 243–264 (1987)
18. Muller, F., Valette, F.: High-order attacks against the exponent splitting protection. In: Yung, M., Dodis, Y., Kiayias, A., Malkin, T. (eds.) PKC 2006. LNCS, vol. 3958, pp. 315–329. Springer, Heidelberg (2006). https://doi.org/10.1007/11745853_21
19. Proton Technologies AG: Protonmail v3.6 release notes
20. Roche, T., Imbert, L., Lomné, V.: Side-channel attacks on blinded scalar multiplications revisited. In: Belaïd, S., Güneysu, T. (eds.) CARDIS 2019. LNCS, vol. 11833, pp. 95–108. Springer, Cham (2020). https://doi.org/10.1007/978-3-030-42068-0_6

21. Taylor, D., Wu, T., Mavrogiannopoulos, N., Perrin, T.: Using the secure remote password (SRP) protocol for TLS authentication. RFC **5054**, 1–24 (2007). https://doi.org/10.17487/RFC5054

22. Vanhoef, M., Ronen, E.: Dragonblood: analyzing the dragonfly handshake of WPA3 and EAP-pwd. In: 2020 IEEE Symposium on Security and Privacy, SP 2020, pp. 517–533. IEEE (2020). https://doi.org/10.1109/SP40000.2020.00031

23. Wilson, E.B.: Probable inference, the law of succession, and statistical inference. J. Am. Stat. Assoc. **22**(158), 209–212 (1927). https://doi.org/10.1080/01621459.1927.10502953

24. Wu, T.: The SRP authentication and key exchange system. RFC **2945**, 1–8 (2000). https://doi.org/10.17487/RFC2945

25. Wu, T.D.: The secure remote password protocol. In: NDSS 1998. The Internet Society (1998). https://www.ndss-symposium.org/ndss1998/secure-remote-password-protocol/

Secure Computations

Privacy-Preserving Data Aggregation with Probabilistic Range Validation

F. W. Dekker(✉)(iD) and Zekeriya Erkin(iD)

Cyber Security Group, Delft University of Technology, Delft, The Netherlands
{f.w.dekker,z.erkin}@tudelft.nl

Abstract. Privacy-preserving data aggregation protocols have been researched widely, but usually cannot guarantee correctness of the aggregate if users are malicious. These protocols can be extended with zero-knowledge proofs and commitments to work in the malicious model, but this incurs a significant computational cost on the end users, making adoption of these protocols less likely.

We propose a privacy-preserving data aggregation protocol for calculating the sum of user inputs. Our protocol gives the aggregator confidence that all inputs are within a desired range. Instead of zero-knowledge proofs, our protocol relies on a probabilistic hypergraph-based detection algorithm with which the aggregator can quickly pinpoint malicious users. Furthermore, our protocol is robust to user dropouts and, apart from the setup phase, it is non-interactive.

Keywords: Privacy · Data aggregation · Applied cryptography · Hypergraphs

1 Introduction

Data aggregation gives us many valuable insights into the real world in the form of machine learning [1], participatory sensing [2], software telemetry [3,4], and smart metering [5]. Although the usefulness of these methods depends on the amount of available data, privacy concerns make users reluctant to share their sensitive data with a third party [6,7]. This poses a significant threat to the viability of large-scale data analysis.

To overcome this problem, privacy-preserving data aggregation (PDA) protocols have been proposed which allow an aggregator to calculate statistics on privacy-sensitive data without being able to determine private values. There are various ways to achieve this. For example, several proposals use techniques such as homomorphic encryption [6,8] and secret sharing [9,10] to guarantee that user contributions cannot be decrypted unless they have been aggregated. Other proposals use differential privacy [11–13] to ensure that the connection between the observed value and the actual value is perturbed. Either way, PDA protocols provide the same expressiveness as non-PDA protocols, but without sacrificing user privacy. These guarantees usually come at the cost of increased computational complexity, increased bandwidth usage, or decreased accuracy.

© Springer Nature Switzerland AG 2021
K. Sako and N. O. Tippenhauer (Eds.): ACNS 2021, LNCS 12727, pp. 79–98, 2021.
https://doi.org/10.1007/978-3-030-78375-4_4

A shortcoming of many existing proposals is that they assume that all users are honest-but-curious, for example as in [8,14,15]. As a result, these proposals cannot be used to defend against dishonest users that want to invalidate the aggregate or nudge it in their favour. This means that dishonest users could tamper with their smart meter to reduce their reported electricity consumption [16] or inject false data to increase their score in a ranking system [17]. The aggregator would have been able to detect these attacks by looking at the users' private values, but the privacy-preserving properties of the PDA protocol prevent this.

Transitioning from the honest-but-curious model to the malicious model can be achieved using zero-knowledge proofs and commitments, as suggested in proposals such as [8,13,14]. In particular, range proofs [18] can be used to prove in zero knowledge that a committed value is within a given range. However, range proofs—and zero-knowledge proofs in general—often either require a trusted setup or a significant amount of resources from the user [19]. This makes these approaches unappealing or even infeasible for resource-constrained users.

In this paper, we present an efficient PDA protocol for finding the sum of all private user values at a regular interval. The protocol lets an aggregator probabilistically identify private values that are not within a desired range without the need for zero-knowledge proofs. First, the aggregator divides all users into multiple overlapping groups such that every user is in a unique set of groups. Then, in each interval, each user sends their encrypted values to the aggregator, who determines the sum of private values per group. Finally, the aggregator pinpoints malicious users by looking at the intersection of groups that violate the range. By memorising which groups have out-of-range aggregates, the aggregator can combine detections from different rounds to further enhance its detection rate.

Our protocol boasts several important properties. Firstly, the scheme can be configured to customise the balance between privacy, complexity, and detection rate. For example, one can increase the work the aggregator needs to perform per round to increase the protocol's resistance to user collusions. Secondly, our protocol does not require a trusted setup and is non-interactive apart from the registration phase: Users simply send their encrypted values to the aggregator, who then aggregates and validates asynchronously. Thirdly, our protocol is an efficient solution for aggregators relying on resource-constrained users; users are subject to $\mathcal{O}(\log n)$ complexity per round in the number of users n. Fourthly, the grouping structure of our protocol gives the protocol robustness as the aggregator can continue to operate even when users fail to submit their measurements. Finally, our protocol can be used as a primitive to build complex algorithms such as principal component analysis, singular-value decomposition, and decision tree classifications by writing the inputs as aggregate-sum queries, like in [20].

The remainder of this paper is structured as follows. In Sect. 2 we look at related work. Then, in Sect. 3 we present our protocol in detail, and in Sect. 4 we analyse its security, privacy, complexity, and detection rate. Finally, in Sect. 5 we present our conclusions.

2   Related Work

We discuss various protocols for range validation of malicious inputs. First, we consider PDA protocols that have range validation built in. Then, we consider several alternative approaches not inherent to PDA protocols.

Kursawe [9] proposes a scheme in which the aggregator verifies that all private values are valid by checking that the sum of inputs approximates the true aggregate. However, it cannot identify which user sent the invalid value and requires knowledge of the true aggregate beforehand, which is not always feasible.

Sun et al. [21] present APED, a PDA protocol that detects defective smart meters using a method similar to ours. In APED, a trusted third party divides all users into w random sets of disjoint pairs such that each user is in w pairs at once, and creates a random key k_i for each user i. Then, for each pair of users (i, j), the third party sends $k_{i,j} = -(k_i + k_j)$ to the aggregator. In each round, each user i sends a ciphertext of their measurement, encrypted with the key k_i. After receiving the ciphertexts for that round, the aggregator decrypts the product of the ciphertexts of each pair in one of the w pairing sets of users using that pair's combined key $k_{i,j}$. If a pair cannot be decrypted, at least one of the two users must be defective, and the aggregator will use a different pairing set in the next round. After some rounds, the aggregator infers from the overlap of invalid pairs which users are defective. An extension of the protocol, DG-APED [22], uses groups of arbitrary size. Both protocols have two drawbacks. Firstly, they rely on a trusted third party to create groups and generate key material. Secondly, because the protocols are tailored to defective users, the detection algorithms are unsuitable for users that do not always send invalid users.

Ahadipour, Mohammadi, and Keshavarz-Haddad [23] propose a protocol that reduces the amount of private data the aggregator has access to. Users are divided into disjoint groups, and the aggregator obtains the sum of each group's values in addition to a random subset of the users' private values. The aggregator then looks at the collected private values to determine which users sent invalid values. While this reduces the privacy impact on its users, giving the aggregator access to even a single private value is not tolerable for sensitive data.

Yang and Li [15] propose a protocol that can identify out-of-range values using re-encryption. The aggregator divides users into disjoint groups, and when it finds that the aggregate of a group is out of range, it re-encrypts and shuffles the values of the violating group and sends them to a random user in that group. The random user decrypts the values and reports which values are out of range. The main drawback of this scheme is that it is especially vulnerable to collusions, as a single collusion between the aggregator and the random user suffices to reveal all private values of an entire group to the aggregator.

Finally, there is a multitude of proposals that assume that users are honest-but-curious, but note that zero-knowledge proofs could be used to perform input validation [8,13,14]. With zero-knowledge proofs, users can mathematically prove that their value is within a particular range without having to reveal their value. Generic zero-knowledge proofs such as SNARKs require a trusted setup, which is often not a realistic assumption. Its cousin, the STARK [24], resolves this problem, but this comes at the cost of increased communication complexity. Corrigan-Gibbs and Boneh [25] introduce SNIPs to allow users to prove that input is valid according to an arbitrary circuit, but this solution requires a multitude of cooperating servers, of which all must be honest to guarantee correctness and at least one must be honest to guarantee privacy for the user; furthermore, client-side communication costs grow linearly with the complexity of the validation circuit. Range proofs [18] are a specific form of zero-knowledge proof specific to range checking. Even though range proofs such as Bulletproofs [26] are more efficient than generic zero-knowledge proofs, they still incur a relatively high complexity for the users (i.e. the provers) [19], and must also be used in addition to the privacy-preserving data aggregation protocol and a cryptographic link between the two such as a commitment scheme.

3   Probabilistically Range-Limited Private Data Aggregation

We consider a setting with n users and a single aggregator, similar to related work in Sect. 2. Users continuously submit new privacy-sensitive measurements to the aggregator at regular intervals called rounds; we assume that users and the aggregator have access to a synchronised clock. We work in the standard model under the assumption that the discrete log problem is intractable. Some users are malicious and may deviate from the protocol; these are exactly the users the aggregator wants to identify. All other users are honest-but-curious (also known as semi-honest). We assume that the aggregator is honest-but-curious, an assumption made in several other related works including [8,10]. This assumption makes sense in a business-driven setting, in which a malicious aggregator would be faced with negative publicity and a loss in consumer trust if its behaviour were discovered. Still, we allow for collusions between users and the aggregator. We assume that the sets of malicious and colluding users do not change throughout the protocol. Finally, we assume that the security, integrity, and authenticity of all messages is guaranteed. The notation used to describe our protocol is shown in Table 1. Our protocol broadly works as follows.

1. *Registration*: Each user sends a message to the aggregator indicating that they want to register. Once all users have registered, the aggregator divides the users into overlapping groups. It then sends information such as the public parameters and the group configuration to all registered users.
2. *Submission*: Every round, each user creates a new secret share of the value 0 for each group they are in. The user takes copies of their private value and blinds each copy with a different secret share. The user sends the blinded copies in addition to commitments to the secret shares to the aggregator.
3. *Aggregation*: The aggregator verifies that the secret shares of each group sum to 0 and verifies that each user used copies of a single private value, remembering which users and groups failed verification. Next, the aggregator computes the sum of private values of each group, and remembers which groups have aggregates that are out of bounds. Finally, the aggregator combines all group aggregates to find the sum of all private values.

4. *Detection*: Eventually, the aggregator looks back at which groups exhibited malicious activity over the past several rounds, and derives from their overlap which users caused the malicious behaviour. As the protocol progresses, the aggregator is able to identify more and more malicious users.

Table 1. The notation used in the description of our protocol

Symbol	Meaning
n	Number of users
b	Grouping base/radix = users per group
ℓ	Grouping dimensionality = groups per user
$[min, max]$	Valid range of a single private value
g	Generator for commitments
pp	Public parameters, contains all of the above
U	Set of all user identifiers
G	Set of all group identifiers
G_i	Set of identifiers of groups of user i
U_j	Set of identifiers of users of group j
N_i	Set of identifiers of neighbours of user i
(sk_i, pk_i)	User i's key pair
t	Round number
$m_{i,t}$	User i's private value in round t
$c_{i,j,t}$	User i's encryption of $m_{i,t}$ for group j
$M_{j,t}$	Sum of private values of users in group j in round t
M_t	Sum of all private values in round t
$r_{i\to j,t}$	User i's random value for neighbour j in round t
$s_{i,j,t}$	User i's secret share for group j in round t
$d_{i,j,t}$	User i's commitment to $s_{i,j,t}$
V	Set of group identifiers aggregator marked as malicious
W	Set of user identifiers aggregator marked as malicious

3.1 Registration

The goal of the registration phase is to determine the parameters under which the protocol will run and to exchange the necessary information for subsequent rounds. Firstly, the honest-but-curious aggregator chooses a random generator g of an algebraic structure in which the discrete log problem is hard, such as a specific elliptic curve. Additionally, the aggregator chooses application-specific values for n and $min < max$. Then, each user sends a message to the aggregator indicating the desire to participate in the protocol. Once n users have registered, the aggregator sends the public parameters pp and some additional information to all users. The remaining public parameters and additional information are chosen based on the following grouping algorithm and secret sharing scheme.

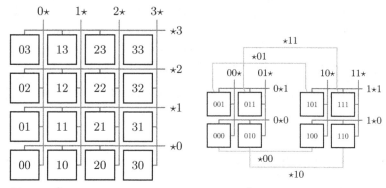

(a) A 4^2-hypermesh, which has 16 nodes and 8 hyperedges

(b) A 2^3-hypermesh (which is the graph of a regular cube), which has 8 nodes and 12 hyperedges

Fig. 1. Examples of hypermeshes

Parameters for the Grouping Algorithm. The grouping algorithm divides users into groups such that the aggregator can pinpoint malicious users based on which groups exhibit malicious behaviour. We base our algorithm on the structure of a hypermesh [27]. A b-ary ℓ-dimensional hypermesh is a hypergraph with b^ℓ nodes, where each node is assigned an ℓ-digit identifier $d_{\ell-1}d_{\ell-2}\ldots d_0$ such that $d_i \in [0, b)$ for all $0 \leq i < \ell$. Two nodes are neighbours if and only if their identifiers differ in exactly one digit. Nodes are connected by b-edges, i.e. edges with b endpoints. Edge identifiers have the same format as node identifiers, except that exactly one digit is replaced by the wildcard symbol $\star$. Every edge then connects the b nodes of which the identifier matches that of the edge, ignoring the digit in the wildcard's position. Identifiers can be considered coordinates in an ℓ-dimensional Euclidean space, with $b^{\ell-1}$ edges aligned along each dimension for a total of $\ell b^{\ell-1}$ edges. We give some examples of hypermeshes in Fig. 1.

In our protocol, the aggregator generates a b-ary ℓ-dimensional hypermesh after all n users have registered, with the requirements that $n = b^\ell$, $b \geq 2$, and $\ell \geq 2$. The edges in the hypermesh are then exactly the groups that users are in. Generating such a hypermesh constitutes choosing values for b and ℓ, and assigning to each user a unique identifier in $[0, b^\ell)$, which can be converted to a unique ℓ-digit b-ary identifier. These three variables are sufficient for a user to reconstruct the hypermesh and determine their own position. The ℓ groups that user i is in, denoted G_i, can be found by replacing the respective ℓ digits in i by the wildcard symbol $\star$. The b users in group j, denoted U_j, can be found by replacing the wildcard symbol $\star$ with the respective values $[0, b)$. The neighbours of user i, denoted N_i, can be found by taking the union of $\{j \in U_i \mid G_j\}$, minus i.

Parameters for Secret Sharing. Our scheme uses secret sharing to prevent the aggregator from decrypting ciphertexts unless all ciphertexts of a group have been aggregated. We apply the procedure for creating 0-sum additive secret shares used in [8] to each group in G. We avoid direct communication between users by forwarding messages through the (honest-but-curious) aggregator, but use public-key encryption to ensure that the aggregator cannot see the actual random values being transmitted. Our goal is to obtain secret shares $s_{i,j,t}$ for each user $i \in U$ in each group $j \in G_i$ in each round t such that

$$\forall j \in G : \sum_{i \in U_j} s_{i,j,t} = 0. \tag{1}$$

While the following description assumes that users exchange random numbers each round, such excessive communication can be avoided by having users exchange seeds for random number generators once during registration.

First, each user i generates an asymmetric key pair (sk_i, pk_i), and includes pk_i when sending the registration message to the aggregator. Once all n users have registered, the (honest-but-curious) aggregator sends to each user i the public keys $\{pk_k \mid k \in N_i\}$. These key pairs can be reused and do not need to be exchanged again in future rounds. Then, in each round t, user i generates a random number $r_{i \to k,t}$ for each neighbour $k \in N_i$, encrypts it with pk_k, and sends this value to the aggregator, who forwards the message to user k. Once user i has obtained $r_{k \to i,t}$ for each neighbour k, user i creates the secret share

$$s_{i,j,t} = \sum_{k \in G_j} \left(r_{i \to k,t} - r_{k \to i,t} \right) \tag{2}$$

for each $j \in G_i$. We consider the privacy of this construction in Sect. 4.2. We present a communication diagram that includes registration in Fig. 2.

3.2   Submission

In round t, each user i submits the private value $m_{i,t}$ such that the aggregator can obtain the group aggregates without seeing $m_{i,t}$. We use encryption function $c_{i,j,t} = m_{i,t} + s_{i,j,t}$ to have each user i send $\{c_{i,j,t} \mid j \in G_i\}$ to the aggregator, with the secret share $s_{i,j,t}$ as described in Sect. 3.1. To prevent malicious users from avoiding detection by using a different $m_{i,t}$ in different groups, users must additionally send commitments to their secret shares. We use a simple homomorphic commitment scheme that is computationally binding and computationally hiding: To commit to a value x, a user sends g^x. Then, each user i computes commitments $d_{i,j,t} = g^{s_{i,j,t}}$ and sends $\{(c_{i,j,t}, d_{i,j,t}) \mid j \in G_i\}$ to the aggregator.

3.3   Aggregation

The aggregation phase is asynchronous to user submissions and may be invoked by the aggregator at any time. Before aggregating the submissions for round t, the aggregator verifies for each group $j \in G$ of which all users have submitted their values by checking that

$$\prod_{i \in U_j} d_{i,j,t} = \prod_{i \in U_j} g^{s_{i,j,t}} = g^{\sum_{i \in U_j} s_{i,j,t}} = g^0 = 1 \tag{3}$$

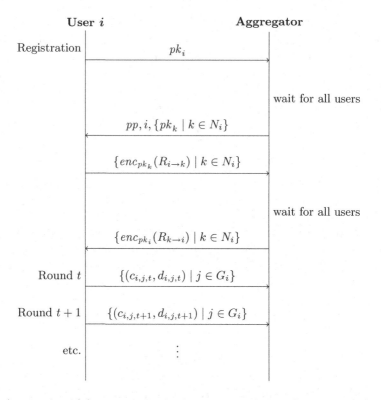

Fig. 2. An overview of the communication in our protocol. To reduce per-round communication, users exchange seeds $R_{i \to k}$ during registration to generate $r_{i \to k,t}$ in round t.

to ensure that users committed to secret shares of the value 0. If a group j fails this check, at least one user in this group must have been malicious, so the aggregator adds j to V. Next, the aggregator constructs for each user i the set

$$\{g^{c_{i,j,t}}(d_{i,j,t})^{-1} \mid j \in G_i\} = \{g^{m_{i,t}+s_{i,j,t}}g^{-s_{i,j,t}} \mid j \in G_i\} = \{g^{m_{i,t}} \mid j \in G_i\} \quad (4)$$

and checks that all values in the set are equal. This ensures that each $c_{i,j,t}$ for user i uses the same $m_{i,t}$. If user i fails this check, all groups in G_i are added to V, effectively marking this user as malicious once the detection algorithm runs. Users that fail to submit measurements similarly have their groups added to V. If desired, a level of lenience can be introduced by only adding these groups once a user fails to submit in multiple rounds.

After the aggregator has completed its verifications, aggregation can start. For each group $j \in G$, the aggregator calculates

$$M_{j,t} = \sum_{i \in U_j} c_{i,j,t} = \sum_{i \in U_j} (m_{i,t} + s_{i,j,t}) = \sum_{i \in U_j} m_{i,t}. \quad (5)$$

If an aggregate $M_{j,t}$ is not in the range $[b \cdot min, b \cdot max]$, at least one user must have sent a value that is not in $[min, max]$, so the aggregator adds j to V. This check can be adjusted to support use cases in which ranges differ per user or per round by checking that the aggregate is in the sum of the users' current ranges.

The sum of all private values can be calculated by taking the sum of all group aggregates. However, the aggregator should refrain from including invalid groups. Therefore, the aggregator calculates

$$M_t = \frac{\sum_{j \in G \setminus V} M_{j,t}}{\ell}, \tag{6}$$

which is the average of the total sums along each of the hypermesh's ℓ dimensions, excluding groups in V. This approximates the sum of only the honest-but-curious users; if all users behave honestly this approximation is perfect. If desired, the aggregator can estimate the sum of all users by including a fake group aggregate for each group in V based on the average of $\{M_{j,t} \mid G \setminus V\}$.

3.4 Detection

The detection algorithm lets the aggregator identify which users are malicious. Throughout the protocol and across rounds, the aggregator adds groups that exhibit malicious behaviour to the set V. In particular, the set V contains all groups in which at least one user sent a wrongly constructed secret share or sent different private values to different groups in the same round, and contains a subset of groups in which at least one user sent an out-of-bounds value. By looking at the overlaps of groups in V, the aggregator can infer which users caused the malicious behaviour; users that are in exactly ℓ different groups in V are malicious and are added to W. Over time, the set V becomes more and more complete until all groups containing malicious users have been detected. We prove that this method does not result in false-positive detections in Sect. 4.1, even if some malicious users collude. We analyse the detection rate in Sect. 4.4.

4 Analyses

4.1 Security Analysis

In this section we prove that the aggregator does not incorrectly identify users, we prove that malicious users cannot submit different measurements to different groups, and we analyse the impact of missing users to the aggregate.

Proof of No False Positives. It is important that the aggregator correctly identifies which users are malicious. We prove that malicious users cannot frame an honest-but-curious user, even if they coordinate the values they send.

Theorem 1. *In our protocol, the aggregator will never identify an honest-but-curious user as a malicious user if there are fewer than ℓ malicious users.*

Proof. For the sake of contradiction, let there be an honest-but-curious user whom the aggregator falsely identifies as malicious. Then this user must be in ℓ groups of V, so this user shares ℓ groups with malicious users. Because a group contains those users that differ by exactly one digit, two users can at most share a single group. The wrongly-identified user must therefore share groups with ℓ different malicious users. However, by assumption of the theorem's antecedent, there are strictly fewer than ℓ malicious users. Therefore, the honest-but-curious user could not have been identified as a malicious user.   □

Proof of Aggregate Consistency. Users blind their private measurements $m_{i,t}$ using secret shares $s_{i,j,t}$ to obtain $c_{i,j,t}$. It is important that the aggregator verifies that a user's $c_{i,j,t}$ values use the same underlying $m_{i,t}$, malicious users could avoid detection by causing inconsistencies between aggregates otherwise. We show that it is infeasible for users to do this under our security model, regardless of how many users are malicious. Working in the standard model, every user i sends $(c_{i,j,t}, d_{i,j,t})$ for each $j \in G_i$ to the aggregator, constructed in any way the users want. Let $s_{i,j,t} = dlog_g(d_{i,j,t})$ and $m_{i,j,t} = c_{i,j,t} - s_{i,j,t}$ for all users i and for all $j \in G_i$, regardless of whether values are constructed honestly.

Theorem 2. *In our protocol, a malicious user i cannot send messages in round t to the aggregator such that $m_{i,j,t} \neq m_{i,j',t}$ for any two groups $j, j' \in G_i$ such that the aggregator's verification does not fail, assuming that the discrete log problem is intractable in the group generated by g.*

Proof. Firstly, if either user i or any neighbour $k \in N_i$ fails to send their messages, the aggregator's verification fails right away and the malicious user does not succeed. Now, it follows from the aggregator's verification of Eq. 3 that $\sum_{i \in U_j} s_{i,j,t} = 0$. Subsequently, we know from the verification of Eq. 4 that, for fixed $i \in U$ and $t \in \mathbb{N}$, all $c_{i,j,t} - s_{i,j,t}$ for $j \in G_i$ are equal. Therefore, by definition of $m_{i,j,t}$, all $m_{i,j,t}$ for fixed $i \in U$ and $t \in \mathbb{N}$ are also equal.   □

Impact of Missing User Values. The influence of malicious users on M_t decreases as the aggregator adds more groups to V. At the same time, groups in V contain honest-but-curious users. We quantify the effect that malicious users have on the correctness of the total aggregate.

Each user effectively contributes their measurement ℓ times, and, by Theorem 2, each contribution is the same. An ideal protocol would remove only the ℓ contributions of each malicious user. Our protocol also removes the $(b-1)\ell$ contributions of each malicious user's neighbours. The total impact of any set of fewer than ℓ malicious users is greatest when these malicious users do not share any groups, in which case V contains $(\ell-1)\ell$ groups. The aggregator then removes $b(\ell-1)\ell$ contributions instead of the optimal $(\ell-1)\ell$; a factor of b more than optimal. With a total of ℓb^ℓ contributions amongst all users, the effect of malicious users on M_t therefore diminishes as ℓ increases.

4.2 Privacy Analysis

We argue that our protocol is a secure data summation protocol in the setting described in Sect. 3. In particular, we argue that when executing the protocol using a b^ℓ-hypermesh, both the joint view of any set of users and the
joint view of the aggregator and a set of fewer than $(b-1)^\ell$ users do not
leak any information about honest-but-curious users' inputs, besides what can
be inferred from the group aggregates. We should note that we assume that
each group with an honest-but-curious user also contains at least one other
non-colluding honest-but-curious user so as to prevent trivial attacks on the
aggregates. This assumption is naturally present in many group-based aggregation schemes, including [8,10,14]. Also recall that the aggregator is honest-but-
curious and will therefore assign users to random positions honestly.

Firstly, we consider the joint view of any set of users $U_A \subset U$. The view
consists only of the public parameters pp, the users' private data, and the public
keys pk_i and random seeds $r_{i \to k,t}$ other users have sent to users in U_A. Confidentiality is trivial because the view does not contain any data derived from the
private values $m_{i,t}$ of any user $i \notin U_A$.

Next, we consider the joint view of the honest-but-curious aggregator and any
set $U_A \subset U$ of fewer than $(b-1)^\ell$ users. The view consists of the same data as
before, now in addition to the aggregator's private information and the data that
are sent to the aggregator. We proceed to dissect the implications of this view.
Firstly, malicious users in U_A differ only from honest-but-curious users in U_A in
that they can interact dishonestly with other users, but this does not give them
an advantage. If a malicious user refuses to interact with or sends malformed
data to a user, then this user halts and privacy is maintained. Otherwise, if a
malicious user sends non-random data to user i, then this is no worse than an
honest-but-curious user in U_A sharing their data with the aggregator. Secondly,
users that are not in U_A receive sensitive information through the aggregator,
but privacy is ensured by encrypting data such that the decryption key is not in
the adversary's view. Thirdly, the private values $m_{i,t}$ of user $i \notin U_A$ are masked
using the secret shares $s_{i,j,t}$ constructed from values $r_{i \to k,t}$. Because at least one
user $k \neq i$ of each group $j \in G_i$ is not in U_A, both $r_{i \to k,t}$ and $r_{k \to i,t}$ are chosen
honestly and remain unknown to the adversary. Because additive secret sharing
is trivially secure, the secret shares $s_{i,j,t}$ properly mask $m_{i,j,t}$. Finally, we observe
that each submission occurs in multiple linearly dependent aggregates, which is
equivalent to a system of linear equations. We prove that it is infeasible for the
adversary to solve this system because it is not full rank.

Theorem 3. *The rank of the incidence matrix of a b^ℓ-hypermesh is $b^\ell - (b-1)^\ell$.*
(Equivalently, the number of unknowns in the incidence matrix is $(b-1)^\ell$.)

Proof. We model the incidence matrix such that each row describes a group and
each column describes a user. We construct the incidence matrix recursively, similar to how the hypermesh itself can be constructed. Given a b-ary 1-dimensional
hypermesh, its incidence matrix $C_{b,1}$ is a $(1 \times b)$-matrix containing only 1s. Then,
a b-ary ℓ-dimensional hypermesh can be constructed from b copies of the b-ary

$(\ell - 1)$-dimensional hypermesh, where all nodes are additionally connected to their counterparts in the other copies using b-edges. This allows us to construct the incidence matrix $C_{b,\ell}$ for $\ell > 1$ as

$$
\begin{bmatrix}
C_{b,\ell-1} & 0 & \cdots & 0 \\
0 & C_{b,\ell-1} & \cdots & 0 \\
\vdots & \vdots & \ddots & \vdots \\
0 & 0 & \cdots & C_{b,\ell-1} \\
I_{b^{\ell-1}} & I_{b^{\ell-1}} & \cdots & I_{b^{\ell-1}}
\end{bmatrix},
\tag{7}
$$

where each 0 represents a matrix of the same size as $C_{b,\ell-1}$ containing only 0s, and I_x denotes an identity matrix of size $x \times x$.

We now use complete induction on ℓ to prove that $\mathrm{rank}(C_{b,\ell}) = b^\ell - (b-1)^\ell$. For the base case, we take $\ell = 1$ and find that $\mathrm{rank}(C_{b,1}) = 1$, which matches our theorem:

$$
b^\ell - (b-1)^\ell = b - (b-1) = 1.
\tag{8}
$$

For the recursive case, take as our induction hypothesis that $r = \mathrm{rank}(C_{b,\ell-1}) = b^{\ell-1} - (b-1)^{\ell-1}$. We write $C_{b,\ell}$ in column echelon form as follows to determine its rank. Firstly, consider the column operations necessary to write $C_{b,\ell-1}$ in column echelon form, and apply them to each instance of $C_{b,\ell-1}$ in $C_{b,\ell}$. Note that this also transforms the $I_{b^{\ell-1}}$s located beneath the $C_{b,\ell-1}$s. After applying these steps, each instance of $C_{b,\ell-1}$ has $b^{\ell-1} - r$ empty columns on the right, while each instance of $I_{b^{\ell-1}}$ has no zero columns because it is full rank. The rightmost $b^{\ell-1} - r$ columns of each $I_{b^{\ell-1}}$ are now identical, however, and have nothing but 0s above them. As such, we cancel out these columns except in the rightmost instance of $I_{b^{\ell-1}}$ using simple column operations. This cancels out $(b-1)(b^{\ell-1} - r)$ columns, while all other columns are non-zero. After moving these zero columns to the right of the matrix, $C_{b,\ell}$ is in column echelon form. The rank of $C_{b,\ell}$ is then the number of non-zero columns, which is

$$
b^\ell - (b-1)\left(b^{\ell-1} - r\right) = b^\ell - (b-1)\left(b^{\ell-1} - \left(b^{\ell-1} - (b-1)^{\ell-1}\right)\right)
\tag{9}
$$

$$
= b^\ell - (b-1)(b-1)^{\ell-1} = b^\ell - (b-1)^\ell,
\tag{10}
$$

proving our theorem. □

With fewer than $(b-1)^\ell$ users in the view, the adversary always has at least one unknown in this system. To give an intuition into the growth of $(b-1)^\ell$, consider Fig. 3, where we show the maximum ratio of users that may collude with the aggregator as a function of b and ℓ without breaking confidentiality. For example, a system with $b = \ell = 2$ could not tolerate a single colluding user, while a system with $b = \ell = 5$ could tolerate up to $\frac{4^5}{5^5} \approx 33\%$ of all users colluding. As the number of groups per user grows, the collusion resistance decreases. This can be compensated for by increasing the number of users per group, but, as we discuss in Sect. 4.4, this decreases the detection rate.

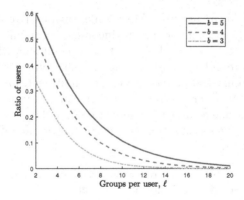

Fig. 3. Maximum proportion of users that can collude with the aggregator as a function of b (users per group) and ℓ (groups per user)

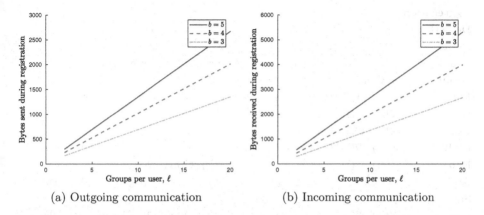

(a) Outgoing communication   (b) Incoming communication

Fig. 4. Per-user communication during registration. We assume 4 bytes per (masked) private value and 256-bit EC-cryptography. With point compression, this results in 33-byte keys, ciphertexts (for seeds), and commitments.

4.3 Complexity Analysis

We quantify the complexity of our protocol in terms of the number of users n. Then, we compare our protocol to a selection of related PDA protocols. We express complexity in terms of the amount of encryptions, decryptions, multiplications, exponentiations, additions, subtractions, and outgoing messages, separately for each user and the aggregator, similar to the analysis in [10].

Complexity of Our Protocol. Firstly, note that in our protocol, $b = n^{\frac{1}{\ell}}$. This amount is maximal when $\ell = 2$, so we say that b is $\mathcal{O}\left(\sqrt{n}\right)$. Meanwhile, $\ell = \log_b(n)$ is $\mathcal{O}(\log n)$. We show a time diagram of our protocol in Fig. 2.

During the registration, each user sends one encrypted seed for each neighbor and a fixed-size key to the aggregator, resulting in an outgoing communication complexity of $\mathcal{O}\left(\sqrt{n}\log n\right)$ per user. Meanwhile, each user receives one key and one encrypted seed per neighbor, for an incoming communication complexity of $\mathcal{O}\left(\sqrt{n}\log n\right)$ per user. We visualize registration communication complexity in Fig. 4. Later, in each round, each user sends for each group it is in a constant-size message containing a masked plaintext and a commitment, for a communication complexity of $\mathcal{O}(\log n)$. Users do not receive anything during rounds. Creating a submission requires one commitment and one masked private value for each of the user's groups, for a total of $\mathcal{O}(\log n)$ exponentiations and $\mathcal{O}(\log n)$ additions per user per round.

Table 2. Complexity analysis of several privacy-sensitive data aggregation protocols, separated by party: User (U) or Aggregator (A), given total number of users n and range size 2^r.

Protocol	[15]		[25]		[26]		Ours	
Aggregation	✓		✓				✓	
Detection	✓		✓		✓		✓	
Robust			✓		✓		✓	
Topology	Tree		Arbitrary		Arbitrary		Hypermesh	
Group	ElGamal		FFT field		EC		EC	
Party	U	A	U	A	U	A	U	A
Enc	$\mathcal{O}(1)$	$\mathcal{O}(1)$	–	–	–	–	–	–
Dec	$\mathcal{O}(1)$	$\mathcal{O}(1)$	–	–	–	–	–	–
Mult	$\mathcal{O}(1)$	$\mathcal{O}(1)$	$\mathcal{O}(r\log r)$	$\mathcal{O}(r\log r)$	–	–	–	$\mathcal{O}(n\log n)$
Exp	$\mathcal{O}(1)$	$\mathcal{O}(1)$	–	–	$\mathcal{O}(r)$	$\mathcal{O}(nr)$	$\mathcal{O}(\log n)$	$\mathcal{O}(n\log n)$
Add	–	–	–	–	–	–	$\mathcal{O}(\log n)$	$\mathcal{O}(n\log n)$
Sub	–	–	–	–	–	–	–	–
Com	$\mathcal{O}(1)$	$\mathcal{O}(1)$	$\mathcal{O}(\log r)$	$\mathcal{O}(1)$	$\mathcal{O}(r)$	$\mathcal{O}(nr)$	$\mathcal{O}(\sqrt{n}\log n)$	$\mathcal{O}(n\sqrt{n}\log n)$

The aggregator forwards each user message during the registration, resulting in a factor of n more communication. After the registration, however, the aggregator does not need to communicate with users other than sending acknowledgements. During aggregation, the aggregator verifies user inputs, requiring one exponentiation and one multiplication for each group for each user, for a total of $n\ell b^{\ell-1}$ of either operation. The calculation of the aggregate itself requires only that the aggregator sums together all $n\ell b^{\ell-1}$ submissions. The detection phase does not require complex operations, as the aggregator need only find which users are in ℓ groups of V.

Comparison to Related Protocols. We compare our protocol to a selection of related PDA protocols, as shown in Table 2. Our analysis is subject to several limitations. Firstly, because our protocol is tailored to identifying malicious users, we restrict our analysis to detection protocols for malicious users, thus also excluding APED [21] and DG-APED [22]. Secondly, in our analysis of the protocol in [25], we assume that the number of multiplication gates is linear in the size of the range, which corresponds to the size of an integer comparison circuit. Finally, for the protocol in [15], we assume a binary tree topology for simplicity, and include operations related to the detection sub-protocol for fairness.

The protocol in [15] provides by far the lowest complexity by validating in a decentralised fashion, but requires long periods of interactivity and has the weakest security model: An honest-but-curious aggregator and any single user can collude to obtain all private values. Prio [25] and Bulletproofs [26] have a complexity that depends on the size r of the valid range; meanwhile, our complexity is independent of r. Additionally, with Bulletproofs, the size of the range must be of the form $[0, 2^r)$ for some natural number r, whereas our protocol supports arbitrary ranges, as does Prio. Finally, Bulletproofs can verify user submissions in bulk, but only if all users have the same valid range. Otherwise, the verification complexity grows linearly with the number of different ranges. While an alternative would be to verify the widest range in bulk, this is not practical. Our protocol supports different ranges for all users without an increase in complexity, instead affecting the detection rate, as we discuss in Sect. 4.4.

We conclude that the complexities of these protocols must be considered in the context of the application. If users have different, personalised use cases, the computation and communication complexities of our protocol scale better than competing protocols.

4.4   Detection Rate Analysis

Values submitted by honest-but-curious users in the same group as a malicious user may coincidentally compensate for the malicious transgression. As a result, our detection algorithm is probabilistic. In this section we analyse how the detection rate varies as a function of the protocol's parameters. In our analysis we model each honest-but-curious user's value as a truncated binomial distribution X with $\mu = \frac{min+max}{2}$ and a support of $[min, max]$. For the sake of illustration, we use $\sigma = 2$, $min = 5$, and $max = 15$. We model the sum of n independent honest-but-curious users' values, denoted X_n, by approximating X with a non-truncated binomial distribution, multiplying the distribution by n, and truncating this distribution to the range $[n \cdot min, n \cdot max]$.

Detection Rate of a Single Malicious User. Consider a system with a single malicious user i who submits the out-of-range measurement m. We assume that $m > max$, without loss of generality because X and X_{b-1} are symmetrical. Recall that user i is detected only once all ℓ groups in G_i are in V.

First, we consider the detection rate of an individual group. The aggregate of a group $j \in G_i$ does not exceed its upper bound if and only if $M_{j,t} = X_{b-1}+m \leq b \cdot max$, or, equivalently, if $X_{b-1} \leq b \cdot max - m$. We illustrate the probability that this relation holds as a function of m and b in Fig. 5a. The figure shows that fixing a particular detection rate results in the corresponding malicious value growing linearly with the group size. Note that the detection rate is exactly 0% at $m = max$ and exactly 100% at $m = b(max - min) + min$.

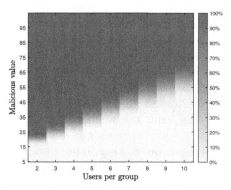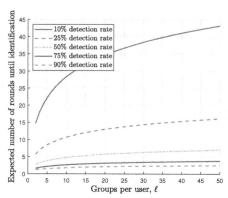

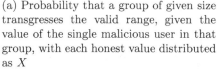

(a) Probability that a group of given size transgresses the valid range, given the value of the single malicious user in that group, with each honest value distributed as X

(b) Expected number of rounds until a given number of the malicious user's groups has been detected by the aggregator, given the per-group detection rate for any single round

Fig. 5. Detection rate of a single malicious user

We can thus model the detection rate of a group as a geometric variable to express the expected number of rounds until it is detected. Because the groups G_i overlap only in user i, their detection rates are independent for fixed m. The expected number of rounds until all ℓ groups have been detected at least once is then the expected maximum of ℓ iid geometric variables, which is [28]

$$f(\ell, p) = \sum_{k=0}^{n} \left(\binom{\ell}{k} p^k (1-p)^{\ell-k} (1 + f(\ell - k, p)) \right), \tag{11}$$

where ℓ is the number of groups and p is the per-round detection probability of each group. Figure 5b shows $f(\ell, p)$ for various combinations of ℓ and p. We conclude that increasing the number of groups per user necessitates a higher per-group detection rate to retain the number of expected rounds, which can be done by reducing the group size, for example.

Detection Rate of Multiple Malicious Users. When a group contains multiple malicious users, these users can either intensify or diminish the sum effect they have on their group's aggregate. This means that, depending on the usage scenario, multiple malicious users either become harder to detect (if malicious users have equal reason to transgress the range in either direction) or easier to detect (if malicious users have more reason to transgress the range in a particular detection). Therefore, our protocol is best suited for applications where users are most likely to transgress in a particular direction.

We can reuse our results from Sect. 4.4 to quantify the detection rate of a group with multiple malicious users. Given a group of size b with n malicious

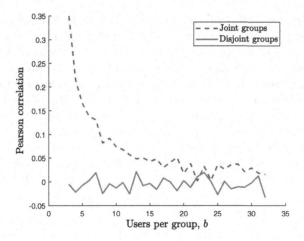

Fig. 6. The correlation of the detection rate of two groups, each with a different malicious user and overlapping in one honest-but-curious user. Simulated in Matlab by sampling honest values from truncated normal distribution $\mathcal{N}(10, 9)$ with support $[8, 19]$. Malicious users send $10 + 5b$, which ensures the groups are not always detected. Correlation was calculated with 5000 trials per group size.

users, the detection rate of the sum of malicious values m is

$$\Pr[X_{b-n} + m \leq b \cdot max] = \Pr[X_{b-n} + m - (n-1) \cdot max \leq (b - (n-1)) \cdot max]. \quad (12)$$

That is, this detection rate is the same as that of a single malicious user that sends the value $m - (n-1) \cdot max$ in a group with only $b - (n-1)$ users.

Users may coordinate the malicious values they send to avoid being detected by the aggregator in some groups. However, it follows from Eq. 12 that complete avoidance is possible only if the sum of their values is valid. Because values are consistent between groups by Theorem 2, this type of avoidance detection requires that the sum effect on the total aggregate is valid, so malicious users do not gain any significant advantages by working together.

An important observation regarding the interplay of group aggregates is that malicious users that do not share a group may still have an overlap in the users that they share groups with. In this case, the detection rates of these groups become covariant because of the common user. As shown in Fig. 6, the impact of this covariance depends on the group size b and quickly becomes negligible. Therefore, the expected number of rounds until detection as expressed in Eq. 5b holds for multiple users up to covariance.

5   Conclusion

Data aggregation is an immensely useful tool for various applications, but introduces a number of privacy concerns. Existing privacy-preserving data aggregation protocols tend to assume that the users are honest-but-curious rather than malicious, or use zero-knowledge proofs, which impose significant computational requirements on the users. Either way, adoption of these much-needed protocols is difficult. We present a data aggregation protocol that probabilistically detects out-of-range user values without giving the aggregator access to these values. Our protocol imposes only $\mathcal{O}(\log n)$ per-round computational complexity on its users without relying on expensive cryptography. The protocol is also robust to missing data because it can exclude any number of groups that have exhibited malicious behaviour. Furthermore, given b^ℓ users for positive integers b and ℓ, the aggregator will not misidentify an honest-but-curious user as malicious as long as there are strictly fewer than ℓ malicious users. Finally, our protocol continues to guarantee privacy even when up to $(b-1)^\ell$ users collude with the aggregator.

References

1. Bonawitz, K., et al.: Practical secure aggregation for privacy-preserving machine learning. In: Proceedings of the ACM Conference on Computer and Communications Security, New York, New York, USA, pp. 1175–1191. ACM Press (2017). ISBN 9781450349468. https://doi.org/10.1145/3133956.3133982
2. Burke, J., et al.: Participatory sensing. In: The 4th ACM Conference on Embedded Networked Sensor Systems, p. 5 (2006). https://escholarship.org/uc/item/19h777qd
3. Fanti, G., Pihur, V., Erlingsson,Ú.: Building a RAPPOR with the unknown: privacy-preserving learning of associations and data dictionaries. Proc. Priv. Enhancing Technol. **2016**(3), 41–61 (2016). ISSN 2299–0984. https://doi.org/10.1515/popets-2016-0015
4. Bittau, A., et al.: PROCHLO: strong privacy for analytics in the crowd. In: SOSP 2017 - Proceedings of the 26th ACM Symposium on Operating Systems Principles, New York, New York, USA, pp. 441–459. ACM Press (2017). ISBN 9781450350853. https://doi.org/10.1145/3132747.3132769
5. LeMay, M., Gross, G., Gunter, C.A., Garg, S.: Unified architecture for large-scale attested metering. In: Proceedings of the Annual Hawaii International Conference on System Sciences, pp. 1–10 (2007). ISSN 15301605. https://doi.org/10.1109/HICSS.2007.586
6. Garcia, F.D., Jacobs, B.: Privacy-friendly energy-metering via homomorphic encryption. In: Cuellar, J., Lopez, J., Barthe, G., Pretschner, A. (eds.) STM 2010. LNCS, vol. 6710, pp. 226–238. Springer, Heidelberg (2011). https://doi.org/10.1007/978-3-642-22444-7_15
7. Christin, D.: Privacy in mobile participatory sensing: current trends and future challenges. J. Syst. Software **116**, 57–68 (2016). ISSN 01641212. https://doi.org/10.1016/j.jss.2015.03.067
8. Erkin, Z., Tsudik, G.: Private computation of spatial and temporal power consumption with smart meters. In: Bao, F., Samarati, P., Zhou, J. (eds.) ACNS 2012. LNCS, vol. 7341, pp. 561–577. Springer, Heidelberg (2012). https://doi.org/10.1007/978-3-642-31284-7_33
9. Kursawe, K.: Some Ideas on Privacy Preserving Meter Aggregation. Radboud Universiteit Nijmegen, Technical report, ICIS-R11002, pp. 1–15 (2010)

10. Erkin, Z.: Private data aggregation with groups for smart grids in a dynamic setting using CRT. In: 2015 IEEE International Workshop on Information Forensics and Security, WIFS 2015 - Proceedings, vol. 30, pp. 1–6. IEEE, 11 2015. ISBN 9781467368025. https://doi.org/10.1109/WIFS.2015.7368584

11. Rastogi, V., Nath, S.: Differentially private aggregation of distributed time-series with transformation and encryption. In: Proceedings of the ACM SIGMOD International Conference on Management of Data, New York, New York, USA, pp. 735–746. ACM Press (2010). ISBN 9781450300322. https://doi.org/10.1145/1807167.1807247

12. Ács, G., Castelluccia, C.: I Have a DREAM! (DiffeRentially privatE smArt Metering). In: Filler, T., Pevný, T., Craver, S., Ker, A. (eds.) IH 2011. LNCS, vol. 6958, pp. 118–132. Springer, Heidelberg (2011). https://doi.org/10.1007/978-3-642-24178-9_9

13. Shi, E., Hubert Chan, T.-H., Rieffel, E., Chow, R., Song, D.: Privacy-preserving aggregation of time-series data. In: Annual Network & Distributed System Security Symposium (NDSS) (2011)

14. Kursawe, K., Danezis, G., Kohlweiss, M.: Privacy-friendly aggregation for the smart-grid. In: Fischer-Hübner, S., Hopper, N. (eds.) PETS 2011. LNCS, vol. 6794, pp. 175–191. Springer, Heidelberg (2011). https://doi.org/10.1007/978-3-642-22263-4_10

15. Yang, L., Li, F.: Detecting false data injection in smart grid in-network aggregation. In: 2013 IEEE International Conference on Smart Grid Communications, SmartGridComm 2013, pp. 408–413. IEEE, October 2013. ISBN 9781479915262. https://doi.org/10.1109/SmartGridComm.2013.6687992

16. McLaughlin, S., Holbert, B., Fawaz, A., Berthier, R., Zonouz, S.: A multi-sensor energy theft detection framework for advanced metering infrastructures. IEEE J. Sel. Areas Commun. 31(7), 1319–1330 (2013). ISSN 07338716. https://doi.org/10.1109/JSAC.2013.130714

17. Lie, D., Maniatis, P.: Glimmers: resolving the privacy/trust quagmire. In: Proceedings of the Workshop on Hot Topics in Operating Systems - HOTOS, volume Part F1293, New York, New York, USA, 2017, pp. 94–99. ACM Press. ISBN 9781450350686. https://doi.org/10.1145/3102980.3102996

18. Boudot, F.: Efficient proofs that a committed number lies in an interval. In: Preneel, B. (ed.) EUROCRYPT 2000. LNCS, vol. 1807, pp. 431–444. Springer, Heidelberg (2000). https://doi.org/10.1007/3-540-45539-6_31

19. Morais, E., Koens, T., van Wijk, C., Koren, A.: A survey on zero knowledge range proofs and applications. SN Appl. Sci. 1(8), 1–17 (2019). ISSN 2523-3963. https://doi.org/10.1007/s42452-019-0989-z

20. Blum, A., Dwork, C., McSherry, F., Nissim, K.: Practical privacy: the SulQ framework. In: Proceedings of the ACM SIGACT-SIGMOD-SIGART Symposium on Principles of Database Systems, pp. 128–138 (2005). https://doi.org/10.1145/1065167.1065184

21. Sun, R., Shi, Z., Lu, R., Lu, M., Shen, , X.: APED: an efficient aggregation protocol with error detection for smart grid communications. In: GLOBECOM - IEEE Global Telecommunications Conference, pp. 432–437 (2013). https://doi.org/10.1109/GLOCOM.2013.6831109

22. Shi, Z., Sun, R., Lu, R., Chen, L., Chen, J., Shen, X.S.: Diverse grouping-based aggregation protocol with error detection for smart grid communications. IEEE Trans. Smart Grid 6(6), 2856–2868 (2015). ISSN 19493053. https://doi.org/10.1109/TSG.2015.2443011

23. Ahadipour, A., Mohammadi, M., Keshavarz-Haddad, A.: Statistical-based privacy-preserving scheme with malicious consumers identification for smart grid, pp. 1–9, April 2019
24. Ben-Sasson, E., Bentov, I., Horesh, Y., Riabzev, M.: Scalable, transparent, and post-quantum secure computational integrity. IACR Cryptol. ePrint Arch., 2018:46 (2018). URL https://eprint.iacr.org/2018/046.pdf
25. Corrigan-Gibbs, H., Boneh, D.: Prio: private, robust, and scalable computation of aggregate statistics. In: Proceedings of the 14th USENIX Symposium on Networked Systems Design and Implementation, NSDI 2017, pp. 259–282, March 2017. ISBN 9781931971379
26. Bünz, B., Bootle, J., Boneh, D., Poelstra, A., Wuille, P., Maxwell, G.: Bulletproofs: short proofs for confidential transactions and more. In: Proceedings - IEEE Symposium on Security and Privacy, volume 2018-May, pp. 315–334. IEEE, May 2018. ISBN 9781538643525. https://doi.org/10.1109/SP.2018.00020
27. Szymanski, T.: "Hypermeshes": optical interconnection networks for parallel computing. J. Parall. Distrib. Comput. **26(1)**, 1–23 (1995). ISSN 07437315. https://doi.org/10.1006/jpdc.1995.1043
28. Eisenberg, B.: On the expectation of the maximum of IID geometric random variables. Stat. Probabil. Lett. **78**(2), 135–143 (2008). ISSN 01677152. https://doi.org/10.1016/j.spl.2007.05.011

LLVM-Based Circuit Compilation
for Practical Secure Computation

Tim Heldmann, Thomas Schneider, Oleksandr Tkachenko,
Christian Weinert[✉], and Hossein Yalame

Technical University of Darmstadt, Darmstadt, Germany
tim.heldmann@stud.tu-darmstadt.de,
{schneider,tkachenko,weinert,yalame}@encrypto.cs.tu-darmstadt.de

Abstract. Multi-party computation (MPC) allows two or more parties to jointly and securely compute functions over private inputs. Cryptographic protocols that realize MPC require functions to be expressed as Boolean or arithmetic circuits. Deriving such circuits is either done manually, or with hardware synthesis tools and specialized MPC compilers. Unfortunately, such existing tools compile only from a single front-end language and neglect decades of research for optimizing regular compilers.

In this paper, we make MPC practical for developers by automating circuit compilation based on the compiler toolchain LLVM. For this, we develop an LLVM optimizer suite consisting of multiple transform passes that operate on the LLVM intermediate representation (IR) and gradually lower functions to circuit level. Our approach supports various front-end languages (currently C, C++, and Fortran) and takes advantage of powerful source code optimizations built into LLVM. We furthermore make sure to produce circuits that are optimized for MPC, and even offer fully automated post-processing for efficient post-quantum MPC.

We empirically measure the quality of our compilation results and compare them to the state-of-the-art specialized MPC compiler HyCC (Büscher et al. CCS'2018). For all benchmarked HyCC example applications (e.g., biomatch and linear equation solving), our highly generalizable approach achieves similar quality in terms of gate count and composition.

Keywords: MPC · Circuit compilation · LLVM · Hardware synthesis

1 Introduction

Multi-party computation (MPC) allows two or more parties to jointly compute functions over their respective inputs, while the privacy of the inputs is ensured and nothing but the functions' output is revealed. First cryptographic protocols to realize MPC were proposed already in the 1980's by Yao [63] and Goldreich, Micali, and Widgderson [23]. However, it took until 2004 for MPC to be implemented efficiently [41] and see adoption for privacy-preserving applications, e.g., private set intersection [28,49] and privacy-preserving machine learning (PPML) [7,20,46,48].

© Springer Nature Switzerland AG 2021
K. Sako and N. O. Tippenhauer (Eds.): ACNS 2021, LNCS 12727, pp. 99–121, 2021.
https://doi.org/10.1007/978-3-030-78375-4_5

The widespread adoption of MPC is unfortunately compromised by the requirement to implement the functions to be computed as Boolean or arithmetic circuits. This process is tedious and error-prone when done by hand, and additionally requires an extensive understanding of the underlying cryptographic protocols to build circuits that can be evaluated efficiently.

To address this issue, previous works tried to develop toolchains for automatic compilation of high-level code to circuit representations. Most notably, the specialized MPC compiler HyCC [13] compiles ANSI C to optimized Boolean and arithmetic circuits. However, works like HyCC allow compilation only from a very limited subset of a *single front-end language* and more importantly neglect decades of research that went into building and optimizing conventional compilers like GCC and the versatile LLVM toolchain [38], which we leverage in this paper.

Other works like TinyGarble [17,56] rely on logic synthesis tools (e.g., Synopsis Design Compiler [57] or Yosys-ABC [1,62]) to generate net lists of Boolean circuits. However, logic synthesis tools require knowledge of hardware description languages like Verilog or VHDL, and were built to optimize electronic circuits in terms of clock cycle usage, routing, and placing [58]. To match the cost metrics relevant for efficient MPC and restrict circuit generation to the supported basic gate types, it is nevertheless possible to re-purpose such tools by providing custom constraints and technology libraries.

Our Contributions. In this paper, we aim at making MPC practical for software developers by automating circuit compilation based on the compiler toolchain LLVM [38]. For this, we design and implement an LLVM optimizer suite consisting of multiple transform passes that gradually lower functions to circuit level. For example, the passes remove conditional branching and array accesses, eliminate constant logic, and replace low-level instructions with optimal building blocks that we obtain via logic synthesis tools.

Our LLVM optimizer suite operates entirely on the level of the LLVM intermediate representation (IR). Thus, we naturally facilitate compilation from numerous existing front-ends for a wide range of programming languages. We currently support a subset of C, C++, and Fortran, and give a road map for extensions to additional high-level languages like Rust. Furthermore, our approach takes advantage of powerful source code optimizations built into LLVM, which can swiftly deliver significant improvements in terms of resulting circuit sizes and therefore MPC performance.

To bridge the gap from LLVM-IR to MPC frameworks, we provide a converter to the widely known Bristol circuit format [59] that can be evaluated, e.g., by ABY [18] and MOTION [11]. Instead of converting LLVM-IR to Bristol, it is also possible to further compile via LLVM back-ends to a conventional architecture like x86. Besides testing for functional correctness, such circuit-based binaries have further applications in mitigating cache side-channel attacks [42].

Even though we construct our circuits from optimal building blocks, the assembled result might not be overall optimal. Therefore, to compete with sophisticated circuit-level optimizations delivered by specialized MPC compilers like HyCC [13], we add fully automated post-processing. For this, we convert Bristol to Verilog net lists, apply optimization passes of synthesis tools [1,57,62], and convert back to Bristol. By defining different constraint sets and technology libraries, we not only support size-optimized Boolean circuits considering the free-XOR [35] and half-gates technique [65], but also cost metrics for post-quantum secure MPC [12]. Our approach is generic and can easily be adjusted for further cost metrics that might be of interest, e.g., garbling under standard assumptions [24].

Finally, we empirically measure the quality of our compilation results and compare them to the specialized MPC compiler HyCC [13]. For this, we benchmark example applications similar as in the HyCC repository (e.g., biomatch and linear equation solving via Gaussian elimination) as well as additional implementations. Our LLVM-based approach achieves similar or even better quality in terms of gate count and composition, while also providing a richer feature set and the benefits of extensibility to other high-level languages as well as MPC cost metrics.

In short, we summarize our contributions as follows:

1. Design and implementation of an LLVM-based toolchain for circuit compilation from various high-level languages (currently a subset of C, C++, and Fortran) publicly available at https://encrypto.de/code/LLVM.
2. Fully automated post-processing of Bristol circuits via logic synthesis tools to optimize for (post-quantum) MPC-relevant cost metrics [12,35,65].
3. Empirical performance evaluation showing similar or better quality compared to the specialized MPC compiler HyCC [13].

Outline. We introduce the necessary MPC as well as compiler background in Sect. 2 and discuss related works in Sect. 3. In Sect. 4, we present our LLVM-based circuit compilation toolchain and propose fully automated post-processing in Sect. 5. We evaluate our results in Sect. 6 before concluding with a comprehensive outlook in Sect. 7.

2 Preliminaries

We introduce the necessary background on MPC (cf. Sect. 2.1), LLVM (cf. Sect. 2.2), and logic synthesis (cf. Sect. 2.3).

2.1 Multi-party Computation

Multi-party computation (MPC) allows N mutually distrusting parties to jointly compute functions over their respective inputs. In addition to the correctness of the function output, MPC guarantees privacy of the inputs as nothing but the function output is revealed. Two seminal cryptographic protocols that realize MPC and are still highly relevant are Yao's garbled circuits [63] and the protocol by Goldreich, Micali, and Wigderson (GMW) [23]. The work by Beaver, Micali, and Rogaway (BMR) [5] extends the idea of Yao from the two- to the multi-party case. All these protocols obliviously evaluate Boolean circuit representations of the desired functionality. While Yao/BMR evaluate the circuit in a constant-round protocol, the number of communication rounds for GMW depends on the multiplicative depth of the circuit. In this work, we for now

focus on the compilation of size-optimized Boolean circuits for the first approach (Yao/BMR), while an extension to depth-optimized circuits for GMW is
straightforward.

Yao's Garbled Circuits/BMR. In Yao's protocol [63], one party (the garbler) generates a garbled circuit corresponding to a Boolean circuit by encrypting the truth table of each gate. The other party (the evaluator) then evaluates (decrypts) the circuit received from the garbler. Transferring the required
keys corresponding to the chosen inputs is done via a cryptographic protocol
called oblivious transfer (OT) [30]. Today's most efficient solution for garbled
circuits is a combination of free-XOR [35] and half-gates [65]. With these optimizations, each AND gate requires the transfer of two ciphertexts, whereas XOR
gates are essentially free (no communication necessary). BMR [5] is an extension
of Yao's protocol to the multi-party case, where all parties garble and evaluate
the circuit such that no subset of parties learns anything about the intermediate
values.

Post Quantum Yao. A post-quantum version of Yao's protocol was recently
proposed in [12], where the adversary has access to a quantum computer. The
authors proved Yao's protocol in the quantum world under the assumption that
the used encryption scheme is PQ-IND-CPA. They assume the quantum adversary has only access to a quantum random oracle and does not make queries
to the encryption oracle in superposition. Since the free-XOR optimization [35]
was established under a weaker assumption, it cannot be applied in the quantum
world, and thus the cost of XOR is the same as for AND gates.

Bristol Circuit Format. Circuit descriptions specify either the transfer of data
on register level (RTL) or a list of gates, wires, and their connections (net list).
The most commonly used circuit format for MPC is the Bristol format [3,59],
which is a plain text net list format. Each line in a Bristol file represents a
single INV, AND or XOR gate. Each gate can have one or two inputs and has
exactly one output, all of which are specified via IDs. Every output ID is unique,
in static single assignment (SSA) form, and all IDs are in ascending order. The
number of input as well as output wires is specified in the header of the file.

Frameworks. There exist many MPC frameworks [52] implementing different
protocols and considering different adversaries w.r.t. the ratio of honest/dishon-
est parties (honest/dishonest majority or full threshold) and the behaviour (semi-
honest, covert, malicious). MPC frameworks take either a (subset) of a high-level
language language, a domain specific programming language, or a net list as
input. Our approach generates circuits in the Bristol net list format, which we
empirically evaluate using the state-of-the-art framework MOTION [11].

2.2 LLVM

LLVM started as a research project in 2004 with the goal to enable lifelong program analysis and transformation for arbitrary software [38]. While originally
being an acronym for low-level virtual machine, the LLVM project now spans

different sub projects including, e.g., the specification for the LLVM intermediate representation (LLVM-IR), the LLVM-IR optimizer, and the Clang C/C++ front-end. The intended LLVM workflow to generate binaries is as follows:

1. Compile source code with a compatible front-end to LLVM-IR.
2. Use the LLVM optimizer to optimize the LLVM-IR.
3. Use a back-end to compile the optimized LLVM-IR to an executable binary.

Due to the strict separation between the toolchain steps, LLVM is highly extensible. Especially the default optimization passes can be extended with custom language- or hardware-specific passes. In the following, we introduce the LLVM-IR and optimization passes in more detail.

LLVM Intermediate Representation (LLVM-IR). The LLVM-IR is the connection between the front- and back-ends. It exists in three forms: as (i) in-memory IR used by the compiler, (ii) bytecode for just-in-time compilers, and (iii) a human readable assembly language. While all of them are equivalent, and can be converted losslessly, all further mentions of LLVM-IR refer to the assembly language.

LLVM-IR is a static single assignment (SSA)-based, strictly typed representation of the translated source code. For translating to LLVM-IR, features common in non-SSA-based languages must to be transformed. One typical problem here is the differing state of variables depending on previously run parts of the program, as occurs with branching. The solution for SSA restrictions in LLVM-IR are so-called φ-nodes. Such nodes are instructions that evaluate differently depending on which part of the program was executed last. The same problem occurs when dealing with loops, which often can also be resolved via loop unrolling.

LLVM Optimizer. The LLVM optimizer is intended to perform LLVM-IR to LLVM-IR transformations. It utilizes optimizer passes that run on specific parts of the LLVM-IR. The optimizer comes with a set of language independent optimizations [40], but can be extended with additional passes. Passes can be categorized as analysis and transform passes. Analysis passes generate additional information about LLVM-IR code without any modifications. Transform passes, on the other hand, are allowed to modify the LLVM-IR, possibly invalidating previously run analyses in the process.

2.3 Logic Synthesis for MPC Circuit Compilation

Logic synthesis tools take a function description in a hardware description language (HDL) such as Verilog or VHDL as input, and transform it to the respective target technologies, e.g., look-up tables (LUTs) for field programmable gate arrays (FPGAs) or Boolean gates for application-specific integrated circuits (ASICs). Since creating hand-optimized Boolean circuits for MPC is an error-prone and time-consuming task, it is a promising and natural approach to utilize existing logic synthesis tools. However, software developers are rarely familiar with HDLs and re-purposing such tools for performing MPC-specific optimizations requires the development of custom ASIC technology libraries. In this work, we utilize the open-source Yosys-ABC synthesis tool [1, 62]. In contrast to previous works [17, 19], we not only create optimized building blocks, but provide a fully automated compilation and MPC-optimization workflow from several high-level programming languages. Furthermore, we are the first to develop a custom ASIC technology library for post-quantum MPC [12].

3   Related Work

Our LLVM-based circuit compilation toolchain allows software developers to use multiple different general-purpose programming languages to produce circuits for MPC. To the best of our knowledge, we are the first to utilize LLVM for such an endeavour. The recently initiated CIRCT project [39] instead aims at replacing HDLs like Verilog with IR as a portable format between hardware design tools and utilizes the LLVM infrastructure for offering transform passes between different abstractions as well as architectures. On the other hand, there exist multiple tools that allow developers to generate circuits from a *single* high-level or domain-specific language. In the following, we first give an overview of and comparison between these tools. Then, we briefly review MPC frameworks that evaluate such generated circuits or can be programmed with custom MPC-specific languages, and choose one of them for benchmarking circuits generated via our LLVM toolchain (cf. Sect. 6.2).

3.1   Circuit Generation

The following approaches generate circuits from high-level code, but like our LLVM-based circuit compilation approach abstract away the circuit evaluation.

Dedicated Compilers for MPC. TinyGarble [17, 56] uses logic synthesis to generate efficient Boolean circuits for MPC from Verilog net lists. However, since TinyGarble's optimization process requires a Verilog net list, it is reliant on an external high-level synthesis (HLS) tool to compile high-level code. Our approach is designed to be compatible with various LLVM front-ends for compiling high-level languages, and focuses on the generation of circuits from LLVM-IR. Since many programmers are unfamiliar with HDLs, we target a much larger community of software developers.

CBMC-GC is an extension of CBMC [15]. It converts ANSI C to a Boolean circuit [27] and proves that the generated circuit is equivalent to the input program. While being compatible with ANSI C, CBMC-GC has limitations in terms of variable naming and is restricted to inputs from two parties. Not only is our approach input and variable name agnostic, as the circuit's inputs are generated depending on the function's signature, but it is also not limited to ANSI C. Furthermore, we make use of the source code optimization suite of LLVM. Starting circuit synthesis from optimized code can be very advantageous (cf. Sect. 4.1).

Although our implementation does not have a formal verification proof, the correctness of our compiler can be tested easily, e.g., by running a test suite after compiling the transformed LLVM-IR code via LLVM back-ends to x86 binaries.

HyCC [13] is a compiler that extends CBMC-GC for hybrid circuits that contain Boolean and arithmetic parts for efficient mixed-protocol evaluation. For this, it partitions an ANSI C program into modules using a heuristic and then assigns the most suitable MPC protocol in terms of runtime and/or communication. Furthermore, HyCC applies sophisticated circuit-level optimizations to increase efficiency. Currently, our toolchain generates only Boolean circuits and does not support automatic protocol selection. Manual switching of protocols can be implemented in the "gateify" pass (cf. Sect. 4.3), and automated protocol selection can be added by developing an optimization pass based on the work of [31] (cf. Sect. 7). Instead of transform passes that perform circuit-level optimizations, we optimize circuits via post-processing by utilizing logic synthesis tools (cf. Sect. 5).

The portable circuit format (PCF) compiler [36] generates circuits in the PCF format using bytecode generated by LCC [22] from ANSI C. This allows for optimizations on the bytecode level such as dead gate removal and constant propagation. Then, it uses an internal language to translate instructions from the bytecode to a Boolean circuit. In comparison to net list formats, PCF features loops and recursion, removing the need for recursive function inlining as well as loop unrolling. We also make use of bytecode-level optimizations and additionally feature circuit-level post-processing. In contrast to our toolchain, PCF relies on the LCC compiler, which supports only ANSI C.

High-Level Synthesis. High-level synthesis (HLS) is an approach for designing circuits in a high-level language by specifying the desired behavior. The exact translation into a chip design is controlled by a compiler. HLS systems usually require expert knowledge, as they rely on domain-specific programming languages like Verilog [16,60] instead of C, C++, or Fortran.

Another difference between HLS tools and our approach is that their goal is to create electrical circuits, which have different cost metrics than MPC. In HLS, much thought is given to routing and placement algorithms, which is of limited use for optimizing circuits for MPC. Being designed with MPC applications in mind, our approach leads to better extensibility and less overhead.

Domain-Specific Languages. PAL [45] compiles a domain-specific language (DSL) into a size-optimized Boolean circuit. The scalable KSS compiler [37] generates Boolean circuits from a DSL by employing a constant propagation optimization method. SMCL [47], L1 [55], and Wysteria [50] are custom high-level languages for describing MPC that support the combination of different MPC protocols. Wysteria additionally provides a tool for circuit compilation. However, it is based on functional programming and therefore tedious to learn by developers who are trained in imperative programming.

Obliv-C [64] and EzPC [14] extend a general-purpose programming language with MPC-specific functionality descriptions, e.g., secret/public variables and oblivious if, and automatically compile executables. Also, EzPC supports automatic protocol assignment for mixed-protocol computation and uses the ABY framework [18] to compile executable binaries.

3.2 MPC Frameworks for Circuit Evaluation

There exist many MPC frameworks that allow users to run MPC protocols. They take as input a circuit description or a domain-specific language for MPC. For a comprehensive overview, we refer to [25]. Here, we briefly describe popular MPC frameworks and justify the choice for our benchmarks (cf. Sect. 6.2).

Fairplay [41] was the first framework for secure two-party computation and FairplayMP [6] is its extension to multiple parties. Both use the secure function description language (SFDL) to describe functions and convert to the secure hardware description language (SHDL). Sharemind [8] implements 3-party additive secret sharing with honest majority and is a proprietary software programmed with SecreC. TASTY [26] is a framework for two parties that allows to mix garbled circuits with homomorphic encryption for applications implemented using a subset of Python. FastGC [29] is a two-party framework that is implemented in Java and uses garbled circuits. It allows gate-level pipelining of the circuit, which reduces the memory overhead. Frigate [44] consists of an efficient compiler and an interpreter. The compiler takes a custom C-style language and ensures the correctness of the generated circuits.

ABY [18] and ABY3 [43] are mixed-protocol MPC frameworks written in C++ for two- and three-party computation, respectively. FRESCO is a Java MPC framework that implements additive secret sharing schemes. EMP toolkit [61] implements a few MPC protocols and oblivious transfer in C++, and provides a low-level API for cryptographic primitives. PICCO [66] compiles an input description written in a custom extension of C to C and runs it using N-party threshold MPC. JIFF [9] is a framework for information-theoretically secure MPC written in JavaScript, which allows to use it in web applications. MPyC [54] is a Python framework for N-party computation based on secret sharing protocols. MP-SPDZ [33] implements multiple MPC protocols and cryptographic primitives in different security models. SCALE-MAMBA [2] is a framework for N-party mixed-protocol maliciously secure MPC that compiles a Python-like language to bytecode that is parsed by a "virtual machine" that runs MPC protocols.

In this work, we use the MOTION framework [11] for benchmarking the circuits generated by our LLVM toolchain (cf. Sect. 6.2). MOTION is an N-party mixed-protocol MPC framework implemented as a C++ library. It supports the BMR [5] as well as the GMW protocol [23] (cf. Sect. 2.1). It guarantees semi-honest security against all but one corrupted parties (full threshold). MOTION provides a user-friendly API for evaluating circuits in the Bristol format [3,59], which is also the format our toolchain produces.

4   LLVM-Based Circuit Compilation

We now present our LLVM-based circuit compilation approach. For this, we first give an intuitive overview of our optimizer suite of LLVM transform passes that ultimately compile high-level programs to Bristol circuit representations. Afterwards, each transform pass is described in detail.

4.1   Overview

In this section, we give an intuition for our transformation pipeline that consists of a suite of LLVM-IR transform passes.

Using a compatible LLVM front-end (e.g., Clang for C and C++, or Flang for Fortran), we first compile the given code to LLVM-IR code. At this point, we can apply all source code optimizations shipped by LLVM and additionally perform loop unrolling. For example, the control flow simplifying pass "simplify-cfg" removes unused branches and pre-computes constant branching logic. The instruction combine pass "instcombine" simplifies Boolean or arithmetic instructions. For example, the function return b^(a*b/a); operating on integers a and b always returns 0. The LLVM optimizer detects this in 117 ms , while HyCC [13] takes 25 s to generate a circuit with 6416 gates. The output of this stage is the basis for circuit generation and will be referred to as the "base function".

As branching is not trivially supported on circuit level, we then proceed with eliminating all branches. This is done by our so-called "phi remove" pass, described in Sect. 4.2. For this, we have to inline all basic blocks (i.e., blocks of sequentially executed instructions), and swap φ-nodes to select instructions (the LLVM-IR representation of a ternary expression).

Now that all code is contained in one basic block, our "gateify" pass, described in 4.3, replaces all instructions with "circuit-like" functions. A circuit-like function is a function that first disassembles the inputs into single bits, evaluates the function exactly as a circuit consisting of primitive gates, and reassembles the result to the required datatype.

Next in line is the "array to multiplexer" pass. Its basic concept is similar to the gateify pass as it swaps arrays for calls to functions that behave like multiplexers and thus enable *oblivious* data accesses on circuit level. The exact differences are described in Sect. 4.4.

Since at this point the program's code is distributed over various external functions, we now apply the "merge function" pass (cf. Sect. 4.5). It takes all the different external function calls, merges their content into a single function, and wires the outputs to inputs accordingly. The resulting function behaves very similar to a circuit consisting of primitive gates that represents the same function.

To further reduce the size of the generated function, and therefore the circuit, a final pass is applied. The "constant logic elimination" pass, described in Sect. 4.6, simplifies logic instructions, by either pre-computing the result in case of two constant operands, or passing the corresponding value or constant in case of one constant operand, or both operands being the same. Lastly, if the result of an instruction is never used, it is removed entirely.

The LLVM-IR code consisting of only gate-like instructions can then be trivially converted to the Bristol format, using our LLVM-to-Bristol converter (cf. Sect. 4.7). Then, we convert Bristol to a Verilog net list and apply our postprocessing using logic synthesis tools (cf. Sect. 5). This results in an even smaller circuit that we convert back to Bristol. The latter constitutes the final result of our toolchain.

4.2 Phi Remove Pass

The LLVM-IR is in static single assignment (SSA) form (cf. Sect. 2.2). Therefore, conditional branching is difficult to represent, as variables can have different values depending on COMPthe evaluation of condition statements. The LLVM-IR solution for this problem are φ-nodes that take different values depending on the COMPpreviously evaluated basic block. While the basic premise of SSA holds true for circuits, φ-nodes must be replaced. Instead of calculating only one path depending on the branch condition and generating the value in the φ-node depending on the source basic block, we evaluate both branches regardless of the condition and replace φ-nodes with a multiplexer. The selection bit of the multiplexer is the result of the branching condition.

This approach works flawlessly for two-way branching, e.g., regular if/else instructions. The LLVM-IR specification, however, allows for an arbitrary number of values to be taken by a φ-node, as a basic block can be branched to by any number of other basic blocks. This can be especially useful when trying to represent switch/case instructions. It requires analysis of the conditions leading to the branch, as well as a multiplexer tree instead of a single multiplexer.

To summarize, the phi remove pass identifies two-way branches, recursively descends the basic blocks, replaces φ-nodes with ternary select instructions (which are handled later), and splices the instruction lists of the basic block together with the goal to ultimately achieve a function that only has one basic block.

4.3 Gateify Pass

The "gateify" pass iterates through every function of the module and identifies supported instructions. Once such an instruction is found, the pass creates a new "circuit-like" function with the same behavior. The exact instructions of this new function are defined by our building blocks. In Appendix A we elaborate on how we utilized hardware synthesis tools similar to [17,56] in order to obtain optimal circuits for primitive instructions that can serve as building blocks.

As Boolean MPC circuits rely on bitwise operations while LLVM-IR uses static types larger than one bit, it is necessary to disassemble the static compound types like i8 or i32 into 8 or 32 i1 types, respectively. This disassembly process is done as a prephase inside the new function. The computation of the result is then done by applying the instructions specified in the circuit description of the building block. Once all circuit instructions have been copied, the result is then given as i1 types that have to be reassembled to a compound type. This reassembly process is the postphase of the building block.

The newly created function signature and return value are matched to be equal to the operands and result of the replaced instruction. The original instruction is then deleted and all uses of the calculated result are replaced with the result returned by the newly created function. Internally, the new function is assigned the attribute "gate" to mark it as a circuit-like function. This will be important to identify mergeable functions later.

4.4   Array to Multiplexer Pass

The "array to multiplexer" pass is required for source languages that support arrays as a construct and corresponding front-ends use the LLVM-IR array construction to represent them. For example, LLVM-IR code generated by Clang for C and C++ will use the LLVM-IR array construct. On the other hand, Fortran instead of arrays has the concept of multidimensional fields, which behave similar but are not represented as arrays in LLVM-IR.

The pass first analyzes the array usage of a given function. During this analysis, all stores to constant positions are mapped out. If the same position is written multiple times, the updated values are saved as well.

However, if a value should be stored to a position unknown at compile time, every single position could be affected. To support stores to variable positions, every position of the array can be updated with the result of a ternary instruction, similar to this: i == unkownPos ? newValue : array[i]. This updates every position with its own value, except the one position where the condition evaluates to true, leading to this position being updated to the new value.

Once all stores are mapped out, the analysis result is used to replace all reads from a constant position with the value that is at the corresponding position at the time the read occurs. This value is the last update that happened to that position before the read occurred. If a value is loaded from a position that is not known during the compilation, the whole array is given to a multiplexer tree, with the position disassembled to bits as the decision bits of the multiplexer tree in the corresponding layer.

4.5   Merge Pass

The "merge" pass creates a single circuit from all circuit-like functions. It first creates its own prephase, disassembling every parameter of the base function to provide as primitives for the merged function. Then, it clones the instructions of all circuit-like functions in the new merged function, excluding the pre- and postphase. As the instructions of the base function were topologically sorted, it is guaranteed that the first instruction to clone will only access primitives or constants. Following functions will either reference primitives or intermediate results that have already been disassembled.

After successfully cloning every instruction of a building block, it is necessary to map the cloned instructions such that their references match the context of the function they got cloned into. The output bits of every instruction are saved and mapped to the corresponding inputs of any instruction that references them. Once the return statement is reached, a postphase is added that reassembles the output bits to match the return type of the base function.

4.6   Constant Logic Elimination Pass

The "constant logic elimination" pass cleans up the merged function. It iterates through every instruction in the merged function. Due to the gateify pass, every instruction is either an AND, XOR, or INV instruction. In case both operands for an AND or XOR instruction are constants, the result is computed, and every instruction referencing the result updated to use the pre-computed value instead. The original instruction is then removed. In case one operand is a constant, a lookup table determines whether to keep the instruction or replace it with a constant or the operand. Once all logic gates with constant operands are eliminated, a last pass is done to remove instructions with unused results.

4.7   Export to Bristol Format

After all passes are executed, the resulting LLVM-IR file contains a fully merged function with exactly one basic block. This file can then be passed to our "LLVM-IR to Bristol" converter. The converter will skip past the disassembly phase and locate the gate operations. Each line is then converted to a line in the Bristol file, until the end of the gate section is reached. As it is idiomatic to the Bristol format to state the amount of gates and wires in the beginning of the file, as well as the amount of parameters and the bit width of the result, they are calculated and prepended. Finally, the unique references between LLVM-IR instructions are mapped to wire identifiers in ascending order while ensuring that result bits are mapped to the highest numbered wire identifiers.

5   Post-processing Circuits for MPC

In Sect. 4, we described our LLVM-based circuit compilation approach that gradually lowers high-level implementations to circuit level. Specifically, our "gateify" transform pass (cf. Sect. 4.3) replaces all low-level LLVM-IR instructions with functionally equivalent building blocks. We designed these building blocks to be optimal according to MPC-relevant cost metrics, as was previously done in [17,19,32,56] (cf. Appendix A). However, we did not develop a transform pass that performs optimizations on the overall circuit, i.e., across building blocks. Therefore, our generated circuits are likely larger than those generated by specialized MPC compilers like HyCC [13] that include such optimizations, e.g., to replace highly redundant circuit parts.

To not reinvent the wheel, we instead propose to utilize HDL synthesis tool on the output of our LLVM-based circuit compilation for global optimizations. For this, we create a fully automated pipeline that first converts Bristol circuit descriptions to Verilog net lists, applies optimization passes of logic synthesis tools [1,57,62], and converts back to Bristol. By defining different constraint sets and technology libraries, we not only support size-optimized Boolean circuits considering the free-XOR [35] and half-gates technique [65], but also cost metrics for post-quantum secure MPC [12] (cf. Sect. 6). Additionally, this approach is generic and can easily be adjusted for further cost metrics that might be of interest, e.g., garbling under standard assumptions [24].

The conversion from Bristol to Verilog net lists is trivial due to their similarity in terms of structure and abstraction level. Yosys-ABC [1,62] then generates a net list output under synthesis objectives, which are provided by the developer to optimize the parameters like minimizing the delay or limiting the area of a synthesized circuit. We therefore develop customized technology libraries of basic gates, which include synthesis parameters like timing and area to guide the mapping. Concretely, we want to output a functionally equivalent yet optimized Boolean circuit net list consisting of only 2-input AND and XOR as well as INV gates. For the conversion back to Bristol, we utilize existing tooling from SCALE-MAMBA [2], which we extend to parse custom Verilog modules.

In the following, we detail our custom constraints and technology libraries. The performance (both in terms of runtime and circuit quality improvement) is evaluated in Sect. 7.

5.1   Customized Logic Synthesis for MPC

Regarding MPC protocols, we focus on Yao and BMR in this work (cf. Sect. 2.1), and therefore Boolean circuits. The relevant cost metric for both protocols is the multiplicative size, i.e., the number of AND gates in the circuit. In contrast, the cost of XOR evaluation is negligble [35]. We configure Yosys-ABC to minimize the multiplicative size by setting the XOR and INV gate area to 0 and for AND gates to a high non-zero value.

5.2   Customized Logic Synthesis for Post-quantum MPC

In the post-quantum setting, the previously discussed free-XOR optimization [35] is not applicable (cf. Sect. 2.1). Therefore, the relevant cost metric shifts from multiplicative size to the total gate count.

In order to meet our goal in post-quantum MPC, we design a customized library containing 2-input XOR as well as non-XOR gates. We set the area of all gates to an equal non-zero value and synthesize circuits considering area optimization as the main restriction. By doing so, we provide highly optimized circuits for post-quantum MPC that can moreover be conveniently compiled from various high-level languages.

6   Evaluation

We evaluate our LLVM-based approach to MPC circuit compilation in two aspects. First, we provide a complexity analysis of our transform passes. Then, we measure the quality of the generated circuits with respect to MPC cost metrics in comparison with HyCC [13] and provide concrete runtime as well as communication overheads when executing such circuits with the recent MPC framework MOTION [11]. The implementation of our toolchain is publicly available at https://encrypto.de/code/LLVM.

6.1   LLVM Transform Passes Complexity Analysis

The runtime of our transform passes depends on the number of instructions, basic blocks, and the size of the required building blocks. A summary of all complexities analyzing the worst case for each pass can be found in Table 1. Note that it is impossible for the worst case to occur simultaneously in all passes.

Let I be the number of instructions in the base function, B the number of basic blocks, N the size of the biggest utilized building block, and A the largest number of elements in an array.

Table 1. Complexity of our passes. I is the number of instructions, B the number of basic blocks, A the number of array slots, and N the size of the largest building block.

Pass	φ-Remove	Gateify	Array2MUX	Merge	C. Log. Elim.	**Total**
Complexity	$O(I+B)$	$O(I \cdot N)$	$O(I \cdot A)$	$O(I^2 \cdot N^2)$	$O(I \cdot N)$	$O(I^2 \cdot N^2)$

Phi Remove Pass. The phi remove pass's runtime mainly depends on the size and the number of basic blocks in the function. It recursively descends through all B basic blocks, replacing each φ-instruction with a ternary one. Once all the φ-instructions are replaced, the basic block merging is linear in complexity, as all instructions are saved in a doubly linked list, where we can splice the instructions of any basic block into any other basic block. Since in the worst case all I instructions are φ-instructions, this leads to a complexity of $O(I+B)$.

Gateify Pass. The gateify pass's runtime depends on the number of instructions and the size of the building blocks replacing them. Once an instruction has been replaced at least once, we can reference the building block for all identical instructions later on. But since we cannot universally assume duplicate instructions, the complexity class is $O(I \cdot N)$.

Array to Multiplexer Pass. The array to multiplexer pass iterates through all I instructions to identify `getelementptr` instructions. The modification step can then either forward constant reads with a complexity of $O(1)$, or create a multiplexer tree. For arrays with A elements, this tree has size $2^{\lceil \log_2(A) \rceil} - 1 \approx A$. The total complexity is therefore $O(I \cdot A)$.

Merge Pass. The merge gate function pass copies all instructions from the building blocks into a single function. While all other passes operate on the base function, this pass copies and re-maps every instruction in the building block functions. It can also not rely on the same splicing technique as the phi remove pass as the splice instruction is moving and not copying the instructions, and we might need to reference the building block again later. This leads to a complexity of $O(I^2 \cdot N^2)$, which makes the merge pass the bottleneck.

Constant Logic Elimination Pass. The constant logic elimination pass goes through all now $O(I \cdot N)$ instructions and pre-computes as well as propagates the logic if possible. Then, all unused computations are removed. This means $O(I \cdot N)$ instructions are inspected/modified.

6.2 LLVM Compilation Performance and Quality Analysis

We now measure the quality of the circuits generated by our LLVM-based toolchain (cf. Sect. 4) with respect to MPC cost metrics, and especially the benefits of our fully automated post-processing (cf. Sect. 5). Furthermore, we benchmark these circuits with the recent MPC framework MOTION [11] to analyze concrete runtime as well as communication overheads.

All these aspects we also compare to the HyCC compiler [13] to demonstrate that our very extensible approach can compete with or even outperform specialized MPC tools. Therefore, we mainly base our evaluation on applications written in C from the HyCC repository that we detail below.

Table 2. Compile time of different programs in seconds, compiled with HyCC [13] and LLVM, and with post-processing for minimizing the number of AND gates (LLVM$^+$) and the total number of gates for more efficient post-quantum MPC (LLVM PQ$^+$).

Program	HyCC [13]	LLVM	LLVM$^+$	LLVM PQ$^+$
Euclid	1.34	0.68	5.59	5.26
Dummy	2.20	1.32	10.73	10.88
Gauss	11.81	11.08	127.76	125.14
Biomatch	12.20	14.11	152.16	147.80

Benchmark Applications. The "Euclid" benchmark calculates the squared Euclidean distance between two points. This is a small and simple program, which shows basic translation capabilities.

The "biomatch" benchmark is similar to Euclid, but additionally calculates the square root of the result using Heron's method [21] with a cutoff at 20 iterations. This benchmark is used to show loop unroll handling and how highly repetitive functions can be greatly optimized with our post-processing approach.

The "Gauss" benchmark is a linear equation solver for up to 4 variables. It implements a forward elimination and backward substitution. This shows the difference if non-repetitive loops are unrolled and translated.

Additionally, we implement a "dummy" application that showcases as many supported features as possible in a comprehensive manner. The code for this application is attached in Appendix B.

Compile Time. In Table 2, we provide the runtime of the compilation for HyCC and our LLVM toolchain as well as the post-processing steps, measured on four cores of an Intel Xeon Gold 6144 CPU @ 3.50 GHz and 32 GB of RAM.

The compilation times of both approaches are comparable. For smaller applications (Euclid, dummy), LLVM is about twice as fast as HyCC. On the other hand, for a larger application (biomatch), HyCC is slightly faster. This is due to the comparatively high complexity of our merge pass (cf. Sect. 6.1) when handling large and redundant circuits, which is currently the bottleneck in our optimizer suite. Finally, we observe that the respective post-processing steps add a significant overhead of factor 10x on top of the basic compilation. However, we note that this is a one-time cost that occurs only before deployment when the development of an application is finalized.

Circuit Size and Composition. In Table 3, we show the circuit sizes and the composition of the compilation results. The basic compilation step with LLVM based on our transform passes already delivers circuits in the same order of magnitude as HyCC. However, they are concretely less efficient for MPC in terms non-free AND gates (by factor 1.3x to 2.1x). Especially the biomatch circuit is only half the size when compiled with HyCC. This is due to the fact that HyCC has circuit-level optimizations, making it possible to remove the highly redundant instructions coming from loop unrolling.

However, our fully automatic post-processing significantly lowers this disadvantage, making the Gauss application even more efficient than when compiled with HyCC. In terms of post-processing for post-quantum MPC, we have to compare the total number of gates (cf. Sect. 2.1). There, our post-quantum post-processing manages to reduce the size by up to factor 1.7x compared to the regular LLVM output and improves up to factor 1.3x upon the already post-processed version for MPC considering free-XOR [35].

Concrete Efficiency. In Table 4, we present the performance measurements when executing the circuits with the BMR protocol (cf. Sect. 2.1) in the recent MOTION framework [11] for up to $N = 5$ parties. The goal of this evaluation is to determine how the differences in circuit quality effect concrete performance, especially in comparison with the circuits generated by HyCC [13]. All benchmarks were performed on machines with an Intel Core i9-7960X CPU @ 2.80 GHz and 128 GB of RAM. Each party has a dedicated machine, communicating via 10 Gbit/s Ethernet with 1.25 ms RTT. Additionally, we simulate a 100 Mbit/s WAN connection with 100 ms RTT to model secure computation over the Internet.

Table 3. Circuit size of different programs compiled with HyCC and LLVM, and with post-processing for minimizing the number of AND gates (LLVM$^+$) and the total number of gates for more efficient post-quantum MPC (LLVM PQ$^+$).

Program	HyCC [13]	LLVM	LLVM$^+$	LLVM PQ$^+$
	Number of gates in thousands formatted as "non-XOR/total"			
Euclid	1.47 / 5.24	1.99 / 6.46	1.47 / 6.97	1.47 / 5.26
Dummy	1.59 / 5.30	2.19 / 6.05	1.74 / 7.40	1.74 / 5.78
Gauss	39.15 / 114.18	39.40 / 114.33	38.91 / 133.49	38.91 / 113.42
Biomatch	22.67 / 67.93	47.14 / 135.99	27.66 / 81.72	27.69 / 78.23

Table 4. Communication and runtime for running our applications using the BMR protocol [5] in the MOTION framework [11] with N parties.

Program	N	Communication [MB]			Runtime LAN [s]			Runtime WAN [s]		
		HyCC [13]	LLVM	LLVM$^+$	HyCC [13]	LLVM	LLVM$^+$	HyCC [13]	LLVM	LLVM$^+$
Euclid	2	0.88	1.17	0.88	0.18	0.22	0.19	1.14	1.20	1.17
	3	0.97	1.29	0.97	0.24	0.26	0.22	1.32	1.37	1.26
	4	1.06	1.41	1.06	0.27	0.33	0.28	1.38	1.56	1.40
	5	1.15	1.54	1.15	0.34	0.36	0.31	1.57	1.86	1.58
Dummy	2	0.95	1.29	1.03	0.19	0.23	0.20	1.13	1.26	1.20
	3	1.04	1.42	1.14	0.24	0.26	0.26	1.22	1.31	1.32
	4	1.14	1.55	1.24	0.29	0.30	0.29	1.37	1.59	1.43
	5	1.24	1.69	1.35	0.35	0.37	0.33	1.57	1.84	1.76
Gauss	2	22.45	22.59	22.31	1.79	1.92	1.80	3.97	3.98	3.90
	3	24.84	24.99	24.68	1.86	1.90	1.90	7.44	7.67	7.65
	4	27.23	27.40	27.06	2.16	2.19	2.16	12.14	11.65	10.95
	5	29.62	29.80	29.43	2.47	2.51	2.56	15.79	16.24	15.48
Biomatch	2	13.01	27.01	15.86	1.97	3.69	1.79	3.81	6.43	4.00
	3	14.39	29.88	17.55	1.94	3.73	2.04	6.20	10.32	6.30
	4	15.78	32.76	19.24	2.15	4.05	2.14	8.35	15.53	9.23
	5	17.16	35.64	20.93	2.50	4.57	2.46	11.34	19.67	12.23

As expected, the performance strongly correlates with the size of the generated circuit. We can observe that while the runtime and communication for LLVM-generated circuits is already in the same ballpark as HyCC, our post-processing diminishes the additional overhead such that our circuits perform almost equally (Euclid, dummy, biomatch), and sometimes even better (Gauss). The biggest impact of post-processing can again be seen for the biomatch application, where we are able to cut runtime and communication almost by half by removing highly redundant parts of the circuit.

7   Conclusion and Outlook

Our LLVM-based approach to MPC circuit compilation is promising, especially in terms of extensibility, usability, and circuit quality. Supporting different non-domain specific programming languages (currently C, C++, and Fortran), we make MPC practical for various software developer communities.

In the following, we give a comprehensive outlook by discussing remaining limitations regarding LLVM-IR language support, extensions to other front-ends, and the generation of hybrid circuits for mixed-protocol MPC.

Language Support. Our LLVM optimizer-based approach currently does not support structs and recursive functions. Struct support can be added as part of the gateify pass (cf. Sect. 4.3), or a dedicated struct remove pass. Partial inlining of recursive functions has been a field of interest of the LLVM community since 2015 [4] as it can increase performance of recursive programs [53]. With exception of tail call optimized recursion, however, no optimization pass has been developed until now.

Extension to Other Front-Ends. The highlight of our approach is its independence of the compiled high-level language, as we only operate on LLVM-IR, which is shared among all front-ends. Unfortunately, front-ends for different programming languages compile to vastly different LLVM-IR code. For example, a simple program that returns the addition of two integers compiles to ~17 kB of LLVM-IR code when written in Rust, while a C version is only ~2 kB. This is because Clang almost directly translates C code to LLVM-IR, while Rust makes heavy use of LLVM's intrinsic functions (e.g., `llvm.sadd.with.overflow.*`). In case of errors like overflow, underflow, type errors, out of bounds memory accesses, or similar, probably unwanted behavior, the code tries to recover or terminate the program with a meaningful error message. Translating all these extra steps in a circuit would lead to massive circuits.

We suggest to develop a transform pass that tries to remove most of the checks and error states. Thus, only circuit logic for essential parts of the program is generated, while keeping the program and circuit equivalent for valid inputs.

Hybrid Circuits. HyCC [13] generates Boolean and arithmetic circuits for mixed-protocol MPC. In contrast, our work only studies size-optimized Boolean circuits. A first step for achieving parity in this regard would be to equip the gateify pass with suitable building blocks (e.g., depth-optimized Boolean circuits for GMW [23]) and to allow direct translation of arithmetic LLVM-IR operations like `add`. As for finding the optimal protocol selection, we propose to implement a suitable heuristic that gathers and analyzes all relevant information during an immutable pass and divides/annotates the program in a module/analysis pass. Any of this would also require a significant extension of the Bristol format to support arithmetic operations and annotations for protocol conversions.

Acknowledgment. We thank the anonymous reviewers for their helpful comments. This project was co-funded by the Deutsche Forschungsgemeinschaft (DFG) – SFB 1119 CROSSING/236615297 and GRK 2050 Privacy & Trust/251805230, and by the German Federal Ministry of Education and Research and the Hessian Ministry of Higher Education, Research, Science and the Arts within their joint support of the National Research Center for Applied Cybersecurity ATHENE. It has received funding from the European Research Council (ERC) under the European Union's Horizon 2020 research and innovation program (grant agreement No. 850990 PSOTI).

A   Optimized Building Blocks

We provide details of the building blocks used by our LLVM toolchain during the gateify pass (cf. Sect. 4.3). To obtain these building blocks, we utilize logic synthesis tools [1,57,62] with our custom technology libraries (cf. Sect. 5.2) to optimize (multiplicative) size and restrict the types of basic gates. The most common building blocks are addition, subtraction, multiplication, and (integer) division, multiplexer for array accesses, and comparator, which we detail in the following. Table 5 shows a summary of the circuit size complexities, i.e., the number of non-linear (AND) gates. Moreover, we show the actual circuit sizes for standard 32 bit integers generated by the synthesis tool.

Table 5. Multiplicative complexity of building blocks for bit length l. Concrete sizes for $l = 32$ as used in Sect. 4.3.

Building block	ADD	SUB	MULT	DIV	MUX	CMP
Multiplicative complexity (# non-XOR)	$l-1$	$l-1$	$l^2 - l$	$l^2 + 2l + 1$	l	l
Concrete size ($l = 32$)	31	31	993	1264	32	32

Addition/Subtraction. To perform addition of two l-bit values, the traditional ripple carry adder (RCA), in which the carry out of one stage is fed directly to the carry-in of the next stage, has a multiplicative size of $l-1$ [10,34]. The subtractor can be viewed as a special case of adder as the subtraction of two values a and b can be represented as $a - \bar{b} + 1$ where $\bar{b}$ denotes the two's complement representation of b.

Multiplication. In classic logic synthesis, a multiplier outputs a $2l$-bit product of two l-bit inputs. The best approach for this multiplier is the textbook method with the size of $2l^2 - l$ [34]. However, in many programming languages and MPC protocols, multiplication is defined as a $l \rightarrow l$ operation, where the product of two l unsigned integers is l-bit. Generating a $l \rightarrow l$ multiplication with logic synthesis tools give us a circuit size of $l^2 - l$ [27,44].

Division. The division operation computes the quotient and remainder of two binary integer numbers. The standard approach for the division is similar to the text-book multiplication, where the divisor is iteratively shifted and subtracted from the remainder. By doing so, one division operation can be built with complexity of $2l^2$ AND gates. Restoring division can help us in hardware synthesis to have a complexity of $l^2 + 2l + 1$ [51].

Multiplexer. A 2-to-1 MUX was proposed in [35] with a size of l. The tree architecture for an m-to-1 MUX has size $(m - 1)l$.

Comparator. The standard comparator circuit checks whether one l-bit number is greater than another with a size of l. We implement this comparator as described in [35].

B   Dummy Application

In Listing 1 we provide the C++ code for our dummy application that we use for benchmark purposes in addition to applications from the HyCC repository (cf. Sect. 6.2). It showcases as many supported features as short as possible.

Listing 1. Dummy application that covers many supported features.

```
1   #include <stdio.h>
2
3   int dummy (int a, int b, int c) {
4       int array[8];
5       for (int i=0; i<8; i++) {
6           array[i] = a + b * i;
7       }
8       int ret=0;
9       if (c < array[c]) {
10          ret = array[2] + array[3];
11      }
12      else {
13          ret = array[0] * array[1];
14      }
15      return ret;
16  }
17
18  int main(){
19      int a, b, c;
20      scanf("%d\n%d\n%d", &a, &b, &c);
21      printf("DummyFunction: %d\n", dummy(a, b, c));
22  }
```

References

1. ABC: A system for sequential synthesis and verification. http://www.eecs.berkeley.edu/~alanmi/abc/
2. Aly, A., et al.: SCALE-MAMBA v1. 10: Documentation (2020)
3. Archer, D., et al.: Bristol Fashion MPC circuits (2020). https://homes.esat.kuleuven.be/~nsmart/MPC/
4. Barrio, P., Carruth, C., Molloy, J.: Recursion inlining in LLVM (2015). https://www.llvm.org/devmtg/2015-04/slides/recursion-inlining-2015.pdf
5. Beaver, D., Micali, S., Rogaway, P.: The round complexity of secure protocols (extended abstract). In: STOC (1990)
6. Ben-David, A., Nisan, N., Pinkas, B.: FairplayMP: a system for secure multi-party computation. In: CCS (2008)
7. Boemer, F., Cammarota, R., Demmler, D., Schneider, T., Yalame, H.: MP2ML: a mixed-protocol machine learning framework for private inference. In: ARES (2020)
8. Bogdanov, D., Laur, S., Willemson, J.: Sharemind: a framework for fast privacy-preserving computations. In: Jajodia, S., Lopez, J. (eds.) ESORICS 2008. LNCS, vol. 5283, pp. 192–206. Springer, Heidelberg (2008). https://doi.org/10.1007/978-3-540-88313-5_13

9. Boston University: JIFF: JavaScript implementation of federated functionalities (2015). https://github.com/multiparty/jiff/
10. Boyar, J., Damgård, I., Peralta, R.: Short non-interactive cryptographic proofs. J. Cryptol. **13**, 449–472 (2000)
11. Braun, L., Demmler, D., Schneider, T., Tkachenko, O.: MOTION - A framework for mixed-protocol multi-party computation. ePrint (2020). https://ia.cr/2020/1137
12. Büscher, N., et al.: Secure two-party computation in a quantum world. In: Conti, M., Zhou, J., Casalicchio, E., Spognardi, A. (eds.) ACNS 2020. LNCS, vol. 12146, pp. 461–480. Springer, Cham (2020). https://doi.org/10.1007/978-3-030-57808-4_23
13. Büscher, N., Demmler, D., Katzenbeisser, S., Kretzmer, D., Schneider, T.: HyCC: compilation of hybrid protocols for practical secure computation. In: CCS (2018)
14. Chandran, N., Gupta, D., Rastogi, A., Sharma, R., Tripathi, S.: EzPC: programmable, efficient, and scalable secure two-party computation for machine learning. In: EuroS&P (2019)
15. Clarke, E., Kroening, D., Lerda, F.: A tool for checking ANSI-C programs. In: Jensen, K., Podelski, A. (eds.) TACAS 2004. LNCS, vol. 2988, pp. 168–176. Springer, Heidelberg (2004). https://doi.org/10.1007/978-3-540-24730-2_15
16. Coussy, P., Morawiec, A.: High-Level Synthesis: From Algorithm to Digital Circuit. Springer, Dordrecht (2008). https://doi.org/10.1007/978-1-4020-8588-8
17. Demmler, D., Dessouky, G., Koushanfar, F., Sadeghi, A., Schneider, T., Zeitouni, S.: Automated synthesis of optimized circuits for secure computation. In: CCS (2015)
18. Demmler, D., Schneider, T., Zohner, M.: ABY - a framework for efficient mixed-protocol secure two-party computation. In: NDSS (2015)
19. Dessouky, G., Koushanfar, F., Sadeghi, A.R., Schneider, T., Zeitouni, S., Zohner, M.: Pushing the communication barrier in secure computation using lookup tables. In: NDSS (2017)
20. Fereidooni, H., et al.: SAFELearn: secure aggregation for private federated learning. In: Deep Learning and Security Workshop (2021)
21. Fowler, D., Robson, E.: Square root approximations in old Babylonian mathematics: YBC 7289 in context. Historia Mathematica (1998)
22. Fraser, C.W., Hanson, D.R.: A Retargetable C Compiler: Design and Implementation. Addison-Wesley (1995)
23. Goldreich, O., Micali, S., Wigderson, A.: How to play any mental game or a completeness theorem for protocols with honest majority. In: STOC (1987)
24. Gueron, S., Lindell, Y., Nof, A., Pinkas, B.: Fast garbling of circuits under standard assumptions. In: CCS, pp. 567–578. ACM (2015)
25. Hastings, M., Hemenway, B., Noble, D., Zdancewic, S.: SoK: general purpose compilers for secure multi-party computation. In: S&P (2019)
26. Henecka, W., Kögl, S., Sadeghi, A., Schneider, T., Wehrenberg, I.: TASTY: tool for automating secure two-party computations. In: CCS (2010)
27. Holzer, A., Franz, M., Katzenbeisser, S., Veith, H.: Secure two-party computations in ANSI C. In: CCS (2012)
28. Huang, Y., Evans, D., Katz, J.: Private set intersection: are garbled circuits better than custom protocols? In: NDSS (2012)
29. Huang, Y., Evans, D., Katz, J., Malka, L.: Faster secure two-party computation using garbled circuits. In: USENIX Security (2011)
30. Ishai, Y., Kilian, J., Nissim, K., Petrank, E.: Extending oblivious transfers efficiently. In: Boneh, D. (ed.) CRYPTO 2003. LNCS, vol. 2729, pp. 145–161. Springer, Heidelberg (2003). https://doi.org/10.1007/978-3-540-45146-4_9

31. Ishaq, M., Milanova, A.L., Zikas, V.: Efficient MPC via program analysis: a framework for efficient optimal mixing. In: CCS (2019)
32. Javadi, M., Yalame, H., Mahdiani, H.: Small constant mean-error imprecise adder/-multiplier for efficient VLSI implementation of MAC-based applications. IEEE Trans. Comput. (2020)
33. Keller, M.: MP-SPDZ: a versatile framework for multi-party computation. In: CCS (2020)
34. Kolesnikov, V., Sadeghi, A.-R., Schneider, T.: Improved garbled circuit building blocks and applications to auctions and computing minima. In: Garay, J.A., Miyaji, A., Otsuka, A. (eds.) CANS 2009. LNCS, vol. 5888, pp. 1–20. Springer, Heidelberg (2009). https://doi.org/10.1007/978-3-642-10433-6_1
35. Kolesnikov, V., Schneider, T.: Improved garbled circuit: free XOR gates and applications. In: Aceto, L., Damgård, I., Goldberg, L.A., Halldórsson, M.M., Ingólfsdóttir, A., Walukiewicz, I. (eds.) ICALP 2008. LNCS, vol. 5126, pp. 486–498. Springer, Heidelberg (2008). https://doi.org/10.1007/978-3-540-70583-3_40
36. Kreuter, B., Shelat, A., Mood, B., Butler, K.: PCF: a portable circuit format for scalable two-party secure computation. In: USENIX Security (2013)
37. Kreuter, B., Shelat, A., Shen, C.H.: Billion-gate secure computation with malicious adversaries. In: USENIX Security (2012)
38. Lattner, C., Adve, V.S.: LLVM: a compilation framework for lifelong program analysis & transformation. In: Code Generation and Optimization (2004)
39. LLVM Community: CIRCT / Circuit IR compilers and tools (2020). https://github.com/llvm/circt
40. LLVM Project: LLVM's analysis and transform passes (2020). https://llvm.org/docs/Passes.html
41. Malkhi, D., Nisan, N., Pinkas, B., Sella, Y.: Fairplay - Secure two-party computation system. In: USENIX Security (2004)
42. Mantel, H., Scheidel, L., Schneider, T., Weber, A., Weinert, C., Weißmantel, T.: RiCaSi: rigorous cache side channel mitigation via selective circuit compilation. In: Krenn, S., Shulman, H., Vaudenay, S. (eds.) CANS 2020. LNCS, vol. 12579, pp. 505–525. Springer, Cham (2020). https://doi.org/10.1007/978-3-030-65411-5_25
43. Mohassel, P., Rindal, P.: ABY3: a mixed protocol framework for machine learning. In: CCS (2018)
44. Mood, B., Gupta, D., Carter, H., Butler, K.R.B., Traynor, P.: Frigate: a validated, extensible, and efficient compiler and interpreter for secure computation. In: Euro S&P (2016)
45. Mood, B., Letaw, L., Butler, K.: Memory-efficient garbled circuit generation for mobile devices. In: Keromytis, A.D. (ed.) FC 2012. LNCS, vol. 7397, pp. 254–268. Springer, Heidelberg (2012). https://doi.org/10.1007/978-3-642-32946-3_19
46. Nguyen, T.D., et al.: FLGUARD: secure and private federated learning. ePrint (2021). https://ia.cr/2021/025
47. Nielsen, J.D., Schwartzbach, M.I.: A domain-specific programming language for secure multiparty computation. In: Workshop on Programming Languages and Analysis for Security (2007)
48. Patra, A., Schneider, T., Suresh, A., Yalame, H.: ABY2.0: improved mixed-protocol secure two-party computation. In: USENIX Security (2020)
49. Pinkas, B., Rosulek, M., Trieu, N., Yanai, A.: PSI from PaXoS: fast, malicious private set intersection. In: Canteaut, A., Ishai, Y. (eds.) EUROCRYPT 2020. LNCS, vol. 12106, pp. 739–767. Springer, Cham (2020). https://doi.org/10.1007/978-3-030-45724-2_25

50. Rastogi, A., Hammer, M.A., Hicks, M.: Wysteria: a programming language for generic, mixed-mode multiparty computations. In: S&P (2014)
51. Robertson, J.E.: A new class of digital division methods. Trans. Electron. Comput. (1958)
52. Rotaru, D.: awesome-mpc (2020). https://github.com/rdragos/awesome-mpc# frameworks
53. Rugina, R., Rinard, M.: Recursion unrolling for divide and conquer programs. In: Midkiff, S.P., et al. (eds.) LCPC 2000. LNCS, vol. 2017, pp. 34–48. Springer, Heidelberg (2001). https://doi.org/10.1007/3-540-45574-4_3
54. Schoenmakers, B.: MPyC: secure multiparty computation in Python (2018). https://github.com/lschoe/mpyc/blob/master/README.md
55. Schropfer, A., Kerschbaum, F., Muller, G.: L1 - an intermediate language for mixed-protocol secure computation. In: Computer Software and Applications Conference (2011)
56. Songhori, E.M., Hussain, S.U., Sadeghi, A., Schneider, T., Koushanfar, F.: Tiny-Garble: highly compressed and scalable sequential garbled circuits. In: S&P (2015)
57. Synopsis: DC Ultra (2020). https://www.synopsys.com/implementation-and-signoff/rtl-synthesis-test/dc-ultra.html
58. Tatsuoka, M., et al.: Physically aware high level synthesis design flow. In: DAC (2015)
59. Tillich, S., Smart, N.: (Bristol Format) Circuits of basic functions suitable for MPC and FHE (2020). https://homes.esat.kuleuven.be/~nsmart/MPC/old-circuits.html
60. Verilog.com: Verilog Resources (2020). https://verilog.com/
61. Wang, X., Malozemoff, A.J., Katz, J.: EMP-toolkit: Efficient multiparty computation toolkit (2016). https://github.com/emp-toolkit
62. Wolf, C.: Yosys open synthesis suite. http://www.clifford.at/yosys/
63. Yao, A.C.: How to generate and exchange secrets (extended abstract). In: FOCS (1986)
64. Zahur, S., Evans, D.: Obliv-C: a language for extensible data-oblivious computation. ePrint (2015). https://ia.cr/2015/1153
65. Zahur, S., Rosulek, M., Evans, D.: Two halves make a whole. In: Oswald, E., Fischlin, M. (eds.) EUROCRYPT 2015. LNCS, vol. 9057, pp. 220–250. Springer, Heidelberg (2015). https://doi.org/10.1007/978-3-662-46803-6_8
66. Zhang, Y., Steele, A., Blanton, M.: PICCO: A general-purpose compiler for private distributed computation. In: CCS (2013)

An Efficient Passive-to-Active Compiler for Honest-Majority MPC over Rings

Mark Abspoel[1], Anders Dalskov[2]([✉]), Daniel Escudero[3], and Ariel Nof[4]

[1] CWI, Amsterdam, The Netherlands
abspoel@cwi.nl
[2] Partisia, Aarhus, Denmark
[3] Aarhus University, Aarhus, Denmark
escudero@cs.au.dk
[4] Technion, Haifa, Israel
ariel.nof@cs.technion.ac.il

Abstract. Multiparty computation (MPC) over rings such as $\mathbb{Z}_{2^{32}}$ or $\mathbb{Z}_{2^{64}}$ has received a great deal of attention recently due to its ease of implementation and attractive performance. Several actively secure protocols over these rings have been implemented, for both the dishonest majority setting and the setting of three parties with one corruption. However, in the honest majority setting, no *concretely* efficient protocol for arithmetic computation over rings has yet been proposed that allows for an *arbitrary* number of parties.

We present a novel compiler for MPC over the ring $\mathbb{Z}_{2^k}$ in the honest majority setting that turns a semi-honest protocol into an actively secure protocol with very little overhead. The communication cost per multiplication is only twice that of the semi-honest protocol, making the resultant actively secure protocol almost as fast.

To demonstrate the efficiency of our compiler, we implement both an optimized 3-party variant (based on replicated secret-sharing), as well as a protocol for n parties (based on a recent protocol from TCC 2019). For the 3-party variant, we obtain a protocol which outperforms the previous state of the art that we can experimentally compare against. Our n-party variant is the first implementation for this particular setting, and we show that it performs comparably to the current state of the art over fields.

1 Introduction

Multiparty computation (MPC) is a cryptographic tool that allows multiple parties to compute a given function on private inputs whilst revealing only its output; in particular, parties' inputs and the intermediate values of the computation remain hidden. MPC has by now been studied for several decades, and different protocols have been developed throughout the years.

Most MPC protocols are "general purpose", meaning that they can in principle compute *any* computable function. This generality is typically obtained by

---

A. Dalskov—Work done while author was a student at Aarhus University.

K. Sako and N. O. Tippenhauer (Eds.): ACNS 2021, LNCS 12727, pp. 122–152, 2021.
https://doi.org/10.1007/978-3-030-78375-4_6

representing the function as an arithmetic circuit modulo some integer p. Note that implied in this representation, is a set of integers on which computation can be performed. Traditionally, MPC protocols are classified as being either *boolean* or *arithmetic*, where the former have $p = 2$ and the latter has $p > 2$. However, most of the existing arithmetic MPC protocols, independently of their security, require the modulus to be a prime (and for some protocols this prime must be large) [5,6,14,18,22,29,31].

1.1   Secure Computation over Rings

It was only recently that practical protocols in the arithmetic setting for a non-prime modulus were developed. The SPDZ$_{2^k}$ protocol securely evaluates functions in the dishonest majority case [15], while several other works focus on honest majority case for small number of parties [2,14,21,22]. Computation over $\mathbb{Z}_{2^k}$ is appealing as it is generally more natural than computation modulo a prime, especially for powers like 2^{32}, 2^{64} or 2^{128}. This type of computation has the potential to lead to more efficient protocols with respect to computation over fields, as in practical settings it avoids a software implementation of a modular reduction operation by using native data-types existing in modern architectures. For example, computing fast reductions modulo an n-bit Mersenne prime requires computing a product of two n-bit numbers without overflow.[1] Thus, for a $\approx$128-bit prime, this requires arithmetic on 256-bit numbers. In contrast, arithmetic in $\mathbb{Z}_{2^{128}}$ is supported by most modern compilers. Furthermore, many MPC applications require bitwise operations, like secure comparison to be able to perform branching, or secure truncation to be able to handle fixed-point data. This is particularly relevant for machine learning applications, for example. Protocols based on computation modulo 2^k have the potential to execute these operations much more efficiently, given the existing compatibility between binary computation, that is, computation modulo 2, and operations modulo a larger power of 2.

  The improvement in performance of ring-based protocols was observed experimentally for the aforementioned SPDZ$_{2^k}$ protocol in [17]. More recently, the work by Dalskov et al. [16] demonstrated that the same applies for honest majority protocols, where the protocols over rings presented in that work outperform similar ones over fields by a factor of around 2.

1.2   Our Contributions

As discussed above, it is a natural and well-motivated question to study the efficiency of MPC protocols over $\mathbb{Z}_{2^k}$. In spite of the benefits that this algebraic structure may provide, protocol design becomes much harder due to the undesired properties of this ring, like the existence of zero-divisors. For example, to date, no concretely-efficient protocol over $\mathbb{Z}_{2^k}$ that works for any number of parties has been proposed in the honest majority setting. This is particular critical when active adversaries are considered, as techniques to ensure security in this

---

[1] This reduction uses the identity $x \cdot y = a2^n + b \equiv a + b \bmod 2^n - 1$ for some a, b. However this requires computing and storing the product $x \cdot y$ without overflow.

case typically rely on properties of fields. In this work, we push the knowledge barrier on this area by presenting a generic compiler that transforms a passively secure protocol for computation over $\mathbb{Z}_{2^{k+s}}$ in the honest majority setting, to a protocol over the ring $\mathbb{Z}_{2^k}$ that is actively secure with abort and provides roughly s bits of statistical security. Summarizing our contributions:

- Our compiler simplifies protocol design by only requiring that the underlying passively secure protocol is secure up to an additive attack, which is a condition that is much easier to ensure. For example, this was shown to hold for multiple well-known protocols over fields in [24], a result which we extend in our paper to recent protocols over rings.
- Our compiler is highly efficient and the overhead is essentially just twice that of the passively secure protocol. More precisely, each multiplication just needs to be evaluated twice.
- Our compiler preserves all the properties of the passively secure protocol. In particular, we obtain the first actively secure protocols where the cost of dot products is *independent* of their length without relying on expensive function dependent preprocessing such as is the case for prior work [13,21,22,34].
- Finally, we provide two instantiations and show through experiments that they are concretely efficient:

  1. Our first instantiation is for 3 parties and is based on replicated secret sharing. We show experimentally as well as theoretically that it outperforms other 3 party protocols both over the ring $\mathbb{Z}_{2^{k+s}}$ and over fields $\mathbb{Z}_p$ with $\log(p) \approx k + s$. This gap of s bits for the field case is necessary when considering applications that require more complex primitives like secure comparison or truncation, as traditional techniques for these tasks (e.g. [12]) require such a gap to guarantee privacy.
  2. Our second instantiation is for an arbitrary number n of parties, and is based on the work by Abspoel et al. [2]. It is the first *practical* (in the sense of having been experimentally demonstrated to be concretely efficient) example of such a protocol for $\mathbb{Z}_{2^k}$ with active security and an honest majority. The protocol from [2] requires $3(k + s) \log n$ bits per multiplication in the online phase; however we describe a novel optimization that removes the $\log n$ factor that might be of independent interest. Although our protocol does not outperform its field counterpart from [14] (it is merely comparable), our results illustrate that the *a priori* benefits of working over $\mathbb{Z}_{2^k}$ may be outweighed by the complexity of computing over the so-called Galois ring extensions, which are required to make these protocols work. This observation is relevant as many recent works, such as [8,9,34], rely on Galois ring extensions of large degree without taking into account their computational overhead.

Outline. Section 2 introduces some of the definitions we will be needing and Sect. 3 introduces the building blocks we need in our compiler. In Sect. 4 our main protocol (i.e., our compiler) is presented, as well as the formal statements of security and security proofs. We then present the n party instantiation in

Sect. 5, and a three party instantiation in Sect. 6. Finally, in Sect. 7 we present our experimental results and compare our results with prior works.

1.3 Related Work

The only previous general compiler with concrete efficiency over rings, to the best of our knowledge, is the compiler of [20], which was improved by [21]. However, their compiler does not preserve the adversary threshold when moving from passive to active security. In addition, in [20] and [21] the compiler was instantiated for the 3-party case only.

The only concretely efficient protocol for arithmetic computation over rings that works for *any* number of parties is the SPDZ_{2^k} protocol [15] which was proven to be practical in [17]. This protocol is for the dishonest majority and thus requires the use of much heavier machinery, which makes it orders of magnitudes slower than ours. However, they deal with a more complicated setting and provide stronger security.

The work of [30] provides a method for working over small fields (e.g., $\mathbb{F}_2$) which improves upon the Chida et al. protocol [14]. However, their method is not suited for the rings that we consider in our work.

In the three-party setting with one corruption, there are several works which provide high efficiency for arithmetic computations over rings. The Sharemind protocol [7] is being used to solve real-world problems but provides only passive security. The actively secure protocol of [22], which was optimized and implemented in [3], is based on the "cut–and–choose" approach and will be favorable when working over small rings. The actively secure three-party protocol of [21] is the closest to our protocol in the sense that they also focus on efficiency for large rings. The overall communication per multiplication gate of their protocol is $3(k+s)$ bits sent by each party, which is higher than ours by $(k+s)$ bits. We provide a detailed empirical comparison with [21] in Sect. 7.3. Finally, a new promising direction was presented by [9], but their verification step takes several seconds for a 1-million gate over fields, and this is expected to be orders of magnitude worse for rings due to the need of large-degree Galois ring extensions. The protocols of [13,34] have a slightly higher bandwidth overall than [3], but they focus on minimizing online (input-dependent) cost and they tailor their protocols to specific applications for machine learning. Also, [34] uses the techniques from [9] for the preprocessing, so it is unlikely to provide any efficiency in practice.

Finally, it is important to mention that the techniques from [9], which work for 3 parties, can be generalized to multiple parties as a passive-to-active compiler. This has been done in [28] over fields, and it is not hard to see that these techniques can be made to work over $\mathbb{Z}_{2^k}$ by considering large-degree Galois ring extensions, as done in [9]. However, this method is not practical as even a small degree extension can quite expensive, as shown in this work. Furthermore, the round complexity of the passively secure protocol is not preserved by this transformation.

2   Preliminaries and Definitions

Notation. Let $P_1, \ldots, P_n$ denote the n parties participating in the computation, and let t denote the number of corrupted parties. In this work, we assume an honest majority, hence $t < \frac{n}{2}$. Throughout the paper, we use H to denote the subset of honest parties and $\mathcal{C}$ to denote the subset of corrupted parties. We use $[n]$ to denote the set $\{1, \ldots, n\}$. $\mathbb{Z}_M$ denotes the ring of integers modulo M, and the congruence $x \equiv y \bmod 2^\ell$ is denoted by $x \equiv_\ell y$.

We use the standard definition of security based on the ideal/real model paradigm [10,25], with security formalized for non-unanimous abort. This means that the adversary first receives the output, and then determines for each honest party whether they will receive abort or receive their correct output. It is easy to modify our protocols so that the honest parties unanimously abort by running a single (weak) Byzantine agreement at the end of the execution [26]. For simplicity, we omit this step from the description of our protocols. Our protocol is cast in the synchronous model of communication, in which it is assumed that the parties share a common clock and protocols can be executed in rounds.

2.1   Linear Secret Sharing and Its Properties

Let ℓ be a positive integer. A perfect (t, n)-secret-sharing scheme (SSS) over $\mathbb{Z}_{2^\ell}$ distributes an input $x \in \mathbb{Z}_{2^\ell}$ among the n parties $P_1, \ldots, P_n$, giving *shares* to each one of them in such a way that any subset of at least $t + 1$ parties can reconstruct x from their shares, but any subset of at most t parties cannot learn anything about x from their shares. We denote by $\mathsf{share}(x)$ the sharing interactive procedure and by $\mathsf{open}(\llbracket x \rrbracket)$ the procedure to open a sharing and reveal the secret. The share procedure may take also in addition to x, a set of shares $\{x_i\}_{i \in J}$ for $J \subset [n]$ and $|J| \leq t$, such that $\mathsf{share}(x, \{x_i\}_{i \in J})$ satisfies $\llbracket x \rrbracket = (x_{1'}, \ldots, x_{n'})$, with $x_{i'} = x_i$ for $i \in J$. The open procedure may take an index i as an additional input. In this case, the secret is revealed to P_i only. In case the sharing $\llbracket x \rrbracket$ is not correct as defined below, $\mathsf{open}(\llbracket x \rrbracket)$ will output $\bot$. An SSS is linear if it allows the parties to obtain shares of linear combinations of secret-shared values without interaction.

Our compiler applies to any linear SSS over $\mathbb{Z}_{2^k}$ that has a multiplication protocol that is secure against additive attacks, as defined in Sect. 2.2. The only extra, non-standard properties required by our compiler are the following (for a formalization of the requirements of the SSS, see the full version of this work):

Modular Reduction. We assume that the open procedure is compatible with modular reduction, meaning that for any $0 \leq \ell' \leq \ell$ and any $x \in \mathbb{Z}_{2^\ell}$, reducing each share in $\llbracket x \rrbracket_\ell$ modulo $2^{\ell'}$ yields shares $\llbracket x \bmod 2^{\ell'} \rrbracket_{\ell'}$. We denote this by $\llbracket x \rrbracket_\ell \to \llbracket x \rrbracket_{\ell'}$.

Multiplication by $1/2$. Given a shared value $[\![x]\!]_\ell$, we assume if all the shares are even then shifting these shares to the right yields shares $[\![x']\!]_{\ell-1}$, where $x' = x/2$.[2]

Throughout the entire paper, we set the threshold for the secret-sharing scheme to be $\lfloor \frac{n-1}{2} \rfloor$, and we denote by t the number of corrupted parties. Now we define what it means for the parties to have *correct* shares of some value. Let J be a subset of honest parties of size $t + 1$, and denote by $\mathsf{val}([\![v]\!])_J$ the value obtained by these parties after running the open protocol, where no corrupted parties or additional honest parties participate, i.e. $\mathsf{open}([\![v]\!]^J)$. Note that $\mathsf{val}([\![v]\!])_J$ may equal $\perp$ and in this case we say that the shares held by the honest parties are not valid. Informally, a secret sharing is correct if every subset of $t + 1$ honest parties reconstruct the same value (which is not $\perp$).

2.2 Secure Multiplication up to Additive Attacks [23,24]

Our construction works by running a multiplication protocol (for multiplying two values that are shared among the parties) that is *not* fully secure in the presence of a malicious adversary and then running a verification step that enables the honest parties to detect cheating. In order to achieve this, we start with a multiplication protocol with the property that the adversary's ability to cheat is limited to carrying out a so-called "additive attack" on the output. Formally, we say that a multiplication protocol is secure up to an additive attack if it realizes the functionality $\mathcal{F}_{\mathsf{mult}}$, which receives input sharings $[\![x]\!]$ and $[\![y]\!]$ from the honest parties, and an additive error value d from the adversary, and outputs a sharing of $x \cdot y + d$. Since the corrupted parties can determine their own shares in the protocol, the functionality allows the adversary to provide the shares of the corrupted parties, but this reveals nothing about the secret-shared value.

The requirements defined by this functionality can be met by several semi-honest multiplication protocols over $\mathbb{Z}_{2^\ell}$. In this work we focus on two of them in particular: one based on replicated secret sharing, and the other a more recent protocol of Abspoel et al. [2], which extends Shamir's secret sharing to the setting of $\mathbb{Z}_{2^\ell}$.

In addition to the above, we consider a similar functionality $\mathcal{F}_{\mathsf{DotProduct}}$ that, instead of computing one single multiplication, allows the parties to securely compute the dot product of two vectors of shares, where the adversary is allowed to inject an additive error to the final output. As in [14], we will show that the functionality can be realized at almost the same cost as $\mathcal{F}_{\mathsf{mult}}$.

---

[2] If all the shares $[\![x]\!]_\ell$ are even then these shares may be written as $[\![x]\!]_\ell = 2 \cdot [\![y]\!]_\ell$, which, by the homomorphism property, are shares of $2 \cdot y$. Since these are shares of x as well, this shows that $x \equiv_\ell 2 \cdot y$, so x is even.

3   Building Blocks and Sub-protocols

Our compiler requires a series of building blocks in order to operate. These include generation of random shares and public coin-tossing, as well as broadcast. Furthermore, a core step of our compiler is checking that a secret-shared value is zero, leaking nothing more than this binary information. This is not easy to instantiate over $\mathbb{Z}_{2^k}$, and we discuss this in Sect. 3.1. We stress that our presentation here is very general and it assumes nothing about the underlying secret-sharing scheme beyond the properties stated in Sect. 2.1.

$\mathcal{F}_{\mathsf{rand}}$ – **Generating Random Coins.** We define the ideal functionality $\mathcal{F}_{\mathsf{rand}}$ to generate a sharing of a random value unknown to the parties. The functionality lets the adversary choose the corrupted parties' shares, which together with the random secret chosen by the functionality, are used to compute the shares of the honest parties. The way to compute this functionality depends on the specific secret-sharing scheme that is being used, and we discuss concrete instantiations later on.

$\mathcal{F}_{\mathsf{coin}}$ – **Generating Random Coins.** $\mathcal{F}_{\mathsf{coin}}(\ell)$ is an ideal functionality that chooses a random element from $\mathbb{Z}_{2^\ell}$ and hands it to all parties.

$\mathcal{F}_{\mathsf{bc}}$ – **Broadcast with Abort.** With this functionality, a given party sends a message to all other parties, with the guarantee that all the honest parties agree on the same value. Furthermore, if the sender is honest, the agreed-upon value is precisely the one that the sender sent. The protocol may abort, and can be instantiated using the well-known echo-broadcast protocol, where the parties echo the message they received and send it the other parties.

$\mathcal{F}_{\mathsf{input}}$ – **Secure Sharing of Inputs.** This is a functionality that allows a party to distribute consistent shares of its input. This can be instantiated generically by sampling $[\![r]\!]$ using $\mathcal{F}_{\mathsf{rand}}$, reconstructing this value to the party who will provide input x, and letting this party broadcast the difference $x - r$. The parties can then compute the shares $[\![x]\!] = (x - r) + [\![r]\!]$.

3.1   Checking Equality to 0

For our compiler we require a functionality $\mathcal{F}_{\mathsf{CheckZero}}(\ell)$, which receives $[\![v]\!]_\ell^H$ from the honest parties, uses them to compute v and sends accept to all parties if $v \equiv_\ell 0$. Else, if $v \not\equiv_\ell 0$, the functionality sends reject.

A simple way to approach this problem when working over a field is sampling a random multiplicative mask $[\![r]\!]$, multiply $[\![r \cdot v]\!] = [\![r]\!] \cdot [\![v]\!]$, open $r \cdot v$ and check that it is equal to zero. Clearly, since r is random then $r \cdot v$ looks also random if $v \neq 0$. However, this technique does not work over the ring $\mathbb{Z}_{2^\ell}$: for example, if v is a non-zero even number then $r \cdot v$ is always even, which reveals too much about v. In this section we present a generic protocol to solve the problem of checking equality of zero over the ring, which is unfortunately more expensive and complicated than the protocol over fields described above. On the upside, this check is only called *once* in a full execution of the main protocol and so the complexity of this technique is amortized away. Furthermore, for 3 parties for example, one can get a much more efficient solution, as we show in Sect. 6.

Our general protocol to compute $\mathcal{F}_{\mathrm{CheckZero}}$ is described in Protocol 1. We consider two functionalities, $\mathcal{F}_{\mathrm{CorrectMult}}$ and $\mathcal{F}_{\mathrm{randBit}}$, that compute correct multiplications and sample shared random bits, respectively.

We have the following proposition.

Proposition 1. *Protocol 1 securely computes* $\mathcal{F}_{\mathrm{CheckZero}}$ *with abort in the* $(\mathcal{F}_{\mathrm{randBit}}, \mathcal{F}_{\mathrm{CorrectMult}})$*-hybrid model in the presence of malicious adversaries who control* $t < n/2$ *parties.*

Protocol 1 Checking Equality to 0

Input: The parties hold a sharing $[\![v]\!]_\ell$.

The protocol:

1. The parties call $\mathcal{F}_{\mathrm{randBit}}$ to get ℓ random shared bits $[\![r_0]\!]_\ell, \ldots, [\![r_{\ell-1}]\!]_\ell$.
2. The parties bit-decompose v:
   (a) The parties compute $[\![r]\!]_\ell = \sum_{i=0}^{\ell-1} 2^i \cdot [\![r_i]\!]_\ell$.
   (b) The parties call $c = \mathsf{open}([\![v]\!]_\ell + [\![r]\!]_\ell)$ and bit-decompose this value as $(c_0, \ldots, c_{\ell-1})$.
   (c) The parties locally convert $[\![r_i]\!]_\ell \to [\![r_i]\!]_1$ for $i = 1, \ldots, \ell - 1$.
3. The parties check that all the bits of $v \bmod 2^\ell$ are zero:
   (a) The parties use $\mathcal{F}_{\mathrm{CorrectMult}}(1)$ to compute $\bigvee_{i=0}^{\ell-1}([\![r_i]\!]_1 \oplus c_i)$ and open this result.
   (b) If the opened value above is equal to 0 then the parties output accept. Otherwise they output reject.

Correct Multiplication. We consider a functionality $\mathcal{F}_{\mathrm{CorrectMult}}$, that is similar to $\mathcal{F}_{\mathrm{mult}}$, except it does not allow additive errors. Our protocol to instantiate this functionality is based on a technique known as "sacrificing". The idea is to generate correct random multiplication triples, which are then consumed to multiply the inputs. This is done by calling $\mathcal{F}_{\mathrm{rand}}$ three times to obtain random shares $[\![a]\!]$, $[\![b]\!]$, $[\![a']\!]$, calling $\mathcal{F}_{\mathrm{mult}}$ twice to obtain $[\![a \cdot b]\!]$ and $[\![a' \cdot b]\!]$, and using one triple to check the correctness of the other. Some modifications are needed in order to make this work over the ring $\mathbb{Z}_{2^\ell}$ for which we use the "SPD$\mathbb{Z}_{2^k}$ trick" from [15]. This requires us to perform the check over the ring $\mathbb{Z}_{2^{\ell+s}}$, thereby achieving a statistical error of 2^{-s}. The construction is presented in detail in Protocol 2.

Note that the protocol can be divided into two stages: an offline phase where the multiplication triple is generated, and an online phase where the triple is used to compute the product of the given shares. Thus, an efficient implementation would batch all the preprocessing together, and then proceed to consume these triples when the actual multiplication is required.

We remark that other approaches to produce random triples, such as "cut–and–choose", would work here as well. However, the "cut–and–choose" method becomes efficient only when many triples are being generated together—much more than what is needed by our protocol (for example, in [22], to achieve good parameters for the "cut–and–choose" process which yield low bandwidth, 2^{20}

triples are generated together). Thus, the sacrificing approach is favorable in our setting.

It can be easily checked that w in the protocol equals $d' - r \cdot d$, where d' and d are the additive errors from the two calls to $\mathcal{F}_{\mathsf{mult}}$. The following lemma shows that d cannot be non-zero with non-negligible probability, which shows that the triple $(\llbracket a \rrbracket_{\ell+s}, \llbracket b \rrbracket_{\ell+s}, \llbracket c \rrbracket_{\ell+s})$ is correct modulo 2^k. From this, the security of Protocol 2 follows.

Lemma 1 ([15]). *If the check at the end of the first step in Protocol 2 passes, then the additive error $d \in \mathbb{Z}_{2^{\ell+s}}$ that $\mathcal{A}$ sent to $\mathcal{F}_{\mathsf{mult}}$ is zero modulo 2^ℓ with probability at least $1 - 2^{-s}$.*

Protocol 2 Correct Multiplication

Inputs: Two shares $\llbracket x \rrbracket_\ell$ and $\llbracket y \rrbracket_\ell$ to be multiplied.

The protocol:
1. Generate a multiplication triple via sacrificing.
   (a) The parties call $\mathcal{F}_{\mathsf{rand}}(\ell + s)$ three times to obtain sharings $\llbracket a \rrbracket_{\ell+s}, \llbracket a' \rrbracket_{\ell+s}, \llbracket b \rrbracket_{\ell+s}$.
   (b) The parties call $\mathcal{F}_{\mathsf{mult}}(\ell + s)$ on input $\llbracket a \rrbracket_{\ell+s}$ and $\llbracket b \rrbracket_{\ell+s}$ to obtain shares $\llbracket c \rrbracket_{\ell+s}$, and on input $\llbracket a' \rrbracket_{\ell+s}$ and $\llbracket b \rrbracket_{\ell+s}$ to obtain shares $\llbracket c' \rrbracket_{\ell+s}$.
   (c) The parties call $\mathcal{F}_{\mathsf{coin}}(s)$ to obtain a random element $r \in \mathbb{Z}_{2^s}$.
   (d) The parties execute $\mathsf{open}(r \cdot \llbracket a \rrbracket_{\ell+s} - \llbracket a' \rrbracket_{\ell+s}) = a''$.
   (e) The parties execute $\mathsf{open}(a'' \cdot \llbracket b \rrbracket_{\ell+s} - r \cdot \llbracket c \rrbracket_{\ell+s} + \llbracket c' \rrbracket_{\ell+s}) = w$ and check that $w \equiv_{\ell+s} 0$.
   (f) If the check in the previous step has failed, the parties abort. Otherwise they compute $\llbracket \pi \rrbracket_{\ell+s} \rightarrow \llbracket \pi \rrbracket_\ell$ for $\pi \in \{a, b, c\}$, take $(\llbracket a \rrbracket_\ell, \llbracket b \rrbracket_\ell, \llbracket c \rrbracket_\ell)$ as a valid triple and continue to the next step.
2. Use the generated triple to multiply the input shares.
   (a) The parties execute $\mathsf{open}(\llbracket x \rrbracket_\ell - \llbracket a \rrbracket_\ell) = u$ and $\mathsf{open}(\llbracket y \rrbracket_\ell - \llbracket b \rrbracket_\ell) = v$.
   (b) The parties locally compute $\llbracket z \rrbracket_\ell = \llbracket c \rrbracket_\ell + u \cdot \llbracket b \rrbracket_\ell + v \cdot \llbracket a \rrbracket_\ell + u \cdot v$.

Outputs: The parties output the shares $\llbracket z \rrbracket_\ell$.

Proof: Since $\mathcal{F}_{\mathsf{mult}}$ is used in the first step, we have that $c = a \cdot b + d$ and $c' = a' \cdot b + d'$, where $d, d' \in \mathbb{Z}_{2^{\ell+s}}$ are the additive attacks chosen by the adversary in the first and second call to $\mathcal{F}_{\mathsf{mult}}$ respectively. It follows that $a'' \cdot b - r \cdot c + c' \equiv_{\ell+s} d' - r \cdot d$. Hence, if 2^v is the largest power of 2 dividing d, it holds that if $w \equiv_{\ell+s} 0$ then $\frac{r}{2^v} \equiv_{\ell+s-v} \left(\frac{d}{2^v}\right)^{-1} \frac{d'}{2^v}$, which holds with probability at most $2^{-(\ell+s-v)}$. If $d \not\equiv_\ell 0$, then $v > \ell$ and therefore this probability is upper bounded by 2^{-s}, which concludes the proof. ∎

Generating Random Shared Bits. We also consider a functionality $\mathcal{F}_{\mathsf{randBit}}$ that operates in a similar way to $\mathcal{F}_{\mathsf{rand}}$, but ensures the random shared value is in $\{0, 1\}$. We instantiate this functionality essentially by showing that the bit-generation procedure from [17], which is presented in the setting of SPDZ-type of shares, also extends to more general secret-sharing schemes. The main tool needed here is the "multiplication by 1/2" property presented in Sect. 2.1, which states that parties can locally divide their shares of a secret $x \bmod 2^\ell$ by 2 to obtain shares of $x/2 \bmod 2^{\ell-1}$, as long as the shares and the secret are even.

Proposition 2. *Protocol 3 securely computes functionality $\mathcal{F}_{\mathsf{randBit}}$ with abort in the $(\mathcal{F}_{\mathsf{rand}}, \mathcal{F}_{\mathsf{CorrectMult}})$-hybrid model in the presence of malicious adversaries controlling $t < n/2$ parties.*

Proof: First, observe that simulation here is straightforward. Since the protocol has no inputs, the simulator $\mathcal{S}$ can perfectly simulate the honest parties in the execution (including aborting the protocol if the honest parties output $\bot$ when running the open procedure). In addition, $\mathcal{S}$ receives the corrupted parties' shares when playing the role of $\mathcal{F}_{\mathsf{rand}}$ and $\mathcal{F}_{\mathsf{CorrectMult}}$ and thus it can compute locally $[\![b]\!]_\ell^{\mathcal{C}}$ and hand it to $\mathcal{F}_{\mathsf{randBit}}$.

Next, we show that the honest parties' output is identically distributed in both the real and ideal executions. In the simulation, the honest parties' output is random shares of a random bit (computed given the corrupted parties' shares). We now show that this is the same for the real world execution.

To see this, first observe that $c \equiv_{\ell+2} a^2$ (with no additive errors), since $\mathcal{F}_{\mathsf{CorrectMult}}$ was used. Furthermore, using Lemma 4.1 in [17], we obtain that $d = \sqrt{c}^{-1} \cdot a \bmod 2^{\ell+2}$ satisfies $d \in \{\pm 1, \pm 1 + 2^{\ell+1}\}$, so in particular $d \equiv_{\ell+1} \pm 1$, with each one of these cases happening with equal probability. This implies that $b = b'/2 \bmod 2^\ell$ satisfies $b \equiv_\ell 0$ or $b \equiv_\ell 1$, each case with the same probability.

The final observation is that all the shares of $b' = d + 1 \bmod 2^{\ell+1}$ are even, which is required to ensure that the parties can execute the right-shift operation in step 5. This is implied by the following argument. First of all, notice that $[\![d]\!]_{\ell+2} + 1 = 2 \cdot \sqrt{c}^{-1}[\![r]\!]_{\ell+2} + (\sqrt{c}^{-1} + 1)$. Now, the shares $2 \cdot \sqrt{c}^{-1}[\![r]\!]_{\ell+2}$ are even since these are obtained by multiplying the constant 2. Furthermore, the constant $(\sqrt{c}^{-1} + 1)$ is even since $\sqrt{c}^{-1}$ is odd, and by the assumptions of the secret-sharing scheme each canonical share of it is either 0 or the constant itself (see the "shares of a constant" property in Sect. 2.1), so in particular all of its shares are even.

The above implies that at the end of the protocol, the parties hold a sharing of a random bit, exactly as in the simulation. This concludes the proof. ∎

Protocol 3 Random Shared Bits Generation

The protocol:

1. The parties call $\mathcal{F}_{\mathsf{rand}}(\ell + 2)$ to obtain a shared value $[\![r]\!]_{\ell+2}$. Then, the parties set $[\![a]\!]_{\ell+2} = 2 \cdot [\![r]\!]_{\ell+2} + 1$.
2. The parties call $\mathcal{F}_{\mathsf{CorrectMult}}(\ell + 2)$ on input $[\![a]\!]_{\ell+2}$ and $[\![a]\!]_{\ell+2}$ to obtain shares $[\![c]\!]_{\ell+2} = [\![a^2]\!]_{\ell+2}$. Then, they run $\mathsf{open}([\![c]\!]_{\ell+2})$ to obtain c.
3. The parties compute $[\![d]\!]_{\ell+2} = \sqrt{c}^{-1} \cdot [\![a]\!]_{\ell+2}$, where $\sqrt{c}$ is a fixed square root of c modulo $2^{\ell+2}$, and the inverse is taken modulo $2^{\ell+2}$.
4. The parties locally convert $[\![d]\!]_{\ell+2} \to [\![d]\!]_{\ell+1}$, and compute $[\![b']\!]_{\ell+1} = [\![d]\!]_{\ell+1} + 1$.
5. The parties locally shift their shares of b' one position to the right to obtain shares $[\![b]\!]_\ell$, where $b \equiv_\ell \frac{b'}{2}$.

Outputs: The parties output $[\![b]\!]_\ell$.

4 The Main Protocol for Rings

In this section, we present our construction to compute arithmetic circuits over the ring $\mathbb{Z}_{2^k}$. A formal description appears in Protocol 4. Our protocol follows the paradigm of [14], which roughly works by running a "redundant" copy of the circuit where each shared wire value $[\![w]\!]$ is accompanied by $[\![r \cdot w]\!]$ for some global uniformly random r. In [14] it was shown that such a "dual" execution allows the parties to perform a simple check to ensure that no additive errors were introduced in the multiplication gates. However, such check does not directly work over $\mathbb{Z}_{2^k}$, given that it relies on the fact that every non-zero element must be invertible, which only holds over fields.

In order to reduce the cheating success probability, we borrow the idea of [15] of working on the larger ring $\mathbb{Z}_{2^{k+s}}$. As we will show below, this ensures that a similar check to that in [14] over fields can be carried out over $\mathbb{Z}_{2^{k+s}}$, ensuring no additive attacks over $\mathbb{Z}_{2^k}$ are carried out, except with probability at most 2^{-s}.

At the core of the security of our protocol lies the following lemma, which shows that an additive attack that is non-zero modulo 2^k in any multiplication gate leads to failure in the final check to zero, with overwhelming probability.

Protocol 4 Computing Arithmetic Circuits Over the Ring $\mathbb{Z}_{2^k}$

Inputs: Each party P_j ($j \in \{1, \ldots, n\}$) holds an input $x_j \in \mathbb{Z}_{2^k}^L$.

Auxiliary Input: The parties hold the description of an arithmetic circuit C over $\mathbb{Z}_{2^k}$ that computes f on inputs of length $M = L \cdot n$. Let N be the number of multiplication gates in C. In addition, the parties hold a parameter $s \in \mathbb{N}$.

The protocol:

1. *Secret sharing the inputs:*
   (a) For each input x_j held by party P_j, party P_j represent it as an element of $\mathbb{Z}_{2^{k+s}}^L$ and sends x_j to $\mathcal{F}_{\text{input}}(k + s)$.
   (b) Each party P_j records its vector of shares $(x_1^j, \ldots, x_M^j)$ of all inputs, as received from $\mathcal{F}_{\text{input}}(k + s)$. If a party received $\perp$ from $\mathcal{F}_{\text{input}}$, then it sends abort to the other parties and halts.

2. *Generate randomizing shares:* The parties call $\mathcal{F}_{\text{rand}}(k + s)$ to receive $[\![r]\!]_{k+s}$, where $r \in_R \mathbb{Z}_{2^{k+s}}$.

3. *Randomization of inputs:* For each input wire sharing $[\![v_m]\!]_{k+s}$ (where $m \in \{1, \ldots, M\}$) the parties call $\mathcal{F}_{\text{mult}}$ on $[\![r]\!]_{k+s}$ to receive $[\![r \cdot v_m]\!]_{k+s}$.

4. *Circuit emulation:* The parties traverse over the circuit in topological order. For each gate G_ℓ the parties work as follows:
   - G_ℓ *is an addition gate:* Given tuples $([\![x]\!]_{k+s}, [\![r \cdot x]\!]_{k+s})$ and $([\![y]\!]_{k+s}, [\![r \cdot y]\!]_{k+s})$ on the left and right input wires respectively, the parties locally compute $([\![x + y]\!]_{k+s}, [\![r \cdot (x + y)]\!]_{k+s})$.
   - G_ℓ *is a multiplication-by-a-constant gate:* Given a constant $a \in \mathbb{Z}_{2^k}$ and tuple $([\![x]\!]_{k+s}, [\![r \cdot x]\!]_{k+s})$ on the input wire, the parties locally compute $([\![a \cdot x]\!]_{k+s}, [\![r \cdot (a \cdot x)]\!]_{k+s})$.
   - G_ℓ *is a multiplication gate:* Given tuples $([\![x]\!]_{k+s}, [\![r \cdot x]\!]_{k+s})$ and $([\![y]\!]_{k+s}, [\![r \cdot y]\!]_{k+s})$ on the *left* and *right* input wires respectively:
     (a) The parties call $\mathcal{F}_{\text{mult}}$ on $[\![x]\!]_{k+s}$ and $[\![y]\!]_{k+s}$ to receive $[\![x \cdot y]\!]_{k+s}$.
     (b) The parties call $\mathcal{F}_{\text{mult}}$ on $[\![r \cdot x]\!]_{k+s}$ and $[\![y]\!]_{k+s}$ to receive $[\![r \cdot x \cdot y]\!]_{k+s}$.

5. *Verification stage:* Let $\{([\![z_i]\!]_{k+s}, [\![r \cdot z_i]\!]_{k+s})\}_{i=1}^N$ be the tuples on the output wires of all multiplication gates and let $\{[\![v_m]\!]_{k+s}, [\![r \cdot v_m]\!]_{k+s}\}_{m=1}^M$ be the tuples on the input wires of the circuit.
   (a) For $m = 1, \ldots, M$, the parties call $\mathcal{F}_{\text{rand}}(k + s)$ to receive $[\![\beta_m]\!]_{k+s}$.
   (b) For $i = 1, \ldots, N$, the parties call $\mathcal{F}_{\text{rand}}(k + s)$ to receive $[\![\alpha_i]\!]_{k+s}$.
   (c) *Compute linear combinations:*

>   i. The parties call $\mathcal{F}_{\mathsf{DotProduct}}$ on $(\llbracket\alpha_1\rrbracket_{k+s},\ldots,\llbracket\alpha_N\rrbracket_{k+s},\llbracket\beta_1\rrbracket_{k+s},\ldots,\llbracket\beta_M\rrbracket_{k+s})$ and
> $(\llbracket r\cdot z_1\rrbracket_{k+s},\ldots,\llbracket r,\cdot z_N\rrbracket_{k+s},\llbracket r\cdot v_1\rrbracket_{k+s},\ldots,\llbracket r\cdot v_M\rrbracket_{k+s})$ to obtain
> $\llbracket u\rrbracket_{k+s}=\llbracket\sum_{i=1}^{N}\alpha_i\cdot(r\cdot z_i)+\sum_{m=1}^{M}\beta_m\cdot(r\cdot v_m)\rrbracket_{k+s}$.
>   ii. The parties call $\mathcal{F}_{\mathsf{DotProduct}}$ on $(\llbracket z_1\rrbracket,\ldots,\llbracket z_N\rrbracket,\llbracket\beta_1\rrbracket,\ldots,\llbracket\beta_M\rrbracket)$ and
> $(\llbracket z_1\rrbracket_{k+s},\ldots,\llbracket z_N\rrbracket_{k+s},\llbracket v_1\rrbracket_{k+s},\ldots,\llbracket v_M\rrbracket_{k+s})$ to obtain
> $\llbracket w\rrbracket_{k+s}=\llbracket\sum_{i=1}^{N}\alpha_i\cdot z_i+\sum_{m=1}^{M}\beta_m\cdot v_m\rrbracket_{k+s}$.
>   (d) The parties run $\mathsf{open}(\llbracket r\rrbracket_{k+s})$ to receive r.
>   (e) Each party locally computes $\llbracket T\rrbracket_{k+s}=\llbracket u\rrbracket_{k+s}-r\cdot\llbracket w\rrbracket_{k+s}$.
>   (f) The parties call $\mathcal{F}_{\mathsf{CheckZero}}(k+s)$ on $\llbracket T\rrbracket_{k+s}$. If $\mathcal{F}_{\mathsf{CheckZero}}(k+s)$ outputs reject, the
>   parties output $\perp$ and abort. If it outputs accept, they proceed.
> 6. *Output reconstruction:* For each output wire of the circuit with $\llbracket v\rrbracket_{k+s}$, the parties locally
>   convert to $\llbracket v\rrbracket_k$. Then, they run $v\bmod 2^k=\mathsf{open}(\llbracket v\rrbracket_k,j)$, where P_j is the party whose
>   output is on the wire. If P_j received $\perp$ from the open procedure, then it sends $\perp$ to the
>   other parties, outputs $\perp$ and halts.
>
> **Output:** If a party has not aborted, then it outputs the values received on its output wires.

Lemma 2. *If $\mathcal{A}$ sends an additive value $d\not\equiv_k 0$ in any of the calls to $\mathcal{F}_{\mathsf{mult}}$ in the execution of Protocol 4, then the value T computed in the verification stage of Step 5 equals 0 with probability bounded by $2^{-s+\log(s+1)}$.*

Proof: Suppose that $(\llbracket x_i\rrbracket_{k+s},\llbracket y_i\rrbracket_{k+s},\llbracket z_i\rrbracket_{k+s})$ is the multiplication triple corresponding to the i-th multiplication gate, where $\llbracket x_i\rrbracket_{k+s},\llbracket y_i\rrbracket_{k+s}$ are the sharings on the input wires and $\llbracket z_i\rrbracket_{k+s}$ is the sharing on the output wire. We note that the values on the input wires may not actually be the appropriate values as when the circuit is computed by honest parties. However, in the verification step, each gate is examined separately, and all that is important is whether the randomized result is $\llbracket r\cdot z_i\rrbracket_{k+s}$ for whatever z_i is here (i.e., even if an error was added by the adversary in previous gates). By the definition of $\mathcal{F}_{\mathsf{mult}}$, a malicious adversary is able to carry out an additive attack, meaning that it can add a value to the output of each multiplication gate. We denote by $\delta_i\in\mathbb{Z}_{2^{k+s}}$ the value that is added by the adversary when $\mathcal{F}_{\mathsf{mult}}$ is called with $\llbracket x_i\rrbracket_{k+s}$ and $\llbracket y_i\rrbracket_{k+s}$, and by $\gamma_i\in\mathbb{Z}_{2^{k+s}}$ the value added by the adversary when $\mathcal{F}_{\mathsf{mult}}$ is called with the shares $\llbracket y_i\rrbracket_{k+s}$ and $\llbracket r\cdot x_i\rrbracket_{k+s}$. However, it is possible that the adversary has attacked previous gates and so $\llbracket y_i\rrbracket_{k+s}$ is actually multiplied with $\llbracket r\cdot x_i+\epsilon_i\rrbracket$, where the value $\epsilon_i\in\mathbb{Z}_{2^{k+s}}$ is an accumulated error from previous gates.[3] Thus, it holds that $\mathsf{val}(\llbracket z_i\rrbracket)^H=x_i\cdot y_i+\delta_i$ and $\mathsf{val}(\llbracket r\cdot z_i\rrbracket)^H=(r\cdot x_i+\epsilon_i)\cdot y_i+\gamma_i$. Similarly, for each input wire with sharing $\llbracket v_m\rrbracket$, it holds that $\mathsf{val}(\llbracket r\cdot v_m\rrbracket)^H=r\cdot v_m+\xi_m$, where $\xi_m\in\mathbb{Z}_{2^{k+s}}$ is the value added by the adversary when $\mathcal{F}_{\mathsf{mult}}$ is called with $\llbracket r\rrbracket_{k+s}$ and the shared input $\llbracket v_m\rrbracket_{k+s}$. Thus, we have that

---

[3] Although attacks in previous gates may be carried out on both multiplications, the idea is here is to fix x_i which is shared by $\llbracket x_i\rrbracket_{k+s}$ at the current value on the wire, and then given the randomized sharing $\llbracket x_{i'}\rrbracket_{k+s}$, define $\epsilon_i=x_{i'}-r\cdot x_i$ as the accumulated error on the input wire.

$$\mathsf{val}(\llbracket u \rrbracket)^H = \sum_{i=1}^{N} \alpha_i \cdot ((r \cdot x_i + \epsilon_i) \cdot y_i + \gamma_i)$$

$$+ \sum_{m=1}^{M} \beta_m \cdot (r \cdot v_m + \xi_m) + \Theta_1$$

$$\mathsf{val}(\llbracket w \rrbracket)^H = \sum_{i=1}^{N} \alpha_i \cdot (x_i \cdot y_i + \delta_i) + \sum_{m=1}^{M} \beta_m \cdot v_m + \Theta_2$$

where $\Theta_1 \in \mathbb{Z}_{2^{k+s}}$ and $\Theta_2 \in \mathbb{Z}_{2^{k+s}}$ are the values being added by the adversary when $\mathcal{F}_{\mathsf{DotProduct}}$ is called in the verification step, and so

$$\mathsf{val}(\llbracket T \rrbracket)^H = \mathsf{val}(\llbracket u \rrbracket)^H - r \cdot \mathsf{val}(\llbracket w \rrbracket)^H =$$

$$= \sum_{i=1}^{N} \alpha_i \cdot ((r \cdot x_i + \epsilon_i) \cdot y_i + \gamma_i) + \sum_{m=1}^{M} \beta_m \cdot (r \cdot v_m + \xi_m) + \theta_1$$

$$- r \cdot \left(\sum_{i=1}^{N} \alpha_i \cdot (x_i \cdot y_i + \delta_i) + \sum_{m=1}^{M} \beta_m \cdot v_m + \Theta_2 \right)$$

$$= \sum_{i=1}^{N} \alpha_i \cdot (\epsilon_i \cdot y_i + \gamma_i - r \cdot \delta_i) \tag{1}$$

$$+ \sum_{m=1}^{M} \beta_m \cdot \xi_m + (\Theta_{1-r} \cdot \Theta_2),$$

where the second equality holds because r is opened and so the multiplication $r \cdot \llbracket w \rrbracket_{k+s}$ always yields $\llbracket r \cdot w \rrbracket_{k+s}$. Let $\Delta_i = \epsilon_i \cdot y_i + \gamma_{i-r} \cdot \delta_i$.

Our goal is to show that $\mathsf{val}(\llbracket T \rrbracket)^H$, as shown in Eq. (2), equals 0 with probability at most $2^{-s+\log(s+1)}$. We have the following cases.

- *Case 1: There exists $m \in [M]$ such that $\xi_m \not\equiv_k 0$. Let m_0 be the smallest such m for which this holds. Then $\mathsf{val}(\llbracket T \rrbracket)^H \equiv_{k+s} 0$ if and only if*

$$\beta_{m_0} \cdot \xi_{m_0} \equiv_{k+s} \left(-\sum_{i=1}^{N} \alpha_i \cdot \Delta_i - \sum_{\substack{m=1 \\ m \neq m_0}}^{M} \beta_m \cdot \xi_m - (\Theta_{1-r} \cdot \Theta_2) \right).$$

Let 2^u be the largest power of 2 dividing ξ_{m_0}. Then we have that

$$\beta_{m_0} \equiv_{k+s-u} \left(\frac{-\sum_{i=1}^{N} \alpha_i \cdot \Delta_i - \sum_{\substack{m=1 \\ m \neq m_0}}^{M} \beta_m \cdot \xi_m - (\Theta_{1-r} \cdot \Theta_2)}{2^u} \right) \cdot \left(\frac{\xi_{m_0}}{2^u} \right)^{-1}.$$

By the assumption that $\xi_m \not\equiv_k 0$ it follows that $u < k$ and so $k + s - u > s$ which means that the above holds with probability at most 2^{-s}, since β_{m_0} is uniformly distributed over $\mathbb{Z}_{2^{k+s}}$.

– *Case 2: All* $\xi_m \equiv_k 0$. By the assumption in the lemma, some additive value $d \not\equiv_k 0$ was sent to $\mathcal{F}_{\mathsf{mult}}$. Since none was sent for the input randomization, there exists some $i \in \{1, \ldots, N\}$ such that $\delta_i \not\equiv_k 0$ or $\gamma_i \not\equiv_k 0$. Let i_0 be the smallest such i for which this holds. Note that since this is the first error added which is $\not\equiv_k 0$, it holds that $\epsilon_{i_0} \equiv_k 0$. Thus, in this case, $\mathsf{val}(\llbracket T \rrbracket)^H \equiv_{k+s} 0$ if and only if $\alpha_{i_0} \cdot \Delta_{i_0} \equiv_{k+s} Y$, where

$$Y = \left(-\sum_{\substack{i=1 \\ i \neq i_0}}^{N} \alpha_i \cdot \Delta_i - \sum_{m=1}^{M} \beta_m \cdot \xi_m - (\Theta_{1-r} \cdot \Theta_2) \right).$$

Let q be the random variable corresponding to the largest power of 2 dividing Δ_{i_0}, where we define $q = k + s$ in the case that $\Delta_{i_0} \equiv_{k+s} 0$. Let E denote the event $\alpha_{i_0} \cdot \Delta_{i_0} \equiv_{k+s} Y$. We have the following claims.

• *Claim 1: For $k < j \leq k + s$, it holds that* $\Pr[q = j] \leq 2^{-(j-k)}$.
  To see this, suppose that $q = j$ and $j > k$. It holds then that $\Delta_{i_0} \equiv_j 0$, and so $\Delta_{i_0} \equiv_k 0$. We first claim that in this case it must hold that $\delta_{i_0} \not\equiv_k 0$. Assume in contradiction that $\delta_{i_0} \equiv_k 0$. In addition, by our assumption we have that $\gamma_{i_0} \not\equiv_k 0$, $\epsilon_i \equiv_k 0$ and $\Delta_{i_0} = \epsilon_{i_0} \cdot y_{i_0} + \gamma_{i_0} - r \cdot \delta_{i_0} \equiv_k 0$. However, $\epsilon_i \cdot y_{i_0} \equiv_k 0$ and $r \cdot \delta_{i_0} \equiv_k 0$ imply that $\gamma_{i_0} \equiv_k 0$, which is a contradiction.
  We thus assume that $\delta_{i_0} \not\equiv_k 0$, and in particular there exists $u < k$, such that u is the largest power of 2 dividing δ_{i_0}. It is easy to see then that $q = j$ implies that $r \equiv_{j-u} \left(\frac{\epsilon_{i_0} \cdot y_{i_0} + \gamma_{i_0}}{2^u} \right) \cdot \left(\frac{\delta_{i_0}}{2^u} \right)^{-1}$. Since $r \in \mathbb{Z}_{2^{k+s}}$ is uniformly random and $u < k$, we have that this equation holds with probability of at most $2^{-(j-u)} \leq 2^{-(j-k)}$.

• *Claim 2: For $k < j < k + s$ it holds that* $\Pr[E \mid q = j] \leq 2^{-(k+s-j)}$.
  To prove this let us assume that $q = j$ and that E holds. In this case we can write $\alpha_{i_0} \equiv_{k+s-j} \frac{Y}{2^j} \cdot \left(\frac{\Delta_{i_0}}{2^j} \right)^{-1}$. For $k < j < k + s$ it holds that $0 < k + s - j < s$ and therefore this equation can be only satisfied with probability at most $2^{-(k+s-j)}$, given that $\alpha_{i_0} \in \mathbb{Z}_{2^s}$ is uniformly random.

• *Claim 3:* $\Pr[E \mid 0 \leq q \leq k] \leq 2^{-s}$.
  This is implied by the proof of the previous claim, since in the case that $q = j$ with $0 \leq j \leq k$, it holds that $k + s - j \geq s$, so the event E implies that $\alpha_{i_0} \equiv_s \frac{Y}{2^j} \cdot \left(\frac{\Delta_{i_0}}{2^j} \right)^{-1}$, which holds with probability at most 2^{-s}.

Putting these pieces together, we thus have the following:

$$\Pr[E] = \Pr[E \mid 0 \leq q \leq k] \cdot \Pr[0 \leq q \leq k]$$
$$+ \sum_{j=k+1}^{k+s} \Pr[E \mid q = j] \cdot \Pr[q = j]$$
$$\leq 2^{-s} + s \cdot 2^{-s} = (s+1) \cdot 2^{-s} = 2^{-s+\log(s+1)}. \qquad (2)$$

To sum up the proof, in the first case we obtained that $T = 0$ with probability of at most 2^{-s} whereas in the second case, this holds with probability of at most $2^{-s+\log(s+1)}$. Therefore, we conclude that the probability that $T = 0$ in the verification step is bounded by $2^{-s+\log(s+1)}$ as stated in the lemma. This concludes the proof.   ∎

The security of Protocol 4 now follows as Lemma 2 shows that additive errors that are non-zero modulo 2^k cannot take place without leading to abort. However, one non-trivial issue lies in handling additive attacks that are zero modulo 2^k, but not modulo 2^{k+s}, as these do not affect correctness but may lead to selective failure attacks, in which an abort signal can be generated depending on the inputs from honest parties. Our protocol deals with this potential attack by using secret coefficients for the random linear combination taken in the verification step. If we take public coefficients, as done in [14], the following attack can be carried out.

Assume that the adversary has attacked exactly one gate, indexed by i_0, in the following way. When multiplying x_{i_0} with y_{i_0}, the adversary acted honestly, but when multiplying $r \cdot x_{i_0}$ with y_{i_0}, it added the value d_{i_0}. Thus, on the output wire, the parties hold a sharing of the pair $(x_{i_0} \cdot y_{i_0}, r \cdot x_{i_0} \cdot y_{i_0} + d_{i_0})$. Now, assume that this wire enters another multiplication gate, indexed by j_0 with input shares on the second wire being $(w_{j_0}, r \cdot w_{j_0})$ and that the output of this second gate is an output wire of the circuit. Thus, on the output of this gate, the parties will hold the sharing $(x_{i_0} \cdot y_{i_0} \cdot w_{j_0}, (r \cdot x_{i_0} \cdot y_{i_0} + d_{i_0}) w_{j_0})$ (assuming the adversary does not attack this gate as well). In this case, we have that $T = \alpha_{i_0 s} \cdot d_{i_0} + \alpha_{j_0} \cdot (d_{i_0} \cdot w_{j_0}) = d_{i_0}(\alpha_{i_0} + \alpha_{j_0} \cdot w_{j_0})$. Now, if $d_{i_0} = 2^{k+s-1}$ then it follows that $T \equiv_{k+s} 0$ if and only if $\alpha_{i_0} + \alpha_{j_0} \cdot w_{j_0}$ is even.

The attack presented above does not change the k lower bits of the values on the wires, and thus has no effect on the correctness of the output. However, if α_{i_0} and α_{j_0} are public and known to the adversary, then by $\mathcal{F}_{\mathsf{CheckZero}}$'s output the adversary may be able to learn whether w_{j_0} is even or not. In contrast, when α_{i_0} and α_{j_0} are kept secret, learning whether $\alpha_{i_0} + \alpha_{j_0} \cdot w_{j_0}$ is even or odd does not reveal any information about w_{j_0} since it is now perfectly masked by α_{i_0} and α_{j_0}. Therefore, to prevent this type of attack, we are forced to use random secrets for our random linear combination. Here is where the functionality $\mathcal{F}_{\mathsf{DotProduct}}$ becomes handy, as it allows to compute the sum of products of sharings in an efficient way which is exactly what we need to compute $\sum_{i=1}^{N} [\![\alpha_i]\!] \cdot [\![z_i]\!]$.

We state the security of our protocol below. A full simulation-based proof appears in the full version of this work.

Theorem 1. *Let f be an n-party functionality over $\mathbb{Z}_{2^k}$ and let s be a statistical security parameter. Then, Protocol 4 securely computes f with abort in the $(\mathcal{F}_{\mathsf{input}}, \mathcal{F}_{\mathsf{mult}}, \mathcal{F}_{\mathsf{coin}}, \mathcal{F}_{\mathsf{rand}}, \mathcal{F}_{\mathsf{CheckZero}}, \mathcal{F}_{\mathsf{DotProduct}})$-hybrid model with statistical error $2^{-s+\log(s+1)}$, in the presence of a malicious adversary controlling $t < \frac{n}{2}$ parties. The communication complexity in bits of the resulting protocol is*

$$M \cdot \left(2 \cdot \mathcal{C}_{\mathsf{rand}}(k+s) + \mathcal{C}_{\mathsf{mult}}(k+s) + \mathcal{C}_{\mathsf{open(i)}}(k+s) + (k+s)\right)$$
$$+ N \cdot \left(\mathcal{C}_{\mathsf{rand}}(k+s) + 2 \cdot \mathcal{C}_{\mathsf{mult}}(k+s)\right) + O \cdot \mathcal{C}_{\mathsf{open(i)}}(k),$$

where M is the number of inputs, N is the number of multiplication gates in the circuit, O is the number of output wires of the circuit and C_* represents the cost (in bits) of calling the functionality $\mathcal{F}_*$.

5 Instantiation for n Parties

In this section, we present our instantiation based on Shamir's secret sharing over rings, using the techniques from [2]. This technique works for any number of parties, although for 3 parties one can obtain more efficient solutions, such as the one we describe in Sect. 6 that uses replicated secret sharing. Over finite fields, Shamir's scheme requires a distinct evaluation point for each player, and one more for the secret. This is usually not a problem if the size of the field is not too small. However, over commutative rings R the condition on the sequence of evaluation points $\alpha_0, \ldots, \alpha_n \in R$ is that the pairwise difference $\alpha_i - \alpha_j$ is invertible for each pair of indices $i \neq j$. For our ring of interest $\mathbb{Z}_{2^\ell}$, the largest such sequence the ring admits is only of length 2 (e.g., $(\alpha_0, \alpha_1) = (0, 1)$).

The solution from [2] is to embed inputs from $\mathbb{Z}_{2^\ell}$ into a large enough Galois ring R that has $\mathbb{Z}_{2^\ell}$ as a subring. This ring is of the form $R = \mathbb{Z}_{2^\ell}[X]/(h(X))$, where $h(X)$ is a monic polynomial of degree $d = \lceil \log_2 n \rceil$ such that $h(X) \bmod 2 \in \mathbb{F}_2[X]$ is irreducible. Elements of R thus correspond uniquely to polynomials with coefficients in $\mathbb{Z}_{2^\ell}$ that are of degree at most $d - 1$. Note the similarity between the Galois ring and finite field extensions of $\mathbb{F}_2$: elements of the finite field $\mathbb{F}_{2^d}$ correspond uniquely to polynomials of at most degree $d - 1$ with coefficients in $\mathbb{F}_2$.

There is a ring homomorphism $\pi : R \rightarrow \mathbb{Z}_{2^\ell}$ that sends $a_0 + a_1 X + \cdots + a_{d-1}X^{d-1} \in R$ to the free coefficient a_0, which we shall use later on.[4] For more relevant structural properties of Galois rings, see [2].

We adopt the above-mentioned version of Shamir's scheme over R, but restrict the secret space to $\mathbb{Z}_{2^\ell}$. The share space will be equal to R. Let $1 \leq \tau \leq n$ be the privacy parameter of the scheme. Then, the set of *correct* share vectors is

$$C_\tau = \left\{ (f(\alpha_1), \ldots, f(\alpha_n)) \in R^n \ \middle| \ \begin{array}{l} f \in R[X], \ \deg(f) \leq \tau, \\ \text{and } f(\alpha_0) \in \mathbb{Z}_{2^\ell} \subset R \end{array} \right\}. \tag{3}$$

With the restriction that the secret is in $\mathbb{Z}_{2^\ell}$, we have that C_τ is an $\mathbb{Z}_{2^\ell}$-module, i.e., the secret-sharing scheme is $\mathbb{Z}_{2^\ell}$-linear. Since it is based on polynomial interpolation, the properties from Sect. 2.1 can be easily seen to hold. This includes division by 2 if all the shares are even.

In this section, we denote a sharing under C_τ as $[\![x]\!]_\tau = (x_1, \ldots, x_n)$. We call τ the *degree* of the sharing. The reason we are explicit about τ is that we will use sharings of two different degrees. This stems from the critical property of this secret-sharing scheme that enables us to evaluate arithmetic circuits: this secret-sharing scheme is *multiplicative*. This means there is a $\mathbb{Z}_{2^\ell}$-linear map $R^n \rightarrow \mathbb{Z}_{2^\ell}$ that for sharings $[\![x]\!]_\tau, [\![y]\!]_\tau$ sends $(x_1 y_1, \ldots, x_n y_n) \mapsto x \cdot y$.

---

[4] Technically, an element of R is a residue class modulo the ideal $(h(X))$, but we omit this for simplicity of notation.

Put differently, $(x_1y_1, \ldots, x_ny_n) \in C_{2\tau}$ is a degree-2τ sharing with secret $x \cdot y$. We denote it $[\![x \cdot y]\!]_{(2\tau)} = (x_1y_1, \ldots, x_ny_n)$—in particular note the parenthesized subscript refers to the degree of the sharing, as opposed to the modulus. Note that $C_i \subseteq C_j$ for $0 < i < j$; in particular every degree-2τ sharing is also a sharing of degree $n - 1$. A sharing of degree $n - 1$ is related to additive secret sharing, where the secret equals the sum of the shares $x = \sum_i x_i$. The difference is that here there are constants, i.e. we may write $x = \sum_i \lambda_i x_i$, for $\lambda_1, \ldots, \lambda_n \in R$. We shall make use of this in our multiplication protocol, ensuring that parties only need to communicate an element of $\mathbb{Z}_{2^\ell}$ instead of an element of R. However, note that $[\![\cdot]\!]_{(2\tau)}$ does not meet the definition of a secret-sharing scheme in Sect. 2.1, in particular because the corrupted parties shares are not well defined and cannot be computed from the honest parties' shares.

5.1   Generating Randomness

We efficiently realize $\mathcal{F}_{\mathrm{rand}}$ by letting each player P_i sample and secret-share a random element s_i, and then multiplying the resulting vector of n random elements with a particular[5] Vandermonde matrix [19].[6] Of the resulting vector, τ entries are discarded to ensure the adversary has zero information about the remaining ones. Thus, $n - \tau$ random elements are outputted, resulting in an amortized communication cost of $O(n)$ ring elements per element. A priori the adversary can cause the sharings to be incorrect; this is remedied with Protocol 6 by opening a random linear combination of the sharings and verifying the result.

Since our secret-sharing scheme $[\![\cdot]\!]_\tau$ is $\mathbb{Z}_{2^\ell}$-linear, we would like to choose our matrix with entries in $\mathbb{Z}_{2^\ell}$. Unfortunately, the Vandermonde matrix we need does not exist over $\mathbb{Z}_{2^\ell}$, for the same reason secret sharing does not work. However, the secret-sharing scheme which consists of d parallel sharings of $[\![\cdot]\!]_\tau$ be interpreted as an R-linear secret-sharing scheme [2,11]. This secret-sharing scheme, which we denote as $\langle \cdot \rangle$, has share space S^d (since the scheme is identical to sharing d independent secrets in S in parallel using $[\![\cdot]\!]_\tau$), and secret space R^d. The scheme is R-linear because the module of share vectors, which is $(C_\tau)^d$, is an R-module via the tensor product $(C_\tau)^d \cong C_\tau \otimes_S S^d \cong C_\tau \otimes_S R$. In practice, a single secret-shared element $\langle x \rangle$ may be interpreted as a secret-shared column vector $([\![x_1]\!]_\tau, \ldots, [\![x_d]\!]_\tau)^T$. To compute the action of an element $r \in R$ on $\langle x \rangle$ in this representation, we first need to fix a basis of R over S. Recall $R = \mathbb{Z}_{2^\ell}[X]/(h(X))$, so we may pick the canonical basis $1, X, \ldots, X^{d-1} \in R$. This allows us to represent an element $a \in R$ as a column vector $(a_0, \ldots, a_{d-1})^T \in S^d$, i.e., explicitly: $a = a_0 + a_1X + \cdots + a_{d-1}X^{d-1}$. Multiplication by $r \in R$ is an S-linear map of vectors $S^d \to S^d$, i.e., it can be represented as a $d \times d$ matrix M_r with entries in S. The product $r \langle x \rangle = \langle rx \rangle$ is then equal to $M_r([\![x_1]\!]_\tau, \ldots, [\![x_d]\!]_\tau)^T$. If a single party P has a vector of shares $(s_1, \ldots, s_d) \in R$ for $\langle x \rangle = ([\![x_1]\!]_\tau, \ldots, [\![x_d]\!]_\tau)^T$, then $M_r(s_1, \ldots, s_d)^T$ is their vector of shares corresponding to $\langle rx \rangle$.

---

[5] Over fields this can be a general Vandermonde matrix, but this is not sufficient over R.

[6] In general, any R-linear code with good distance and dimension suffices to get $O(n)$ complexity in the protocol, but the Vandermonde construction is optimal.

In our protocol, the parties compute $(\langle r_1 \rangle, \ldots, \langle r_{n-\tau} \rangle)^T = A(\langle s_1 \rangle, \ldots, \langle s_n \rangle)^T$, where A has entries in R. This can be computed by writing out the R-linear combinations $\langle r_i \rangle = \sum_{k=1}^{n} a_{ik} \langle s_k \rangle = \sum_{k=1}^{n} M_{a_{ik}} \langle s_k \rangle$, with $\langle s_k \rangle = (\llbracket s_{k1} \rrbracket_\tau, \llbracket s_{kd} \rrbracket_\tau)^\intercal$. Fix a sequence $\beta_1, \ldots, \beta_n \in R$ such that for each pair of indices $i \neq j$ we have that $\beta_i - \beta_j$ is invertible.[7] We let A be the $(n - \tau) \times n$ matrix such that the j-th column is $(1, \beta_j, \beta_{j^2}, \ldots, \beta_j^{n-\tau-1})^T$. This matrix is super-invertible, i.e. any square submatrix obtained by sampling a subset of $n - \tau$ columns is invertible [2].

Protocol 5 Generating random sharings of $\llbracket \cdot \rrbracket_\tau$

The protocol:

1. Each party P_i samples an element $s_i \leftarrow (\mathbb{Z}_{2^\ell})^d$ and secret-shares it as $\langle s_i \rangle$ among all parties.
2. The parties locally compute the linear matrix-vector product to obtain $(\langle r_1 \rangle, \ldots, \langle r_{n-\tau} \rangle)^T := A(\langle s_1 \rangle, \ldots, \langle s_n \rangle)^T$.
3. The parties execute Protocol 6 $\lceil \kappa/d \rceil$ times in parallel on $\langle r_1 \rangle, \ldots, \langle r_{n-\tau} \rangle$ If any execution fails, they abort. Otherwise, for each $j = 1, \ldots, n - \tau$ they interpret $\langle r_j \rangle = (\llbracket r_{j1} \rrbracket_\tau, \ldots, \llbracket r_{jd} \rrbracket_\tau)$ and output $\llbracket r_{11} \rrbracket_\tau, \ldots, \llbracket r_{1d} \rrbracket_\tau, \llbracket r_{21} \rrbracket_\tau, \ldots, \llbracket r_{(n-\tau)d} \rrbracket_\tau$.

Lemma 3. *Protocol 5 securely computes $(n - \tau)d$ parallel invocations of $\mathcal{F}_{\text{rand}}$ for $\llbracket \cdot \rrbracket_\tau$ with statistical error of at most $2^{-\kappa}$ in the presence of a malicious adversary controlling $t < n/2$ parties.*

Proof: Let $\mathcal{A}$ be the real-world adversary. The simulator $\mathcal{S}$ interacts with $\mathcal{A}$ by simulating the honest parties in an execution of the protocol. In doing so, $\mathcal{S}$ obtains honest parties' shares $\langle r_1 \rangle_H, \ldots, \langle r_{n-\tau} \rangle_H$.

We distinguish three cases:

1. If at least one of the simulated honest parties aborts in any of the executions of Protocol 6, then $\mathcal{S}$ sends abort to $\mathcal{F}_{\text{rand}}$.
2. If the checks pass but the honest parties' shares are inconsistent, $\mathcal{S}$ outputs fail. By Lemma 4 this only happens with probability at most $2^{-\kappa}$, allowed by the claim.
3. In the remaining case, the checks of Protocol 6 pass and the honest parties' shares are consistent. $\mathcal{S}$ calculates the corrupted parties' shares $\langle r_1 \rangle_C, \ldots, \langle r_{n-\tau} \rangle_C$ from the honest parties' shares, and sends them to $\mathcal{F}_{\text{rand}}$.

Before the invocation of $\mathcal{F}_{\text{rand}}$, the honest parties have no private inputs, hence $\mathcal{S}$ simulates them perfectly and $\mathcal{A}$'s view will be identical to the real execution. Thus, the simulated honest parties will abort in the ideal execution precisely when they would in the real execution.

The only thing it remains to prove is that if the parties do not abort, the output shares are identically distributed in the real and ideal executions. In particular, we need to prove that in the real execution, the *sharings* are independent and uniformly sampled from $\langle \cdot \rangle$.

---

[7] We may just use $(\beta_1, \ldots, \beta_n) = (\alpha_1, \ldots, \alpha_n)$.

Let $H \subseteq \mathcal{H}$ be a subset of honest parties of size $n - \tau$, and let $C := \{1, \ldots, n\} \backslash H$ denote its complement. Let A_H, A_C denote the submatrices of A corresponding to the columns indexed by H and C respectively. Let $\langle \mathbf{s}_H \rangle$ denote the vector $\langle s_i \rangle_{i \in H}$ of length $n - \tau$, and correspondingly $\langle \mathbf{s}_C \rangle := \langle s_i \rangle_{i \in C}$. Then $(\langle r_1 \rangle, \ldots, \langle r_{n-\tau} \rangle)^T = A_H \langle \mathbf{s}_H \rangle + A_C \langle \mathbf{s}_C \rangle$. Since $\langle \mathbf{s}_H \rangle$ is wholly generated by the honest parties, it consists of $n - \tau$ independent and uniformly random sharings of $\langle \cdot \rangle$. A_H is invertible (since A is super-invertible), hence we also have that $\langle \mathbf{s}_H \rangle$ consists of independent and uniformly random sharings. Adding a fixed $A_C \langle \mathbf{s}_C \rangle$ will not affect the distribution, hence the sharings $\langle r_1 \rangle, \ldots, \langle r_{n-\tau} \rangle$ are independent and uniformly random sharings. ∎

5.2   Checking Correctness of Sharings

We check whether sharings are correct by taking a random linear combination of the sharings, masking it with a random sharing, and opening the result to all parties.

This protocol does not securely compute an ideal functionality, because privacy is not preserved if the sharings are incorrect. The way we use it this does not matter, since we only verify correctness of sharings of random elements.

Protocol 6 Checking correctness of sharings of $\langle \cdot \rangle$

Inputs: possibly incorrect sharings $\langle x_1 \rangle, \ldots, \langle x_N \rangle$, and a possibly incorrect sharing $\langle r \rangle \leftarrow (\mathbb{Z}_{2^\ell})^d$ of a random element.

The protocol:
1. The parties call $\mathcal{F}_{\mathsf{coin}}$ N times to get $a_1, \ldots, a_N \leftarrow (\mathbb{Z}_{2^\ell})^d$.
2. The parties compute $\langle u \rangle := a_1 \langle x_1 \rangle + \cdots + a_N \langle x_N \rangle + \langle r \rangle$.
3. The parties run $\mathsf{open}(\langle u \rangle)$. If it returns $\bot$, output $\bot$. Else, output $\mathsf{correct}$.

Lemma 4. *If at least one of the input sharings* $\langle x_1 \rangle, \ldots, \langle x_N \rangle$ *is incorrect, Protocol 6 outputs* $\mathsf{correct}$ *with probability at most* $\frac{1}{2^d}$.

To show correctness, we use the following consequence from [2, Lemma 3].

Lemma 5. *Let* $C \subseteq R^n$ *be a free* R-*module. Then for all* $x \notin C$ *and* $u \in R^n$, *we have that*
$$\Pr_{r \leftarrow R}[rx + u \in C] \leq \frac{1}{2^d}$$
where r *is chosen uniformly at random from* R.

Proof: [Proof of Lemma 4]. Let C denote the R-module of correct share vectors (such as in (3)). One of the input sharings is incorrect; without loss of generality assume it is $\langle x_1 \rangle$. The protocol $\mathsf{open}(\langle u \rangle)$ returns a value not equal to $\bot$ if and only if $\langle u \rangle = a_1 \langle x_1 \rangle + (a_2 \langle x_2 \rangle + \cdots + a_n \langle x_n \rangle + \langle r \rangle)$ is in C. By Lemma 5 this probability is bounded by $1/2$, since a_1 was chosen uniformly at random. Since $\langle u \rangle$ is masked with $\langle r \rangle$, the protocol is private. ∎

5.3 Secure Multiplication up to Additive Attacks

Multiplication follows the outline of the passively secure protocol of [19]. The protocol begins with a preprocessing phase, where *random double sharings* are produced, i.e. a pair of sharings $(\llbracket r \rrbracket_\tau, \llbracket r \rrbracket_{(2\tau)})$ of the same uniformly random element r shared using polynomials of degree τ and degree 2τ, respectively.

We denote a double sharing as $\llbracket r \rrbracket_{(\tau,2\tau)} := ((r_1, r'_1), \ldots, (r_n, r'_n))$. It is a $\mathbb{Z}_{2^\ell}$-linear secret-sharing scheme with secret space $\mathbb{Z}_{2^\ell}$ and share space $R \oplus R$. The set of correct share vectors is the $\mathbb{Z}_{2^\ell}$-module

$$\left\{ ((f(\alpha_1), g(\alpha_1)), \ldots, (f(\alpha_n), g(\alpha_n))) \,\middle|\, \begin{array}{l} f, g \in R[X], \\ f(\alpha_0) = g(\alpha_0) \in \mathbb{Z}_{2^\ell}, \\ \deg(f) \leq \tau, \ \deg(g) \leq 2\tau \end{array} \right\}.$$

Secret-sharing an element r under $\llbracket \cdot \rrbracket_{(\tau,2\tau)}$ involves selecting two uniformly random polynomials of degrees at most τ and 2τ respectively.

To generate sharings in $\llbracket \cdot \rrbracket_{(\tau,2\tau)}$, we essentially use Protocol 5. However, this protocol does not securely realize $\mathcal{F}_{\mathsf{rand}}$, since in Lemma 3 we use the fact that the simulator can compute the corrupted parties' shares from the honest parties' shares, which is not the case for the degree-2τ part (hence why $\llbracket \cdot \rrbracket_{(2\tau)}$, therefore also $\llbracket \cdot \rrbracket_{(\tau,2\tau)}$, does not meet the definition of a secret-sharing scheme in Sect. 2.1). This will only lead to an additive attack in the online phase, which is why we can still use the protocol.

Protocol 7 Secure multiplication up to an additive attack

Inputs: Parties hold correct sharings $\llbracket x \rrbracket_\tau$, $\llbracket y \rrbracket_\tau$.

Preprocessing: The parties execute Protocol 5 for $\llbracket \cdot \rrbracket_{(\tau,2\tau)}$ instead of $\llbracket \cdot \rrbracket_\tau$. They only check correctness for the $\llbracket \cdot \rrbracket_\tau$ part, and not for the $\llbracket \cdot \rrbracket_{(2\tau)}$ part. They obtain a random double sharing $(\llbracket r \rrbracket_\tau, \llbracket r \rrbracket_{(2\tau)})$.

The protocol:

1. The parties locally calculate $\llbracket \delta \rrbracket_{(2\tau)} := \llbracket x \rrbracket_\tau \cdot \llbracket y \rrbracket_\tau - \llbracket r \rrbracket_{(2\tau)}$.
2. Each P_i for $i = 1, \ldots 2\tau+1$ sends $u_i := \pi(\lambda_i \delta_i)$ to P_1 (recall $\pi(a_0 + a_1 X + \cdots + a_{d-1} X^{d-1}) = a_0 \in \mathbb{Z}_{2^\ell}$, and the λ_i are constants such that $\sum_{i=1}^n \lambda_i \delta_i = \delta$)
3. P_1 can now reconstruct δ as $\delta = \sum_{i=1}^n u_i$.
4. P_1 broadcasts δ.
5. The parties locally compute $\llbracket x \cdot y \rrbracket_\tau = \llbracket r \rrbracket_\tau + \delta$.

The reason each party sends u_i instead of δ_i to P_1 is two-fold. It saves bandwidth, since only an element of $\mathbb{Z}_{2^\ell}$ needs to be communicated instead of an element of R. More importantly though, if the inputs $\llbracket x \rrbracket_\tau$, $\llbracket y \rrbracket_\tau$ are not guaranteed to be correct, then sending full shares δ_i can compromise privacy.

Note that it is important that the random double sharing $\llbracket r \rrbracket_{(\tau,2\tau)}$ is guaranteed to be correct. I.e., the shares are degree τ and 2τ respectively.

Lemma 6. *Protocol 7 securely computes $\mathcal{F}_{\mathsf{mult}}$ with statistical error $\leq 2^{-\kappa}$ in the $\mathcal{F}_{\mathsf{rand}}$-hybrid model in the presence of a malicious adversary controlling $t < n/2$ parties.*

Proof: Without loss of generality, assume $2\tau + 1 = n$ (recall that τ is the secret sharing threshold and not the number of corrupted parties, and so the proof still holds for any $t < n/2$).

For the offline phase, the simulator acts as in Lemma 3. By the proof, we have that $[\![r]\!]_\tau$ is a correct sharing. The sharing $[\![r']\!]_{(2\tau)}$ is not well-defined, because the adversary can change its mind about its shares at any time. However, the adversary always knows the additive error $r' - r$ that it introduces by changing its shares.

For the online phase, $\mathcal{S}$ simulates the honest parties towards $\mathcal{A}$.

We distinguish two cases:

- *Case 1: P_1 is not corrupt.* The simulated P_1 receives $\{u_i\}_{i\in\mathcal{C}}$ from $\mathcal{A}$. If it receives $\perp$ for any value u_i, it sends abort to $\mathcal{F}_{\mathsf{mult}}$ and simulates P_1 aborting. Otherwise, it calls $\mathcal{F}_{\mathsf{mult}}$ and receives $\{x_i\}_{i\in\mathcal{C}}, \{y_i\}_{i\in\mathcal{C}}$. For any $i \in \mathcal{C}$, since $\mathcal{S}$ knows x_i, y_i, r'_i, it may calculate $\delta_i = x_i y_i - r'_i$ and thus the value $\pi(\lambda_i\delta_i)$ the adversary is supposed to send if it behaves honestly. The simulator can therefore extract $d = \sum_{i\in\mathcal{C}} u_i - \pi(\lambda_i\delta_i)$. $\mathcal{S}$ does not know the true value of δ, however it may sample $\delta \leftarrow \mathbb{Z}_{2^\ell}$, send it to the corrupted parties, and calculate the corrupted parties' shares as $z_i = r_i + \delta + d$.

  It then simulates the broadcast of δ. If the broadcast aborts, $\mathcal{S}$ simulates the parties aborting and sends abort to $\mathcal{F}_{\mathsf{mult}}$. Otherwise, it sends $d, \{z_i\}_{i\in\mathcal{C}}$ to $\mathcal{F}_{\mathsf{mult}}$, and outputs whatever $\mathcal{A}$ outputs.

  In the ideal execution, $\mathcal{A}$ receives a random δ. It cannot distinguish this from the real value $x \cdot y - r$, since r is uniformly random and by privacy of the secret-sharing scheme it does not have any information on it.

- *Case 2: P_1 is corrupt.* $\mathcal{S}$ samples $[\![\delta]\!]_{(2\tau)} \leftarrow [\![\cdot]\!]_{(2\tau)}$. For $i \in \mathcal{H}$ it sends $u_i = \pi(\lambda_i\delta_i)$ to the corrupted P_1. The simulated honest parties receive an identical broadcasted value δ', otherwise the broadcast protocol aborts.

  Since $\mathcal{S}$ knows δ, it can extract $d := \delta' - \delta$, and calculate the corrupted parties' shares as $z_i = r_i + \delta'$. It then sends $d, \{z_i\}_{i\in\mathcal{C}}$ to $\mathcal{F}_{\mathsf{mult}}$, and it outputs whatever $\mathcal{A}$ outputs.

As mentioned above, the adversary cannot distinguish whether it is talking to a simulator or the real parties, hence its output will be identical.

In the ideal execution where no abort took place, the actual (non-simulated) parties receive their shares $\{z_i\}_{i\in\mathcal{H}}$ directly from $\mathcal{F}_{\mathsf{mult}}$. The shares are consistent and will reconstruct to the secret $z = x \cdot y + d$. In the ideal execution, the shares are generated by the probabilistic function $\mathsf{share}(z, \{z_i\}_{z\in\mathcal{C}})$, such that the shares are uniformly random subject to the constraints on the shares.[8] In the real execution, the shares also correspond to z. The sharing in the real execution is calculated as $[\![r]\!]_\tau + \delta$, where $[\![r]\!]_\tau$ is a uniformly random sharing. Therefore, the outputs are identical in both executions. ∎

When evaluating a circuit gate-by-gate using Protocol 7, we consider an optimization in which we do not need to execute the broadcast (which might

---

[8] Depending on the privacy threshold the constraints may fully determine the shares.

be expensive) for each multiplication, but instead they will perform a broadcast just before opening the values. In the multiplication protocol, P_1 will just send a value (not guaranteed to be the same) to all other parties. Each party P_i keeps track of a hash value h_i of all received values in step 4 of the protocol far. Before opening their outputs, each party P_i sends its hash h_i to all other parties. If any party detects a mismatch, they abort. Note that security up to additive attack is guaranteed only after this procedure succeeds, which is executed before opening the output.

In doing so, we lose the invariant that all secret-shared values are guaranteed to be correct. In other scenarios, as for example the $t < n/3$ setting, this completely breaks the security of the protocol as shown in [27]. However, this is not a problem in our case since the degree-2τ sharings have no redundancy in them. As shown in [27], this is enough to guarantee the security of the protocol with the deferred check, and the reason is essentially that the shares that the potentially corrupt party P_1 receives are now uniformly random and independent of each other.

5.4 Reducing Communication Using Pseudo-Randomness [8,33]

Our protocol as described so far is information-theoretically secure. We can reduce communication by using a pseudo-random generator in the following way. Assume that each pair of parties hold a joint random seed. Then, when party P_i shares an element with degree t, it is possible to derive t shares from the seed known to P_i and the corresponding party, and set the remaining $t + 1$ shares (including the dealer's own share) given the pseudo-random shares and the value of the secret. Thus, only t shares need to be transmitted, thereby reducing communication by half. Using the same reasoning, it is possible to share a secret using degree $2t$ without any interaction. Here $n - 1 = 2t$ shares are computed using the seed known to the dealer and each party, and then the dealer sets its own share such that all shares will reconstruct to the secret. We can use this idea to also reduce communication in the multiplication protocol. Instead of broadcasting δ, party P_i can share it to the parties with degree t, and use the above optimization, so that P_1 will have to send t elements instead of $n - 1$. We note that here instead of comparing δ (to ensure correctness of output sharings), the parties can perform a batch correctness check (Protocol 6) for all sharings dealt by P_1 before the verification step in the main protocol.

6 Instantiation for 3 Parties

We now present in detail the efficient three party instantiation of our compiler from replicated secret sharing. Sharing a value $x \in \mathbb{Z}_{2^\ell}$ is done by picking at random $x_1, x_2, x_3 \in \mathbb{Z}_{2^\ell}$ such that $\sum_i x_i \equiv_\ell x$. P_i's share of x is the pair (x_i, x_{i+1}) and we use the convention that $i + 1 = 1$ when $i = 3$. To reconstruct a secret, P_i receives the missing share from the two other parties. Note that reconstructing a secret is robust in the sense that parties either reconstruct the correct value x or they abort.

Replicated secret sharing satisfies the properties described in Sect. 2.1, and one can efficiently realize the required functionalities described in the same section. Below we discuss some of these properties/functionalities.

6.1   Generating Random Shares

Shares of a random value can be generated non-interactively, as noted in [31,32], by making use of a setup phase in which each party P_i obtains shares of two random keys k_i, k_{i+1} for a pseudorandom function (PRF) F. The parties generate shares of a random value for the j-th time by letting P_i's share to be (r_i, r_{i+1}), where $r_i = F_{k_i}(j)$. These are replicated shares of the (pseudo)random value $r = \sum_i F_{k_i}(j)$. Proving that this securely computes $\mathcal{F}_{\mathsf{rand}}$ is straightforward and we omit the details.

6.2   Secure Multiplication up to an Additive Attack

To multiply two secret-shared values, we use the protocol from [4,32], which is described in 8. The shares of 0 that this protocol needs can be obtained by using correlated keys for a PRF, in similar fashion to the protocol for $\mathcal{F}_{\mathsf{rand}}$ sketched above.

Protocol 8 Secure multiplication up to an additive attack.

Inputs: Parties hold sharings $[\![x]\!]$, $[\![y]\!]$ and additive sharings $(\alpha_1, \alpha_2, \alpha_3)$ where $\sum_{i=1}^{3} \alpha_i = 0$.

The protocol:

1. P_i computes $z_i = x_i y_i + x_{i+1} y_i + x_i y_{i+1} + \alpha_i$ and sends z_i to P_{i-1}.
2. P_j, upon receiving z_{j+1}, defines its share of $[\![x \cdot y]\!]$ as (z_j, z_{j+1}).

The above protocol is secure up to an additive attack as noted in [31]. We note that this can be extended to instantiate $\mathcal{F}_{\mathsf{DotProduct}}$ at the communication cost of one single multiplication, as shown in [14].

6.3   Efficient Checking Equality to 0

Checking that a value is a share of 0 can be performed very efficiently in this setting by relying on a random oracle $\mathcal{H}$. The observation we rely on is that, if $\sum_i x_i \equiv_\ell 0$, then $x_{i-1} \equiv_\ell -(x_i + x_{i+1})$ and so P_i can send $z_i = \mathcal{H}(-(x_i + x_{i+1}))$ which will be equal to x_{i-1} which is held by P_{i+1} and P_{i-1}. Since only one party is corrupted, it suffices that each P_i will send it only to P_{i+1}. Upon receiving z_i from P_i, P_{i+1} checks that $z_i = \mathcal{H}(x_{i-1})$ and aborts if this is not the case.

This protocol is formalized in Protocol 9 in the $\mathcal{F}_{\mathsf{RO}}$-hybrid model. The $\mathcal{F}_{\mathsf{RO}}$ functionality is described in Functionality 1. We remark that this protocol does not instantiate $\mathcal{F}_{\mathsf{CheckZero}}$ exactly. In order for the proof of security to work, we need to allow the adversary to cause the parties to reject also when $v = 0$. We denote this modified functionality by $\mathcal{F}_{\mathsf{CheckZero}}'$. This is minor change since the main requirement from $\mathcal{F}_{\text{CheckZero}}$ in our compiler is that the parties won't accept a value as 0 when it is not, which is still satisfied by the modified functionality.

Functionality 1 $\mathcal{F}_{\text{RO}}$ – Random Oracle functionality

Setup: Let M be an initially empty map.
The protocol:
- On input x from a party P, if $(x, y) \in M$ for some y, return y. Otherwise pick y at random and set $M = \{(x, y)\} \cup M$ and return y.
- On (x, y) from $\mathcal{S}$ and if $(x, \cdot) \notin M$ set $M = \{(x, y)\} \cup M$.

Protocol 9 Checking Equality to 0 in the $\mathcal{F}_{\text{RO}}$-Hybrid Model

Inputs: Parties hold a sharing $[\![v]\!]$.
Protocol:
1. Party P_i queries $\beta_i \leftarrow \mathcal{F}_{\text{RO}}(-(v_i + v_{i+1}))$ and sends β_i to P_{i+1}.
2. Upon receiving β_{i-1} from P_{i-1}, each party P_i checks that $\beta_{i-1} = \mathcal{F}_{\text{RO}}(v_{i+1})$. If this is not the case, then P_i outputs reject. Otherwise, it outputs accept.

We have the following proposition.

Proposition 3. *Protocol 9 securely computes* $\mathcal{F}_{\text{CheckZero}}$ *in the* $\mathcal{F}_{\text{RO}}$*-hybrid model in the presence of one malicious corrupted party.*

Proof: Let $\mathcal{A}$ be the real adversary who corrupts at most one party and $\mathcal{S}$ the ideal world simulator. Let P_i be the corrupted party. The simulation begins with $\mathcal{S}$ receiving the shares of P_i, i.e., (v_i, v_{i+1}). Then, $\mathcal{S}$ proceed as follows:

- If $\mathcal{S}$ receives accept from $\mathcal{F}_{\text{CheckZero}}'$, then it knows that $v \equiv_\ell 0$ and so it can compute the share $v_{i-1} = -(v_i + v_{i+1})$ and so it knows the honest parties' shares and can perfectly simulate the execution, while playing the role of $\mathcal{F}_{\text{RO}}$. If $\mathcal{A}$ cause the parties to reject by using different shares, then $\mathcal{S}$ sends reject to $\mathcal{F}_{\text{CheckZero}}'$.
- If $\mathcal{S}$ receives reject, then it chooses a random $v_{i-1} \in \mathbb{Z}_{2^\ell} \setminus \{-(v_i + v_{i+1})\}$ and defines the honest parties' shares accordingly. Then, it plays the role of $\mathcal{F}_{\text{RO}}$ simulating the remaining of the protocol. By the definition of $\mathcal{F}_{\text{RO}}$, the view of $\mathcal{A}$ is distributed identically in the simulated and the real execution. ∎

7 Implementation and Evaluation

We implement both protocols in C++ and rely on uint64_t and unsigned int128 types for arithmetic over $\mathbb{Z}_{2^\ell}$, where the former is used when $\ell = 64$ and the latter when $\ell = 128$. This choice allows us to investigate two sets of parameters: $\ell = 64$ can be viewed as 32 bit computation with 32 bits of statistical security, while $\ell = 128$ gives us 64 bits of computation with 64 bits of statistical security. We rely on libsodium for hashing and the PRG we use is based on AES.

For the Galois-ring variant our implementation uses the ring $R = \mathbb{Z}_{2^\ell}[X]/(h(x))$ with $h(X) = X^4 + X + 1$ and denote this by $\mathsf{GR}(2^\ell, d = 4)$. This ring supports $2^4 - 1 = 15$ parties and the act of hard-coding the irreducible polynomial allows us to implement multiplication and division in the ring using lookup tables. It is worth remarking that operations in $\mathsf{GR}(2^\ell, d)$ are more expensive than certain prime fields (in particular, Mersenne primes as the ones used in [14]). Concretely, a multiplication in $\mathsf{GR}(2^{64}, 4)$ requires 20 `uint64_t` multiplications and 18 additions, while a multiplication in $\mathbb{Z}_{2^{64}}$ requires only a couple of `uint64_t` multiplications as well as a few bitwise operations. So while some MPC primitives in $\mathbb{Z}_{2^\ell}$ may be cheaper (for example, masking a value in $\mathbb{Z}_{2^\ell}$ is cheaper), this gain in efficiency is greatly reduced by the complexity of operating over the Galois ring.

Experimental Setup. We run our experiments on AWS `c5.9xlarge` machines, which have 36 virtual cores, 72 GB of memory and a 10 Gbps network. We utilize 3 separate machines and so for experiments with $n > 3$, some parties run on the same machine. However, the load on each machine is distributed evenly (e.g., with 5 parties, the first two machines each run 2 parties each while the last run only 1 party).

7.1   Experiments

For our experiments, we focus on two instantiations.

First we compare our Shamir based instantiation (cf. Sect. 5) against the field protocol of [14]. For this, we use the implementation at [1]. We perform the same benchmarks as reported on in [14]; that is, circuits of varying depth with a fixed number of parties. Each experiment is repeated for n set to 3, 5, 7 and 9. The main goal here is to understand the overhead of working with $\mathsf{GR}(2^\ell, d)$ as opposed to working over $\mathbb{Z}_p$. As [1] supports different choices of the prime p we set p to be a 61-bit Mersenne prime, as this is the most efficient field that also allows for a reasonable expressive computations.

Our second set of experiments will compare our replicated secret-sharing based instantiation (cf. Sect. 6) against the protocols for computation over rings presented in [21]. In these experiments we measure the throughput of multiplications in our protocol; that is, how many multiplications our protocol can compute per second. Since we do not have access to the implementations of [21], we opt instead to use the same experimental setup as theirs in order to obtain a fair comparison. We report here on benchmarks run in a LAN setting. Secondly, we compare our 3-party protocol against the 3-party instantiation from [14]. The 3-party protocol in [14] can be considered state-of-the-art, and thus a comparison against our protocol is in order.

While the protocol of [14] is the natural choice for comparing our n-party instantiation, a number of efficient specialized 3 party protocols exist which we briefly mention here. We choose the protocols of [21] for comparison as their experiments and setup is straightforward to replicate with our protocol, thus allowing us to make a fair comparison. Concurrently with [21], several other proposals for 3 party protocols have been published, such as [13] or [34]. However, no public implementation exists for these works, and the nature of the experiments they perform makes it very hard to perform a fair comparison (as we do later with the results from [21]). More precisely, both [13] and [34] evaluate their protocols relative to an implementation of ABY3 [32] that was also implemented by the authors themselves (as no public implementation of ABY3 was available at that time).

While [34] have better amortized communication cost, we estimate that their *concrete* running time (when considering end-to-end times, as we do in this work) will be worse. We base this conjecture on the fact that [34] uses the interpolation based check from [8]. For the case of fields, this check was shown in [9] to take several seconds in order to check 1 million multiplications (which is the benchmark we use). Running the same check, but over a ring, requires computation over a fairly large extension of $\mathbb{Z}_{2^k}$, which we have no reason to expect would be significantly faster than the field based check. Concluding, we would not be surprised if [34] is faster *in the online phase*; however, preprocessing the triples needed to get this would be much slower than our protocol. We stress that our protocol (for the 3 party case) has *no preprocessing*, so we expect our protocol to perform much better when measuring end-to-end times.

7.2   Results: Shamir Instantiation

The results of our experiments can be seen in Table 1. Across the board, we see that preprocessing is more expensive in our protocol than in [14]. However, the overhead is in line with the observation made above that operating in $\mathsf{GR}(2^\ell, d)$ is about 4 times as expensive than in $\mathbb{Z}_p$ when $\ell = 64$ and p is a 61-bit Mersenne prime. This motivates a line of research in improving the efficiency of computing over Galois rings, given the relevance of these structures as highlighted in Sect. 1.2. This is in particular true when the number of parties is small, as here local computation is the dominant factor. Moving to a larger number of parties, the overhead decreases, which we attribute to differences in the efficiency of the communication layer between our protocol and the one in [14].

Interestingly, we see that for a lower number of parties combined with very deep circuits, our protocol performs better in the online phase. E.g., [14] takes 7.3 s, while both of our version is below 4.5 s. This could again be explained by differences in the communication layer (since both our protocols communicate roughly the same amount of information due to the fact that we only need to send a $\mathbb{Z}_{2^\ell}$ element during reconstruction). However, our protocol is again less efficient when the number of parties increases, which would be due to the fact that the king needs to send more data during a reconstruction, as well as broadcast being more costly when more parties are involved. We remark that it is possible to distribute the broadcast load of the king among several parties, which may close the gap to some extent.

We see an expected overhead of roughly ×2 between $\ell = 64$ and $\ell = 128$ (consider the depth 20 row in Table 1, as this is the setting where differences in local computation is most prominent). This more or less confirms the intuition

Table 1. LAN running times in seconds for circuits with 10^6 multiplications, different depth and for varying number of parties, evaluated using Shamir SS-based MPC. Each value is a tuple a/b where a is the preprocessing time and b is the time it takes to evaluate the circuit.

Depth	Protocol	3	5	7	9
20	Ours $\ell = 64$	1.56/0.18	2.12/0.28	2.46/0.37	2.70/0.47
	Ours $\ell = 128$	2.79/0.52	4.28/0.74	4.73/0.91	5.10/1.11
	[14]	0.43/0.18	0.63/0.22	0.93/0.45	1.03/0.28
100	Ours $\ell = 64$	1.50/0.23	1.97/0.30	2.30/0.37	2.76/0.41
	Ours $\ell = 128$	2.80/0.51	3.78/0.61	4.15/0.77	5.02/0.95
	[14]	0.42/0.42	0.64/0.22	0.90/0.52	1.04/1.27
1,000	Ours $\ell = 64$	1.58/0.67	1.95/1.08	2.23/1.43	2.62/1.84
	Ours $\ell = 128$	2.80/1.23	3.68/1.81	4.23/2.08	5.03/2.47
	[14]	0.41/0.96	0.63/0.68	0.89/0.95	1.05/1.17
10,000	Ours $\ell = 64$	1.50/3.85	2.01/8.55	2.41/13.41	2.65/16.76
	Ours $\ell = 128$	2.81/4.43	3.71/8.07	4.38/13.31	5.03/16.43
	[14]	0.38/7.30	0.61/7.32	0.89/8.40	1.05/12.88

that an operation in $\mathbb{Z}_{2^{128}}$ is around 2–3 times as expensive compared to an operation in $\mathbb{Z}_{2^{64}}$.[9]

As a more general conclusion, we observe that working over these Galois ring extensions does indeed incur an overhead—even for small extensions such as the one we use.

7.3 Results: Replicated-Based Instantiation

We also compare our replicated secret-sharing based instantiation with the protocols of [21], and present the results in Fig. 1a and Fig. 1b.[10] As we do not have access to the code of all the protocols considered in [21], we run our protocol in the same setup. With the exception of the Sharemind postprocessing protocol, we observe that we outperform all protocols of [21]. We may attribute this to the fact that both Sharemind and MP-SPDZ are more mature codebases and thus it is likely that a greater effort has been put into optimizations.

---

[9] Indeed, while a multiplication in $\mathbb{Z}_{2^{64}}$ is one unsigned 64-bit multiplication, a multiplication on 128-bit types compile to three $\mathbb{Z}_{2^{64}}$ multiplications. That the overhead is less than ×3 can be attributed to the compiler being able to easier vectorize 64-bit multiplications in the $\mathbb{Z}_{2^{128}}$ case.

[10] We thank the authors of [21] for giving us the tikzcode of their graph, as well as their raw experimental data which allows us to make a fair comparison in this section.

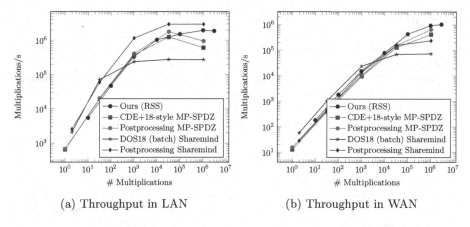

(a) Throughput in LAN   (b) Throughput in WAN

Fig. 1. Throughput benchmarks for replicated secret-sharing with 3 parties.

Table 2. LAN times in seconds for circuits with 10^6 multiplications and varying depth with three parties.

	Protocol	20	100	1,000	10,000
RSS	Ours $\ell = 64$	0.23	0.23	0.49	2.36
	Ours $\ell = 128$	0.4	0.41	0.56	2.47
	[14]	0.26	0.33	0.59	2.53

However, when we consider our protocol running in a WAN, we see that we outperform all protocols in [21]. This concurs with the fact that our protocol only needs to send 2 ring elements per multiplication, while the postprocessing protocols of [21] needs to send 3 (Table 2).

We also run our 3-party protocol against the similar field based one from [14]. Given the similarities between the 3-party instantiation in that work and ours, it is not surprising that the two protocols perform very similar. Similar to our Shamir based instantiation, we observe the largest difference (in our favor) with deeper circuits, which we can again attribute to slight differences in the communication layer. On the other hand, the difference is smaller for the more shallow circuits where local computation matters more. For this case, our protocol with $\ell = 64$ is comparable in terms of speed to [14], which uses a 64-bit prime. On the other hand, our protocol with $\ell = 128$ is slightly slower. However, as highlighted in the introduction, the need of an s-gap in field-based protocols to support more complex primitives like secure comparison or truncation implies that comparing a 64-bit prime with $\ell = 64$ is fair.

Acknowledgment. This work has been supported by the European Research Council (ERC) under the European Unions's Horizon 2020 research and innovation programme under grant agreement No. 669255 (MPCPRO); and the Danish Independent Research Council under Grant-ID DFF-6108-00169 (FoCC).

References

1. Fast large-scale honest-majority MPC for malicious adversaries (2017). https:// github.com/cryptobiu/MPCHonestMajorityNoTriples
2. Abspoel, M., Cramer, R., Damgård, I., Escudero, D., Yuan, C.: Efficient information-theoretic secure multiparty computation over $\mathbb{Z}/p^k\mathbb{Z}$ via Galois rings. In: Hofheinz, D., Rosen, A. (eds.) TCC 2019. LNCS, vol. 11891, pp. 471–501. Springer, Cham (2019). https://doi.org/10.1007/978-3-030-36030-6_19
3. Araki, T., et al.: Optimized honest-majority MPC for malicious adversaries - breaking the 1 billion-gate per second barrier, pp. 843–862 (2017)
4. Araki, T., Furukawa, J., Lindell, Y., Nof, A., Ohara, K.: High-throughput semi-honest secure three-party computation with an honest majority, pp. 805–817 (2016)
5. Beerliová-Trubíniová, Z., Hirt, M.: Efficient multi-party computation with dispute control. In: Halevi, S., Rabin, T. (eds.) TCC 2006. LNCS, vol. 3876, pp. 305–328. Springer, Heidelberg (2006). https://doi.org/10.1007/11681878_16
6. Ben-Sasson, E., Fehr, S., Ostrovsky, R.: Near-linear unconditionally-secure multiparty computation with a dishonest minority. In: Safavi-Naini, R., Canetti, R. (eds.) CRYPTO 2012. LNCS, vol. 7417, pp. 663–680. Springer, Heidelberg (2012). https://doi.org/10.1007/978-3-642-32009-5_39
7. Bogdanov, D., Laur, S., Willemson, J.: Sharemind: a framework for fast privacy-preserving computations. In: Jajodia, S., Lopez, J. (eds.) ESORICS 2008. LNCS, vol. 5283, pp. 192–206. Springer, Heidelberg (2008). https://doi.org/10.1007/978-3-540-88313-5_13
8. Boneh, D., Boyle, E., Corrigan-Gibbs, H., Gilboa, N., Ishai, Y.: Zero-knowledge proofs on secret-shared data via fully linear PCPs. In: Boldyreva, A., Micciancio, D. (eds.) CRYPTO 2019. LNCS, vol. 11694, pp. 67–97. Springer, Cham (2019). https://doi.org/10.1007/978-3-030-26954-8_3
9. Boyle, E., Gilboa, N., Ishai, Y., Nof, A.: Practical fully secure three-party computation via sublinear distributed zero-knowledge proofs, pp. 869–886 (2019)
10. Canetti, R.: Security and composition of multiparty cryptographic protocols. J. Cryptol. **13**(1), 143–202 (2000)
11. Cascudo, I., Cramer, R., Xing, C., Yuan, C.: Amortized complexity of information-theoretically secure MPC revisited. In: Shacham, H., Boldyreva, A. (eds.) CRYPTO 2018. LNCS, vol. 10993, pp. 395–426. Springer, Cham (2018). https:// doi.org/10.1007/978-3-319-96878-0_14
12. Catrina, O., de Hoogh, S.: Improved primitives for secure multiparty integer computation. In: Garay, J.A., De Prisco, R. (eds.) SCN 2010. LNCS, vol. 6280, pp. 182–199. Springer, Heidelberg (2010). https://doi.org/10.1007/978-3-642-15317-4_13
13. Chaudhari, H., Choudhury, A., Patra, A., Suresh, A.: ASTRA: high throughput 3PC over rings with application to secure prediction. In: Proceedings of the 2019 ACM SIGSAC Conference on Cloud Computing Security Workshop, CCSW@CCS 2019, London, UK, November 11, 2019, pp. 81–92 (2019)
14. Chida, K., et al.: Fast large-scale honest-majority MPC for malicious adversaries. In: Shacham, H., Boldyreva, A. (eds.) CRYPTO 2018. LNCS, vol. 10993, pp. 34–64. Springer, Cham (2018). https://doi.org/10.1007/978-3-319-96878-0_2
15. Cramer, R., Damgård, I., Escudero, D., Scholl, P., Xing, C.: SPD$\mathbb{Z}_{2^k}$: efficient MPC mod 2^k for dishonest majority. In: Shacham, H., Boldyreva, A. (eds.) CRYPTO 2018. LNCS, vol. 10992, pp. 769–798. Springer, Cham (2018). https://doi.org/10.1007/978-3-319-96881-0_26

16. Dalskov, A.P.K., Escudero, D., Keller, M.: Secure evaluation of quantized neural networks, vol. 2020, no. 4, pp. 355–375 (2020)
17. Damgård, I., Escudero, D., Frederiksen, T.K., Keller, M., Scholl, P., Volgushev, N.: New primitives for actively-secure MPC over rings with applications to private machine learning, pp. 1102–1120 (2019)
18. Damgård, I., Keller, M., Larraia, E., Pastro, V., Scholl, P., Smart, N.P.: Practical covertly secure MPC for dishonest majority – or: breaking the SPDZ limits. In: Crampton, J., Jajodia, S., Mayes, K. (eds.) ESORICS 2013. LNCS, vol. 8134, pp. 1–18. Springer, Heidelberg (2013). https://doi.org/10.1007/978-3-642-40203-6_1
19. Damgård, I., Nielsen, J.B.: Scalable and unconditionally secure multiparty computation. In: Menezes, A. (ed.) CRYPTO 2007. LNCS, vol. 4622, pp. 572–590. Springer, Heidelberg (2007). https://doi.org/10.1007/978-3-540-74143-5_32
20. Damgård, I., Orlandi, C., Simkin, M.: Yet another compiler for active security or: efficient MPC over arbitrary rings. In: Shacham, H., Boldyreva, A. (eds.) CRYPTO 2018. LNCS, vol. 10992, pp. 799–829. Springer, Cham (2018). https://doi.org/10.1007/978-3-319-96881-0_27
21. Eerikson, H., Keller, M., Orlandi, C., Pullonen, P., Puura, J., Simkin, M.: Use your brain! Arithmetic 3PC for any modulus with active security, pp. 5:1–5:24 (2020)
22. Furukawa, J., Lindell, Y., Nof, A., Weinstein, O.: High-throughput secure three-party computation for malicious adversaries and an honest majority. In: Coron, J.-S., Nielsen, J.B. (eds.) EUROCRYPT 2017. LNCS, vol. 10211, pp. 225–255. Springer, Cham (2017). https://doi.org/10.1007/978-3-319-56614-6_8
23. Genkin, D., Ishai, Y., Polychroniadou, A.: Efficient multi-party computation: from passive to active security via secure SIMD circuits. In: Gennaro, R., Robshaw, M. (eds.) CRYPTO 2015. LNCS, vol. 9216, pp. 721–741. Springer, Heidelberg (2015). https://doi.org/10.1007/978-3-662-48000-7_35
24. Genkin, D., Ishai, Y., Prabhakaran, M., Sahai, A., Tromer, E.: Circuits resilient to additive attacks with applications to secure computation, pp. 495–504 (2014)
25. Goldreich, O.: Foundations of Cryptography: Basic Applications, vol. 2. Cambridge University Press, Cambridge (2004)
26. Goldwasser, S., Lindell, Y.: Secure multi-party computation without agreement. J. Cryptol. 18(3), 247–287 (2005)
27. Goyal, V., Liu, Y., Song, Y.: Communication-efficient unconditional MPC with guaranteed output delivery. In: Boldyreva, A., Micciancio, D. (eds.) CRYPTO 2019. LNCS, vol. 11693, pp. 85–114. Springer, Cham (2019). https://doi.org/10.1007/978-3-030-26951-7_4
28. Goyal, V., Song, Y., Zhu, C.: Guaranteed output delivery comes free in honest majority MPC. In: Micciancio, D., Ristenpart, T. (eds.) CRYPTO 2020. LNCS, vol. 12171, pp. 618–646. Springer, Cham (2020). https://doi.org/10.1007/978-3-030-56880-1_22
29. Keller, M., Orsini, E., Scholl, P.: MASCOT: faster malicious arithmetic secure computation with oblivious transfer, pp. 830–842 (2016)
30. Kikuchi, R., et al.: Field extension in secret-shared form and its applications to efficient secure computation. In: Jang-Jaccard, J., Guo, F. (eds.) ACISP 2019. LNCS, vol. 11547, pp. 343–361. Springer, Cham (2019). https://doi.org/10.1007/978-3-030-21548-4_19
31. Lindell, Y., Nof, A.: A framework for constructing fast MPC over arithmetic circuits with malicious adversaries and an honest-majority, pp. 259–276 (2017)
32. Mohassel, P., Rindal, P.: ABY^3: a mixed protocol framework for machine learning, pp. 35–52 (2018)

33. Nordholt, P.S., Veeningen, M.: Minimising communication in honest-majority MPC by batchwise multiplication verification. In: Preneel, B., Vercauteren, F. (eds.) ACNS 2018. LNCS, vol. 10892, pp. 321–339. Springer, Cham (2018). https://doi.org/10.1007/978-3-319-93387-0_17
34. Patra, A., Suresh, A.: BLAZE: blazing fast privacy-preserving machine learning (2020)

Cryptanalysis

Experimental Review of the IKK Query Recovery Attack: Assumptions, Recovery Rate and Improvements

Ruben Groot Roessink[✉], Andreas Peter, and Florian Hahn

University of Twente, Enschede, The Netherlands
r.grootroessink@alumnus.utwente.nl, {a.peter,f.w.hahn}@utwente.nl

Abstract. In light of more data than ever being stored using cloud services and the request by the public for secure, privacy-enhanced, and easy-to-use systems, Searchable Encryption schemes were introduced. These schemes enable privacy-enhanced search among encrypted documents yet disclose (encrypted) queries and responses. The first query recovery attack, the IKK attack, uses the disclosed information to (partly) recover what plaintext words the client searched for. This can also leak information on the plaintext contents of the encrypted documents. Under specific assumptions, the IKK attack has been shown to potentially cause serious harm to the security of Searchable Encryption schemes.

We empirically review the IKK query recovery attack to improve the understanding of its feasibility and potential security damage. In order to do so, we vary the assumed query distribution, which is shown to have a severe (negative) impact on the accuracy of the attack, and the input parameters of the IKK attack to find a correlation between these parameters and the accuracy of the IKK attack. Furthermore, we show that the recovery rate of the attack can be increased up to 10% points, while decreasing the variance of the recovery rate up to 78% points by combining the results of multiple attack runs. We also show that the including deterministic components in the probabilistic IKK attack can increase the recovery rate up to 21% points and decrease its variance up to 57% points.

Keywords: Searchable Encryption · IKK · Query recovery

1 Introduction

The use of currently available encryption schemes allows users to securely upload and retrieve documents anywhere in the world using cloud services. A user encrypts a set of documents and sends these encrypted documents to a server for storage. The server can return documents upon request by the user, which the user can decrypt to obtain the original documents, while the server is not capable of reading the contents of the documents. A downside of using encryption schemes is that they, in general, limit the functionalities of the cloud service. One such functionality is the possibility to search for word occurrences among documents. To overcome this loss in functionality, while also taking into regard data

© Springer Nature Switzerland AG 2021
K. Sako and N. O. Tippenhauer (Eds.): ACNS 2021, LNCS 12727, pp. 155–183, 2021.
https://doi.org/10.1007/978-3-030-78375-4_7

confidentiality, Song et al. [15] introduced the notion of Searchable Encryption (SE).

In general, SE schemes provide a client with a way to search for the occurrence of a certain (plaintext) word, a *keyword*, among a set of encrypted documents, while neither the client nor the server has to decrypt all documents which the client wants to search among. A client generates a search token, a *query*, which it sends to a server hosting a set of (encrypted) documents. The server uses the query to find a subset of the encrypted documents corresponding with the search token and returns this subset to the client.

Nearly all of these SE schemes leak at least some information, usually in the form of *data access patterns* [8,9,15]. This means that an adversary can observe the issued queries from the client and the document identifiers of documents corresponding to said queries in the response by the server. This allows the client to make a connection between the queries and the corresponding documents. Some schemes were proposed [8,10] that hide these access patterns. However, these schemes are quite inefficient as they require an extensive number of computations after each query. Other schemes propose to obfuscate the access patterns which can both lead to inconsistencies in the search results (false positives or false negatives) and an increase in communication and storage overhead [7].

Islam et al. [12] elaborate on the implications of the leakage of access patterns by proposing the first *query recovery attack*, dubbed IKK attack in subsequent research after the first initials of the authors of the paper. Their attack is a statistical attack which tries to map queries to their corresponding real-world keywords. This mapping process is dubbed *query recovery*. A correctly 'recovered' query tells an adversary what the client searched for and possibly even tells something about the contents of (encrypted) documents stored on the server. In their attack Islam et al. use the relative co-occurrence counts of queries, which denotes the number of documents a certain number of queries occur in together, relative to the total number of documents. These counts can be calculated from leaked access patterns. The IKK attack also assumes the adversary has access to (a close approximation of) the co-occurrence counts of the plaintext (key)words in these documents, dubbed *background knowledge*. Islam et al. show that a large percentage of queries is recoverable, expressed as the *(query) recovery rate*, if the adversary has perfect background knowledge, meaning that the co-occurrence counts of keywords exactly match the co-occurrence counts of their corresponding queries. They also briefly show that the recovery rate drops significantly in simulations with non-perfect background knowledge.

We revisit the IKK attack and empirically evaluate assumptions Islam et al. make in their proposal of the IKK attack. Additionally, we research correlations between certain parameters and the accuracy/recovery rate of the IKK attack and propose improvements to the attack that increase the recovery rate of the attack.

Our Contributions

- We show that assumptions on the (Zipfian) distribution of queries/natural search behavior Islam et al. made positively influences the accuracy of the IKK attack.
- We show that there is a correlation between input parameters of the IKK attack and the accuracy of attack runs, independent of the (email) dataset used in the targeted Searchable Encryption scheme, potentially allowing an adversary to reuse the same values of parameters across different datasets.
- We show that the accuracy of the IKK attack can be increased significantly when combining multiple runs using a majority voting scheme as the median recovery rate is increased up to 10% points, whereas the variance of the recovery rate is decreased up to 78% points.
- We show that a more deterministic approach to select new states in the IKK attack, inspired by the Count attack [6], increases the accuracy of the attack, while decreasing the average number of states visited. The median recovery rate is increased up to 21% points and the variance of recovery rates is decreased up to 57% points, while the average visited number of states is decreased by 28%.

2   The IKK Query Recovery Attack

2.1   Searchable Encryption (SE)

The first SE scheme was proposed by Song et al. [15] to provide a client with a way to search for the occurrence of a plaintext word among a set of encrypted documents stored on a server without an adversary being able to learn the (plaintext) contents of these documents.

The server stores a set of encrypted documents, for example email files. The client wants to retrieve emails that contain information on an upcoming merger and thus requests all emails that contain the (plaintext) word *merger*. It does so by generating a so-called query using a keyed trapdoor function, $Trapdoor_{sk}(merger)$, for example, a keyed hash function. Only users with key sk can generate valid queries. More formally, a user knowing key sk can generate query token q_i for a keyword k_i. We assume, just like Islam et al. [12], that queries are deterministic, i.e. $Trapdoor_{sk}(k_i) = Trapdoor_{sk}(k_j)$ if $k_i = k_j$.

In order to retrieve the corresponding documents, the client sends the query to the server, which on its turn, performs a matching algorithm. Most proposed SE schemes either encrypt every single word in a document (*In-place SE* [6]) to encrypt a document or encrypt every document using a traditional encryption scheme, such as AES, while also generating an encrypted inverted index of documents and trapdoors (*Encrypted-index SE* [6]) to allow the server to perform the search query. No matter the SE scheme, the server returns all the documents that match the search query, which can be decrypted by the client.

2.2 Access Pattern Disclosure

Just like Cash et al. [6], we deem the server the most likely adversary as it has access to the most information. Nonetheless, any adversary with access to the communication channels is able to connect a query to the identifiers of the documents that were returned and thus is able to see which documents were *accessed* upon the query of the client. This has been dubbed *(data) access pattern disclosure* in the literature [12]. Almost all SE schemes, except schemes that re-encrypt the documents or the encrypted index stored on the server after each query [8,10], disclose access patterns of particular queries, and thus each query gives an adversary more information on which queries are connected to which documents. Some schemes propose to obfuscate access patterns which can lead to inconsistencies in the search results (false positives or false negatives) or an increase in communication and storage overhead [7]. In our research, we assume no such inconsistencies were added to the search results.

Although we note that different SE schemes leak different levels of information, we only research the disclosure of access patterns and assume that the adversary is able to get ⟨*query, response*⟩ pairs, where *response* is a list of documents that matched the issued query. The leaked ⟨*query, response*⟩ pairs allow the adversary to construct an inverted index from queries/trapdoors and documents. Each cell in the matrix contains a 1 if the document matched the query, i.e. the plaintext keyword occurs at least once in said document, or a 0 if not. An example of an (observed) query inverted index is shown in Table 1.

Table 1. Example of a query inverted index

Query	Documents		
	Doc_1	Doc_2	Doc_3
$q_1 = Trapdoor_{sk}(merger)$	1	1	0
$q_2 = Trapdoor_{sk}(corporate)$	1	1	0
$q_3 = Trapdoor_{sk}(report)$	0	1	1

2.3 Statistical Processing

The IKK attack is grounded on the assumption that some words are more likely to occur together in any piece of natural language than others. Islam et al. [12] give the example of the words *New, York* and *Yankees*, where the words *New* and *York* are more likely to occur together than *New* and *Yankees* or *York* and *Yankees* because they are also used to refer to the city and the state and not only the baseball team. Islam et al. propose a model where the co-occurrence counts of 2 queries are used to recover which plaintext words correspond to which queries. The authors use a so-called co-occurrence matrix to express all co-occurrence counts of the queries in an attack run, as an co-occurrence matrix lists the (relative) co-occurrence count for each of the queries with all other queries and with itself. The probability that two words appear together in a given document is expressed using the following formula by Islam et al.:

$$\beta = \frac{R_{Q_s} \cdot R_{Q_t}}{n} \tag{1}$$

In this formula, Q_s and Q_t are two queries, and R_{Q_x} denotes a vector with ones and zeros indicating whether the word corresponding to the query occurs at least once in the document corresponding with the place in the vector (1) or not (0). The co-occurrence count is calculated by taking the *dot* product of R_{Q_s} and R_{Q_t}. To get the relative co-occurrence count this value is simply divided by n, which denotes the total number of documents in the dataset. A query co-occurrence matrix simply lists all the co-occurrences of queries, is symmetric by nature and is easily generated using an inverted index as every row in the index, corresponding to query Q_x, is already represented as vector R_{Q_x}. The relative co-occurrence count of a query with itself is the total number of documents said query occurs in divided by n. The example inverted index in Table 1 gives us the co-occurrence matrix in Table 2.

Table 2. Example of a query co-occurrence matrix

Queries	q_1	q_2	q_3
q_1	0.67	0.67	0.33
q_2	0.67	0.67	0.33
q_3	0.33	0.33	0.67

Table 3. Example of a (perfect) background knowledge co-occurrence matrix

Keywords	*Corporate*	*Merger*	*Report*
corporate	0.67	0.67	0.33
merger	0.67	0.67	0.33
report	0.33	0.33	0.67

2.4 Background Knowledge Assumptions

In most of their simulations Islam et al. [12] assume the adversary has perfect background knowledge of the co-occurrence counts of plaintext words in the documents stored encrypted on the server. They mention that it is difficult, if not impossible, to obtain perfect background knowledge and briefly experiment on the accuracy of their attack in simulations with non-perfect background knowledge by adding various degrees of Gaussian noise to a co-occurrence matrix corresponding to perfect background knowledge.

Cash et al. [6] further research the effect of non-perfect background knowledge, but instead of adding various degrees of Gaussian noise to a perfect representation of the background knowledge (of the adversary) the authors assume the adversary (server) has access to a *fraction* of the plaintext documents and thus the adversary is capable of calculating both inverted indices and co-occurrence matrices from the documents it knows. The authors report that the IKK attack performs quite poorly if the background knowledge is made up of less than 99% of the documents. An example of a background knowledge co-occurrence matrix is shown in Table 3.

2.5 Simulated Annealing

Islam et al. [12] use two algorithms to recover queries from a query co-occurrence matrix and a background knowledge co-occurrence matrix: Their *Optimizer* (Algorithms 1 and 2) algorithm assigns a random 1-to-1 mapping for each query to a random keyword in the background co-occurrence matrix as the *initial state* variable. The mapping corresponds to a mapping between the query co-occurrence matrix and a subset of the background knowledge co-occurrence matrix which is equal in its dimensions to the query co-occurrence matrix. Each cell in the query co-occurrence matrix is therefore mapped to a single cell in the background knowledge co-occurrence matrix. The *initial state* is given as input to their ANNEAL (Algorithms 3 and 4) algorithm. This algorithm is a *Simulated Annealing* algorithm [13], which first copies the *initial state* to a *current state* variable and enters a while loop. Each iteration the algorithm randomly selects both a mapping (of a single query to a single keyword, i.e. $q_1 \mapsto k_1$) and a keyword (k_2) from the list of potential keywords. If the selected keyword is already mapped to another query, i.e. $q_2 \mapsto k_2$ is in *current state*, the mappings are simply interchanged, i.e. $q_1 \mapsto k_2$ and $q_2 \mapsto k_1$, otherwise the selected mapping is changed to $q_1 \mapsto k_2$ to obtain the *next state*.

The algorithm determines whether it should accept or reject *next state* in favor of or against *current state* respectively. The algorithm calculates the sum of the squared Euclidean distance of the co-occurrence counts of each of the mappings with other mappings for both *current state* and *next state*. Depending on the calculated squared Euclidean distance either *next state* is accepted (and becomes *current state* in the iteration of the while loop) or is rejected. If the Euclidean distance of *next state* is lower than that of *current state* *next state* is accepted. A *next state* with a higher Euclidean distance is not necessarily rejected, but might be accepted with a small probability, depending how close the Euclidean distance is to 0. This is included to decrease the possibility of the algorithm finishing its run in a local optimum state as opposed to finding the global optimum state.

The *ANNEAL* algorithm takes three input parameters, next to the co-occurrence matrices. These input parameters *initial temperature, cool down rate* and *rejection rate* are used to ensure the algorithm has a finite run time. The *initial temperature* initializes the internal *current temperature* variable of the algorithm. Each iteration in the while loop *current temperature* is decreased by multiplying it with *cool down rate* (a value between 0 and 1, close to 1). The algorithm returns *current state* as the final mapping if the system *freezes*, i.e. *current temperature becomes 0. initial temperature* and *current temperature* therefore together determine the maximum number of loops the algorithm goes through. The algorithm can also finish before it freezes if no *next state* has been accepted for a certain (consecutive) number of iterations, which is determined by the value of *rejection rate*. The *current temperature* variable is also used also in deciding whether to accept a worse *next state* with a small probability.

2.6   Simulations

Datasets Used. Both Islam et al. [12] and Cash et al. [6] use the _sent_mail_ data folder of the ENRON dataset [2] (containing 30109 emails) as the dataset to run simulations on. Additionally, Cash et al. use the Apache Lucene project's _java-user_ mailing list [1] (containing 50116 emails) in their simulations.

Tokenization/Stemming Algorithm. Both papers tokenize all emails in the dataset to specific words before they are able to stem individual words, but neither elaborate on the tokenization algorithm used in their simulations. Stemming is done using Porter's stemming algorithm [14] to get the stem of each word, meaning that words like 'has' and 'have', which in principle have the same meaning, are stemmed to the same word.

Keyword Generation. The stemmed keywords are sorted in decreasing order of overall occurrence. The 200 most occurring (stemmed) words in a dataset, that are likely to occur in every file (for example 'a' and 'the'), are removed as they are not deemed useful in a Searchable Encryption scheme. The next x words are regarded as the keyword set.

Query Generation. Both Islam et al. and Cash et al. simulate a certain number of queries by using the Zipfian distribution on the keyword set. Due to the nature of the Zipfian distribution words with a higher occurrence count are more likely to be simulated as a query.

Reported Results. Islam et al. report recovery rates ranging from 60%–100% depending on the number of keywords, number of queries and the % of queries 'known' before the attack run. With different levels of Gaussian noise added to the background knowledge, the accuracy of the attack ranges between 40% and 85%. Cash et al. report recovery rates of the IKK attack ranging between 0% and 100% and show an exponentially decreasing correlation between the size of the input matrices (query and background knowledge co-occurrence matrices) and the recovery rate. Cash et al. also report recovery rates ranging between 0% and 60% for different percentages of documents 'known' to the adversary.

3   Revisiting the IKK Attack

Islam et al. [12] introduced the study on query recovery attacks by proposing the IKK query recovery attack. The authors report high query recovery rates that would allow an adversary to determine what a user searched for. More importantly, as Cash et al. [6] note in their paper, correctly recovered queries are inherently a part of the plaintext of encrypted documents and thus disclose part of the plaintext of the document stored on the server. We therefore stress that it is important to get a more broad understanding of query recovery attacks. In this research we revisit the following facets of the IKK attack:

- We evaluate the assumption on query distribution following the Zipfian distribution made by Islam et al. while simulating runs of the IKK attack (Sect. 4).
- We look at the correlation between the *initial temperature, cool down rate* and the *rejection rate* input parameters and the accuracy of the IKK attack (Sect. 5).

Furthermore, we propose and research the following improvements to the IKK attack:

- We propose to use a majority voting scheme to increase the accuracy of the IKK attack by combining the results of multiple runs (Sect. 6).
- We propose to (more) deterministically choose the next state of the ANNEAL algorithm to increase the accuracy of and decrease the number of visited states by the IKK attack. This method incorporates the (relative) word occurrence method, as proposed by Cash et al. in their Count attack (Sect. 6).

In order to run simulations of the IKK attack to address the points above we implemented the IKK attack as proposed by Islam et al. in Python3 and published it on Github [3]. The implementation allows the user to select:

- the distribution used to simulate queries (*Zipfian, reverse Zipfian, Uniform*)
- values for the parameters of the ANNEAL algorithm (*initial temperature, cool down rate, rejection rate*)
- sizes of the query and background knowledge co-occurrence matrices (resp. *number of queries, number of keywords*)
- datasets/email folders to use in the simulation (*ENRON/ _sent_mail, ENRON/inbox, ApacheLucene-java-user (Apache)*)
- different methods to simulate non-perfect background knowledge (*Gaussian noise addition, using a fraction of the keywords, using a fraction of the documents*)
- the number of consecutive runs with exactly the same input parameters
- whether to more deterministically select new states using word occurrences as also proposed in the Count attack by Cash et al.

To give the reader an idea of the input parameters used in our simulations we mention the standard values for the different parameters of the IKK attack in Table 4.

We briefly capture our generalized method below. Simulation specific methodologies are elaborated upon in their correlated sections (Sects. 4, 5 and 6).

1. Tokenize and stem the words in all documents in a specific dataset. Tokenization is done by splitting the document on whitespaces. Stemming is done using Porter's stemming algorithm [14].
2. Sort all unique (stemmed) words in decreasing order of occurrence (count) (the total number of times a word occurs in the dataset, not the number of matching documents).

Table 4. Standard parameter values in the IKK attack simulations

Variable	Value	Variable	Value	Variable	Value
initial temperature	1.0	*nr of keywords*	1500	*dataset /*	*ENRON /*
cool down rate	0.999	*nr of queries*	150	*email folder*	*_sent_mail*
rejection rate	50000				
		nr of runs	1	*keyword percentage*	1.0
Gaussian	0.0			*document percentage*	1.0
noise scaling factor		*distribution*	*Zipfian*		

3. Disregard the first 200 most occurring words, just like Islam et al., and take the subsequent x words as *keyword set*. x is equal to the *number of keywords* input variable in our simulations.
4. Simulate y queries from the x selected keywords using a specified query distribution as the *query set*. y is equal to the *number of queries* input variable in our simulations.
5. Generate the query and background knowledge inverted indices from the selected queries and keywords, and the list of documents.
6. Generate the query and background knowledge co-occurrence matrices from the inverted indices.
7. Input the co-occurrences matrices and the input parameters *initial temperature*, *cool down rate* and *rejection rate* in the ANNEAL algorithm.
8. Calculate the (query) recovery rate by dividing the number of correctly mapped queries, where *query = keyword*, by the total number of queries.

Islam et al. also use a *known queries* variable in their experiments, a method also adopted by Cash et al. This variable denotes ⟨*query, keyword*⟩ pairs that the adversary knows to be mapped correctly before the attack run. We argue that the actual value of this variable is likely to be (close to) 0 and we therefore excluded this variable from our experiments.

4   Assumptions Evaluation

In their simulations, Islam et al. [12] make an assumption on distribution of queries in a real-world SE scheme in order to estimate real-world search behavior of users. They assume natural search behavior can be estimated by simulating queries using the Zipfian distribution as they argue that search behavior might follow a Zipfian distribution as the simulations are run on a natural language corpus. In their paper, the authors state that 'according to Zipf's law, in a corpus of natural language utterances, the frequency of appearance of an individual word is inversely proportional to its rank' [17]. The Zipfian distribution is also used by Cash et al. [6] to simulate queries for their simulations.

In order to simulate queries, from the simulated keyword set (of size x), Islam et al. first sort the words in the keyword set in decreasing order of overall occurrence. For the word in the jth position in this list (rank j) the following formulas are used to determine the probability the word is selected as a query:

$$Pr_j = \frac{\frac{1}{j}}{N_x} = \frac{1}{j \times N_x}, \qquad N_x = \sum_{i=1}^{x} \frac{1}{i} \qquad (2)$$

A word with a higher total occurrence count is therefore more likely to be simulated as a query. Islam et al. also note that duplicate queries are removed. We argue that the assumption that search behavior follows a Zipfian distribution is counter-intuitive in the sense that users are more likely to search for a specific email in their mail archive and thus issue a (single word) query that is likely to return the sought after document while also not returning too much other emails (false positives). We therefore argue that search behavior might instead follow a reverse Zipfian distribution and thus a word that has a lower occurrence count has a higher chance of being selected as a query. The reverse Zipfian distribution can be calculated using the same formulas as the Zipfian distribution, but the list of word occurrences is sorted in ascending order of occurrence as opposed to descending order.

To compare the effect of the distribution used to simulate the queries we conducted three different simulations for the Zipfian distribution, reverse Zipfian Distribution and Uniform distribution respectively. The Uniform distribution denotes the setting where queries are simulated from the keyword set uniformly at random. The results of our simulations are shown in Fig. 1, where each box plot is the aggregation of 20 simulations.

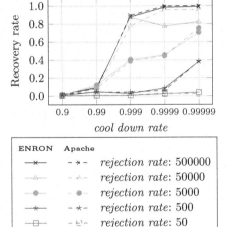

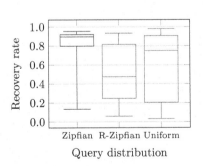

Fig. 1. Correlation of different query distribution and recovery rate

Fig. 2. Correlation between *cool down rate* and recovery rate, with different values of *rejection rate*

It can be seen that the distribution chosen to simulate queries influences the results of the IKK attack quite a lot and that simulations where the queries were simulated using the Zipfian distribution in general have a much higher recovery rate than simulations where a different distribution was used. Unfortunately, we simply do not know what distribution real-world search behavior follows in a Searchable Encryption scheme as, to the best of our knowledge, there exists no dataset which contains query search behavior of real-world users in an SE setting. We can only conclude that the actual distribution determines the accuracy of the IKK attack and therefore whether using a Searchable Encryption scheme poses a risk for search privacy and potentially data confidentially. These results are in line with a similar notion (high-selectivity keywords vs. low-selectivity keywords) as made in [4], which was published during our research.

5   Recovery Rate Quantification

Islam et al. [12] show that their IKK attack allows an adversary to recover (most of the) queries in a simulated setting. Their ANNEAL algorithm (Algorithms 3, 4), which is part of their attack algorithm, takes three input parameters *initial temperature*, *cool down rate* and *rejection rate* to ensure the algorithm has a finite run time. These parameters are further explained in Sect. 2.5.

The values of these parameters have a significant influence on the number of visited states of the IKK attack as the *initial temperature* and *cool down rate* together determine the maximum number of states the algorithms visits, whereas the value of *rejection rate* determines whether the algorithm finishes before the *current temperature* reaches 0 or not. We argue that the accuracy of the IKK attack is therefore dependent on the values of these input parameters. This means that a proven correlation between these three input parameters, independent of the underlying dataset, and the recovery rate might allow an adversary to use simulations on another dataset to find the optimal input parameters for the IKK attack.

To answer the question whether there is a correlation between the three input parameters and the recovery rate, independent of the dataset, we used the same datasets as used by Islam et al. and Cash et al. as these datasets are most common in literature. The first dataset is the ENRON dataset [2], specifically its _sent_mail data folder which contains 30109 emails. Cash et al. also experiment on the *java-user* mailing list of the Apache Lucene project (henceforth Apache) [1] (reportedly containing about 38.000 emails). However, the exact dataset they used was unavailable and thus we crawled the archive site of the java-user mailing list and retrieved 50116 emails. The crawled Apache dataset is included in our Python3 implementation of the IKK attack on Github [3]. In order to test our hypothesis we conducted three different experiments. In all of the experiments we kept one of the input parameters (*initial temperature, cool down rate, rejection rate*) constant while varying the other two. The experiments were repeated for both the Apache and ENRON dataset, with both the query and background knowledge co-occurrence matrix from the same dataset and with perfect background knowledge. Each point in Figs. 2, 3 and 4 is the average of 5 simulations of the IKK attack.

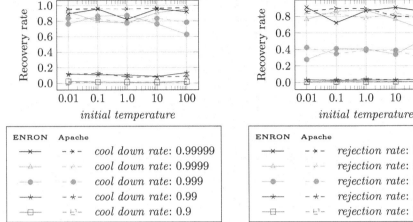

Fig. 3. Correlation between *initial temperature* and Recovery rate, with different values of *cool down rate*

Fig. 4. Correlation between *initial temperature* and Recovery rate, with different values of *rejection rate*

Figure 2 shows the aggregation of simulation results with a constant *initial temperature*. The results of simulations on the ENRON dataset and the Apache dataset are roughly the same. The only exceptions are the simulations with a *rejection rate* of 50000 and a *cool down rate* of 0.9999 respectively 0.99999, which we attribute to the relatively low number of simulations (5) aggregated in each data point. With more simulations these results might become more similar. Furthermore, the recovery rate increases with both the *cool down rate* and the *rejection rate*. This makes sense as the maximum number of loops is increased with a *cool down rate* closer to 1 and a higher *rejection rate* increases the likelihood of finding the best mapping as the algorithm does not halt prematurely.

Figure 3 shows the aggregation of simulations with a constant *rejection rate*. We see that the value of recovery rate is only dependent on the value of *cool down rate* as the correlation between *initial temperature* and recovery rate is relatively constant. The recovery rate is also not dependent on the underlying dataset used as the results for both the ENRON and Apache dataset are roughly the same.

Figure 4 shows the aggregation of simulations with a constant *cool down rate*. We see that the value of recovery rate is dependent on the value of *rejection rate* and not on the value of *initial temperature* as we again see a constant correlation between *initial temperature* and recovery rate. We can also see that the value of recovery rate is not dependent on the underlying dataset used as the results are quite similar for both the ENRON and Apache datasets.

We conclude that the values of *rejection rate* and *cool down rate* significantly influence the recovery rate of the IKK attack. Furthermore, we conclude that it is possible for an adversary to find the optimal values for *cool down rate* and *recovery rate* using simulations on a different dataset as the recovery rate is independent of the underlying dataset used. This means that it is possible to use simulations on the ENRON dataset to select the optimal input parameter values for runs on the Apache dataset and vice versa. We argue that email datasets are quite similar due to the nature of the files they contain as emails are structured in a certain way, are limited in length and are used for specific purposes and thus might contain similar data. More research should be conducted to find out whether our findings hold true for completely different datasets as well.

6   Improvements

6.1   Combining Multiple Runs

The IKK attack returns a 1-to-1 mapping between queries and keywords. An adversary cannot, from the mapping alone, determine which queries were recovered correctly and which were not, as even with perfect background knowledge the IKK attack shows a lot of variance. For example, Fig. 5 shows that the recovery rates of 20 simulations of the IKK attack with equal input parameters and perfect background knowledge return recovery rates ranging between 0.1 and 0.98, which almost spans the entire range of possible recovery rates.

The IKK attack is a probabilistic algorithm in the sense that the algorithm uniformly at random selects a new mapping to change in the current state to determine the next state to explore. We argue that the IKK attack shows a large variance in the recovery rate as the algorithm merely approximates the optimal state yet does not necessarily always return it. A deterministic algorithm that simply visits every possible mapping is less likely to show a large variance, but the single attack runs will have to evaluate far more different states in order to be successful, making such an algorithm quite inefficient as the total number of potential states is given using the following equation:

$$\text{nr. of states} = \frac{(\text{nr. of keywords})!}{(\text{nr. of keywords} - \text{nr. of queries})!}. \tag{3}$$

For 50 observed queries and 500 keywords in the background knowledge this would mean that there are already $7.039 * 10^{133}$ potential states to explore.

As every single run of the IKK attack still approximates the optimal mapping, we argue that it is possible to combine the results of different attack runs using a simple majority voting scheme to better approximate the optimal solution. We conducted 20 simulations each consisting of 20 attack runs on the same query co-occurrence matrix and background knowledge co-occurrence matrix (representing perfect knowledge) per simulation. In each of the simulations, we combined a certain number of runs by selecting the most prevalent keyword mapped to each of the queries. If no prevalent keyword could be found (two or more keywords are most prevalent) the majority voting scheme did not assign a most prevalent keyword to a query and instead assigned the *None* value.

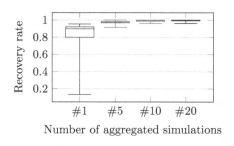

Fig. 5. Aggregation of a number of different runs of the same simulation using a majority voting scheme

Figure 5 shows the results of combining multiple runs on the same query and background co-occurrence matrices. It can be seen that the accuracy of the attack significantly decreases the variance that is observed with single runs of the IKK attack. When combining 5 runs per simulation (#5) the results are already very promising, which is even more the case when the aggregation contains either 10 or 20 runs per simulation. Our proposed aggregation method also has the advantage that the single attack runs can executed in parallel and then aggregated, ensuring the execution time overhead is limited. The median recovery rate between 1 run per simulation (#1) and 20 runs per simulation (#20) is increased with more than 10% points, whereas the variance is decreased with 78% points.

6.2   Deterministic IKK Attack

As the IKK attack is a probabilistic algorithm, it does not necessarily return the optimal query-to-keyword mapping. We argue a more deterministic approach to finding the right mapping might increase the recovery rates of the IKK attack.

The Count attack, as proposed by Cash et al. [6], takes a more deterministic approach to map queries to keywords, by eliminating candidate mapping keywords using the relative document occurrence count of keywords. Cash et al. assume the adversary has access to not only the co-occurrence counts of queries and keywords, but is also in possession of the (relative) document occurrence counts from queries and keywords, i.e. the number of documents a query or keyword occurs in (relative to the total number of documents in the dataset). The theory behind this is that, while assigning a keyword to a query, a lot of potential keywords can already be eliminated as their relative document occurrence count is not within a certain range of the relative document occurrence count of the query. These keywords therefore are not likely to be the right keyword corresponding to the query and thus can be disregarded.

The Count attack incorporates eliminating candidate keywords using their document occurrence count 'and brute-forces all possible mappings for a small number of queries and returns the mapping which maximizes the number of disambiguated queries'. Cash et al. report much higher recovery rates from their deterministic Count attack as opposed to the probabilistic IKK attack. We propose to incorporate the candidate keyword elimination method of the Count attack while selecting new mappings in the IKK attack to both decrease the number of potential states to visit as well as increase its accuracy. We also argue that the accuracy of the attack will increase as the algorithm is likely to visit better states on average as the worst potential states are eliminated. Our method still differs from the method as used by Cash et al. as they propose a deterministic algorithm, whereas our algorithm still makes use of the probabilistic nature of the IKK attack.

In order to eliminate candidate keywords Cash et al. construct a confidence interval for the document occurrence count of each of the keywords using Hoeffding's inequality [11]. The lowerbound (LB) and upperbound (UB) of the confidence interval per keyword k are calculated using the following formula(s):

$$LB_k,\ UK_k = \frac{c_k^s}{p_{pk}} \mp \sqrt{0.5\, n\, log\, 40} \tag{4}$$

In this formula c_k computes the document occurrence count of keyword k in the background knowledge dataset and p_{pk} denotes the size relativity between the query and background knowledge dataset. $\frac{c_k}{p_{pk}}$ therefore denotes the expected document occurrence count of k in the query dataset. $\epsilon = \sqrt{0.5\, n\, log\, 40}$ is used by Cash et al. to ensure the confidence interval has a confidence level of 95%. n denotes the number of documents in the query dataset. After calculating a confidence interval for each of the keywords the candidate keywords for a query can be calculated as $S_q = \{k' \in K | LB_{k'} \leq c_q \leq UB_{k'}\}$. S_q denotes the candidate keyword set, K the keyword set and c_q denotes the document occurrence count of query q.

The Original IKK attack maps queries to keywords in two places in the algorithm, namely when selecting the *initial state* (Algorithms 1 and 2) and while selecting a *next state* (Algorithms 3, 4 and 5). We therefore incorporated the method of Cash et al. in two places in our Deterministic IKK attack:

While selecting the initial state we first assign a *None* value to queries of which S_q is an empty set, meaning that no keywords are in range. These queries are left unchanged throughout the entire algorithm run and thus are assigned *None* in the final mapping as well. This also allows an adversary to determine which queries were not mapped to a keyword. Then all queries with a non-empty candidate set S_q are ordered in ascending order of the size of S_q and each of the queries, starting at the query with the lowest size of S_q, is assigned a random keyword in S_q that was not yet assigned to another query. As we enforce the 1-to-1 mapping property of the IKK attack this potentially creates the edge case where all keywords in S_q of a query are already assigned to other queries. The algorithm tries, with a depth of one, whether it is possible to re-assign one of the other queries to 'free up' a keyword in S_q. If it succeeds the 'freed' keyword is assigned to the query, otherwise the query is assigned *None* and is thus disregarded during the rest of the algorithm run.

While selecting a new state we choose a random query, keyword mapping, e.g. $q_1 \mapsto k_1$, from the queries in the *current state* that were not assigned *None* and we select a random keyword k_2 from S_{q_1} as opposed to the full keyword set, while ensuring $k_1 \neq k_2$. Then, just like in the Original IKK attack there are two possibilities:

If k_2 was mapped to a query q_2 we try whether keyword k_1 is in range of query q_2 and interchange the mapping if so. If not, we keep (uniformly at random) selecting a new keyword k_2 and checking whether the new k_2 adheres to the right properties. If we cannot find a satisfactory candidate k_2 for a certain number of loops (2 times the size of the keyword set in our simulations) the algorithm returns the current state as the next state, which is rejected as the Euclidean distance is not better than the old current state (as they are the same). If k_2 was not mapped to any query in the current state we change the next state so that $q_1 \mapsto k_2$.

In order to compare our deterministic version of the IKK attack to the Original IKK attack, especially in cases where the adversary does not have full background knowledge, we defined a metric that captures the correlation between the similarity between the co-occurrence matrices and the recovery rate as we argue that it is important to research the effect of our improvements on simulations with different levels of background knowledge to get a broad understanding of the effects of our improvements. We have used four different methods to simulate non-perfect background knowledge (omitting a percentage of the selected keywords, omitting a percentage of the documents in a dataset, adding Gaussian noise and using a different dataset as background knowledge). These methods, the defined metric and the results with the original IKK attack are included in Appendix A.

Table 5. Nr. of states visited by the IKK and Deterministic IKK attack

Parameters	IKK version	Min.	Max.	Avg.
# Total loops	Original	531,733	737,741	733,213
	Deterministic	196,790	737,741	526,038
# Accepted loops	Original	7783	9535	8533
	Deterministic	7287	101,145	14,252
$\frac{\text{\# Accepted loops}}{\text{\# Total loops}}$	Original	0.0105	0.0159	0.0117
	Deterministic	0.0099	0.1371	0.0263

Table 5, the aggregation of 500 simulations of both algorithms, shows that the Deterministic IKK algorithm visits much less total states on average than the Original IKK attack. Additionally, the average number of iterations where the next state is accepted is much higher and the ratio between the number of *accepted* loops and total loops is more than twice as high for the Deterministic IKK attack. It is useful to note that both attacks at most visit 737,741 different states and then return their current state as the final mapping. This is due to the chosen values of the input parameters of the ANNEAL algorithm and explains the values in the **Max.** column of the *# Total loops* row.

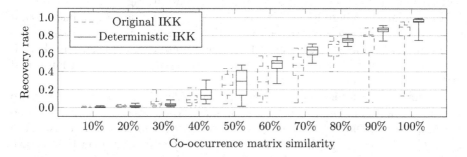

Fig. 6. Original/Deterministic IKK recovery rates and recovery rate, simulating non-perfect background knowledge by regarding a *percentage* of keywords

In Fig. 6 we compare recovery rate of the Original and Deterministic IKK attack when only a fraction of the actual keywords simulates background knowledge. The recovery rates of the Original IKK attack and methods to generate non-perfect background knowledge are the same as expressed in Fig. 8 and each bucket in the figure is the aggregation of 20 simulations. We see the same linear correlation for the Deterministic IKK attack as we saw before for the Original IKK attack, however, recovery rates of the Deterministic IKK attack show much less variance as well as a higher median value.

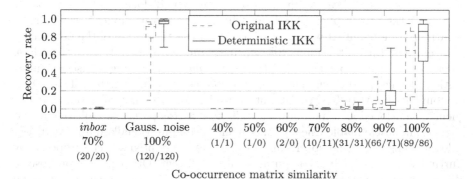

Fig. 7. Original/Deterministic IKK recovery rates and recovery rate, simulating non-perfect background knowledge using other methods

Figure 7 shows the comparison of the Original and Deterministic IKK attack when non-perfect background knowledge is simulated using other methods than using a percentage of all keywords. Figure 7 therefore also contains the same information as Figs. 9 and 10. The (non-percentage) numbers between brackets denote the number of simulations aggregated in that box plot. Due to the way in which we generate non-perfect background knowledge these are not the round number of 20 simulations per box plot as is the case in Fig. 6.

In simulations where we took a different, but similar dataset as background knowledge (*ENRON/inbox*) we see that both attacks have recovery rates close to 0 and in simulations where we added Gaussian noise to the background knowledge we see that the Deterministic IKK attack again shows less variance and higher recovery rates.

In simulations where a percentage of user folders in a dataset was used to simulate background knowledge we see the same exponential correlation between co-occurrence similarity and the recovery rate as we see for simulations using the Original IKK attack. Additionally, we see that the Deterministic IKK attack achieves higher recovery rates on average, but we do not see the drop in variance that we saw in simulations using the other methods to simulate non-perfect background knowledge.

All in all, we conclude that using components of the Count attack by Cash et al. [6], that make the IKK attack more deterministic, is a promising method to both decrease the number of states visited in a single attack run (28% decrease) and increase the recovery rate, as the median recovery rate is increased up to 21% points (Fig. 7, 100% box plot) and the variance is decreased up to 57% points (Fig. 6, 100% box plot).

7   Related Work

The first Searchable Encryption scheme was introduced by Song et al. [15] to allow for (plaintext) search among a set of encrypted documents. Their paper introduces the first In-place SE scheme which uses a stream cipher to scan for the occurrence of a plaintext word as well as introduces the notion of the potentially more efficient Encrypted-Index SE schemes. Song et al. already note that these schemes leak access patterns and that statistical attacks might disclose information of encrypted documents, but do not research this further. The notion of Oblivious RAM (ORAM) [10], introduced before the first SE scheme, is frequently mentioned as a method to not disclose access patterns. Oblivious RAM, however, in a Searchable Encryption scheme is computationally quite expensive. A less expensive version specifically targeted for encrypted search, proposed by Curtmola et al. [8], still is computationally inefficient. Other papers propose to obfuscate access patterns by introducing inconsistencies in the search results by modifying the internal encrypted index of the SE scheme [7] or by using Bloom filters [5,9]. These schemes are reportedly computationally expensive as well.

The first statistical attack, the IKK attack, on Searchable Encryption schemes that leak access patterns was proposed by Islam et al. [12]. This attack uses co-occurrence counts of observed queries to determine what plaintext word(s) the client searched for. Cash et al. [6] recognize that a recovered query inherently discloses part of the plaintext of encrypted documents and propose their Count attack as a response to the IKK attack. The Count attack uses the (relative) document occurrence counts next to the co-occurrence counts of queries to deliver better results faster as opposed to the IKK attack. Cash et al. also define different levels of leakage of SE schemes and coin the term *leakage-abuse attacks* to more broadly describe attacks that are intended to disclose information on the contents of encrypted documents in SE schemes as opposed to attacks that only disclose what the client searched for. Leakage-abuse attacks were further researched by Blackstone et al. [4].

Both the IKK attack and the Count attack are passive attacks, meaning that the adversary acts according to the protocol of the SE scheme, but tries to additionally obtain as much information and potentially runs calculations in parallel. Zhang et al. [16] show that an adversary capable of injecting files into a Searchable Encryption scheme that leaks access patterns 'is devastating for query privacy'.

Blackstone et al.[4], which was published during our research, deserves a special mention. This paper focuses on new attacks, but also includes experiments using the IKK and Count attacks as these experiments are used for the comparison to newer attacks. Our paper, instead, studies the IKK attack in-depth to shed more light on its assumptions and practicality. The reported IKK recovery scores align with the results in this paper.

8   Conclusion

In this paper, we revisited the IKK query recovery attack on Searchable Encryption schemes as proposed by Islam et al. [12].

We show that the assumption that queries in a Searchable Encryption scheme follow a Zipfian (query) distribution, as Islam et al. made while simulating queries, positively influences the recovery rate of the IKK attack. Furthermore, we show a correlation between input parameters of the IKK attack, of which the values were left unexplained by Islam et al. and the recovery rate of the IKK attack, independent of the underlying dataset used in the SE scheme. This potentially allows the adversary to optimize the parameter values using a different dataset before executing the actual attack.

We also propose improvements to the IKK attack by showing that the accuracy of the attack can be improved significantly by combining multiple attack runs, as we show that median recovery rates can be increased up to 10% points, whereas the variance of recovery rates of simulation can be decreased up to 78% points. In addition, we show that the accuracy of the IKK attack can be increased, while the number of states visited can be decreased by incorporating deterministic components, based on notions made by Cash et al. [6] in their Count attack, to the IKK attack. The average number of states visited is decreased by 28%, the median recovery rate is shown to be increased up to 21% points in different simulations, whereas its variance is decreased up to 57% points.

In recent literature, e.g. [7], obfuscation methods have been proposed to combat the effectiveness of the IKK attack. We leave research into the effects of these obfuscation methods on the effectiveness of our Deterministic IKK open for the reader.

Appendices

A   Co-occurrence Matrix Correlation (Partial Background Knowledge)

Both Islam et al. [12] and Cash et al. [6] both briefly elaborate on the recovery rate of the IKK attack in the case where the adversary only has partial background knowledge. Islam et al. add various degrees of Gaussian noise to individual cells in the co-occurrence matrix representing perfect background knowledge to simulate this setting, whereas Cash et al. simulate non-perfect background knowledge co-occurrence matrix by taking a fraction of all documents in the dataset. Both papers show that the accuracy of the attack is greatly dependent on the level of background knowledge the adversary has. We therefore argue that it is important to get a better understanding of the correlation between the level of background knowledge the adversary has and the recovery rate of the IKK attack. We also argue that the level of background knowledge can be expressed as a similarity between the query and background knowledge co-occurrence matrices, i.e. the *co-occurrence matrix similarity*.

In order to express co-occurrence matrix similarity we propose a metric that returns a similarity score between 0 (no similarity) and 1 (equivalent matrices) between two co-occurrence matrices of the same dimensions. For two matrices M_1 and M_2 and arbitrary words a, b (corresponding to a row and column) the following formulas are used:

$$\Delta^2_{a,b} = \begin{cases} (M_1[a,b] - M_2[a,b])^2, & \text{if } a,b \in M_1 \text{ and } a,b \in M_2 \\ 0, & \text{otherwise} \end{cases} \tag{5}$$

$$\Delta^2_{total} = \sum_{\forall a,b \in M_1} \Delta^2_{a,b} \tag{6}$$

$$\epsilon_{a,b} = \begin{cases} 1, & \text{if } a,b \in M_1 \text{ and } a,b \in M_2 \\ 0, & \text{otherwise} \end{cases} \tag{7}$$

$$\epsilon_{total} = \sum_{a,b \in M_1} \epsilon_{a,b} \tag{8}$$

$$Co - ocsim. = \left(1 - \frac{\Delta^2_{total}}{\epsilon_{total}}\right) * \left(\frac{K_{\text{overlap}}}{K_{\text{total}}}\right) \tag{9}$$

Equations 5 and 6 are used to calculate the total squared Euclidean distance of cells that occur both in M_1 and M_2.

Table 6. Example co-occurrence matrices

M_1	a	b	c
a	1	1	1
b	1	1	1
c	1	1	1

M_2	a	b	c
a	1	1	1
b	1	1	1
c	1	1	1

M_3	a	b	c
a	0	0	0
b	0	0	0
c	0	0	0

M_4	a	b	d
a	1	1	1
b	1	1	1
d	1	1	1

Equations 7 and 8 are used to calculate the number of cells that occur in both M_1 and M_2.

In Eq. 9 we calculate the average squared Euclidean distance of cells that occur in both matrices and multiply this by the ratio of *row identifiers that occur in both matrices* ($K_{overlap}$) to the *total number of rows in both matrices* (K_{total}).

In Table 6 matrices M_1 and M_2 are exactly the same. Δ^2_{total} is 0 as the squared Euclidean distance between each of the cells is $(1-1)^2 = 0$. The average is therefore also 0. As all keywords in both matrices also occur in the other matrix, $\frac{K_{overlap}}{K_{total}} = 3/3 = 1$. The similarity between the matrices is calculated as $co - ocsim. = (1-0) * 1 = 1$ meaning that the matrices are exactly the same. The calculation for the similarities between matrices M_1 and M_3, and M_1 and M_4 gives the values 0 and 2/3 respectively. In our simulations we calculate the co-occurrence matrix similarity using the perfect background knowledge co-occurrence matrix M_F (which corresponds with an unquerified query co-occurrence matrix) and a non-perfect background knowledge co-occurrence matrix M_P. Both matrices have the same dimensions. In order to simulate partial background co-occurrence matrix M_P we use the following methods:

Gaussian noise addition - We use the method by Islam et al. to add Gaussian noise in various degrees to the cells in M_F to obtain M_P.

Document percentage - In this setting we use 10% to 100% of the user folders in a dataset to generate M_P. This method differs a bit from the method by Cash et al. as we argue that the adversary is more likely to obtain a percentage of the mail boxes of users (and all documents that are in these folders) than a percentage of all documents, selected uniformly at random, in a dataset. We believe that this choice might influence the results as different users are likely to use specific language in (all of) their emails.

Keyword percentage - In this setting we, uniformly at random, select 10% to 100% of the keywords in M_F to obtain M_P. To keep the dimensions of M_P consistent throughout all our simulations we supplement the selected keywords with words with a lower occurrence count in the dataset used, i.e. that were not in the keyword set.

Different input folder - In this setting we use a different, but similar dataset to generate M_P. In our simulations we use the *inbox* folder (containing 44859 emails) of the ENRON dataset.

The results of the different methods are shown in Figs. 8, 9 and 10. In these figures we group the values into certain buckets to group similarity scores. If a co-occurrence similarity score is between 0 and 0.1 it is put in the 10% similarity bucket, a value between 0.1 and 0.2 is put in the 20% bucket and so on.

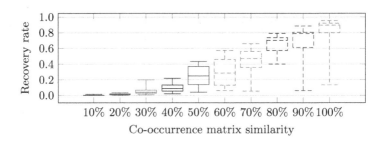

Fig. 8. Correlation between co-occurrence matrix similarity and recovery rate, simulating non-perfect background knowledge by regarding a *percentage* of keywords

Figure 8 shows the correlation between the co-occurrence similarity and the recovery rate in the setting where we use a certain percentage of the keywords in the keyword set to simulate partial background knowledge. Each bucket represents 20 simulations. Due to the nature of our similarity score using 90% of keywords from the keyword set will result in a similarity score of exactly 90%. The figure shows a clear linear correlation between the co-occurrence similarity score and the recovery rate. This makes sense as in this setting entire rows (and thus also columns) that are present in M_F are changed while simulating M_P. The highest possible percentage of recoverable queries therefore is linearly dependent on the percentage of keywords regarded. As the individual cell values are not changed while simulating M_P (as opposed to the other methods) the algorithm is likely to recover (most of the) queries of which the corresponding keywords were selected in M_P as these have the optimal Euclidean distance of 0.

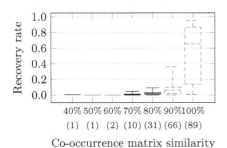

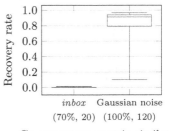

Fig. 9. Correlation between co-occurrence matrix similarity and recovery rate, simulating non-perfect background knowledge by regarding a *percentage* of user folders in the dataset

Fig. 10. Correlation between co-occurrence matrix similarity and recovery rate, simulating non-perfect background knowledge by using the *ENRON/inbox* data or by adding Gaussian noise

Figure 9 shows the correlation between the co-occurrence matrix similarity and the recovery rate in simulations where non-perfect background knowledge is simulated by taking a percentage of user folders in a dataset to generate M_P. We ran 20 simulations for each percentage ranging from 10%, 20% to 100% each. The first thing that we notice is that the buckets do not contain the same number of simulations per bucket, which is shown in the figure as the number between brackets. This is due to the fact that we uniformly at random select a percentage of all user folders in a dataset and these user folders do not contain the same number of documents. Different writing styles can also be of influence to the overall co-occurrence similarity. The results in Fig. 9 show a different correlation than the results in Fig. 8. This makes sense as in these simulations both row/column identifiers as well as individual cell values are changed. The algorithm is less likely to correctly map queries to keywords that do occur in M_P as the changed individual cell values, in Fig. 9, make it less likely to find the optimal mapping. We note that the results in the 40%-60% bucket do not give much information, as each bucket consists of a single simulation. We conclude from the rest of the results that the co-occurrence matrix similarity and the recovery rate show an exponential correlation in Fig. 9.

The results in Fig. 10 show the correlation between the co-occurrence matrix similarity and the recovery rate of simulations where M_P was generated using a similar, but different dataset ($ENRON/inbox$) and when we add Gaussian noise to various degrees. First of all, if we generate M_P using the $ENRON/inbox$ data folder we obtain a similarity score of approximately 70% to the $ENRON/\_sent\_mail$ dataset. The recovery rate of almost 0 is consistent with our results in Fig. 9.

With the addition of various degrees of Gaussian noise (with C values 0.0, 0.2, ..., 1.0) the similarity of the co-occurrences matrices is always between 0.999 and 1.0. This can be explained as this method does not change the row/column identifiers, but only changes the individual cell values (co-occurrence counts). As only a little noise is added most of these cell values stay relatively the same. The recovery rate distribution among 120 simulations is relatively high as opposed to other methods to generate non-perfect background knowledge.

We conclude that it is not possible to use our matrix similarity metric to find a single correlation between the similarity of co-occurrence matrices and the recovery rate. The different methods change non-perfect background knowledge M_P in different manners and this influences the results of the IKK attack a lot. The IKK attack correctly recovers queries if the co-occurrence counts in M_P exactly match (or are close to) those in M_F, which is shown in Figs. 8 and 10 ($Gaussian\ noise\ addition$). If the co-occurrence counts in M_P are further away from those in M_F, which is the case in Figs. 9 and 10 ($Inbox\ folder$) the accuracy of the IKK attack decreases drastically.

We argue that the scenario where the background knowledge, represented as M_P, is generated by taking a percentage of the user folders in a dataset is the most realistic one in a real-world scenario. It is not unlikely that an adversary, somehow, gets access to a certain set of the plaintext contents of the email boxes of specific users. The IKK attack proves to be a powerful attack which can break the privacy of queries as well as data confidentially of documents stored encrypted of the server, yet it is only exploitable by a powerful adversary, which has access to a dataset which results in background knowledge that is at least 90% similar the actual dataset encrypted on the server, as can be seen in Fig. 9.

B IKK Algorithms

In this section, we cite (part of) the Simulated Annealing (SA) algorithms as proposed by Islam et al.[12] as well as formalize our proposed algorithms for the Deterministic version of the IKK attacks. In short:

- Algorithm Optimizer (Algorithms 1 and 2) is used to select the initial state of the ANNEAL algorithm.
- Algorithm ANNEAL (Algorithms 3 and 4) is the heart of the IKK attack and is the actual algorithm that maps queries to keywords (apart from setting the initial state). The algorithms displayed are a simplified version of the ANNEAL algorithm as presented by Islam et al. and are mainly included to illustrate changes we made to more deterministically select the nextState.

Algorithm 1: Optimizer

input
    V : variable list
    // List of all (non-mapped) queries
    D : domain list
    // List of all (non-mapped) keywords
    K : known assignments
    // Known query-keyword mappings
    Mc   // Query co-occurrence matrix
    Mp   // Background knowledge co-oc matrix
    $Q = \{q: S_q\}$ // Queries and their candidate keywords
1 initState ← {} // Initial state
2 valList ← copy D
  // Copies values in D to variable valList
3 foreach $var \in V$ do
4   val ← random.choice(valList)
       // Randomly selects a keyword from valList
5   add {var ↦ val} to initState
       // Adds mapping to initState
6   remove val from valList
       // As query to keyword mappings are 1-to-1
  end
7 nonAssignableQueries ← {}
  // Var. containing None-assigned queries
8 sortedQ ← sort(Q, key=len(S_q), ascending=True)
  // Sorts Q on number of candidate keywords

Algorithm 2: Optimizer (cont.)

```
 9  foreach var, S_var ∈ sortedQ do
10      candKeywords ← S_var
        // Gets candidate keywords for query v
11      if len(candKeywords) == 0 then
12          add v to nonAssignableQueries
            // Query v added to nonAssignable Queries
        else
13          assignedKWs = []
            // Every candidate keyword per query is
14          nonAssignedKWs = []
            // already assigned to another query or not
15          foreach cand ∈ candKeywords do
16              if cand ∈ valList then
17                  add cand to nonAssignedKWs
                    // cand not assigned to another query
                else
18                  add cand to assignedKWs
                    // cand assigned to another query
                end
            end
19          if len(nonAssignedKWs) ≠ 0 then
20              val ← random.choice(nonAssignedKWs)
                // Selects keyword from nonAssignedKWs
21              add {var ↦ val} to initState
                // Adds mapping to initState
22              remove val from valList
                // Query/keyword mappings are 1-to-1
            else
23              foreach k ∈ assignedKWs do
24                  q ← initState.getByValue(k)
                    // Get query q, mapped to keyword k
25                  if k ∈ S_q then
26                      remove { q ↦ k } from initState
                        // Removes old mapping from initState
27                      add { q ↦ val } to initState
                        // Adds new mapping to initState
28                      add { var ↦ k } to initState
                        // Adds new mapping to initState
                        break
                    end
                end
29              if initState.get(var) == None then
                    add var to nonAssignableQueries
                    // If no suitable mapping could be found
                end
            end
        end
    end
end
30  add K to initState
    // Adds known mappings to initState
31  return ANNEAL(initState, D, Mp, Mc)
    // Returns result of function ANNEAL()
32  return ANNEAL(initState, D, Mp, Mc, nonAssignableQueries, Q)
```

Algorithm 3: ANNEAL

input	// Simulated Annealing parameters

  initState
  D
  Mc, Mp
  initTemperature
  // *initial temperature* variable
  coolingRate // *cool down rate* variable
  rejectThreshold
  // *rejection rate* variable
  nonAssignableQueries
  // List of None assigned queries
  $Q = \{q: S_q\}$ // Queries and their candidate keywords
1 currentState ← initState
  // Search continues until temp. reaches 0
2 succReject ← 0 // or the system is frozen (no new state
3 currT ← initTemperature
  // is accepted for large number of times)

Algorithm 4: ANNEAL (cont.)

1 **while** *(currT ≠ 0 and succReject < rejectThreshold)* **do**
2   currentCost, nextCost ← 0, 0
3   nextState ← findNextState(currentState, D)
    // Selects nextState using the method by Islam et al.
4   nextState ← findNextStateDet(currentState, D, Q)
    // Selects **nextState** deterministically
5   E ← costCalculation(nextState, currentState)
    // Calculates cost difference of two states,
6   probability = exp(-E/currT)
    // using the method by Islam et al.
7   acceptNewState = $(E < 0)$ or (random.choice ¡ probability)
    //nextState accepted if $E < 0$ or with prob. exp(-E/currT)
8   **if** *acceptNewState* **then**
9   succReject, currentState ← 0, nextState
   else
10   succReject++
   end
11   currT = coolingRate*currT
    // temperature is decremented each loop
   end
12 **foreach** *query ∈ nonAssignableQueries* **do**
13   add {query ↦ None} to currentState
    // Maps non-assignable queries to None
   end
14 **return** currentState

Algorithm 5: findNextStateDet

---

input
    currentState   // 1-to-1 mapping of all queries to keywords
    $Q = \{q: S_q\}$ // Queries and their candidate keywords
    D

1 nextState ← copy currentState
2 $\{x \mapsto y\}$ ← random.choice(nextState)
3 S_x ← Q.get(x) // Gets candidate keywords for query x
4 cands ← S_x.remove(y)
    // Keyword y cannot be selected again
5 y' ← None   // Initializes y'
6 **if** $len(cands) \neq 0$ **then**
    | y' = random.choice(cands)
    | // Selects random keyword from candidates
  else
    | return currentState
    | // No new mapping could be found
  end
7 count ← 0   // Initializes count variable
8 **while** $\{z \mapsto y'\} \in currentState$ and $y \notin S_z$ **do**
9 | y' = random.choice(cands)
    | // Selects a new candidate keyword y'
    | **if** $len(count) \leq 2 * len(D)$ **then**
    | | return currentState
    | | // No new mapping could be found
    | **end**
10 | count += 1
  end
11 remove $\{x \mapsto y\}$ from nextState
12 add $\{x \mapsto y'\}$ to nextState
13 **if** $\{z \mapsto y'\} \in currentState$ **then**
14 | remove $\{z \mapsto y'\}$ from nextState
    | // If y' is already mapped to query z
15 | add $\{z \mapsto y\}$ to nextState
    | // Map query z to y instead of y'
  end
16 **return** nextState

– Algorithm findNextStateDet (Algorithm 5) is our proposed sub algorithm of the ANNEAL algorithm which selects a new state of the algorithm more deterministically.

In order to easily annotate differences between the Original IKK attack (as proposed by Islam et al.) and our proposed Deterministic IKK attack we use the following colors:

– **Black** annotates lines that are present in both the Original and Deterministic IKK attack.

– **Red** annotates lines that are present in the Original IKK attack, but not in the Deterministic IKK attack. Red lines are replaced by blue lines.
– **Blue** annotates lines that are not present in the Original IKK attack, but are in the Deterministic IKK attack. Blue lines replace red lines.

The Original IKK attack and the Deterministic IKK attack are elaborated upon in Sects. 2.6 and 6 respectively.

We note that the pseudo code in the algorithms as shown below does not fully match with our implementation of the Original/Deterministic IKK attack [3]. First of all, we used Python3 specific methods to easily implement both attacks and, in order to reduce the number of lines we re-used as much of the code of the Original IKK attack as possible to implement our Deterministic IKK attack.

References

1. Apache Lucene java-user email dataset, September 2001-July 2011. http://mail-archives.apache.org/mod_mbox/lucene-java-user/. Accessed 19 May 2020
2. ENRON email dataset, version 7th May 2015. https://www.cs.cmu.edu/~./enron/. Accessed 19 May 2020
3. IKK query recovery attack implementation (Python). https://github.com/rubengrootroessink/IKK-query-recovery-attack. Accessed 27 June 2020
4. Blackstone, L., Kamara, S., Moataz, T.: Revisiting leakage abuse attacks. IACR Cryptol. ePrint Arch. **2019**, 1175 (2019)
5. Boneh, D., Kushilevitz, E., Ostrovsky, R., Skeith, W.E.: Public key encryption that allows PIR queries. In: Menezes, A. (ed.) CRYPTO 2007. LNCS, vol. 4622, pp. 50–67. Springer, Heidelberg (2007). https://doi.org/10.1007/978-3-540-74143-5_4
6. Cash, D., Grubbs, P., Perry, J., Ristenpart, T.: Leakage-abuse attacks against searchable encryption. In: Proceedings of the 22nd ACM SIGSAC Conference on Computer and Communications Security, pp. 668–679. ACM (2015)
7. Chen, G., Lai, T.H., Reiter, M.K., Zhang, Y.: Differentially private access patterns for searchable symmetric encryption. In: IEEE INFOCOM 2018-IEEE Conference on Computer Communications, pp. 810–818. IEEE (2018)
8. Curtmola, R., Garay, J., Kamara, S., Ostrovsky, R.: Searchable symmetric encryption: improved definitions and efficient constructions. J. Comput. Secur. **19**(5), 895–934 (2011)
9. Goh, E.J.: Secure indexes. IACR Cryptology ePrint Archive, 216 (2003)
10. Goldreich, O., Ostrovsky, R.: Software protection and simulation on oblivious rams. J. ACM (JACM) **43**(3), 431–473 (1996)
11. Hoeffding, W.: Probability inequalities for sums of bounded random variables. In: The Collected Works of Wassily Hoeffding, pp. 409–426. Springer (1994)
12. Islam, M.S., Kuzu, M., Kantarcioglu, M.: Access pattern disclosure on searchable encryption: ramification, attack and mitigation. In: NDSS. vol. 20, p. 12. Citeseer (2012)
13. Kirkpatrick, S., Gelatt, C.D., Vecchi, M.P.: Optimization by simulated annealing. Science **220**(4598), 671–680 (1983)
14. Porter, M.F.: Snowball: A language for stemming algorithms (2001)

15. Song, D.X., Wagner, D., Perrig, A.: Practical techniques for searches on encrypted data. In: Proceeding 2000 IEEE Symposium on Security and Privacy. S&P 2000, pp. 44–55. IEEE (2000)
16. Zhang, Y., Katz, J., Papamanthou, C.: All your queries are belong to us: the power of file-injection attacks on searchable encryption. In: 25th USENIX Security Symposium (USENIX Security 16), pp. 707–720 (2016)
17. Zipf, G.K.: Selected studies of the principle of relative frequency in language (1932)

Efficient Methods to Search for Best Differential Characteristics on SKINNY

Stéphanie Delaune[1]([✉]), Patrick Derbez[1], Paul Huynh[2], Marine Minier[2], Victor Mollimard[1], and Charles Prud'homme[3]

[1] Univ. Rennes, CNRS, IRISA, Rennes, France
{stephanie.delaune,patrick.derbez,victor.mollimard}@irisa.fr
[2] Université de Lorraine, CNRS, Inria, LORIA, 54000 Nancy, France
{paul.hyunh,marine.minier}@loria.fr
[3] IMT-Atlantique, TASC, LS2N, Nantes, France
charles.prudhomme@imt-atlantique.fr

Abstract. Evaluating resistance of ciphers against differential cryptanalysis is essential to define the number of rounds of new designs and to mount attacks derived from differential cryptanalysis.

In this paper, we propose automatic tools to find the best differential characteristics on the SKINNY block cipher. As usually done in the literature, we split this search in two stages denoted by Step 1 and Step 2. In Step 1, we aim at finding all truncated differential characteristics with a low enough number of active Sboxes. Then, in Step 2, we try to instantiate each difference value while maximizing the overall differential characteristic probability. We solve Step 1 using an ad-hoc method inspired from the work of Fouque *et al.* whereas Step 2 is modelized for the Choco-solver library as it seems to outperform all previous methods on this stage.

Notably, for SKINNY-128 in the **SK** model and for 13 rounds, we retrieve the results of Abdelkhalek *et al.* within a few seconds (to compare with 16 days) and we provide, for the first time, the best differential related-tweakey characteristics up to 14 rounds for the **TK1** model. Regarding the **TK2** and the **TK3** models, we were not able to test all the solutions Step 1, and thus the differential characteristics we found up to 16 and 17 rounds are not necessarily optimal.

Keywords: Differential cryptanalysis · Automatic tools · SKINNY

1 Introduction

Differential cryptanalysis [5] evaluates the propagation of an input difference $\delta X = X \oplus X'$ between two plaintexts X and X' through the ciphering process. Indeed, differential attacks exploit the fact that the probability of observing a

The research leading to these results has received funding from the French National Research Agency (ANR) under the project Decrypt ANR-18-CE39-0007.

K. Sako and N. O. Tippenhauer (Eds.): ACNS 2021, LNCS 12727, pp. 184–207, 2021.
https://doi.org/10.1007/978-3-030-78375-4_8

specific output difference given a specific input difference is not uniformly distributed. Today, differential cryptanalysis is public knowledge, and block ciphers such as AES have proven bounds against differential attacks. A classical extension of differential cryptanalysis is the so called related-key differential cryptanalysis [4] that allows an attacker to inject differences not only between the plaintexts X and X' but also between the keys K and K' (even if the secret key K stays unknown from the attacker). This attack has been recently extended to tweakable block ciphers [3]. Those particular ciphers allow in addition to the key, a public value called a tweak. Thus, related-tweakey differential attacks allow related-key differences but also related-tweak differences (i.e. differences in a pair of tweaks (T, T')). In differential attacks, two notions are considered: first, differentials where only the input and the output differences are known; and differential characteristics where each difference after each round is completely specified. A classical approach to evaluate the resistance against differential attacks is to compute the probability of the best differential characteristic of the cipher.

Finding optimal (related-tweakey) differential characteristics is a highly combinatorial problem that hardly scales. To limit this explosion, a common solution consists in using a truncated representation [16] for which cells are abstracted by single bits that indicate whether sequences contain differences or not. Typically, each cell (i.e. byte or nibble) is abstracted by a single bit (or, equivalently, a Boolean value). In this case, the goal is no longer to find the exact input and output differences, but to find the positions of these differences, i.e., the presence or absence of a difference for every cell. When a difference is present at the input of an S-box, we talk about an active S-box or an active byte/nibble. However, some truncated representations may not be valid (i.e., there do not exist actual byte values corresponding to these difference positions) because some constraints at the byte level are relaxed when reasoning on difference positions.

Hence, the optimal (related-tweakey) differential characteristic problem is usually solved in two steps [1,6]. In the first one, every differential byte is abstracted by a Boolean variable, denoted by Δ, that indicates whether there is a difference or not at this position, and we search for all truncated representations of low weight as the less differences passing through S-boxes there are, the more the probability is increased. Then, for each of these low weight truncated representations, the second step aims at deciding whether it is valid (i.e., whether it is possible to find actual cell values, denoted δ, for every Boolean variable) and, if it is valid, at finding the actual cell values that maximize the probability of obtaining the output difference given the input difference.

Related Work. Many techniques have been proposed to search for the Step 1 solutions using automatic tools such as Boolean satisfiability (SAT) [21,26,27] or Mixed Integer Linear Programming (MILP) [3,24,30] and Satisfiability Modulo Theories (SMT) [17]. Dedicated solutions have also been proposed [20].

Regarding the search of the best instantiation of a truncated characteristic, most of the approaches were ad-hoc and dedicated to a precise cipher [6,9–11,18,28]. Concerning the use of SAT solvers, [28] implements a SAT model for differential cryptanalysis based on Cryptominisat5 [26] for Midori64 and LED64. This model implies a sufficiently small number of clauses to model the non-zero values of the DDT and to be applicable. However, no result concerning 8-bit S-boxes are given. As SAT uses Boolean formulas, it seems that the same problem than for MILP appears for modeling S-box: a huge number of Boolean formulas will be necessary to correctly model this step even if dedicated tools as Logic Friday or the Expresso algorithm [1] are used. In [1], 16 days are needed to find the best related tweakey differential characteristics on SKINNY-128 for the **SK** model. Recently, in [11,12], the authors introduce Constraint Programming (CP) models for Step 2 and the performance results are really promising regarding AES-192 and AES-256.

Our Contribution. In this paper, we refine the security bounds on the SKINNY-n tweakable block cipher regarding differential cryptanalysis for the four following attack models according to the size of the tweakey: the **SK** model focuses on single-key attack, the **TK1** model considers related-tweakey attack when the tweakey has only one component, the **TK2** model in the related-tweakey settings considers 2 components and the **TK3** model, 3 components.

To do so, we implement Step 1 using an ad-hoc method inspired from [10]. We also propose a CP model for Step 2 taking as input the solutions outputted by Step 1. Thus, we provide, for the first time, the best differential related-tweakey characteristics up to 14 rounds for the **TK1** model. We also consider the **TK2** and **TK3** models and we were able to found some differential characteristics up to 16 rounds for the **TK2** model and up to 17 rounds for the **TK3** model of SKINNY-128. However, we were not able to test all the solutions Step 1, and thus these differential characteristics are not necessarily optimal. This is an important improvement compared to previous results. For instance, in [19] Liu *et al.* could only find the best differential characteristics up to 7 and 9 rounds for **TK1** and **TK2**. Finally we also show there is no differential characteristic with probability higher than 2^{-128} against 15 rounds in the **TK1** model, 19 rounds for **TK2** and 23 rounds for **TK3**. All those results clearly show that SKINNY is much more resistant to differential cryptanalysis than one would expect while counting the number of active S-boxes.

As a feedback, we also provide the time results we obtain when implementing the Step 1 using another tool, a MILP model for the 4 attack settings. As a result we show that MILP is not always the best choice. First, for Step 1, the ad-hoc method is able to surpass the MILP model. Second, the CP model proposed for Step 2 is incomparably much faster than the MILP model proposed in [1] that requires 16 days according their paper.

All the codes to reproduce these results can be found at [7].

Organization of the Paper. Section 2 gives a short description of SKINNY-n; Sect. 3 presents our Ad-Hoc tool and gives performance results comparing our Ad-Hoc model with a MILP one; Sect. 4 presents our dedicated modeling for Step 2 based on CP and analyzes the obtained results. Finally, Sect. 5 concludes this paper.

2   Cipher Under Study: SKINNY-n

In this section, we briefly review the tweakable block cipher SKINNY-n where n denotes the block size and can be equal to 64 or 128 bits. All the details that have been overlooked can be found in [3].

As its name indicates, it enciphers blocks of length 64 or 128 bits seen as a 4×4 matrix of cells (nibbles for $n = 64$ or bytes for $n = 128$). We denote $x_{i,j,k}$ the cell at row i and column j of the internal state at the beginning of round k (i.e. $0 \le i, j \le 3$ and $0 \le k \le r + 1$ where r is the number of rounds depending on the tweak length and on the key length). SKINNY-n follows the TWEAKEY framework from [15]. SKINNY-n has three main tweakey size versions: the tweakey size can be equal to $t = 64$ or 128 bits, $t = 128$ or 256 bits and $t = 192$ or 384 bits and we denote $z = t/n$ the tweakey size to block size ratio. Then, the number of rounds is directly derived from the z value: between 32 rounds for the 64/64 version up to 56 for the 128/384 version.

The tweakey state is also viewed as a collection of z 4×4 square arrays of cells (nibbles for $n = 64$ or bytes for $n = 128$). We denote these arrays $TK1$ when $z = 1$, $TK1$ and $TK2$ when $z = 2$, and finally $TK1$, $TK2$ and $TK3$ when $z = 3$. We also denote by $TKk_{i,j}$ the nibble or the byte at position $[i, j]$ in TKk. Moreover, we define the associated adversarial model **SK** (resp. **TK1**, **TK2** or **TK3**) where the attacker cannot (resp. can) introduce differences in the tweakey state.

One encryption round of SKINNY is composed of five operations applied in the following order: SubCells (SC), AddConstants (AC), AddRoundTweakey (ART), ShiftRows (SR) and MixColumns (MC) (see Fig. 1).

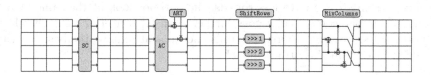

Fig. 1. The SKINNY round function with its five transformations [14].

SubCells. A 4-bit ($n = 64$) or an 8-bit ($n = 128$) S-box is applied to each cell of the state. See [3] for the details of the S-boxes.

AddConstants. A 6-bit affine LFSR is used to generate round constants c_0 and c_1 that are XORed to the state at position $[0, 0]$ and $[1, 0]$ whereas the constant $c_2 = \texttt{0x02}$ is XORed to the position $[2, 0]$.

AddRoundTweakey. The first and second rows of all tweakey arrays are extracted and bitwise exclusive-ored to the cipher internal state, respecting the array positioning. More formally, we have:
- $x_{i,j} = x_{i,j} \oplus TK1_{i,j}$ when $z = 1$,
- $x_{i,j} = x_{i,j} \oplus TK1_{i,j} \oplus TK2_{i,j}$ when $z = 2$,

– $x_{i,j} = x_{i,j} \oplus TK1_{i,j} \oplus TK2_{i,j} \oplus TK3_{i,j}$ when $z = 3$.

Then, the tweakey arrays are updated. First, a permutation P_T is applied on the cells positions of all tweakey arrays: if $\ell = 4 * i + j$ where i is the row index and j is the column index, then the cell ℓ is moved to position $P_T(\ell)$ where $P_T = [9, 15, 8, 13, 10, 14, 12, 11, 0, 1, 2, 3, 4, 5, 6, 7]$. Second, every cell of the first and second rows of $TK2$ and $TK3$ are individually updated with an LFSR on 4 bits (when $n = 64$) or on 8 bits (when $n = 128$) with a period equal to 15.

ShiftRows. The rows of the cipher state cell array are rotated to the right. More precisely, the second (resp. third and fourth) cell row is rotated by 1 position (resp. 2 and 3 positions).

MixColumns. Each column of the cipher internal state array is multiplied by the 4×4 binary matrix M:

$$\begin{pmatrix} 1\ 0\ 1\ 1 \\ 1\ 0\ 0\ 0 \\ 0\ 1\ 1\ 0 \\ 1\ 0\ 1\ 0 \end{pmatrix}$$

Since 2016 and the birth of SKINNY-128, the cryptographic world never stopped trying to attack it. Among all the cryptanalysis results, we could cite the following ones in the related-tweakey settings and classified according the type of attacks. First, in [19, 25, 31], boomerang and rectangle related-tweakey attacks are considered. The best result is on 28 rounds with a complexity of 2^{315} in time based on a boomerang distinguisher of 23 rounds in the **TK3** scenario. Concerning impossible related-tweakey attack [19, 29], the best attack has 23 rounds using a distinguisher with 15 rounds in the **TK2** scenario. Even if the distinguishers presented here have less rounds, they do not look at the same attack scenario. This paper essentially goes further than [1] concerning the search of the best related-tweakey differential trails and aims at refining the best security bounds of SKINNY in this attack model.

3   Models and Results for Step 1

As explained in the introduction, in a first step called Step 1, we abstract each possible difference at cell (nibble or byte) level by a binary variable which symbolizes the presence/absence of a difference value at a given position of the cipher. The main concern regarding this step is the combinatorial explosion induced by the abstract XOR operation for which the sum of two non-zero values can lead to the presence or the absence of a difference.

3.1   Possible Transitions

Since the S-box is bijective and the ShiftRows operation only permutes cells, both those operations do not affect truncated differences. But for the AddRoundTweakey and MixColumns transformations we need to take care of the

XOR operation. More precisely, given two truncated differences a and b we know that the possible values of $(a, b, a \oplus b)$ are:

$$(0, 0, 0), (0, 1, 1), (1, 0, 1), (1, 1, 0), (1, 1, 1)$$

However we have to pay attention to uninstantiable solutions. For instance, given three truncated differences a, b and c, $(1, 1, 1, 0, 0, 1)$ is a possible value for $(a, b, c, a \oplus b, a \oplus c, b \oplus c)$ but it is impossible to instantiate it because if $a = b$ and $a = c$ then $b = c$.

Hence we rewrite the equation $y = \texttt{MixColumns} \circ \texttt{AddRoundTweakey}(x, k)$ to avoid such patterns:

- $y[1] = x[0] \oplus k[0]$,
- $y[3] = y[1] \oplus x[2]$,
- $y[0] = y[3] \oplus x[3]$,
- $y[2] = x[1] \oplus k[1] \oplus x[3]$

We experimentally verified that each truncated solution of this system can be instantiated.

Keyschedule. When looking at the key schedule of SKINNY at the cell level and for truncated differential characteristics it is mostly a simple cell permutation. In the model **SK**, there are no differences in the round keys. In the **TKx** models, differences in the round keys are possible. If the number of rounds targeted is at most 30, the rule for active cells on the round keys is quite simple: either the cell is inactive for all round keys, either it is active for all round keys but one (**TK2**) or two (**TK3**).

3.2   Ad-hoc Models for Step 1

To the best of our knowledge, the most efficient algorithm to search for truncated differential characteristics on SPN ciphers is the one described in [10] by Fouque *et al.* which was applied on the 3 versions of AES. It is mostly dynamic programming as Round i is independent of the paths of rounds $0, 1, \ldots, i-1$ and at each step we only have to save, for each truncated state, the minimal number of active S-boxes to reach it. Hence, the complexity of this algorithm is exponential in the state size but linear in the number of rounds. The algorithm is specified in Algorithm 1. At the end of the algorithm we obtain an array C such that $C[r][s]$ contains the minimal number of active S-boxes required to reach state s after r rounds. Retrieving the truncated representations is then done quite easily using C, starting from the last state to the first. Let say we want to exhaust all truncated differential characteristics on R rounds with at most b active S-boxes ending with state s. From $C[R-1][s]$, we know whether such characteristic exists or not. If $C[R-1][s] \leq b$ we exhaust all states s' such that the transition $s' \to s$ through one round is possible and, for each of them, we now need to exhaust all truncated differential characteristics on $R-1$ rounds with at most $b - |s|$ active S-boxes ending with state s'.

Algorithm 1: Search for the best truncated representation (**SK**).

---

foreach *state s* **do**
  | $M[s] \longleftarrow$ list of states s' reachable from s through one round
end
foreach *state s* **do**
  | $C[0][s] \longleftarrow$ number of active cells of s
end
for $1 \le r < R$ **do**
  | **foreach** *state s* **do** $C[r][s] \longleftarrow \infty$
  | **foreach** *state s* **do**
  | | **foreach** *state s' in $M[s]$* **do**
  | | | $c \longleftarrow C[r-1][s] +$ number of active cells of s'
  | | | **if** $c < C[r][s']$ **then** $C[r][s'] \longleftarrow c$
  | | **end**
  | **end**
end
return C

The complexity of the algorithm in the single key model is very low, and we experimentally counted around $(R-1) \times 2^{20}$ simple operations for R rounds. A naive solution to search for truncated representations in the **TK1**, **TK2** and **TK3** models would be to apply the previous algorithm for each possible configuration of the key. While for **TK1** this would only increase the overall complexity by a factor 2^{16}, the search would not be practical for both the **TK2** and **TK3** models. Indeed, because of the possible cancellations occurring in the round keys, the number of configurations is very high:

$$\left(\sum_{k=0}^{8} \binom{8}{k} \left(\sum_{i=0}^{tk-1} \binom{\lfloor (R-1)/2 \rfloor}{i} \right)^k \right) \left(\sum_{k=0}^{8} \binom{8}{k} \left(\sum_{i=0}^{tk-1} \binom{\lceil (R-1)/2 \rceil}{i} \right)^k \right).$$

For instance, for $R = 30$, there are more than 2^{64} configurations in the **TK2** model.

In the following we present the first practical algorithm which tackles down the problem for the **TK** models without relying on a black box solver as MILP, SAT or CP solvers. Actually this is the only algorithm fast enough to generate all the Step 1 solutions required to perform the Step 2. Indeed, the best differential characteristic is rarely based on the truncated differential characteristics minimizing the number of active S-boxes and thus we need to generate a large number of truncated characteristics to find the one instantiating with the best probability. As we will explain in Sect. 3.4, all other approaches we tried to generate them failed.

The idea of our ad-hoc method is quite similar to the one used in the single key model. Actually, to compute the minimal number of active S-boxes at round $r + 1$ we only need to know the minimal number of active S-boxes for each possible state at round r together with the number of cancellations for each key cell occurred so far. Indeed, we do not need to know at which rounds the cancellations occurred but only how many times they did. A simplified version of this algorithm is described in Algorithm 2. The most important part is related to the variable *cancelled* which count how many times each key cell is cancelled through the encryption. It is a vector of 16 cells, each cell taking values among $\{0, 1, \ldots, x-1, r\}$ for the **TKx** model. The main advantage of our representation is that at each step of the algorithm, $C[r][s]$ contains at most $(x+1)^{16}$ elements for the **TKx** model which is much lower than the number of possible sequences of round keys.

Algorithm 2: Search for the best truncated representation (**TK**).

---

foreach *state s, round key k* **do**
  $\quad M[k][s] \longleftarrow$ list of states s' reachable from s and k through one round
end
foreach *state s* **do**
  $\quad C[0][s] \longleftarrow \{(\text{number of active cells of } s, 0)\}$
end
for $1 \leq r < R$ **do**
  $\quad$ **foreach** *state s* **do** $C[r][s] \longleftarrow \emptyset$
  $\quad$ **foreach** *state s* **do**
  $\quad\quad$ **foreach** $(cost, cancelled) \in C[r-1][s]$ **do**
  $\quad\quad\quad$ **foreach** *round key k compatible with cancelled* **do**
  $\quad\quad\quad\quad$ **foreach** *state s' in $M[k][s]$* **do**
  $\quad\quad\quad\quad\quad$ $c \longleftarrow$ cost + number of active cells of s'
  $\quad\quad\quad\quad\quad$ $C[r][s'] \longleftarrow C[r][s'] \cup \{(c, \text{update}(cancelled, k))\}$
  $\quad\quad\quad\quad$ **end**
  $\quad\quad\quad$ **end**
  $\quad\quad$ **end**
  $\quad$ **end**
  $\quad$ **foreach** *state s* **do** keepOptimals($C[r][s]$)
end
return C

Finally we introduce a new improvement which greatly speeds up the search procedure. It is based on the so-called *early abort technique* principle and the idea is to handle the key cell by cell. Indeed, we expect that the best truncated differential characteristics do not involve many active cells in the round key and so we want to quickly cut those branches during the search. To do so we first pick a key cell and guess whether it is active or not. At this step we have not decided yet if any cancellations occur nor their positions but only if it is always 0 or at least once 1. Then we apply the algorithm partially and guess another key cell if and only if it seems possible to find a truncated differential characteristic with a small enough number of active S-boxes. More precisely, along the search we have the relation $y = x \oplus k$ where k is the round key. We introduce a new 16-bit variable g such that $g_i = 0$ if we made a choice for bit i of k and 1 otherwise. To compute the possible truncated transitions from x to y through k for all the possible key (according to g) we can restrict ourself at looking at the possible truncated transitions from $(x|g)$ to y through $(k|g)$ where $|$ is the bitwise OR. Indeed, we use the fact that in truncated setting $1 \oplus 1$ is 0 or 1 and thus our technique allows to handle all the possible keys by looking only at few transitions.

3.3   Results for Step 1

For Step 1, we run our ad-hoc tool on the four attack scenarios (**SK**, **TK1**, **TK2**, and **TK3**) when varying the number of rounds between 3 and 20. We conducted all our experiments on our server composed of 2× AMD EPYC 7742 64-Core and 1TB of RAM. In particular, we were able to complete the security analysis made in [2,3] and claim that the minimal number of active S-boxes in **TK1** for 28, 29 and 30 rounds are 105, 109 and 113 respectively (as shown in Table 1).

Table 1. Lower bounds on the number of active S-boxes in SKINNY.

# Rounds	28	29	30
TK1	105	109	113

However, the optimal solution of Step 2, in terms of differential characteristic probability, could be obtained for a number of active S-boxes which is not the optimal one. Hereafter, we denote Obj_{Step1} the number of active S-boxes we consider when solving the problems. For example, assume that, when processing Step 2, one obtains a differential characteristic with the best probability equal to $2^{-3 \times 6} = 2^{-18}$ with $Obj_{Step1} = 6$ and whereas the optimal differential probability of the S-box is 2^{-2}. It means that one has to test all solutions outputted by Step 1 until $Obj_{Step1} < 18/2 = 9$ to be sure that none has a better differential characteristic probability. This is exactly what happened for the case of SKINNY-128 in the **TK** models. We only want to stress here that computing the optimal bounds is often not enough and we need to go further. However, increasing the value of Obj_{Step1} induces an increase of the possible number of Step 1 solutions as illustrated in the third column of Table 4. As one can see, this number of solutions tends to grow exponentially when we increase v. For example, for SKINNY-128 with 14 rounds in the **TK1** model, for the optimal value $v^* = 45$, Step 1 outputs only 3 solutions; whereas we have 897 solutions for $v = v^* + 5 = 50$; 137 019 solutions for $v = v^* + 10 = 55$ and finally 7 241 601 solutions for $v = 59$. So, the time required to output all those Step 1 solutions and the time required for the Step 2 computations on 1 solution outputted by the Step 1 become the bottleneck of the overall process.

3.4   Other Approaches

We tried different approaches to solve the Step 1 problem, including MILP, SAT and CP models.

Our SAT model is encoded through the high level modeling language MiniZinc while our CP model is based on the Choco-solver. Unfortunately, the results of both the SAT and the CP models are really bad: for example, for all instances greater than 16 rounds we were unable to obtain the solutions in reasonable time. This is mainly due to the need to enumerate solutions for SAT, which implies to prohibit all solutions previously found. For CP, on the other hand, this has to do with the nature of the Boolean variables themselves where the Choco-solver can not efficiently propagate lower bounds and upper bounds on Boolean variables.

Our MILP model was much better than our SAT and CP ones. We started from the original model presented in [3] but made several optimizations. First, we added constraints in the **SK** model to obtain all solutions up to column shifts in order to remove symmetries. Moreover, as the original model only describes the way to find the minimal number of active S-boxes, we added a constraint in each model to set a lower bound on the number of active S-boxes and thus, be able to enumerate all the Step 1 solutions given a particular lower bound for the number of active S-boxes. Then, in the original MILP model all xor operations were modeled using dummy variables which is known to be inefficient. Thus we replaced the corresponding inequalities, using that $x \oplus y \oplus z = 0$ can be described with the three inequalities:

$$\{x + y \geq z\}, \ \{x + z \geq y\}, \ \{y + z \geq x\}.$$

Finally, regarding the resolutions of the MILP models, the parallelization were left to the Gurobi solver.[1]

We compared the MILP model to our ad-hoc tool and we found that our MILP model is much slower in most cases and actually too slow to output all the Step 1 solutions needed to perform Step 2. Running times are given in Table 2.

Table 2. Comparison of the running times required to generate all Step 1 solutions between our MILP and ad-hoc approaches.

Rounds	Model	Obj_{Step1}	MILP	Ad-hoc
14	**TK1**	$45 \rightarrow 59$	>6 h	5 m
19	**TK2**	$52 \rightarrow 63$	>6 h	19 m
20	**SK**	96	342 m	16 s
20	**TK1**	70	38 m	28 s
20	**TK2**	57	745 s	193 s
20	**TK3**	45	998 s	326 s

---

[1] see: https://www.gurobi.com/documentation/9.0/refman/threads.html .

Note that while our ad-hoc tool gave very good running times, it may require a lot of memory to store the array C. For instance, for 30 rounds in **TK3** mode, our tool required up to 500 GB of RAM to finish the search. It is also important to note that it did not take fully advantage of the 128 cores of our server, and most often used less than 40 cores.

4   Modeling Step 2 with CP

The aim of Step 2 is to try to instantiate the abstracted solutions provided by Step 1 while maximizing the probability of the differential characteristic. Thus, Step 2 takes as input a solution of Step 1 with the objective function of maximizing the probability of the differential characteristic. However, some solutions of Step 1 could not be instantiated in Step 2 as refining the abstraction level of Step 2 will induce *non-consistent* solutions. In the literature, this step has been modeled using ad-hoc methods [6], MILP [1], SAT [28] or CP [12]. As MILP [1] and SAT [28] seem to hardly scale due to prohibitive computational times (linked with the size of the 8-bit S-boxes that must be represented in the form of linear inequalities or of clauses), we focus here on a dedicated CP method implemented using the Choco solver [22]. We also provide, in the second part of this section, the results we obtain when instantiating the differential characteristics in the 4 attack scenarios.

4.1   Constraint Programming

Although less usual than MILP to tackle cryptanalytic problems, CP has already been used in e.g. [9,13]. We recall some basic principles of CP and we refer the reader to [23] for more details.

CP is used to solve Constraint Satisfaction Problems (CSPs). A CSP is defined by a triple (X, D, C) such that $X = \{x_1, x_2, \ldots, x_n\}$ is a finite set of variables, D is a function that maps every variable $x_i \in X$ to its domain $D(x_i)$ and $C = \{c_1, c_2, \ldots, c_m\}$ is a set of constraints. $D(x_i)$ is a finite ordered set of integer values to which the variable x_i can be assigned to, whereas c_j defines a relation between some variables $vars(c_j) \subseteq X$. This relation restricts the set of values that may be assigned simultaneously to $vars(c_j)$. Each constraint is equipped with a filtering algorithm which removes from the domains of $vars(c_j)$, the values that cannot satisfy c_j.

In CP, constraints are classified in two categories. *Extensional constraints*, also called *table constraints*, explicitly define the allowed (or forbidden) tuples of the relation. *Intentional constraints* define the relation using mathematical operators. For instance, in a CSP with $X = \{x_1, x_2, x_3\}$ such that $D(x_1) = D(x_2) = D(x_3) = \{0, 1\}$, a constraint ensuring that the sum of the variables in X is different from 1 can be either expressed in extension (1) or in intention (2):

1. TABLE($\langle x_1, x_2, x_3 \rangle, \langle (0,0,0), (0,1,1), (1,0,1), (1,1,0), (1,1,1) \rangle$)
2. $x_1 + x_2 + x_3 \neq 1$

Actually, any intentional constraint can be encoded with an extensional one provided enough memory space, and conversely [8]. However, they may offer different performances.

The purpose of a CSP is to find a *solution*, i.e. an assignment of all variables to a value from their respective domains such that all the constraints are simultaneously satisfied. When looking for a solution, a two-phase mechanism is operated: the *search space exploration* and the *constraint propagation*. The exploration of the search space is processed using a *depth-first search*. At each step, a decision is taken, i.e. a non-assigned variable is selected and its domain is reduced to a singleton. This modification requires to check the satisfiability of all the constraints. This is achieved thanks to constraint propagation which applies each constraint filtering algorithm. Any application may trigger modifications in turn; the propagation ends when either no modification occurs and all constraints are satisfied or a failure is thrown, *i.e.*, at least one constraint cannot be satisfied. In the former case, if all variables are assigned, a solution has been found. Otherwise a new decision is taken and the search is pursued. In the latter case, a backtrack to the first refutable decision is made and the search is resumed.

Turning a CSP into a Constrained Optimisation Problem (COP) is done by adding an objective function. Such a function is defined over variables of X, the purpose is then to find the solution that optimizes the objective function. Finding the optimal solution is done by repeatedly applying the two-phase mechanism above, and by adding a *cut* on the objective function that prevents from finding a same cost solution in the future.

4.2   Modeling Step 2 with CP

Given a Boolean solution for Step 1, Step 2 aims at searching for the byte-consistent solution with the highest (related-tweakey) differential characteristic probability (or proving that there is no byte-consistent solution). In this section, Model 1 describes the CP model we used for SKINNY-128 (**SK**). Actually, the ones used to model the other variants, as well as SKINNY-64 are rather similar.

For each Boolean variable $\Delta X_{r,i,j}$ of Step 1, we define an integer variable $\delta X_{r,i,j}$. The domain of this integer variable depends on the value of the Boolean variable in the Step 1 solution: If $\Delta X_{r,i,j} = 0$, then the domain is $D(\delta X_{r,i,j}) = \{0\}$ (*i.e.*, $\delta X_{r,i,j}$ is also assigned to 0); otherwise, the domain is $D(\delta X_{r,i,j}) = [1, 255]$. For each byte that passes through an S-box, we define an integer variable $\delta SB_{r,i,j}$ which corresponds to the difference after the S-box. Its domain is $\{0\}$ if $\Delta X_{r,i,j}$ is assigned to 0 in the Step 1 solution; otherwise, it is $D(\delta SB_{r,i,j}) = [1, 255]$. This is expressed in (3) of Model 1.

Finally, as we look for a byte-consistent solution with maximal probability, we also add an integer variable $P_{r,i,j}$ for each byte in an S-box: this variable corresponds to the absolute value of the base 2 logarithm of the probability of the transition through the S-box. Actually, a factor 10 has been applied to avoid considering floats. Thus we define a TABLE constraint (4) composed of valid triplets of the form $(\delta X_{r,i,j}, \delta SB_{r,i,j}, P_{r,i,j})$. Note that these triplets only

Minimize

$$Obj_{Step2} = \sum_{r=1}^{R} \sum_{i=1}^{4} \sum_{j=1}^{4} P_{r,i,j} \tag{1}$$

subject to

$$20 \times n \leq \sum_{r=1}^{R} \sum_{i=1}^{4} \sum_{j=1}^{4} P_{r,i,j} \leq \min(70 \times n, O^*) \tag{2}$$

$\forall r \in 1..R, \forall i \in 1..4, \forall j \in 1..4$

$$\begin{cases} \delta X_{r,i,j} = 0 \wedge \delta SB_{r,i,j} = 0 \wedge P_{r,i,j} = 0 & \text{if } \Delta X_{r,i,j} = 0 \\ \delta X_{r,i,j} \geq 1 \wedge \delta SB_{r,i,j} \geq 1 \wedge P_{r,i,j} \geq 20 & \text{otherwise} \end{cases} \tag{3}$$

$\forall r \in 1..R, \forall i \in 1..4, \forall j \in 1..4$

$$\text{TABLE}(\langle \delta X_{r,i,j}, \delta SB_{r,i,j}, P_{r,i,j} \rangle, \langle \text{SBox} \rangle) \quad \text{if } \Delta X_{r,i,j} \neq 0 \tag{4}$$

$\forall r \in 1..R - 1, \forall j \in 1..4 \qquad \delta SB_{r,0,j} = \delta X_{r+1,1,j}$

$$\tag{5}$$

$\forall r \in 1..R - 1, \forall j \in 1..4$

$$\begin{cases} \delta SB_{r,2,(2+j)\%4} = \delta X_{r+1,2,j} & \text{if } \Delta SB_{r,1,(3+j)\%4} = 0 \\ \delta SB_{r,1,(3+j)\%4} = \delta X_{r+1,2,j} & \text{if } \Delta SB_{r,2,(2+j)\%4} = 0 \\ \delta SB_{r,1,(3+j)\%4} = \delta SB_{r,2,(2+j)\%4} & \text{if } \Delta X_{r+1,2,j} = 0 \\ \text{TABLE}(\langle \delta SB_{r,1,(3+j)\%4}, \delta SB_{r,2,(2+j)\%4}, \delta X_{r+1,2,j} \rangle, \langle \text{XOR} \rangle) & \text{otherwise} \end{cases} \tag{6}$$

$\forall r \in 1..R - 1, \forall j \in 1..4$

$$\begin{cases} \delta SB_{r,2,(2+j)\%4} = \delta X_{r+1,3,j} & \text{if } \Delta SB_{r,0,j} = 0 \\ \delta SB_{r,0,j} = \delta X_{r+1,3,j} & \text{if } \Delta SB_{r,2,(2+j)\%4} = 0 \\ \delta SB_{r,0,j} = \delta SB_{r,2,(2+j)\%4} & \text{if } \Delta X_{r+1,3,j} = 0 \\ \text{TABLE}(\langle \delta SB_{r,0,j}, \delta SB_{r,2,(2+j)\%4}, \delta X_{r+1,3,j} \rangle, \langle \text{XOR} \rangle) & \text{otherwise} \end{cases} \tag{7}$$

$\forall r \in 1..R - 1, \forall j \in 1..4$

$$\begin{cases} \delta X_{r+1,0,j} = \delta X_{r+1,3,j} & \text{if } \Delta SB_{r,3,(1+j)\%4} = 0 \\ \delta SB_{r,3,(1+j)\%4} = \delta X_{r+1,3,j} & \text{if } \Delta X_{r+1,0,j} = 0 \\ \delta SB_{r,3,(1+j)\%4} = \delta X_{r+1,0,j} & \text{if } \Delta X_{r+1,3,j} = 0 \\ \text{TABLE}(\langle \delta SB_{r,3,(1+j)\%4}, \delta X_{r+1,0,j}, \delta X_{r+1,3,j} \rangle, \langle \text{XOR} \rangle) & \text{otherwise} \end{cases} \tag{8}$$

where $\forall r \in R..n, \forall i \in 1..4, \forall j \in 1..4,$

$$\delta X_{r,i,j} \in 0..255, \ \delta SB_{r,i,j} \in 0..255, \ P_{r,i,j} \in \{0, 20, .., 70\},$$

and $\langle \text{XOR} \rangle$ encodes $\oplus$ relation and $\langle \text{SBox} \rangle$ the S-box constraint.

Model 1: Formulation of **SK** Step2.

contain non-zero values and that $P_{r,i,j}$ takes only 2 different values for the 4-bit S-box (SKINNY-64) and 7 different values for the 8-bit S-box (SKINNY-128). There are roughly 2^{14} triplet elements in the Table constraint for the SKINNY-128 case. As the S-box layer is the only non-linear layer, the other operations could be directly implemented in a deterministic way at the cell level. The associated constraints thus follow the SKINNY-128 linear operations. When possible, i.e. when one element is known to be zero, we replace XOR constraints (encoded using TABLEconstraints) by a simple equality constraint. This corresponds to TABLE constraints (5), (6), (7) and (8) in Model 1.

The overall goal is finally to find a byte-consistent solution which maximizes differential characteristic probability. Thus, we define an integer variable Obj_{Step2} to minimize the sum of all $P_{r,i,j}$ variables (1). This value mainly depends on the number of S-boxes outputted by Step1 Obj_{Step1} and can be bounded to $\lceil 20 \cdot Obj_{Step1}, 70 \cdot Obj_{Step1} \rfloor$ (2).

The differences for the models **TK1**, **TK2** and **TK3** are the modeling of the XORs induced by the lanes of the tweakey through XOR table constraints. Each XOR constraint depicted in Model 1 provides high quality filtering but requires 65536 tuples to be stored which results in prohibitive memory usage. This may limit the number of threads that can be used for the resolution, which was the case for **TK2** and **TK3**. To get around this issue, we encoded the XOR constraint in intention (by defining filtering rules), providing a more memory efficient algorithm, at the expense of filtering strength. This last choice was applied for **TK2** and **TK3** (SKINNY-128 only). We also rely on TABLEconstraints to model the LFSRs applied on TK2 and TK3.

Concerning the search space strategy, for the **TK2** and the **TK3** attack settings, the Step 1 only outputs the truncated value of the sum of the TKi. Thus, the search space strategy first looks at the cancellation places of the sum of the TKi and then instantiates the TKi values according to those positions. For the **TK1** setting, we simply apply the default Choco-solver strategy.

Concerning the parallelization, we affect one solution outputted by Step 1 per thread and we share between the threads the value of Obj_{Step2}.

4.3 Step 2 Performance Results

We run our Step 2 model on the two versions of SKINNY (SKINNY-64 and SKINNY-128) using our CP models written in Choco-solver. We conduct all our experiments on our server composed of $2\times$ AMD EPYC 7742 64-Core and 1TB of RAM. All the reported times are **real** system times.

Up to our knowledge, we only found [1] that gives time results concerning finding the best **SK** differential characteristic probability on SKINNY-128 using a MILP tool based on Gurobi.

More precisely, the authors say: "In our experiments, we used Gurobi Optimizer with Xeon Processor E5-2699 (18 cores) in 128 GB RAM." and, for 13 rounds, "in our environment, the test of 6 classes [Step 1 solutions with 58 active S-boxes without symmetries] finished in 16 days. Finally, it is proven that the tight bound on the probability of differential characteristic for 13 rounds is 2^{-123}" in the **SK** model.

Regarding the **TK** models, the best known results were obtained by Liu *et al.* also using MILP models [19]. They could only find the best differential characteristics up to 7, 9 and 13 rounds for **TK1**, **TK2** and **TK3** respectively.

Results for SKINNY-64. We sum up in Table 3 all the results we obtain for SKINNY-64 in the four different attack models (**SK,TK1,TK2** and **TK3**). The overall time, in this case, is not a bottleneck. We only give results concerning number of rounds that are at the limit (just under and just upper) when regarding the number of active S-boxes which is equal to 32 in the case of SKINNY-64 as the state size is 64 bits and as the best differential probability of the S-box is equal to 2^{-2}. Thus, the best overall differential characteristic probability must be under 2^{-64}.

Note that sometimes, we need to browse several Obj_{Step1} bounds to find the optimal differential characteristic probability when the number of rounds is fixed. Indeed, we need to proactively adapt the probability bound we found. For example, in the case of **TK2** SKINNY-64 with 13 rounds, the optimal Obj_{Step1} is equal to 25 and when providing the Step 2 process with this Obj_{Step1} bound, we find a best differential characteristic probability equal to 2^{-55}. Thus, we need to enumerate all the Step 1 solutions with $Obj_{Step1} = 26$ and $Obj_{Step1} = 27$ to be sure that the previous probability is really the best one. Then, before running again Step 2 on those new results we adapt the best probability to the new bound equal to 2^{-55} instead of the old bound equal to 2^{-64}.

We also provide in Appendix A the details of the best found differential characteristics.

Table 3. Overall results concerning SKINNY-64 in the four attack models. Step 2 time corresponds to the Step 2 time taken over all Step 1 solutions when Obj_{step1} takes the values precise in the first column. Best Pr corresponds to the best found probability of a differential characteristic.

	Nb Rounds	Obj_{Step1}	Nb sol. Step 1	Step 2 time	Best Pr
SK	7	26	2	1 s	2^{-52}
SK	8	36	17	1 s	$<2^{-64}$
TK1	10	23	1	1 s	2^{-46}
TK1	11	32	2	1 s	$=2^{-64}$
TK2	13	$25 \to 27$	10	1 s	2^{-55}
TK2	14	31	1	1 s	$<2^{-64}$
TK3	15	$24 \to 26$	46	2 s	2^{-54}
TK3	16	$27 \to 31$	87	4 s	$=2^{-64}$
TK3	17	31	2	1 s	$<2^{-64}$

Results for SKINNY-128. In the same way, we provide in Table 4 the best differential characteristic probability with the total time required for this search for the 4 different attack models. As one can see, we also verify all the possible values for Obj_{Step1} for a given number of rounds, depending on the probability value previously found. Thus, this time, the number of solutions outputted by Step 1 could be huge when we move away from the optimal Step 1 value v^*. However, as the time spent to solve one solution is reasonable (at least when considering **SK** and **TK1**), our model scales reasonably well: the worst case requires 25 days of `real` time on our server on 8 threads and 31 GB of RAM[2].

Table 4. Overall results concerning SKINNY-128 in the four attack models. Step 2 time corresponds to the Step 2 time taken over all solutions of *Step1-enum* when Obj_{step1} takes the values precise in the first column. Best Pr corresponds to the best found probability of a differential characteristic.

	Nb Rounds	Obj_{step1}	Nb sol. Step 1	Step 2 time	Best Pr
SK	9	$41 \rightarrow 43$	52	16 s	2^{-86}
SK	10	$46 \rightarrow 48$	48	11 s	2^{-96}
SK	11	$51 \rightarrow 52$	15	4 s	2^{-104}
SK	12	$55 \rightarrow 56$	11	6 s	2^{-112}
SK	13	$58 \rightarrow 61$	18	2 m 27 s	2^{-123}
SK	14	$61 \rightarrow 63$	6	21 s	$\leq 2^{-128}$
TK1	8	$13 \rightarrow 16$	14	4 s	2^{-33}
TK1	9	$16 \rightarrow 20$	6	3 s	2^{-41}
TK1	10	$23 \rightarrow 27$	6	4 s	2^{-55}
TK1	11	$32 \rightarrow 36$	531	37 s	2^{-74}
TK1	12	$38 \rightarrow 46$	186 482	213 m	2^{-93}
TK1	13	$41 \rightarrow 53$	2 385 482	2 days	$2^{-106.2}$
TK1	14	$45 \rightarrow 59$	11 518 612	20 days	2^{-120}
TK1	15	$49 \rightarrow 63$	7 542 053	25 days	$\leq 2^{-128}$
TK2	9	$9 \rightarrow 10$	7	3 s	2^{-20}
TK2	10	$12 \rightarrow 17$	132	11 s	$2^{-34.4}$
TK2	11	$16 \rightarrow 25$	4203	6 m	$2^{-51.4}$
TK2	12	$21 \rightarrow 35$	1 922 762	512 m	$2^{-70.4}$
TK2	19	$52 \rightarrow 63$	530 693	280 m	$\leq 2^{-128}$
TK3	10	6	3	3 s	2^{-12}
TK3	11	10	3	10 s	2^{-21}
TK3	12	$13 \rightarrow 17$	373	1 h	$2^{-35.7}$
TK3	13	$16 \rightarrow 25$	34 638	85 h	$2^{-51.8}$
TK3	23	$55 \rightarrow 63$	47 068	11 h	$\leq 2^{-128}$

---

[2] It seems that the use of the 128 threads was prohibited by the memory usage of XOR tables (i.e. XOR in extension).

Table 5. Overall results concerning SKINNY-128 with exactly one active cell in the tweakey.

	Nb Rounds	Obj_{step1}	Best Pr
TK2	13	$25 \rightarrow 44$	$2^{-86.2}$
TK2	14	$31 \rightarrow 54$	$\geq 2^{-105.8}$
TK2	15	$35 \rightarrow 56$	$\geq 2^{-113.8}$
TK2	16	$40 \rightarrow 63$	$\geq 2^{-127.6}$
TK3	14	$19 \rightarrow 33$	2^{-67}
TK3	15	$24 \rightarrow 40$	2^{-81}
TK3	16	$27 \rightarrow 48$	2^{-98}
TK3	17	$31 \rightarrow 54$	2^{-110}
TK3	19	$43 \rightarrow 63$	$\leq 2^{-128}$
TK3	20	$45 \rightarrow 63$	$\leq 2^{-128}$
TK3	21	$48 \rightarrow 63$	$\leq 2^{-128}$
TK3	22	$51 \rightarrow 63$	$\leq 2^{-128}$

Our **TK2** and **TK3** models are based on XOR constraints encoded in intention (and not using tables) and these experiences have been launched using the 128 threads of our server.

Concerning **TK2** and **TK3**, we were not able to perform all the computations due to the huge number of Step 1 solutions. Hence we decided to handle only the Step 1 solutions with exactly one active byte in the round keys in order to limit the number of truncated characteristics to instantiate. Those results are given in Table 5. We provide in Appendix B the best **TK2** differential characteristic we found for 16 rounds, and the best **TK3** differential characteristic we found for 17 rounds. Note that we do not know if these differential characteristics are optimal in terms of probability as we were not able to test all the solutions Step 1.

Lessons Learnt. The overall gap is not to find the optimal value of $Obj_{Step1} = v^*$ for a given number of rounds and to enumerate the corresponding overall solutions if the Step 1 model is sufficiently tight. The real gap is if the value obtained for Obj_{Step2} (here equal to $2 \times v^*$ as the best differential probability for the S-box is equal to 2^{-2}) is far from the optimal bound then we have to increase Obj_{Step1} up to the bound $\lfloor Obj_{Step2}/2 \rfloor$. Further we are from v^* in the Step 1 resolution, more numerous are the Step 1 solutions (in fact this number grows exponentially as could be seen in Table 4). Thus, the time for the Step 2 resolution becomes the bottleneck.

5   Conclusion

In this paper, we improve the security bounds regarding differential characteristics search on the block cipher SKINNY. As usually done, we have divided the search procedure into two steps: Step 1 which abstracts the difference values into Boolean variables and finds the truncated characteristics with the smallest number of active S-boxes; and Step 2 which inputs the results of Step 1 to output the best possible probability instantiating the abstract solutions outputted by Step 1. Of course, each solution of Step 1 could not always be instantiated in Step 2.

For Step 1, an ad-hoc method which heavily uses the structure of the problem is proposed. For solving Step 2, we have implemented a Choco-solver model. Regarding Step 2, our Choco-solver model is much faster than any other approaches. It allowed us to find, for the first time, the best (related-tweakey) differential characteristics in the **TK1** model up to 14 rounds for SKINNY-128 and to show there is no differential trail on 15 rounds with a probability better than 2^{-128}. Regarding the **TK2** model, we were able to find the best differential trails up to 16 rounds. For **TK3**, we are able to exhibit a differential characteristic up to 17 rounds. Note that in [19] Liu *et al.* were only able to reach 7 and 9 rounds in the **TK1** and **TK2** model respectively. Our approach is thus an important improvement.

A   Best (Related-Tweakey) Differential Characteristics for SKINNY-64

The best **SK** differential characteristics on 7 rounds of SKINNY-64 with probability equal to 2^{-52} is given in Table 6. The best **TK1** differential characteristics on 10 rounds of SKINNY-64 with probability equal to 2^{-46} is given in Table 7. The Best **TK2** differential characteristics on 13 rounds of SKINNY-64 with probability equal to 2^{-55} is given in Table 8. Best **TK3** differential characteristics on 15 rounds of SKINNY-64 with probability equal to 2^{-54} is given in Table 9.

Table 6. The Best **SK** differential characteristics on 7 rounds of SKINNY-64 with probability equal to 2^{-52}. The four words represent the four rows of the state and are given in hexadecimal notation.

Round	$\delta X_i = X_i \oplus X_i'$ (before SB)	δSBX_i (after SB)	Pr(States)
$i = 1$	0040 4444 4440 4400	0020 2222 2220 2200	$2^{-2\cdot10}$
2	0000 0020 0200 2002	0000 0010 0100 1001	$2^{-2\cdot4}$
3	0010 0000 0000 0001	0080 0000 0000 0008	$2^{-2\cdot2}$
4	0000 0080 0000 0080	0000 0040 0000 0040	$2^{-2\cdot2}$
5	0400 0000 0004 0000	0200 0000 0002 0000	$2^{-2\cdot2}$
6	0000 0200 0200 0000	0000 0100 0100 0000	$2^{-2\cdot2}$
7	0001 0000 0011 0001	0008 0000 0088 0008	$2^{-2\cdot4}$

Table 7. The Best **TK1** differential characteristics on 10 rounds of SKINNY-64 with probability equal to 2^{-46}. The four words represent the four rows of the state and are given in hexadecimal notation.

Round	$\delta X_i = X_i \oplus X_i'$ (before SB)	δSBX_i (after SB)	$\delta TK1_i$	Pr(States)
$i = 1$	0000 0002 0020 0200	0000 0001 0010 0100	1000 0000 0B80 0000	$2^{-2.3}$
2	1000 1000 0000 0000	B000 8000 0000 0000	B000 8000 1000 0000	$2^{-2.2}$
3	0000 0000 0000 0000	0000 0000 0000 0000	0010 0000 B000 8000	–
4	0010 0010 0000 0010	00B0 00A0 0000 00B0	00B0 0080 0010 0000	$2^{-2.3}$
5	0B00 0000 0002 0000	0100 0000 0001 0000	0000 1000 00B0 0080	$2^{-2.2}$
6	0000 0100 0000 0000	0000 0800 0000 0000	0000 B800 0000 1000	$2^{-2.1}$
7	0000 0000 0B00 0000	0000 0000 0100 0000	0000 0010 0000 B800	$2^{-2.1}$
8	0001 0000 0000 0001	0008 0000 0000 0008	0008 00B0 0000 0010	$2^{-2.2}$
9	0080 0000 000B 0000	0040 0000 0001 0000	0000 0100 0008 00B0	$2^{-2.2}$
10	0140 0040 0110 0140	0820 0020 0880 0820	0000 0B08 0000 0100	$2^{-2.7}$

Table 8. The Best **TK2** differential characteristics on 13 rounds of SKINNY-64 with probability equal to 2^{-55}. The four words represent the four rows of the state and are given in hexadecimal notation.

Round	$\delta X_i = X_i \oplus X_i'$ (before SB)	δSBX_i (after SB)	$\delta TK1_i$	$\delta TK2_i$	Pr(States)
$i = 1$	0000 8200 0080 0000	0000 4100 0040 0000	0000 0008 0502 0000	0000 000C 060C 0000	$2^{-2.3}$
2	4000 0000 0410 4000	2000 0000 02A0 2000	5000 0002 0000 0008	D000 0008 0000 000C	$2^{-2.4}$
3	0000 A000 0002 0002	0000 6000 0006 0003	0800 0000 5000 0002	0800 0000 D000 0008	$2^{-2.3}$
4	0630 0000 0000 0600	03F0 0000 0000 0100	0250 0000 0800 0000	01A0 0000 0800 0000	$2^{-3.3}$
5	1000 0000 0000 0000	9000 0000 0000 0000	8000 0000 0250 0000	1000 0000 01A0 0000	2^{-2}
6	0000 0000 0000 0000	0000 0000 0000 0000	2000 5000 8000 0000	2000 5000 1000 0000	–
7	0000 0000 0000 0000	0000 0000 0000 0000	0080 0000 2000 5000	0020 0000 2000 5000	–
8	00A0 00A0 0000 00A0	0060 0050 0000 0050	0020 0050 0080 0000	0040 00B0 0020 0000	$2^{-2.3}$
9	0500 0000 000B 0000	0C00 0000 000C 0000	0000 8000 0020 0050	0000 4000 0040 00B0	$2^{-3.2}$
10	0000 0C00 0000 0000	0000 0200 0000 0000	0000 2500 0000 8000	0000 9700 0000 4000	2^{-2}
11	0000 0000 0B00 0000	0000 0000 0100 0000	0000 0080 0000 2500	0000 0090 0000 9700	2^{-2}
12	0001 0000 0000 0001	000A 0000 0000 0008	0005 0020 0000 0080	000F 0030 0000 0090	$2^{-2.2}$
13	0080 0000 0001 0000	0040 0000 0008 0000	0000 0800 0005 0020	0000 0300 000F 0030	$2^{-2.2}$

Table 9. The Best **TK3** differential characteristics on 15 rounds of SKINNY-64 with probability equal to 2^{-54}. The four words represent the four rows of the state and are given in hexadecimal notation.

Round	$\delta X_i = X_i \oplus X_i'$ (before SB)	δSBX_i (after SB)	$\delta TK1_i$	$\delta TK2_i$	$\delta TK3_i$	Pr(States)
$i = 1$	0000 0001 4000 0004	0000 0008 2000 0002	0000 080D 0000 0800	0000 0408 0000 0500	0000 0E0D 0000 0C00	$2^{-2.3}$
2	0000 0000 0000 0020	0000 0000 0000 0010	0008 0000 0000 080D	000B 0000 0000 0408	000E 0000 0000 0E0D	2^{-2}
3	010D 000D 0000 000D	0A0E 0002 0000 0002	0D08 0000 0008 0000	0109 0000 000B 0000	060F 0000 000E 0000	$2^{-2.3}2^{-3}$
4	0020 0000 2000 0000	0030 0000 3000 0000	0000 0008 0D08 0000	0000 0007 0109 0000	0000 000F 060F 0000	$2^{-2.2}$
5	0000 0030 0030 0000	0000 00C0 00C0 0000	D000 0008 0000 0008	2000 0003 0000 0007	3000 0007 0000 000F	$2^{-3.2}$
6	0000 C000 000C 0000	0000 2000 0002 0000	0800 0000 D000 0008	0F00 0000 2000 0003	0700 0000 3000 0007	$2^{-2.2}$
7	0200 0000 0000 0200	0500 0000 0000 0300	08D0 0000 0800 0000	0640 0000 0F00 0000	0B90 0000 0700 0000	$2^{-2.2}$
8	3000 0000 0000 0000	D000 0000 0000 0000	8000 0000 08D0 0000	E000 0000 0640 0000	B000 0000 0B90 0000	2^{-3}
9	0000 0000 0000 0000	0000 0000 0000 0000	8000 D000 8000 0000	D000 9000 E000 0000	5000 4000 B000 0000	−
10	0000 0000 0000 0000	0000 0000 0000 0000	0080 0000 8000 D000	00C0 0000 D000 9000	0050 0000 5000 4000	−
11	0010 0010 0000 0010	0080 0090 0000 00A0	0080 00D0 0080 0000	00A0 0030 00C0 0000	00A0 0020 0050 0000	$2^{-2.3}$
12	0A00 0000 0005 0000	0A00 0000 000A 0000	0000 8000 0080 00D0	0000 8000 00A0 0030	0000 A000 00A0 0020	$2^{-2}2^{-3}$
13	0000 0A00 0000 0000	0000 0A00 0000 0000	0000 8D00 0000 8000	0000 5600 0000 8000	0000 D100 0000 A000	2^{-3}
14	0000 0000 0000 0000	0000 0000 0000 0000	0000 0080 0000 8D00	0000 0010 0000 5600	0000 00D0 0000 D100	−
15	0000 0000 0004 0000	0000 0000 0002 0000	000D 0080 0000 0080	000D 00B0 0000 0010	0008 0060 0000 00D0	2^{-2}

B Best (Related-Tweakey) Differential Characteristics for SKINNY-128

Concerning the best **SK** differential characteristics on 13 rounds of SKINNY-128, We obtain the same best **SK** differential characteristics on 13 rounds of SKINNY-128 with probability equal to 2^{-123} given in Table 11 of Appendix D of [1]. The best **TK1** differential characteristics on 14 rounds of SKINNY-128 with probability equal to 2^{-120} is given in Table 10. The best **TK2** differential characteristics on 16 rounds of SKINNY-128 with probability equal to $2^{-127.6}$ we found is given in Table 11. The best **TK3** differential characteristics on 17 rounds of SKINNY-128 with probability equal to 2^{-110} we found is given in Table 12.

Table 10. The Best **TK1** differential characteristics on 14 rounds of SKINNY-128 with probability equal to 2^{-120}. The four words represent the four rows of the state and are given in hexadecimal notation.

Round	$\delta X_i = X_i \oplus X_i'$ (before SB)	δSBX_i (after SB)	$\delta TK1_i$	Pr(States)
$i=1$	02000002 00000200 00020000 00020040	08000008 00000800 00080000 00080004	00000000 00000000 01000000 00000000	$2^{-2.6}$
2	00000400 08000008 00000000 08000000	00000100 10000010 00000000 10000000	00000100 00000000 00000000 00000000	$2^{-2.4}$
3	00000010 00000000 10100000 00000000	00000040 00000000 40400000 00000000	00000000 00000000 00000100 00000000	$2^{-2.3}$
4	00004000 00000040 00004040 00004000	00000400 00000004 00000404 00000400	00000000 01000000 00000000 00000000	$2^{-2.5}$
5	04000400 00000400 00050000 04040400	05000500 00000100 00050000 05050500	00000000 00000000 00000000 01000000	$2^{-3.6}2^{-2}$
6	00050500 05000500 00000004 05000505	00050500 01000100 00000005 05000505	00000000 00000100 00000000 00000000	$2^{-3.6}2^{-2.2}$
7	00050005 00050500 00040000 00000500	00050005 00050500 00050000 00000500	00000000 00000000 00000000 00000100	$2^{-3.6}$
8	00000000 00050005 00000500 00050000	00000000 00010005 00000500 00050000	00000000 00010000 00000000 00000000	$2^{-3.3}2^{-2}$
9	00000000 00000000 00000000 05000000	00000000 00000000 00000000 05000000	00000000 00000000 00000000 00010000	2^{-3}
10	00000005 00000000 00000000 00000000	00000001 00000000 00000000 00000000	00000001 00000000 00000000 00000000	2^{-2}
11	00000000 00000000 00000000 00000000	00000000 00000000 00000000 00000000	00000000 00000000 00000001 00000000	–
12	00000000 00000000 00000000 00000000	00000000 00000000 00000000 00000000	00000000 00000001 00000000 00000000	–
13	00000000 00000000 01000000 00000000	00000000 00000000 20000000 00000000	00000000 00000000 00000000 00000001	2^{-2}
14	00002000 00000000 00002000 00002000	00008000 00000000 00008000 00008000	00010000 00000000 00000000 00000000	$2^{-2.3}$

Table 11. The Best **TK2** differential characteristics we found on 16 rounds of SKINNY-128 with probability equal to $2^{-127.6}$. The four words represent the four rows of the state and are given in hexadecimal notation.

Round	$\delta X_i = X_i \oplus X_i'$ (before SB) / δSBX_i (after SB)	$\delta TK1_i$ / $\delta TK2_i$	Pr(States)
$i=1$	00000000 00404010 40400000 40000000 00000000 00040440 04040000 04000000	00000000 00000000 00000000 00007700 00000000 00000000 00000000 00003900	$2^{-2.6}$
2	00000400 00000000 40000000 00000404 00000500 00000000 04000000 00000101	00000000 00770000 00000000 00000000 00000000 00730000 00000000 00000000	$2^{-2.3}2^{-3}$
3	00010000 00000500 00000000 00000100 00200000 00000500 00000000 00002000	00000000 00000000 00000000 00770000 00000000 00000000 00000000 00730000	$2^{-2.2}2^{-3}$
4	00000000 00200000 00000005 00200000 00000000 00800000 00000005 00800000	00000077 00000000 00000000 00000000 000000E7 00000000 00000000 00000000	$2^{-2.2}2^{-3}$
5	80050090 00000090 00058000 00050090 03010002 00000002 00010200 00010003	00000000 00000000 00000077 00000000 00000000 00000000 000000E7 00000000	$2^{-2.8}$
6	00010303 03010002 00000001 01010003 00202020 20200009 00000020 20200020	00000000 00000077 00000000 00000000 00000000 000000CE 00000000 00000000	$2^{-2.6}2^{-3.4}$
7	20000000 00202020 B0002000 00002020 80000000 00808080 80008000 00009380	00000000 00000000 00000000 00000077 00000000 00000000 00000000 000000CE	$2^{-2.6}2^{-2.4}2^{-3}$
8	00930000 80000000 00000080 00008000 00EA0000 03000000 00000003 00000300	00770000 00000000 00000000 00000000 009D0000 00000000 00000000 00000000	$2^{-2.3}2^{-6}$
9	00000000 00000000 00000000 00030000 00000000 00000000 00000000 00BC0000	00000000 00000000 00770000 00000000 00000000 00000000 009D0000 00000000	2^{-5}
10	BC000000 00000000 00000000 00000000 4C000000 00000000 00000000 00000000	77000000 00000000 00000000 00000000 3B000000 00000000 00000000 00000000	2^{-6}
11	00000000 00000000 00000000 00000000 00000000 00000000 00000000 00000000	00000000 00000000 77000000 00000000 00000000 00000000 3B000000 00000000	–
12	00000000 00000000 00000000 00000000 00000000 00000000 00000000 00000000	00007700 00000000 00000000 00000000 00007700 00000000 00000000 00000000	–
13	00000000 00000000 00000000 00000000 00000000 00000000 00000000 00000000	00000000 00000000 00007700 00000000 00000000 00000000 00007700 00000000	–
14	00000000 00000000 00000000 00000000 00000000 00000000 00000000 00000000	00000000 77000000 00000000 00000000 00000000 EF000000 00000000 00000000	–
15	00000000 00000000 00980000 00000000 00000000 00000000 00420000 00000000	00000000 00000000 00000000 77000000 00000000 00000000 00000000 EF000000	2^{-5}
16	00000042 00000000 00000042 00000042 00000008 00000000 00000008 00000008	–	$2^{-2.4\cdot3}$

Table 12. The Best **TK3** differential characteristics we found on 17 rounds of SKINNY-128 with probability equal to 2^{-110}. The four words represent the four rows of the state and are given in hexadecimal notation.

Round	$\delta X_i = X_i \oplus X'_i$ (before SB) / δSBX_i (after SB)	$\delta TK1_i$ / $\delta TK2_i$ / $\delta TK3_i$	Pr(States)
$i=1$	00000200 00320000 08000000 00000808 00000800 00920000 18000000 00001010	00000000 00BA0000 00000000 00000000 00000000 00430000 00000000 00000000 00000000 00730000 00000000 00000000	$2^{-2\cdot3}2^{-3\cdot2}$
2	00100000 00000800 00000000 00001000 00400000 00001000 00000000 00004000	00000000 00000000 00000000 00BA0000 00000000 00000000 00000000 00430000 00000000 00000000 00000000 00730000	$2^{-2\cdot3}$
3	00000000 00400000 00000010 00400000 00000000 00040000 00000040 00040000	000000BA 00000000 00000000 00000000 00000086 00000000 00000000 00000000 00000039 00000000 00000000 00000000	$2^{-2\cdot3}$
4	04400005 00000005 00400400 00400005 05040001 00000001 00040100 00040005	00000000 00000000 000000BA 00000000 00000000 00000000 00000086 00000000 00000000 00000000 00000039 00000000	$2^{-2\cdot6}2^{-3\cdot2}$
5	00040505 05040001 00000004 04040005 00010101 01010028 00000001 01010001	00000000 000000BA 00000000 00000000 00000000 0000000D 00000000 00000000 00000000 0000009C 00000000 00000000	$2^{-2\cdot9}2^{-3}$
6	01000000 00010101 03000100 00000101 20000000 00202020 20002000 0000B320	00000000 00000000 00000000 000000BA 00000000 00000000 00000000 0000000D 00000000 00000000 00000000 0000009C	$2^{-2\cdot6}2^{-3}2^{-4}$
7	00B30000 20000000 00000020 00002000 00EE0000 80000000 00000080 00008000	00BA0000 00000000 00000000 00000000 001A0000 00000000 00000000 00000000 004E0000 00000000 00000000 00000000	$2^{-2\cdot3}2^{-7}$
8	00000000 00000000 00000000 00800000 00000000 00000000 00000000 00030000	00000000 00000000 00BA0000 00000000 00000000 00000000 001A0000 00000000 00000000 00000000 004E0000 00000000	2^{-2}
9	03000000 00000000 00000000 00000000 29000000 00000000 00000000 00000000	BA000000 00000000 00000000 00000000 34000000 00000000 00000000 00000000 A7000000 00000000 00000000 00000000	2^{-4}
10	00000000 00000000 00000000 00000000 00000000 00000000 00000000 00000000	00000000 00000000 BA000000 00000000 00000000 00000000 34000000 00000000 00000000 00000000 A7000000 00000000	—
11	00000000 00000000 00000000 00000000 00000000 00000000 00000000 00000000	0000BA00 00000000 00000000 00000000 00006900 00000000 00000000 00000000 0000D300 00000000 00000000 00000000	—
12	00000000 00000000 00000000 00000000 00000000 00000000 00000000 00000000	00000000 00000000 0000BA00 00000000 00000000 00000000 00006900 00000000 00000000 00000000 0000D300 00000000	—
13	00000000 00000000 00000000 00000000 00000000 00000000 00000000 00000000	00000000 BA000000 00000000 00000000 00000000 D3000000 00000000 00000000 00000000 69000000 00000000 00000000	—
14	00000000 00000000 00000000 00000000 00000000 00000000 00000000 00000000	00000000 00000000 00000000 BA000000 00000000 00000000 00000000 D3000000 00000000 00000000 00000000 69000000	—
15	0000000 00000000 00000000 00000000 00000000 00000000 00000000 00000000	00000000 0000BA00 00000000 00000000 00000000 0000A700 00000000 00000000 00000000 00003400 00000000 00000000	—
16	00000000 00000000 00000029 00000000 00000000 00000000 00000030 00000000	00000000 00000000 00000000 0000BA00 00000000 00000000 00000000 0000A700 00000000 00000000 00000000 00003400	2^{-3}
17	00300000 00000000 00300000 00300000 00400000 00000000 00400000 00400000	—	$2^{-2\cdot3}$

References

1. Abdelkhalek, A., Sasaki, Y., Todo, Y., Tolba, M., Youssef, A.M.: MILP modeling for (large) s-boxes to optimize probability of differential characteristics. IACR Trans. Symmetric Cryptol. **2017**(4), 99–129 (2017)
2. Alfarano, G.N., Beierle, C., Isobe, T., Kölbl, S., Leander, G.: ShiftRows alternatives for AES-like ciphers and optimal cell permutations for Midori and SKINNY. IACR Trans. Symmetric Cryptol. **2018**(2), 20–47 (2018). https://doi.org/10.13154/tosc. v2018.i2.20-47
3. Beierle, C., et al.: The SKINNY family of block ciphers and its low-latency variant MANTIS. In: Robshaw, M., Katz, J. (eds.) CRYPTO 2016. LNCS, vol. 9815, pp. 123–153. Springer, Heidelberg (2016). https://doi.org/10.1007/978-3-662-53008-5_5
4. Biham, E.: New types of cryptanalytic attacks using related keys. In: Helleseth, T. (ed.) EUROCRYPT 1993. LNCS, vol. 765, pp. 398–409. Springer, Heidelberg (1994). https://doi.org/10.1007/3-540-48285-7_34
5. Biham, E., Shamir, A.: Differential cryptanalysis of feal and n-hash. In: Davies, D.W. (ed.) EUROCRYPT 1991. LNCS, vol. 547, pp. 1–16. Springer, Heidelberg (1991). https://doi.org/10.1007/3-540-46416-6_1
6. Biryukov, A., Nikolić, I.: Automatic search for related-key differential characteristics in byte-oriented block ciphers: application to AES, Camellia, Khazad and others. In: Gilbert, H. (ed.) EUROCRYPT 2010. LNCS, vol. 6110, pp. 322–344. Springer, Heidelberg (2010). https://doi.org/10.1007/978-3-642-13190-5_17
7. Delaune, S., Derbez, P., Huynh, P., Minier, M., Mollimard, V., Prud'Homme, C.: SKINNY with scalpel comparing tools for differential analysis (April 2021). https:// hal.archives-ouvertes.fr/hal-03040548, working paper or preprint
8. Demeulenaere, J., et al.: Compact-table: efficiently filtering table constraints with reversible sparse bit-sets. In: Rueher, M. (ed.) CP 2016. LNCS, vol. 9892, pp. 207–223. Springer, Cham (2016). https://doi.org/10.1007/978-3-319-44953-1_14
9. Eichlseder, M., Nageler, M., Primas, R.: Analyzing the linear keystream biases in AEGIS. IACR Trans. Symmetric Cryptol. **2019**(4), 348–368 (2019)
10. Fouque, P.-A., Jean, J., Peyrin, T.: Structural evaluation of AES, and chosen-key distinguisher of 9-Round AES-128. In: Canetti, R., Garay, J.A. (eds.) CRYPTO 2013. LNCS, vol. 8042, pp. 183–203. Springer, Heidelberg (2013). https://doi.org/ 10.1007/978-3-642-40041-4_11
11. Gérault, D., Lafourcade, P., Minier, M., Solnon, C.: Revisiting AES related-key differential attacks with constraint programming. Inf. Process. Lett. **139**, 24–29 (2018)
12. Gerault, D., Lafourcade, P., Minier, M., Solnon, C.: Computing AES related-key differential characteristics with constraint programming. Artif. Intell. **278**, 103183 (2020)
13. Gerault, D., Minier, M., Solnon, C.: Constraint programming models for chosen key differential cryptanalysis. In: Rueher, M. (ed.) CP 2016. LNCS, vol. 9892, pp. 584–601. Springer, Cham (2016). https://doi.org/10.1007/978-3-319-44953-1_37
14. Jean, J.: TikZ for cryptographers (2016). https://www.iacr.org/authors/tikz/
15. Jean, J., Nikolić, I., Peyrin, T.: Tweaks and keys for block ciphers: the TWEAKEY framework. In: Sarkar, P., Iwata, T. (eds.) ASIACRYPT 2014. LNCS, vol. 8874, pp. 274–288. Springer, Heidelberg (2014). https://doi.org/10.1007/978-3-662-45608-8_15
16. Knudsen, L.R.: Truncated and higher order differentials. In: Preneel, B. (ed.) FSE 1994. LNCS, vol. 1008, pp. 196–211. Springer, Heidelberg (1995). https://doi.org/ 10.1007/3-540-60590-8_16

17. Kölbl, S., Leander, G., Tiessen, T.: Observations on the SIMON block cipher family. In: Gennaro, R., Robshaw, M. (eds.) CRYPTO 2015. LNCS, vol. 9215, pp. 161–185. Springer, Heidelberg (2015). https://doi.org/10.1007/978-3-662-47989-6_8

18. Lafitte, F.: Cryptosat: a tool for sat-based cryptanalysis. IET Inf. Secur. **12**(6), 463–474 (2018)

19. Liu, G., Ghosh, M., Song, L.: Security analysis of SKINNY under related-tweakey settings (long paper). IACR Trans. Symmetric Cryptol. **2017**(3), 37–72 (2017). https://doi.org/10.13154/tosc.v2017.i3.37-72

20. Matsui, M.: On correlation between the order of S-boxes and the strength of DES. In: De Santis, A. (ed.) EUROCRYPT 1994. LNCS, vol. 950, pp. 366–375. Springer, Heidelberg (1995). https://doi.org/10.1007/BFb0053451

21. Mouha, N., Preneel, B.: A proof that the ARX cipher salsa20 is secure against differential cryptanalysis. IACR Cryptol. ePrint Arch. **2013**, 328 (2013). http://eprint.iacr.org/2013/328

22. Prud'homme, C., Fages, J.G., Lorca, X.: Choco documentation. TASC, INRIA Rennes, LINA CNRS UMR 6241, COSLING S.A.S. (2016). http://www.choco-solver.org

23. Rossi, F., Beek, P.V., Walsh, T.: Handbook of Constraint Programming (Foundations of Artificial Intelligence). Elsevier Science Inc., New York (2006)

24. Sasaki, Yu., Todo, Y.: New impossible differential search tool from design and cryptanalysis aspects. In: Coron, J.-S., Nielsen, J.B. (eds.) EUROCRYPT 2017. LNCS, vol. 10212, pp. 185–215. Springer, Cham (2017). https://doi.org/10.1007/978-3-319-56617-7_7

25. Song, L., Qin, X., Hu, L.: Boomerang connectivity table revisited. Application to SKINNY and AES. IACR Trans. Symmetric Cryptol. **2019**(1), 118–141 (2019). https://doi.org/10.13154/tosc.v2019.i1.118-141

26. Soos, M., Nohl, K., Castelluccia, C.: Extending SAT solvers to cryptographic problems. In: Kullmann, O. (ed.) SAT 2009. LNCS, vol. 5584, pp. 244–257. Springer, Heidelberg (2009). https://doi.org/10.1007/978-3-642-02777-2_24

27. Sun, L., Wang, W., Wang, M.: Automatic search of bit-based division property for ARX ciphers and word-based division property. In: Takagi, T., Peyrin, T. (eds.) ASIACRYPT 2017. LNCS, vol. 10624, pp. 128–157. Springer, Cham (2017). https://doi.org/10.1007/978-3-319-70694-8_5

28. Sun, L., Wang, W., Wang, M.: More accurate differential properties of LED64 and Midori64. IACR Trans. Symmetric Cryptol. **2018**(3), 93–123 (2018)

29. Sun, S., et al.: Analysis of AES, SKINNY, and others with constraint programming. In: 24th International Conference on Fast Software Encryption (2017)

30. Sun, S., Hu, L., Wang, P., Qiao, K., Ma, X., Song, L.: Automatic security evaluation and (related-key) differential characteristic search: application to SIMON, PRESENT, LBlock, DES(L) and other bit-oriented block ciphers. In: Sarkar, P., Iwata, T. (eds.) ASIACRYPT 2014. LNCS, vol. 8873, pp. 158–178. Springer, Heidelberg (2014). https://doi.org/10.1007/978-3-662-45611-8_9

31. Zhao, B., Dong, X., Meier, W., Jia, K., Wang, G.: Generalized related-key rectangle attacks on block ciphers with linear key schedule: applications to SKINNY and GIFT. Des. Codes Cryptogr. **88**(6), 1103–1126 (2020). https://doi.org/10.1007/s10623-020-00730-1

Towards Efficient LPN-Based Symmetric Encryption

Sonia Bogos[1], Dario Korolija[2], Thomas Locher[3](✉), and Serge Vaudenay[4]

[1] ELCA, Lausanne, Switzerland
sonia.duc@elca.ch
[2] ETH, Zurich, Switzerland
dario.korolija@inf.ethz.ch
[3] ABB Research, Baden, Switzerland
thomas.locher@ch.abb.com
[4] EPFL, Lausanne, Switzerland
serge.vaudenay@epfl.ch

Abstract. Due to the rapidly growing number of devices that need to communicate securely, there is still significant interest in the development of efficient encryption schemes. It is important to maintain a portfolio of different constructions in order to enable a quick transition if a novel attack breaks a construction currently in use. A promising approach is to construct encryption schemes based on the learning parity with noise (LPN) problem as these schemes can typically be implemented fairly efficiently using mainly "exclusive or" (XOR) operations. Most LPN-based schemes in the literature are asymmetric, and there is no practical evaluation of any LPN-based symmetric encryption scheme.

In this paper, we propose a novel LPN-based symmetric encryption scheme that is more efficient than related schemes. Apart from analyzing our scheme theoretically, we provide the first practical evaluation of a symmetric LPN-based scheme, including a study of its performance in terms of attainable throughput depending on the selected parameters. As the encryption scheme lends itself to an implementation in hardware, we further evaluate it on a low-end SoC FPGA. The measurement results attest that our encryption scheme achieves high performance rates in terms of throughput on such hardware, providing evidence that symmetric encryption schemes based on hard learning problems may be constructed that can compete with state-of-the-art encryption schemes.

Keywords: Symmetric encryption · Learning parity with noise · LPN · FPGA implementation

1 Introduction

There has been a substantial amount of work in recent years on the development of encryption schemes whose security relies on the hardness of solving a difficult *learning problem*. In fact, there is a strong connection between cryptography

© Springer Nature Switzerland AG 2021
K. Sako and N. O. Tippenhauer (Eds.): ACNS 2021, LNCS 12727, pp. 208–230, 2021.
https://doi.org/10.1007/978-3-030-78375-4_9

and learning problems as shown in the seminal work by Impagliazzo and Levin who quite generally proved that cryptography is only possible if and only if efficient learning is not [20]. A well studied example of such a learning problem is *learning parity with noise* (LPN). In short, it is the problem of identifying an unknown binary vector given only noisy scalar products of this vector and other vectors chosen uniformly at random. Since computations are carried out in $\mathbb{Z}_2$, the scalar product is a single bit. The scalar products are noisy in the sense that the resulting bit is flipped with a certain probability.[1]

Building encryption schemes based on the LPN problem is appealing because they are expected to achieve decent throughput measured in the number of bytes processed per second. In recent years, several encryption schemes based on LPN have been proposed; however, barring a few exceptions, the focus has been primarily on asymmetric cryptography (see Sect. 6 for details on related work). All proposed schemes have in common that they require fresh, cryptographically strong random bits for the encryption of each piece of plaintext. This requirement can be disadvantageous for multiple reasons: First, the generation of secure random bits itself may be computationally expensive. Second, low-power embedded devices often have a limited number of entropy sources, which makes it challenging to produce random bits [17]. Moreover, extracting randomness from sources with low entropy incurs a significant computational overhead [29]. Finally, if each invocation of the encryption process requires fresh randomness, this additional randomness must either be appended to the encrypted data or it is embedded in it. In the former case, the space complexity (or bandwidth requirement) increases and in the latter case, we get a more complex decryption routine and thus a lower throughput for decryption.

We propose a *synchronous stream cipher*, called *Firekite*, which uses an LPN-based pseudo-random number generator (PRNG) with a simple structure [3] to generate its keystream. The PRNG used in Firekite differs from the PRNG introduced by Blum et al. [3] in that it handles the noise vector differently and uses a different noise distribution. Firekite further uses a Ring-LPN hardness assumption to reduce the key size. Unlike other proposed encryption schemes based on the LPN problem, our scheme only requires a source of cryptographically strong random bits for key generation but not for encryption. We further discuss how to use our scheme in practice by proposing concrete sets of parameters to instantiate it. As an additional contribution, the attainable throughput based on our software implementation is measured for various parameter sets. While the potential for efficient LPN-based cryptography has been noted before, this is the first work that measures the actual performance of such an encryption scheme. Moreover, as our scheme can greatly benefit from dedicated hardware, we implemented and evaluated it on a low-power field-programmable gate array (FPGA). To the best of our knowledge, this is also the first time any LPN-based encryption scheme is tested and evaluated on an FPGA.

---

[1] Note that the problem is not difficult to solve without any noise, using Gaussian elimination.

Although it is unlikely that current symmetric encryption schemes such as AES, which is nowadays employed ubiquitously, will be broken in the near future, we believe that a portfolio of cryptographic constructions must be at our disposal for multiple reasons. First, fallback solutions are required in case one construction is broken. Second, encryption is used in devices with different capabilities and constraints in a multitude of scenarios, which entails that different schemes are appropriate depending on the use case. LPN-based cryptography may prove to be a sensible approach for specific use cases.

The paper is structured as follows. Background on LPN is provided in Sect. 2. Our encryption scheme is introduced in Sect. 3 and analyzed in terms of security and performance in Sect. 4 and Sect. 5, respectively. A summary of related work is provided in Sect. 6, and Sect. 7 concludes the paper.

2   Background

LPN is a well studied problem in cryptography and machine learning. It is appealing in cryptography as it is a strong candidate for post-quantum cryptography: while efficient algorithms for quantum computers have been found to solve the factorization and the discrete logarithm problem [28], which are the foundation of asymmetric encryption schemes used in practice, no efficient quantum algorithm that solves the LPN problem is known. Moreover, the LPN problem is a promising candidate because only simple operations such as "exclusive or" (XOR) and scalar products are required, which can be implemented efficiently.

Informally, the LPN problem is asking to solve a noisy binary system of equations. We will now provide the formal definition, which uses an LPN *oracle*. Let $x \xleftarrow{U} \mathcal{X}$ denote the event that x is drawn uniformly at random from the domain $\mathcal{X}$.

Definition 1. (LPN Oracle). *Let $s \xleftarrow{U} \mathbb{Z}_2^n$ and Ber_τ be the Bernoulli distribution with a noise parameter $\tau \in]0, \frac{1}{2}[$. Let $D_{s,\tau}$ further denote the distribution defined as*

$$\{(u,c) \mid u \xleftarrow{U} \mathbb{Z}_2^n, c = u^T s + d, d \leftarrow \mathsf{Ber}_\tau\} \in \mathbb{Z}_2^{n+1}.$$

An LPN oracle $\mathcal{O}_{s,\tau}^{\mathsf{LPN}}$ outputs independent random samples according to $D_{s,\tau}$.

Given this definition, we are now in the position to define the LPN problem and the notion of an LPN solving algorithm.

Definition 2. (Search LPN). *Given access to an LPN oracle $\mathcal{O}_{s,\tau}^{\mathsf{LPN}}$, find the vector s. Let $n' \leq n$. We say that an algorithm $\mathcal{M}$ (q, t, μ, θ, n')-solves the search LPN problem, where the secret has size n and the noise parameter is τ, if*

$$\Pr[\mathcal{M}^{\mathcal{O}_{s,\tau}^{\mathsf{LPN}}}(1^n) = (s_1 \ldots s_{n'}) \mid s \xleftarrow{U} \mathbb{Z}_2^n] \geq \theta,$$

$\mathcal{M}$ runs in time t, uses memory μ, and queries the LPN oracle at most q times.

In the decisional LPN problem, the objective is to distinguish between output from the LPN oracle and uniformly distributed random vectors of size $n + 1$. It has been proven that the search LPN and the decisional LPN problem are equivalent [3, 22].

Looking at the history of solving LPN, the first specific LPN solving algorithm is BKW [4], which recovers the LPN secret bit by bit. An important improvement was presented by Levieil and Fouque [25] whose algorithm uses the Walsh-Hadamard transform, which makes it possible to recover several bits of the secret at once and requires fewer initial queries. The use of covering codes, introduced by Guo et al. [16], further improves the performance of LPN solving algorithms [5, 32]. An analysis of the best LPN solving algorithms for a wide range of parameters can be found in the work of Bogos and Vaudenay [5].

All these algorithms are characterized by the fact that their time complexity is sub-exponential, $2^{O\left(\frac{n}{\log(n)}\right)}$, and they require a sub-exponential number of queries, $2^{O\left(\frac{n}{\log(n)}\right)}$, when the noise parameter τ is constant.[2]

Trading off the time complexity in favor of the number of queries, Lyubashevsky [26] uses BKW as a black box and adds a processing phase at the beginning of the LPN solving algorithm. With this modification, the LPN problem can be solved requiring only a polynomial number of queries ($n^{1+\varepsilon}$ for a constant $\varepsilon > 0$) at the expense of an increased time complexity of $2^{O\left(\frac{n}{\log(\log(n))}\right)}$.

3 PRNG and Firekite Construction

We first provide an overview of the LPN-based PRNG construction in Sect. 3.1. It is important to note that the basic construction has been proposed before [3]. However, the level of detail provided in Sect. 3.1 should help the reader to better understand how our PRNG differs from the general construction. Our PRNG is introduced formally and in detail in Sect. 3.2. Subsequently, our encryption scheme *Firekite*, which is based on this PRNG, is presented in Sect. 3.3.

3.1 Overview

The challenge of the LPN problem, as defined in Sect. 2, is to distinguish between a source providing either random bit vectors of length $n+1$ or vectors containing n random bits plus a single bit that is the noisy scalar product of these n bits and a secret vector s of length n. This definition can naturally be extended to matrices and vectors: the noisy scalar product of a secret $m \times n$-matrix M and a random vector v, i.e., $M^T v + e$, where e denotes a sparse n-bit noise vector, is hard to distinguish from a random n-bit vector. Note that addition is carried out in $\mathbb{Z}_2$, i.e., addition corresponds to computing the XOR of the inputs.

---

[2] A simple guessing strategy has a complexity of $O\left(n^3 e^{n^{1-\delta}}\right)$ using $O\left(n e^{n^{1-\delta}}\right)$ queries if $\tau = n^{-\delta}$.

The PRNG construction exploits the fact that noisy matrix-vector products are indistinguishable from random vectors. In order to solve the problem that LPN-based constructions require a source of randomness, we proceed as follows: rather than having a separate mechanism, the output of a noisy matrix-vector product is used iteratively as a source of randomness for the next noisy matrix-vector multiplication. Concretely, given a secret matrix M and secret initial vector v and e, the vector $M^T v + e$ can be used to generate the input for the next iteration.

Obviously, simply iterating this process alone does not yield a PRNG because there is no output. This problem is addressed as follows. If $n \gg m$, the noisy matrix-vector product of length n can be split into three pieces: m bits are used as the next vector v', some bits are interpreted as a compact encoding $c_{e'}$ of the next noise vector e', and the remaining bits, denoted by g, constitute the output.

While the length of the noise vector is n, a concise representation of the noise vector e' is possible because e' is sparse. Formally, $\mathcal{H}(e')$ bits are needed to encode e', where $\mathcal{H}(e')$ denotes the entropy of the bit string e' [3]. This process is depicted in Fig. 1.

$$
\begin{pmatrix} & M & \end{pmatrix}^T \cdot \begin{pmatrix} v \end{pmatrix} + \begin{pmatrix} e \end{pmatrix} = \begin{pmatrix} g \\ \hline v' \\ \hline c_{e'} \end{pmatrix}
$$

Fig. 1. The output of the noisy matrix-vector product is split into three components g, v', and $c_{e'}$. The vector g is the output of the PRNG, whereas v' and $c_{e'}$ are used iteratively to compute the next noisy matrix-vector product.

3.2 PRNG

Having a basic understanding of the general PRNG construction, we proceed by giving a formal specification of our PRNG. The *state* of the PRNG is the pair (M, w), where M is a binary $m \times n$-matrix, for some integer parameters m and n, where $n \gg m$ and n is a power of 2, and w is a vector of length $m + k \cdot \log(n) < n$ for some integer parameter k.[3] The matrix M is called the *secret key*, which never changes. Unlike the secret M, the vector w, which is kept secret as well, is updated during the execution of the PRNG. Appropriate choices for the parameters m, n, and k are discussed in Sect. 4.3.

Let $\|$ denote concatenation of vectors, i.e., for two vectors v and v' of lengths ℓ and ℓ', respectively, $v\|v'$ denotes the vector of length $\ell + \ell'$ for which

$$
(v\|v')[i] = \begin{cases} v[i] & \text{if } i < \ell \\ v'[i - \ell] & \text{otherwise} \end{cases}
$$

---

[3] Note that $\log(\cdot)$ always denotes logarithm base 2 throughout this paper.

for all $i \in \{0, \ldots, \ell + \ell' - 1\}$. We define $w = v\|c_e$, where v and c_e are vectors of length m and $k \cdot \log(n)$, respectively. The vector c_e is to be understood as the concise formulation of a sparse vector of length n. Let b_i be the unit vector of length n where only the bit at position i is set to 1 (and all other bits are 0). If $c_e = i_1\|i_2\|\ldots\|i_k$, the noise vector e is defined as $e = \bigvee_{j=1}^{k} b_{i_j}$, where i_j denotes the binary representation of a non-negative integer using $\log(n)$ bits. In other words, c_e encodes the positions in e where the bit is set to 1.[4] As an illustrative example, consider the case when $n = 16$, $k = 3$, and $c_e = (1001\|0100\|1100)$, i.e., the bits at indices 9, 4, and 12 are to be set (reading from left to right). Thus, the decoded noise vector is $e = (0001001000010000)$ (with the lowest-order bit on the right). It is important to note that it is possible that the same index occurs more than once, i.e., $i_j = i_{j'}$, for some $j, j' \in \{1, \ldots, k\}$. Consequently, the number of bits set in e is upper bounded by k.

We are now in the position to describe the PRNG algorithm. In the first step, vector v is set to the first m bits in w, and the remaining $k \cdot \log(n)$ bits of w are interpreted as the concise formulation $c_e = i_1\|i_2\|\ldots\|i_k$ of the noise vector e. Next, the noise vector is set to the decoded form of c_e, i.e., $e := \bigvee_{j=1}^{k} b_{i_j}$, where each index i_j is extracted from $c_e = i_1\|i_2\|\ldots\|i_k$. In the main step, the n-bit vector $M^T v + e$ is computed, which is interpreted as the concatenation of vectors g and w' of lengths $n - (m + k \cdot \log(n))$ and $m + k \cdot \log(n)$, respectively. Finally, the internal state (M, w) is updated to (M, w') and the output of the PRNG is simply the vector g.

From the description of the algorithm it follows that the algorithm can be implemented using only XOR operations, except for the decoding of the noise vector. The steps of the PRNG algorithm are summarized in Algorithm 1.

Algorithm 1. PRNG with state (M, w)

1: Parse $v\|i_1\|i_2\|\ldots\|i_k := w$
2: Set $e := \bigvee_{j=1}^{k} b_{i_j}$
3: Compute $g\|w' := M^T v + e$
4: $w := w'$
5: **return** g

3.3   Firekite

The PRNG described in Sect. 3.2 can theoretically be used as the basis of several cryptographic constructions. Firekite is a synchronous stream cipher that uses this PRNG, initialized with the secret state (M, w), to produce the keystream directly. Formally, the encryption of a data item d of length $n - (m + k \cdot \log(n))$ is $\mathrm{PRNG}() + d$, where $\mathrm{PRNG}()$ is to be understood as the invocation of the PRNG returning the next random vector g of length $n - (m + k \cdot \log(n))$. Thus,

---
[4] Intuitively, the length of c_e is an approximation of the entropy $\mathcal{H}(e)$ of e.

the plaintext vectors are processed sequentially, and the output g of the PRNG depends on the internal vector w, which is updated for each invocation of the PRNG. As for any synchronous stream cipher, a ciphertext can be decrypted by simply applying Algorithm 1 again on the ciphertext to obtain the plaintext.

As we will see, when setting the parameters m, n, and k to appropriate values, the matrix M becomes quite large. For the sake of a low memory footprint and efficient key distribution and management, it is preferable to have short keys. This problem can be addressed by moving from the LPN problem to a variant of the Ring-LPN problem [18]: Consider the ring R of all polynomials in X over $\mathbb{Z}_2$ with binary coefficients reduced modulo $X^b - 1$ for a suitable parameter $b > n$, i.e., a parameter b for which it holds that $(X^b - 1)/(X - 1)$ is irreducible. Let $q_1 \xleftarrow{U} \mathbb{Z}_2^b$ and $q_i := X^{i-1}q_1$ for $i \in \{2, \ldots, b\}$. The $b \times b$-matrix Q consists of the rows $q_1, \ldots, q_b$. In other words, the ith row of Q can be constructed by rotating the first row to the left by $i - 1$ positions. The Ring-LPN conjecture states that the problem remains hard when using the matrix Q in place of a fully random matrix, subject to the constraint that the polynomial is irreducible. Thus, the key used in Firekite is the random b-bit vector q_1. It is worth noting that an attacker might obtain the parity of the secret due to the factor $X - 1$ but no more information about the secret is revealed.

As described in Sect. 3.1, we require that $m \ll n$ and for n to be a power of 2. Thus, the matrix Q from the Ring-LPN instance cannot be used directly. Instead, given desired parameters n and m and the b-bit key, the matrix M is derived from the key by generating the first m rows of Q and dropping the last $b - n$ columns.

The security implications of this transformation and details on the security of Firekite in general are provided in Sect. 4. Moreover, for the Ring-LPN construction, we show in Sect. 4.3 that the key size is reduced from mn to $n + c$, where c is a small constant, for suggested parameter sets.

As mentioned before, the internal state w has to be kept secret. If an attacker can control the initialization of w as part of a chosen-ciphertext attack, the attacker can mount a key recovery attack to obtain the secret matrix M. The initial vector w can be derived from a public m-bit nonce N using a standard technique: Let $C_0 = c\|c + 1\| \cdots \|c + k - 1$ be a vector of length $k \log(n)$, where $c := n - m - k \log(n)$, and let $w_0 := N\|C_0$. Given the secret key M and the vector w_0 derived from the nonce N, we compute

1. $v\|i_1\| \ldots \|i_k := w_{\ell-1}$
2. $e := \bigvee_{j=1}^{k} b_{i_j}$
3. $g\|w_\ell := M^T v + e$

iteratively for $\ell \in \{1, \ldots, r\}$ for some constant r (defined below) and define $w := w_\ell$. Thus, the procedure essentially consists of r successive executions of Algorithm 1, discarding the vector g in each iteration.

We set the value of r as follows: In each iteration, the noise vector contributes $k\frac{m}{n}$ bits on average to vector v because the length of v is m and the noise bits are spread uniformly across n bits. The number of possibilities to choose $k\frac{m}{n}$

positions in vector v (with replacement) is $m^{k\frac{m}{n}}$. During r trials, we assume that $r-1$ of the corresponding noise vectors look random, which implies that the total number of combinations is $m^{k\frac{m}{n}(r-1)}$. Thus, the number of combinations exceeds $(2^m)^2$ by setting $r := 1 + \left\lceil \frac{2n}{k\log(m)} \right\rceil$. This heuristic argument suggests that v is fully random for this choice of r.[5]

This nonce-based variant can also be utilized to turn Firekite into a non-sequential stream cipher by providing a new nonce after a certain number of invocations of the PRNG. It is worth pointing out, however, that the number of invocations must be significantly larger than r to ensure that the cost of processing the nonce does not introduce a substantial overhead.

4   Security Analysis

In order to solve Ring-LPN based on irreducible polynomials, we can apply the same algorithms that solve LPN. It is intuitive that instances where the matrix M is also secret, which is the case in Firekite, require more effort from an attacker compared to the traditional LPN or Ring-LPN instances that are instantiated with the same parameters. On the other hand, utilizing only the top m rows of the Ring-LPN matrix Q as described in Sect. 3.2 to generate matrix M can only have a negative impact on security. As there are no known techniques to break Ring-LPN instances for irreducible polynomials faster than standard LPN instances, we conjecture that using a secret matrix M derived from the b-bit key Q_1 does not result in a substantially reduced security compared to using a fully random $m \times n$-matrix M. Therefore, we do not distinguish between these two constructions in the following and simply consider a secret matrix M.

However, we must analyze the implication of generating the noise vector as described in Sect. 3.2. While the PRNG proposed in prior art [3] is based on an LPN instance where the noise vector has a Hamming weight of k, the noise vector has a Hamming weight of *at most* k in our case. In this section, we first show that an LPN instance based on our distribution of noise bits is still hard.

In order to be able to study the performance of Firekite in practice, we need to instantiate it with secure parameters. To this end, we transform the problem of breaking our scheme into the LPN problem in Sect. 4.2. This transformation allows us to find concrete parameters for our scheme based on the best known attacks against the well-studied LPN problem. In Sect. 4.3, we then discuss how to derive parameters for practical use and provide exemplary parameters.

4.1   Security Reduction for Noise Distribution

A well-known result about PRNGs states that it suffices to show the pseudo-randomness of a single application of the PRNG (e.g., §3.3.2 in [15]). Hence, we need to prove that it is hard to distinguish the output $M^T v + e$ from bits chosen uniformly at random. We will now prove that we get an LPN variant that is hard

---

[5] Note that the square in $(2^m)^2$ is a safety margin.

when using the noise distribution of Firekite as opposed to setting each bit in the vector e independently according to the noise parameter $\tau \in \left]0, \frac{1}{2}\right[$ as defined in Definition 1.

Let N_τ denote the Hamming weight of the noise vector, i.e., the number of bits that are set to 1 in the n-bit noise vector. In the standard LPN setting, it holds that $\mathbb{E}\left[N_\tau^{\mathsf{LPN}}\right] = \tau n$. In Firekite (FK), the Hamming weight of the noise vector corresponds to the number of distinct elements when picking k out of n elements uniformly at random with replacement. Hence, we have that

$$\mathbb{E}\left[N_\tau^{FK}\right] = n \cdot \left(1 - \left(1 - \frac{1}{n}\right)^k\right). \tag{1}$$

Using the inequality

$$(1 + x)^r \leq 1 + \frac{rx}{1 - (r-1)x} \tag{2}$$

for $x \in (-1, \frac{1}{r-1}]$ and $r > 1$, we obtain that

$$\mathbb{E}\left[N_\tau^{FK}\right] \stackrel{(1)}{=} n \cdot \left(1 - \left(1 - \frac{1}{n}\right)^k\right) \stackrel{(2)}{\geq} \frac{n \cdot k}{n + k - 1}. \tag{3}$$

Furthermore, observing that $\frac{k}{n} < \frac{1}{2}$,[6] we obtain that

$$k > \mathbb{E}\left[N_\tau^{FK}\right] \stackrel{(3)}{>} \frac{2}{3}k. \tag{4}$$

We assume for the sake of contradiction that an LPN instance with the Firekite noise distribution can be broken, i.e., solved efficiently. Given a standard LPN instance where the size of the secret is n and the noise parameter is τ, we set k such that $\tau n \leq k$, e.g., by setting $k := \frac{3}{2}\tau n$.

Since N_τ^{LPN} follows a binomial distribution, we have that $\Pr[N_\tau^{\mathsf{LPN}} = \lfloor \mathbb{E}\left[N_\tau^{\mathsf{LPN}}\right]\rfloor] \in \Omega(1/n)$. For the chosen parameters, it is thus likely that the number of noise bits set to 1 is less than k. If we assume that LPN with our noise distribution can be solved efficiently, then LPN with noise parameter τ can be solved efficiently too: the noise of any given LPN instance could come from our noise distribution with probability at least $\Omega(1/n)$. Hence it follows that the attacker can solve LPN with a complexity that is $O(n)$ times larger than the complexity needed to break LPN with the Firekite noise distribution.

Thus, we can use essentially the same proof as for a constant Hamming weight [3] to show that the Firekite noise distribution is secure under the assumption that LPN is a hard problem.

---

[6] While this inequality is true for any LPN instance, the ratio k/n is much smaller for parameters we propose in Sect. 4.3. Thus, tighter bounds on $\mathbb{E}\left[N_\tau^{FK}\right]$ can be derived for recommended parameters.

4.2   Transformation to LPN Problem

In the standard LPN problem, the goal is to reconstruct a secret vector s given pairs of the form (u, c), where u is a random vector and $c = u^T s + e$, with $e \in \{0, 1\}$, is a noisy scalar product of u and s. The basic problem underlying Firekite restricts the input provided to an attacker. Specifically, the attacker sees only (parts of) $c = M^T v + e$, i.e., both M and v are kept secret. We show in this section that Firekite is based on a problem that can be transformed into the LPN problem.

Let $H = I \| X$ be a parity-check matrix of dimensions $(n - m) \times n$, where I is the $(n - m) \times (n - m)$-identity matrix and X is a $(n - m) \times m$-matrix such that $HM^T = 0$. Furthermore, let M_1 and M_2 denote the matrices comprising the first $(n - m)$ and last m columns of M, respectively. Thus, it holds that $M = M_1 \| M_2$ and $X = M_1^T (M_2^T)^{-1}$. Since $HM^T = 0$, we have that

$$(HM^T)v = H(M^T v) = H(c + e) = (I \| X)c + (I \| X)e = 0. \tag{5}$$

Let $\bar{c}$ and $\bar{e}$ denote the subvectors consisting of the last m elements of c and e, respectively. For the jth component c_j of c it holds that

$$c_j \overset{(5)}{=} x_j^T \bar{c} + e_j + x_j^T \bar{e}, \tag{6}$$

where x_j is the jth row of X, for any $j \in \{1, \ldots, n - m\}$. By defining $\eta_j := e_j + x_j^T \bar{e}$, we get

$$c_j \overset{(6)}{=} x_j^T \bar{c} + \eta_j.$$

Since c_j and $\bar{c}$ are known, x_j is a secret, and η_j is a noise bit, this corresponds to a standard LPN problem with the goal of recovering x_j for all $j \in \{1, \ldots n - m\}$. The noise bit η_j consists of noise bit e_j plus $\frac{m}{2}$ additional noise bits in expectation because the expected number of bits set in x_j is $\frac{m}{2}$. Once all vectors $x_1, \ldots, x_{n-m}$ (and thus X) are recovered, M can be recovered as well. Hence, the problem can be transformed into an equivalent LPN problem with higher noise.

While this transformation merely shows that the problem underlying Firekite is *at most* as hard as LPN, we believe the inverse to be true as well, i.e., we conjecture that the two problems are equivalent. As the above transformation is the best available method to attack the problem, we use it to derive secure parameters based on the most efficient known attacks against the standard LPN problem in the next section.

4.3   Parameters

The parameters n, m, and k must be carefully chosen to maximize security and performance while keeping the size of the key and internal state small. In order to determine a level of security for a specific set of parameters, we use the following approach. Since the expected number of noise bits set in e is $n \left(1 - \left(\frac{n-1}{n} \right)^k \right)$ according to Eq. (1), we define the probability that any specific bit in e is set as $\tau := 1 - \left(\frac{n-1}{n}\right)^k$. Recall, however, that the noise bits are not set according to a binomial distribution.[7] Since the noise η_j is the combination of $\frac{m}{2} + 1$ noise terms in expectation, the *bias* is approximately $(1 - 2\tau)^{\frac{m}{2}+1}$, which is small for a reasonably large m. Given that the bias is low, the most efficient method to solve the LPN problem is the algorithm by Levieil and Fouque [25]. This algorithm can be seen as a Gaussian elimination algorithm performed on blocks of bits (instead of single bits) where at the end the Walsh-Hadamard transform is applied to retrieve a block of the secret. Since τ approximately determines the ratio of k over n, suitable parameters can easily be computed based on their algorithm. Although the execution of the algorithm by Levieil and Fouque solely retrieves a single vector x_j, we use the resulting computational complexity as a bound to derive the entire matrix M. This is a conservative estimate as it may be possible to retrieve all $n - m$ with the same amortized complexity.

Table 1. Parameters for 80-bit security and the resulting key sizes (corresponding to parameter b), α and r values, and computed security levels.

Parameters			Properties			
m	n	k	Key Size (b)	α	r	Sec. Level
216	1024	16	1061	0.63	18	82.76
216	2048	32	2053	0.72	18	82.76
216	4096	54	4099	0.79	21	80.69
216	8192	112	8219	0.80	20	82.60
216	16,384	216	16,421	0.80	21	80.68
224	32,768	416	32,771	0.80	22	80.66
224	65,536	834	65,539	0.79	22	80.82

The fact that the choice of parameters has a direct impact on performance must also be taken into account. Naturally, the larger the vector g is in relation to n, the more bits are used directly for encryption and fewer invocations of Algorithm 1 are needed. Let

$$\alpha = \alpha(m, n, k) := \frac{n - (m + k \log n)}{n}$$

denote the fraction of the output of Algorithm 1 that is used for encryption. A simple model of the amortized cost of Algorithm 1 in terms of the number of instructions that need to be executed *per bit* is

$$I(m, n, k) := \frac{m}{2p} \frac{1}{\alpha(m, n, k)} + N(n, k), \tag{7}$$

where p is the number of bits for which an XOR operation can be computed in a single instruction and $N(n, k)$ captures the amortized per-bit overhead to

---

[7] In particular, the variance is substantially lower.

compute and apply the noise vector. The factor $\frac{m}{2p}$ is due to the fact that in expectation $m/2$ bits in vector v are set and p bits are processed together. The term $N(n,k)$ is roughly proportional to k/n and thus only marginally increases the amortized cost. Profiling of our implementation confirms that this model is fairly accurate in that 95% of the computation is spent on the matrix-vector multiplication, which corresponds to the first term in Eq. (7). Evidently, m contributes directly to the amortized cost and must be minimized. However, a reduction of m must be compensated with an increase of the number k of noise bits in order to keep the same level of security. Since every increment of k requires an additional $\log(n)$ bits, α becomes smaller, which negatively affects the amortized cost according to Eq. (7). In practice, the search space can be restricted quite well because an efficient implementation imposes additional constraints, e.g., all vectors should fit into an integer number of bytes.

Table 2. Parameters for 128-bit security and the resulting key sizes (corresponding to parameter b), α and r values, and computed security levels.

Parameters			Properties			
m	n	k	Key Size (b)	α	r	Sec. Level
352	1024	16	1061	0.50	17	129.07
352	2048	32	2053	0.66	17	129.07
352	4096	58	4099	0.74	18	128.95
352	8192	120	8219	0.77	18	128.99
352	16,384	228	16,421	0.78	18	128.93
352	32,768	456	32,771	0.78	18	128.93
352	65,536	906	65,539	0.77	19	128.92

Table 1 and Table 2 provide parameters for 80-bit and 128-bit security, respectively, for an increasing length n. As mentioned before, the values in the table are derived analytically, based on the algorithm by Levieil and Fouque. A first observation is that the security level remains basically the same when scaling n and k in the same manner while keeping m constant. This behavior is expected because a constant ratio of n and k implies that the probability that any bit is flipped remains constant as well. The effect of scaling the parameter n will be examined more closely in Sect. 5.1. The tables further show that it is possible to have keys lengths, which correspond to the length b of Q_1 as defined in Sect. 3.2, that are comparable to the lengths of keys in standard asymmetric encryption schemes. However, it is impossible to have key lengths similar to the lengths of standard symmetric encryption schemes because m must be in the order of hundreds of bits, and it must hold that n is significantly larger than m to ensure that α is not too small. Moreover, we see that increasing n only leads to an increase of α up to a certain point because more bits are needed to encode a single noise bit index as n grows larger. The tables also provide the number r of rounds needed to initialize vector w for the nonce-based variant for each set of parameters. We see that r only varies slightly for the proposed sets of parameters. Finally, it is important to note that increasing the security level does not affect the key size. Still, the increase of m invariably leads to a larger computational cost. Hence it follows that the right choice of parameters highly depends on the requirements in terms of performance and memory constraints. A general recommendation would be to use $n = 4096$ (i.e., $b = 4099$) and m and k as given in the two tables for either 80-bit or 128-bit security. These parameters achieve a decent trade-off between performance and space. As we will see in Sect. 5.2, the memory requirements for these parameters are small enough for use on a standard low-end FPGA. For certain architectures with plenty of memory and wide buses, the last row in the two tables, i.e., the parameters for $n = 65,536$ (i.e., $b = 65,539$) might be preferable for performance reasons. The actual performance for specific parameter ranges is investigated in the subsequent section, which will provide further justification for our choice of recommended parameters.

5   Performance Evaluation

The primary objective is to evaluate the performance in terms of throughput, which is the number of bytes that can be encrypted or decrypted per second. As discussed in Sect. 4, the choice of parameters crucially affects not only the attained level of security but also the performance. Therefore, performance is evaluated for a range of parameters corresponding to different security levels.

The procedure to obtain the desired measurement results is the same for all experiments: Random input data is allocated in memory, which is then encrypted and the time required for this encryption is measured. This process is repeated 20 times and all measured times are recorded. The reported throughput is simply the ratio of the input size and the *median* of all recorded times in seconds required to process the input. Note that we solely report the median value because the variance is so small that the differences would hardly be visible in the figures. Similarly, the input size was varied from tens of kilobytes up to one gigabyte without any significant impact on performance on all considered platforms, suggesting that the measured throughput reflects the throughput that would be observed in real-world applications.

The impact of the parameters on performance is analyzed in Sect. 5.1 using our software implementation. We further explore the potential of parallelization and evaluate performance gains in a multi-threaded environment. It is important to note that this implementation is neither tested nor analyzed sufficiently for practical use. In particular, it might be susceptible to side-channel attacks because the implementation uses direct memory access and executes XOR operations conditional on the bits in the secret state w. While an optimized, well-tested implementation might yield somewhat different numbers, we believe that the evaluation results capture the relative performance with respect to parameterization reasonably well. Since Firekite is better suited to be run on dedicated hardware, we further implemented it on a low-power FPGA. The evaluation results on this platform are presented in Sect. 5.2. Unlike the software implementation, the constant-time FPGA implementation is significantly better protected against side-channel attacks.

Naturally, a base of comparison is needed to put the performance numbers into perspective. We chose to compare our software and hardware implementation against the *Advanced Encryption Standard* (AES) [8] due to its ubiquity and high level of efficiency. This comparison is meant to illustrate how close an LPN-based scheme can come to a state-of-the-art symmetric encryption scheme in terms of performance on the given hardware. A thorough comparison against multiple state-of-the-art stream ciphers on different hardware platforms is beyond the scope of this work.

5.1 Performance on a Desktop Computer

The experiments to analyze the impact of the parameters on performance were conducted on a quad-core Intel Core i5-4570 at 3.2 GHz with 8 GB of DDR3 memory (at 1.6 GHz). Our Firekite implementation is written in C++ and consists of roughly 2000 lines of code. It is compiled using the optimization flags `-O3` and `-funroll-loops` for most classes. The additional compilation flag `-mavx2` is added for the core classes that perform XOR operations in order to make use of *Advanced Vector Extensions* (AVX),[8] which add several SIMD instructions that operate on 256 bit inputs. Thus, an XOR operation can be applied to $p = 256$ bits per cycle. Recall that the amortized number of instructions to encrypt a single bit is roughly proportional to $1/p$ according to Eq. (7), i.e., any non-trivial increase of p leads to a substantial improvement of throughput.

The level of security is raised primarily by increasing the number m of n-bit vectors. Equation (7) states that the computational effort grows linearly with m, which implies that a greater level of security results in a lower throughput. In order to test this hypothesis, values for m and k have been chosen that maximize throughput while achieving a security level of $80, 90, \ldots, 150$ for the two recommended values for n, i.e., $n = 4096$ and $n = 65,536$. As discussed in Sect. 4.3, the algorithm by Levieil and Fouque is used to determine the security level of a specific set of parameters m, n, and k based on the transformation to the standard LPN problem (see Sect. 4.2).

The measured throughput for the chosen parameter sets is given in Fig. 2. It is evident from this figure that the hypothesis is true in that the performance degrades when increasing the security level. While the rate of degradation slightly decreases for larger levels of security, the simplified model that assumes a linear relationship between security level and throughput is fairly accurate.

An interesting observation is that there is a substantial gap in the attained throughput for $n = 4096$ and $n = 65,536$. A plausible explanation for this gap is that a larger n is likely to result in fewer cache misses. The effect of increasing

---

[8] Note that the flag `-mavx` can be used instead, in which case the `PXOR` instruction is used in place of `VPXORS`, resulting in 256-bit operations but with fewer execution ports.

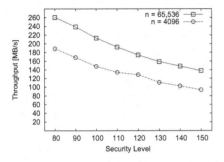 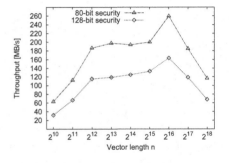

Fig. 2. The change in throughput is shown for $n = 4096$ and $n = 65,536$ when increasing the security level from 80 to 150 in increments of 10.

Fig. 3. The effect on the throughput when increasing the vector length from $n = 2^{10}$ to $n = 2^{18}$ is shown for the security levels 80 and 128.

n is studied in a second experiment. Specifically, all valid values for n in the range from $n = 2^{10}$ to $n = 2^{18}$ are tested. The parameters m and k have been set to values that maximize throughput for the two security levels 80 and 128. The result of this experiment is depicted in Fig. 3.

The figure shows that the vector length n considerably affects performance. When n is small, there are frequent cache misses, leading to a low throughput. The rate at which performance improves slows down when reaching $n = 4096$. Thus, this value for n is a good choice when memory is limited. However, there is a substantial improvement when increasing n from 2^{15} to 2^{16}. This improvement is due to the fact that 16 is a power of 2, which enables multiple optimizations: First, the noise vector can be constructed efficiently as 16 bits can efficiently be read sequentially. Moreover, when setting m and k to values so that αn is divisible by 256, *aligned memory access* is possible for efficient use of the AVX instructions. On the given test machine, throughput dropped significantly when increasing n further for two reasons. First, the optimizations for $n = 2^{16}$ are not possible for these vector lengths. Second, if the vectors become too long, cache misses become more frequent and parts of the vectors need to be loaded repeatedly. In fact, the drop is so steep that the throughput for $n = 2^{17}$ is lower than for $n = 2^{12}$. Naturally, results may vary depending on the given hardware architecture. In particular, the peak may occur for a different value of n.

Having discussed how the parameters affect performance in terms of throughput, we proceed to analyze the potential for parallelization. It is easy to see that the computation of $M^T v + e$ can be parallelized well. The basic principle is to partition M into t matrices $M_1, \ldots, M_t$ of dimension $\frac{m}{t} \times n$ and assigning each partition to one of t threads. Additionally, vector v and c_e are also partitioned into smaller vectors roughly of size m/t and $k \log(n)/t$, respectively. Each thread $i \in \{1, \ldots, t\}$ then computes $M_i^T v_i$ and e_i, which requires a fraction of $1/t$ of the entire computational effort. Subsequently, the t matrix-vector products are added together and the *logical or* of all t noise vectors is computed. Finally, the resulting noise vector is added to the computed matrix-vector product.

In reality, this process is slightly more complex because there are several constraints that must be respected when partitioning M, v, and e. Obviously, m/t may not be an integer number, therefore it must be guaranteed that the partitioning uniquely assigns each bit in v to a thread. The splitting of c_e is more involved because care has to be taken that each partition consists of a multiple of $\log(n)$ bits as these many bits encode a single index in the noise vector.

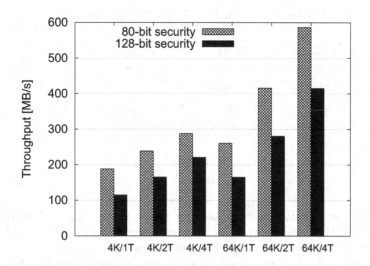

Fig. 4. The effect of using multiple threads on throughput is shown. One, two, and four threads (1T, 2T, 4T) are used for vector lengths $n = 4096$ (4K) and $n = 65,536$ (64K). The results are provided for security levels 80 and 128.

In our next experiment, one, two, and four threads (denoted by 1T, 2T, and 4T, respectively) are used to process the provided input and the processing time is measured. Figure 4 summarizes the results for both recommended vector lengths, $n = 4096$ (4K) and $n = 65,536$ (64K), and security levels 80 and 128. The measurement results indicate that spreading the computational task across multiple threads indeed leads to a higher throughput. The improvement is more substantial for vectors of larger size and for higher security levels, i.e., when parameters n and m are larger. This is due to the fact that increasing these parameters results in more work that can be partitioned among the threads. As an example, throughput increases by merely 26% (21%) when using two threads instead of one (four threads instead of two) for 80-bit security and a vector length n of 4096. By contrast, for $n = 65,536$ and 128-bit security, the throughput improves by 70% and 48% when increasing the number of threads from one to two and from two to four, respectively, resulting in an overall speed-up factor of approximately 2.5. While a multi-threaded execution evidently improves performance, the overhead to synchronize the threads and the effort to merge the partial results from all threads limits the potential of parallelization.

Finally, Table 3 compares the performance numbers against the performance of the AES implementation of OpenSSL.

Table 3. The throughput of AES-128 in CBC and CTR mode with and without hardware acceleration (HWA) are listed, as well as throughput of Firekite for the configurations 4K/1T, 4K/4T, 64K/1T, and 64K/4T for 128-bit security.

Algorithm	Mode	HWA	Throughput [MB/s]
AES-128	CBC	✓	738
AES-128	CTR	✓	2864
AES-128	CBC	✗	357
AES-128	CTR	✗	258
Firekite (128-bit)	4K/1T	✗	115
Firekite (128-bit)	4K/4T	✗	221
Firekite (128-bit)	64K/1T	✗	165
Firekite (128-bit)	64K/4T	✗	415

Hardware acceleration was disabled for some experiments to show the huge effect of having hardware support in the form of the AES_NI instruction. Firekite only reaches a similar performance level when hardware acceleration is disabled, $n = 65,536$, and when using multiple threads. While Firekite makes use of AVX/AVX2 instructions, we conjecture that support for operands the size of n, e.g., $n = 4096$, would be required to become competitive. Naturally, Firekite would further greatly benefit from hardware support for the decoding of the noise vector. Thus, we conclude that hardware support is a general requirement for high performance.

5.2 Performance on an FPGA

Both AES and Firekite have been implemented for execution on a *Cyclone V* FPGA, which is a low-cost and low-power system on a chip with a dual-core ARM Cortex-A9 MPCore processor at 925 MHz.[9] It offers 41,910 adaptive logic modules, 166,036 registers, and 553 RAM blocks. Even though 1GB of external RAM is available and accessible through a dedicated controller, only on-chip RAM is used in our implementation for performance reasons as the access latency for on-chip RAM is lower. Encryption modules were added to the system with a softcore *NIOS II* CPU instantiated in the FPGA fabric. Specifically, version f of the CPU is used, which is characterized by high-speed pipelined data paths and available on-board data and instruction caches. Each of the encryption modules

---

[9] https://www.verical.com/datasheet/intel-fpga-5CSXFC6D6F31C6-N-5759991.pdf.

contains read and write direct memory access (DMA) units to minimize memory access latencies. The frequency of the clock supplied to all units is 50 MHz.

The goal for the implementation of both AES and Firekite is to utilize the available resources to the largest extent possible in order to maximize performance in terms of the number of bytes that are encrypted per cycle. A custom implementation of AES with the S-box implemented as a lookup table is used in our experiments. We distinguish between single port (SP) and dual port (DP) memory access: for SP memory access it is only possible to read from memory or write to memory but not in the same cycle, whereas DP memory access uses two ports to enable reading and writing at the same time. Consequently, the implementation for SP and DP memory access differ substantially, notably in that only the DP implementation is *pipelined*, i.e., data is scheduled for encryption (or decryption) as soon as it is fetched from memory.

For AES, we consider a parallelizable mode (CTR) and a non-parallelizable mode (CBC). In non-parallelizable modes, batches of data must be encrypted sequentially; moreover, the encryption of the next batch can only be started after it has been fetched from memory. However, it is important to note that both modes are pipelined for DP memory access. For the more complex version with DP memory access, four stages can be executed in parallel on this FPGA, whereas it is possible to execute 32 stages in parallel for the simpler version with a single-port DMA component. Thus, the sole advantage of the parallelizable modes is that more data can be fetched in parallel, resulting in larger bursts, fewer memory accesses, and consequently higher memory performance. We therefore expect parallelizable modes to perform slightly better, in particular when coupled with dual port memory access.

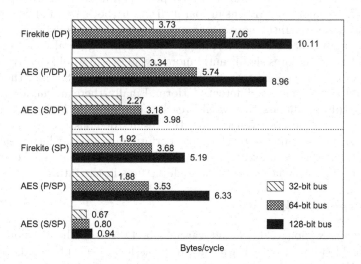

Fig. 5. The number of encrypted bytes/cycle is shown for AES and Firekite using DP (top) and SP (bottom) memory access, for a bus size of 32, 64, and 128 bit. Results are provided for both sequential (S) and parallelized (P) AES executions.

The parameters that are used for the Firekite implementation are $m = 512$, $n = 4096$, and $k = 64$, which corresponds to a security level of 183. These parameters have been chosen because parameters that are powers of 2 simplify the design. The key advantage in comparison to AES is that all computations can, in theory, be carried out in parallel. The top-level diagram is similar to the diagram for AES and is omitted. The implementation uses numerous registers on the datapath. In order to save space, the rows of matrix M are constructed when needed as described in Sect. 3.2. The largest amount of space in the FPGA fabric is consumed by the computational blocks that are used to perform the XOR operations and decode the noise vectors. Since the resources on this FPGA do not suffice to perform all operations of Algorithm 1 in one cycle, the computation is executed in 32 cycles. In addition to an SP DMA version, a version with DP memory access was developed as well, which introduces extra registers to enable the parallelization of all operations.

As mentioned before, performance is measured in terms of the number of bytes that are encrypted per cycle. The numbers are derived by encrypting a payload of 48KB and dividing 49,152 by the number of used cycles. Figure 5 summarizes the results for AES, with and without parallelization, and Firekite for SP and DP memory access. Furthermore, the effect of using different bus sizes is presented as well.

The results are encouraging as Firekite encrypts more bytes per cycles when using either DP or SP DMA components, except for SP memory access and a bus size of 128 bits. The throughput of Firekite is higher by a factor of 1.64 to 2.54 (depending on the bus size) for DP memory access, and even 2.87 to 5.5 times larger for SP memory access. As far as resource consumption is concerned, Firekite uses more registers than AES as expected (roughly 20–25K vs. 4–11K). However, the versions of AES using parallelization (both DP and SP memory access) actually use slightly more combinational logic elements (34K vs. 35–36K).

These numbers naturally do not imply that Firekite generally performs better. First of all, it requires significantly more registers and would clearly not perform well when constrained to a small number of registers. Second, the results might be quite different on a different platform. Finally, there are numerous lightweight encryption schemes that would reach a considerably higher throughput given the same resources. Nonetheless, the results demonstrate that an LPN-based encryption scheme can reach decent performance levels, which means that such schemes can potentially become viable alternatives to state-of-the-art symmetric encryption schemes for specific architectures in the future.

6   Related Work

One main application of LPN and variants of LPN is authentication, and a plethora of LPN-based authentication protocols have been proposed: HB [19], HB$^+$ [21], HB^{++} [6], HB$^{\#}$ [14], AUTH [24], and Lapin [18] among others [7,27]. Several encryption schemes also base their security on the hardness of LPN [1,9–13,23,31]. Constructions of *pseudo-random number generators* [2,3] and *pseudo-random functions* [30] based on LPN have been presented as well.

Alekhnovich [1] proposed two constructions for public-key encryption schemes that encrypt a given plaintext bit for bit. Improvements were introduced by Damgård et al. [9] and by Döttling et al. [11]. A more efficient scheme building on top of the work of Döttling et al. was presented by Kiltz et al. [23]. HELEN [12] is another encryption scheme that bases its security on LPN and the decisional minimum distance problem. More recently, Yu and Zhang [31] illustrated how LPN can be used in a tag-based encryption scheme.

The work that is most closely related to ours presents the symmetric encryption scheme LPN-C [13]. The secret key in their scheme is a random matrix M. It uses an error correcting code $\mathcal{C}$ with generator matrix G to encrypt a plaintext vector d: the ciphertext is (v, y) for a random vector v and $y := M^T v + e + G \cdot d$, where e is a noise vector whose bits are sampled from a Bernoulli distribution. In order to decrypt (v, y), $y + M^T v = e + G \cdot d$ is computed and then d is recovered by running the decoding algorithm of $\mathcal{C}$.

Clearly, there are similarities between LPN-C and Firekite: both schemes use a random matrix M as the secret key and the computation of a ciphertext includes a term of the form $M^T v + e$. However, the two encryption schemes are quite different in several respects. First of all, LPN-C uses an error-correcting code $\mathcal{C}$, which is not required for Firekite. Another differentiating factor is the distribution of the bits in the noise vectors. It is a binomial distribution in the case of LPN-C, whereas the distribution for Firekite has a lower variance, and the hamming weight of the noise vector is upper bounded by k. Since the error-correcting code can only successfully recover the plaintext if the number of noise bits does not exceed a given threshold, it is possible that decryption fails with a certain (small) probability. Alternatively, the authors suggest to truncate the binomial distribution to ensure that the Hamming weight of noise vectors does not exceed the correction capacity of $\mathcal{C}$. However, this modification can have a negative impact on the security of the scheme. By contrast, there are no decryption failures for Firekite. What is more, unlike Firekite, LPN-C must generate fresh random numbers for each messages.

While the work introducing LPN-C does not contain any measurement results, it is evident from the specification that LPN-C is unlikely to reach the same level of performance as Firekite for recommended parameters. The lower performance is partly due to the use of an error-correcting code, which may incur a substantial overhead. More importantly, LPN-C requires a much larger m, e.g., $m = 512$ for a security level of 80, because the vector v is made public. According to current knowledge, state-of-the-art attacks can exploit this additional information to recover the secret key more efficiently.

7   Conclusion

We introduced a novel LPN-based synchronous stream cipher, called Firekite, that has a simple structure and is parallelizable, particularly when given hardware support. This is the first work that presents performance numbers of any

LPN-based scheme by benchmarking both a software and a hardware implementation. Moreover, it is the first LPN-based scheme that achieves decent throughput numbers on dedicated hardware, albeit at the cost of higher resource usage than state-of-the-art symmetric encryption schemes.

We hope that these results stimulate interest and trigger more research in this direction in order to further explore the potential of practical encryption based on LPN, which may lead to the development of viable alternatives to commonly used symmetric encryption schemes.

References

1. Alekhnovich, M.: More on average case vs approximation complexity. In: Proceedings 44th Symposium on Foundations of Computer Science (FOCS), pp. 298–307 (2003)
2. Applebaum, B., Cash, D., Peikert, C., Sahai, A.: Fast cryptographic primitives and circular-secure encryption based on hard learning problems. In: Halevi, S. (ed.) CRYPTO 2009. LNCS, vol. 5677, pp. 595–618. Springer, Heidelberg (2009). https://doi.org/10.1007/978-3-642-03356-8_35
3. Blum, A., Furst, M., Kearns, M., Lipton, R.J.: Cryptographic primitives based on hard learning problems. In: Stinson, D.R. (ed.) CRYPTO 1993. LNCS, vol. 773, pp. 278–291. Springer, Heidelberg (1994). https://doi.org/10.1007/3-540-48329-2_24
4. Blum, A., Kalai, A., Wasserman, H.: Noise-tolerant learning, the parity problem, and the statistical query model. In: Proceedings 32nd Annual ACM Symposium on Theory of Computing (STOC), pp. 435–440 (2000)
5. Bogos, S., Vaudenay, S.: Optimization of LPN solving algorithms. In: Proceedings 22nd International Conference on the Theory and Application of Cryptology and Information Security (ASIACRYPT), pp. 703–728 (2016)
6. Bringer, J., Chabanne, H., Dottax, E.: HB^{++}: a lightweight authentication protocol secure against some attacks. In: Proceedings 2nd International Workshop on Security, Privacy and Trust in Pervasive and Ubiquitous Computing (SecPerU), pp. 28–33 (2006)
7. Cash, D., Kiltz, E., Tessaro, S.: Two-round man-in-the-middle security from LPN. In: Kushilevitz, E., Malkin, T. (eds.) TCC 2016. LNCS, vol. 9562, pp. 225–248. Springer, Heidelberg (2016). https://doi.org/10.1007/978-3-662-49096-9_10
8. Daemen, J., Rijmen, V.: The Design of Rijndael: AES - The Advanced Encryption Standard. Springer, Heidelberg (2013). https://doi.org/10.1007/978-3-662-04722-4
9. Damgård, I., Park, S.: Is Public-Key Encryption Based on LPN Practical? IACR Cryptology ePrint Archive (2012)
10. Döttling, N.: Low noise LPN: KDM secure public key encryption and sample amplification. In: Katz, J. (ed.) PKC 2015. LNCS, vol. 9020, pp. 604–626. Springer, Heidelberg (2015). https://doi.org/10.1007/978-3-662-46447-2_27
11. Döttling, N., Müller-Quade, J., Nascimento, A.C.A.: IND-CCA secure cryptography based on a variant of the LPN problem. In: Wang, X., Sako, K. (eds.) ASIACRYPT 2012. LNCS, vol. 7658, pp. 485–503. Springer, Heidelberg (2012). https://doi.org/10.1007/978-3-642-34961-4_30
12. Duc, A., Vaudenay, S.: HELEN: a public-key cryptosystem based on the LPN and the decisional minimal distance problems. In: Youssef, A., Nitaj, A., Hassanien, A.E. (eds.) AFRICACRYPT 2013. LNCS, vol. 7918, pp. 107–126. Springer, Heidelberg (2013). https://doi.org/10.1007/978-3-642-38553-7_6

13. Gilbert, H., Robshaw, M.J.B., Seurin, Y.: How to encrypt with the LPN problem. In: Aceto, L., Damgård, I., Goldberg, L.A., Halldórsson, M.M., Ingólfsdóttir, A., Walukiewicz, I. (eds.) ICALP 2008. LNCS, vol. 5126, pp. 679–690. Springer, Heidelberg (2008). https://doi.org/10.1007/978-3-540-70583-3_55

14. Gilbert, H., Robshaw, M.J.B., Seurin, Y.: HB#: increasing the security and efficiency of HB+. In: Smart, N. (ed.) EUROCRYPT 2008. LNCS, vol. 4965, pp. 361–378. Springer, Heidelberg (2008). https://doi.org/10.1007/978-3-540-78967-3_21

15. Goldreich, O.: Foundations of Cryptography: Volume 1. Basic Tools. Cambridge University Press, Cambridge (2007)

16. Guo, Q., Johansson, T., Löndahl, C.: Solving LPN using covering codes. In: Sarkar, P., Iwata, T. (eds.) ASIACRYPT 2014. LNCS, vol. 8873, pp. 1–20. Springer, Heidelberg (2014). https://doi.org/10.1007/978-3-662-45611-8_1

17. Heninger, N., Durumeric, Z., Wustrow, E., Halderman, J.A.: Mining Your Ps and Qs: detection of Widespread Weak Keys in Network Devices. In: Proceedings 21st USENIX Security Symposium, p. 35 (2012)

18. Heyse, S., Kiltz, E., Lyubashevsky, V., Paar, C., Pietrzak, K.: Lapin: an efficient authentication protocol based on ring-LPN. In: Canteaut, A. (ed.) FSE 2012. LNCS, vol. 7549, pp. 346–365. Springer, Heidelberg (2012). https://doi.org/10.1007/978-3-642-34047-5_20

19. Hopper, N.J., Blum, M.: Secure human identification protocols. In: Boyd, C. (ed.) ASIACRYPT 2001. LNCS, vol. 2248, pp. 52–66. Springer, Heidelberg (2001). https://doi.org/10.1007/3-540-45682-1_4

20. Impagliazzo, R., Levin, L.A.: No better ways to generate hard NP instances than picking uniformly at random. In: Proceedings 31st Annual Symposium on Foundations of Computer Science (FOCS), pp. 812–821 (1990)

21. Juels, A., Weis, S.A.: Authenticating pervasive devices with human protocols. In: Shoup, V. (ed.) CRYPTO 2005. LNCS, vol. 3621, pp. 293–308. Springer, Heidelberg (2005). https://doi.org/10.1007/11535218_18

22. Katz, J., Shin, J.S., Smith, A.: Parallel and concurrent security of the HB and HB+ protocols. J. Cryptol. 23(3), 402–421 (2010)

23. Kiltz, E., Masny, D., Pietrzak, K.: Simple chosen-ciphertext security from low-noise LPN. In: Krawczyk, H. (ed.) PKC 2014. LNCS, vol. 8383, pp. 1–18. Springer, Heidelberg (2014). https://doi.org/10.1007/978-3-642-54631-0_1

24. Kiltz, E., Pietrzak, K., Cash, D., Jain, A., Venturi, D.: Efficient authentication from hard learning problems. In: Paterson, K.G. (ed.) EUROCRYPT 2011. LNCS, vol. 6632, pp. 7–26. Springer, Heidelberg (2011). https://doi.org/10.1007/978-3-642-20465-4_3

25. Levieil, É., Fouque, P.-A.: An improved LPN algorithm. In: De Prisco, R., Yung, M. (eds.) SCN 2006. LNCS, vol. 4116, pp. 348–359. Springer, Heidelberg (2006). https://doi.org/10.1007/11832072_24

26. Lyubashevsky, V.: The parity problem in the presence of noise, decoding random linear codes, and the subset sum problem. In: Chekuri, C., Jansen, K., Rolim, J.D.P., Trevisan, L. (eds.) APPROX/RANDOM -2005. LNCS, vol. 3624, pp. 378–389. Springer, Heidelberg (2005). https://doi.org/10.1007/11538462_32

27. Lyubashevsky, V., Masny, D.: Man-in-the-middle secure authentication schemes from LPN and weak PRFs. In: Canetti, R., Garay, J.A. (eds.) CRYPTO 2013. LNCS, vol. 8043, pp. 308–325. Springer, Heidelberg (2013). https://doi.org/10.1007/978-3-642-40084-1_18

28. Shor, P.W.: Polynomial-time algorithms for prime factorization and discrete logarithms on a quantum computer. SIAM J. Comput. 26(5), 1484–1509 (1997)

29. Trevisan, L.: Extractors and pseudorandom generators. J. ACM **48**(4), 860–879 (2001)
30. Yu, Yu., Steinberger, J.: Pseudorandom functions in almost constant depth from low-noise LPN. In: Fischlin, M., Coron, J.-S. (eds.) EUROCRYPT 2016. LNCS, vol. 9666, pp. 154–183. Springer, Heidelberg (2016). https://doi.org/10.1007/978-3-662-49896-5_6
31. Yu, Y., Zhang, J.: Cryptography with auxiliary input and trapdoor from constant-noise LPN. In: Robshaw, M., Katz, J. (eds.) CRYPTO 2016. LNCS, vol. 9814, pp. 214–243. Springer, Heidelberg (2016). https://doi.org/10.1007/978-3-662-53018-4_9
32. Zhang, B., Jiao, L., Wang, M.: Faster algorithms for solving LPN. In: Fischlin, M., Coron, J.-S. (eds.) EUROCRYPT 2016. LNCS, vol. 9665, pp. 168–195. Springer, Heidelberg (2016). https://doi.org/10.1007/978-3-662-49890-3_7

System Security

A Differentially Private Hybrid Approach to Traffic Monitoring

Rogério V. M. Rocha[1](✉)[iD], Pedro P. Libório[1][iD], Harsh Kupwade Patil[2][iD], and Diego F. Aranha[1,3][iD]

[1] Institute of Computing, University of Campinas, Campinas, Brazil
`rogerio.rocha@ic.unicamp.br`, `liborio@lrc.ic.unicamp.br`
[2] LG Electronics, Santa Clara, USA
`harsh.patil@lge.com`
[3] Department of Computer Science, Aarhus University, Aarhus, Denmark
`dfaranha@cs.au.dk`

Abstract. In recent years, privacy research has been gaining ground in vehicular communication technologies. Collecting data from connected vehicles presents a range of opportunities for industry and government to perform data analytics. Although many researchers have explored some privacy solutions for vehicular communications, the conditions to deploy them are still maturing, especially when it comes to privacy for sensitive data aggregation analysis. In this work, we propose a hybrid solution combining the original differential privacy framework with an instance-based additive noise technique. The results show that for typical instances we obtain a significant reduction in outliers. As far as we know, our paper is the first detailed experimental evaluation of differentially private techniques applied to traffic monitoring. The validation of the proposed solution was performed through extensive simulations in typical traffic scenarios using real data.

Keywords: Differential privacy · Smooth sensitivity · Hybrid approach · Intelligent Transportation Systems (ITS)

1 Introduction

Mobility is a major concern in any city, and deploying Intelligent Transportation Systems (ITS) can make cities more efficient by minimizing traffic problems [1]. The adoption of ITS is widely accepted in many countries today. Because of its high potential, ITS has become a multidisciplinary field of connective work and therefore many organizations around the world have developed solutions to provide ITS applications to meet growing demand [2].

This study was financed in part by the Coordenação de Aperfeiçoamento de Pessoal de Nível Superior - Brasil (CAPES) - Finance Code 001, Conselho Nacional de Desenvolvimento Científico e Tecnológico (CNPq) and LG Electronics via Unicamp Development Foundation (FUNCAMP) Agreement 5296.

© The Author(s) 2021
K. Sako and N. O. Tippenhauer (Eds.): ACNS 2021, LNCS 12727, pp. 233–256, 2021.
https://doi.org/10.1007/978-3-030-78375-4_10

Data collection in connected vehicles presents numerous opportunities through aggregated data analysis for companies, industries, and governments. Among these opportunities, one can highlight investigation of the driver behavior, which helps vehicle manufacturers and insurers to improve and develop new services. Another interesting application is the monitoring of traffic conditions which allows transport departments to manage mobility and improve services [5].

Regarding traffic management, it is increasingly important to understand the behavior of urban mobility. It includes presenting the travel profile of drivers for future mobility planning and testing in new scenarios. A Traffic Data Center (TDC) is a vital component in the mobility management. All collected data is processed and analyzed by a TDC in order to manage traffic in real-time or simply store it for additional operations [4]. A vehicle periodically sends *beacons* collected by sensors to its neighbors, including base stations, which are then sent directly to a TDC. The vehicle sensors collect data such as identification, timestamp, position, speed (direction), acceleration, among other about 7700 signals, some of which are treated as sensitive [4,5].

It is undeniable that analyzing this volume of data brings substantial social benefits, but also concerns about data breaches and leakage. Disclosure of this data poses a serious threat to the privacy of contributors, and creates a liability for industry and governments. In Europe, the General Data Protection Regulation (GDPR) imposes stricter rules on the storage and management of personally identifiable information, with non-compliance resulting in severe penalties [5].

To put it in context, it is worth mentioning that any type of monitoring can lead to a privacy breach through tracking. The main privacy concerns for drivers are disclosure, vehicle tracking and commercial use of personal data [5]. The speed, object of study in this paper, is a vector quantity which has a module (numerical value) and direction. In this way, the speed is considered as confidential data, as it is possible to deduce the driver's absolute value on a specific time and, more importantly, what is the driver's direction at that time and place.

In recent years, a strong mathematical definition of privacy in the context of statistical databases became increasingly accepted as a standard privacy notion. The original differential privacy framework was introduced by Dwork et al. in 2006 [3]. Since then, there was a lot of progress, including the sample and aggregate framework developed by Nissim et al. [9]. Based on this framework, our main research question is *how to preserve the privacy of drivers while providing accurate aggregated information to a TDC, such as the average speed?*

This paper addresses the problem of calculating the average speed in a road segment under a differentially private solution while maintaining the utility of aggregated data. Our main contributions are the following:

- We propose a hybrid approach exploring the characteristics of the original differential privacy [3] and the sample and aggregate frameworks [9].
- We present a formal proof showing that the proposed approach satisfies the differential privacy definition.
- We validate the hybrid approach through extensive empirical evaluation in some typical traffic scenarios, focusing on accuracy of the average speed.

1.1 Related Work

In recent years, researchers have explored numerous solutions to the problem of preserving privacy in the context of ITS. Pseudonym change strategies are the main local privacy-preserving solutions found in the literature, where contributors do not trust service providers. However, due to the precise space-time information contained in beacons, these strategies are still vulnerable to tracing, even supposedly anonymous [6]. In addition, due to safety applications, which require availability and accurate information, the design of alternative local privacy-preserving solutions is very restricted.

Regardless of local privacy-preserving solutions, our purpose is to focus on centralized solutions for data aggregation analysis, where the database is held by a trusted party. In this direction, the main contribution is due to Kargl et al. [4] in 2013, which investigated how differential privacy can be applied to ITS. Specifically, they propose an architecture that enables differential privacy when using beacons for some ITS applications and services. This architecture integrates a differentially private module through an extension of the PRECIOSA PeRA policy enforcement framework. To illustrate the functioning of the proposed module and how it addresses the accuracy and privacy requirements, Kargl et al. designed a simple algorithm for average speed calculation, based on the original framework of differential privacy.

A comprehensive survey on introduction of differential privacy in the automotive domain is presented by Nelson and Olovsson [5], where they claim that one of the main problems to introduce differential privacy in the automotive domain is maintaining high utility for the analyses. Another important work in this direction is due to Hassan et al. [7]. They survey differential privacy techniques and their application to cyber-physical systems, including ITS, as basis for the development of modern differential privacy techniques to address various problems and data privacy scenarios. Both works claim that the most prominent study relating differential privacy and vehicular domain is due to Kargl et al. [4].

Regarding data, most of collected signals by vehicle sensors are numeric and, specially in traffic monitoring, the aggregation functions sum, count and average capture many of calculations utilized in ITS applications [4]. These aggregation functions tend to have high distortion for small databases, mainly, for the sum and average due to variable global sensitivity that may not be diluted at a small database [5]. ITS applications typically have defined accuracy standards for reported values. For example, U.S. standardization determines that the distortion (error) presented at the reported average speed should be up to 20%, depending on the application [4]. It represents an upper bound on the noise introduced by a differentially private mechanism.

Given these surveys, our aim is to explore the peculiarities of the addressed problem and associate them to the characteristics of differentially private techniques, in order to obtain more accurate results while maintaining the same level of privacy. Although in most situations the instances are misbehaved, our hypothesis is that well-behaved instances are produced in some situations. This is due to the fact that the addressed problem is dynamic. The main difference compared to [4] is that while they focus on a differentially private architecture applied to ITS, this article aims to deepen in this architecture by proposing a robust and effective differentially private algorithm to calculate the average speed in a realistic scenario that meets privacy and accuracy requirements.

The remainder of this paper is organized as follows. In Sect. 2, we present the theoretical foundations related to the differential privacy required to build our approach. Section 3 describes the proposed solution. After that, the experimental evaluation is presented in Sect. 4. Finally, we conclude and give direction to future work in Sect. 5.

2   Background

Differential privacy emerged from the problem of performing statistical studies on a population while maintaining the privacy of its individuals. The definition models the risk of disclosing data from any individual belonging to a database by performing statistical analyses on it.

Definition 1. DIFFERENTIAL PRIVACY [3]. *A randomized algorithm A taking inputs from the domain D^n gives (ϵ, δ)-differential-private analysis if for all data sets $D_1, D_2 \in D^n$ differing on at most one element, and all $U \subseteq Range(A)$, denoting the set of all possible outputs of A,*

$$\left| ln \left\{ \frac{Pr[A(D_1) \in U] - \delta}{Pr[A(D_2) \in U]} \right\} \right| \leq \epsilon \tag{1}$$

where the probability space is over the coin flips of the mechanism A and $\frac{p}{0}$ is defined as 1 for all $p \in \mathbb{R}$.

The parameters ϵ and δ, known respectively as *privacy loss parameter* and *relaxation parameter*, control the level of privacy and, consequently, the level of utility in the model. While ϵ determines the level of indistinguishability between the two databases, δ allows negligible leakage of information from individuals under analysis.

The protection of the individual's privacy in a database is done by adding carefully-crafted noise to the individual contribution or the aggregated data. In this way, it is sufficient to mask the maximum possible contribution (upper bound) in the database, which is the maximum difference between the analyses performed over two databases differing only in one element. This difference is known as global sensitivity, denoted by Δ_f.

One of the main models of computation is the centralized model (also known as output perturbation). In this model, there is a trusted party that has access to the raw individuals' data and uses it to release noisy aggregate analyses. The Laplace and exponential [8,11] mechanisms are two of the main primitives in the differential privacy framework used to perturb the output analysis. The first, is the most widely used mechanism and it is based on sampling continuous random variables from Laplace distribution. In order to sample a random variable, one should calibrate the Laplace distribution by centering the location parameter at either zero or the aggregated value and setting the scale parameter as the ratio between Δ_f and ϵ.

On the other hand, the exponential mechanism is used to handle both numerical and categorical analysis [8,16]. This mechanism outputs an element $o \in O$ with probability $\propto e^{\left(\frac{\epsilon q(D,o)}{2\Delta_q}\right)}$, where O is a set of all possible outputs and Δ_q is the sensitivity of the quality function.

McSherry and Talwar [16] observed that the Laplace mechanism can be viewed as a special case of the exponential mechanism, by using the quality function as $q(D,o) = -|f(D) - o|$, which provides $\Delta_q = \Delta_f$. In this way, we can use the continuous exponential distribution and it is sufficient to assume $q(D,o) = -[f(D) - o]$, whereas the output o can be set as zero, which gives the true value of the analysis. Li et al. [8] proves that if a quality function is monotonic we can omit the constant two in the exponential mechanism.

Regarding the composability, the composition theorems are essential to design differentially private solutions. It allows to combine multiple mechanisms or perform multiple analyses over the same database by controlling the privacy and relaxation parameters, that is, the privacy budget. The sequential and parallel composition theorems are the main ones present in the literature.

In sequential composition, the parameters will be accumulated according to the number of performed analyses. On the other hand, in parallel composition, the resulting differentially private analysis will take into account only the maximum values of the parameters.

In the original differential privacy framework [3], the noise magnitude depends on the global sensitivity (Δ_f) but not on the instance D. For many functions, such as the median, this framework yields high noise compromising the utility of the analysis. The smooth sensitivity framework [9] allows to add significantly less noise than calibration with global sensitivity.

The smooth sensitivity is the smallest upper bound on the local sensitivity (LS), which is a local measure of sensitivity, and takes into account only the two instances involved in the analysis [9]. Nissim et al. proved that adding noise proportional to this upper bound is safe.

Definition 2. SMOOTH SENSITIVITY [9]. *For $\beta > 0$, the β-smooth sensitivity of f is:*

$$S^*_{f,\beta}(D_1) = \max_{k=0,\ldots,n} e^{-k\beta} \left(\max_{D_2:d(D_1,D_2)=k} LS_f(D_2) \right). \tag{2}$$

The following definition states that if a probability distribution that does not change too much under translation and dilation it can be used to add noise proportional to $S^*_{f,\beta}$.

Definition 3. ADMISSIBLE NOISE DISTRIBUTION [9]. *A probability distribution $h \in \mathbb{R}$ is (α, β)-admissible for $\alpha(\epsilon, \delta)$ and $\beta(\epsilon, \delta)$ if it satisfies the following inequalities:*

$$\left| ln \left[\frac{Pr_{X \sim h}(X \in U) - \frac{\delta}{2}}{Pr_{X \sim h}(X \in U + \Delta)} \right] \right| \leq \epsilon/2 \tag{3}$$

$$\left| ln \left[\frac{Pr_{X \sim h}(X \in U) - \frac{\delta}{2}}{Pr_{X \sim h}(X \in U \cdot e^{\lambda})} \right] \right| \leq \epsilon/2 \qquad (4)$$

for all $\|\Delta\| \leq \alpha$, $|\lambda| \leq \beta$ and all subsets $U \subseteq \mathbb{R}$.

The following lemma arises from Definitions 2 and 3.

Lemma 1. [9]. *The Laplace distribution on $\mathbb{R}$ with scale parameter b is (α, β)-admissible with $\alpha = b\frac{\epsilon}{2}$ and $\beta = \frac{\epsilon}{2ln(1/\delta)}$.*

Proof. The proof can be found in the Appendix A.   □

Claim. [9]. In order to get an (ϵ, δ)-differentially-private algorithm, one can add noise proportional to $\frac{S^*_{f,\beta}(D)}{\alpha}$.

Let a database $D = \{d_1, ..., d_n\}$ in non-decreasing order and $f_{med} = median(D)$ where $d_i \in \mathbb{R}$, with $d_i = 0$ for $i \leq 0$ and $d_i = \Delta_f$ for $i > n$. Nissim et al. [9] proved that the β-smooth sensitivity of *Median* function is

$$S^*_{f,\beta}(D) = \max_{k=0,...,n} \left[e^{-k\beta} \max_{t=0,...,k+1} (d_{m+t} - d_{m+t-k-1}) \right], \qquad (5)$$

where m is the rank of median element and $m = \frac{n+1}{2}$ for odd n. It can be computed in time $O(n^2)$.

The intuition behind the sample and aggregate framework [9] is to replace an aggregate function f by f^*, a smoothed and efficient version of it. This framework evaluates f over random partitions of the original database and releases f^* over the results by calibrating the noise magnitude with smooth sensitivity.

In this work, we deal with an unbounded stream of events as a database. An event may be an interaction between a particular person and an arbitrary term [10]. In this way, we focus on event-level privacy where the protection is centered on a single reported beacon. As the data set is dynamic, the attribute will change for each interaction making an event unique where its ID (identification) is the combination of timestamp and user ID.

3   Hybrid Approach

In this section, we describe the proposed approach to calculate the average speed on a road segment satisfying the definition of differential privacy. This approach combines the original differential privacy framework (ODP) [3] to the sample and aggregate framework (SAA) [9]. The adoption of the latter was inspired by the hypothesis that most speed values are close to the average when measured in a short time interval and road segment yielding some well-behaved instances. The hybrid approach is justified by the dynamism of the application, which yields misbehaved instances leading to very high sensitivity in the SAA framework.

The noise magnitude from the original and smooth sensitivity techniques are not related. While the differences among the instance and its neighbors are taken into account to get the noise magnitude in the smooth sensitivity, the original technique considers only the global sensitivity without examining the instance itself. The core of our contribution is to propose a formulation relating these techniques in order to obtain the lowest noise magnitude, which results in more accurate analyses.

From now on, we will refer to the collected set of beacons as a prefix, a finite length chain from an unbounded stream of beacons. In our approach, we calculate the noisy prefix size by using the exponential mechanism, since we are not interested in negative values. To calculate the average speed, we use the Laplace mechanism in both ODP and SAA frameworks.

A trivial procedure to calculate the differentially private average function using the ODP framework is to add a random variable, sampled from the Laplace distribution, to the true sum function, then divide it by the set size N to obtain the average. In this case, the scale parameter is set as $\frac{\Delta_f}{\epsilon}$. The following algorithmic construction illustrates this procedure.

Algorithm 1: Trivial-ODP $(prefix, N, \Delta_f, \epsilon)$

---

1 # Calculate the scale of Laplace distribution
2 $b \leftarrow \frac{\Delta_f}{\epsilon}$
3 # Calculate sum from prefix
4 $sum \leftarrow 0$
5 for $e \in prefix$ do
6 $\quad | \quad sum \leftarrow sum + e_{speed}$
7 end
8 # Sample random variable from Laplace distribution
9 $Y_s \leftarrow Laplace(b)$
10 # Calculate noisy sum
11 $sum_{noisy} \leftarrow sum + Y_s$
12 # Calculate the noisy average speed
13 $avg_{noisy} \leftarrow \frac{sum_{noisy}}{N}$
14
15 return avg_{noisy}, b

On the other hand, using the SAA framework, we can divide the prefix into random partitions and evaluate the average function over each partition. After this process, we must sort the resulting data set where we will select the central element (median) as the average speed. The main idea is to reduce the impact of anomalies present in the prefix when calculating the aggregation. It allow us to introduce less but significant noise to protect the maximum element in well-behaved instances. This procedure is presented in more details in Algorithm 2.

The Hybrid approach is based in the following lemma and theorem.

Lemma 2. *Let a prefix $P = \{x_1, x_2, ..., x_{n-1}, x_n\}$ be a set of points over $\mathbb{R}$, such that $x_i \in [0, \Delta_f]$ for all i. Sampling a random variable from the Laplace*

Algorithm 2: SAA $(prefix, N, M, \Delta_f, \epsilon, \delta)$

1 # Partition prefix into M random samples of size N/M
2 $count \leftarrow 0$
3 $average_{speeds} \leftarrow \emptyset$
4 **while** $count < M$ **do**
5   # Extract the partition using a uniformly random sample
6     $partition \leftarrow RandomSample(prefix, N/M)$
7   # Calculate average speed from partition adding to a list
8     $avg \leftarrow \frac{Sum(partition)}{N/M}$
9     $average_{speeds} \leftarrow Append(avg)$
10     $count \leftarrow count + 1$
11 **end**
12 # Sort average speeds set in non-decreasing order
13 $sorted_{average_{speeds}} \leftarrow Sort(average_{speeds})$
14 # Calculate the scale of Laplace distribution
15 $b \leftarrow \frac{\Delta_f}{\epsilon}$
16 # Calculate alpha and beta parameters
17 $\alpha \leftarrow b\frac{\epsilon}{2}; \beta \leftarrow \frac{\epsilon}{2ln(1/\delta)}$
18 # Calculate smooth sensitivity of median function by Eq. (5)
19 $smooth_{sensitivity_{median}} \leftarrow S^*_{f_{median},\beta}(sorted_{average_{speeds}}, M, \Delta_f)$
20 # Get random variable from Laplace distribution
21 $Y_m \leftarrow Laplace\left(\frac{smooth_{sensitivity_{median}}}{\alpha}\right)$
22 # Calculate noisy average speed
23 $avg_{noisy} \leftarrow Median(sorted_{average_{speeds}}) + Y_m$
24
25 **return** $avg_{noisy}, \frac{smooth_{sensitivity_{median}}}{\alpha}$

---

distribution with scale parameter set as $\frac{\Delta_f/N}{\epsilon}$ and add it to the true average function is equivalent to Algorithm 1, both performed over P.

Proof. Consider the cumulative distribution function of the Laplace distribution with mean $(\mu = 0)$ [17]. Suppose S is the sum of P and $r_s = \lambda \cdot S$ represents a proportion of S. The probability of sampling any value greater than r_s is given by

$$p_s(X > r_s) = \frac{1}{2}e^{-\frac{r_s}{b_s}} \qquad (6)$$

where $b_s = \frac{\Delta_f}{\epsilon}$.

Now, suppose A is the average of P and $r_a = \lambda \cdot A$ represents a proportion of A. The probability of sampling any value greater than r_a is given by

$$p_a(X > r_a) = \frac{1}{2}e^{-\frac{r_a}{b_a}} \qquad (7)$$

In order to conclude the proof, we need to determine b_a. So, it is a fact that $S = A \cdot N$. Thus, we have $r_s = \lambda \cdot A \cdot N$, which results in $r_s = r_a \cdot N$.

By substituting it in Eq. (6) and equaling to Eq. (7), i.e., $p_s = p_a$, we obtain $b_a = \frac{\Delta_f/N}{\epsilon}$.   □

Based on Lemma 2, the following algorithmic construction is an alternative to Algorithm 1.

Algorithm 3: ODP $(prefix, N, \Delta_f, \epsilon)$

---

1 # Calculate the scale of Laplace distribution
2 $b \leftarrow \frac{\Delta_f/N}{\epsilon}$
3 # Calculate sum from prefix
4 $sum \leftarrow 0$
5 **for** $e \in prefix$ **do**
6 | $sum \leftarrow sum + e_{speed}$
7 **end**
8 # Calculate true average
9 $avg \leftarrow \frac{sum}{N}$
10 # Sample random variable from Laplace distribution
11 $Y_s \leftarrow Laplace(b)$
12 # Calculate the noisy average speed
13 $avg_{noisy} \leftarrow avg + Y_s$
14
15 **return** avg_{noisy}, b

Theorem 1. *Let a prefix $P = \{x_1, x_2, ..., x_{n-1}, x_n\}$ be a set of points over $\mathbb{R}$, such that $x_i \in [0, \Delta_f]$ for all i. Then, Algorithm 2 provides more accurate results than Algorithm 3, if $S^*_{f_{median}, \beta}(D) < \alpha \cdot \frac{\Delta_f/N}{\epsilon}$, both performed over P.*

Proof. Let b_{SAA} and b_{ODP} be the scale parameter of the Laplace distribution in Algorithms 2 and 3, respectively. Then, we obtain

$$b_{SAA} = \frac{S^*_{f_{median}, \beta}(D)}{\alpha} \tag{8}$$

$$b_{ODP} = \frac{\Delta_f/N}{\epsilon} \tag{9}$$

Rearranging Eq. (8) and setting b_{ODP} as an upper bound on b_{SAA}, we get $S^*_{f_{median}, \beta}(D) < \alpha \cdot b_{ODP}$, which results in

$$S^*_{f_{median}, \beta}(D) < \alpha \cdot \frac{\Delta_f/N}{\epsilon}. \tag{10}$$

In order to prove this theorem, assume for the sake of contradiction that Algorithm 3 provides more accurate results than Algorithm 2, both performed over P. Then, b_{ODP} is less than b_{SAA}. By Eq. (10), it is a contradiction.

Therefore, if Eq. (10) holds, then Algorithm 2 provides more accurate results than Algorithm 3.   □

From Theorem 1 and Lemma 2, the noise magnitude of the Hybrid approach is formulated as follows:

$$b_{Hybrid} = \begin{cases} b_{SAA}, & \text{if } S^*_{f_{\text{median}},\beta}(D) < \alpha \cdot \frac{\Delta_f/N}{\epsilon} \\ b_{ODP}, & \text{otherwise.} \end{cases} \qquad (11)$$

The algorithmic construction of the Hybrid approach is presented in Algorithm 4. This algorithm calculates the average speed in a differentially private way using all beacons reported in a short time interval in a specific road segment. It gets as input a privacy budget ϵ related to each received event in the base station, the prefix size N to calculate the average speed, the number of partitions for SAA framework, the global sensitivity of the average function (speed limit in the road segment), the privacy loss parameters for count and average functions, and the relaxation parameter for average function (non-zero).

The algorithm starts by checking the privacy budget of the privacy loss and relaxation parameters. After that, it initializes an empty list called *beacons* used to store all beacons received through the base station. Next, the base station starts collecting data (beacons/events) adding each of them to the list. The collection control is made by a differentially private *Count* function which uses the exponential mechanism, Algorithm 5. The event collection is performed by the *Receive Beacon* function. Each beacon includes the vehicle speed (m/s) between 0 and Δ_f. It is worth mentioning that, in a realistic scenario, some values can be above the speed limit Δ_f but these values are intentionally not protected in proportion to their magnitude, since in our scenario they are reckless drivers. After collecting enough data to compose the prefix, the algorithm selects the most recent beacons to calculate the average speed. The next step is to calculate the noisy average speed through the two frameworks, *ODP* and *SAA*. Then, we choose the average noisy speed calculated with the lowest noise magnitude. Finally, the privacy loss and relaxation parameters are deducted from the privacy budget for each event in the prefix.

3.1   Security Analysis

A Threat Model. Differential privacy was designed considering a very strong adversary, with an infinite computational power, who has the knowledge of the entire data set, except a single element. It is considered that the adversary cannot glean any additional information about this element beyond what it known before interacting with the privacy mechanism. This assumption is not unrealistic since differential privacy is supposed to provide privacy given adversaries with arbitrary background knowledge. Then, the adversary tries to obtain additional information about this element using the knowledge of the entire data set except it and the auxiliary information about it before the data set analysis.

In our scenario, for simplicity, consider that there are two service providers (carriers A and B) that provide aggregate information to customers (drivers), such as average speed on a road segment. Also, we consider that all drivers on a road segment are customers of both carriers except by a single customer e who is a customer of only one of them, B, for example. As we are dealing with a strong adversary, it is supposed that they have knowledge about all others customers except by e. That is, the speed of all drivers which are customers of carrier A. Then, from the entire data set (the selected prefix by carrier A) which has length N, the adversary can obtain the sum of all speeds and calculate the difference between this sum and the result of the product between the average speed from B, which includes the driver es speed, multiplied by $N + 1$. This procedure gives the correct contribution of e.

Algorithm 4: Hybrid $(\epsilon,\ \delta,\ N,\ M,\ \Delta_f,\ \epsilon_c,\ \epsilon_a,\ \delta_a)$

```
1  if ϵc + ϵa ≤ ϵ and δa ≤ δ then
2  |   # Initialize beacon list
3  |   beacons ← ∅
4  |   # Receive first event and add it to the beacon list
5  |   e ← ReceiveBeacon()
6  |   beacons ← Append(e)
7  |   # Receive the remaining events and add them to the beacon list
8  |   while Count(beacons, ϵc) < N do
9  |   |   e ← ReceiveBeacon()
10 |   |   beacons ← Append(e)
11 |   end
12 |   # Select the N more recent events
13 |   prefix ← SelectLatestBeacons(beacons, N)
14 |   # Calculate the noisy average speed through ODP and SAA
15 |   avgODP, bODP ← ODP(prefix, N, Δf, ϵa)
16 |   avgSAA, bSAA ← SAA(prefix, N, M, Δf, ϵa, δa)
17 |   # Choosing the lowest noise magnitude
18 |   if bSAA < bODP then
19 |   |   avgnoisy ← avgSAA
20 |   end
21 |   else
22 |   |   avgnoisy ← avgODP
23 |   end
24 |   # Deduce count and average privacy loss parameter from each event
   |   privacy budget in prefix
25 |   for e ∈ prefix do
26 |   |   ϵ ← ϵ − ϵc − ϵa
27 |   |   δ ← δ − δa
28 |   end
29 |
30 |   return avgnoisy
31 end
32 else
33 |   write "Privacy budget exceeded!"
34 end
```

Algorithm 5: Count (*beacons*, ϵ)

1 # Calculate the scale of Exponential distribution
2 $\lambda \leftarrow \epsilon$
3 # Calculate count from beacon list
4 $count \leftarrow 0$
5 for $e \in prefix$ do
6 | $count \leftarrow count + 1$
7 end
8 # Get random variable from exponential distribution
9 $Y_c \leftarrow Exponential(\lambda)$
10 # Calculate noisy count
11 $count_{noisy} \leftarrow count - Y_c$
12
13 return $count_{noisy}$

Privacy Analysis. The security of the Hybrid approach is supported by the following lemmas and theorem. In Lemma 3, we prove that the randomized *Count* function, presented in Algorithm 5, is differentially private. After that, Lemma 4 shows that Algorithm 3 satisfies differential privacy. Next, we prove through Lemma 5 by parallel composition that Algorithm 2 is differentially private. Finally, in Theorem 2, we prove that the Hybrid approach presented in Algorithm 4 satisfies differential privacy by sequential composition.

Lemma 3. *From the beacon list, let $B = \{x_1, x_2, ..., x_{n-1}, x_n\}$ be a set of points over $\mathbb{R}$ such that $x_i \in [0, \Delta_f]$ for all i and $|B|$ be the length of the beacon list. Then, Algorithm 5 satisfies $(\epsilon, 0)$-differential privacy.*

Proof. Assume that, without loss of generality, A represents Algorithm 5. Let B_1 and B_2 be two neighboring beacon lists differing at most one event, i.e., $||B_1| - |B_2|| = 1$. From Eq. (1) in the differential privacy definition, we must evaluate two cases: when the ratio is greater than 1 and less or equal to 1. Since the quality of the *Count* function is monotonic [11], we get:

– When $\frac{Pr[A(B_1) \in U]}{Pr[A(B_2) \in U]} \geq 1$, we have

$$\frac{Pr[A(B_1) \in U]}{Pr[A(B_2) \in U]} = \frac{\epsilon \int_a^b e^{-\epsilon x} dx}{\epsilon \int_a^b e^{-\epsilon(x+1)} dx} = \frac{\frac{e^{-(\epsilon a)} - e^{-(\epsilon b)}}{\epsilon}}{\frac{e^{-\epsilon}[e^{-(\epsilon a)} - e^{-(\epsilon b)}]}{\epsilon}} \leq e^\epsilon. \quad (12)$$

– When $\frac{Pr[A(B_1) \in U]}{Pr[A(B_2) \in U]} < 1$, we have by symmetry that the ratio is $\geq e^{-\epsilon}$.

□

Lemma 4. *Let P be a prefix from a beacon list $B = \{x_1, ..., x_n\}$ such that $N = |P| \leq |B|$ and $x_i \in [0, \Delta_f]$ for all i. Then, Algorithm 3 satisfies $(\epsilon, 0)$-differential privacy.*

Proof. Assume now, without loss of generality, that A represents Algorithm 3. Let P_1 and P_2 be two neighboring prefixes differing at most one event, $|A(P_1) - A(P_2)| = \Delta_f/N$. From the definition of differential privacy, we obtain

- When $\frac{Pr[A(P_1) \in U]}{Pr[A(P_2) \in U]} \geq 1$, we have

$$\frac{Pr[A(P_1) \in U]}{Pr[A(P_2) \in U]} = \frac{\frac{\epsilon_s N}{2\Delta_f} \int_U e^{-\frac{\epsilon_s N |x|}{\Delta_f}} dx}{\frac{\epsilon_s N}{2\Delta_f} \int_U e^{-\frac{\epsilon_s N |x + \Delta_f/N|}{\Delta_f}} dx} = \frac{\int_a^b e^{-\frac{\epsilon_s N |x|}{\Delta_f}} dx}{\int_a^b e^{-\frac{\epsilon_s N |x + \Delta_f/N|}{\Delta_f}} dx}. \tag{13}$$

We will solve this ratio in two parts. First, considering numerator of Eq. (16), evaluating the cases when $x \geq 0$ and $x < 0$, we obtain respectively

$$\int_a^b e^{\mp \frac{\epsilon_s N x}{\Delta_f}} dx = \pm \frac{\Delta_f [e^{\mp(\epsilon_s aN)/\Delta_f} - e^{\mp(\epsilon_s bN)/\Delta_f}]}{\epsilon_s N}. \tag{14}$$

Now, considering denominator of Eq. (16), evaluating the cases when $x \geq -\Delta_f/N$ and $x < -\Delta_f/N$, we obtain respectively

$$\int_a^b e^{\mp \frac{\epsilon_s N(x + \Delta_f/N)}{\Delta_f}} dx = \pm \frac{e^{-\epsilon_s N} \Delta_f [e^{\mp(\epsilon_s aN)/\Delta_f} - e^{\mp(\epsilon_s bN)/\Delta_f}]}{\epsilon_s N}. \tag{15}$$

By replacing Eq. (14) and Eq. (15) in Eq. (16), we obtain

$$\frac{\pm \frac{\Delta_f [e^{\mp(\epsilon_s aN)/\Delta_f} - e^{\mp(\epsilon_s bN)/\Delta_f}]}{\epsilon_s N}}{\pm \frac{e^{-\epsilon_s N} \Delta_f [e^{\mp(\epsilon_s aN)/\Delta_f} - e^{\mp(\epsilon_s bN)/\Delta_f}]}{\epsilon_s N}} \leq e^{\epsilon_s}. \tag{16}$$

- When $\frac{Pr[A(P_1) \in U]}{Pr[A(P_2) \in U]} < 1$, we have by symmetry that the ratio is $\geq e^{-\epsilon_s}$.

$\square$

Lemma 5. *Let P be a prefix from a beacon list $B = \{x_1, ..., x_n\}$ such that $N = |P| \leq |B|$ and $x_i \in [0, \Delta_f]$ for all i. Then, Algorithm 2 is ϵ-differentially private with probability $1 - \delta$.*

Proof. Our construction is based on uniformly distributed samples from the prefix P. These random samples are extracted without replacement, producing M partitions of size N/M. The M partitions form a set from which we can calculate the average speed. In order to do it, we first need to sort this set of partitions in a non-decreasing order and then calculate the smooth sensitivity of *Median* function from Eq. (5). Thus, Algorithm 2 follows the sample and aggregate framework.

The proof of this lemma follows directly by combination of Definition 3, Lemma 1 and parallel composition theorem [8]. $\square$

Theorem 2. *Let P be a prefix from a beacon list $B = \{x_1, ..., x_n\}$ such that $N = |P| \leq |B|$ and $x_i \in [0, \Delta_f]$ for all i. Then, Algorithm 4 satisfies (ϵ, δ)-differential privacy.*

Proof. From Lemma 3, Lemma 4 and Lemma 5 we have that Algorithm 5, 3 and 2 are differentially private. By the sequential composition theorem [8], the combination of Algorithm 5, 3 or 2 occurs when $\epsilon_c + \epsilon_a \leq \epsilon$ and $\delta_a \leq \delta$ in Algorithm 4. Therefore, Algorithm 4 satisfies (ϵ, δ)-differential privacy.   □

4   Empirical Evaluation

In this section, we present and discuss the results obtained from the evaluation of the Hybrid approach for differentially private computation of average speed. Since the evaluation focuses on the accuracy of the proposed solution, the two fundamental parameters were fixed and calibrated as suggested in the literature [11]. In this evaluation, we set the privacy loss parameter as $ln(2) - 0.15$ for *average* function and 0.15 for *count* function. Since we have defined the prefix size in this evaluation as 55, it is sufficient to calibrate the relaxation parameter with 0.01, which allows negligible leakage information in the size of the prefix, $o(1/N)$. For the SAA approach, we partition the prefix into 11 random partitions with 5 elements each.

In order to evaluate the approach, we adopted the open source traffic mobility (SUMO) [13] and the discrete event-based (OMNeT++) [15] simulators. In addition, as a interface of the two simulators, we use the open source framework for running vehicular network simulations (Veins) [14]. The evaluation was performed on a realistic mobility scenario provided by Codeca et al. in [12], using the SUMO simulator. The realistic mobility scenario is able to meet all basic requirements in size, realism and duration of a real-world city (Luxembourg) with a typical topology in mid-size European cities. From now on, we will refer to the realistic mobility scenario as the Luxembourg scenario. This scenario is available to industrial and scientific communities working on vehicular traffic congestion, intelligent transportation systems and mobility patterns.

As a utility metric, we adopt the absolute deviation and create filters on the reported original average speed. The values to calibrate the filters are in line with US standardization (in Subsect. 1.1). The scenario of evaluation and the numerical and graphical results are presented in following sections.

4.1   Luxembourg Scenario

As mentioned before, the realistic mobility scenario is based on the city of Luxembourg and contains residential or arterial roads and highways, see Fig. 1a. The Luxembourg scenario has an area of 156 km^2, 930 km of roads, 4,500 intersections, 200 traffic lights, and 290,000 cars. This scenario works on two types of mobility traces, which have duration of about 88,000 s (24 h), and peaks of traffic in about 8AM, 13PM and 6PM, as it can be seen in Fig. 1b.

DUA-T (Dynamic User Assigned Traces) is one of the mobility traces, which provides the optimal path for each origin-destination pair in terms of time and length. It is not very realistic because it does not take other vehicles and congestion into account. DUE-T (Dynamic User Equilibrium Traces) is the other

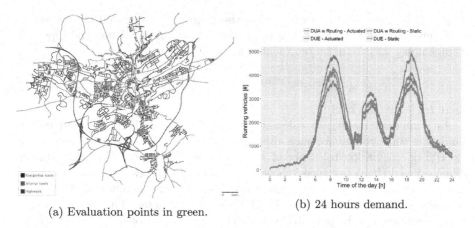

(a) Evaluation points in green.

(b) 24 hours demand.

Fig. 1. Luxembourg scenario and traffic demand. **Source:** (a) https://www. vehicularlab.uni.lu/lust-scenario/   (b)   https://github.com/lcodeca/LuSTScenario/ tree/master (Color figure online)

mobility trace that provides the approximated equilibrium for the scenario's traffic demand [12]. The latter can be combined with static or actuated traffic light systems. The static case isolates the impact of routing, while the actuated case would imply two independent optimization problems, the traffic light timing and the vehicular rerouting [12]. The combination of DUE-T and actuated traffic lights seems more realistic. However, we opt by combination of DUA-T and static traffic lights because this setting cause more traffic congestion and it fits well with our problem.

We evaluate the Hybrid approach in four strategic points of the Luxembourg scenario (green points in Fig. 1) in a rush period, between about 6AM and 10AM, as it can be seen in Fig. 1b. The Road Side Units (RSU's) or base stations were positioned using the Geodetic (Longitude/Latitude) coordinate system. The first and third points are located on a highway with low vehicle density. The first point has an RSU with a range of 250 m monitoring traffic on the road with no congestion. At the third point, we have a substantial traffic jam caused by a maintenance on the road, which has an RSU with a range of 150 m. The second and fourth points are located at the center of the city containing high vehicle density and traffic lights. RSU's are monitoring arterial roads with a respective range of 75 and 42.5 m, all congested in different levels. The second point has a regular traffic flow, with very little jam caused by traffic lights and the last point has a lot of congestion because it is the main avenue in the city center where several streets lead to it. The next subsection summarizes our numerical results.

4.2   Experimental Results

The filters were created with deviation tolerances (tol) of 5, 10 and 20% over the reported original average speed ($avg_{original}$). The reported noisy average speed

(avg_{noisy}) is expected to remain within the respective range and any measurement reported outside this range is considered an outlier. Thus, the reported average noisy speed can be represented as

$$avg_{noisy} = avg_{original} \cdot (1 \pm tol) \qquad (17)$$

where *tol* is divided by 100.

As numerical result, we calculate the number of outliers obtained in the simulation time window for each approach: ODP, SAA (all deviation tolerances) and Hybrid (deviation tolerance of 10%). In addition, we calculate the number of misbehaved (bad) instances, those that produce SAA scale parameters larger than the expected SAA scale parameter, and also the number of SAA scale parameters that are lower than the ODP scale parameter. The expected SAA scale parameter is calculated based on $Pr(-avg_{original} \cdot tol \leq X \leq avg_{original} \cdot tol) = 0.95$, where the random variable X is the noise to be added to the original average speed. Furthermore, in order to enrich our discussion, we present the following graphic results: the behavior of the real average speed, the quality of the instances by presenting the scale parameter for each instance and the relative deviation between the results of the hybrid approach and the original average speed. Table 1 summarizes the numerical results.

Table 1. Results of the Luxembourg scenario evaluation. The coordinates and speed limits (m/s) of the points correspond respectively to (49.579464, 6.100917), limit of 36.11; (49.617679, 6.132573), 13.89; (49.575654, 6.131255), 36.11; and (49.611492, 6.126152), 13.89.

Point	Number of events	Bad instances (%)	Lower b_{SAA} (%)	Outliers (%)								
				ODP			SAA			Hybrid		
				5%	10%	20%	5%	10%	20%	5%	10%	20%
1st	3,648	65.25	41.31	25.54	9.46	4.52	25.94	9.51	4.54	9.33	1.05	0.00
2nd	2,046	77.74	25.34	32.08	15.59	7.37	33.52	15.98	7.50	13.36	3.42	0.68
3rd	4,210	99.34	34.17	77.17	57.98	36.89	80.23	65.96	47.68	45.77	30.19	15.29
4th	5,068	99.70	62.23	96.01	87.24	84.78	90.53	77.13	75.13	87.89	72.37	70.35

We initiate our discussion by pointing out that the number of outliers is decreasing when it varies among the deviation tolerances from 5% to 20% in all points of evaluation. It is an expected behavior since we expand the tolerance range. Although we are getting an improvement in the number of outliers in all cases when moving among deviation tolerances, the rate of variation when switching among the evaluation points are decreasing. For example, this rate varies from about 8.88 in the 1st point (cell Hybrid 5% divided by cell Hybrid 10% in Table 1) until about 1.21 in the 4th point of evaluation (cell Hybrid 5% divided by cell Hybrid 10% in Table 1). This shows that the greater the congestion, the lower the rate of variation among the deviation tolerances.

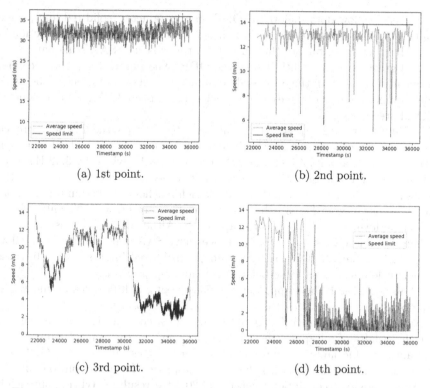

Fig. 2. Average and limit speed behavior during the simulation time window.

At the first and second point of evaluation, which are respectively located in a highway and an arterial road, we can see that ODP and SAA provide virtually the same result (number of outliers) for all deviation tolerance. For instance, it is about 9.5% and 16% in the 1st point and 2nd point, respectively, for a deviation tolerance of 10%. The good result at these points is due to the ideal flow both on the highway and on the arterial road, so that the ODP has the same behavior as the SAA. Observe in Fig. 2a and 2b that the behavior of the average speed is very close to the speed road limit. The results of the 2nd point are worse than the 1st due to the traffic lights present in the second point yielding a small traffic jam. Note that in the Fig. 2b there are measurements far below the speed limit.

Still in the 1st and 2nd evaluation points, the results related to the Hybrid approach show that we obtain a significant reduction in outliers. At the 1st point, in Table 1, the number of outliers is reduced from about 9.5% (ODP and SAA) to about 1% (Hybrid) for a deviation tolerance of 10%, a reduction rate of more than nine times. When we move to the deviation tolerance of 20% the number of outliers is reset to zero (Hybrid) from about 4.5% (ODP and SAA). Figure 3a shows the behavior of the relative deviation for all measurements and from it we can see that all deviation are below 20%. Note, in Fig. 4a, that even with more than 65% of badly behaved instances, we get about 41% of the SAA scale parameters (yellow dots) below the ODP scale parameter (solid red line), these smaller obtained scale parameters is sufficient to obtain a significant reduction in the outliers. Observe further that in Fig. 4a, the expected SAA scale parameter (dashed green line) is slightly below the ODP scale parameter (solid red line) and most of the 41% of the SAA scale parameters (yellow dots) below the ODP scale parameter (solid red line) are also below the expected SAA scale parameter (dashed green line).

In Table 1, at the 2nd point, the reduction rate related to the Hybrid approach compared to ODP and SAA for the deviation tolerance of 10% is a bit lower than at the 1st point, around 4.5 (15.59 ODP or 15.98 SAA divided by 3.42 Hybrid), half of the 1st point but still a great result, especially when we consider the results for the deviation tolerance of 20% which reaches a reduction rate of more than 11 times. See in Fig. 3b that most deviation are below 15% which shows a good performance of the Hybrid approach. Although 78% of instances are misbehaved, more than 25% of all instances have SAA scale parameters (yellow dots) smaller than the ODP scale parameter (solid red line), see Fig. 4b, these smaller scale parameters are crucial to get this improvement.

The reason the Hybrid approach provides great results is because most outliers do not overlap between the ODP and SAA approaches.

Now, considering the 3rd evaluation point located in a highway, we can see that the results of all approaches suffered a huge negative impact caused by a substantial traffic jam. The number of outliers reached about 80% (ODP and SAA) and almost half of it with the Hybrid approach for deviation tolerance of 5%. When moving to deviation tolerance of 20% the result of Hybrid approach is less than a half of the ODP and SAA results. Figure 2c shows the behavior of the average speed in this point. Observe that all the measurements are too far from the speed limit (36.11). There are two declines in the average speed behavior, one at the beginning of the simulation reaching about 6 m/s and another after 30000 s that reaches about 2 m/s. This is due to the high traffic demand at around 8AM where vehicles will abruptly reduce their speed when they are very close to road maintenance in order to avoid collisions, contributing to congestion.

Still in the 3rd evaluation point, the SAA result has a considerable worsening in relation to the ODP result, about 8% points in the deviation tolerance of 10% reaching until about 11% in the deviation tolerance of 20%. This is explained by the traffic jam yielding misbehaved instances which directly impacts the good performance of the SAA approach. From Table 1 we obtain about 99% of badly behaved instances, this lead to very little measurements below the expected scale parameter (dashed green line), see Fig. 4c. Even so, we get about 34% of the SAA scale parameters (yellow dots) below the ODP scale parameter (solid red line), sufficient to obtain a reduction rate of about 2 times in the number of outliers for the deviation tolerance of 5% and 10% with Hybrid approach compared to ODP and SAA, and reaching more than 3 times for the deviation tolerance of 20%.

Finally, in the 4th evaluation point, the growth in the number of outliers is even more evident when compared to the 3rd evaluation point, reaching about

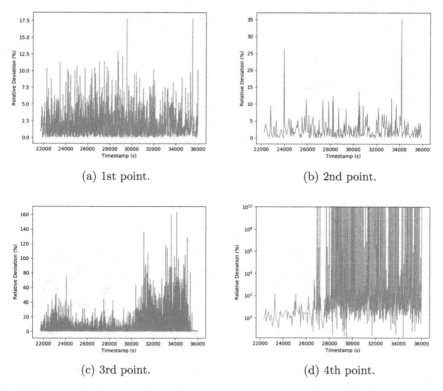

(a) 1st point.   (b) 2nd point.

(c) 3rd point.   (d) 4th point.

Fig. 3. Relative deviation between the hybrid approach and the original average speed for each instance during the simulation time window.

2.3 times more in the ODP approach and about 4.6 times in Hybrid approach for the deviation tolerance of 20%. This worsening occurs because most of SAA scale parameters when applied over an average speed very close to zero leads to an outlier. See, in Fig. 2d, that most measurements are close to zero. We can also see in Fig. 3d that the relative deviation is very high in most measurements in the simulation time window.

The SAA result improves considerably compared to the ODP result at the 4th valuation point, about 10% below in the deviation tolerance of 10%. Although almost all (99.7%) instances are misbehaved, close to 63% of the SAA scale parameters (yellow dots) are below the ODP scale parameter (solid red line) as it can be seen in Fig. 4d, which explains this improvement. However, it was not sufficient to help the Hybrid approach provide good results (significant reduction in outliers), this is due to the huge number of average speed very close to zero. We can conclude that all approaches are very sensitive to an average speed close to zero.

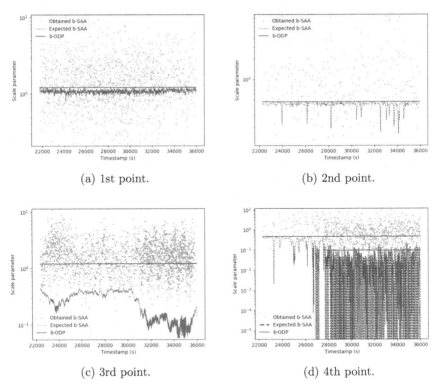

(a) 1st point.   (b) 2nd point.

(c) 3rd point.   (d) 4th point.

Fig. 4. Scale parameter for each instance during the simulation time window. (Color figure online)

5   Conclusion

We proposed in this paper a hybrid privacy-preserving data aggregation solution for traffic monitoring focusing on event-level privacy. This solution was designed to calculate the average speed on a road segment combining the original differential privacy to the sample and aggregation frameworks.

Experimental results have shown that the Hybrid approach is superior to the singular use of ODP and SAA approaches in situations that present none or at most some congestion, following the hypothesis that vehicles will travel in the same speed in a short period of time and space. The results of the first and second points of evaluation confirm this statement. However, at points where there is a lot of traffic jam, the performance of the Hybrid approach is negatively affected by the misbehaved produced instances. This shows how dependent the Hybrid approach is on the SAA approach.

As future work, we intend to propose a concurrent solution to this proposal by looking for improvements on the smooth sensitivity framework or alternatives to this one, or by using other techniques to get the median of a set with little noise, such as combining the sample and aggregate framework with exponential mechanism. Furthermore, we plan to evaluate the performance and security results of proposed approaches against a solution in a local model of computation.

A   Proof Lemma 1

The Laplace distribution on $\mathbb{R}$ *with scale parameter* b *, is (* α, β *)-admissible with* $\alpha = b\frac{\epsilon}{2}$ *and* $\beta = \frac{\epsilon}{2ln(1/\delta)}$.

Proof. From Definition 3, we can obtain parameters α and β. Since the Laplace distribution is not a heavy tail distribution, then $\delta > 0$.

– Considering Eq. 3, we have
  • When $\frac{Pr_{X \sim h}(X \in U) - \frac{\delta}{2}}{Pr_{X \sim h}(X \in U + \Delta)} \geq 1$, we have

$$
\begin{aligned}
\frac{Pr_{X \sim h}(X \in U) - \frac{\delta}{2}}{Pr_{X \sim h}(X \in U + \Delta)} &= \frac{\int_U \frac{1}{2b} e^{-\frac{|x|}{b}} dx - \frac{\delta}{2}}{\int_{U+\Delta} \frac{1}{2b} e^{-\frac{|x|}{b}} dx} \\
&= \frac{\frac{1}{2b} \int_c^d e^{-\frac{|x|}{b}} dx - \frac{\delta}{2}}{\frac{1}{2b} \int_c^d e^{-\frac{|x+\Delta|}{b}} dx} = \frac{\int_c^d e^{-\frac{|x|}{b}} dx - \frac{\delta}{2}}{\int_c^d e^{-\frac{|x+\Delta|}{b}} dx}
\end{aligned}
\tag{18}
$$

Considering numerator of Eq. (18), we have to evaluate interval $[c, d]$ in two cases,
  * when $x \geq 0$:

$$
\int_c^d e^{-\frac{x}{b}} dx = b(e^{-c/b} - e^{-d/b}),
\tag{19}
$$

  * and when $x < 0$:

$$
\int_c^d e^{\frac{x}{b}} dx = -b(e^{c/b} - e^{d/b}).
\tag{20}
$$

Now, considering denominator of Eq. (18), we have
  * when $x \geq -\Delta$:

$$
\int_c^d e^{-\frac{x+\Delta}{b}} dx = e^{-\Delta/b} b(e^{-c/b} - e^{-d/b}),
\tag{21}
$$

  * and when $x < -\Delta$:

$$
\int_c^d e^{\frac{x-\Delta}{b}} dx = -e^{-\Delta/b} b(e^{c/b} - e^{d/b}).
\tag{22}
$$

By substituting Eq. (19) and Eq. (21) in Eq. (18) we obtain

$$
\frac{b(e^{-c/b} - e^{-d/b}) - \frac{\delta}{2}}{e^{-\Delta/b} b(e^{-c/b} - e^{-d/b})}
$$

$$
= e^{\Delta/b} \frac{b(e^{-c/b} - e^{-d/b}) - \frac{\delta}{2}}{b(e^{-c/b} - e^{-d/b})} \leq e^{\epsilon/2}
\tag{23}
$$

$$
\Leftrightarrow e^{\Delta/b} \leq e^{\epsilon/2} \frac{b(e^{-c/b} - e^{-d/b})}{b(e^{-c/b} - e^{-d/b}) - \frac{\delta}{2}}.
$$

When δ tends to zero in Eq. (23), the ratio tends to 1. Thus, assuming a negligible δ, we get

$$\Delta \leq b(\epsilon/2) + ln\left[\frac{b(e^{-c/b} - e^{-d/b})}{b(e^{-c/b} - e^{-d/b}) - \frac{\delta}{2}}\right] \tag{24}$$

$$\approx b(\epsilon/2).$$

Similarly, by replacing Eq. (20) and Eq. (22) in Eq. (18) we get the same result, $\Delta \leq b(\epsilon/2)$.

- When $\frac{Pr_{X\sim h}(X \in U) - \frac{\delta}{2}}{Pr_{X\sim h}(X \in U + \Delta)} < 1$, we have by symmetry that

$$\frac{Pr_{X\sim h}(X \in U) - \frac{\delta}{2}}{Pr_{X\sim h}(X \in U + \Delta)} \geq e^{-\epsilon/2}$$

$$\approx e^{-\Delta/b} \geq e^{-\epsilon/2} \tag{25}$$

$$\approx \Delta \leq b(\epsilon/2).$$

Therefore, it is sufficient to admit $\alpha = b(\epsilon/2)$, so that the translation property is satisfied with probability $1 - \frac{\delta}{2}$.

- Considering Eq. (4), we have
  - When $\frac{Pr_{X\sim h}(X \in U) - \frac{\delta}{2}}{Pr_{X\sim h}(X \in U \cdot e^\lambda)} \geq 1$, we have

$$\frac{Pr_{X\sim h}(X \in U) - \frac{\delta}{2}}{Pr_{X\sim h}(X \in U \cdot e^\lambda)} = \frac{\int_U \frac{1}{2b}e^{-\frac{|x|}{b}} dx - \frac{\delta}{2}}{\int_{U \cdot e^\lambda} \frac{1}{2b}e^{-\frac{|x|}{b}} dx}$$

$$= \frac{\int_c^d e^{-\frac{|x|}{b}} dx - \frac{\delta}{2}}{\int_c^d e^{-\frac{|e^\lambda x|}{b}} dx} \tag{26}$$

Numerator of Eq. (26) is given by Eq. (19) and (20). On the other hand, denominator of Eq. (26) is given by evaluating interval $[c, d]$ in two cases,
  - when $x \geq 0$:

$$\int_c^d e^{-\frac{e^\lambda x}{b}} dx = e^{-\lambda}b[e^{-(e^\lambda c)/b} - e^{-(e^\lambda d)/b}], \tag{27}$$

  - and when $x < 0$:

$$\int_c^d e^{\frac{e^\lambda x}{b}} dx = -e^{-\lambda}b[e^{(e^\lambda c)/b} - e^{(e^\lambda d)/b}]. \tag{28}$$

By replacing Eq. (19) and Eq. (27) in Eq. (26) we obtain

$$\frac{b(e^{-c/b} - e^{-d/b}) - \frac{\delta}{2}}{e^{-\lambda}b[e^{-(e^\lambda c)/b} - e^{-(e^\lambda d)/b}]} \leq e^{\epsilon/2}$$

$$e^\lambda \leq e^{\epsilon/2}\frac{b[e^{-(e^\lambda c)/b} - e^{-(e^\lambda d)/b}]}{b(e^{-c/b} - e^{-d/b}) - \frac{\delta}{2}}. \tag{29}$$

From an analysis of Eq. (29), we can conclude that, regardless of values of b, c and d, where $d > c$, the ratio tends to zero when we get high values of λ. This is because the value of δ is negligible. When we get λ tending to zero, the ratio tends to 1. Thus, an acceptable upper bound for λ, so that Eq. (29) is satisfied with high probability, is $\epsilon/(2ln(1/\delta))$. This value tends to zero when we get a very small value for δ.

Similarly, by replacing Eq. (20) and Eq. (28) in Eq. (26) we obtain the same result, $\lambda \leq \epsilon/(2ln(1/\delta))$.

- When $\frac{Pr_{X \sim h}(X \in U) - \frac{\delta}{2}}{Pr_{X \sim h}(X \in U \cdot e^{\lambda})} < 1$, we have by symmetry that

$$\frac{Pr_{X \sim h}(X \in U) - \frac{\delta}{2}}{Pr_{X \sim h}(X \in U \cdot e^{\lambda})} \geq e^{-\epsilon/2}, \tag{30}$$

which results in $-\lambda \geq -\epsilon/(2ln(1/\delta))$.

Therefore, to satisfy the dilation property with probability $1 - \frac{\delta}{2}$, it is enough to assume $\beta = \epsilon/(2ln(1/\delta))$.

$\square$

References

1. Xiong, Z., Sheng, H., Rong, W., Cooper, D.: Intelligent transportation systems for smart cities: a progress review. Sci. China Inf. Sci. **55**(12), 2908–2914 (2012)
2. Research and Consultation Summary Report. https://www.transport.gov.scot/medi-a/41636/its-strategy-research-and-consultation-summary-report-july-2017.pdf. Accessed 21 Oct 2019
3. Dwork, C., McSherry, F., Nissim, K., Smith, A.: Calibrating noise to sensitivity in private data analysis. In: TCC 2006, pp. 265–284 (2006)
4. Kargl, F., Friedman, A., Boreli, R.: Differential privacy in intelligent transportation systems. In: WiSec 2013, pp. 107–112 (2013)
5. Nelson, B., Olovsson, T.: Introducing differential privacy to the automotive domain: opportunities and challenges. In: IEEE 86th VTC-Fall, pp. 1–7 (2017)
6. Jemaa, I., Kaiser, A., Lonc, B.: Study of the impact of pseudonym change mechanisms on vehicular safety. In: IEEE Vehicular Networking Conference (VNC), pp. 259–262 (2017)
7. Hassan, M., Rehmani, M., Chen, J.: Differential privacy techniques for cyber physical systems: a survey. arXiv:1812.02282 (2018)
8. Li, N., Lyu, M., Su, D.: Differential Privacy: From Theory to Practice. 1st edn. Morgan & Claypool Publishers (2016)
9. Nissim, K., Raskhodnikokova, S., Smith, A.: Smooth sensitivity and sampling in private data analysis. In: 39th ACM STC, pp. 75–84 (2007)
10. Dwork, C., Naor, M., Pitassi, T., Rothblum, G.: Differential privacy under continual observation. In: Association for Computing Machinery Symposium on Theory of Computing, pp. 715–724 (2010)
11. Dwork, C., Roth, A.: The algorithmic foundations of differential privacy. Found. Trends Theoret. Comput. Sci. **9**, 211–407 (2014)
12. Codeca, L., Frank, R., Faye, S., Engel, T.: Luxembourg SUMO traffic (LuST) scenario: traffic demand evaluation. IEEE Intell. Transp. Syst. Mag. **9**, 52–63 (2017)

13. Krajzewicz, D., Behrisch, M., Bieker, L., Erdmann, J.: Recent development and applications of SUMO - Simulation of Urban MObility. Int. J. Adv. Syst. Measur. **5**(3 & 4), 128–138 (2012)
14. Sommer, C., German, R., Dressler, F.: Bidirectionally coupled network and road traffic simulation for improved IVC analysis. IEEE Trans. Mob. Comput. **10**(1), 3–15 (2011)
15. OMNeT++. https://omnetpp.org/. Accessed 22 Aug 2019
16. McSherry, F., Talwar, K.: Mechanism design via differential privacy. In: FOCS 2007, pp. 94–103 (2007)
17. Jaynes, E.: Probability Theory: The Logic of Science. Cambridge University Press, Cambridge (2003)

Proactive Detection of Phishing Kit Traffic

Qian Cui[1,2(✉)], Guy-Vincent Jourdan[1,2(✉)], Gregor V. Bochmann[1(✉)], and Iosif-Viorel Onut[2(✉)]

[1] University of Ottawa, Ottawa, Canada
gjourdan@uottawa.ca, bochmann@uottawa.ca
[2] IBM Centre for Advanced Studies, Ottawa, Canada
vioonut@ca.ibm.com

Abstract. Current anti-phishing studies mainly focus on either detecting phishing pages or on identifying phishing emails sent to victims. In this paper, we propose instead to detect live attacks through the messages sent by the phishing site back to the attacker. Most phishing attacks exfiltrate the information gathered from the victim by sending an email to a "drop", throwaway email address. We call these messages **exfiltrating emails**. Detecting and blocking exfiltrating emails is a new tool to protect networks in which a number of largely unmonitored websites are hosted (universities, web hosting companies etc.) and where phishing sites may be created, either directly or by compromising existing legitimate sites. Moreover, unlike most traditional antiphishing techniques which require a delay between the attack and its detection, this method is able to block the attack as soon as it starts collecting data.

It is also useful for email providers who can detect the presence of drop mailbox in their service and prevent access to it. Gmail deployed a simple rule-based detection system and detected over 12 million exfiltrating emails sent to more than 19,000 drop Gmail addresses in one year [52].

In this work, we look at this problem from a new perspective: we use a Recurrent Neural Network to learn the structure of exfiltrating emails instead of their content. We compare our implementation, called **DeepPK**, against word-based and pattern-based methods, and tested their robustness against evasion techniques. Although all three models are shown to be very effective at detecting unmodified messages, **DeepPK** is the overall more resistant and remains quite effective even when the messages are altered to avoid detection. With DeepPK, we also introduce a new message encoding technique which facilitates scaling of the classifier and makes detection evasion harder.

Keywords: Phishing kit · Exfiltrating emails · Network traffic detection

K. Sako and N. O. Tippenhauer (Eds.): ACNS 2021, LNCS 12727, pp. 257–286, 2021.
https://doi.org/10.1007/978-3-030-78375-4_11

1   Introduction

A so-called "phishing attack" is a cyber crime in which an attacker (the *phisher*) deploys a website that mimics another site in order to induce victims to provide sensitive information. Although significant efforts to the defend against phishing attacks have been made both in academia and in industry, the fight between attackers and defenders keeps going on. The Anti-Phishing Working Group (APWG) reports having detected 266,387 phishing sites during the third quarter of 2019, the highest number in three years, with more than two third using SSL, the highest percentage seen since this is being tracked [5]. Phishers keep improving their techniques to avoid detection, for example using SSL or adding multiple redirections [6].

Most of the literature on anti-phishing focuses either on detecting phishing emails sent to the victims (e.g. [11,22,26,36,49,53] and many more) or on detecting phishing web pages(e.g. [2,12,13,18,23,32,44,45,59] and many more). These solutions are centered around the victims, the goal is to protect the victims from the attacks, that is, to cut off the channel between victims and attacks. However, very little work has been done focusing on the channel between the attackers and the attacks. However, that channel is as critical as the other ones: breaking it defeats the attack. This is the topic of this paper, and more specifically the channel through which the attacker collects the stolen information from the phishing site. This approach helps web hosting provider and network owner to combat phishing by detecting immediately that an attack is being deployed on their network. It is a new idea that is not centered around the actual victims (most victims have no connection to the network on which the attack is being deployed) and thus this is a new tool which can work in combination with existing ones.

In most phishing attacks, the stolen information is exfiltrated back to the phisher by email: the code of the phishing site simply sends an email to a "drop address" each time someone submits something to the phishing site. Each email contains the data submitted by one victim. In the case of a multi-page phishing site, it is even often the case that several emails are sent for a single victim. Therefore, detecting and blocking these emails is a different and complementary means to combat phishing attacks. In the following, we call these emails sent by the phishing site to the phisher "**exfiltrating emails**".

In this paper, we evaluate three different machine learning technique to detect exfiltrating emails: word-based, pattern-based and structure-based detection. We test the robustness of our three models against potential attacks. Although all three models are shown to be very effective at detecting these messages, the model using a deep-learning approach, which is called **DeepPK**, is the one that is the overall best since it remains quite effective even when the messages are altered to avoid detection. The key idea of **DeepPK** is to deal with the email structure as a sequence of components that follows specific grammar rules. The key component of **DeepPK** is a bidirectional Long Short-Term Memory (LSTM) network [46]. It allows **DeepPK** to automatically learn the difference between the structural grammar rules of exfiltrating emails and regular emails. In order to effectively represent email structure, we propose a new encoding method, the **structure token**, which uses a small corpus containing only 14 symbols.

We train and test our models on a realistic database of exfiltrating emails. These emails are built from the combination of two real datasets: a database of exfiltrating emails generated by actual "phishing kits", which gives us the patterns of the exfiltration emails, but not the data provided by the victims, and a database of values that have been submitted to real phishing sites. By meshing up these two databases, we end up with a system that can generate a large number of exfiltrating emails. In this paper, we use almost 65,000 such messages to train and test our models.

The solution described in this paper has a key advantage over most of the existing ones: it does not require the attack to be first reported, or to be somehow actively discovered. Instead, it is the attack's own network traffic that is being detected and stopped. Therefore, this technique can be used to stop a phishing attack immediately, preventing a single delivery of stolen information to the phisher.

The paper is organized as follows: In Sect. 2 we explain what detecting exfiltrating email achieves that current phishing detection method do not. In Sect. 3, we present our exfiltrating emails database. Then in Sect. 4, we introduce our machine learning-based approaches. In Sect. 5, we present the evaluation of our models, which is followed by the robustness test in Sect. B. We provide an overview of the literature in Sect. 6 before concluding in Sect. 7. All of the source code and some of the non-sensitive data used in this paper will be made available after the anonymous review.

2 Motivations

As already mentioned, most of the antiphishing efforts are directed at protecting victims, either by preventing the attacker's message from reaching its target, or by detecting that a site is not genuine. However, not every potential victim uses these mechanisms, and even when they do, these mechanisms are not perfect: for instance, Hu et al. [29] have shown that even email providers that do apply anti-spoofing detection techniques fail to always prevent forged emails from reaching the victims. It is therefore also important to help network administrators to proactively detect that a phishing site has been deployed on their network, without being notified of the URL fist. Such a phishing site can be deployed on a network because the attacker has compromised one of the servers, or because the attacker as a legitimate right to deploy a website there. Very little work has been done in this area. Of course, one could use any phishing site detection method and scan the network to look for such sites, but this can be difficult due to the network's size and the lack of control over what is being deployed there. More importantly, scanning would probably yield limited success without first somehow knowing the actual URL of the phishing site on the server. Waiting to be notified about the attack has the obvious disadvantage of being out of the control of the network's administrator, and of opening a window of time during which the attack is live on the network. Closing that gap is necessary to prevent victims from providing data to the phishing site, and to preserve the reputation of the network, which may otherwise end up being blacklisted.

Detecting exfiltrating emails is a new tool which provides a web hosting providers a new way to learn that a phishing attack is hosted on their network and stop it immediately, by monitoring outgoing emails instead of scanning their own network. It addresses the problem of having to find out or to be informed of the exact URL of the phishing attack, since that is instead the network traffic of the phishing site itself that triggers the detection. Another considerable advantage of such a system is that it can detect and block the attack as soon as someone submits data to the site, preventing the attackers from collecting any information. In addition, drop email addresses are uncovered and can be reported to the email providers and suitable authorities.

This tool will be useful to web hosting companies, but also to any entities managing a large and relatively open network, such as a university for example.

As already demonstrated in [52], our work can also be useful to email providers: it is possible to reliably and rapidly detect that one of the mailboxes is the recipient of such exfiltrating emails and block its access immediately, also completely preventing the attacker from accessing the data. This is of particular interest to free email providers, which are used extensively by phishers to create dedicated drop email addresses.

In this research, we focus on phishing attacks that are using clear-text drop emails as exfiltration techniques. It is always surprising to the academic community that such a basic and vulnerable exfiltration technique could be used in practice. A vast array of other techniques are of course possible to exfiltrate the data, including but not limited to simple email encryption, pushing the data out using another protocol such as http(s) or (s)ftp, more covert methods such as DNS-based exfiltration [38], or storing the data on the server and switching from a push-based model to a pull-based model. Several easy-to-find implementations of phishing-kit proof-of-concepts do in fact provide alternate ways of exfiltering data. In practice, the almost exclusive reliance on plain-text emails is well documented by practitioners [20,31,34,39,42,52,57]. Most recently, in [52] it is reported that all of the 10,000 kits analyzed in that study use the PHP *mail()* command to exfiltrate data. In [31] an analysis of 1,000 Phishing Kits done in 2018 found that "the vast majority of kits (98%) used email to exfiltrate stolen data to attackers". Another study from 2018, [39], does not mention any other mean of data exfiltration. This is certainly also our empirical evidence having worked with well over 10,000 live attacks over the past couple of years: attackers today use almost exclusively clear-text drop emails for data exfiltration. Even when the phishing kit offers other alternative (usually some level of encryption), these alternatives are almost never enabled in live attacks. One explanation for this is that phishing attacks are very low-skill attacks, and any complication would negatively impact the model (see Sect. 7 for some more discussion about this). It is also possible that only some of the attacks are using clear-text drop emails, and for some reasons these are the attacks that we discover.[1] Even if that is the case, it remains that a large number of attacks are using clear-text drop emails as exfiltration techniques and stopping these ones is a step in the right direction.

Our tool is not meant to replace existing ones. Detecting classical phishing emails is still necessary but serves a different purpose: it prevents email users of the domain from being victimized by phishing sites that are usually hosted somewhere else. Our tool is as a new and effective mechanism to secure networks against hosting phishing attacks themselves. Classical phishing email detection does not provide any direct protection against that.

We believe that there are two main contributions in this paper: first, we provide a new direction for detecting exfiltrating emails using neural networks trained on the structural information of the message. We introduce a encoding method which effectively extracts that structural information with only 14 characters. Second, we identify a missing piece in the fight against phishing. The hosting mechanism and the data exfiltration techniques are an essential and somewhat overlooked part of the equation. The detection models that we present here do work very effectively on current phishing attacks. Other detection models might be as effective, and attackers will certainly take countermeasure to prevent detection in the future. Nevertheless, it remains that web hosting providers must now be included in the defense against phishing, and that proactive techniques such as the one presented here must be developed and maintained as the situation evolves.

3   Exfiltrating Emails Generations

One difficulty with this research is to access to exfiltrating emails to train and test the models. We are not aware of any such database prior to this work. Some prior work could have indirectly access to some exfiltrating emails (e.g. using honeypots [27]) but in limited quantity.

In this work, the starting point for the generation of exfiltrating emails is two datasets that the forensic teams of our industry partners have collected from real attacks:

1. A set of 3,162 distinct **Phishing Kits** which are actual phishing websites written in the PHP language,
2. and a collection of 370 files containing various amount of data collected by real phishing sites.

The generation process involves three stages: Phishing Kit Deployment, Files Parsing, and Email Generation described in the next subsections.

---

[1] Maybe because these are low-skill attacks, and some higher-skill attacks are evading our detection.

3.1 Phishing Kit Deployment

Each phishing kit is deployed in a custom sandbox environment. By redefining functions and certain global objects of the standard library (PHP language) used by the phishing kits, it is arranged that the calls requesting values for HTTP GET/POST request variables and cookies will return special placeholder values which we can later use to identify the value which is requested e.g. a POST request variable named "username".

Any email messages sent are captured. These messages are parsed, identifying all special placeholder values in addition to a small number of special patterns including IP address, date/time and user agent, with the end result being a sequence of static strings and dynamic value specifications termed an **email template**. A sample is shown in Fig. 1. A total of 6,448 unique email templates acceptable for use in subsequent steps are generated from the data. As previously noted, phishing kits often send more than one message, either because the attack is done in several steps and each step triggers a separated message, or because the phishing kit contains more than one phishing sites.

```
———=F3dreport 2018=———
Em@il: <EMAIL>
pass: <PASSWORD>
pass2: <PASSWORD>
———=IP Address & Date=———
IP Address: <IP>
Country: <COUNTRY>
Date: <DATE>
```

Fig. 1. Sample exfiltrating email template extracted from a phishing kit (manually modified for obfuscation)

3.2 Data File Parsing

Our data files contain sets of values that have been collected during phishing attacks and recovered by forensics teams. These values correspond to what the victims provide to the phishing site (and thus what is then exfiltrated in the emails). The type of data found in this dataset is what one expects from a phishing site: mostly credentials for websites and other systems, but also credit cards information and other personal information. In addition, the IP address of the victim, time of access, type of browser etc. is often collected by phishers.

It is worth noting that in a typical phishing attack, the majority of the values submitted to the site are not genuine. Instead, the majority of the inputs seem to come from users attempting to "get back" at the phishers by submitting a flurry of random data, insults and denial-of-service attempts. Nevertheless, these are the values that a typical phishing attack will receive and exfiltrate, and thus all of these values are valid and indeed necessary for our purpose.

We did parse all of our data files to extract the individual values and match them to the values requested by the phishing kits. The end result of this process is the population of an **Exfiltration Database** with data for 115,713 entries comprising 332,224 values.

3.3 Email Generation

The general idea is to generate emails from each email template by filling in placeholders using data from the exfiltration database. For each of the 6,448 email templates, we generate 10 email messages randomly filling in placeholders using data from the exfiltration database. When doing so, we require that all template values are populated, although we do not insist that the data all belongs to a single entry or even to data from the same file. This resulted in 64,480 exfiltration emails, two examples are provided in Fig. 2.[2] To ensure that our models are trained and tested on different datasets, email messages coming from the same template are either all used for training or all used for testing.

```
————=F3dreport 2018=————         ————=F3dreport 2018=————
Em@il: victim1@gmail.com         Em@il: victim2@hotmal.com
pass: victim1pass                pass: victim2test11
pass2: victim1pass2              pass2: victim2test11
————=IP Address & Date=——        ————=IP Address & Date=————
—                                —
IP Address: 123.123.123.222      IP Address: 123.123.12.12
Country: Unknown                 Country: Unknown
Date: 2018-12-14 04:16:11        Date: 2018-12-12 01:23:19
```

Fig. 2. Two instances of exfiltrating emails generated from the template of Fig. 1, values manually obfuscated.

4 Methodology

We have trained three different models to recognize exfiltrating emails. In this Section, we first introduce two approaches that are commonly used in email classification: word-based and pattern-based detection model. We then introduce our structure-based model.

---

[2] Because these files do contain some sensitive data, we cannot publish this database as is. We will however make available the encoded version of the emails on which our deep learning algorithm works upon request and after verification.

4.1 Word-Based Detection Model

Naive Bayes approaches have been shown to be very successful in text classification task [8,58]. Therefore, we included one such implementation in our exfiltrating email classifiers.

Specifically, the model learns the conditional probability and the independent probability of each word from the training set, and uses these probabilities to predict the probability that a new text belongs to a certain category. Formally, we work from a set of documents consisting of n unique word tokens $[w_1, w_2, \ldots, w_n]$. These documents are classified into p categories $[C_1, C_2, \ldots, C_p]$. Each document can be represented as a vector $x = (x_1, ..., x_n)$, where x_i represents the relative weight of w_i in that document.

In our case, to effectively represent word features, we first extract consecutive alphanumeric characters using the regexp [0-9A-Za-z] to get a "word" list. We then apply 1-gram and 2-gram to create word tokens. The corpus of the model is built using the 5,000 most frequent tokens. We apply a "scaled term frequency" to calculate the frequency of the token. Formally, the scaled term frequency of the word token w_i in the document d_j is

$$1 + \log(\# \text{ of occurrences of } w_i \text{ in the document } d_j).$$

We then apply tf-idf using the scaled tf to vectorize the tokens. For vector normalization, we apply an "L2" normalization: the sum of squares of vector elements is 1. Finally, for each document (email), we end up with a 5,000-dimension vector.

The probability that a document of vector $(x_1, ..., x_n)$ belongs to the category C_k is $p(C_k|x_1, ..., x_n) = \frac{p(C_k) \prod_{i=1}^{n} p(x_i|C_k)}{p(x_1, ..., x_n)}$.

Note that x_i is a TF-IDF value of the word token w_i, which is only related to the set of documents. In other words, given a set of documents, $p(x_1, ..., x_n)$ is a constant for each category C_k. Therefore, $p(C_k|x_1, ..., x_n)$ is proportional to $p(C_k) \prod_{i=1}^{n} p(x_i|C_k)$. We apply the Gaussian Naive Bayes algorithm to estimate the likelihood of features, $p(x_i|C_k) = \frac{1}{\sqrt{2\pi\sigma_{C_k}{}^2}} \exp\left(-\frac{(x_i - \mu_{C_k})^2}{2\sigma_{C_k}{}^2}\right)$, where the parameters σ_{C_k} and μ_{C_k} are learnt by the model during training. $p(C_k)$ is also a learnable parameter, which is equal to

$$\frac{\# \text{ of documents in } k^{th} \text{ category}}{\# \text{ of documents}}$$

Once the model is trained, it is used to assign a new document of vector $x'_1, ..., x'_n$ to the category C_i which maximizes $p(C_k|x'_1, ..., x'_n)$. In the following sections, we name this model **NB**.

4.2 Pattern-Based Detection Model

In addition to using different set of words (when compared to regular emails), exfiltrating emails also tend to use singular patterns. For instance, they are often organized following the format: \<header\> + \<field name\> + \<delimiter\> +

<value>. Therefore, we also trained a classifier to look for patterns. We first encode the content of the messages using only five character classes: letters (L), digits (D), punctuation (P), newline (N) and whitespace other than newline (W). Each email is first encoded using these five classes. We then compute all n-grams of lengths 10 to 16 on the encoded email sets, exfiltrating emails and regular emails, and we keep only the n-grams that appear only in one of the two sets, that is, n-grams that are found at least once in the exfiltrating (resp. regular) training set but never appear in the regular (resp. exfiltrating) training set. A greedy set cover algorithm is applied to obtain a token cover set, which only covers the same set of documents. We derive a classifier using only the token cover set for the class of exfiltrating emails which classifies a document as exfiltrating if and only if its token set contains one of the tokens in the exfiltrating token cover set.

Formally, let t be a tokenizer function and A and B be email classes. Let $D(A, B) = \bigcup t(A) \setminus \bigcup t(B)$ and similarly let $D(B, A) = \bigcup t(B) \setminus \bigcup t(A)$. Finally, using a set cover algorithm, select a small subset $C(A, B) \subseteq D(A, B)$ such that $\{m \in A \mid t(m) \cap D(A, B) \neq \emptyset\} = \{m \in A \mid t(m) \cap C(A, B) \neq \emptyset\}$ and similarly for $C(B, A)$. Let C_0 be the set of clean messages, and C_1 be the exfiltrating emails. Define a classifier c by

$$c(M) = \begin{cases} 1 & \text{if } t(M) \cap C(C_1, C_0) \neq \emptyset \\ 0 & \text{otherwise} \end{cases}$$

In the following sections, we name this model **Set-cover**.

4.3   Structure-Based Detection Model

As discussed in Sect. 4.2, exfiltrating emails tend to follow a specific format that is rarely used in regular emails. If we look at the structure of the document as a grammar, exfiltrating emails and regular emails follow two different grammars. Deep learning algorithms are known to be effective at learning underlying grammars of text documents [7,14,51], therefore we also include a deep learning-based classifier.

As we did in Sect. 4.2, we first encode the message using using a new **structure token** using 14 symbols. The details of that encoding is provided in Appendix A.1. In addition to the structure token, our model also include two "semantic" features: the **content entropy** and the **text proportion**, which are detailed in Appendix A.2.

Recurrent Neural Networks (RNN) are often used for problems with sequential information as input and have been shown to be effective in a variety of natural language processing problems [9,35]. For this model, we use a Long Short-Term Memory (LSTM) RNN, which has been proved to perform well in dealing with complex patterns and long sequences [28,50]. The details of our use of LSTM, which we call **DeepPK**, are provided in Appendix A.3.

5 Experiment

We now report our basic results, starting with a description of our experiment environment.

5.1 Experiment Environment

We have developed DeepPK using Keras[3] with Tensorflow as the back end. For HTML emails preprocessing, we use Beautifulsoup[4] to extract the text from the HTML emails. Our models NB and Set-cover are implemented using Scikit-learn[5]. Our experiments are performed on a Windows-based system with an Intel i5 CPU at 3.5 Ghz and 16 GB RAM. DeepPK is trained and tested on a NVIDIA Geforce GTX 1060 with 6 GB RAM. Our source code can be found on our website, http://ssrg.site.uottawa.ca/phishing_kit/.

5.2 Exfiltration Email and Regular Email Database

We obtained our regular emails database from the **Enron email dataset**[6], which was collected and prepared by a third party organization, and contains about 0.5 million messages coming from 150 users. Our exfiltrating emails database, which consists of 64,480 messages from 6,448 unique exfiltration email templates are generated by the approach discussed in Sect. 3.

To ensure that training and testing data is separated, we first split our 6,448 unique exfiltration email templates into two sets at a ratio of 4:1: 5,158 templates are randomly selected for training, and the remaining 1,290 are used for testing. This yield 51,580 email instances for training, and 12,900 email instances are for testing. For the regular email database, we create a balanced training set by randomly sampling 51,580 messages from the Enron email dataset. For the regular email test set, we use 5 times the number of test exfiltrating emails, for a total of 64,500 regular emails. This unbalance is to mimic a real-life scenario in our tests, since exfiltration emails would be a fraction of the mail traffic in reality.

As described in Appendix A.3, we inject into some of the (encoded) exfiltration emails some length of tokens taken from regular emails in order to avoid learning only the prefix of these messages. Specifically, we inject into 8 of the 10 instances generated from the each template a token segment randomly sampled from the regular training set. The size of the segment is randomly selected between 1 and 50 characters.

In order to avoid overfitting during training, we further split our training set: 80% is used for the actual training, while 20% is used for validation. Accordingly, we end up with 41,260 messages in each exfiltration email set and regular email

[3] https://keras.io/.
[4] https://www.crummy.com/software/BeautifulSoup/bs4/doc/.
[5] https://scikit-learn.org/stable/.
[6] http://www.cs.cmu.edu/~enron/.

set used for training, and 10,320 messages in each set used for validation. During training, we store the model which yields the best performance on the validation set and then evaluate it on the test set.

5.3 Model Evaluation

In order to evaluate the effectiveness of our models, we compared them on similar experiments and report here the results. By default, we use the following parameters for DeepPK: input length is 600 and number of memory units is 128. Since DeepPK uses tumbling windows to process the data, to ensure a fair comparison, we also test the NB model with tumbling windows (that model is noted **NB-Window** below). We tried window sizes of 5 to 10 lines and report only the one with the best performance.

We apply five standard metrics to evaluate the performance of the models: false positive[7] (FP), false negative (FN), precision (pre)=$\frac{TP}{TP+FP}$ (TP stands for true positive), recall (rec)=$\frac{TP}{TP+FN}$ and f-score=$\frac{2*pre*rec}{pre+rec}$. The results are shown Table 1.

Table 1. Performance comparison between models

Performance comparison					
Model	# false positive (%)	# false negative (%)	Precision	Recall	F1 score
NB	728 (1.13%)	115 (0.89%)	94.61%	99.11%	96.81%
NB-window	2,596 (4.02%)	99 (0.77%)	83.14%	99.23%	90.48%
Set-cover	261 (0.40%)	285 (2.21%)	97.97%	97.79%	97.88%
Single LSTM	626 (0.97%)	**37 (0.29%)**	95.36%	**99.71%**	97.49%
Bidirectional LSTM w/o content feature	343 (0.53%)	65 (0.50%)	97.40%	99.50%	98.44%
Bidirectional LSTM with content feature	**221 (0.34%)**	63 (0.49%)	**98.31%**	99.51%	**98.91%**

For the NB model, we note that using a tumbling window improves the false negatives rate but at the expense of the false positives rate. For DeepPK, the model that only uses a single LSTM yields the best false negative rate (0.29%) but the worst false positive rate (0.97%). Through manual inspection of these false positives, we found that most of them are very short regular emails. The model that uses bidirectional LSTM fixes this issue thanks to the additional information provided by the backward direction. The performance is further improved by using our semantic features, which help the model correctly classify regular emails with a structure similar to that of the exfiltrating emails (e.g. the case shown in Fig. 3). In general, the model which uses bidirectional LSTM and semantic feature yields the best false positive rate (0.34%) and the best F1 score (98.91%) across all models.

---

[7] Here, a "positive" classification means that the message is flagged as exfiltrating email.

5.4   Model Robustness

Our results in the Sect. 5.3 show that all three proposed models perform well in detecting exfiltrating emails. In this section, we discuss several possible ways an attacker could modify exfiltrating emails to evade detection, and we evaluate how resilient the models are to these modifications. When looking at these potential detection evasion techniques, we specifically focus on solutions that would be relatively easy to implement for the attacker and would modify the exfiltrating emails without preventing automatic processing at the receiving end. More advanced evasion techniques are of course possible, but they would likely impact negatively the "business model" of phishing by requiring more advanced technical skills from attackers (see Sect. 7). Here, we consider two potential attacks:

– **Injection attack.** In this attack, the phisher injects additional noise into the exfiltrating email, which is otherwise unchanged. In practice, the injected text can be random strings, or pieces of text extracted from regular emails. The latter is a more effective attack because it introduces "negative" noise (segments possibly matching what the model has learned from the regular emails), which is more likely to result in misclassification. In our study, we consider a worst case scenario and use actual text segments from our regular email database to increase the chances of defeating the models. We test four different ways of injecting "negative" noise : injecting at the top of the message, at the bottom of the message, in the middle of the message, and finally scattering the injected text throughout the exfiltrating email.
  We run several experiments. When injecting top, middle or bottom of the message, we injected a size of text ranging from 10% to 100% of the original exfiltration email, measured by the length of the resulting structure token. So in the worst case, 50% of the resulting structure token comes from injected text. When scattering the injection throughout the text, the injection is measured in terms of number of lines in the original text. In our experiment, we increase the number of injected lines, going from one line randomly inserted in the original text to one line inserted between each line of the original text.
– **Replacement attack.** In this attack, the phisher replaces the text of the structure of the exfiltrating emails with strings that the model has rarely or never seen. The purpose of the attack is to eliminate "positive" indicators. An easy way to perform such an attack is to systematically replace existing field names with other strings. Note that because DeepPK detects exfiltrating emails based on our structure token and not on the message itself, this model is not impacted by this attack if the strings used for replacement are of the same length as the strings they replace (since it would yield the same structure token). In order to have an effective attack against our model, we apply what we have called "incremental injection", where the size of the injected stings is gradually increased.
  We run several experiments with this attack as well. First, as mentioned we change the length of consecutive tokens, trying various increments from 17 to 101. This ensures that each experiment produces a different structure token

Table 2. Attack test sets

Injection attack (injection proportion: from 0.1 to 1.0 by steps of 0.1)	
Label	Description
Inject_header	Injection of "negative" noise at the top
Inject_middle	Injection of "negative" noise in the middle
Inject_tail	Injection of "negative" noise at the bottom
Inject_line	Injection of "negative" noise scattered throughout the message
Replacement attack (incremental injection length: [17, 20, 33, 45, 52, 64, 78, 89, 96, 101])	
Replace_word	Replace words (continuous alphabetical characters) with randomly generated ones
Replace_non_word	Replace non-words with randomly generated non-words
Replace_all	Word and non-word replacement

fragments. For each length, we try three different types of replacements: we try to replace only "words" (that is, sequences encoded as C in the structure token). We then try to replace only "non-words" (that is, sequences encoded as N, L or S in the structure token), and finally, we try to replace everything.

In these experiments we use the model trained on the original database, so the modified exfiltration messages have never been seen by the models before. We do not report the results on the regular emails again, since these would not be impacted by these experiments. We use the test set discussed in Sect. 5.2. Instead of using 10 instances per template, we randomly choose one instance from each template, and end up with 1,290 exfiltrating emails that we modify for the experiments. As explained, the injected text segments are randomly sampled from the regular test set. In order to facilitate the comparison, we use the same random seed for all our experiments (Table 2).

When faced with injection attacks, in general, DeepPK performs well, with an error rate of at most 5%, except with the test set inject_line. On that test, the error rate increases with the proportion of injected text, to reach 28% at the top. This is because, as expected, this injection destroys the sequence of structure tokens, eliminating some key tokens. The Set-cover model is stable in the injection test, with an error rate of at most 6%. This is not surprising since the Set-cover model only looks for learned "bad" token in the message. Injecting noise does not impact the presence of these tokens and the noise is just ignored by this model. Still, except for the test set inject_line, the Set-cover model performs worse than DeepPK even with a relatively high proportion of injected text (up to 70 to 90% of the original message depending on the test). The NB model does not perform well in the injection test. The model breaks down significantly as more "negative" content is injected. The use of tumbling windows does help, but the performance is still worse than the other two models. More details are available in Fig. 9 of Appendix B.

The word replacement attacks has almost no effect to the performance of DeepPK, with an error rate peaking at 5%. On the other hand, the performance of DeepPK on the test sets replace_non_word and replace_all is quite inconsistent: it sometimes performs very well with an error rate of less than 2%, but in some cases the error rate goes above 80% (Fig. 10 of Appendix B). To better analyze this phenomenon, we have conducted a complete set of tests on the test set replace_all, ranging the injection proportion from 1 to 100, step by step. Out of these 100 tests, the error rate is below 10% 42 times, and below 5% 31 times. The explanation might be that "non-words" in the template are important indicators of exfiltrating email for DeepPK. However, to successfully conduct such an attack, the attacker needs to successfully break up the part of the structure that happens to have been learned by DeepPK, which is quite challenging and a process of trial and error. Generating such exfiltrating emails would be significantly more difficult than what is currently done. What is more, interpreting these emails once that are received would also be orders of magnitude harder than the current situation. Therefore, this attack, however effective, seems of limited practicality. Set-cover and NB are basically defeated by this attack, see Appendix B for more details.

6   Related Works

Most of studies on phishing attack detection focus on identifying phishing pages and phishing emails that are used to spread phishing links.

Most proposed phishing sites detection techniques look for some intrinsic characteristics of the attack. For instance, [16,24,33,37,40,54,55] use an array of machine learning models to train a binary classifier. Some work has also been done to compare these approaches [1,36]. But as mentioned in Sect. 2, detecting that a site is a phishing site does not address the needs of a network administrator if, as is the case in these papers, the site's exact URL is needed for the detection.

The main general approach for detecting phishing emails is to apply machine learning techniques to detect the characteristics of a content that is designed to deceive the victim. Fette et al. [22] propose such as method. The feature of their model mainly focus on the phishing link embedded in the email, such as the number of dots and the number of domains in URL, rather than the email content. They report a 99.5% accuracy and 0.13% false positive on a dataset of 860 phishing emails and 6,950 regular emails. In [48,53], the authors suggest to combine natural language processing techniques and contextual information to identify phishing emails. In [53], the authors report a 98% true positive rate and 0.7% false positive rate on a dataset of 2,000 phishing emails and 1,000 regular emails. In [48], the authors report an accuracy of 92.2% and a 4.9% false positive rate on a dataset of 14,370 phishing emails and 14,370 regular emails. Some researchers suggest to also use delivery information to detect phishing emails. In [11,26], sets of features such as the consistency between sender domain and the embedded link are used. Stringhini et al. [49] propose a detection model for spear phishing attacks by profiling the email sender: writing habits, composing habits, and interaction habits. Such behavioral-based detection would not be directly suitable for our purpose, since in our case no impersonation is taking place. However, none of these techniques would probably be very effective at detecting exfiltrating emails because exfiltrating emails do not contain URLs or deceptive text, and are sent to the attacker's drop email address and from the header's viewpoint are not different from regular emails.

The work most related to ours is [52], in which a large scale analysis on credential theft is conducted. The author work on a source of about 10,000 kits, and propose a method to extract phishing templates by parsing the kits source code. They then look for instances of these templates on Gmail, using Gmail's built-in anti-abuse detection system. They detect over 12 millions exfiltration emails between March 2016 and March 2017. This works confirms that most phishing attackers (who use Gmail 75% of the time for drop email address) simply use plain-text when exfiltrating emails and thus detecting and blocking these messages at the hosting site would currently be extremely effective. The detection method that they use is however based on text matching; as we have shown in the Sect. 5.4, attacker could simply evade detection merely by using different keywords. Our method is more resistant and is aimed primarily at hosting provider.

One general problem with the above methods is that the attacks need to be first discovered and reported, and this means some delay between the attack and its detection (about 10 h according to the report from APWG [25]). Our method can identify a phishing attack as soon as it starts to collect information. It basically prevents the attack to succeed at all if exfiltrating emails are scanned in real time, at the source or at the receiving end. In [17], two "zero delay" phishing attack detection methods are presented: one uses domain names to infer that a site will host an attack, and the other does proactive "blind" scanning of the network. By contrast, the method proposed here works regardless of the domain name used (in particular it works even when the domain name is not related to the attack) and will work without knowing nor guessing the URL of the attack.

The main difference between our work and all the above methods is that the goal of these methods is to protect a victim from an attack. Although it could indirectly help network administrators to detect a phishing site on their network, it usually requires the URL of the attack to be known, which usually means that someone needs to first report the attack to the administrator. In contrast, the goal of our work is to directly help the administrator to detect a phishing site on their network, and it does it automatically and without delay. In [27], a system is presented in which honeypots are safely deployed and phishing kit are monitored. This is probably the closest work to ours, but the aim is quite different. That system does not provide a way to detect an attack being deployed on a live network. It is however one possible way to learn new email exfiltration patterns and thus it can work and combination to our system. In [43,56], the authors propose to monitor spam botnets and infer regular expressions matching the messages sent by these botnets. A similar approach may also achieve good performance in our context. However, as explained before, in our case the attacker controls the entire channel, from the message creation to the message consumption, and thus simple rule-based systems would be easier to be defeated by simply changing the messages body, as we did in Sect. B. As we showed, the models that we propose, in particular our deep learning-base model, can be quite resistant to simple pattern modifications of the messages.

In addition to phishing detection, there is a significant body of academic work focusing on email classification for several purposes, such as spam detection. For instances, Blanzieri et al. [10] present a survey of supervised machine learning algorithms for spam detection in 2008. These methods treat the email content either as a set of word tokens, or as a text in natural language. A binary classifier is then trained based on the extracted features to identify spam. Some methods also combine other information, such as attachments, headers and embedded images to improve the performance. Elssied et al. [21] apply a k-means clustering technique to identify spam. Not all solutions rely on machine learning-based classifier, e.g. Pérez-Díaz et al. [41] propose a method using a set of rules.

In general, all these spam detection methods mainly focus on email content and use semantic features to build classifiers. To the best of our knowledge, we are the first to propose a machine learning method which uses structural features of the messages to classify emails.

7   Limitations and Conclusion

One clear limitation of our empirical evaluation is that the attacker does control the entire exfiltration system and therefore can in theory very easily change it to avoid detection. As previously mentioned, using simple email encryption or switching to a completely different exfiltration technique would defeat the detection methods evaluated in this paper. Such a switch would not be terribly difficult to achieve from the attacker viewpoint. We argue that forcing phisher to step-up their game and implement more advanced exfiltration techniques is a good thing that will hurt the business of phishing attacks. The main reason for this is that phishing attacks are very low-skill attacks. In [15], 15 phishing attack "vendors" are surveyed. In general, these individuals have very low technical skills, and are only claiming the most basic web-programming abilities. Their clients, who are the actual attackers, presumably have even lower technical skills. Empirically, we can confirm that the code that we have seen in thousands of phishing kits is of very low quality and does not suggest any kind of programming understanding. In [19], an analysis of the evolution of phishing attacks over time also shows that only the most basic updates are performed on live attacks by the attackers. Raising the technical bar even slightly will likely exclude many of the current players. Another reason is the low return that phishing attacks yield, and the poor quality of the data collected. In [15], it is reported that the cost of a tailor-made phishing site ranges from 15\$ to 250\$. As mentioned in Sect. 3.2, in our experience the vast majority of the data sent to a phishing site is bogus[8] and thus processing the data to identify usable information is a time consuming process. Adding a decryption step, or using less structured exfiltration format

---

[8] Anecdotally, the more advanced technical steps that we regularly see in phishing kits are techniques to prevent returning visitors from submitting data again, presumably in an attempt to limit the amount of fake data submission.

will complicate data processing further and reduce profitability even more. We can report that in practice, we have almost never seen an attack in which the phisher bothered encrypting the content of the exfiltration emails.

Of course, if our system or a similar one becomes widely adopted, this will force attackers to step up their game and e.g. start encrypting their messages. As explained, we think that this will hurt their business. Nevertheless, when that time comes, new detection techniques will have to be found, depending on the new exfiltration trends. For example, several approaches have been proposed to work on encrypted traffic by comparing the traffic pattern ending to the same destination [3,4,30]. If the main exfiltration technique remains email-based, then some protection could be expected from a wide adoption of standards such as SPF[9] and DKIM[10], which will limit the ability to successfully send email from hacked servers that are not meant to send emails.

Another possible criticism to our work is that we will not be able to detect exfiltrating emails that follow a completely different pattern. This criticism is mitigated by the fact that this new pattern can simply be added to our training set once known, and that we see much fewer patterns than there are attacks, suggesting a vast amount of code-sharing among phishers. It is in practice likely that our current model would catch many actual exfiltrating emails sent in North America and Europe at the time of writing. System such as the one described in [27] could also be used to discover new patterns as they are introduced.

We also acknowledge that our database is heavily biased toward North-American and European attacks. This is not a limitation of our method but a limitation of our database. Training our model on a larger database should address this issue.

The solution proposed here is, as far as we know, the first one that suggests to detect exfiltrating emails using structural information. This method has the advantage of working very well in our experiments, and being robust against evasion techniques trying to avoid detection by modifying the email content. We also introduce a new "structure token" which proves to be very effective when combined with our deep learning algorithm. Our work is also the first one to our knowledge to be tested on synthetic but realistic exfiltration emails, using a combination of two real datasets.

Unlike usual solutions that can be deployed at the end-user end, our solution needs to be deployed by host providers, where the phishing sites are being deployed, or by email providers, where the exfilrating emails are being received. This can be seen as a limitation, but also as a strength, since a handful of very large scale players could deploy our system and have a significant and immediate impact on phishing activities.

---

[9] https://tools.ietf.org/html/rfc7208.
[10] https://tools.ietf.org/html/rfc6376.

A   Details About DeepPK

A.1   Structure Tokens

In order to compare the "structure" of the body of emails, we introduce what we call the **structure token**, which is a symbolic representation of that email structure. Formally, we encode the text of the message using four categories: letters ([a-zA-Z]), encoded as C, digits ([0–9]), encoded as N, line breaks ([\n\r]), encoded as L, and finally any character that does not belong to the previous categories, encoded as S. In addition, we count consecutive occurrences of characters in the same category and append the number of occurrences to the category symbol. For compactness, we do not append that number if it is 1. For instance, the text "Hi Yvonne\n This is John, please call me back." is represented as the structure token "C2SC6LSC4SC2SC4S2C6SC4SC2SC4S" (where single instances of a category where the number 1 is omitted are underlined).

There are several advantages to using such a structure token. First, it does not capture the actual text (the words) used in the message, and instead captures the structure of the content. For instance, in the example above, if some words are changed (e.g., greetings or names are modified), we still get a similar structure token. The number of consecutive occurrences of a particular category might change a little bit when a word is changed, but the sequence of categories will remain relatively stable. This adds significant value in our context because in exfiltrating emails, what will change between messages is the part containing the victim's data. The remaining content is the **template**, which doesn't change across messages sent by the same phishing attack. Figure 2 shows two instances of the same template. The "template" part (separators, fields name, line breaks) remains identical in both messages, and the corresponding structure tokens will match. In addition, it is often the case that the structure token will still be quite similar across messages in the parts containing victim's data. For instance, all IP addresses end up with the structure token "NXSNXSNXSNX" where X ∈ [", 2, 3]. It is also true that using a structure token makes is more difficult for the attacker to evade detection, since it is not enough to modify the text of the template. A new template needs to be introduced to significantly change the structure token. Finally, last but not least, using a structure token insures that model learns patterns from one-way encoded inputs rather than directly from data containing sensitive information. This protects users data privacy both during training and at run time, since actual email content is never sent to the system.

But a very important practical consequence of using structure token instead of traditional encoding methods, such as using words as encoding units, is that our method uses a very small corpus containing only 14 symbols[11] which allows our tokens to be applied to large datasets. In order to vectorize structure tokens, we apply the so-called "one-hot encoding", which is a vector of bits of the same size as the encoding corpus, 14 bits in our case. Each bit corresponds to the

---

[11] Our four categories, C, N, L and S, and the 10 digits, 0 to 9.

index of one of the symbols in the corpus, and each character is being encoded with a vector in which only one bit is set to 1. As an example, given a corpus {a,b,c}, 'a' could be encoded [1, 0, 0], 'b' encoded [0, 1, 0] and 'c' encoded [0,0,1]. The one-hot encoding string of the text "aacb" would then be [[1, 0, 0], [1, 0, 0], [0, 0, 1], [0, 1, 0]].

A.2   Semantic Feature of Email

Our initial intent was to use only structure tokens to identify exfiltrating emails. However, we noticed that this resulted in a handful of false positives in the odd cases where regular emails follow a structure similar to exfiltrating emails. Figure 3 shows one such example.

CALENDAR ENTRY: APPOINTMENT

Description: Cleveland Cliffs Mtg/Bob Stevens 4180

Date: 7/19/2000
Time: 1:00 PM - 4:30 PM (Central Standard Time)

Chairperson: Outlook Migration Team

Detailed Description:

Fig. 3. One example of false positives

In order to correctly classify these messages, we enhance our method by introducing two "semantic" features: the **content entropy** and the **text proportion**.

Entropy is a commonly used metric in information theory. It measures the uncertainty of a piece of information produced by a source of data [47]. Formally, given a string S consisting of n characters $\{c_1, c_2, ..., c_n\}$ that are generated by a corpus of k unique symbols, the entropy of S, $ent(S) = -\sum_{i=1}^{m} p(s_i) * log(p(s_i))$, where m is the number of symbols used in the string S, and $p(s_i)$ is the probability of symbol s_i appearing in S. The higher the value of entropy, the more disordered or uncertain the string generated by the corpus. However, entropy has a tendency to generate greater values for the string that uses a large variety of symbols. In order to alleviate this tendency, we divide the initial number by the logarithm of the number of symbols in the string. Finally, we end up with a normalized entropy in the range [0,1]: $ent_{normal}(s) = -\sum_{i=1}^{m} \frac{p(s_i)*log(p(s_i))}{log(m)}$.

In our case, we use the above normalized entropy and a corpus of 26 English letters ([a–z]) and 10 digits ([0–9]) to build what call the **content entropy**. Specifically, we first convert email text into lowercase. We then calculate the normalized entropy for the processed content and get the content entropy. Since a regular email is mainly composed of English words, which has a higher certainty than the content of an exfiltrating email (e.g. username and password), it yields a lower content entropy.

Another difference between exfiltrating emails and regular emails is that exfiltrating emails tend to use a greater proportion of non-numeric and non-letter symbols. In order to quantify this difference, we propose another context feature, the **text proportion**. Formally, given a string S consisting of n characters $\{c_1, c_2, ..., c_n\}$, the **text proportion** $TP(S)$ is defined with the following formula:

$$TP(S) = \frac{\sum_{i=1}^{n} LN(c_i)}{n}$$

$$\text{where } LN(c) = \begin{cases} 1 & \text{if } c \in [\text{a-zA-Z0-9}] \\ 0 & \text{otherwise} \end{cases}$$

As an example, the text proportions of the exfiltrating emails in Fig. 2 are 0.7065 (left) and 0.7097 (right), while the text proportion of the regular email in Fig. 3 is 0.7703, higher than Fig. 2.

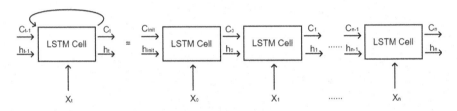

Fig. 4. LSTM cell and its unrolled form

A.3 Long Short-Term Memory Model

A Recurrent Neural Network (RNN) is a neural network where cells are connected in a round-robin fashion. Long Short-Term Memory (LSTM) is a type if RNN. As shown in Fig. 4, an LSTM cell has three inputs: X_t, C_{t-1} and h_{t-1}. X_t is the tth character in the input sequence X. C_{t-1} is the state passed from the previous step, which stores the "memory" of what has been learned from the previous sequence. h_{t-1} is the output of the LSTM cell in the previous step, representing the latest prediction based on the previous sequence. The LSTM cell uses these values to calculate outputs, which are taken as the input in the next step.

Formally, $C_t = f_t * C_{t-1} + i_t * \tilde{C}_t$, where $f_t = \text{sigmoid}(W_f \cdot [h_{t-1}, x_t] + b_f)$, $i_t = \text{sigmoid}(W_i \cdot [h_{t-1}, x_t] + b_i)$ and $\tilde{C}_t = \text{tanh}(W_C \cdot [h_{t-1}, x_t] + b_C)$. It can be seen that the new cell state C_t is equal to the partial previous status C_{t-1} plus the scaled update candidate $\tilde{C}_t$, and controlled by two gating components

f_t and i_t, that are the functions of the current element x_t and the output in the previous step h_{t-1}. In our context, these two gating components control the memory focus of the model during training: it keeps the memory of the key sequence and ignores the parts that do not contribute meaningful indicators for the model.

The output of the LSTM cell h_t is a function of the new cell state C_t. Formally, $h_t = o_t * \tanh(C_t)$, where $o_t = \text{sigmoid}(W_o \cdot [h_{t-1}, x_t] + b_o)$. The gating component o_t controls the output scale of the cell status. In our context, h_t is a vector indicator that identifies whether the currently processed token comes from an exfiltrating email.

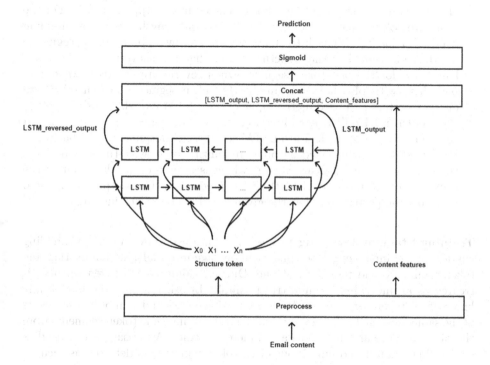

Fig. 5. System design of DeepPK

Detection Model. In order to construct our detection model, we pass the structure token through the LSTM cell and combine the LSTM output in the final step with the content features to yield the final prediction. A problem with using a single LSTM cell is that the output of the LSTM cell in the final step may not provide complete information of email structure. To overcome this issue, we apply a variant of LSTM: the **Bidirectional LSTM**, which uses a reversed copy of the input sequence to train an additional LSTM cell. Therefore, the model is able to know the complete information of the input in both directions [46]. We call this detection model **DeepPK**. The complete overview is shown Fig. 5. Additional information about **DeepPK**'s parameters are provided Appendix A.4.

– **Preprocessing Model.** When an email is classified, the first step is the preprocessing model. In this model, we first parse the text of the email body. If it is a HTML email, we scan all HTML tags and extract the text from each tag. We then generate the structure token and the semantic features based on the text content. Different message bodies yield structure tokens of different lengths. However, LSTM cell requires fixed-length input. By trial and error, we have selected a "reasonable" size as the input length (the details of the selection of the input length is discussed in the Appendix A.5). For the structure tokens that are longer than this input length, we use a tumbling window of the input length to create several non-overlapping token segments for that message. For the structure token that are shorter than the input length (or for the last token segment when several are created), we simply pad them with placeholders. Finally, the token segments are encoded into one-hot vectors and used as the input of our LSTM model.
– **Bidirectional LSTM.** A Bidirectional LSTM model consists of two LSTM cells. The output of the forward LSTM cell (LSTM_output) and the backward LSTM cell (LSTM_reversed_output) are joint together with the semantic features to form a new feature vector, which is later used as the input of the sigmoid output layer to yield the final prediction. The output of Sigmoid indicates the probability that the given email is an exfiltrating email.

Training Stage and Testing Stage. As mentioned above, we use a tumbling window of the input length to split each message into multiple non-overlapping token segments, and pad the last one. During training, each token segment is treated as an individual ground-truth sample. In other words, the model only knows if the token segments are from exfiltrating emails and cannot link segments of the same message back together. On the test set, multiple token segments from the same message are treated as a complete identifier. A message is classified as exfiltrating email if and only if one of its token segments is detected as such.

Injection on Training Set. As discussed in Sect. A.3, the function of the LSTM cell is to extract and learn key structure tokens from exfiltrating emails. However, when the training set is not sufficiently diverse, the model may fail to learn useful token sequences and instead may only remember some sequence or symbols at a specific position. For instance, exfiltrating emails often contain some series of dashes at the beginning. As a consequence, the structure token of these exfiltrating emails starts with the symbol S. In contrast, regular emails normally start with greetings, so the structure token of most regular emails starts with C. If such a training set is used to train the model, it causes the model to only use the first symbol as a strong indicator of exfiltrating emails and ignore the subsequent sequence. It causes the model to be very vulnerable in practice because an attacker can easily fool it, e.g. by embedding the exfiltrating email into a regular email.

In order to solve this issue, we randomly inject structure token fragments of different lengths, that are sampled from regular emails. To prevent learning these injected fragments, we inject the fragments that are sampled from the regular training set.

A.4   Analysis of DeepPK

In this section, we discuss the impact of various parameters in DeepPK's performance.

Our results are shown Fig. 6. In general, we can see that the precision increases but the recall decreases with the number of memory cells and the size of the input. The recall is still quite stable and stays above 99% across the board. The input length plays an important role: a shorter input allows the model to recognize more exfiltrating emails (higher recall), but increases the false positive rate. This indicates that the model requires enough structural information to accurately classify the messages.

The model is less sensitive to the number of memory units (the precision remains above 94% across the board). The model with 128 memory units and an input length of 600 yields the highest F1 score.

A.5   Analysis of Structure Token Length

As discussed in Sect. A.3, we needed to select a "reasonable" length for the structure token, since the LSTM cell requires fixed-length input. A reasonable length is the length that is able to cover "enough" context for the model to learn the required information from the structure token. To determine that, we first look at the length distribution of the structure token length in the exfiltrating email database, as shown in the Fig. 7.

We can see that save a few instances that end up with a very long structure token, most exfiltrating tokens have fewer than 600 characters. Through manual inspection, we find that these instances with long structure tokens can be divided into two categories: one category comes from instances produced by a specific template that collects 70 fields, as shown in Fig. 8. It comes from a phishing attack targeting a Brazilian bank https://www.bradescoseguranca.com.br. The other category are instances of exfiltrating emails that are coming from end users that have attacked back the phishing site: in these messages, the fields are populated with extremely long dummy strings. We thus chose 600 as the input length for DeepPK, since this length can cover most exfiltrating emails. In fact, even for the instance that exceeds this length, the cropped part is often a repeat of the previous part.

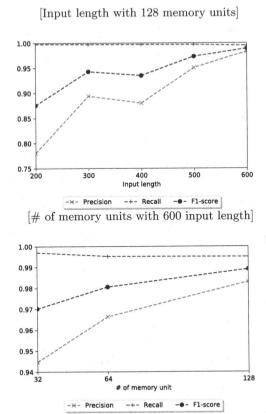

Fig. 6. DeepPK performance with different parameters

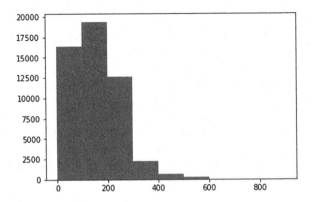

Fig. 7. Distribution of structure token length in the phishing database

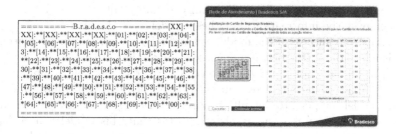

Fig. 8. Email template with long structure tag and its screenshot (In the actual exfiltration email, the data is where the "**" are in the figure.)

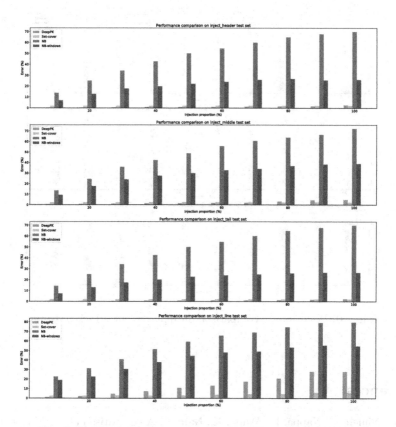

Fig. 9. Performance comparison on injection attack test sets

B   Model Robustness

Set-cover does not fare well at all against replacement attacks, because this attack removes the information that these models have learned.

The apparent success of the model NB and NB-windows against replacement attack is misleading. It is because in these attacks, the model does not recognize anything at all and ends up with a zero vector. Since the model can only provide 2 outputs (exfiltrating email or non exfiltrating emails), this simply indicates that our model happens to defaults to an "exfiltrating email" output when the input is completely unknown. It also indicates that this model would flag as "exfiltrating emails" any message for which it knows none of the word.

It is noted that the replacement attack test we conduct is very strict: each structure token fragment in the attack instance is totally different from the original one, which may rarely occur in practice. Our results show that even under this extreme test, DeepPK can still provide reasonable performances.

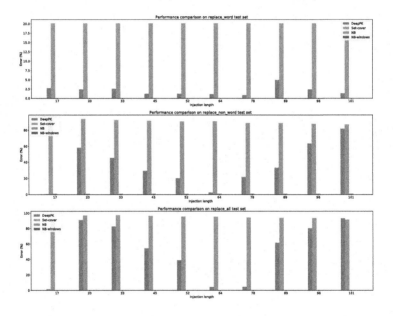

Fig. 10. Performance comparison on replacement attack test sets

References

1. Abu-Nimeh, S., Nappa, D., Wang, X., Nair, S.: A comparison of machine learning techniques for phishing detection. In: Proceedings of the Anti-phishing Working Groups 2nd Annual eCrime Researchers Summit, pp. 60–69. ACM (2007)

2. Afroz, S., Greenstadt, R.: Phishzoo: detecting phishing websites by looking at them. In: 2011 Fifth IEEE International Conference on Semantic Computing (ICSC), pp. 368–375. IEEE (2011)

3. Al-Obeidat, F., El-Alfy, E.S.: Hybrid multicriteria fuzzy classification of network traffic patterns, anomalies, and protocols. Personal and Ubiquitous Computing, pp. 1–15 (2017)

4. Alshammari, R., Zincir-Heywood, A.N.: Machine learning based encrypted traffic classification: identifying SSH and skype. In: 2009 IEEE Symposium on Computational Intelligence for Security and Defense Applications, pp. 1–8. IEEE (2009)

5. Anti-Phishing Working Group: Phishing Activity Trends Report 3rd Quarter in 2019. docs.apwg.org/reports/apwg_trends_report_q3_2019.pdf

6. Anti-Phishing Working Group: Phishing Activity Trends Report 4th Quarter in 2018. https://docs.apwg.org//reports/apwg_trends_report_q4_2018.pdf

7. Bahdanau, D., Cho, K., Bengio, Y.: Neural machine translation by jointly learning to align and translate. arXiv preprint arXiv:1409.0473 (2014)

8. Behdad, M., Barone, L., Bennamoun, M., French, T.: Nature-inspired techniques in the context of fraud detection. IEEE Trans. Syst. Man Cybernet. Part C (Applications and Reviews) **42**(6), 1273–1290 (2012)

9. Bengio, Y., Ducharme, R., Vincent, P., Jauvin, C.: A neural probabilistic language model. J. Mach. Learn. Res. **3**, 1137–1155 (2003)

10. Blanzieri, E., Bryl, A.: A survey of learning-based techniques of email spam filtering. Artif. Intell. Rev. **29**(1), 63–92 (2008)

11. Chandrasekaran, M., Narayanan, K., Upadhyaya, S.: Phishing email detection based on structural properties. In: NYS Cyber Security Conference, vol. 3. Albany, New York (2006)

12. Chang, E.H., Chiew, K.L., Sze, S.N., Tiong, W.K.: Phishing detection via identification of website identity. In: 2013 International Conference on IT Convergence and Security, ICITCS 2013, pp. 1–4. IEEE (2013)

13. Chen, T.C., Dick, S., Miller, J.: Detecting visually similar web pages: application to phishing detection. ACM Trans. Internet Technol. **10**(2), 5:1–5:38 (2010)

14. Cho, K., et al.: Learning phrase representations using RNN encoder-decoder for statistical machine translation. arXiv preprint arXiv:1406.1078 (2014)

15. ClearSky Cyber Security: The Economy Behind the Phishing Websites Creation. https://www.clearskysec.com/wp-content/uploads/2017/08/The_Economy_behind_the_phishing_websites_-_White.pdf (2017)

16. Corona, I., et al.: DeltaPhish: detecting phishing webpages in compromised websites. In: Foley, S.N., Gollmann, D., Snekkenes, E. (eds.) ESORICS 2017. LNCS, vol. 10492, pp. 370–388. Springer, Cham (2017). https://doi.org/10.1007/978-3-319-66402-6_22

17. Cui, Q.: Detection and Analysis of PhishingAttacks. Ph.D. thesis, University of Ottawa (2019)

18. Cui, Q., Jourdan, G.V., Bochmann, G.V., Couturier, R., Onut, I.V.: Tracking phishing attacks over time. In: Proceedings of the 26th International Conference on World Wide Web, pp. 667–676. International World Wide Web Conferences Steering Committee (2017)

19. Cui, Q., Jourdan, G.-V., Bochmann, G.V., Onut, I.-V., Flood, J.: Phishing attacks modifications and evolutions. In: Lopez, J., Zhou, J., Soriano, M. (eds.) ESORICS 2018. LNCS, vol. 11098, pp. 243–262. Springer, Cham (2018). https://doi.org/10.1007/978-3-319-99073-6_12

20. EC-Council: How Strong is your Anti-Phishing Strategy? (2018). https://blog.eccouncil.org/how-strong-is-your-anti-phishing-strategy/

21. Elssied, N.O.F., Ibrahim, O., Abu-Ulbeh, W.: An improved of spam e-mail classification mechanism using k-means clustering. J. Theoret. Appl. Inf. Technol **60**(3), 568–580 (2014)
22. Fette, I., Sadeh, N., Tomasic, A.: Learning to detect phishing emails. In: Proceedings of the 16th international conference on World Wide Web, pp. 649–656. ACM (2007)
23. Geng, G.G., Lee, X.D., Wang, W., Tseng, S.S.: Favicon - a clue to phishing sites detection. In: eCrime Researchers Summit (eCRS), pp. 1–10, September 2013
24. Gowtham, R., Krishnamurthi, I.: A comprehensive and efficacious architecture for detecting phishing webpages. Comput. Secur **40**, 23–37 (2014)
25. Group, A.P.W.: Global Phishing Report 2H 2014 (2014). http://docs.apwg.org/reports/APWG_Global_Phishing_Report_2H_2014.pdf
26. A. Hamid, I.R., Abawajy, J.: Hybrid feature selection for phishing email detection. In: Xiang, Y., Cuzzocrea, A., Hobbs, M., Zhou, W. (eds.) ICA3PP 2011. LNCS, vol. 7017, pp. 266–275. Springer, Heidelberg (2011). https://doi.org/10.1007/978-3-642-24669-2_26
27. Han, X., Kheir, N., Balzarotti, D.: Phisheye: Live monitoring of sandboxed phishing kits. In: Proceedings of the 2016 ACM SIGSAC Conference on Computer and Communications Security, pp. 1402–1413. ACM (2016)
28. Hochreiter, S., Schmidhuber, J.: Long short-term memory. Neural Comput. **9**(8), 1735–1780 (1997)
29. Hu, H., Wang, G.: End-to-end measurements of email spoofing attacks. In: 27th {USENIX} Security Symposium ({USENIX} Security 2018), pp. 1095–1112 (2018)
30. Husák, M., Čermák, M., Jirsík, T., Čeleda, P.: Https traffic analysis and client identification using passive SSL/TLS fingerprinting. EURASIP J. Inf. Secur. **2016**(1), 6 (2016)
31. Imperva: Our Analysis of 1,019 Phishing Kits (2018). https://www.imperva.com/blog/our-analysis-of-1019-phishing-kits/
32. Liu, W., Liu, G., Qiu, B., Quan, X.: Antiphishing through phishing target discovery. IEEE Internet Comput. **16**(2), 52–61 (2012)
33. Ludl, C., McAllister, S., Kirda, E., Kruegel, C.: On the effectiveness of techniques to detect phishing sites. In: M. Hämmerli, B., Sommer, R. (eds.) DIMVA 2007. LNCS, vol. 4579, pp. 20–39. Springer, Heidelberg (2007). https://doi.org/10.1007/978-3-540-73614-1_2
34. McCalley, H., Wardman, B., Warner, G.: Analysis of back-doored phishing kits. In: Peterson, G., Shenoi, S. (eds.) DigitalForensics 2011. IAICT, vol. 361, pp. 155–168. Springer, Heidelberg (2011). https://doi.org/10.1007/978-3-642-24212-0_12
35. Mikolov, T., Karafiát, M., Burget, L., Černocky̌, J., Khudanpur, S.: Recurrent neural network based language model. In: Eleventh Annual Conference of the International Speech Communication Association (2010)
36. Miyamoto, D., Hazeyama, H., Kadobayashi, Y.: An evaluation of machine learning-based methods for detection of phishing sites. In: Köppen, M., Kasabov, N., Coghill, G. (eds.) ICONIP 2008. LNCS, vol. 5506, pp. 539–546. Springer, Heidelberg (2009). https://doi.org/10.1007/978-3-642-02490-0_66
37. Mohammad, R.M., Thabtah, F., McCluskey, L.: mohammad2014. Neural Computi. Appl **25**(2), 443–458 (2014)
38. Nadler, A., Aminov, A., Shabtai, A.: Detection of malicious and low throughput data exfiltration over the DNS protocol. Comput. Secur. **80**, 36–53 (2019)

39. Oest, A., Safei, Y., Doupé, A., Ahn, G., Wardman, B., Warner, G.: Inside a phisher's mind: Understanding the anti-phishing ecosystem through phishing kit analysis. In: 2018 APWG Symposium on Electronic Crime Research (eCrime), pp. 1–12, May 2018. https://doi.org/10.1109/ECRIME.2018.8376206
40. Pan, Y., Ding, X.: Anomaly based web phishing page detection. In: null. pp. 381–392. IEEE (2006)
41. Pérez-Díaz, N., Ruano-Ordas, D., Mendez, J.R., Galvez, J.F., Fdez-Riverola, F.: Rough sets for spam filtering: Selecting appropriate decision rules for boundary e-mail classification. Appl. Soft Comput. 12(11), 3671–3682 (2012)
42. PhishLabs: How to Fight Back against Phishing (2013). https://info.phishlabs. com/hs-fs/hub/326665/file-558105945-pdf/White_Papers/How_to_Fight_Back_ Against_Phishing_-_White_Paper.pdf
43. Pitsillidis, A., et al.: Botnet judo: Fighting spam with itself. In: NDSS (2010)
44. Ramesh, G., Krishnamurthi, I., Kumar, K.S.S.: An efficacious method for detecting phishing webpages through target domain identification. Decis. Support Syst. 61(1), 12–22 (2014)
45. Rosiello, A.P.E., Kirda, E., Kruegel, C., Ferrandi, F.: A layout-similarity-based approach for detecting phishing pages. In: Proceedings of the 3rd International Conference on Security and Privacy in Communication Networks, SecureComm, pp. 454–463. Nice (2007)
46. Schuster, M., Paliwal, K.K.: Bidirectional recurrent neural networks. IEEE Trans. Signal Process. 45(11), 2673–2681 (1997)
47. Shannon, C.E.: A mathematical theory of communication. Bell Syst. Tech. J. 27(3), 379–423 (1948)
48. Smadi, S., Aslam, N., Zhang, L., Alasem, R., Hossain, M.: Detection of phishing emails using data mining algorithms. In: 2015 9th International Conference on Software, Knowledge, Information Management and Applications (SKIMA), pp. 1–8. IEEE (2015)
49. Stringhini, G., Thonnard, O.: That ain't you: blocking spearphishing through behavioral modelling. In: Almgren, M., Gulisano, V., Maggi, F. (eds.) DIMVA 2015. LNCS, vol. 9148, pp. 78–97. Springer, Cham (2015). https://doi.org/10.1007/978-3-319-20550-2_5
50. Sundermeyer, M., Schlüter, R., Ney, H.: LSTM neural networks for language modeling. In: Thirteenth Annual Conference of the International Speech Communication Association (2012)
51. Sutskever, I., Vinyals, O., Le, Q.V.: Sequence to sequence learning with neural networks. In: Advances in Neural Information Processing Systems, pp. 3104–3112 (2014)
52. Thomas, K., et al.: Data breaches, phishing, or malware?: understanding the risks of stolen credentials. In: Proceedings of the 2017 ACM SIGSAC Conference on Computer and Communications Security, pp. 1421–1434. ACM (2017)
53. Verma, R., Shashidhar, N., Hossain, N.: Detecting phishing emails the natural language way. In: Foresti, S., Yung, M., Martinelli, F. (eds.) ESORICS 2012. LNCS, vol. 7459, pp. 824–841. Springer, Heidelberg (2012). https://doi.org/10.1007/978-3-642-33167-1_47
54. Whittaker, C., Ryner, B., Nazif, M.: Large-scale automatic classification of phishing pages. In: In Proceedings of the Network & Distributed System Security Symposium (NDSS 2010), San Diego, CA, pp. 1–14 (2010)
55. Xiang, G., Hong, J., Rose, C.P., Cranor, L.: Cantina+: a feature-rich machine learning framework for detecting phishing web sites. ACM Trans. Inf. Syst. Secur. 14(2), 21:1–21:28 (2011)

56. Xie, Y., Yu, F., Achan, K., Panigrahy, R., Hulten, G., Osipkov, I.: Spamming botnets: signatures and characteristics. ACM SIGCOMM Comput. Commun. Rev. **38**(4), 171–182 (2008)
57. Zawoad, S., Dutta, A.K., Sprague, A., Hasan, R., Britt, J., Warner, G.: Phish-net: investigating phish clusters using drop email addresses. In: 2013 APWG eCrime Researchers Summit, pp. 1–13, September 2013. https://doi.org/10.1109/eCRS.2013.6805777
58. Zhang, H., Li, D.: Naïve Bayes text classifier. In: 2007 IEEE International Conference on Granular Computing (GRC 2007), p. 708. IEEE (2007)
59. Zhang, Y., Hong, J., Lorrie, C.: Cantina: a content-based approach to detecting phishing web sites. In: Proceedings of the 16th International Conference on World Wide Web, Banff, AB, pp. 639–648 (2007)

VESTIGE: Identifying Binary Code Provenance for Vulnerability Detection

Yuede Ji$^{(\boxtimes)}$, Lei Cui, and H. Howie Huang

Graph Computing Lab, George Washington University, Washington, D.C., USA
{yuedeji,leicui,howie}@gwu.edu

Abstract. Identifying the compilation provenance of a binary code helps to pinpoint the specific compilation tools and configurations that were used to produce the executable. Unfortunately, existing techniques are not able to accurately differentiate among closely related executables, especially those generated with minor different compiling configurations. To address this problem, we have designed a new provenance identification system, VESTIGE. We build a new representation of the binary code, i.e., attributed function call graph (AFCG), that covers three types of features: idiom features at the instruction level, graphlet features at the function level, and function call graph at the binary level. VESTIGE applies a graph neural network model on the AFCG and generates representative embeddings for provenance identification. The experiment shows that VESTIGE achieves 96% accuracy on the publicly available datasets of more than 6,000 binaries, which is significantly better than previous works. When applied for binary code vulnerability detection, VESTIGE can help to improve the top-1 hit rate of three recent code vulnerability detection methods by up to 27%.

Keywords: Compilation provenance · Code similarity · Vulnerability · Binary code · Graph neural network

1 Introduction

A binary code is generated from source code through the compilation process. The source code can be compiled to completely different binary codes, when different compilers, coupled with different configuration settings, are used. The process of identifying the compiler and configuration is referred to as the compilation provenance identification [35]. Knowing the compilation provenance is very helpful for binary code analysis, especially for malware analysis [16,21,41], code vulnerability detection [14,17,40], and code authorship identification [29,30]. In this context, compilation provenance identification aims to find out the used compiler family, compiler version, and optimization level. Note that in this paper we do not take into account the computer architecture for which the code is compiled, because it can be accurately identified by existing tools, e.g., the *file* software.

© Springer Nature Switzerland AG 2021
K. Sako and N. O. Tippenhauer (Eds.): ACNS 2021, LNCS 12727, pp. 287–310, 2021.
https://doi.org/10.1007/978-3-030-78375-4_12

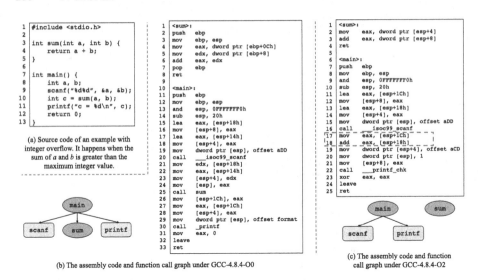

(a) Source code of an example with integer overflow. It happens when the sum of *a* and *b* is greater than the maximum integer value.

(b) The assembly code and function call graph under GCC-4.8.4-O0

(c) The assembly code and function call graph under GCC-4.8.4-O2

Fig. 1. Code example. (a) shows an example source code with integer overflow, (b) (c) show the assembly code and function call graph by compiling the source code with compiler GCC-4.8.4 but different optimization levels O0 vs. O2.

Prior works transform this problem to a machine learning-based classification problem [35,36]. That is, they regard the compilation provenance as the label, extract features from the binary code, and leverage machine learning methods, e.g., conditional random field, to predict (classify) the provenance. The key component in this design is the feature, as one needs to mine the useful features that are able to show the difference between various compilation provenance. Two types of features have been used in prior works, that is, the normalized instruction patterns, and the control flow graph [35,36].

1.1 Motivation

However, we observe that these features focus only on the instruction and function levels, and as a result, are unable to differentiate closely related provenances. For the example source code with integer overflow (happens when the sum of *a* and *b* exceeds the maximum value of *int*) shown in Fig. 1(a), one may compile with the same compiler but with different optimization levels (O0 vs. O2). The assembly codes (disassembled with IDA-Pro [4]) are presented in Fig. 1(b) and (c), respectively. For the control flow graph (CFG) features, as there are no branch instructions in both *sum* and *main* functions, their CFGs remain the same (one node) in both cases. Similarly, for the instruction features, after normalization, e.g., unifying the register and memory address, the patterns will be the same with the minor difference in the occurred frequency. As a result, using the aforementioned features alone will unlikely to produce the correct provenance for these two binary codes.

In this paper, we have observed that a new feature, i.e., the function call graph at the binary code level, can be used to significantly improve the accuracy of provenance identification, especially for those binary codes generated with different optimization levels. As we will show in Sect. 2, the optimization level has the largest impact in binary code similarity detection, compared with compiler family and version. Figure 1 also shows the function call graphs of the binaries. With optimization level O0, the *main* function calls three functions, i.e., the *sum* function and two library functions (*scanf* and *printf*). In contrast, with optimization level O2, the *main* function only calls the two library functions as the *sum* function is inlined shown in lines 17 and 18 in Fig. 1(c). Clearly, the function call graphs will be able to help differentiate these two cases.

1.2 Contribution

To take advantage of this observation, we have designed a new code provenance identification method, VESTIGE. Given a binary, VESTIGE transforms it to a new representation, i.e., attributed function call graph, that covers code features from three levels, instruction, function, and binary. Later, VESTIGE applies an attention-based graph neural network to generate a representative embedding to predict the compilation provenance.

In summary, we make the following contributions.

- **New representation and method.** We design a new representation for binary code, i.e., attributed function call graph (AFCG). The AFCG takes the function call graph from the binary level as the graph structure. Later, we attribute each node in the AFCG as a vector with the features from both instructions and functions. Further, VESTIGE applies the attention-based graph neural network (GAT) [39] to generate more accurate embeddings by directly learning from the attributed graph. GAT can learn a representative embedding by automatically highlighting the important nodes, which are, in this case, the more representative functions for the correct compilation provenance.
- **Implementation and evaluation.** We have implemented a prototype of VESTIGE and tested it on several publicly available datasets with more than six thousand binaries. For provenance identification, VESTIGE achieves 96% accuracy for overall provenance, which significantly outperforms previous work's 90% accuracy. Particularly for the optimization level, VESTIGE achieves 99% accuracy over previous work's 92%.
- **Applying to code vulnerability detection.** We successfully apply VESTIGE as a pre-processing step to binary code similarity detection and vulnerability detection. In both cases, given an unknown binary, prior works would compare it with the *known* vulnerable code from a pre-built database [11,13,14,40,43]. Such a strategy often leads to comparing two binary codes compiled with different provenances. Instead, with VESTIGE, one can first identify the compilation provenance of the unknown binary. Then, one only needs to compare it with the known vulnerable code compiled with the same provenance. In this way, one avoids the blind comparison

and thus can improve accuracy. Particularly, for code similarity detection, we apply VESTIGE to three recent works, BGM [14], Genius [14], and Gemini [40]. VESTIGE can improve the top-1 hit rate by 27%, 13%, and 22% for BGM, Genius, and Gemini, respectively. On detecting 20 OpenSSL vulnerabilities, VESTIGE helps improve the top-1 hit rate by 16%, 19%, and 26% for BGM, Genius, and Gemini, respectively.

Paper Organization. Section 2 explains the use case of VESTIGE on binary code similarity detection. Section 3 presents the design of VESTIGE, and Sect. 4 shows experimental results. Section 5 summarizes related work. Section 6 discusses and concludes the paper.

2   Use Case: Binary Code Similarity Detection

This section studies the use case of VESTIGE in binary code similarity detection. In the following, we discuss the background, challenge of code difference, and VESTIGE solution.

In this work, we focus on the static code similarity detection methods. The dynamic methods that leverage the dynamic execution behaviors, but face the scalability challenge [12] are left for future work. It is also worthy to point out that in this work we assume a binary is compiled with one compilation provenance. Although it is possible to compile a binary with different settings, the real-world software usually uses one configuration for easy maintenance and usability [7]. Further, the binary code is assumed to be stripped, which means one can not get helper information, such as section names, debugging symbols and sections, symbol and relocation information, and compiler-generated symbols.

2.1   Background

A lot of executable binary code performing different functionalities run in the servers, mobile devices, and Internet-of-Thing (IoT) devices [9,27,33]. Unfortunately, a large number of vulnerabilities exist in these binaries and have become the major attacking vectors [23]. For example, the researchers from Independent Security Evaluators (ISE) find 124 vulnerabilities from 13 routers and network-attached storage (NAS) devices in 2019 [5]. Also, in February 2020, Cisco confirms the existence of five critical vulnerabilities that have affected tens of millions of network devices [1].

Binary code similarity detection is a commonly used method to detect vulnerabilities [11,13,14,17,25,40,43]. Given an unknown binary, such a method would compare it with the vulnerable code from a pre-built vulnerability database. If the unknown code were similar to one vulnerable code, it would be considered as a positive which might share the same vulnerability. The identified similar code will be further investigated either manually or by automatic verification methods to confirm the vulnerability. The detection of an unknown binary is regarded as the online phase. Meanwhile, these methods usually need an offline phase, which includes preparing the known vulnerable code database and building the model, e.g., training for machine learning-based methods.

Here we illustrate the details of binary code similarity detection with a recent work Gemini [40]. First, for any function in the binary code, Gemini represents it as an attributed control flow graph (ACFG), where each node in the control flow graph is attributed as an eight-dimension feature vector, including betweenness centrality value and the number of string constants, numeric constants, transfer instructions, calls, instructions, arithmetic instructions, and offspring. Second, Gemini collects n (by default 154) vulnerable functions and extracts their ACFGs to build the known vulnerability database. Third, for an unknown binary, Gemini extracts the ACFG of each function, creates query pairs with the vulnerable functions in the vulnerability database, and computes their similarities. Assume there are m functions in the unknown binary, Gemini would create $m * n$ query pairs. Fourth, Gemini computes the similarity score of each function pair with a neural network-based embedding generation method. Particularly, Gemini applies a graph embedding network to firstly generate embeddings for the ACFGs. Later, Gemini uses the Siamese network to compute the similarity score. For each vulnerability function, Gemini would extract top-k (e.g., k equals 50) similar functions as positive. Finally, the security experts would verify the positive code to confirm the vulnerability.

2.2   Code Variance from Compilation

The same source code can be compiled to completely different binary codes, as various compilation toolchains can be used. Therefore, binary code similarity detection methods face the challenge of code variance brought by the compilation process. To figure out the impacts, we have studied a commonly used binary code representation, i.e., control flow graph (CFG), under different compilation provenances. The node in CFG denotes the basic block and the edge denotes the control flow. It is directly or indirectly used as the key data representation in the code similarity detection methods [11,14,40,43].

In this study, we compile the OpenSSL software (version 1.0.1f) with different compilation configurations. The default provenance is GCC-4.8.4 with optimization level O0 on architecture x86. Further, we compare with a higher optimization level O3, and a different compiler Clang-3.5. Figure 2 shows the cumulative distribution function of the similarity score between two CFGs of the same function but from differently compiled binaries. The similarity score is measured by the DSC similarity defined in Eq. (1), where $|A|, |B|$ denote the vertex count of CFG A and B, $|A \cap B|$ denotes the minimum vertex count between the two CFGs.

$$DSC(A, B) = \frac{2 * |A \cap B|}{(|A| + |B|)} \tag{1}$$

From Fig. 2, one can observe that both the optimization level and compiler affect the CFGs. In particular, the optimization level shows a bigger impact, only 42% CFGs share the same size and 20% CFGs show a similarity score of less than 0.53, in which the CFGs are already quite different. The compiler also affects the CFGs but with a smaller effect. That is, 71% CFGs share the same size.

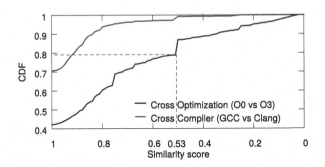

Fig. 2. The cumulative distributed function (CDF) of CFG size similarity for different optimizations and compilers.

2.3   Solution with VESTIGE

To tackle this challenge, existing binary code similarity detection methods focus on developing algorithms to eliminate these variances. For example, Genius uses clustering and locality sensitive hashing [14], Gemini uses graph embedding network and Siamese network [40], InnerEye uses recurrent neural networks [43], and Asm2Vec uses PV-DM model [11]. These methods have been shown to work well in their experiments, but the number of tested compilation provenances is limited. For example, excluding architecture variance, they tested 12, 4, 4, and 8 for Genius, Gemini, InnerEye, and Asm2vec, respectively.

Clearly, the complete coverage of compilation provenance poses a significant challenge. As of this writing, GCC has released 202 versions [3] and LLVM has 53 versions [2]. Each version has at least 4 optimization levels, which makes the number of compilation provenances for these two compilers more than one thousand, not to mention other factors that can also affect compilation provenance.

Besides capturing the code variance from different compilation provenances, the all-in-one models in these methods also need to identify the difference between the binary code compiled from different source code, which is also challenging. When the compilation provenance scales up, the performance of existing works will drop further as a result.

The key tenet of this work is that *identifying compilation provenance accurately will help produce better detection results of binary code similarity.* As shown in Fig. 3, one can leverage VESTIGE to first identify the compilation provenance of the unknown binary. With the provenance information, the following code similarity detector only needs to compute the similarity between the unknown binary code and the known vulnerable code (from the vulnerability database) having the same compilation provenance. That means, existing code similarity detection methods only need to worry about the challenge from different source codes. Further, such a solution can scale up as VESTIGE takes over the burden of handling a large number of compilation provenances. With VESTIGE, the performance of code similarity and vulnerability detection can be significantly improved as we will show in Sect. 4.

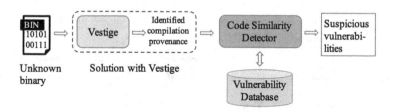

Fig. 3. Applying VESTIGE to binary code similarity detection. The dotted rectangle shows the preprocessing step with provenance identification.

3   VESTIGE Design

This section presents the design of VESTIGE, including attributed function call graph construction, provenance identification with graph neural network, and implementation.

3.1   Overview

The architecture of VESTIGE is shown in Fig. 4. Given a binary, VESTIGE first disassembles it to assembly code. Later, VESTIGE extracts three types of features, i.e., the idiom features from the instruction level, the graphlet features on the control flow graph from the function level, and the function call graph from the binary level. With all these features, we build a new representation, named attributed function call graph (AFCG). Next, VESTIGE generates the graph embedding for AFCG with an attention-based graph neural network.

During the training stage, VESTIGE tunes the graph neural network model by the downstream task, i.e., multi-graph classification. In this case, the label is the compilation provenance combined by compiler family, compiler version, and optimization level.

During the inference stage, VESTIGE will go through the same process of disassembling binary code and constructing AFCG, but output the predicted compilation provenance.

3.2   Representing Binary Code as Attributed Function Call Graph

The key to provenance identification is to find the appropriate features that can show the difference between various compilation provenances. We find there are three levels of features that can be used in combination to identify provenance. Together, we construct a new representation for the binary code as attributed function call graph (AFCG). Below, we will discuss why the features are useful for provenance identification and how we extract them.

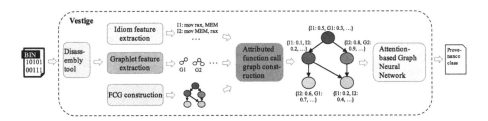

Fig. 4. The architecture of VESTIGE. Given a binary code, VESTIGE first builds the attributed function call graph by disassembling it and extracting three types of features, i.e., idiom, graphlet, and function call graph. Later, VESTIGE applies the attention-based graph neural network to predict the provenance.

1) Instruction level features are used because different compilers and configurations usually have different approaches in terms of instruction usage, register usage, instruction ordering, etc. For example, for the source code *"tbio = BIO_pop(f)"* in line 3 of Fig. 5(a), GCC-4.8.4-O0 would use the accumulator register *eax* and two *mov* instructions before calling the *BIO_pop* function. On the other hand, GCC-4.8.4-O2 would use the base address register *ebx* and just one *mov* instruction.

To identify the differences, we take the instruction patterns, known as idioms, as the instruction features for provenance identification [35,37]. These features are generated in two steps, instruction normalization, and feature extraction.

Instruction normalization will keep the essential opcode and normalize the operands to a general shape. Particularly, we will normalize the register, memory address, and other user-controlled operands, such as constant and function name. For the assembly code in Fig. 5(b), we will normalize them to the code shown in Fig. 6(a).

In the second step, we extract the unique instruction patterns and their combinations as the feature whose size is the number of covered instructions. To improve the representativeness of the patterns, we add the wildcard to represent any instruction. For the example code, the extracted features are shown in Fig. 6(a) with '|' as the instruction split symbol.

2) Function level features. Similarly, different compilation process will affect how the basic blocks form the control flow graph (CFG). As a CFG is extracted from a function, we consider such features at the function level. For the example code in Fig. 5(a), it is one node with GCC-4.8.4-O0 shown in Fig. 5(b), while it is split into two nodes with GCC-4.8.4-O2 shown in Fig. 5(c).

Again, we extract the function features in two steps, CFG normalization and feature extraction. First, we normalize the CFG by assigning a type value to each node and edge. As each node is a basic block, its type value will be decided by the category of contained instructions, e.g., string, branch, and logic operation [24]. We classify the instructions into 14 categories and use a 14-bit integer to represent the type, where each bit denotes whether the specific instruction category exists or not. For the edges initiated by branch operations, we label them based on the different types of branch operations, e.g., *jnz, jge*. The normalized CFG of the example function is shown in Fig. 6(b).

Second, we extract different subgraphs from the normalized CFG as features. A subgraph is regarded as a subset of the connected nodes with the corresponding edges. For the example CFG in Fig. 6(b), its subgraphs included G1, G2, G3, and others. As the goal here is to mine useful subgraph patterns that can represent the compilation provenance, we set a threshold to the interested subgraph size (number of nodes) to avoid mining all the possible subgraphs, which is not scalable as it is an NP problem [15].

3) Binary level features. In this work, we especially focus on the fact that the compilers will optimize the program from the *binary level* to achieve the optimal global performance. Many compiler optimizations work on the binary level, such as, function inlining, interprocedural dead code elimination, interprocedural constant propagation, and procedure reordering [6]. Taking the *function inlining* (usually enabled in *O2* and *O3*) as an example, it heuristically selects

```
1 ...
2 do {
3         tbio = BIO_pop(f);
4         BIO_free(f);
5         f = tbio;
6 } while (f != upto)
7 ...
```

(a) Source code fragment of CVE-2015-1792

```
loc_81A85B6:
mov    eax, [esp+2Ch+arg_0]
mov    [esp+2Ch+var_2C], eax
call   BIO_pop
mov    [esp+2Ch+var_10], eax
...
```

(b) Compiled with GCC-4.8.4-O0

```
loc_816C6F2:
mov    [esp+1Ch+var_1C], ebx
call   BIO_pop
mov    [esp+1Ch+var_1C], ebx
...

loc_816C6F0:
...
```

(c) Compiled with GCC-4.8.4-O2

```
loc_824A343:
mov    eax, [esp+1Ch+arg_0]
mov    [esp+1Ch+var_1C], eax
call   BIO_pop
mov    [esp+1Ch+var_1C], eax
...
```

(d) Compiled with Clang-5.0-O0

Fig. 5. A running example code and its assembly code with different compilation provenance. (a) shows the source code fragment of CVE-2015-1792, (b) (c) (d) show its assembly code with GCC-4.8.4-O0, GCC-4.8.4-O2, and Clang-5.0-O0, respectively.

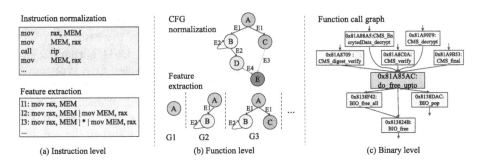

Fig. 6. The features in three levels for provenance identification, using the assembly code from Fig. 5(b) as an example.

the functions worth inlining. From the binary level, one can clearly see the difference from a feature like the call relationships between functions.

We find that the function call graph (FCG), generated in the binary level, is an effective representation to show the changes brought by different compilation provenances. In an FCG, the node denotes a function, and the edge denotes the call relationship. It is able to capture the difference from function changes in terms of number, call relationship, etc. Thus, we construct the FCG as the binary level feature.

*4) **Attributed function call graph (AFCG).*** To combine the features from three different levels together, we newly design a representation, namely attributed function call graph (AFCG). Taking the function call graph (FCG) as the core structure, it attributes each node (function in this case) as an initial feature vector.

At the training phase, we need to extract the features from a number of binaries. Since we are extracting the patterns from both instruction and CFG, the resulted number of features is massive. One can get an impression of the instruction features in Fig. 6(a). For the first two instructions, we construct 4 features in total, 2 for single instruction, 1 for the two instructions, and 1 for the two instructions with wildcard in-between. In our experiment with only 600 binaries, the number of extracted features is up to millions. This is known as the feature explosion challenge, which would cause the machine learning algorithms to take an incredibly long time to converge [26].

To solve that, we employ the feature selection technique. Particularly, we use the mutual information method to select a reasonable number of *good* features. In this case, a feature is *good* if it is important to classify different classes, which can be quantified by the mutual information between the feature and class. In the end, we select the top-k highly ranked features. Further, for the feature value, which is initialized as the frequency, we will normalize it to [0: 1] to avoid feature bias. Particularly, we divide each feature frequency to the maximum frequency value among all the binaries. To this end, we build the AFCG with a reasonable number of attributes. An example of the final AFCG is shown in Fig. 4.

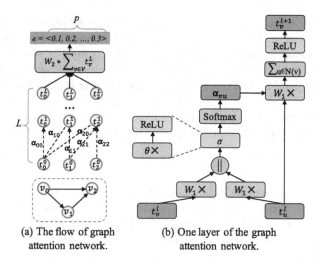

(a) The flow of graph attention network.

(b) One layer of the graph attention network.

Fig. 7. Graph attention network (GAT). (a) shows the workflow, (b) explains one layer.

3.3 Identifying Provenance with Graph Neural Network

After we generate the AFCG for each binary, the problem is transformed into a multi-class graph classification problem. Such a problem is a perfect fit for the graph neural network (GNN) [8,10,22,39], which is able to learn an embedding for a graph and further tune the model based on the downstream task, i.e., multi-graph classification.

For provenance identification, we apply a recently developed graph neural network, i.e., graph attention network (GAT) [39]. Conventional graph neural networks, e.g., GCN [22] and structure2vec [10], iteratively learn a model by accumulating the neighbor embeddings based on the fixed graph structure, i.e., equally or degree-based. However, in this application, the neighbor nodes or edges on the AFCG have different impacts on the final embedding. For example, when generating the embedding of a node in the AFCG, the function with critical compilation features that can be used to identify the provenance should be more representative, and thus should be weighted more for embedding generation. Fortunately, the graph attention network (GAT) with the attention mechanism satisfies our requirement. GAT is able to automatically identify the important nodes and edges and will assign larger weights to the more important ones and smaller weights to the less important ones. We will elaborate on the details below.

GAT takes a graph g as input, iteratively computes the node embedding by attention on its neighbor nodes, and outputs a learned embedding e for the whole graph as shown in Fig. 7(a). GAT is stacked with L layers. Each layer (except the input layer) takes the node embeddings from the previous layer as input and outputs the computed node embeddings from this layer. Below, we will discuss the details of GAT.

Attention Mechanism. For the $(l+1)$-th layer, the node embedding computation for node v is shown in Fig. 7(b). For every neighbor node of v (including itself), GAT first learns an attention coefficient, and later computes the embedding for node v. We use t_v^l to represent the embedding for node v at the l-th layer which has d-dimension, and t_v^{l+1} to represent the embedding at the $(l+1)$-th layer which has d'-dimension. For every edge connecting u and v, we use α_{vu} to denote the attention coefficient, which is computed from a single-layer feedforward neural network. The formalized equation is shown in Eq. (2),

$$\alpha_{vu} = \text{softmax}\left(\sigma\left(\theta\left[W_1 t_v^l \parallel W_1 t_u^l\right]\right)\right) \tag{2}$$

where softmax($\cdot$) represents the standard softmax function which normalizes the input vector into a probability distribution, $\sigma(\cdot)$ represents the activation function which is the ReLU function in our setting, θ is a weight vector with $2d'$ dimensions, W_1 is a shared weight matrix with $d' \times d$ dimensions, and $\parallel$ is the concatenation operation.

Graph Convolution. After obtaining the attention coefficients from the neighbors of node v, GAT will accumulate the neighbor embedding, which is the graph convolution operation [22]. The formalized equation is shown in Eq. (3).

$$t_v^{l+1} = \sigma\left(\sum_{u \in N(v)} \alpha_{vu} W_1 t_u^l\right) \tag{3}$$

Here for each edge connecting u and v, its accumulated value will be the multiplication of the attention coefficient α_{vu}, weight matrix W_1, and embedding t_u^l of node u. Followed by another activation function, one will get the node embedding t_v^{l+1} with d'-dimension.

Graph Embedding. At the output layer, we will accumulate all the node embeddings in this graph to one embedding as in Eq. (4),

$$e = W_2\left(\sum_{v \in V} t_v^L\right) \tag{4}$$

where W_2 is a weight matrix with dimension $p \times p$ and p equals to d' of the previous layer, e is a p dimension vector. We use the cross-entropy loss function to compute the loss value between graph embedding and the provenance class. Later, it backward propagates the loss value to the previous layers and optimizes the learned model with Adam optimizer aiming at minimizing the loss value.

3.4   Implementation

VESTIGE includes two major components, AFCG constructor and graph attention network. The AFCG constructor is implemented on top of a binary analysis platform, Dyninst [38]. We set the pattern size of instruction and function level features to be 3 since larger features are slow to generate and usually have low importance ranks. This setting already yields a million scale feature count for the evaluated dataset (discussed in Sect. 4). We set the selected number of features for instruction and function to be $1,024$ (studied in Sect. 4.3).

We implement the graph attention network with TensorFlow (v1.3.0) and set the intermediate and final embedding size as 128, the number of epochs 100, the number of iterations 4, the number of heads 2, the learning rate 0.0001. The parameters are selected based on both accuracy and runtime (Sect. 4.3).

4   Experiment

In this section, we conduct extensive experiments to answer the following research questions:

- **(RQ1)** How does VESTIGE compare with other works on provenance identification?
- **(RQ2)** How do the two key designs in VESTIGE, i.e., attributed function call graph (AFCG) and graph attention network (GAT), affect the performance?
- **(RQ3)** How do various parameters impact the performance of VESTIGE, including the number of features for constructing AFCG and the hyperparameters in graph attention network?
- **(RQ4)** How can we apply VESTIGE to binary code similarity detection as well as vulnerability detection?

4.1   Experiment Setting and Dataset

We run the experiments on an internal server, which has two Intel Xeon E5-2683 (2.00 GHz) CPUs. Each CPU has 14 cores and enables hyper-threading. It is also equipped with four Nvidia K40 GPUs, while only one is used for each run.

We use the following three datasets for the experiment.

Dataset I: Baseline dataset. We build a baseline dataset with five standard software, i.e., GNU Bash (v4.3), Diffutils (v3.3), Grep (v2.16), Tar (v1.27.1), and Wget (v1.15). We compiled them with 24 different compilation provenances, including six compilers, i.e., GCC-{4.6.4, 4.8.4, 5.4.1} and Clang-{3.3, 3.5, 5.0}, and four optimization levels (O0-O3) on x86 architecture. In the end, we are able to collect 336 binaries as some software may generate multiple binaries, e.g., 4 for Diffutils. We use this dataset for evaluating provenance identification.

Dataset II: Code similarity dataset. We build a code similarity dataset with six software, SNNS-4.2, PostgreSQL-7.2, Binutils-{2.25, 2.30}, and Coreutils-{8.21, 8.29}. They are compiled with the same 24 compilation provenances. In total, we get 6,168 binaries. This dataset is used for both provenance identification and code similarity detection.

Dataset III: Vulnerability dataset. We build a vulnerability dataset with three versions of OpenSSL (0.9.7f, 1.0.1f, and 1.0.1n) by collecting 20 CVEs.

They are also compiled with the same 24 provenances. This dataset is used for vulnerability detection.

The **evaluation metric** used for provenance identification is accuracy, which is defined as the number of correctly classified samples over the total. As the label distribution is balanced, the accuracy is a valid metric. For the experiments of code similarity and vulnerability detection, the used metric is hit rate. Among the top-k similar code, if the targeted code is included, it is a hit, otherwise, it is a miss. Since the top-k similar codes are usually manually investigated by the security analysts, a higher hit rate with a smaller k would be valued.

4.2   Accuracy of Provenance Identification

This section studies the accuracy of VESTIGE and related works on provenance identification, which answers research questions **RQ1** and **RQ2**. This experiment uses the 6,504 binaries from the baseline (dataset I) and code similarity dataset (dataset II). We perform 10-fold cross-validation. For each binary, we guarantee that all of its 24 provenance varieties are split into the same group so that we can justify the generalization of the trained model. In this experiment, all the methods use 1,024 instruction, and function level features.

We compare with two implementations, i.e., a recent work Origin [35] and a baseline of VESTIGE with a different graph neural network model, structure2vec (S2V) [10]. We get the source code of Origin from the Dyninst group. Both implementations are configured with the parameters leading to their best performance.

Table 1. Accuracy of binary code provenance identification (The best are highlighted).

	Origin	VESTIGE-S2V	VESTIGE-GAT
Optimization level	92.2%	98.7%	**99.0%**
Compiler version	96.8%	95.5%	**97.9%**
Compiler family	**99.5%**	**99.5%**	**99.5%**
Overall accuracy	90.2%	93.3%	**96.1%**

Table 1 presents the accuracy for overall provenance, and specific compilation configurations, i.e., optimization level, compiler version, and compiler family. Each case is studied independently while keeping the other two unchanged. We can get three consistent observations. First, VESTIGE outperforms other works on provenance identification for the overall and specific provenance (**RQ1**). For the overall provenance, VESTIGE with GAT is able to achieve 96.1% accuracy over Origin's 90.2%. For the specific provenances, VESTIGE achieves 99% accuracy over Origin's 92.2% for optimization levels. For compiler versions, VESTIGE achieves 97.9% accuracy over Origin's 96.8%. For compiler family, both methods achieve a rather high accuracy at 99.5%.

Second, GAT is effective for provenance identification (**RQ2**). With the same input, VESTIGE with GAT outperforms VESTIGE with S2V for both overall and specific compilation provenances as shown in Table 1. The improvement demonstrates the effectiveness of the attention mechanism on capturing the important nodes and features towards the correct compilation provenance.

Third, AFCG is an efficient representation for the binary code towards compilation provenance identification, especially for optimization level (**RQ2**). We intend to compare two implementations with the only difference in AFCG, while the machine learning method in Origin can not take AFCG as input and the graph neural network can not sustain the input of Origin. From both Table 1 and Fig. 8, we can see the effectiveness of AFCG. From Table 1, one can see VESTIGE-S2V gets 98.7% accuracy over Origin's 92.2% for optimization level.

Further, Fig. 8 shows the accuracy changes for overall and specific compilation provenance with a different number of instruction and function features. Interestingly, with only 16 features, VESTIGE can achieve 98% accuracy for optimization level, up to 31% higher than Origin. This clearly shows the impact of binary-level features for provenance identification. AFCG is able to identify optimization level differences since many optimizations work on the binary level. Origin crashes when adding more features beyond 1, 024 due to the large intermediate data size crashes the used tool, CRFsuite [31].

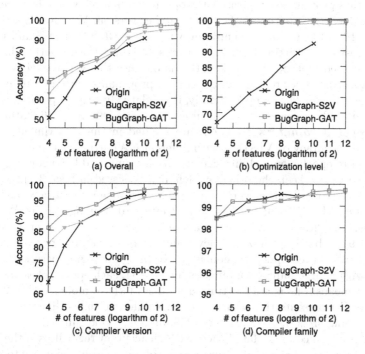

Fig. 8. Accuracy of binary provenance identification with different number of features for (a) overall, (b) optimization level, (c) compiler version, and (d) compiler family.

4.3 Sensitivity Study

This section conducts sensitivity study for the feature count in AFCG and the hyper-parameters in GAT (**RQ3**). We use the same dataset from the previous experiment and also perform 10-fold cross validation.

1) Feature count in AFCG denotes the total number of instruction and function level features. This is the major parameter for constructing AFCG, as only a small number (thousand scale) of the total features (million scale) will be selected. We perform an extensive study on this parameter by selecting different number of features. Particularly, we test the provenance accuracy of overall, optimization level, compiler version, and compiler family for the number of features from 16 to 4,096 with the power of two. The results are shown in Fig. 8.

We can get two consistent observations in this experiment. First, VESTIGE and the two compared works mostly converge with around 1,024 features. For the overall accuracy, VESTIGE-GAT achieves 96.1% with 1,024 features. With 4,096 features, the accuracy only improves a little bit 0.8%. Similar observation can be concluded on the accuracy of VESTIGE-S2V. To this end, we can conclude that 1,024 instruction and function level features are sufficient for provenance identification.

Second, the binary level feature can help to effectively identify the changes from different provenance, especially the optimization level, which has been studied in the previous experiment. For the compiler version, VESTIGE is able to get 86% with 16 initial features, comparing with VESTIGE-S2V's 81% and Origin's 68%. Interestingly, starting from 128 features, Origin performs better than VESTIGE-S2V-based method. We believe this is because the S2V model is not able to emphasize the nodes relating to the correct provenance since it equally weighs the neighbor nodes. For compiler family, it is relatively easy to predict as all the methods are able to achieve high accuracy, i.e., over 98% from 16 features.

2) Hyper-parameters in GAT are studied in this experiment. Figure 9 presents the accuracy of VESTIGE with different GAT hyper-parameters, including number of epochs, embedding size, iteration count, and head count. For each parameter test, we keep the others as default (discussed in Sect. 3.4).

Figure 9(a) presents the overall and specific provenance accuracy against the number of epochs. We run the test dataset every 10 training epochs. With only 20 epochs, VESTIGE already reaches a stable state, where the overall accuracy is around 95%, both optimization level and compiler family are close to 100% accuracy, and the compiler version is above 95%. In this experiment, we are training with a large number of binaries, i.e., 5,854, each epoch takes about 10.3 min. That means, one is able to train a usable VESTIGE model within 206 min.

Figure 9(b) presents the accuracy against different embedding size. We test five embedding sizes, i.e., 32, 64, 128, 256, and 512. One can see that the optimization level and compiler family achieve high accuracy regardless of the embedding size. However, the overall accuracy and compiler version increase to a stable state from embedding size 128. As larger embedding sizes take longer time to

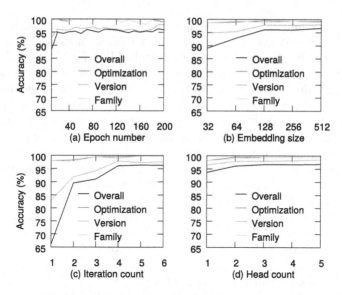

Fig. 9. Sensitivity study of hyper-parameters in GAT, including (a) epoch number, (b) embedding size, (c) iteration count, and (d) head count.

train, e.g., embedding size 512 costs 26% more time than size 128 per epoch, we select 128 as the embedding size.

Figure 9(c) shows the accuracy against different number of iterations. We test six iteration counts from 1 to 6. The optimization level and compiler family achieve high accuracy from 3 iterations, while the overall and compiler version achieve high accuracy from 4 iterations. Although the iteration count does not significantly affect the runtime, training with 6 iterations still costs 3% more time than 4 iterations per epoch. Therefore, we set the iteration count to be 4.

Figure 9(d) shows the accuracy against different number of heads from 1 to 5. One can observe that starting from 2 heads, the model achieves high accuracy for the overall provenance as well as each specific provenance. For the runtime, training with 5 heads would incur 11% more time per epoch. Therefore, we set the head count to 2.

4.4 Case Study: Code Similarity Detection

This section applies VESTIGE to binary code similarity detection, and later vulnerability detection (**RQ4**). Particularly, we apply three recent code similarity detection methods, i.e., Gemini [40], Genius [14], and BGM [14]. They convert each binary function as an attributed control flow graph (ACFG), which is presented in §2. We illustrate their details in the following.

- *Bipartite graph matching (BGM)* is a baseline method to evaluate the pairwise graph-based matching approaches [14,40]. BGM regards the similarity score of two binary functions as the graph edit distance-based similarity between the two ACFGs. We get its source code from the authors of Genius [14].

- *Genius* is the first work of using graph embedding for binary code similarity detection [14]. Since each function is represented as an ACFG, Genius uses graph edit distance to compute the similarity of two functions. Later, it applies the *bag-of-words* method to create a high-level embedding for each function. During online searching, it uses semantic hashing on the embeddings to quickly get the similar code. We get part of the source code from the authors and reimplement the rest.
- *Gemini* presents the first work of using a graph neural network to generate embeddings for binary code similarity detection [40]. It uses the Siamese network to supervise the embedding generation. The Siamese network takes two embeddings as input with the label as either +1 for similar and −1 for different, computes the loss value, and back propagates it to embedding generation. We get its source code from the authors.

1) Case #1: Code Similarity Detection.

The code similarity dataset (Dataset II) is used for this experiment. BGM does not need training, but it needs tuning the cost weight for the eight attributes in ACFG. We use the default values from [40] as they get them through large scale testing. Both Genius and Gemini need the training to be able to identify similar code. Realizing the binaries from the same software may share similar code, we split the dataset into training and testing from the software level. That is, we use the 600 binaries from software SNNS and PostgreSQL as training dataset, and the 5,568 binaries from Binutils-{2.25, 2.30} and Coreutils-{8.21, 8.29} as testing dataset. VESTIGE uses the same split for the training and testing dataset. Such dataset splitting would show the generability of both VESTIGE and code similarity detection methods.

Table 2. Top-1 and top-5 hit rate for the original methods and new solutions with VESTIGE on binary code similarity detection.

	Top-1		Top-5	
	Original	+ VESTIGE	Original	+ VESTIGE
BGM	29%	56%	45%	89%
Genius	51%	64%	69%	91%
Gemini	66%	87%	77%	94%

During testing, we randomly select 1,000 different query functions from the testing dataset. For each query function, we will search the targeted binaries, which are known to have matches to the query function. In the end, we compute the average hit rate of the 1,000 queries under different top-k values.

To integrate with the code similarity methods, during the online phase, we first use VESTIGE to figure out the compilation provenance of the query binary, and later apply the code similarity methods to compute function similarities with the predicted provenance. In this case, Vestige gets 82% accuracy for the whole compilation provenance, and 100%, 96% and 84% accuracy for compiler family, compiler version, and optimization level, respectively. Although the performance drops compared with cross validation result from Sect. 4.2, it is reasonable as the training and testing are on a completely different dataset and the size of the testing dataset is much larger than the training. In fact, this shows the generability of our method in a practical scenario.

Table 2 shows the hit rate of top-1 and top-5 for the three code similarity detection methods without and with our provenance identifier. We can observe that provenance identification is able to significantly improve the performance of all the works. Particularly, for the top-1 hit rate, the original code similarity detection methods, BGM, Genius, and Gemini get 29%, 51%, and 66%, respectively. Vestige is able to improve the hit rate by 27%, 13%, and 22%, for BGM, Genius, and Gemini, respectively. Top-1 hit rate is most important because the security analysts would start the manual investigation from the first one. Further, for the top-5 hit rate, the provenance identifier is able to improve BGM, Genius, and Gemini by 44%, 22%, and 17%, respectively. Interestingly, the simple baseline method, BGM, with Vestige is able to reach a rather high 89% hit rate. Note that, the hit rates of prior works align with their original reports since we only pick up the most strict and meaningful top-1 and top-5 hit rates.

2) Case #2: Vulnerability Detection.

In this study, we extend the evaluation of general code similarity detection to the specific case of vulnerability detection. Particularly, we reuse the trained models of the three code similarity works and Vestige from the previous experiment.

We use the vulnerability dataset (Dataset III), and take the ACFGs from OpenSSL-1.0.1f as the vulnerability database. For each binary, we will query against the binaries with 24 different compilation provenances from OpenSSL-1.0.1f. We report the average results of all the binaries with different compilation provenances for that OpenSSL version. Our provenance identifier is able to get 71% accuracy for the overall provenance, and 94%, 78%, 75% for compiler family, compiler version, and optimization level, respectively.

Table 3 shows the top-1 hit rate of the three works without and with Vestige for the 20 CVEs. Interestingly, the provenance identification of Vestige is able to significantly improve the performance of the original works on code similarity detection. One can see that, the original code similarity works get 50%, 39%, 33% top-1 hit rate for Gemini, Genius, and BGM, respectively. With Vestige, the top-1 hit rate improves to 76%, 58%, and 49% for Gemini, Genius, and BGM, respectively.

To understand the false positives of vulnerability detection, we take a deep look at the specific cases. A false positive is likely to happen if a queried normal function shares similar ACFG with the vulnerable function. Although it is uncommon for two completely different functions to have similar ACFGs, we do observe some occurrences, e.g., CVE-2016-0705 which is a double free vul-

Table 3. The average hit rate (%) of top-1 candidates on the 20 CVEs. +P represents adding our provenance identifier VESTIGE to their methods.

CVE	Query	BGM : +P	Genius : +P	Gemini : +P
2015-0209	1.0.1f	46 : 67	50 : 71	50 : 88
2014-0195	1.0.1f	33 : 42	42 : 58	54 : 92
2016-2106	1.0.1f	58 : 63	58 : 63	63 : 83
2012-0027	1.0.1f	42 : 58	58 : 67	63 : 88
2014-3513	1.0.1f	46 : 71	50 : 83	67 : 92
2015-1791	1.0.1f	50 : 67	50 : 83	71 : 96
2015-3196	1.0.1f	42 : 67	38 : 75	58 : 92
2014-3567	1.0.1f	22 : 56	33 : 67	50 : 79
2016-0797	1.0.1n	21 : 41	25 : 41	38 : 83
2016-2180	1.0.1n	25 : 42	29 : 83	46 : 95
2016-2105	0.9.7f	58 : 67	47 : 58	58 : 83
2016-2176	1.0.1n	38 : 42	38 : 46	50 : 67
2016-2109	0.9.7f	10 : 29	30 : 38	40 : 54
2015-3195	0.9.7f	25 : 42	50 : 63	58 : 83
2016-2182	0.9.7f	25 : 42	33 : 50	46 : 58
2016-2178	0.9.7f	13 : 25	19 : 42	25 : 63
2015-0292	0.9.7f	37 : 42	46 : 54	50 : 67
2016-2105	0.9.7f	58 : 63	58 : 63	67 : 71
2016-2842	1.0.1n	5 : 25	10 : 33	19 : 50
2016-0705	1.0.1n	13 : 21	17 : 21	19 : 42
Average	–	33 : 49	39 : 58	50 : 76

nerability in function dsa_priv_decode. In this case, another function, named d2i_ECPrivateKey, is ranked as top-1 for some queries, which encodes and decodes functions for saving and reading a key data structure. We have identified two factors that explain this false positive. First, although the source codes of the two functions are different, they share some similarities. Both of them are related to private key decode, which results in them both invoking a number of similar private key related functions. And the two functions have similar coding characteristics, i.e., both have many conditional branches (including if and goto), and neither has loop operations. Thus, their structures and code features are similar. Second, from the binary level, these two functions share quite similar graph structures. For example, for OpenSSL version 1.0.1f compiled with Clang-3.3-O0, the CFG of dsa_priv_decode has 44 nodes and 61 edges, while d2i_ECPrivateKey has 40 nodes and 58 edges. In short, in this case, the best traditional solution, i.e., Gemini, shows the top-1 hit rate of 50% across 24 varieties. However, with VESTIGE, the hit rate improves to 76%.

5   Related Work

The first work on binary code compilation provenance identification is done by Rosenblum *et al.* [36]. They extract the instruction level features, i.e., idioms, and train a provenance identification model with the linear conditional random fields (CRF) method. Further, they design Origin by adding another type of feature, i.e., the graphlet features from function level [35]. They still use the same linear CRF model. Although there are two more proposed works, Origin still achieves the best performance [28]. BinComp builds a three-layer provenance identification model [34]. The first layer learns the code transformation rules with supervised learning. The second layer extracts the statistical features and labels compiler-related functions. The third layer identifies the compiler version and optimization level from the semantic features. BinComp relies on compiler helper information, which is affected by a complete strip. Massarelli *et al.* design a graph embedding neural network for provenance identification [28]. They build an attributed control flow graph by representing each basic block as an embedding with natural language processing (NLP) models. Using NLP model is promising, but they also miss the important binary level features. o-glassesX [32] identifies the compilation provenance from a short code fragment using a deep learning model with attention mechanism and convolutional neural network. However, the compiler version and optimization level are not well differentiated. For example, the optimization level is only classified as either low (O0) or high (O3). We only compared with Origin and a variant of VESTIGE for two reasons. First, we were not able to find the source code of some other works, e.g., BinComp [34]. Second, even if we got the source code, e.g., o-glassesX [32] (we really appreciate their efforts of releasing them), we were not able to run them on our dataset due to failures on configuring the required disassembly tools.

6   Discussion and Conclusion

The interpretation of machine learning methods, especially neural networks, is an open challenge. VESTIGE uses one graph-based neural network, i.e., graph attention network. We have tried to interpret VESTIGE from the perspective of extracting useful features towards code provenance identification, i.e., the three-level features investigated in Sect. 3. Recently, we see several interesting methods for graph neural network explanation [42]. In the future, we would try to explain VESTIGE with such methods. Though VESTIGE uses a graph neural network, it takes reasonable time for training and inference. We also see some interesting works on accelerating the computation of graph algorithms [18–20], which we would like to leverage in the future to further improve the runtime performance.

In this work, we designed VESTIGE, a binary code provenance identification framework with a graph neural network. VESTIGE designs a new representation of binary code, i.e., attributed function call graph (AFCG) and applies an attention-based graph neural network, graph attention network. We have tested VESTIGE on several publicly available datasets with more than six thousand binaries. VESTIGE outperforms state-of-the-art by 6% for overall provenance.

Acknowledgment. The authors would like to thank the anonymous reviewers from ACNS'21 for their help in improving this paper. We would also like to express our grateful thanks to the authors of Genius, Gemini, and Origin (including Xiaozhu Meng) for sharing the source code and dataset with us. Lei Cui participated in this work while working as a postdoctoral researcher at the George Washington University from June 2017 to July 2018. This work was supported in part by DARPA under agreement number N66001-18-C-4033 and National Science Foundation CAREER award 1350766 and grants 1618706 and 1717774. The views, opinions, and/or findings expressed in this material are those of the authors and should not be interpreted as representing the official views or policies of the Department of Defense, National Science Foundation, or the U.S. Government.

References

1. Cisco confirms 5 serious security threats to 'tens of millions' of network devices, February 2020. https://www.forbes.com/sites/daveywinder/2020/02/05/cisco-confirms-5-serious-security-threats-to-tens-of-millions-of-network-devices
2. Download LLVM releases, December 2019. https://releases.llvm.org/
3. GCC releases - GNU project, March 2020. https://gcc.gnu.org/releases.html
4. Ida pro - interactive disassembler. https://www.hex-rays.com/products/ida/
5. Researchers uncover 125 vulnerabilities across 13 routers and NAS devices (2019). https://www.helpnetsecurity.com/2019/09/17/vulnerabilities-iot-devices/
6. Using the GNU compiler collection (GCC): Optimize options. https://gcc.gnu.org/onlinedocs/gcc/Optimize-Options.html
7. Batchelor, J., Andersen, H.R.: Bridging the product configuration gap between PLM and ERP–an automotive case study. In: 19th International Product Development Management Conference (2012)
8. Bowman, B., Laprade, C., Ji, Y., Huang, H.H.: Detecting lateral movement in enterprise computer networks with unsupervised graph AI. In: Proceedings of the 23rd International Symposium on Research in Attacks, Intrusions and Defenses (RAID) (2020)
9. Dabrowski, A., Echizen, I., Weippl, E.R.: Error-correcting codes as source for decoding ambiguity. In: 2015 IEEE Security and Privacy Workshops (2015)
10. Dai, H., Dai, B., Song, L.: Discriminative embeddings of latent variable models for structured data. In: International Conference on Machine Learning (2016)
11. Ding, S.H., Fung, B.C., Charland, P.: Asm2Vec: boosting static representation robustness for binary clone search against code obfuscation and compiler optimization. In: Proceedings of the IEEE Symposium on Security and Privacy (2019)
12. Egele, M., Woo, M., Chapman, P., Brumley, D.: Blanket execution: dynamic similarity testing for program binaries and components. In: USENIX Security (2014)
13. Eschweiler, S., Yakdan, K., Gerhards-Padilla, E.: discovRE: efficient cross-architecture identification of bugs in binary code. In: Proceedings of NDSS (2016)
14. Feng, Q., Zhou, R., Xu, C., Cheng, Y., Testa, B., Yin, H.: Scalable graph-based bug search for firmware images. In: Proceedings of ACM CCS (2016)
15. Grochow, J.A., Kellis, M.: Network motif discovery using subgraph enumeration and symmetry-breaking. In: Speed, T., Huang, H. (eds.) RECOMB 2007. LNCS, vol. 4453, pp. 92–106. Springer, Heidelberg (2007). https://doi.org/10.1007/978-3-540-71681-5_7

16. Ji, Y., Bowman, B., Huang, H.H.: Securing malware cognitive systems against adversarial attacks. In: International Conference on Cognitive Computing (ICCC). IEEE (2019)
17. Ji, Y., Cui, L., Huang, H.H.: BugGraph: differentiating source-binary code similarity with graph triplet-loss network. In: 16th ACM ASIA Conference on Computer and Communications Security (ASIACCS) (2021)
18. Ji, Y., Huang, H.H.: Aquila: adaptive parallel computation of graph connectivity queries. In: Proceedings of the 29th International Symposium on High-Performance Parallel and Distributed Computing (HPDC) (2020)
19. Ji, Y., Liu, H., Huang, H.H.: iSpan: parallel identification of strongly connected components with spanning trees. In: International Conference for High Performance Computing, Networking, Storage and Analysis (SC), pp. 731–742. IEEE (2018)
20. Ji, Y., Liu, H., Huang, H.H.: SWARMGRAPH: analyzing large-scale in-memory graphs on GPUs. In: International Conference on High Performance Computing and Communications (HPCC). IEEE (2020)
21. Kharaz, A., Arshad, S., Mulliner, C., Robertson, W., Kirda, E.: UNVEIL: a large-scale, automated approach to detecting ransomware. In: USENIX Security (2016)
22. Kipf, T.N., Welling, M.: Semi-supervised classification with graph convolutional networks. arXiv preprint arXiv:1609.02907 (2016)
23. Kotzias, P., Bilge, L., Vervier, P.A., Caballero, J.: Mind your own business: a longitudinal study of threats and vulnerabilities in enterprises. In: NDSS (2019)
24. Kruegel, C., Kirda, E., Mutz, D., Robertson, W., Vigna, G.: Polymorphic worm detection using structural information of executables. In: Valdes, A., Zamboni, D. (eds.) RAID 2005. LNCS, vol. 3858, pp. 207–226. Springer, Heidelberg (2006). https://doi.org/10.1007/11663812_11
25. Liu, B., Huo, W., Zhang, C., Li, W., Li, F., Piao, A., Zou, W.: α Diff: cross-version binary code similarity detection with DNN. In: Proceedings of ASE (2018)
26. Liu, H., Motoda, H.: Feature selection for knowledge discovery and data mining (2012)
27. Marcantoni, F., Diamantaris, M., Ioannidis, S., Polakis, J.: A large-scale study on the risks of the HTML5 WebAPI for mobile sensor-based attacks. In: WWW (2019)
28. Massarelli, L., Di Luna, G.A., Petroni, F., Querzoni, L., Baldoni, R.: Investigating graph embedding neural networks with unsupervised features extraction for binary analysis. In: Proceedings of the 2nd Workshop on Binary Analysis Research (2019)
29. Meng, X., Miller, B.P.: Binary code multi-author identification in multi-toolchain scenarios (2018)
30. Meng, X., Miller, B.P., Jun, K.-S.: Identifying multiple authors in a binary program. In: Foley, S.N., Gollmann, D., Snekkenes, E. (eds.) ESORICS 2017. LNCS, vol. 10493, pp. 286–304. Springer, Cham (2017). https://doi.org/10.1007/978-3-319-66399-9_16
31. Okazaki, N.: CRFsuite: a fast implementation of conditional random fields (CRFs) (2007). http://www.chokkan.org/software/crfsuite/
32. Otsubo, Y., Otsuka, A., Mimura, M., Sakaki, T., Ukegawa, H.: o-glassesX: compiler provenance recovery with attention mechanism from a short code fragment. In: Proceedings of the 3nd Workshop on Binary Analysis Research (2020)
33. Possemato, A., Lanzi, A., Chung, S.P.H., Lee, W., Fratantonio, Y.: ClickShield: are you hiding something? Towards eradicating clickjacking on android. In: Proceedings of ACM CCS (2018)

34. Rahimian, A., Shirani, P., Alrbaee, S., Wang, L., Debbabi, M.: Bincomp: a stratified approach to compiler provenance attribution (2015)
35. Rosenblum, N., Miller, B.P., Zhu, X.: Recovering the toolchain provenance of binary code. In: Proceedings of ISSTA (2011)
36. Rosenblum, N.E., Miller, B.P., Zhu, X.: Extracting compiler provenance from program binaries. In: Proceedings of the 9th ACM SIGPLAN-SIGSOFT Workshop on Program Analysis for Software Tools and Engineering (2010)
37. Rosenblum, N.E., Zhu, X., Miller, B.P., Hunt, K.: Learning to analyze binary computer code. In: AAAI, pp. 798–804 (2008)
38. Open Source: Dyninst: an application program interface (API) for runtime code generation (2016). http://www.dyninst.org
39. Veličković, P., Cucurull, G., Casanova, A., Romero, A., Liò, P., Bengio, Y.: Graph attention networks. arXiv preprint arXiv:1710.10903 (2017)
40. Xu, X., Liu, C., Feng, Q., Yin, H., Song, L., Song, D.: Neural network-based graph embedding for cross-platform binary code similarity detection. In: Proceedings of ACM CCS (2017)
41. Xu, Z., Zhang, J., Gu, G., Lin, Z.: GOLDENEYE: efficiently and effectively unveiling malware's targeted environment. In: Stavrou, A., Bos, H., Portokalidis, G. (eds.) RAID 2014. LNCS, vol. 8688, pp. 22–45. Springer, Cham (2014). https://doi.org/10.1007/978-3-319-11379-1_2
42. Ying, Z., Bourgeois, D., You, J., Zitnik, M., Leskovec, J.: GNNExplainer: generating explanations for graph neural networks. In: Proceedings of NeurIPS (2019)
43. Zuo, F., Li, X., Zhang, Z., Young, P., Luo, L., Zeng, Q.: Neural machine translation inspired binary code similarity comparison beyond function pairs. In: NDSS (2019)

SoK: Auditability and Accountability in Distributed Payment Systems

Panagiotis Chatzigiannis[1]([envelope]), Foteini Baldimtsi[1], and Konstantinos Chalkias[2]

[1] George Mason University, Fairfax, VA, USA
{pchatzig,foteini}@gmu.edu
[2] Novi Financial/Facebook Research, Menlo Park, CA, USA
kostascrypto@fb.com

Abstract. Enforcement of policy regulations and availability of auditing mechanisms are crucial building blocks for the adoption of distributed payment systems. In this work we review a number of existing proposals for distributed payment systems that offer some form of auditability for regulators. We identify two major distinct lines of work: payment systems that are not privacy-preserving such as Bitcoin, where regulation functionalities are typically tailored for organizations controlling many accounts, and privacy-preserving payment systems where regulation functionalities are typically targeted to user level. We provide a systematization methodology over several axes of characteristics and performance, while highlighting insights and research gaps that we have identified, such as lack of dispute-resolution solutions between the regulator and the entity under audit, and the incompatibility of ledger pruning or off-chain protocols with regulatory requirements. Based on our findings, we propose a number of exciting future research directions.

Keywords: Distributed payments · Regulation · Auditing · Privacy · Cryptocurrencies · Blockchain

1 Introduction

Distributed payment systems have emerged as an alternative to the centralized banking system. Starting with Bitcoin [51], a number of schemes have been proposed with the common characteristic of relying on a globally distributed, append-only public ledger (which is sometimes in the form of a blockchain), to record monetary transactions in a publicly verifiable and immutable way. These systems utilize various cryptographic primitives to secure transactions, as well as a *consensus* protocol to guarantee agreement on the ledger's state by all participants. User participation can be controlled or unrestricted, categorizing such systems in *permissioned* and *permissionless* respectively. While such systems

P. Chatzigiannis—did part of this work during an internship at Novi Financial/Facebook Research. Foteini Baldimtsi and Panagiotis Chatzigiannis were supported by NSF #1717067, NSA #204761 and a Facebook research Award.

K. Sako and N. O. Tippenhauer (Eds.): ACNS 2021, LNCS 12727, pp. 311–337, 2021.
https://doi.org/10.1007/978-3-030-78375-4_13

are increasingly growing in popularity, they are often associated with fraudulent transactions [27] or with loss of user funds due to lack of regulation [50].

The distributed nature of the ledger, typically accessible by the open public or by a wide base of participants (even in permissioned systems), enables external observers to access transaction information, for example sender/receiver addresses or transaction amounts. These addresses are essentially random looking strings and provide their owners a sense of anonymity, especially in permissionless payment systems where anyone can easily create multiple addresses. However, it has been shown it is possible to associate these "pseudo-anonymous" addresses with real identities, for instance using clustering techniques [49]). These concerns led to a number of privacy enhancing proposals. Some were standalone cryptocurrencies offering strong privacy guarantees such as Zcash [17] or Monero [57], while others were add-on functionalities to existing systems, such as CoinJoin [48] or TumbleBit [43]. But these systems in turn raised concerns for the regulatory and law-enforcement authorities, since the abuse of such strong privacy guarantees provides users the potential to circumvent regulatory controls (e.g. tax evasion or unauthorized money transmission) or even engage in fraudulent/illegal activities (e.g. money laundering, extortion or drug trafficking [6]).

Needed Features and Regulatory Goals. Ensuring compliance with regulations is crucial for any widely-accepted payment system, even in a system that is designed to preserve user privacy. The goal is to ensure that the system and/or its participants comply with financial regulations and laws (e.g. cannot conduct illicit activities such as money laundering without being accountable to the authorities). In this setting, state authorities or audit firms (e.g. Deloitte or KPMG [4,13]) will need to be convinced that the auditee "follows the rules" by meeting certain regulatory requirements. For example, all participants in a payment system should be compliant with Anti-Money Laundering and Counter-Terrorism Financing (AML/KYC) per Financial Action Task Force (FATF) Travel Rule [5], while an auditor should be able to verify compliance with regulations such as the European General Data Protection Regulation [12] or industry-specific requirements such as the Health Insurance Portability and Accountability Act (HIPAA).

Regulation in Distributed Payment Systems. As mentioned above, pseudoanonymous distributed payment systems such as Bitcoin do not hide transaction information. However, the posted information is not enough to provide regulatory control and additional regulation functionalities are still needed. For instance, in the cryptocurrency world there exist numerous types of centralized organizations which hold users' coins (e.g. online wallets, exchanges, interest accounts etc.) or even "stablecoins" that are backed by fiat currency [9]. These third-party intermediaries are typically opaque to their internal operations, and several infamous examples exist where users lost their funds without holding these intermediaries accountable [50] or organizations investing users' funds instead of focusing on solvency [10]. In fact, the Conference of State Bank Supervisors proposed a model regulatory framework including cryptographic solvency proofs as a means of demonstrating solvency [3]. In that end, some works [23,28] focused on making these services more transparent to earn users trust, and provide auditability functionalities to authorities (i.e., proving that they are solvent) without disclosing additional information or exposing their users' privacy[1]. However preserving privacy does not come for free, as this makes proof manipulation or collusion possible to falsely convince an auditor on the organization's claims.

In the privacy-preserving setting, enforcing regulation is even more challenging, as the notions of privacy and regulation seem contradictory. In such distributed payment systems, regulation implies auditability and accountability at user level (e.g. disclosing the user's assets or past transactions) or transaction level (e.g. disclosing the participants or value associated with some transaction), while the public ledger entries hide such information from parties not associated with it. A handful of academic works attempted to provide some basic accountability or auditability functionalities, either on top of existing privacy-preserving payment systems [28,37], or as new stand-alone ones [52,59]. However, at the time of writing, no such work has attempted to provide a complete solution that would satisfy all needs from its users and regulators, and there is still a research gap for addressing regulatory concerns (e.g. enforce regulation in permissionless systems [29]).

Our Contributions. We review and unify the landscape of distributed payment systems that offer some form of auditability or accountability. Such forms can range from simple audit protocols where an auditor learns some hidden information posted on the public ledger (e.g. hidden value of a transaction), up to system policies that are automatically executed based on a system participant's behavior, while remaining consistent with the system basic security properties. We provide a non-exhaustive list of such functionalities in Sect. 2.2. We then categorize related work into two distinct groups: schemes that do not have underlying privacy characteristics, and schemes that preserve some privacy. These groups in turn create two major categories of regulatory functionalities: at an organization level and at a user/transaction level. Our systematization framework considers the following three axes: (1) the security guarantees of each scheme for organization-level auditing (as such audits can be easily abused or leak information), and their audit functionalities for user/transaction-level auditing (as we identify a plethora of such functionalities in privacy-preserving systems), (2) the efficiency asymptotics and (3) the overall properties and attributes. Through our systemic categorization, we identify a number of insights and research gaps which pave the path for future research directions.

Systematization Scope. We focus on *distributed* payment systems (using a common public ledger) offering *some* form of auditability or accountability as regulation functionalities with any level of privacy guarantees.

We include related works that either propose the above functionalities as stand-alone systems [52,59] or as extensions/add-ons to existing systems [28,37].

---

[1] In some scenarios, non-private auditing might suffice. However, such a protocol would be trivial from a security standpoint, and to our knowledge no related proposal exists.

We include both permissioned and permissionless systems and with different "bookkeeping" formats (e.g. UTXO or account-based). Our work remains orthogonal to the underlying data structures used by the common ledger and to the underlying consensus protocol.

The rest of this paper is organized as follows. In Sect. 2 we provide the definitions and security properties used for our systematization. In Sect. 3 we discuss our categorization for the works we consider. In Sects. 4 we present regulation in works that do not have any underlying privacy preserving mechanisms and highlight insights and research gaps, while in Sect. 5 we follow a similar pattern for privacy preserving systems. We conclude in Sect. 6 with a summary of proposed research directions in this field.

2   Background

We informally present the necessary concepts and definitions required throughout this paper and provide a more detailed cryptographic background in Appendix A.

2.1   (Private) Distributed Payment Systems

Assuming the existence of a consensus layer, we define a basic distributed payment system (DPS) to consist of the following algorithms: Setup(), CreateAcc(), CreateTx() and VerifyTx() with a public ledger L as common input and output. A DPS can be *permissioned* where all participants are known (typically controlled by a single entity or organization), or *permissionless* where participation is open to anyone, resulting in more decentralization (in the above generic definition we do not distinguish between a permissioned and a permissionless system). Note that although participation in the system is typically consistent with the consensus protocol (i.e. transacting in a permissioned payment system implies a permissioned consensus, similarly for permissionless), this is not always the case. For example, it is possible to run a permissionless payment system with a permissioned consensus layer, such as a permissionless "Fabcoin" on top of Hyperledger Fabric [14].

A distributed payment system *must* satisfy the following core properties, which are typically safeguarded by verifiers participating in the consensus algorithm (e.g. often called "miners"):

- *Theft prevention:* Spending values from a sender account S requires knowledge of private information associated with that account (typically a secret key sk_S).
- *Balance:* A transaction which transfers a value v from a sender S to a receiver R, should always increase a receiver's total assets by v and adjust S's total assets by $-v$.
- *Non-negative assets:* A transaction that spends v from sender's total assets, should not result in negative assets for S which would allow S to overspend.

Private DPSs come with the following "privacy-preserving" properties:

- *Confidentiality:* Only the sender S and the receiver R of a transaction tx can learn the value associated with tx.
- *Anonymity:* An external observer of tx cannot derive the public keys or identifiers of S and R associated with that transaction[2].

We note that some systems might offer only one of the above privacy characteristics, but not both. However, if the system provides both confidentiality and anonymity, we say that it is *fully private*. We also call a system *pseudoanonymous* if it does not provide any of the above.

2.2 Enforcing Regulation in Distributed Payment Systems

We now organize the different types of regulation that we encounter in the related literature. These are protocols or policies that disclose information to the auditor, where as an auditor we consider some type of a regulation authority or an audit firm.

Disclosed information can include (but not limited to) [26,52,59]:

- Transaction sender and/or receiver
- Transaction value
- Tax compliance
- Total value of assets

Note that as we discuss below, some functions are mostly applicable to private DPS (e.g. transaction value) while others are applicable to pseudoanonymous systems as well (e.g. total value of assets).

Transaction and User-Level Regulation. As a starting point, an auditor or a regulation authority would focus on inquiries that involve single transactions or the transaction history of certain system participants[3]. At first glance it might seem that a privacy-preserving system (which hides transaction values and/or transacting parties) cannot comply with such regulatory requirements. However, via the use of cryptographic techniques we can allow for auditability and/or accountability properties. We informally define such properties as follows:

- *Auditability:* There exists a protocol where an external auditor A having access to the common public ledger can provably learn the requested information to be audited (e.g. the participating parties in a transaction). This protocol can be either interactive with the audited parties (requiring their consent) or non-interactive (where A learns the information at will).

---

[2] This property is sometimes referred to as "transaction graph obfuscation".

[3] In typical DAPs, a "human user" might control multiple payment addresses. By user/participant regulation below we refer to address-level regulation, unless we explicitly explain otherwise in certain permissioned schemes.

- *Accountability:* There exists a system functionality which enforces automatic execution of policies (as defined in its parameters) when a certain predicate is satisfied. For instance, these policies might automatically reject transactions from a specific user or transactions that do not comply with a spending limit and potentially also automatically disclose private information to a designated authority.

Auditability vs Accountability. In general, accountability does not require active participation of an auditor, and accountability policies are typically enforced during the verification phase of a transaction (which usually happens at the consensus layer). For instance, the system might perform certain actions based on the value of the transaction or the cumulative value of recent ones, such as involuntary leakage of information from that transaction or prevent acceptance of subsequent transactions. The system might also enforce other system-wide policies (e.g. tax payment to a pre-determined address). Therefore, accountability can be thought of as a stronger version of auditability, as defined in a general context in [34,38,42,46]. Another distinctive characteristic is that accountability is *proactive* in nature, while auditability is *reactive*.

Auditability and Accountability vs. System Security. We note that in some works, the notions of auditability and accountability are implicitly used as a "dishonesty" detection mechanism (e.g. breaking the ledger's immutability property), aimed to incentivize a party to "follow the rules" and holding it accountable when it attempts to violate the system's security [11,22,39]. For instance, in Bitfury's whitepaper on Blockchain auditability [11] both of these notions are used interchangeably, and are associated with a system service that detects such malicious activities even in case of collusion with ledger maintainers. However, we don't include such a role for an auditor within our scope, and we assume any such activity would be promptly detected and/or prevented by the consensus layer. In fact, in a regulatory context a party might violate laws or regulations (e.g. launder money, transfer more than $10k in a day etc.) without ever violating the system protocols or breaking its security properties.

Organization-Level Regulation. In the case of an organization controlling a number of payment system accounts on behalf of its customers (i.e., a bank or custodial service), a regulatory concern is if the organization is *solvent*. Such a proof of solvency can be considered as a form of auditability, which convinces an auditor that the organization indeed controls sufficient funds reflected on the public ledger, without however disclosing more information other than this fact is true (e.g. number of its clients, total assets etc.). A solvency proof typically consists of two parts: a Proof of Assets (PoA) and a Proof of Liabilities (PoL), which when combined prove that an organization's assets exceed its liabilities, thus proving solvency. We discuss both of these proofs below. Note in some cases it might be sufficient to prove "partial" solvency (as it is typically done in the real-world) but from a technical standpoint, it's trivial to convert a full solvency to a partial solvency proof. However, an organization would typically prefer to only prove its solvency without disclosing additional information (e.g.

specific asset amounts or account public keys). Also, while regulation at user or transaction level is trivial, in pseudoanonymous systems there are many factors to consider at organization-level, regardless of the system's privacy properties.

Proof of Assets (PoA). As in auditability protocols, a Proof of Assets needs to convince a verifier that an organization controls *at least* a certain amount of funds. Note than this proof does not necessarily need to disclose the exact amount to the auditor, and a lower bound will be sufficient. In some cases however, an upper bound could be provided as well (e.g. in a tax scenario, an organization might want to prove its total assets value lies within a "tax bracket").

For a pseudoanonymous payment system, a naive PoA is to provide signatures to the auditor for some (or all) of the accounts it controls, by also including some challenge value or nonce-timestamp in the signature to ensure freshness. Proving Assets in privacy-preserving systems however might require more complex protocols that involve cryptographic primitives such as ZK proofs.

Proof of Liabilities (PoL). Here the organization needs to periodically publish information on its liabilities (e.g. user balances in banks or exchanges [8]). This information can be either provided directly from the organization, or stored in a public bulletin board. However, with this information publicly available, it is desirable to leak as little side-information as possible (e.g. without exposing the exact value of the organization's liabilities or other information related to its clients). The published information is verified by clients in a probabilistic fashion (i.e., not all of the clients need to actively check for the validity of the published information). We note that publishing this information can be seen equivalent to an auditor "reply" step (where any client can assume the auditor role), so it is possible to reduce the PoL functionality to an auditability protocol.

2.3 Security Properties and Threats of Regulatory Functions

Based on the above discussion of required regulatory functions for DPS we informally define the related security properties.

- *Regulation Correctness.* An honest auditee following the regulation protocols should always be able to convince an auditor and transact under the correct system policies.
- *Regulation Soundness.* An auditor should always reject false claims for a malicious auditee, while the system should always apply the corresponding policies to the system participants that should be affected by those policies.
- *Minimal Information Disclosure.* When implementing a regulation functionality, the auditee should only disclose the needed information, without suffering any "collateral damage" in terms of privacy. For instance, when a user is asked if ever transacted with a specific party, it should not reveal the associated values; an exchange proving solvency should not leak its number of clients.

Beyond security, some additional desired properties are the following:

Table 1. Organization-level Regulation of pseudoanonymous schemes. By ● we denote support of a functionality or addressing a security or privacy issue, by × the existence of security or privacy issues and by "N/A" non applicability.

	Functions		Auditor security		Auditee security				Gener-alize
	PoA	PoL	PoA Collu-sion	Hid-den Liab.	Value hiding	Popul. hiding	Account Leakage	Multi Proof Leakage	
Provisions [28]	●	●	●	●	●	×	●	●	Y
ZeroLedge [31]	N/A	●	N/A	●	●	×	●	●	Y
DaPoL [23]	N/A	●	N/A	●	●	●	●	●	Y
Maxwell [7]	●	●	×	×	×	×	×	×	Y
Blockstream [56]	●	N/A	×	N/A	×	N/A	×	●	N
Wang [58]	●	N/A	●	N/A	×	N/A	N/A	●	Y

- *Offline Auditors.* A system compatible with offline auditors, who do not need to always maintain and track its entire public state.
- *Out-of-band Communication and Storage.* Regulatory functions are preferably performed using system-maintained information, minimizing the use of out of band protocols.
- *Dispute Resolution.* There exists a mechanism to resolve disputes between an auditor and auditee, in case a malicious auditor falsely accuses the auditee of non-compliance. Such mechanism might even include holding an auditor accountable for its own actions.

3 Systematization Methodology

We first categorize all works and systems we consider into two major taxonomies. The first considers pseudoanonymous DPSs (where audits are typically performed at an organization level), and are discussed in detail in Sect. 4. The second includes schemes that have privacy-preserving attributes (where they typically perform auditing at a transaction or user level), and are discussed in detail in Sect. 5 (from our previous discussion, user or transaction-level auditing in pseudoanonymous systems is trivial from a cryptographic standpoint).

Our core systematization is performed over the following three axes (we consider systems with respect to their privacy guarantees separately within each axis):

Audit Properties Axis: We first consider pseudoanonymous systems. In such schemes the basic audit functionalities are Proof of Assets (PoA) and Proof of Liabilities (PoL) which happen in an organization level. In Table 1 we consider schemes that provide PoA and/or PoL functionalities. Additionally, we also look at security and privacy properties, as existing works in the literature have different security guarantees, both for the auditor and the auditee. From

Table 2. Regulation Functionalities in Private Schemes. By ● we denote supporting functionality, by ○ that although not explicitly defined, the scheme can be trivially extended to support that audit type and by "N/A" no support.

Scheme	Transaction-level					Tx/User level	User level			
	Lim	Trace	Value	Sender-Receiver	Tax	Non-participation	Sum	Blacklist	Stats	Anonym. revocation
Zcash ext [37]	●	●	○	○	●	○	○	○	○	●
ZKLedger [52]	○	N/A	●	●	○	○	●	○	●	N/A
PRCash [59]	●	N/A	N/A	N/A	N/A	N/A	N/A	N/A	N/A	●
PGC [26]	●	○	●	N/A	●	N/A	●	N/A	○	N/A
MiniLedger [25]	●	N/A	●	●	○	●	●	○	●	N/A
ACCDET [15]	N/A	N/A	●	●	N/A	○	N/A	N/A	N/A	N/A
ATRA [19]	N/A	N/A	●	●	N/A	N/A	N/A	N/A	N/A	N/A
MProve [32]	N/A	N/A	N/A	N/A	N/A	N/A	●	N/A	N/A	N/A
Damgård et al. [29]	N/A	N/A	N/A	N/A	N/A	N/A	N/A	N/A	N/A	●
Barki-Gouget [16]	N/A	N/A	N/A	N/A	N/A	N/A	N/A	N/A	N/A	●

the auditor's point of view, security implies Regulation Soundness, i.e. rejecting false PoA due to collusion among organizations (denoted as "PoA Collusion" in Table 1) or false PoL due to "Hidden Liabilities" not included in the proof. From the auditee's point of view, security implies Minimal Information Disclosure, i.e. hiding the actual values of its total assets and liabilities ("Value hiding"), not leaking its total client population ("Population hiding") or other details on its accounts ("Account Leakage"), and preventing a malicious auditor from inferring any additional information from subsequent proof executions ("Multi Proof Leakage"). In Table 1 we present a classification of systems according to the above properties, and discuss them in detail in Sect. 4. We also classify a scheme based on whether it can be generalized to work for any distributed ledger-based payment system or if it is designed for a specific one.

For regulating privacy-preserving systems (at a transaction or user level), we desire a scheme to offer a wide variety of auditability and accountability functionalities. In Table 2, we first distinguish between regulatory functions in a transaction level, which includes if value is under or over a threshold (limit), link different transactions (tracing), revealing the transaction's value, sender and/or receiver) and withhold tax by paying the respective amount to a pre-determined account. We also distinguish them in a user level, which includes auditing a user's total assets (equivalent to PoA in pseudoanonymous systems), applying policies only to users in a "blacklist", deriving statistical information from user's past transactions (e.g. learning the average transacted value in a time period) or revoking a user's anonymity based on some criteria. In some cases it might also be desirable to prove non-participation for some user in some transaction, which is a combined audit both in a transaction and in a user level.

Efficiency Axis: Our second axis is based on the efficiency asymptotics for both pseudoanonymous and private systems, namely their space requirements, transaction creation costs and audit proving and verification costs. We do not

Table 3. Efficiency asymptotics. n: # of owned/system accounts (for pseudoanonymous and privacy preserving schemes respectively). N: maximum number of supported accounts. m: number of recorded transactions. k: size of anonymity set. m_u: Txs of user. For Audit Proofs we consider the most basic audit in each scheme (i.e. proof of a value). If audit proof is non-interactive, cost is embedded in tx creation costs).

Scheme	Proof size		Tx Create	Audit Prove		Audit Verify	
	PoA	PoL		PoA	PoL	PoA	PoL
Provisions [28]	$O(k)$	$O(n)$	N/A	$O(k)$	$O(n)$	$O(k)$	$O(n)$
ZeroLedge [31]	N/A	$O(n)$	N/A	N/A	$O(n)$	N/A	$O(n)$
DAPOL [23]	N/A	$O(1)$	N/A	N/A	$O(\lg N)$	N/A	$O(\lg N)$
Maxwell [7]	$O(n)$	$O(1)$	N/A	$O(n)$	$O(\lg n)$	$O(n)$	$O(\lg n)$
Blockstream [56]	$O(n)$	N/A	N/A	$O(n)$	N/A	$O(n)$	N/A
Wang [58]	$O(n)$	N/A	N/A	$O(n)$	N/A	$O(n)$	N/A

Scheme	Ledger Storage	Tx Create	Audit Prove	Audit Verify
Zcash ext [37]	$O(m)$	$O(\lg m(\lg\lg m))$	Embedded in tx	$O(1)$
ZKLedger [52]	$O(mn)$	$O(n)$	$O(1)$	$O(1)$
PRCash [59]	$O(k)$	$O(k)$	Embedded in tx	$O(1)$
PGC [26]	$O(m)$	$O(1)$	$O(m_u)$	$O(m_u)$
MiniLedger [25]	$O(n)$	$O(n)$	$O(1)$	$O(1)$
ACCDET [15]	$O(m)$	$O(k)$	Embedded in tx	$O(m)$
ATRA [19]	$O(m)$	$O(1)$	Embedded in tx	$O(m)$
MProve [32]	$O(k)$ proof size	N/A	$O(k)$	$O(k)$

consider concrete metrics because of the variety (or absence) of implementations. Regarding space efficiency, we consider the proof size for organization-level auditing and the overall ledger storage costs for privacy-preserving schemes with user or transaction level auditing (denoted as "proof storage" and "ledger storage" respectively in Table 3). Then we capture the transaction creation costs (which are not applicable for schemes under the first category as the transactions have already been created). Finally for capturing the auditee's proving and the auditor's verification costs, we consider the most "basic" audit functionality each scheme offers. We note that not all schemes have the same "basic" audit functionality, thus Table 3 should not be seen as a comparison table. Also, audit proofs are not applicable for schemes offering only accountability, as the necessary information is included in the transaction itself, while transaction creation costs do not apply for auditing at an organization level (as they are always independent of PoA or PoL protocols).

General Properties Axis: This axis is based on several different properties and attributes of all existing proposals. We compare them in terms of audit scope, i.e. user level (U) if auditing information of a particular user, transaction level (T) if auditing a transaction's full details and organization (O) if auditing an organization's assets, liabilities or solvency, underlying system architectures (e.g. UTXO or account-based) consensus and participation models (permissioned vs permissionless). We particularly highlight the need of various trusted centralized authorities (either for identification or for auditing purposes), which is typically not desired. In auditing we also categorize the schemes in terms of interaction between auditor and auditee, as well as the audit granularity. Then we also refine schemes based on their level of privacy, and we list any other assumptions not fitting in the previous categories. The comparison is shown in Table 4. We note that requiring interaction for transaction/user level audits implies auditee consent, while *all* organization-level audits always require consent from the organization. Another observation is that non-interactive user/transaction audits typically require the existence of an auditing authority, as the non-interactive data should only be accessible to such authorities (else this would compromise privacy).

Table 4. General categorization of auditable schemes. Scope: T Transaction level, U User level, O Organization level. Model: Acc: account-based, UTXO: Unspent Transaction Output based. By ● we denote full privacy, by ◖ set anonymity, by ◐ confidentiality and by ○ pseudoanonymity (privacy is against auditor and against all observers for pseudoanonymous and privacy-preserving schemes respectively). By ◉ we denote permissionless, by 🔒 permissioned and by ⊥ orthogonality to consensus layer. By ★ we denote non-academic works.

Scheme	Audit Scope	Model	Consensus	Participation	Identity authority	Auditing Interaction	Auditing authority	Fine-coarse	Privacy	Assumptions
Provisions [28]	O	Both	⊥	N/A	N	Y	N	Coarse	◐	
ZeroLedge [31]	O	Both	⊥	N/A	N	N	N	Coarse	◐	
DAPOL [23]	O	Both	⊥	N/A	N	N	N	Coarse	◐	
Maxwell★ [7]	O	Both	⊥	N/A	N	Y	N	Coarse	○	
Blockstream★ [56]	O	UTXO	◉	◉	N	N	N	Fine	○	
Wang [58]	U/O	Both	⊥	N/A	N	Y	N	Fine	○	Secure channel between prover-auditor
Zcash ext [37]	T/U	UTXO	◉	◉	Y	N	Y	Both	●	Trusted setup, Spending authority
ZKLedger [52]	T/U/O	Acc	⊥	🔒	Y	Y	N	Both	●	Out of band comm
PRCash [59]	T/U	Acc	⊥	🔒	Y	N	Y	Coarse (limit)	◐	Trusted validators, Out of band comm, sender-receiver interaction
PGC [26]	T	Acc	⊥	🔒	Y	Y	N	Fine	◐	
MiniLedger [25]	T/U/O	Acc	⊥	🔒	Y	Y (N)	N (Y)	Both	●	
ACCDET [15]	U	UTXO	🔒	🔒	Y	N	Y	Fine	●	
ATRA [19]	U	N/A	🔒	🔒	Y	N	Y	Fine	●	
MProve [32]	O	UTXO	◉	◉	N	N	N	Fine	◐	
Damgård et al. [29]	U	N/A	⊥	🔒	Y	N	Y	N/A	●	Anonymity revoker
Barki-Gouget [16]	U	N/A	⊥	🔒	Y	Y	Y	N/A	●	Anonymity revoker

4 Regulation Functions in Pseudoanonymous Systems

We now discuss the first major category of payment auditable systems; those with a pseudoanonymous underlying system where the focus is typically on organization level regulation. As discussed in Sect. 2.2 the common goal here is for an organization to prove that is solvent.

Insight 1. *Pseudoanonymous systems inherently expose their users' privacy (due to the public nature of the distributed ledger), making user or transaction-level auditing trivial.*

Perhaps the first attempt to prove an organization's digital assets was Bitstamp's Proof of Reserves [2], a procedure on top of Bitcoin (also applicable to any pseudoanonymous system), involving a single entity asking the organization to provide a signature using its private keys on a message selected by that entity. The obvious drawback of this approach however is lack of auditee privacy, i.e. it does not satisfy Minimal Information Disclosure.

Insight 2. *As a naive PoA method, one might prove ownership of accounts associated with those assets by signing a message using the respective private keys. This method however does not accomplish Minimal Information Disclosure, as it also discloses the organization's exact assets as well as the respective accounts.*

Towards providing a way to prove solvency in a more distributed fashion, Maxwell's PoL [7] consists of a "summation" Merkle tree with each leaf contains a client's balance in plaintext, summing with the siblings up to the root as in a plain Merkle tree. Then, the organization's clients *can* check their inclusion in the organization's liabilities through Merkle proofs, which implies this method of PoL has a probabilistic nature. However Minimal Information Disclosure was still unresolved, as Maxwell's PoL publicly exposes the total liabilites and the number of the users, and leaks information of sibling nodes by multiple execution of proofs. In addition, an attack was identified (and subsequently fixed) in this scheme which could potentially enable a participant to claim less liabilities [44].

Gap 1. *Given the probabilistic nature of PoL, an organization can collect information on client queries in the network or application layer and manipulate subsequent proofs by not including user balances with low-probability retrievals. Can such behavior be prevented without having to publicly disclose liabilities data, thus disclosing the population of an organization's accounts?*

Private Information Retrieval techniques have been proposed [23] to efficiently mitigate Gap 1, however such techniques have not yet been deployed.

As in [2], Maxwell's PoA protocol simply requires signing some message using the private keys associated with the controlled assets. As discussed in Sect. 2.2, Maxwell's PoA and PoL combined constitute a proof of the organization's solvency. We also mention an early implementation for Proof of Solvency using similar cryptographic techniques [1].

Provisions [28] was among the first academic works to present a complete proof of solvency solution, and augmented both PoA and PoL protocols with privacy-preserving characteristics. For the PoA part, the organization chooses adds a number account public keys to those it already controls (Provisions assumes these keys are not hashed), essentially forming an anonymity set, then creates a Pedersen commitment for each (with a commitment to zero for those it does not own) and publishes a homomorphic addition of those commitments. Then using standard Zero Knowledge (ZK) protocols, it proves that it either knows the secret key for the respective commitment public key *or* it is a commitment to zero. This ensures that the verifier does not really learn which accounts the organization owns. Note that using standard, efficient ZK proofs is not compatible with hashed public keys (since in systems like Bitcoin it would be required to spend at least once from a wallet address to reveal the account public key). Customized ZK proofs would have to be created for such statements to overcome this limitation, and works like [24] could serve as a starting point.

For the PoL part, the organization constructs and publishes a Pedersen commitment representing each one of its clients' balances, which can be homomorphically added to form a commitment of the organization's total liabilities. At any point, each client can check it is included in the liabilities commitment by asking for an inclusion proof, while ensuring overall that no commitments have been added with negative amounts though appropriate range proofs. However, as shown in Table 1, subsequent execution can still potentially leak some information to external parties (e.g. number of user accounts of organization at a specific time). Given the two above published commitments, the organization proves that their difference is positive (which constitutes the overall proof of solvency). As [28] was published in 2015, there is room for efficiency improvements by i.e. utilizing recent range proof constructions (Bulletproofs [21]).

Insight 3. *Hashed public keys in systems like Bitcoin are not fully compatible with more complex PoA techniques as in [28] using standard Zero-Knowledge proofs. Customized ZK circuits for SNARKs need to be designed in such cases.*

Gap 2. *During PoA, organizations can collude with each other to manipulate these proofs by including their assets to each other's proofs, violating Regulation Soundness. Does a mitigation strategy exist to prevent this?*

While performing PoA in a synchronous manner could trivially prevent organization collusions, this approach is impractical.

Gap 3. *Can we design a PoA protocol on top of a pseudoanonymous system that is fully private for the auditee with sublinear costs?*

We observe that all current PoA protocols form some anonymity set to hide the actual audited organization's accounts. Implementing a zk-SNARK in a system might enable full privacy and sublinear proof size and verification costs, but at the cost of introducing additional assumptions like trusted setup.

ZeroLedge [31] focuses on the PoL aspect, aiming to address the weaknesses of Maxwell's protocol, most notably its "hidden liabilities" attack. In this approach, the organization creates commitments to identifier-value pairs for each of its accounts along with zero-knowledge proofs of their validity as well as to the total liabilities amount. Through the zero-knowledge properties, it prevents collusion attacks and preserves verifier anonymity, however it still leaks some information about the total number of accounts. Similar to Provisions, this scheme could benefit from newer, more efficient range proof techniques such as Bulletproofs [21]. Even so, as shown in Table 3 its asymptotic costs remain linear in the total number of accounts, which might make it very costly in large deployments.

The recent PoL proposed standard (DAPOL) [23] is inspired by previous works [7,28]. It addresses the majority of their privacy-related issues and currently has the best PoL Minimum Information Disclosure possible, without leaking information about other addresses' balances, total liabilities or total number of addresses (which even the "flat" version of Provisions was leaking). To achieve this, as the Merkle Tree approach always leaks such information, it augments it with more sophisticated primitives and constructions, such as Zero Knowledge Proofs, VRFs, and sparse Merkle Trees, and has a "layered" PoL that supports a very large number of addresses. In addition, it presents itself in use cases outside financial applications and solvency proofs, such as disapproval votes, virus outbreak reports or referral programs.

Insight 4. *To achieve Regulation Soundness and Minimal Information Disclosure, more advanced cryptographic primitives and complex constructions have to be employed, such as Zero Knowledge proofs, VRFs and sparse Merkle trees.*

Wang et al. [58] provides a simple protocol for a potential buyer proving assets to a vendor before conducting a transaction, using that transaction's external data as a "challenge". Although this protocol could be extended for providing PoA at an organization level as well, the use-case of such a protocol seems to be limited to a "buyer-vendor" scenario as it is associated with a specific transaction. More importantly, it does not have strong Minimal Information Disclosure as other PoA/PoL protocols like Provisions or DAPOL [23,28].

Finally we briefly mention a few additional works related to organization-level regulation. Hu et al. [44] highlighted a "mix and match" attack on the Maxwell protocol, while proposing its mitigation technique. Blockstream proof of reserves [56] propose an alternative to the naive PoA approach by creating and signing invalid transactions using all owned UTXOs, which however degrades the organization's privacy. Moore and Christin [50] provide a risk analysis for cryptocurrency exchanges, highlighting the need of Solvency Proofs. Finally, Decker et al. [30] proposed a variant of the Maxwell Protocol based on a trusted platform module (TPM) to securely execute the necessary computations while ensuring honest computation. This approach can also facilitate the computation between PoA and PoL for proving solvency.

An open problem in Proofs of Liabilities approach commonly used in these works is Dispute Resolution, i.e. a client claiming that his balance within the organization is not included in the proof. This is problematic in both ways, i.e. a malicious organization simply rejecting an honest client's claim, or a malicious client falsely accusing an honest organization of misbehavior.

Gap 4. *Can disputes be resolved by a third-party judge at an organization-level regulation, when a client claims that their balance with the organization has not been included in a PoL?*

Mutual contract-signing solutions (i.e. both client and the organization signing a user's transaction and signature) might be helpful to solve this gap, however such an approach also needs to be practically deployable.

5 Regulation Functions in Privacy-Preserving Systems

In this section, we provide an overview of distributed payment systems that have privacy-preserving characteristics *and* some form of auditability and/or accountability functionalities focused on a transaction or user-level. In our discussion, we further divide such systems into two categories: the ones that require designated auditors and the ones where no explicit auditors are assumed, as shown in the "Auditing authority" column in Table 4.

5.1 Centralized - Designated Authority

A common approach when designing audit and accountability functionalities for privacy-preserving DPSs is to add a system-designated, centralized authority (or group of authorities). Such authority could either enforce accountability rules or take the role of an external auditor as defined in Sect. 2.2. This approach was adopted in one of the first works [37] to address regulatory concerns in privacy preserving cryptocurrencies in the permissionless model by extending Zerocash [17]. It assumes the existence of various types of authorities where each one is designated to enforce different policies, offering a wide range of auditability functionalities as seen in Table 2. The main idea is to embed *auxiliary information* to coins, such as counters or coin types, and define policies as algorithms that are executed each time a coin is spent. Then, a designated authority can be used to verify a policy at the time of transaction generation, for example it could check that a transaction value does not exceed a certain limit and sign the transaction to certify it. This is a type of accountability, since it can proactively check transactions before being posted in the ledger. We note that this technique can be easily adapted for pretty much any type of policy but as discussed below comes with efficiency and privacy costs. [37] also presents techniques for coin tracing assuming that coins include tracing information encrypted under an authority's public key. Then, an authority could at will trace those coins (and all subsequent coins resulting from transactions of the original coins) without any interaction with the users. Interestingly, [37] also provides techniques for *accountable authorities*, the actions of which would be transparent to users. For instance, users could check if a tracing authority has traced their coins.

The techniques of [37] are quite effective, easily allowing the implementation of a wide range of policies. However, there exist both efficiency and privacy limitations. Requiring transactions to be validated by an authority *before posted,* requires extra communication and computation costs which can be a burden in practice – especially on top of an already computationally intensive system such as Zerocash. Most importantly though, the main issue with the given approach is that it gives too much power to the designated authorities. Not only such authorities can learn transaction information that would otherwise remain private, but they could also arbitrarily refuse to validate certain transactions.

Insight 5. *Embedding encrypted auxiliary information in transactions that can be decrypted by designated authorities at any point, is a trivial solution for accountability and auditing but has negative impact to user privacy.*

Insight 6. *Accountability policies rely on the transaction verifiers (i.e. the consensus layer) to enforce them. Any reactive auditability functionality can be converted to an equivalent proactive accountability policy through auxiliary data and interaction with an authority in the transaction creation phase.*

Although [37] only included a vague description of how to add audit functionalities in Zerocash (without providing a concrete construction or evaluation), it offered some of the first insights and problems for designing auditable/accountable privacy-preserving payment systems. PRCash [59] was developed as a *stand-alone* fully-private payment system with built-in accountability for spending limits. Specifically, it only allows transactions up to a specified amount, while leaving the option for users to de-anonymize themselves against a centralized authority if wishing to transfer larger amounts. PRCash works in a permissioned setting, with an anonymous credential issued by a centralized identity authority to prevent circumventing limits by creating sybil identities. Consequently, this same authority is responsible for both identity management and regulatory functions in the system (although these roles could be decoupled in separate "identity" and "auditing" authorities). PRCash is inspired by the private cryptocurrency Mimblewimble [35,54], however its construction follows a more complex design. Namely it uses two commitments and a public key pair (as opposed to one commitment and no public key cryptography in Mimblewimble) in order to connect participants to identity credentials. The additional commitment is used to generate "re-randomizeable" authority certificates (that permit participating in the system) and a secret key is used to derive a unique transaction ID. For transacting within the limit, the sender would include an appropriate range proof in the transaction. To exceed the limit, instead of the range proof, the sender would need to encrypt his public key under the authority's public key (thus deanonymizing himself to the authority). PRCash as shown in Table 2 is limited to this specific accountability functionality by design, while it relies on a centralized authority for its accountability aspects. In addition, although an external observer of the ledger cannot link transacting parties or learn transaction values, the system is not fully private against transaction Validators in the consensus layer, as each transaction leaks information (pseudo-identifiers) to the Validators which could be used to generate links between transactions.

Insight 7. *In a permissionless setting, identity authorities associating real identities with public keys are required to preserve regulation connected to value limits, or else such regulation can be trivially circumvented through sybil identities.*

In the permissioned setting, an anonymous, auditable payment scheme was presented in [15] (we will refer to it by ACCDET). The goal of ACCDET is to hide the content of transactions without preventing authorized parties from auditing them. The paper considers a centralized identity authority for associating real-world identities with system credentials, similar to PRCash [59], as well as a designated trusted auditor for each system participant who can learn any hidden transaction the participant is involved in at will. This is ensured by including encrypted transaction information under the designated auditor's public key, along with a standard ZK proof of correct encryption under the correct key. Value tokens are hidden using Pedersen commitments, while they are checked for validity and blind-signed by a certifier when spending them. The paper includes an evaluation based on Hyperledger Fabric [14] as a consensus layer and provides an analysis of the computational costs for each required operation. Besides the fact that the trusted auditor is again very powerful, we also note that the auditing verification cost is linear to the number of transactions ever happened in the system, as shown in Table 3. This is because ACCDET does not assume user consent during audit, thus an auditor would have to decrypt the whole ledger in order to trace any user. A more generic approach that does not restrict itself to payment systems [19] (we will refer to it by ATRA), considers the issuance of anonymous credentials in permissioned blockchain systems which could be transformed into a payment scheme. It also implements auditability by assuming the existence of a centralized auditor and encrypting all private transaction information under the auditor's keys. ATRA, similar to ACCDET, has inefficient auditing, as the auditor has to decrypt all ciphertexts in the ledger.

Insight 8. *Auditing a fully-private DPS without any aid from the auditee, is generally inefficient, as the auditor would need to audit the whole ledger to retrieve the desired audits.*

Gap 5. *Can we design a private DPS with centralized authorities that reveal a user identity only when a user misbehaves according to well-defined policies (as done in traditional Chaum e-cash protocols [20])?*

Note that PRCash [59] seems to accomplish this, as it de-anonymizes a user against an authority if the user exceeds a transaction limit. Still PRCash is tailored to support this specific policy, and designing a system that can make users accountable without their consent for arbitrary policies is challenging.

Damgård et al. [29] provide "design principles" for private and accountable distributed payment systems, rather than building a standalone one. Their main focus is to support auditing as anonymity revocation of participants in the identity layer, rather than auditing the aspects of a payment system (e.g. transactions or assets) in the transaction layer. To accomplish this, they propose two kinds of authorities: An Identity provider who provides a digital identity with attributes to account holder and stores registration information, and an anonymity revoker who can revoke anonymity at will on accounts created by the account holder using the registration information. While threshold encryption is proposed to avoid giving too much power to a single anonymity revoker, this approach might be still problematic in the same manner as in Zerocash extension [37]. In a similar manner, Barki-Gouget [16] also focus in a physical entity's anonymity revocation by a centralized authority, while presenting their work as a standalone accountable-anonymous system. As both of above works focus on the identity layer and they only provide an abstract way of building a complete distributed payment system, we omit concrete efficiency asymptotics in Table 3.

5.2   General Auditor

A designated auditor (or set of auditors) makes an implementation simpler, but is a strong assumption for any payment system. Some schemes were proposed making auditing possible by *any* auditing authority typically with the auditee's consent. This approach is generally preferred to address Insight 5 concerns, while still being compatible with regulatory practices as we discuss below.

zkLedger [52] is a *permissioned*, privacy-preserving payment system with built-in auditability functions that does not require a designated auditor. Its shared transaction ledger takes a unique approach, and instead of the typical blockchain format, it employs a two-dimensional table recording all participating parties (columns) and all posted transactions (rows). Transactions are formed via a combination of commitments and ZK proofs and, whenever a transaction happens, a new row is generated in the table including information for *all* system participants, even for those who do not participate in that transaction by committing to a zero value (in order to ensure transaction and participant privacy).

zkLedger's basic auditing functionality is an *interactive* ZK protocol between an account holder and an auditor, where the account holder reveals the value hidden in a commitment in a verifiable manner, without disclosing any other information (such as its private key) or needing to open the commitment. Based on this basic audit functionality, several other audits can be implemented at a transaction or participant level (e.g. transaction limits or statistical information). Statistical audits can be easily derived from the basic value audit using auxiliary bit flags, while limit audits can be implemented using appropriate range proofs. Value audits can also be used to derive participation audits (as well as non-participation proofs) utilizing zkLedger's architecture. zkLedger could be trivially extended to accommodate tax compliance either proactively as an accountability functionality (by verifying a ZK proof that the relation between the total recipient values and the tax authority recipient is equal to a fixed ratio, per Insight 6) or reactively as an auditability functionality (by verifying the same ZK proof as before during the auditing process). Also zkLedger's audits can be seen as organization-level audits (i.e. PoA) due to its participants mainly considered being "Banks". Transaction types and tracing could also be easily added as system add-ons through an additional commitment and an appropriate ZK proof of consistency between sent and received values, but this would further increase storage needs and computational costs. However, its structure circumvents the limitation of Insight 8 which enables efficient auditing with as low as $O(1)$ asymptotic costs (assuming an online auditor tracking ledger state).

However it is obvious from Table 3 that zkLedger suffers from very limited scalability, as requiring each transaction to include a commitment (as well as the needed auxiliary information) for *all* participants, combined with an ever-increasing ledger of such transactions, results in large computational and storage costs, which makes it viable for up to about a hundred participants. It also requires participants to communicate out-of-band and be online at all times, which further limit its practical applications. Nevertheless, it was the first system to depart from the naive approach described in Insight 5 while offering a wide range of auditing functionalities, which inspired subsequent academic works.

Insight 9. *An interactive auditing protocol implies the auditee's consent and cooperation with an auditing authority. This requirement is not necessarily a drawback for such schemes, as refusal to cooperate with authorities can be considered as equivalent to a failed audit. In addition, audit by consent typically enables more efficient auditing.*

Insight 10. *Many audit functions such as transaction limit or tax compliance can be reduced to a "basic" transaction value audit.*

PGC [26] is a confidential payment system with an auditing functionality on transaction values. It uses similar cryptographic techniques to zkLedger. Specifically, it uses an El Gamal encryption variant equivalent to a Pedersen Commitment and the auxiliary information used in zkLedger, and relies on ZK proofs composed of Σ-protocols. PGC by using encryption instead of commitments does not need to rely on out-of-band communication assumptions (which are needed to open the commitments), which could potentially enable it to work in a permissionless setting as well (although not explicitly discussed in the paper). It proposes three different audit functions, namely transaction limit (using appropriate range proofs), value disclosure and tax payments (which can be derived from value disclosure as discussed in Insight 10). Recall that these reactive auditability functions could be converted into equivalent proactive accountability functions enforced by the consensus layer (Insight 6). Since PGC is not anonymous, transaction participant auditing is not applicable. Also transaction types or tracing functionalities can be added in PGC by including the necessary auxiliary information in the transaction structure as in Zcash extension [37]. Although PGC does not suffer from the scalability issues of zkLedger, it requires each transaction to include a unique serial number to prevent replay attacks (as Zcash [17]), which asymptotically results in linearly-increasing blockchain storage to the number of transactions. PGC can be considered as a special case of Insight 8 - by trading off anonymity, it achieves highly efficient auditing only dependent to the number of past user transactions, as shown in Table 3.

Similarly to zkLedger, MiniLedger [25] is a permissioned, fully anonymous system. While it has a similar structure with zkLedger, it identified its vulnerabilities and shortcomings and implements a system without needing out-of-band communication between participants, using a similar encryption scheme with PGC. However the crucial difference is that its ledger size does not grow linearly with the number of recorded transactions, and is only proportional to the number of participants, while preserving efficient auditing (as shown in Table 3). This is accomplished though a transaction pruning process, which however preserves auditability for pruned transactions. In addition, it offers additional regulation functionalities (shown in Table 2) and an option to make non-interactive audits without consent at the cost of having a centralized audit authority (Table 4).

Gap 6. *Is auditing of transactions that do not appear in the ledger (or happen "off the chain") possible?*

While it's desirable to compress a public ledger to improve its scalability, a system that enforces regulation policies is typically incompatible with ledger compression techniques (such as pruning), since auditing in DPSs needs to refer to some published data on the ledger. MiniLedger [25] is a first step towards this in a permissioned setting, however with linear transaction costs in terms of number of participants. At the same time, no system exists that achieves Regulation Correctness and Regulation Soundness for locked funds. While it is unclear how to provide regulatory control for distributed ledger systems implementing payment channels or cross-chain atomic swaps a first approach might be to consider a centralized authority.

Gap 7. *How can a dispute between an auditor and an auditee be resolved?* [4]

We note most of DPSs ignore the problem of dispute resolution in case an auditor misbehaves (e.g. accuses an auditee of failing an audit). While the auditee could publish all their secret information to rebut the accusation, this would fully compromise their privacy.

MProve [32] is a PoA protocol tailored for Monero [57]. As the Provisions protocol won't work for Monero because of ring signature obfuscation, MProve provides a proof that the key images of the one-time addresses controlled by the exchange (which they sum to its total assets) have not previously appeared on the public ledger. This approach provides a proof of non-collusion as well, as the one-time nature of the key images would trivially expose collusion. However it exposes the sender's identity when those key images are spent, which might eventually enable public tracing of transactions (especially in cases where such a PoA protocol is used frequently).

Gap 8. *Can PoA/PoL be implemented on privacy-preserving payment systems without degrading the participant's privacy?*

6   Conclusion

We observe increasing efforts towards implementing regulatory control in distributed payment systems. However, existing lines of research approach the

---

[4] Gap 7 is the equivalent of Gap 4 for privacy-preserving systems.

problem from different angles, with different goals, assumptions and use-cases. Our systematization identifies a number of exciting open problems on providing mechanisms for regulation of DPSs which we summarize below.

Despite auditing in pseudoanonymous systems intuitively being straightforward, no solution exists that prevents collusions among organizations when proving assets, while allowing them to exclude liabilities with low-probability of access (Gaps 1 and 2). In addition, proving assets efficiently, in a fully-anonymous manner and without introducing additional assumptions remains an open problem (Gap 3). In privacy-preserving systems, we note that mapping regulation requirements and laws to automated computations is not trivial, and designing fully-private DPSs supporting many different regulations currently seems out of reach. Proof of solvency on privacy-preserving systems is challenging (Gap 8), while there is no *fully-private* DPS that is scalable, computationally efficient and without strong assumptions such as designated auditing authorities that can violate user privacy. We observe all schemes attempting to enforce regulatory functions are designed for "on-chain" protocols, and are not compatible with information that either lives off the ledger and/or locks funds, or with information that has been pruned entirely from the common ledger (Gap 6). A possible approach is relying on powerful "full nodes" who keep a copy of the full ledger history (regardless of whether it has been pruned or not), and have the auditors use them as query points. While by checking that their history is consistent with the pruned ledger would prevent malicious behavior by those nodes, this approach is still a centralized point of failure for auditing purposes. Finally, dispute resolution without compromising privacy against a third-party judge is an open problem in both pseudoanonymous and privacy-preserving systems (Gaps 4, 7).

Acknowledgements. We thank Kaoutar Elkhiyaoui (IBM Research) for the clarifications on [15] and Dmitry Korneev (Facebook) for his input on needed regulation and compliance.

A   Cryptographic Background

A.1   Consensus

A consensus protocol allows a number of nodes to output a common agreement on input of a sequence of messages. In our setting, the commonly agreed value is typically recorded on a public ledger. The basic properties of a consensus protocol are [36] a) *Consistency:* On some input, all honest nodes make the same output. b) *Liveness:* An input proposed by some honest node will be eventually processed by all honest nodes after a finite number of rounds. A common distinction among consensus protocols is according to their failure model, where *crash tolerant* protocols assume failed nodes may become offline or otherwise stop interacting with the system, while *Byzantine tolerant* [47] protocols assume such nodes might also engage into malicious activity in order to defeat the above properties. These models typically assume different levels of adversarial power needed for the system to fail. Another distinction is based on the participation model, where *permissioned* consensus participation is open only to a closed set of parties, while *permissionless* is open to anyone, which however needs a mechanism to prevent attacks through "sybil" identities such as Bitcoin's Proof of Work [51] or Proof of Stake protocols [45].

A.2   Distributed Payment Systems

A distributed payment system DPS (also known as ledger-based payment system) can be simply defined by the following algorithms and protocols when already assuming the existence of a consensus layer.

- $\mathsf{pp}, L \leftarrow \mathsf{Setup}(\lambda)$: on input of security parameter λ, outputs public parameters pp and initializes a public ledger L to be maintained by the consensus layer. This algorithm is executed once in the setup phase of the system, and is run by either a single party or a quorum of parties in a multi-party computation (MPC) protocol. In the following algorithms and protocols, pp and L are default inputs and are omitted for simplicity.
- $(\mathsf{pk}, \mathsf{sk}) \leftarrow \mathsf{CreateAcc}()$: Run by any party wishing to transact in the system[5], outputs a public key pair.
- $\mathsf{tx} \leftarrow \mathsf{CreateTx}(\mathsf{sk_S}, \mathsf{pk_R}, v)$: Run by a sender wishing to send value v to receiver, and outputs a transaction tx. Although here for simplicity we assume a single sender and receiver, a transaction can generally accommodate multiple senders and receivers. tx is sent to the consensus layer in order to be included in L after verification.
- $\mathsf{VerifyTx}(\mathsf{tx}) := \{0, 1\}$ Verifies the validity of a transaction tx, given the state of the ledger L. Verification is typically performed in a distributed fashion in the consensus layer among all verifiers (often called "miners"), where agreement results in the update of the ledger's state to L' which contains tx.

A.3   Commitment Schemes

Commitment schemes are very commonly used in private DPSs, to hide transaction information. A non-interactive commitment scheme $\mathsf{Com}(\mathsf{pp}, m, r)$ takes as input public parameters pp, a message m and randomness r and outputs a commitment value cm. This value reveals no information about the message (*hiding* property) while it is hard to find (m', r') such that $\mathsf{Com}(\mathsf{pp}, m, r) = \mathsf{Com}(\mathsf{pp}, m', r')$, when $m' \neq m$ (*binding* property). Certain commitment schemes, i.e. Pedersen commitments [53] allow for homomorphic operations over committed values, a useful property in private DPSs.

---

[5] Although participation in payment systems is typically achieved through public key cryptography, some systems achieve it through other primitives (e.g. spending in Mimblewimble [35,54] requires knowledge of a commitment's blinding factor).

A.4   Zero Knowledge Proofs

A Zero Knowledge proof is an interactive protocol between a prover P and a verifier V where P based on a common input statement proves knowledge of a witness w without revealing to V any additional information other than this fact alone. In DPSs, zero-knowledge proofs are used extensively to provide privacy-preserving attributes, with transacting parties proving validity of a transactions based on a public ledger without revealing the full transaction details, while in recent works they are also used to prove compliance with regulatory requirements.

Range Proofs are Zero Knowledge protocols proving that a committed value v lies within some interval (a, b), with v as the witness. In a payment system setting, such proofs are typically used to show that v is positive or does not overflow a maximum presentable value. Most well-known construction families for range proofs include square decomposition [40], multi-base decomposition [55] and Bulletproofs [21], with the latter being the most efficient in terms of proof size. Obviously, one can generate constant size range proofs from trusted-setup based SNARKs like Groth16 [41]. In privacy-preserving DPSs they are often used to ensure their basic core properties discussed in Sect. A.2, but they are also used for regulation purposes (e.g. distinguish between transactions that exceed a value limit).

A.5   Interactive Zero Knowledge Proofs

An interactive zero-knowledge proof (ZKP) for statement $\{w : f(w, x)\}$ where x is publicly known and witness w is known only to prover P, is a protocol between P and verifier V that proves P's knowledge of w such that $f(w, x)$ holds. This protocol needs to satisfy the following:

- **Completeness:** Honest V is always convinced by an honest P who knows a valid witness w.
- **Soundness:** A malicious prover P^* cannot convince a verifier for a false statement.
- **Zero Knowledge:** After executing the protocol, a verifier does not learn any additional information other than the validity of the statement.

An interactive ZKP can be converted to a non-interactive zero knowledge proof (NIZK) using the Fiat-Shamir heuristic [33]. In turn, a ZK - Succinct Non-interactive ARgument of Knowledge (zk-SNARK) is a non-interactive zero-knowledge proof that is succinct, namely its proofs are very short $O(\lambda)$ with efficient verification $O(\lambda|x|)$ [18].

References

1. Bitgo announces "verified by bitgo" proof of asset service. https://www.businesswire.com/news/home/20150630005466/en/BitGo-Announces-%E2%80%9CVerified-BitGo%E2%80%9D-Proof-Asset-Service#.VZKYwO1Viko

2. Bitstamp proof of reserves. https://www.bitstamp.net/s/documents/Bitstamp_proof_of_reserves_statement.pdf
3. CSBS state regulatory requirements for virtual currency activities. https://www.csbs.org/sites/default/files/2017-11/CSBS%20Draft%20Model%20Regulatory%20Framework%20for%20Virtual%20Currency%20Proposal%20-%20Dec.%2016%202014.pdf
4. Deloitte COINIA and the future of audit. https://www2.deloitte.com/us/en/pages/audit/articles/impact-of-blockchain-in-accounting.html
5. FATF travel rule: What you need to know. https://complyadvantage.com/knowledgebase/fatf-travel-rule/
6. IRS is trying to deanonymize privacy coins like monero and zcash. https://www.forbes.com/sites/shehanchandrasekera/2020/07/06/irs-is-trying-to-deanonymize-privacy-coins-like-monero-and-zcash/#4607506c4174
7. Maxwell summation trees. https://bitcointalk.org/index.php?topic=595180.0
8. Proof of solvency: Technical overview. https://medium.com/iconominet/proof-of-solvency-technical-overview-d1d0e8a8a0b8
9. Tether: Fiat currencies on the bitcoin blockchain. https://tether.to/wp-content/uploads/2016/06/TetherWhitePaper.pdf
10. Tether's bank says it invests customer funds in bitcoin. https://www.coindesk.com/tethers-bank-says-it-invests-customer-funds-in-bitcoin
11. On blockchain auditability (2016). https://bitfury.com/content/downloads/bitfury_white_paper_on_blockchain_auditability.pdf
12. Regulation (EU) 2016/679 of the European parliament and of the council of 27 April 2016 on the protection of natural persons with regard to the processing of personal data and on the free movement of such data, and repealing directive 95/46/EC (general data protection regulation). Official Journal of the European Union L119, pp. 1–88 (2016)
13. Deloitte's 2020 global blockchain survey (2020). https://www2.deloitte.com/content/dam/insights/us/articles/6608_2020-global-blockchain-survey/DI_CIR%202020%20global%20blockchain%20survey.pdf
14. Androulaki, E., et al.: Hyperledger fabric: a distributed operating system for permissioned blockchains. In: Proceedings of the Thirteenth EuroSys Conference, EuroSys 2018, Porto, Portugal, 23–26 April 2018, pp. 30:1–30:15 (2018)
15. Androulaki, E., Camenisch, J., Caro, A.D., Dubovitskaya, M., Elkhiyaoui, K., Tackmann, B.: Privacy-preserving auditable token payments in a permissioned blockchain system. In: AFT 2020: 2nd ACM Conference on Advances in Financial Technologies, New York, NY, USA, 21–23 October 2020, pp. 255–267. ACM (2020). https://doi.org/10.1145/3419614.3423259
16. Barki, A., Gouget, A.: Achieving privacy and accountability in traceable digital currency. Cryptology ePrint Archive, Report 2020/1565 (2020). https://eprint.iacr.org/2020/1565
17. Ben-Sasson, E., et al.: Zerocash: decentralized anonymous payments from bitcoin. In: 2014 IEEE Symposium on Security and Privacy, pp. 459–474. IEEE Computer Society Press, May 2014. https://doi.org/10.1109/SP.2014.36
18. Bitansky, N., Chiesa, A., Ishai, Y., Paneth, O., Ostrovsky, R.: Succinct non-interactive arguments via linear interactive proofs. In: Sahai, A. (ed.) TCC 2013. LNCS, vol. 7785, pp. 315–333. Springer, Heidelberg (2013). https://doi.org/10.1007/978-3-642-36594-2_18
19. Bogatov, D., De Caro, A., Elkhiyaoui, K., Tackmann, B.: Anonymous transactions with revocation and auditing in hyperledger fabric. Cryptology ePrint Archive, Report 2019/1097 (2019). https://eprint.iacr.org/2019/1097

20. Brands, S.: Untraceable off-line cash in wallet with observers. In: Stinson, D.R. (ed.) CRYPTO 1993. LNCS, vol. 773, pp. 302–318. Springer, Heidelberg (1994). https://doi.org/10.1007/3-540-48329-2_26
21. Bünz, B., Bootle, J., Boneh, D., Poelstra, A., Wuille, P., Maxwell, G.: Bulletproofs: short proofs for confidential transactions and more. In: 2018 IEEE Symposium on Security and Privacy, pp. 315–334. IEEE Computer Society Press, May 2018. https://doi.org/10.1109/SP.2018.00020
22. Cecchetti, E., Zhang, F., Ji, Y., Kosba, A.E., Juels, A., Shi, E.: Solidus: confidential distributed ledger transactions via PVORM. In: Thuraisingham, B.M., Evans, D., Malkin, T., Xu, D. (eds.) ACM CCS 2017, pp. 701–717. ACM Press, October/November 2017. https://doi.org/10.1145/3133956.3134010
23. Chalkias, K., Lewi, K., Mohassel, P., Nikolaenko, V.: Distributed auditing proofs of liabilities. Cryptology ePrint Archive, Report 2020/468 (2020). https://eprint.iacr.org/2020/468
24. Chase, M., Ganesh, C., Mohassel, P.: Efficient zero-knowledge proof of algebraic and non-algebraic statements with applications to privacy preserving credentials. In: Robshaw, M., Katz, J. (eds.) CRYPTO 2016. LNCS, vol. 9816, pp. 499–530. Springer, Heidelberg (2016). https://doi.org/10.1007/978-3-662-53015-3_18
25. Chatzigiannis, P., Baldimtsi, F.: Miniledger: compact-sized anonymous and auditable distributed payments. In: ESORICS 2021 (2021)
26. Chen, Yu., Ma, X., Tang, C., Au, M.H.: PGC: decentralized confidential payment system with auditability. In: Chen, L., Li, N., Liang, K., Schneider, S. (eds.) ESORICS 2020. LNCS, vol. 12308, pp. 591–610. Springer, Cham (2020). https://doi.org/10.1007/978-3-030-58951-6_29
27. Conti, M., Kumar, E.S., Lal, C., Ruj, S.: A survey on security and privacy issues of bitcoin. IEEE Commun. Surv. Tutor. **20**(4), 3416–3452 (2018). https://doi.org/10.1109/COMST.2018.2842460
28. Dagher, G.G., Bünz, B., Bonneau, J., Clark, J., Boneh, D.: Provisions: privacy-preserving proofs of solvency for bitcoin exchanges. In: Ray, I., Li, N., Kruegel, C. (eds.) ACM CCS 2015, pp. 720–731. ACM Press, October 2015. https://doi.org/10.1145/2810103.2813674
29. Damgård, I., Ganesh, C., Khoshakhlagh, H., Orlandi, C., Siniscalchi, L.: Balancing privacy and accountability in blockchain identity management. Cryptology ePrint Archive, Report 2020/1511 (2020). https://eprint.iacr.org/2020/1511
30. Decker, C., Guthrie, J., Seidel, J., Wattenhofer, R.: Making bitcoin exchanges transparent. In: Pernul, G., Ryan, P.Y.A., Weippl, E. (eds.) ESORICS 2015, Part II. LNCS, vol. 9327, pp. 561–576. Springer, Cham (2015). https://doi.org/10.1007/978-3-319-24177-7_28
31. Doerner, J., Shelat, A., Evans, D.: Zeroledge: proving solvency with privacy (2015)
32. Dutta, A., Vijayakumaran, S.: Mprove: a proof of reserves protocol for monero exchanges. In: 2019 IEEE European Symposium on Security and Privacy Workshops, EuroS&P Workshops 2019, Stockholm, Sweden, 17–19 June 2019, pp. 330–339. IEEE (2019). https://doi.org/10.1109/EuroSPW.2019.00043
33. Fiat, A., Shamir, A.: How to prove yourself: practical solutions to identification and signature problems. In: Odlyzko, A.M. (ed.) CRYPTO 1986. LNCS, vol. 263, pp. 186–194. Springer, Heidelberg (1987). https://doi.org/10.1007/3-540-47721-7_12
34. Frankle, J., Park, S., Shaar, D., Goldwasser, S., Weitzner, D.J.: Practical accountability of secret processes. In: Enck, W., Felt, A.P. (eds.) USENIX Security 2018, pp. 657–674. USENIX Association, August 2018

35. Fuchsbauer, G., Orrù, M., Seurin, Y.: Aggregate cash systems: a cryptographic investigation of mimblewimble. In: Ishai, Y., Rijmen, V. (eds.) EUROCRYPT 2019, Part I. LNCS, vol. 11476, pp. 657–689. Springer, Cham (2019). https://doi.org/10.1007/978-3-030-17653-2_22

36. Garay, J., Kiayias, A.: SoK: a consensus taxonomy in the blockchain era. In: Jarecki, S. (ed.) CT-RSA 2020. LNCS, vol. 12006, pp. 284–318. Springer, Cham (2020). https://doi.org/10.1007/978-3-030-40186-3_13

37. Garman, C., Green, M., Miers, I.: Accountable privacy for decentralized anonymous payments. In: Grossklags, J., Preneel, B. (eds.) FC 2016. LNCS, vol. 9603, pp. 81–98. Springer, Heidelberg (2017). https://doi.org/10.1007/978-3-662-54970-4_5

38. Goldwasser, S., Park, S.: Public accountability vs. secret laws: can they coexist?: a cryptographic proposal. In: Thuraisingham, B.M., Lee, A.J. (eds.) Proceedings of the 2017 on Workshop on Privacy in the Electronic Society, Dallas, TX, USA, 30 October–3 November 2017, pp. 99–110. ACM (2017). https://doi.org/10.1145/3139550.3139565

39. Graf, M., Küsters, R., Rausch, D.: Accountability in a permissioned blockchain: formal analysis of hyperledger fabric, pp. 236–255 (2020). https://doi.org/10.1109/EuroSP48549.2020.00023

40. Groth, J.: Non-interactive zero-knowledge arguments for voting. In: Ioannidis, J., Keromytis, A., Yung, M. (eds.) ACNS 2005. LNCS, vol. 3531, pp. 467–482. Springer, Heidelberg (2005). https://doi.org/10.1007/11496137_32

41. Groth, J.: On the size of pairing-based non-interactive arguments. In: Fischlin, M., Coron, J.-S. (eds.) EUROCRYPT 2016, Part II. LNCS, vol. 9666, pp. 305–326. Springer, Heidelberg (2016). https://doi.org/10.1007/978-3-662-49896-5_11

42. Guts, N., Fournet, C., Zappa Nardelli, F.: Reliable evidence: auditability by typing. In: Backes, M., Ning, P. (eds.) ESORICS 2009. LNCS, vol. 5789, pp. 168–183. Springer, Heidelberg (2009). https://doi.org/10.1007/978-3-642-04444-1_11

43. Heilman, E., Alshenibr, L., Baldimtsi, F., Scafuro, A., Goldberg, S.: TumbleBit: an untrusted bitcoin-compatible anonymous payment hub. In: NDSS 2017. The Internet Society, February/March 2017

44. Hu, K., Zhang, Z., Guo, K.: Breaking the binding: attacks on the merkle approach to prove liabilities and its applications. Comput. Secur. **87** (2019). https://doi.org/10.1016/j.cose.2019.101585

45. Kiayias, A., Russell, A., David, B., Oliynykov, R.: Ouroboros: a provably secure proof-of-stake blockchain protocol. In: Katz, J., Shacham, H. (eds.) CRYPTO 2017. LNCS, vol. 10401, pp. 357–388. Springer, Cham (2017). https://doi.org/10.1007/978-3-319-63688-7_12

46. Küsters, R., Truderung, T., Vogt, A.: Accountability: definition and relationship to verifiability. In: Al-Shaer, E., Keromytis, A.D., Shmatikov, V. (eds.) ACM CCS 2010, pp. 526–535. ACM Press, October 2010. https://doi.org/10.1145/1866307.1866366

47. Lamport, L., Shostak, R.E., Pease, M.C.: The byzantine generals problem. ACM Trans. Program. Lang. Syst. **4**(3), 382–401 (1982)

48. Maxwell, G.: Coinjoin: Bitcoin privacy for the real world (2013). https://bitcointalk.org/index.php?topic=279249.0

49. Meiklejohn, S., et al.: A fistful of bitcoins: characterizing payments among men with no names. In: Papagiannaki, K., Gummadi, P.K., Partridge, C. (eds.) Proceedings of the 2013 Internet Measurement Conference, IMC 2013, Barcelona, Spain, 23–25 October 2013, pp. 127–140. ACM (2013). https://doi.org/10.1145/2504730.2504747

50. Moore, T., Christin, N.: Beware the middleman: empirical analysis of bitcoin-exchange risk. In: Sadeghi, A.-R. (ed.) FC 2013. LNCS, vol. 7859, pp. 25–33. Springer, Heidelberg (2013). https://doi.org/10.1007/978-3-642-39884-1_3
51. Nakamoto, S.: Bitcoin: a peer-to-peer electronic cash system (2009). http://bitcoin.org/bitcoin.pdf
52. Narula, N., Vasquez, W., Virza, M.: zkledger: privacy-preserving auditing for distributed ledgers. In: 15th USENIX Symposium on Networked Systems Design and Implementation (NSDI 2018), Renton, WA, pp. 65–80. USENIX Association, April 2018. https://www.usenix.org/conference/nsdi18/presentation/narula
53. Pedersen, T.P.: Non-interactive and information-theoretic secure verifiable secret sharing. In: Feigenbaum, J. (ed.) CRYPTO 1991. LNCS, vol. 576, pp. 129–140. Springer, Heidelberg (1992). https://doi.org/10.1007/3-540-46766-1_9
54. Poelstra, A.: Mimblewimble (2016). https://download.wpsoftware.net/bitcoin/wizardry/mimblewimble.pdf
55. Poelstra, A., Back, A., Friedenbach, M., Maxwell, G., Wuille, P.: Confidential assets. In: Zohar, A., et al. (eds.) FC 2018. LNCS, vol. 10958, pp. 43–63. Springer, Heidelberg (2019). https://doi.org/10.1007/978-3-662-58820-8_4
56. Roose, S.: Standardizing bitcoin proof of reserves. https://blockstream.com/2019/02/04/en-standardizing-bitcoin-proof-of-reserves/
57. Van Saberhagen, N.: Cryptonote v 2.0 (2013). https://cryptonote.org/whitepaper.pdf
58. Wang, H., He, D., Ji, Y.: Designated-verifier proof of assets for bitcoin exchange using elliptic curve cryptography. Future Gener. Comput. Syst. **107**, 854–862 (2020). https://doi.org/10.1016/j.future.2017.06.028
59. Wüst, K., Kostiainen, K., Čapkun, V., Čapkun, S.: PRCash: fast, private and regulated transactions for digital currencies. In: Goldberg, I., Moore, T. (eds.) FC 2019. LNCS, vol. 11598, pp. 158–178. Springer, Cham (2019). https://doi.org/10.1007/978-3-030-32101-7_11

Defending Web Servers Against Flash Crowd Attacks

Rajat Tandon$^{(\boxtimes)}$ ⓘ, Abhinav Palia ⓘ, Jaydeep Ramani ⓘ, Brandon Paulsen ⓘ,
Genevieve Bartlett ⓘ, and Jelena Mirkovic ⓘ

University of Southern California Information Sciences Institute,
Marina del Rey, CA, USA
{rajattan,palia,jramani,bpaulsen}@usc.edu, {bartlett,mirkovic}@isi.edu
https://steel.isi.edu/Projects/frade/

Abstract. A flash crowd attack (FCA) floods a service, such as a Web
server, with well-formed requests, generated by numerous bots. FCA
traffic is difficult to filter, since individual attack and legitimate service
requests look identical. We propose robust and reliable models of human
interaction with server, which can identify and block a wide variety of
bots. We implement the models in a system called FRADE, and evaluate
them on three Web servers with different server applications and content. Our results show that FRADE detects both naive and sophisticated
bots within seconds, and successfully filters out attack traffic. FRADE
significantly raises the bar for a successful attack, by forcing attackers to
deploy at least three orders of magnitude larger botnets than today.

1 Introduction

Application layer DDoS attacks or flash-crowd attacks (FCAs) are on the rise [23,
25,30]. The attacker floods a popular service with legitimate-like requests, using
many bots. This usually has a severe impact on the server, impairing its ability
to serve legitimate users. The attack resembles a "flash crowd", where many
legitimate clients access popular content. Distinguishing between a flash-crowd
and a FCA is hard, as the attack uses requests whose content is identical to
a legitimate user's content, and each bot may send at a low rate [24,27,44].
Thus, typical defenses against volumetric attacks, such as looking for malformed
requests or rate-limiting clients, do not help against FCAs.

We propose FRADE, a server-based FCA defense, which aims to identify
and block malicious clients, based on a wholistic assessment of their interaction
with the server. FRADE views the problem of distinguishing between legitimate
and attack clients, as distinguishing between humans and bots. Thus, FRADE
is well-suited to protect applications where legitimate service requests are issued
by humans, such as Web servers.

FRADE leverages three key differences between humans and bots. First,
humans browse in a bursty manner, while bots try to maximize their request rate
and send traffic continuously. FRADE learns the dynamics of human interaction
with a given server over several time scales, and builds its *dynamics* models.

© Springer Nature Switzerland AG 2021
K. Sako and N. O. Tippenhauer (Eds.): ACNS 2021, LNCS 12727, pp. 338–361, 2021.
https://doi.org/10.1007/978-3-030-78375-4_14

Second, humans follow popular content across pages, while bots cannot identify popular content. FRADE learns patterns of human browsing over time, and builds its *semantics* model. Third, humans only click on visible hyperlinks, while bots cannot discriminate between hyperlinks based on their visibility. FRADE's *deception* module embeds invisible hyperlinks into the server's replies. When the load on the server is high, FRADE labels as "bot", and blocks clients whose behavior mismatches its dynamics or semantics model, or clients that access deception hyperlinks.

FRADE does not make FCAs impossible, but it successfully mitigates a large range of attack strategies. Our evaluation with real traffic, servers and attacks, shows that FRADE identifies and blocks naive bots after 3–5 requests, and stealthy bots after 15–19 requests, thus significantly raising the bar for attackers. To perform a successful, sustained attack, an attacker must employ more sophisticated bots, and deploy them in waves, retiring old ones as they are blocked by FRADE and enlisting new ones. The attacker needs at least *three orders of magnitude* more bots than used in today's attacks.

Our prior work by Oikonomou and Mirkovic [39] proposed the high-level ideas of differentiating humans from bots using dynamics and semantics models, and decoy hyperlinks. We refer to this work as OM. We build upon the basic ideas in OM, but significantly modify and improve them, to make the system robust against sophisticated adversaries, and practical to implement. Our contributions are (also summarized in Table 1):

Sophisticated Attack Handling: OM cannot handle attacks by an attacker familiar with the defense, while FRADE can (Sect. 3.3).

Stealthier Decoy Hyperlinks: FRADE uses *stealthier deception hyperlinks* than OM (Sect. 2.6), which cannot be detected via automated Web page analysis.

Improved Models: FRADE has *simpler and more robust dynamics and semantics models* (Sect. 2.4 and 2.5), which only require legitimate clients' data to train. OM also required attack data for training, which is hard to obtain and may impair detection of new attacks. FRADE is *much more accurate* than OM in differentiating bots from humans (Sect. 3.5).

Implementation and Evaluation: FRADE is *implemented as a complete system* and *evaluated with real traffic and server content*, while OM was evaluated in *simulation only*. FRADE's implementation-based evaluation helped us *discover and solve major real-time processing issues*, such as enabling the defense to receive and analyze requests during FCAs, and dealing with missed and reordered client requests (Sect. 2.7). FRADE as a complete system, mitigates FCAs about *ten times faster* than OM.

Section 2.8 provides a detailed explanation of the novelties and improvements that FRADE offers over OM. Our code and data are accessible at the link [47].

2   FRADE

We next give an overview of FRADE's goals and operation.

Attacker Model. In our work we consider two attacker models. A *naive attacker* launches FCAs that are observed today and is not familiar with FRADE. A *sophisticated attacker* is familiar with FRADE and actively tries to bypass it.

Design Goals. We aim to design an FCA defense that mitigates both *naive* and *sophisticated* attacks. Our design rests on two premises. First, FRADE's models are based on features that are difficult, albeit not impossible, for an attacker to learn, because they are only observable at the server. Second, if an attacker does successfully learn and mimic our models, it drastically lowers the usefulness of each bot and forces the attacker to employ many more bots to achieve a sustained attack. In our evaluation, FRADE raises the bar for a successful FCA from just a single bot to 8,000 bots. Extrapolating from the botnet sizes observed in contemporary FCAs, FRADE would raise the bar from 3–6 K to 24–48 M bots—far above the size of botnets available today.

Anomaly detection methods regularly learn feature thresholds from training data, and apply them in production. Our contribution lies in (a) selecting which features to learn, to be effective against both naive and sophisticated attacks, (b) implementing and evaluating our approach in three different Web servers, with different content.

2.1   Feature Selection

FRADE aims to differentiate human users from bots during FCAs, and to do so transparently to the human users. Differentiating humans from bots is challenging in an FCA, since legitimate and attack requests can be identical. Our key insight is that *while individual requests are identical, the behavior of traffic sources (humans and bots), observed over sequences of requests differs with regard to dynamics and semantics of interaction with the server, and how they identify content of interest.*

Dynamics: Human users browse server content following their interest, and occasionally pause to read content or attend to other, unrelated tasks (e.g., lunch). Their rate is therefore bursty – it may be high in a small time window, but not sustained over time. Bots are incentivized to generate requests more aggressively, generating a sustained rate of requests over long time. To capture these differences we develop models that encode the dynamics of human user interaction with the server over *multiple time windows*.

The main challenge lies in how to properly model various types of requests to make it hard for bots to avoid detection. Because requests may be generated in different ways and may consume different resources at the server, we develop three dynamics models: (a) *main-page requests* are generated through human action, such as clicking on a hyperlink or scrolling to the bottom of a page – we model their rate directly over multiple time windows, (b) requests for *embedded content*, such as images, are automatically generated by a Web browser, and their rate will vary depending on the browser configuration and the number of embedded objects per page – instead of modeling request *rate* for embedded objects, we associate each object with its parent page, and allow only those objects to load that belong to a recently loaded parent page, (c) requests for dynamic pages can consume many *server resources*, even at low rate – we model the demand for server resources over different time windows.

Semantics: Since humans follow their interests and understand content, they tend to click on popular content more often than not. Bots, on the other hand, must either hard-code a sequence of pages to visit, fabricate requests for non-existing pages, or choose at random from hyperlinks available on the pages, which they previously visited. *The main challenge lies in building a model that properly leverages popularity measures to detect random, fake or hard-coded sequences of bot requests, while being able to handle user sequences that were not seen in training.*

FRADE models sequences of human user's requests, and learns the probabilities of these sequences over time. Clients whose request sequences have low probabilities according to the model will be classified as bots. FRADE has a special *fall-back* mechanism to handle sequences not seen in training.

Deception: We expect human users to visit only those hyperlinks that they can see and that are interesting to them, in the rendered content. *The main challenge in leveraging this difference lies in developing ways to automatically insert decoy hyperlinks in pages, which humans will not visit, and to make it hard for bots to identify them via page source parsing.* FRADE dynamically inserts *decoy* hyperlinks [46], into Web pages, which are linked to anchors invisible to human eye (hidden, small or transparent). FRADE leverages page analysis and CSS files to make these anchors hard to identify by automated analysis. Clients that click on decoy anchors are identified as bots.

We discuss novelty in Sect. 2.8 and demonstrate effectiveness in Sect. 3.

Table 1. Comparison between OM [39] and FRADE.

Feature	OM [39]	FRADE	Section
Web req. FCA	Yes	Yes	Sect. 3.2
Embd. obj. FCA	No	Yes, DYN_e mod	Sect. 3.3
Costly req. FCA	No	Yes, DYN_c mod	Sect. 3.3
Accuracy	$fp \geq 0$, $fn \geq 0$	$fp = 0$, $fn = 0$	Sect. 3.5
Models	DYN_h & sem. mod.	improved	Sect. 2
Honeytokens	Simple	Sophisticated	Sect. 2.6
Training	Leg. & attack data	Leg. data	Sect. 2
Evaluation	Simulation	Real traffic/servers	Sect. 3

2.2   Overview

FRADE runs in parallel with the server and not inline. It includes an attack detection module and three bot identification modules—*dynamics*, *semantics* and *deception*. It interfaces with a firewall (e.g., `iptables`) to implement attack filtering. FRADE learns how human users interact with the Web server that it protects. It builds the semantics and dynamics models by monitoring *Web server access logs* (WAL) in absence of FCAs. Deception objects, invisible to humans in rendered content, are also automatically inserted into each Web page on the server. When a potential FCA is detected, FRADE enters the classification mode. FRADE loads its learned models into memory, and begins tracking each user's behavior. When a user's behavior deviates from one of the learned models, the user is put on the filter list and all their requests are dropped. When attack stops, the detection module deactivates classification. A filtering rule is removed when the traffic matching it declines.

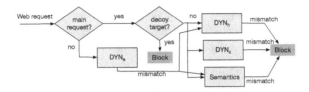

Fig. 1. Overview of FRADE's processing of a Web request.

FRADE uses some customizable parameters for its operation. The parameters and values we used in evaluation are shown in Table 2 and explained below. We perform sensitivity analysis over these parameters in Sect. 3.6.

2.3   Attack Detection

The attack detection module runs separately from the rest of FRADE, and activates and deactivates other modules by starting and stopping processes. Our detection module is intentionally simple, since our focus was on bot identification. We focus on detecting increase in incoming requests, regardless of whether they are due to legitimate flash-crowd event or due to FCA. We then rely on our, very accurate, identification of bots to handle the event. A deploying network can replace our detection module with other mechanisms, such as the Bro Network Security Monitor [40].

Learning. FRADE's attack detection module monitors incoming service requests rate, and learns its smoothed historical mean. If the current incoming rate of requests exceeds the historical mean multiplied by the parameter *attackHigh*, this module raises the alert. Otherwise, the module updates the mean. The update interval, *intDet*, and the parameter *attackHigh*, are configurable (we use $intDet = 1\,\mathrm{s}$ and $attackHigh = 10$).

Table 2. FRADE's parameters and the values we used.

Parameter	Meaning	Value
intDet	Monitoring int	1 s
attackHigh	Incoming req high thresh	10 * avg
attackLow	Incoming req low thresh	2 * avg
windows	Time int. for dyn. models	1 s, 10 s, 60 s, 300 s, 600 s
ρ	Ratio of dec. to vis. obj	1
ThreshPerc	High perc. of a modeled quantity	100

Classification. During an FCA, the detection module continues to collect and evaluate the incoming request rate, but does not update its historical mean. When the current rate falls below the pre-attack historical mean, multiplied by a configurable parameter *attackLow* (we use *attackLow* = 2), FRADE signals the end of the FCA and turns off bot classification modules. Figure 1 shows FRADE's processing of a Web request during attack. In the rest of this section we describe each processing step.

2.4   Request Dynamics

The *dynamics* module models the rate of a user's interaction with a server within a given time interval, and consists of three sub-modules. DYN_h models the rate of main-page requests, such as clicking on a hyperlink or scrolling to the bottom of a page. DYN_e models embedded-object requests, such as loading an image. DYN_c models the rate of a *user's demand for server resources*, where the demand is represented as the total time it took to serve the given user's requests in a given time period.

Learning. DYN_h and DYN_c learn the expected range of the quantity they model (e.g., request rate, processing time, etc.) over all users, by analyzing WAL. We group requests by their source IP address, and assume that each IP address represents one user or a group of users. FRADE classifies each request as either a main-page or embedded. Section 2.10 describes how to detect these two types of requests. DYN_h and DYN_c model the main-page requests and use a high percentile of the range (controlled by *ThreshPerc*, e.g., 99%) as their learned *threshold* for the quantity they model. In our evaluation we use *ThreshPerc* = 100%. The number and sizes of windows are configurable parameters. As humans browse in a bursty manner, having *multiple windows* allows monitoring at different time scales, and drastically raises the bar for a successful FCA. It enables us to correctly classify legitimate bursts and distinguish them from sustained attack floods, even when their peak request rates are equal. We use windows of 1, 10, 60, 300 and 600 s.

DYN_c models the processing time spent to serve a user's requests. This time depends both on the complexity of the user's request, and the current server load. DYN_c models the time to serve a user's request on *lightly loaded server* to capture only that cost to the server that the user can control – the "principal cost". During an attack, we use this principal cost, rather than the actual processing time (inflated cost), to calculate a user's demand on server's resources. This allows us to avoid false positives, where legitimate users hitting a heavily loaded server, experience a large inflated cost through no fault of their own. During learning, each request and its processing time are recorded in a hashmap, called the *ProcessMap*. DYN_c looks up the principal cost for each request in the ProcessMap, and adds it to the running total for the given user. It then learns the *ThreshPerc* value over these totals and for each window.

DYN_e learns which embedded objects exist on each Web page and records this in a hashmap, called the *ObjectMap*.

Classification. During classification, DYN_h and DYN_c collect the same measures of user interaction, per each user, as they did during learning. These measures are continuously updated as new requests arrive. After each update, the module compares the updated measure against its corresponding threshold. If the measure exceeds a threshold, the client's IP is communicated to the filtering module. Whenever a client issues a main-page request, DYN_e loads all the embedded objects related to this request from *ObjectMap* into this user's ApprovedObjectList (AOL). DYN_e checks for the presence of the embedded object requests made by the same user in his AOL. If found, the object is deleted from the AOL. If not found, DYN_e treats this request as a main page request, and forwards it to DYN_h and semantic modules. We do this because a user may bookmark an embedded object, e.g., an image, and request it separately at a future time. Our design allows such requests to be served, while preventing FCAs that create floods of embedded requests.

2.5   Request Semantics

The *semantics* module models the probability of a sequence of requests generated by human users.

Learning. We consider only requests classified as main-page requests. In the learning phase, we compute transition probabilities between each pair of pages (e.g., A to B) on the server using Eq. (1), where $N_{A \to B}$ is the number of transitions from page A to page B, and $N_{A \to *}$ is the number of transitions from page A to any page. We learn $N_{A \to B}$ and $N_{A \to *}$ from WAL. We define the probability of sequence $S = \{u_1, .., u_n\}$ as compound probability of dependent events, which are page transitions, using Eq. (2).

$$P_t(A \to B) = \frac{N_{A \to B}}{N_{A \to *}}, \quad (1); \qquad P(S) = \prod_{i=1}^{n-1} P_t(u_i \to u_{i+1}), \qquad (2)$$

During learning, the semantics model calculates sequence probabilities for each user. Since sequence probability declines with length, we learn the probability for a given range of sequence length (e.g., 5–10 transitions), grouped into a bin. We also ensure that bins are of balanced size. When learning the threshold for each bin, we sort probabilities of all sequences in our training set that fall into that bin and take a low percentile (1-*ThreshPerc*) to be the threshold.

In practice, if a server has very dynamic content, the semantics module may not see all the transitions during learning, leading to false positives in classification. To handle incomplete training data, semantics module has a *fall-back mechanism*. It views Web pages as organized into groups of related content. During learning, it learns transitions from pages to groups, groups to pages, and groups to other groups. We define a group as all the pages that cover the same topic. On some Web sites, the page's topic can be inferred from its file path, while others require analyzing each Web page content to determine the topic (Sect. 2.9). The probability of transition from a page/group to a group, is calculated as the average probability of transition to any file within the group:

$$P_t(A \rightarrow group(b)) = \frac{\sum_{f \in group(b)} P_t(A \rightarrow f)}{N_{A \rightarrow group(b)}}, \tag{3}$$

Classification. FRADE processes the request sequence for each client in the active session list (ASL). When a new request arrives, the module updates the client's sequence probability, just like it did during learning. If a transition from page A → B is not found, FRADE falls back to using groups instead of pages. It attempts to find transitions A → group(B), group(A) → B and group(A) → group(B) in that order. When the first transition is found, its probability is used to multiply the current sequence probability, according to Eq. 2. If no transitions are found, FRADE multiplies the current sequence probability with a constant called *noFileProb* ≪ 1. After each update, it compares the current sequence's probability against the corresponding threshold for the sequence's length. Values lower than the threshold lead to blocking of the client.

2.6   Deception

The *deception* module follows the key idea of honeytokens [46], special objects meant to be accessed only by attackers. The module embeds decoy objects, such as overlapping/small images, into Web pages. In websites with mainly textual content, like Wikipedia, we insert hyperlinks around random pieces of text, but do not highlight them. This makes the hyperlink invisible to humans. In websites with mainly media content, like Imgur, we embed hyperlinks around small images, or small-font text. We insert these decoy objects away from existing hyperlinks, to minimize the chance that they are accidentally visited by humans.

We automatically insert decoy objects into a page's source code so that they do not stand out among other embedded objects in that page. The number of decoy objects to be inserted is guided by the parameter ρ – the ratio of the decoy to original objects on the same page. We make decoy hyperlinks hard to identify from the page's source code by creating separate styles for them in the site's CSS file. We automatically craft the names of the pages, pointed to by decoy hyperlinks, similar to the names of other, non-decoy pages on the server. We introduce some randomness into the deception object's placement, to make it harder to identify them programmatically.

2.7 Using a Proxy to Speed up Servers

FRADE mines data about user payload from WAL, to classify users as humans/ bots, as shown in Fig. 2(a). A server may be so overwhelmed under FCA, that it cannot accept new connections, slowing down logging and delaying FRADE's action.

We explored two approaches to boost the number of requests a server is able to receive and log during FCAs. Our first approach, **transparent proxy (Trans)**, shown in Fig. 2(b), uses a lightweight proxy between clients and the server. It completes the 3-way handshake with the client, receives and logs Web page requests. It then recreates the connection with the backend server. This can speed up logging, but ultimately the target server may overload before we block all bots, and this will back up the Trans server as well. We use http-proxy-middleware [14] as our transparent proxy. It lets us log requests as soon as they arrive, and forward them to the backend server.

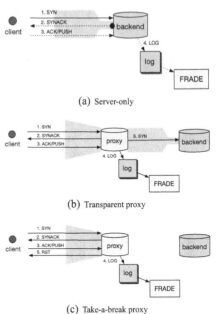

(a) Server-only

(b) Transparent proxy

(c) Take-a-break proxy

Fig. 2. Illustration of high-rate attack handling, (a) by the server itself, (b) by Trans approach and (c) by TAB approach

Our second approach, **take-a-break proxy (TAB)**, shown in Fig. 2(c), uses a dropping proxy between clients and the backend server. FRADE runs on the dropping proxy, which logs and drops all the requests, until our blocking manages to reduce the request rate. Logging requests and dropping them immediately allows for faster blocking, as immediate closure of a connection frees the port and socket on the proxy for reuse. Dropping all requests hurts legitimate clients, but it ensures the fastest bot identification, helping us serve users well for the remaining (possibly lengthy) duration of the FCA. We implement the proxy in http-proxy-middleware [14].

To improve the speed of bot detection, we further stop building the ApprovedObjectList (AOL) once TAB proxy is active. Since no replies are returned to users while the TAB proxy is active, a human user will not issue embedded object requests, while a bot may. This helps us identify bots faster.

2.8 Improvements over OM

We now detail improvements of FRADE over OM – these improvements enable FRADE to be robust against sophisticated attacks, while OM only handles naive attacks.

Stealthier Decoy Hyperlinks: FRADE uses stealthier decoy targets and anchors, and makes the placement of decoy anchors more robust against false positives than OM. FRADE learns the page naming structure from Web server logs, and automatically crafts the names of the target pages for decoy hyperlinks. OM creates target pages with random names, which can be detected by bots.

FRADE inserts the decoy anchors away from the existing, visible anchors to reduce the chance that they are accidentally visited by humans. OM does not address such concerns, and is prone to false positives.

FRADE makes decoy anchors invisible by adding new styles to the site's CSS file, while OM manipulates the anchors in the Web page source, making them small or changing their color or z-index. OM's anchors can be detected more easily by bots.

Improved Dynamics Model: OM models the request dynamics only for main-page requests, while FRADE models it for main-page and embedded requests, and also models each request's principal cost. This helps FRADE handle a variety of sophisticated attacks (see Sect. 3.3) that OM cannot handle.

OM uses decision trees to capture request dynamics, grouping requests into sessions and using four features per session. This makes OM's model more complex than FRADE's, which uses just one feature – the *threshold rate of requests per time window*. OM further requires both legitimate and attack data for training. Attack data is hard to obtain and overfitting can impair detection of new bot variants. FRADE only requires legitimate data for training.

Improved Semantics Model: Both OM and FRADE build the request graph to encode transition probabilities from one Web page to another. But OM focuses only on pages, while FRADE also models transitions between page groups. This fall-back mechanism enables FRADE to handle transitions in production that were not seen in training. Further, OM computes the sequence probability as the average of probabilities on the request graph, while FRADE computes it as a product (compound probability of dependent events), which ensures fast decline with sequence size.

Implementation and Evaluation: FRADE is implemented as a complete system and evaluated in a realistic setting, while OM was evaluated in simulation.

2.9 Deployment Considerations

Customization. To use FRADE, the Web site administrators must (1) categorize their Web pages into groups for the semantics module, and (2) insert decoy hyperlinks into Web pages. This may in some cases require minor human effort, depending on the server's content. Table 3 shows how we classified pages into groups. For Wikipedia, we leveraged its existing categorization of pages into topics. Imgur and Reddit have a folder-based Web site structure, with related files grouped into the same folder. In absence of both, a Web site could use a topic identification tool, such as [2]. We have automated decoy hyperlinks insertion (around 100 lines of code), which can be customized for a new Web site.

User Identification. FRADE currently blocks IP addresses, but this can lead to collateral damage when clients share a NAT. FRADE could use cookies and block users at the application level, but when a server is under FCA, it is too overloaded to process each request and mine its cookie. We thus view IP-based filtering as necessary to relieve the load at the server.

Training Data. FRADE requires training data of legitimate clients and needs to be trained per server. Each server needs to tune the frequency of their training and decoy hyperlink insertion to match the frequency of their content updates. Attackers may introduce adversarial data before the attack to dilute the learned models. One could address this issue by: (1) sampling training data over multiple days, (2) excluding outliers by adopting lower values for *ThreshPerc* parameter, (3) using techniques such as machine unlearning [13].

Dynamic Content and Misclassification. If a server does not update its models on new content, FRADE may miss some transitions in the semantics model, or embedded objects in the AOL. Our fall-back mechanisms for the semantics model and treating embedded requests not found on AOL as main requests, help minimize this effect. We used the data from Internet Archive [34] to measure the daily updates on some frequently-updated Web sites, CNN, NY Times, Imgur and Amazon. On the average, a small percentage of the Web site's content (0.17–0.31%) is added daily, around 6 K–54 K objects and pages. FRADE's models can be incrementally updated this often, without full re-training.

Load Balancers. Larger sites deploy load balancers in front of server farms; we would have to periodically gather web access logs to a central location and run FRADE there to learn models and classify bots. FRADE could then block bot IPs by inserting filtering rules into the load balancer.

2.10 Implementation

FRADE's core engine is written in C++, and runs on the Web server/proxy. Filtering is achieved by interfacing with a host-specific mechanism. We use `iptables` with `ipset` extension, which scale well with large filter lists. We classify each request as either main-page or embedded in the following way. We crawl the full Web site using the Selenium-based [43] crawler. This helps us identify both static and dynamically generated HTML content. We extract main requests by finding elements with tag "a" and attribute "href". We label other requests as embedded. These steps are fully automated.

3   Evaluation

Ideally, we would evaluate FRADE with operational servers, real logs, human users and real FCAs. Unfortunately there are many obstacles to such evaluation: (1) there are no publicly available WAL from modern servers, (2) paying real users to interact with a server during evaluation can get costly and prevent repeatable experiments, (3) there are no publicly-available logs of real FCAs. We test FRADE in emulated experiments on the Emulab testbed [50], using replayed human user traffic and real FCAs. We try to make our experiments as realistic and representative as possible, given the obstacles listed above.

3.1 Emulation Evaluation Setup

We mirror *dynamic* content for three popular Web sites: Imgur, Reddit and Wikipedia. All content is generated dynamically by pulling page information from the server's database, using the original site's scripts. This content is copyright-free and server configuration files were publicly available. We download each full site, modify it by automatically inserting decoy hyperlinks, and deploy the site's original configuration and scripts on our server within Emulab testbed. While we wanted to replicate more servers in our tests, this was impossible because their implementation was either private (e.g., Facebook, YouTube, etc.) or their content was not copyright-free (e.g., major news sites).

We engage human users to browse our Web sites and gather data to train and test FRADE's models. We replay human user data in a controlled environment and launch FCAs, with real traffic, targeting our servers from an emulated botnet. We launch repeated FCAs with various botnet sizes and bot behavior, and measure the time it takes to identify and block bots.

Our chosen Web sites had server software diversity. Imgur runs on Apache, Reddit runs on haproxy, and we deployed Wikipedia on nginx.

Human User Data. We obtained human user data using Amazon Mechanical Turk workers. This study was reviewed and approved by our IRB. In the study we presented an information sheet to each worker, paired the worker with a server at random, and asked the worker to browse naturally. We intentionally did not create specific tasks for workers, as we wanted them to follow their interests and produce realistic data for our semantic models. We also asked each worker to browse at least 20 pages so that we would have sufficient data for training and testing. To keep engagement high, and discourage workers who just click through as fast as possible, we asked each worker to rate each page's loading speed on a 1–5 scale. These ratings were not used in our study. Human behavior may become more aggressive during FCAs (e.g., more attempts to refresh content), which may lead to misclassification. However, QoS studies show that users tend to click less and not more when the server's replies are slow [6]. Our dataset does not capture any adaptation of users to speed of server replies. Each server had 243 unique users for training and 107 users for testing in our dataset.

Legitimate Traffic Generator. During each experiment, we replay user traffic from testing logs. We wrote a custom traffic generator, which extracts timing and URL sequences from logs, and then chooses when to start each sequence based on the desired number of active users. The generator uses many different source IPs. Our replay maintains timing between requests in a sequence, and traffic is replayed at the application level. When a user sequence completes, another sequence is selected and another IP becomes active. If we run out of sequences to replay, we reuse the old ones.

Attack Traffic Generator. Our attack traffic generator is a modified *httperf* tool [37]. We added the ability to choose source IPs from a pool, and to select requests for each IP from a given sequence, in order. Before building our own attack tool, we have investigated popular attack tools, such as HULK [1], LOIC [22] and HOIC [8]. These tools do not allow us to use multiple IP addresses when running on the same physical machine. This feature is important as one can mimic large botnets using few machines. Our tool can generate all attacks generated by HULK, LOIC and HOIC tools, and more.

Table 3. Group assignment for our three Web sites.

Server	Groups
Wikipedia	Topic-based categories
Imgur	Folder-based groups
Reddit	Folder-based groups

Table 4. Time to block all bots

Windows	Time to block all bots		
	Botnet size		
	8 bots	800 bots	8,000 bots
Non-unif-5 (current)	3 s	8 s	16 s
Uniform-5	4 s	15 s	47 s
Uniform-10	3 s	10 s	38 s
Uniform-20	3 s	7 s	23 s

Experiment Topology and Scenarios. Our experiment topology is shown in Fig. 3. It has 8 physical attack nodes (each emulating 1–1,000 virtual attackers each), 1 node emulating 100 legitimate clients, and 3 nodes for mirrored servers. All nodes are of type d430 on Emulab, with 32 cores and the Ubuntu 14.04 OS. We fine-tuned the nodes to maximize the request rate that each client could generate, and to maximize the request rate that our servers could handle. While having a larger topology would have helped us perform larger-scale tests, Emulab is a shared resource and we were limited in how many nodes we could request. Our tests suffice to illustrate trends in FRADE's effectiveness as botnet size increases.

To identify an effective attack rate, we measured the request rate required to slow down each server's processing below 1 request per second. For all the Web sites, this rate was around 1,000 rps. We chose to generate 8 times this rate during an attack – 8,000 rps. We test one server per run. Legitimate clients start sending traffic to the server following the timing and sequences from the testing logs. We main-

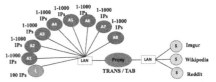

Fig. 3. Attackers: A1–A8 (up to 8,000 virtual bots), Legitimate: L (100 clients), the proxy and 3 Web servers.

tain 100 active, parallel virtual clients throughout the run, each with a separate IP address. After a minute, our virtual attackers (1–1,000 per physical machine) start sending requests to the server at the aggregate rate of 8,000 rps. After 10 min we stop the attackers, and a minute later we stop the clients.

We illustrate FRADE's handling of an FCA in Fig. 4, which shows legitimate and FCA traffic (sent to the server, and allowed by FRADE), and the blocked bots. Legitimate traffic declines at first, until FRADE manages to identify most bots. After 20 s, FRADE blocks all bots and legitimate traffic returns to its pre-attack levels. At that point, although the attacker keeps sending the attack traffic (the *actual attack* area in Fig. 4), the attack requests cannot reach the server, as the bot IP addresses are blocked at the proxy.

3.2 Today's (Naive) Attacks

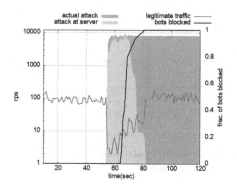

Fig. 4. FRADE's handling of an FCA.

First, we test FCAs, that resemble today's attacks as noted by [16]. Our attackers repeatedly request: (t1) **non-existing URLs,** or (t2) the **base URL.** In the case (t1), we tailor the URL's syntax for it to be identified as main requests. Figures 5(a) and 5(b) show the time that FRADE took to block all the bots, in these FCAs, for each server, and for 8 and 800 bots. Both attacks show similar trends, with the smaller botnet being blocked sooner (around 4 s instead of 8–10 s). All bot classification is done by the DYN_h module.

3.3 Sophisticated Attacks

An attacker familiar with FRADE could attempt to launch a sophisticated FCA, where bots mimic humans to evade detection. To evade DYN_h, bots would send at a lower rate, necessitating a larger botnet. Bots could also attempt to generate requests mimicking a human's semantics, i.e., trying to guess or learning popular sequences. Finally, bots could leverage knowledge of FRADE's different processing pipelines to engage in embedded or costly request floods.

We first explore *fully automated* FCAs. An attacker has previously engaged a crawler to learn about the target server's *Web site graph*, i.e., which pages point to which other pages and to match pages to embedded objects. The attacker knows that lower request rates per bot mean longer detection delays, but does not know each page's popularity and which hyperlinks are decoy links. We only show results for Imgur. FCAs on other servers show a similar trend.

Fully-Automated: Larger Botnet and Smarter Sequences: These FCAs include a larger botnet—8,000 bots. The first two FCAs are using the same (s1) **non-existing** and (s2) **base** URLs as described in Sect. 3.2, with a larger botnet to evade DYN_h detection. The third FCA performs a (s3) **random walk** on the Web site graph, making only main page requests (we investigate FCAs that use embedded links in Sect. 3.3). It cannot differentiate between decoy and non-decoy links.

Figure 6(a) illustrates the time it takes to block all 8,000 bots in s1–s3 attacks, using the TAB proxy approach. The non-existing URL attack (s1) is fully handled within 16 s, with each bot blocked after ≈5.8 requests, by the semantics module. The random walk (s3) is handled within 16 s, with each bot blocked after 3.8 requests on average by the deception module. For the base URL attack (s2) it takes 36 s to block 8,000 bots, with each bot blocked after ≈15 requests by the DYN_h module.

Fully-Automated: Embedded and Costly Request Floods: Attackers could attempt to flood with embedded or costly requests. The **non-existing-object** attack (s4) requests made-up URLs, which end up treated as main page requests by FRADE. Figure 6(b) shows the time to block all 8,000 bots in this FCA. Within a few seconds the FCA is fully handled. Each bot is blocked within 2–3 requests. The semantics module blocks all bots. The **costly** attack (s5) sends the most expensive main page request repeatedly to the server. All bots are blocked by the DYN_c module, within a few seconds.

An attacker could collaborate with some human users to learn popular pages on a server, and decoy objects, and then launch *semi-automated attacks*. The attacker then leverages what they learned to craft sequences of requests, which may evade detection by FRADE's semantics and deception modules. The requests are sent automatically by bots at predetermined timing.

Semi-Automated: Floods that Avoid Deception. The **smart walk** attack (s6) performs a random walk on the Web site graph avoiding decoy links. The **smart-walk-object** (s7) performs a smart walk among all embedded objects on the site, and **smart-walk-site** (s8) performs a smart walk on the site, and requests all non-decoy embedded objects for each

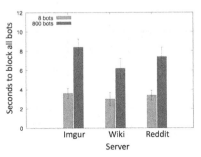

(a) The time FRADE takes to block 8 and 800 bots for *Non-existing URLs Attacks*

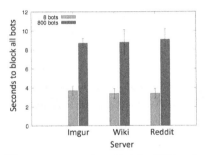

(b) The time FRADE takes to block 8 and 800 bots for *Base URL Attacks*

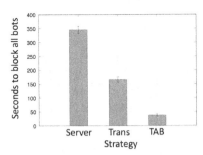

(c) TAB has superior performance for sophisticated attacks

Fig. 5. Today's (Naive) attacks and performance comparison for sophisticated attacks.

main page request. A replay attack [52], where the attacker records and replays legitimate users' requests, is a special example of the smart-walk-site attack. Figure 6(c) shows the time it takes to block all 8,000 bots in these FCAs. In a smart-walk attack (s6), FRADE takes 38 s to block all 8,000 bots. Each bot is blocked after 19 requests on the average, by the DYN_h module. Figure 5(c) illustrates benefits of using a proxy. Without a proxy, it would take around 6 min to block all the bots. With Trans, it takes under 3 min, and with TAB it takes 38 s—almost 10-fold speed-up compared to the server-only approach!

In the smart-walk-object attack (s7), all bots are blocked within a few seconds. Each bot is blocked within 2–3 requests, as it requests embedded objects that are not on the AOL during FCA. All bots are blocked by DYN_e module. The smart-walk-site attack interleaves main page and their corresponding embedded requests, and it avoids decoy links. It thus manages to slip under the radar of DYN_h (main page requests come at a low rate), DYN_c (requests are not costly) and deception (asking for non-decoy links only) modules. All 8,000 bots are blocked within 22 s. Each bot is blocked on the average after 6 requests. The complete blocking is done by the semantics module. Since no replies are returned to users while the TAB proxy is active, a human user will not issue embedded object requests. Hence, FRADE does not keep embedded objects on the AOL while TAB is active. Instead, embedded object requests are treated as main-page requests, and forwarded to DYN_h and semantic modules, which model only main-page requests. The semantics module blocks all the bots, due to the random walk created, leading to low-probability sequences.

Semi-Automated: Floods that Use Popular Sequences. An attacker may learn which sequences are popular among humans and generate main page requests for them. They need to

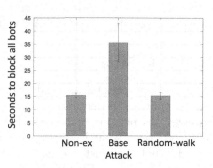

(a) Larger botnets and random-walk

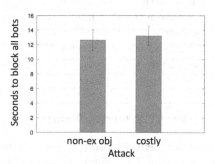

(b) Embedded and costly requests

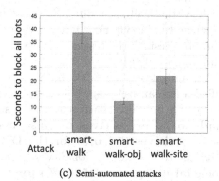

(c) Semi-automated attacks

Fig. 6. The time to block 8,000 bots in sophisticated attacks.

distribute the rate among many bots to evade detection by DYN_h. We evaluate this FCA analytically, using the WAL of a large public network testbed, that serves thousands of users. The logs covered three months of data and around 5 K users. Few users were obvious outliers, making thousands of requests. If we prune the most aggressive 5% of the users and analyze the rest of the user sequences, 95% were shorter than 17 requests. To evade FRADE, the attacker would need to retire each bot after 17 requests. For a 10-min, 1,000 rps FCA, the attacker would need to recruit 35 K bots *to attack this specific server*. Today, a single server can be brought down by a single, aggressive bot. FRADE thus raises the bar for this specific server's FCA 35,000 times.

3.4   Evasion Attacks

It may still be possible to evade FRADE and launch a successful FCA. This would require: (1) Recruiting very large botnets, so each bot is used intermittently. As per our evaluation, FRADE raises the bar from 1 bot to more than 8,000 bots, so at least three orders of magnitude. (2) Leveraging humans instead of bots and instruct users to click on visible, popular content, following their interests. Then, FRADE would not be able to identify malicious (human) clients, but the attacker would need thousands of humans for a sustained FCA. The attacker could combine these two approaches, learning popular sequences from human collaborators, then encoding them in stealthy, low-rate bots. This attack would not be detected by FRADE, but it would require at least 3 orders of magnitude more bots than are in use today (see discussion above of floods that use popular sequences).

3.5   FRADE Outperforms OM

We experimentally compare the accuracy of FRADE versus OM for DYN_h and semantics models. These models exist in both solutions and FRADE improves on OM's design. We use the same legitimate traffic as in Sect. 3.2, interleaved with synthetically generated FCA bot traffic, exploring a range of request rates as suggested in [39]. For OM, we train decision trees using Weka on the training data and test on the testing data. When testing DYN_h we run base-URL FCA, and use 8–8,000 bots. When testing semantics models we run the smart-walk FCA, and also use 8–8,000 bots. A false positive means that the defense classified a human user as a bot. A false negative means that the defense failed to identify a bot. For space reasons we summarize our findings. While **FRADE had no false positives or false negatives** in our tests, **OM had many false positives (7–76%) for the DYN_h model, for Wikipedia and Reddit**, due to high dimensionality [51] of its models and overfitting. OM also had some **false negatives (5–13%) for the semantics model** and the 8,000-bot FCAs, because OM cannot handle transitions not seen in training data, while FRADE can using its *fallback mechanism*. FRADE's models thus outperform those of OM.

In addition to this comparison on attacks they both handle, FRADE also outperforms OM by handling a wider range of attacks (embedded and costly request floods).

3.6 Sensitivity

FRADE uses multiple parameters in its operation, as shown in Table 2. We focus here on analyzing sensitivity of parameters that influence classification accuracy. DYN_h and DYN_c currently use 5 window sizes as time intervals, during which they learn thresholds for their models. These window sizes follow a non-uniform, exponential-like pattern, with increasing gaps between windows. We also tested 3 different uniform distributions: *uniform-5*, *uniform-10* and *uniform-20* with 5, 10 and 20 windows in the 0–600 s range, respectively. We tested non-existing URL FCAs on Imgur with these alternative windowing approaches, and compared the speed of FRADE's response. Results are shown in Table 4. Non-uniform window sizes perform better than uniform sizes, especially for bots that send at a low rate.

Both dynamics and semantics modules use *ThreshPerc* to find the percentage of the quantities they model. In our evaluation, we use 100% as *ThreshPerc*. We chose this value to achieve zero false positives since we had small training data. In reality, a large server would have logs of millions of clients, some of which could be outliers. We have evaluated values of 99%, 95% and 90% for *ThreshPerc* with non-existing URL FCAs on Imgur. For DYN_h model false positives were 3%, 5% and 9% with *ThreshPerc* values of 99%, 95% and 90% respectively. This is mainly because

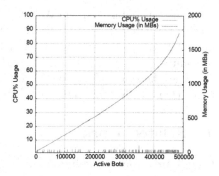

Fig. 7. Memory and CPU cost vs # bots.

our training data is small and does not have outliers, so removing some percentage of aggressive behaviors from training will lead to the similar amount of misclassifications on test data. Semantic model did not generate any false positives with tested *ThreshPerc* values. Another parameter is the decoy object density ρ—the ratio of decoy objects to visible objects on the same page. In our experiments we use $\rho = 1$. The higher the ρ, the faster a bot's identification, but the higher chances that a human user could accidentally access a decoy object and visible distortion to the original page's layout. In our MTurk experiments no humans have clicked on our decoy objects. We also observed no visible distortion. Around $\rho = 1.5$ we observe distortion in Imgur's Web pages, and around $\rho = 5$ distortion becomes severe.

3.7 Operational Cost and Scalability

We tested FRADE with attacks of up to 0.5 M bots to evaluate its scalability. FRADE's operational cost is modest. The CPU load never exceeded 5% and the memory grew linearly to around 1.5 GB for 0.5 M bots (Fig. 7), or around 3 KB per bot or client. Extremely active Web sites like Amazon can see about 4 M active clients per hour [3,4], and would need 12 GBs of memory, which is feasiable today. It takes on the average 0.05 ms to process a Web log request in FRADE. Thus, FRADE could easily process around 20,000 rps on a single core. Since FRADE does not operate in line, it does not add any user-visible delay to request processing.

Table 5. Page serve time in ms

Number of IPs	0	100	1 K	10 K	100 K	1 M
iptables	4.5	4.5	4.5	4.7	4.9	N/A
ipset	4.8	4.8	4.9	4.9	4.9	5.3

We evaluate scalability of FRADE's filtering using `iptables` and `ipset`. We artificially insert a diverse set of IP-rules and send packets matching these rules at a high rate. This emulates the situation when a server is under FCA by numerous bots. We issue Web page requests and measure the time it takes to receive the reply. Table 5 shows the averages over ten runs. `iptables`'s processing time grows modestly until 100 K IPs, but then explodes. We were not able to complete the tests with 1 M IPs. However, `ipset` imposes only a small delay of 8% as the rules table grows from 100 K to 1 M, and no measurable delay for fewer than 100 K rules. Thus, FRADE can block a million IPs using `ipset`.

4 Related Work

Clouds are a common solution for DDoS. They may offer "attack scrubbing" services, but the details of such services are proprietary. Clouds handle volumetric attacks well, but FCAs may fly under their radar. They also use Javascript-based cookies [17,41], to detect if a client is running a browser. These challenges are transparent to humans, and good for detecting automated bots. However, attackers can use the Selenium engine to generate requests. Since Selenium interprets Javascript, it would pass the cookie challenge. FRADE can complement cloud defenses, enabling server-based solutions for FCAs.

CAPTCHAs [7,29] are another popular defense against FCAs. Users, who correctly solve a graphical puzzle have their IPs placed on "allow" list. While a deterrent, CAPTCHAs have some issues. Multiple on-line services offer bulk CAPTCHA solving, using

Table 6. Rel. work comparison, showing the absence or presence of human Web server interaction features, even if present at the very basic level.

Detection mech.	Dyn	Sem	Dec
Jung et al. [28]	✓	✗	✗
Ranjan et al. [42]	✓	✗	✗
Liao et al. [33]	✓	✗	✗
Wang et al. [48]	✗	✓	✗
Xie and Yu [54]	✗	✓	✗
Beitollahi et al. [9]	✓	✓	✗
FRADE	✓	✓	✓

automated and semi-automated methods (e.g. [32]). CAPTCHAs also place a burden on human users, while FRADE does not. Google's reCAPTCHAs [20] and similar approaches for human user detection are transparent to humans, but can still be defeated using deep learning approaches [5,11,45]. These approaches are complementary to FRADE, as they model complementary human user features.

Jan et al. [26] propose a stream-based bot detection model [49] and augment it with a data synthesis method, using Generative Adversarial Networks [36], to synthesize unseen bot behavior distributions. While we lack the data they have, and cannot compare our systems directly, we can comment on their expected relative performance based on their design. Jan et al. system focuses on *eventually detecting advanced bots*, and is well-suited for click bot or chat bot detection. Authors show that it can adapt to new bot behaviors with small re-training, and that it is robust to adversarial attacks. FRADE focuses on *quickly detecting bots involved in an FCA*. Such bots are likely to exhibit specific, aggressive behaviors, since they seek to maximize request rate at the server. When FRADE misses a bot, such bot has a low yield to the attacker, necessitating a large botnet for a sustained attack. Thus FRADE could miss some bots that Jan et al. approach detects, but these bots would not be very useful for flash-crowd attacks.

Comparing reported performance, Jan et al. require long request sequences (30+ requests in a month) to classify a user as benign or bot. This means that new bots will not be detected for at least 30 requests. FRADE can identify and block most bots within 3–6 requests, and sophisticated bots with less than 20 requests. FRADE also achieves higher accuracy – it identifies all bots in our tests and does not misidentify any benign users as bots. Finally, Jan et al. use a small fraction of bot data in training, while FRADE uses only benign user data.

Rampart [35] and COGO [18] build models of resource consumption over time to detect and handle resource exhaustion states. Such defense mechanisms could handle FCAs that employ costly requests, but not other FCA variants.

Like FRADE's *dynamics* model, several efforts use timing requests to detect FCAs [33,42]. Ranjan et al. [42] use the inter-arrival of sessions, requests and the cost profile of a session to assign a suspicion value and prioritize requests. Liao et al. [33] look at the inter-arrival of requests within a window. They use custom classification based on sparse vector decomposition and rely heavily on thresholds derived from their dataset. These works have limited evaluation compared to ours and rely only on modeling human requests, while we also deal with embedded and costly requests, we build semantic models of request sequences and use decoys to bait bots. Yatagai et al. [55] look for repetitive sequences of resources, and clients which spend shorter than normal periods of time between requests. Bharathi et al. [10] use fixed sized windows to examine which, and how many, resources a client accesses and to detect repetitive patterns. Najafabadi et al. [38] use PCA and fixed windows to examine which resources a client requests. Beitollahi et al. [9] propose ConnectionScore, where connections are scored based on history and statistical analysis done during the normal conditions. Models engaged in connection scoring are coarser (e.g., 1 rps vs our rate per several time intervals) than FRADE models, and thus we believe that FRADE would outperform this. Jung et al. [28] learn existing clients of a Web server, and perform network aware clustering [31]. When the server is overloaded, they drop aggressive clients that do not fit in the existing clusters. In comparison to these works, we evaluate timing dynamics at a much finer granularity, and evaluate the strict order of requests, allowing us to detect stealthier FCAs.

Multiple works are related to FRADE's *semantics* model. Wang et al. [48] examine requests over 30-min windows (sessions) and use a click-ratio (page popularity) model and Markov process to model clients. Their detection is highly accurate for bot identification, but has a high false-positive rate, while we have zero false positives. Similar to [48], Xie et al. [54] capture the transition probabilities between requests in a session through a hidden semi-Markov model. Our approach to training and modeling is simpler, while still very accurate.

Our deception model uses honeytokens [46], similar to [12,19,21]. We build on ideas from these prior works (use of decoy links), but we use a variety of decoy objects, configurable object density and automate object insertion code for each site. To our knowledge, our work is the first to combine dynamics, semantics of user requests, and the decoy objects in a single defense, and evaluate its effectiveness using realistic traffic and real servers (Table 6). Our results show that different modules are effective against different FCAs. Thus, a combination is needed to fully handle FCAs. Software and datasets for these prior works are not publicly available, and thus we could not directly compare FRADE to them.

Biometrics solutions (e.g., [15] or [53]) can distinguish bots from humans by capturing mouse movements and keystrokes. These approaches are orthogonal to FRADE, and may suffer from privacy issues.

5   Conclusions

FCAs are challenging to handle. We have presented a solution, FRADE, which models how human users interact with servers and detects bots as they deviate from this expected behavior. Our tests show that FRADE stops naive bots within 3–5 requests and sophisticated bots within 15–19 requests. A bot could modify its behavior to bypass FRADE's detection, but this forces the attacker to use botnets at least three order of magnitude larger than today, to achieve sustained attack. FRADE thus successfully fortifies Web servers against today's FCAs.

Acknowledgment. This material is based upon work supported by the National Science Foundation under grant number 1319215.

References

1. Hulk DDoS tool, May 2018. https://tinyurl.com/y49tze6w. Accessed 31 Mar 2021
2. Classification tools, May 2019. https://tinyurl.com/y6cdav26. Accessed 31 Mar 2021
3. Combined desktop and mobile visits to amazon.com from February 2018 to April 2019 (in millions), May 2019. https://tinyurl.com/y25d8ln8. Accessed 31 Mar 2021

4. Most popular retail websites in the United States as of December 2019, ranked by visitors (in millions), September 2020. https://www.statista.com/statistics/271450/monthly-unique-visitors-to-us-retail-websites/. Accessed 31 Mar 2021
5. Akrout, I., Feriani, A., Akrout, M.: Hacking google reCAPTCHA v3 using Reinforcement Learning (2019)
6. Arapakis, I., Bai, X., Cambazoglu, B.B.: Impact of response latency on user behavior in web search. In: Proceedings of the 37th International ACM SIGIR Conference on Research & Development in Information Retrieval, pp. 103–112. Association for Computing Machinery, New York (2014)
7. Barna, C., Shtern, M., Smit, M., Tzerpos, V., Litoiu, M.: Model-based adaptive DoS attack mitigation. In: Proceedings of the 7th International Symposium on Software Engineering for Adaptive and Self-Managing Systems, SEAMS 2012, pp. 119–128. IEEE Press, Piscataway (2012)
8. Barnett, R.: HOIC, January 2012. https://tinyurl.com/y6en34r3. Accessed 31 Mar 2021
9. Beitollahi, H., Deconinck, G.: Tackling application-layer DDoS attacks. Procedia Comput. Sci. **10**, 432–441 (2012)
10. Bharathi, R., Sukanesh, R., Xiang, Y., Hu, J.: A PCA based framework for detection of application layer DDoS attacks. WSEAS Trans. Inf. Sci. Appl. **9**(12), 389–398 (2012)
11. Bock, K., Patel, D., Hughey, G., Levin, D.: unCAPTCHA: a low-resource defeat of reCAPTCHA's audio challenge. In: 11th {USENIX} Workshop on Offensive Technologies ({WOOT} 2017) (2017)
12. Brewer, D., Li, K., Ramaswamy, L., Pu, C.: A link obfuscation service to detect webbots. In: 2010 IEEE International Conference on Services Computing, pp. 433–440, July 2010
13. Cao, Y., Yang, J.: Towards making systems forget with machine unlearning. In: 2015 IEEE Symposium on Security and Privacy, pp. 463–480. IEEE (2015)
14. Chim, S.: Http proxy middleware, July 2016. https://tinyurl.com/y6td93p4
15. Chu, Z., Gianvecchio, S., Koehl, A., Wang, H., Jajodia, S.: Blog or block: detecting blog bots through behavioral biometrics. Comput. Netw. **57**(3), 634–646 (2013)
16. Cid, D.: Analyzing popular layer 7 application DDoS attacks. Sucuri blog. https://tinyurl.com/y3p7mokb. Accessed 6 Dec 2020
17. Cloudflare. How can an HTTP flood be mitigated?, March 2020. https://www.cloudflare.com/learning/ddos/http-flood-ddos-attack/. Accessed 6 Dec 2020
18. Elsabagh, M., Fleck, D., Stavrou, A., Kaplan, M., Bowen, T.: Practical and accurate runtime application protection against DoS attacks. In: Dacier, M., Bailey, M., Polychronakis, M., Antonakakis, M. (eds.) RAID 2017. LNCS, vol. 10453, pp. 450–471. Springer, Cham (2017). https://doi.org/10.1007/978-3-319-66332-6_20
19. Gavrilis, D., Chatzis, I., Dermatas, E.: Flash crowd detection using decoy hyperlinks. In: 2007 IEEE International Conference on Networking, Sensing and Control, pp. 466–470, April 2007
20. Google. reCAPTCHA v3. https://www.google.com/recaptcha/intro/v3.html. Accessed 31 Mar 2021
21. Han, X., Kheir, N., Balzarotti, D.: Evaluation of deception-based web attacks detection. In: Proceedings of the 2017 Workshop on Moving Target Defense, MTD 2017, pp. 65–73. ACM, New York (2017)
22. Imperva. Low orbit ion cannon. https://tinyurl.com/y3wy32fo. Accessed 31 Mar 2021
23. Imperva. 2020 cyberthreat defense report (2020). https://tinyurl.com/y5jmjuzv. Accessed 31 Mar 2021

24. Imperva Incapsula's. Q1 2017 global DDoS threat landscape report, May 2017. www.incapsula.com. Accessed 6 Dec 2020
25. INDUSFACE (2019). https://tinyurl.com/y4c3ywry. Accessed 6 Dec 2020
26. Jan, S.T., et al.: Throwing darts in the dark? Detecting bots with limited data using neural data augmentation. In: 2020 IEEE Symposium on Security and Privacy (SP), pp. 1190–1206. IEEE (2020)
27. Jonker, M., King, A., Krupp, J., Rossow, C., Sperotto, A., Dainotti, A.: Millions of targets under attack: a macroscopic characterization of the DoS ecosystem. In: Internet Measurement Conference (IMC), November 2017
28. Jung, J., Krishnamurthy, B., Rabinovich, M.: Flash crowds and denial of service attacks: characterization and implications for CDNs and web sites. In: Proceedings of the 11th International Conference on World Wide Web, WWW 2002, pp. 293–304. ACM, New York (2002)
29. Kandula, S., Katabi, D., Jacob, M., Berger, A.: Botz-4-sale: surviving organized DDoS attacks that mimic flash crowds. In: Proceedings of the 2nd Conference on Symposium on Networked Systems Design & Implementation, NSDI 2005, vol. 2, pp. 287–300. USENIX Association, Berkeley (2005)
30. Kaspersky. Report finds 18% rise in DDoS attacks in Q2 2019 (2019). https://tinyurl.com/y258rnpm. Accessed 31 Mar 2021
31. Krishnamurthy, B., Wang, J.: On network-aware clustering of web clients. ACM SIGCOMM Comput. Commun. Rev. $30(4)$, 97–110 (2000)
32. Leyden, J.: Russian serfs paid three dollars a day to break CAPTCHAs, March 2008. https://tinyurl.com/y2czs7xd. Accessed 6 Dec 2020
33. Liao, Q., Li, H., Kang, S., Liu, C.: Application layer DDoS attack detection using cluster with label based on sparse vector decomposition and rhythm matching. Secur. Commun. Netw. $8(17)$, 3111–3120 (2015)
34. Wayback Machine. Internet archive (1996). https://archive.org/web. Accessed 31 Mar 2021
35. Meng, W., et al.: Rampart: protecting web applications from CPU-exhaustion denial-of-service attacks. In: 27th USENIX Security Symposium (USENIX Security 2018) (2018)
36. Mirza, M., Osindero, S.: Conditional generative adversarial nets. arXiv preprint arXiv:1411.1784 (2014)
37. Mosberger, D., Jin, T.: Httperf: a tool for measuring web server performance. SIGMETRICS Perform. Eval. Rev. $26(3)$, 31–37 (1998)
38. Najafabadi, M., Khoshgoftaar, T., Calvert, C., Kemp, C.: User behavior anomaly detection for application layer DDoS attacks. In: 2017 IEEE International Conference on Information Reuse and Integration (IRI), pp. 154–161, August 2017
39. Oikonomou, G., Mirkovic, J.: Modeling human behavior for defense against flash-crowd attacks. In: 2009 IEEE International Conference on Communications, pp. 1–6. IEEE (2009)
40. Paxson, V.: Bro: a system for detecting network intruders in real-time. In: Proceedings of the 7th Conference on USENIX Security Symposium, SSYM 1998, vol. 7, p. 3. USENIX Association, Berkeley (1998)
41. Radware. JS cookie challenges, March 2020. https://tinyurl.com/y2bqmtac. Accessed 6 Dec 2020
42. Ranjan, S., Swaminathan, R., Uysal, M., Knightly, E.: DDoS-resilient scheduling to counter application layer attacks under imperfect detection. In: Proceedings IEEE INFOCOM 2006, pp. 1–13 (2006)
43. Selenium. Selenium webdriver (2012). https://tinyurl.com/y6a4czhe. Accessed 6 Dec 2020

44. V. S. Services. Verisign DDoS trends report q2 2016, June 2016. https://verisign.com/. Accessed 6 Dec 2020
45. Sivakorn, S., Polakis, I., Keromytis, A.D.: I am robot:(deep) learning to break semantic image CAPTCHAs. In: 2016 IEEE European Symposium on Security and Privacy (EuroS&P), pp. 388–403. IEEE (2016)
46. Spitzner, L.: Honeytokens, July 2003. https://tinyurl.com/y4gzbjqz
47. STEEL Lab. Frade: Flash crowd attack defense (2021). https://steel.isi.edu/Projects/frade/
48. Wang, J., Yang, X., Long, K.: Web DDoS detection schemes based on measuring user's access behavior with large deviation. In: 2011 IEEE Global Telecommunications Conference - GLOBECOM 2011, pp. 1–5, December 2011
49. Wang, S., Liu, C., Gao, X., Qu, H., Xu, W.: Session-based fraud detection in online e-commerce transactions using recurrent neural networks. In: Altun, Y., et al. (eds.) ECML PKDD 2017. LNCS (LNAI), vol. 10536, pp. 241–252. Springer, Cham (2017). https://doi.org/10.1007/978-3-319-71273-4_20
50. White, B., et al.: An integrated experimental environment for distributed systems and networks. In: Proceedings of the Fifth Symposium on Operating Systems Design and Implementation, Boston, MA. USENIX Association, December 2002
51. Wikipedia. Curse of dimensionality. https://en.wikipedia.org/wiki/Curse_of_dimensionality/. Accessed 6 Dec 2020
52. Wikipedia. Replay attack. https://en.wikipedia.org/wiki/Replay_attack. Accessed 31 Mar 2021
53. Winslow, E.: Bot detection via mouse mapping, September 2009. https://tinyurl.com/y3kbgwuw
54. Xie, Y., Yu, S.Z.: Monitoring the application-layer DDoS attacks for popular websites. IEEE/ACM Trans. Netw. **17**(1), 15–25 (2009)
55. Yatagai, T., Isohara, T., Sasase, I.: Detection of http-get flood attack based on analysis of page access behavior. In: 2007 IEEE Pacific Rim Conference on Communications, Computers and Signal Processing, pp. 232–235, August 2007

Cryptography and Its Applications

TurboIKOS: Improved Non-interactive Zero Knowledge and Post-quantum Signatures

Yaron Gvili[1], Julie Ha[2], Sarah Scheffler[2], Mayank Varia[2(✉)], Ziling Yang[2], and Xinyuan Zhang[3]

[1] Cryptomnium LLC, Atlanta, USA
yaron.gvili@cs.tau.ac.il
[2] Boston University, Boston, USA
{hajulie,varia,zilyang}@bu.edu
[3] George Mason University, Fairfax, USA
xzhang44@gmu.edu

Abstract. In this work, we present a zero knowledge argument for general arithmetic circuits that is public-coin and constant rounds, so it can be made non-interactive and publicly verifiable with the Fiat-Shamir heuristic. The construction is based on the MPC-in-the-head paradigm, in which the prover jointly emulates all MPC protocol participants and can provide advice in the form of Beaver triples whose accuracy must be checked by the verifier. Our construction follows the Beaver triple sacrificing approach used by Baum and Nof [PKC 2020]. Our improvements reduce the communication per multiplication gate from 4 to 2 field elements, matching the performance of the cut-and-choose approach taken by Katz, Kolesnikov, and Wang [CCS 2018] and with lower additive overhead for some parameter settings. We implement our protocol and analyze its cost on Picnic-style post-quantum digital signatures based on the AES family of circuits.

1 Introduction

Zero knowledge proofs are a useful cryptographic primitive for verifiable yet confidential computing that have found applications in the design of anonymous cryptocurrencies [10,62] and identification schemes [27]. They are also used as a component within other cryptographic protocols like digital signature schemes [8,55] and malicious-secure multiparty computation protocols [43,58]. Both the interactive [44,45] and non-interactive [19,35] variants of zero knowledge (ZK) proofs (respectively, arguments) allow an unbounded (resp., polynomially-bounded) prover $\mathcal{P}$ to convince a verifier $\mathcal{V}$ that a relation C is satisfiable while hiding the witness to this fact. We focus on ZK arguments in this work.

There have been substantial advances over the past decade to improve the efficiency of ZK arguments along several metrics. We categorize these advances into three groups based on their tradeoffs between proof size (or total communication for interactive protocols), RAM requirements, and whether the proofs are verifiable to the general public or a single designated verifier.

© Springer Nature Switzerland AG 2021
K. Sako and N. O. Tippenhauer (Eds.): ACNS 2021, LNCS 12727, pp. 365–395, 2021.
https://doi.org/10.1007/978-3-030-78375-4_15

First, ZK-SNARKs and ZK-STARKs offer sublinear proof size and verification time (between logarithmic and square root of the circuit size $|C|$) but require the prover to use enormous amounts of memory. There is a long line of research into ZK succinct interactive arguments of knowledge (SNARKs), building upon the work of Killian [57]. Initial constructions required superlinear prover time and per-circuit structured setup [11,14,18,21,32,41,46,47,65], and subsequent work achieved linear prover time and permitted universal structured setup [22,30,38,39,48,60,72]. The newest ZK-SNARKs and ZK scalable transparent arguments of knowledge (STARKs) leverage ideas from interactive oracle proofs [13,66] or the sumcheck protocol [29,59] to remove structured setup altogether but have slightly higher proof size [3,12,17,25,26,67,68,70,74]. Moreover, the large RAM requirement remains.

Second, there exist ZK arguments that scale to large statements due to their moderate RAM requirements (approximately security parameter × circuit size) and linear prover and verifier runtime, but that sacrifice public verification because they need a designated verifier to maintain secret randomness. ZK proofs based on privacy-free garbled circuits [37,40,50,53,73] require a designated verifier to garble the circuit and keep the wire labels hidden until the end of the protocol. A separate line of research [5,71] uses vector oblivious linear evaluation (VOLE) [23,24,63] to build proofs with a highly efficient (and optionally non-interactive) online phase, after a one-time interactive preprocessing phase is used to establish correlated randomness between the prover $\mathcal{P}$ and verifier $\mathcal{V}$.

The focus of this work is the remaining situation: when both public verifiability and low RAM utilization are required and a linear proof size is acceptable, the best available constructions are based on the "MPC-in-the-head" paradigm developed by Ishai et al. [51]. These proofs are constructed by executing a secure multiparty computation (MPC) protocol, which only requires fast symmetric key crypto operations and is amenable to the Fiat-Shamir transform [36]. As a result, proofs in the MPC-in-the-head paradigm form the basis of the Picnic digital signature scheme that is currently an "alternate candidate" in round 3 of the NIST post-quantum crypto competition [1,28,55,61].

1.1 Our Contributions

In this work, we contribute a new zero knowledge proof in the MPC-in-the-head paradigm that provides *concretely smaller proof sizes* than prior work. Our construction, called TurboIKOS, retains the benefits of all constructions in the MPC-in-the-head paradigm: low RAM utilization, public verifiability, avoiding structured setup, prover and verifier runtime that are linear in the circuit size $|C|$, and the ability to make the proof non-interactive via the Fiat-Shamir transform.

We describe two variants of TurboIKOS, both of which operate over an NP relation encoded as an arithmetic circuit C over a large field $\mathbb{F}$. The first version is an improvement over Baum-Nof [6] that reduces the number of field elements sent per gate from 4 to 3, and is intended for circuits with large field size (Sect. 3.3). The second version further reduces the number of field elements sent per mult gate from 3 to 2, and uses a modified batched consistency check that allows the technique to be used in smaller fields (Sect. 3.4). We analyze our security in Sect. 4. We describe our implementation of our first variant and evaluate the proof size of our second variant in Sect. 5.

1.2   The MPC-in-the-Head Paradigm

MPC-in-the-head is a method to construct a zero knowledge proof from a secure multiparty computation (MPC) protocol. Given an NP relation encoded as a circuit C, the prover $\mathcal{P}$ runs all parties in a secure computation of C beginning with a sharing of the witness, and the verifier $\mathcal{V}$ challenges $\mathcal{P}$ to open some of the views. Zero knowledge follows from the privacy of the MPC protocol, and soundness is achieved because a malicious $\mathcal{P}$ must have created inconsistent views and $\mathcal{V}$ finds them with noticeable probability. The seminal work of Ishai et al. [51] (also referred to as "IKOS") demonstrated that this transformation works for any MPC protocol. Subsequently, a line of works designed specific protocols with increasingly smaller proof size: ZKBoo [42], ZKB++ [28], Katz et al. [55], and Baum-Nof [6].

Table 1 shows proof sizes for MPC-in-the-head constructions in which the prover $\mathcal{P}$ runs R iterations of an MPC protocol, each of which involves N parties securely evaluating a circuit C with I input wires, O output wires, and M multiplication gates. When using an ordinary MPC protocol like SPDZ [33], a multiplication gate requires all parties to broadcast one message that is stored in the resulting proof, yielding in a proof size of $\Omega(MNR)$. To do better, MPC-in-the-head constructions make optimizations that are not acceptable for "normal" MPC protocols: they design *circuit decompositions* that look like MPC party views, yet can only be computed when a single entity $\mathcal{P}$ knows the inputs of all MPC parties. In circuit decompositions, the emulated MPC parties don't communicate to compute the views, but rather only to check their consistency.

We briefly survey the main ideas in each construction and the impact they have on the proof size per multiplication gate, which tends to be the largest contributor to the proof size.

- ZKBoo [42] and ZKB++ [28] are based on the $N = 3$ party replicated secret sharing MPC protocol of Araki et al. [4]; they do not generalize to arbitrary choices of N. All data is secret shared using 3-out-of-3 additive sharing, and addition can be done locally. Multiplication requires sending 3 messages, each of which is a function of a different subset of 2 of the 3 shares of the input wires. The verifier $\mathcal{V}$ receives two shares, and therefore can verify 1 of the 3 messages sent during each multiplication.
- ZKB++ and all subsequent works sample shares pseudorandomly. Given a seed σ_p for each party p, to share a value v_w on wire w, only the *offset* $e_w = v_w + \sum_p \mathsf{PRF}(\sigma_p, w)$ is recorded in the proof, reducing the cost per multiplication gate but requiring a (cheap) initial setup to distribute seeds.
- Katz et al. [55] extends MPC-in-the-head to accommodate MPC protocols with preprocessing. They build Beaver triples using a cut-and-choose approach, where some triples are opened and checked during preprocessing. The

Table 1. Proof size (in # of field elements) and soundness error (for large fields) for several MPC-in-the-head protocols. Some lower-order terms are omitted for legibility. N is the number of parties, M is the circuit size (number of multiplication gates), I and O are the number of input and output wires for the circuit, respectively, and R is the number of times the protocol is repeated. Note that ZKBoo and ZKB++ are only constructed for $N = 3$. P is a parameter specific to [55] indicating how many Beaver triples are committed to in advance.

Protocol	Proof size	Soundness error
IKOS+SPDZ [33,52]	$R \cdot (6MN + (I+O)N)$	$(1/N)^R$
ZKBoo [42]	$R \cdot (2M + 2I + 2O)$	$(2/3)^R$
ZKB++ [28]	$R \cdot (M + I)$	$(2/3)^R$
Katz et al. [55]	$R \cdot (2M + I + \log N + \log_R(P))$	$\max_{0 \le i \le R} \frac{\binom{P-R+i}{P-R}}{\binom{P}{P-R}N^i}$
Baum-Nof [6]	$R \cdot (4M + I + \log N)$	$(1/N)^R$
$\Pi_{TurboIKOS}$ *(this work)*	$R \cdot (3M + I + \log N)$	$(1/N)^R$
$\Pi_{TurboIKOS}$ *(this work)*	$R \cdot (2M + I + \log N + NU)$	See Theorem 3

proof size $(R \log_R(P))$ required to assist $\mathcal{V}$ in the preprocessing step is independent of the circuit size. The remaining Beaver triples are assumed to be valid and used to verify the real execution.

- Baum-Nof [6] also uses pseudorandom shares and Beaver triples in a variant of the SPDZ MPC protocol, but avoids cut-and-choose in favor of *sacrificing* one Beaver triple to check the validity of each multiplication gate.

For each multiplication gate: ZKB++ requires 1 field element to represent the offset e_w for the output value (but requires more repetitions than the rest), Katz et al. requires 1 more field element to represent the offset for the Beaver triple value, and Baum-Nof requires 2 more field elements to test whether the sacrificed Beaver triple and the circuit values are consistent. In this work, we introduce two new sacrificing-based MPC-in-the-head constructions that require 1 and then 0 field elements to perform this consistency test; the latter introduces an additive overhead that can be smaller than that of Katz et al. for some parameter settings. See Table 1 for more details about the proof size for each protocol.

1.3   Overview of Our Construction

The simplest way to describe our first protocol variant is that we combine the techniques used in the Baum-Nof ZK proof with the Turbospeedz MPC protocol [9] so that sacrificing a Beaver triple costs only one field element instead of two, while preserving the soundness error. Our second variant replaces the remaining field element per multiplication gate with some prover advice about the overall circuit, reducing the proof size so that it is competitive with Katz et al. [55] but with a different set of parameter tradeoffs. In this section, we briefly describe the Turbospeedz construction and explain the challenge when integrating it into MPC-in-the-head.

SPDZ and Turbospeedz. The SPDZ line of works [15,33,64] is a popular family of MPC protocols that offloads the (expensive) generation of Beaver triples into a preprocessing phase so that the online phase has free additions and only requires broadcasting 2 elements per multiplication gate (1 per input wire). Turbospeedz [9] saves 1 element per multiplication gate by exploiting a redundancy: when generating shares of an input wire w pseudorandomly such that the shares of the value are $[v_w] = e_w + [\lambda_w]$, the public offsets e_w can also serve "for free" as the broadcast values for the input wires, and the only effort required is to create the new offset for the 1 output wire.

The Challenge of TurboIKOS. When SPDZ is used in MPC-in-the-head to check a multiplication gate whose input and output wires are claimed to be a Beaver triple $\langle v_x, v_y, v_z \rangle$, it suffices to use the semi-honest protocol without MAC checks, and for the prover $\mathcal{P}$ to cheaply generate an independent Beaver triple $\langle \hat{\lambda}_x, \hat{\lambda}_y, \hat{v}_z \rangle$. However, with Turbospeedz there is a problem: the protocol transmits 2 field elements in the preprocessing stage, in addition to the 1 field element in the online stage. This is fine from an MPC perspective where preprocessing work might be viewed as "free," but is unacceptable for MPC-in-the-head where all elements add equally to the proof size.

To overcome this issue, we turn to another member of the SPDZ family: Overdrive [56]. The Overdrive protocol includes a clever method for generating a partially-correlated Beaver triple $\langle \lambda_x, \hat{\lambda}_y, \hat{v}_z \rangle$ where the shares $[\lambda_x]$ for the first element of the Beaver triple are the *same* as the shares for the true value v_x. With a common element between the two Beaver triples, all of the setup calculations become linear steps that can be computed locally by the parties. Integrating Turbospeedz's function-dependent preprocessing with Overdrive's Beaver triple generation mechanism is one of the accomplishments of our TurboIKOS protocol.

Implementing Picnic Digital Signatures. We provide an open source implementation of our protocol [49] and evaluate our proof size when using a variant of the Picnic post-quantum digital signature scheme [61] that uses AES as its block cipher, following the techniques introduced by BBQ [34]. Picnic signatures are based on an MPC-in-the-head proof of knowledge of a secret key k such that $AES_k(x) = y$, where the corresponding public key is (x, y). As we show in Sect. 5.1, our protocol returns the smallest proof size among streaming- and memory-friendly systems using less than 32 emulated MPC parties. Our signature sizes are also competitive with those of Banquet [7], an independent recent work that involves a memory-intensive polynomial interpolation over the entire circuit.

2 Preliminaries

2.1 Notation

Throughout this work, $\mathcal{P}$ denotes the prover and $\mathcal{V}$ denotes the verifier. We let C denote an arithmetic circuit corresponding to the NP relation with a canonical output message corresponding to logical true (i.e., the witness satisfies the relation). We use ADD, MUL to denote addition and multiplication gates, respectively.

The circuit has a set of gates G of which a subset M are MUL gates, as well as a set W of wires, of which there are subsets I of inputs to the circuit and outputs of MUL gates. $O \subseteq W$ denotes the output wires for the circuit. By abuse of notation, we use the same variables to denote the size of each set; for instance, we let M denote the number of multiplication gates when it is clear from context that we are describing an integer rather than a set.

We consider an MPC-in-the-head protocol execution with N parties that is repeated R times. If a single iteration of a protocol has soundness error δ, then we can run $R = \lceil \frac{\kappa}{\log(1/\delta)} \rceil$ independent iterations to reduce the soundness error to $2^{-\kappa}$ (where all logarithms are taken base-2 in this work).

For computation and equations, we use $\mathbb{F}$ to refer to a finite field and $\mathbb{F}^*$ to refer to the units of that field. We generally use κ as our security parameter and $[v]$ to refer to an additive secret sharing of a value v among the N parties.

We say a party is p.p.t. to denote that it is probabilistic polynomial time.

2.2 Definitions

Pseudorandom Functions and Commitments. We require the existence of a pseudorandom function PRF and a computationally hiding commitment scheme Com in our security analysis in Appendix 4. Our implementation uses hash-based commitments that models the hash function as a random oracle and assumes that AES acts as a PRF. Below we give the formal definitions for PRF and Com:

Definition 1 (Pseudorandom Function). *Let $\mathcal{F} \colon \{0,1\}^* \times \{0,1\}^* \to \{0,1\}^*$ be an efficient, length-preserving, and keyed function. $\mathcal{F}$ is a pseudorandom function with soundness κ if for all adversaries A that run in at most q time steps, A's advantage $Adv_{PRF}(A) = |\Pr_k[A^{\mathcal{F}(k,-)} = 1] - \Pr_H[A^H = 1]|$ at distinguishing the pseudorandom function from a random oracle H is at most $q/2^\kappa$.*

Definition 2 (Commitment). *A commitment scheme is a protocol between two parties $\mathcal{S}$ and $\mathcal{R}$ with the following algorithms:*

- *Com(m): The sender $\mathcal{S}$ has an input message $m \in \{0,1\}^*$ and security parameter 1^n. The algorithm Commit outputs a pair (c,r) where c is the public commitment and r is the private decommitment randomness.*
- *Decom(c, m, r): the sender $\mathcal{S}$ sends (c, m, r) to the receiver $\mathcal{R}$, who then either accepts and outputs m or rejects.*

A computationally secure commitment scheme satisfies the following properties:

- ***Completeness:*** *If $(c,r) = $ Com(m), then in Decom(c, m, r) the receiver $\mathcal{R}$ accepts and outputs m.*
- *(Computational) **Hiding:** For any two message pairs $m, m' \in \{0,1\}^*$, any receiver $\mathcal{R}^*$ running in q time cannot distinguish their respective commitments $Adv_{Com}(\mathcal{R}^*) = |\Pr[\mathcal{R}^*(Com(m,r)) = 1] - \Pr[\mathcal{R}^*(Com(m',r')) = 1]|$ except with probability at most $q/2^\kappa$.*

- *(Computational)* **Binding:** *No adversarial sender S^* running in at most q time has more than probability $q/2^\kappa$ of outputting c, m, m', r, r' such that $m \neq m'$, and $\mathsf{Decom}(c, m, r)$ and $\mathsf{Decom}(c, m', r')$ both accept.*

While our main construction can support arbitrary commitment schemes, in this work we focus on the hash-based commitment scheme in the random oracle model, in which $\mathsf{Com}(m; r) = H(m, r)$ feeds the input message and randomness into the random oracle and $\mathsf{Decom}(c, m, r) = (m, r)$ provides the preimage to the hash. The binding of this scheme follows from a birthday bound analysis: if a random oracle has 2κ bit output length and an adversary makes at most q queries to this oracle, then the probability that the adversary finds a collision in the oracle is at most $q^2/2^{2\kappa}$, and a collision is necessary to break the binding property of the commitment scheme. The hiding property can be proved similarly.

There are a few optimizations that prior works have used here to save space. First, when committing to a list of messages $\langle m_1, m_2, \ldots, m_\ell \rangle$, the sender can provide a succinct commitment $H(\mathsf{Com}(m_1, r_1), \ldots, \mathsf{Com}(m_\ell, r_\ell))$ to the entire list, again thanks to collision resistance. Second, if m is already known to the receiver, then it suffices to send only r during decommitment. Third and most ambitiously, because we will only commit to strings that already have min-entropy κ, when generating a signature scheme we can go further and remove the randomness r from the Com and Decom algorithms to create a deterministic scheme in which decommitments are free. This strategy breaks the hiding property of the commitment and thus the zero knowledge property of the schemes we will construct, but it will suffice for our signature construction; we refer readers to Katz et al. [55, §3.1] for details.

Honest Verifier Zero-Knowledge Argument of Knowledge. Next, we formally define the notion of ZK arguments over an NP-relation $R(x, w)$ as a two-party protocol involving two p.p.t. algorithms, a prover $\mathcal{P}$ and a verifier $\mathcal{V}$. Both parties have the same NP statement x, and only the prover receives its corresponding witness w. The parties interact to determine whether $R(x, w) = 1$ without revealing the witness. We restrict our attention to the honest verifier setting in which $\mathcal{V}$ never deviates from the protocol.

Definition 3. *The protocol $(\mathcal{P}, \mathcal{V})$ is an honest verifier ZK argument for the relation $R(x, w)$ if it satisfies the following properties:*

- **Completeness:** *If $\mathcal{P}$ and $\mathcal{V}$ are honest and $R(x, w) = 1$, $\mathcal{V}$ always accepts.*
- **Soundness:** *For any malicious and computationally bounded prover $\mathcal{P}^*$, there is a negligible function $\mathsf{negl}(\cdot)$ such that a statement x is not in the language (i.e., $R(x, w) = 0$ for all w), then $\mathcal{V}$ rejects on x with probability $\geq 1 - \mathsf{negl}(|x|)$ when interacting with $\mathcal{P}^*$.*
- **Honest verifier computational zero knowledge:** *Let $View_{\mathcal{V}(x,w)}$ be a random variable describing the distribution of messages received by $\mathcal{V}(x)$ from $\mathcal{P}(x, w)$. Then, there exists a p.p.t. simulator Sim such that for all x in the language, $\mathsf{Sim}(x) \approx_c View_{\mathcal{V}(x,w)}$.*

In this work, we will construct a ZK argument of knowledge, which provides a stronger *knowledge soundness* guarantee that if a bounded-time malicious prover $\mathcal{P}^*$ can make the verifier accept a statement x with non-negligible probability, then there exists an extractor $E^{\mathcal{P}^*}(x)$ that can output a witness w such that the relation holds $R(x, w) = 1$.

Additionally, we restrict our attention to honest verifier ZK in this work because our protocol TurboIKOS is also public coin and constant round, so it can be transformed into a non-interactive argument using the Fiat-Shamir transform.

Secure Multi Party Computation (MPC). An MPC protocol allows N players to jointly compute a function of their respective inputs while maintaining the privacy of their individual inputs and the correctness of the output. In addition, the protocol should prevent an adversary who may corrupt a subset of players, from learning additional information or harming the protocol execution. A party's *view* in MPC contains that party's input, randomness, and any messages received by that party. For use in MPC-in-the-head, secure computation protocols must satisfy t-privacy, meaning that the view of any subset $t < N$ of the parties can be simulated (see [51] for a formal definition).

3 Construction

We present our protocol $\Pi_{\text{TurboIKOS}}$ in this section and in Fig. 1. We start by describing the Baum-Nof [6] SPDZ-like protocol and the Turbospeedz MPC protocol. Then, we show how to incorporate Turbospeedz [9] into the MPC-in-the-head paradigm to reduce the amount of communication per MUL gate.

3.1 Starting Point: SPDZ and Baum-Nof

We use the MPC-in-the-head paradigm introduced by Ishai et al. (IKOS) [51] combined with a semi-honest version of the $(N-1)$-private SPDZ MPC protocol [33] as a starting point for our zero-knowledge proof using MPC-in-the-head protocol. In IKOS, a prover simulates an MPC protocol for all parties and commits to a view for each party containing the party's randomness, input, and messages received. To save proof space, an additional "broadcast channel" is committed to for messages that are sent to all parties, rather than writing the same value in all party views. Then the verifier chooses a subset of the parties and challenges the prover to open the committed views of these parties. The verifier then confirms that the views of the opened parties are *consistent*, that is, the message party i sent to party j is the same in views of both those parties. For N-party MPC protocols that *only* send broadcast messages and do not contain any private messages between parties, the verifier opening T parties will have a $\frac{T}{N}$ chance of catching a prover who cheats by creating inconsistent views: the "receiving" half of the message is always revealed in the broadcast channel, and these are checked for consistency with the revealed parties' "sent" messages. By repeating this process R times with fresh randomness, the verifier can shrink the probability of error by a power of R.

We start with the variant of semi-honest SPDZ [33] used by Baum-Nof [6]. Let N denote the set of parties and M denote the set of multiplication gates in the circuit C. The parties hold sharings of the inputs $[x_m]$ and $[y_m]$ for each MUL gate $m \in M$; since this MPC protocol is being emulated by a prover who knows the value on the wire, the parties additionally have a sharing of the gate's output $[z_m]$. The prover generates a random multiplication triple, $\langle a_m, b_m, c_m \rangle$, which will be "sacrificed" to check a multiplication constraint in a MUL gate. The verifier will send a random challenge $\varepsilon_m \leftarrow \mathbb{F}$. Each party does the following:

1. Broadcast $[f_m] = \varepsilon_m[x_m] + [a_m]$ and $[g_m] = [y_m] + [b_m]$
2. Use the recombined f and g to compute

$$[\zeta_m] = \varepsilon_m[z_m] - f_m g_m + f_m[b_m] + g_m[a_m] - [c_m]. \tag{1}$$

Baum and Nof show that if either $\langle a_m, b_m, c_m \rangle$ or $\langle x_m, y_m, z_m \rangle$ is not a valid multiplication triple, this value ζ_m will be nonzero with probability at least $1 - 1/|\mathbb{F}|$ over the choice of ε_m. We will prove similar claims in Lemmas 1–2.

To save proof space, rather than broadcasting the ζ_m values for each MUL gate m, an additional challenge variable $\hat{\varepsilon}_m \in \mathbb{F}$ is sent by the verifier $\mathcal{V}$ and the prover $\mathcal{P}$ responds by sending a linear combination $[Z] = \sum_{m \in M} \hat{\varepsilon}_m[\zeta_m]$ of the secret values and public coefficients. If the prover is honest then $Z = 0$. Baum and Nof show (Proposition 1 of [6]) that Z will be nonzero if at least one mult gate constraint is violated with probability at least $1 - 2/|\mathbb{F}|$. Later in Lemma 2 of this pape we will improve this bound for a batched set of ζ_m values to a $1/|\mathbb{F}|$ error using a very-slightly different batching technique.

If $1/|\mathbb{F}|$ does not yield sufficient soundness error, we can reduce this error by doing multiple batched checks. To do so, we reveal linear combinations $[Z_1], \ldots, [Z_U]$, all over the same $[\zeta_m]$ shares, but using different random $\hat{\varepsilon}_m$ choices provided by the verifier. Let U be the number of these checks.

Naively, this protocol broadcasts $(2M+U)N$ elements since each party broadcasts their f shares and g shares for each multiplication gate, plus $[Z]$. Later in this work we will show multiple ways to reduce this size with different tradeoffs, by taking advantage of the fact that $\mathcal{V}$ has corrupted $N - 1$ parties. We emphasize that all parties' shares must still be committed to before $\mathcal{P}$ knows which party will remain uncorrupted.

To compress the parties' views, we can generate the shares of all values pseudorandomly, with only one public "offset" value per wire. Then, for each multiplication gate, the prover only needs to broadcast the offset values for f and g, along with the offsets of the true output wire z and the Beaver triple product c. Hence, the proof contains 4 field elements per multiplication gate, as shown in Table 1.

3.2 Introducing Turbospeedz

Turbospeedz [9] generally shows how to have only one broadcast per multiplication gate instead of two in normal SPDZ by adding a function-dependent preprocessing step where the circuit to be computed is known, but the input to the circuit need not yet be known. The idea is to add a sharing of a "mask" on each wire, propagated additively (but not multiplicatively) during preprocessing. Then, the masks of the input wires can serve as the first two elements of a Beaver triple, which is also generated during the preprocessing. Let x and y denote the input wire and z denote the output wire of any gate. Let v_x, v_y, v_z denote the real values on the wires. In the preprocessing phase, the prover performs the following:

1. For each party, the prover generates random "masking shares" $[\lambda_w]$ for each input wire and the output wire of each MUL, w.
2. The prover homomorphically computes the mask shares for each ADD gate internal output wire, $[\lambda_z] = [\lambda_x] + [\lambda_y]$.
3. For each wire w, the prover computes external value, $e_w = \lambda_w + v_w$. In MPC, these external values are public to all parties. In MPC-in-the-head, $\mathcal{P}$ will give them to $\mathcal{V}$ in the clear.

In Turbospeedz, given e_x, e_y, and a Beaver triple $\langle a_m, b_m, c_m \rangle$, each party computes their share of MUL gate m's output wire by locally computing

$$[v_z] = e_x e_y - e_y[a_m] - e_x[b_m] + [c_m]$$
$$= (v_x + a_m)(v_x + b_m) - (v_y + b_m)[a_m] - (v_y + a_m)[b_m] + [c_m]$$
$$= [v_x v_y].$$

The parties then proceed to compute and open $[e_z] = [v_z] + [\lambda_z]$. Note that this relies on the parties already possessing a sharing of a *valid* Beaver triple $\langle a_m, b_m, c_m \rangle$ in advance.

The upshot of this method is that multiplication gates can be computed using only one opening (e_z) instead of two (d and e in the previous section).

3.3 Adapting Turbospeedz into Sacrificing-Based MPC-in-the-Head

In this section, we incorporate a modified version of the Turbospeedz method from Sect. 3.2 into the SPDZ-based MPC-in-the-head framework described above from Sect. 3.1. For large field sizes, the resulting MPC-in-the-head protocol $\Pi_{\mathsf{TurboIKOS}}$ will require only 3 field elements per multiplication, rather than the 4 elements used in Baum-Nof [6].

Committing to all Wire Values. The first step of converting Turbospeedz into an MPC-in-the-head protocol is to replace the step of opening shares of e_z by having the $\mathcal{P}$ simply provide e_z in the clear. However, unlike Turbospeedz, we do not wish to have a costly preprocessing process in which the verifier becomes convinced of the validity of all Beaver triples in the circuit; instead we wish to use ζ_m values as in Eq. 1. In order to do this without reusing masks on multiple values, we must make some subtle changes to the original Turbospeedz protocol.

Input: The prover $\mathcal{P}$ and verifier $\mathcal{V}$ receive an input circuit C comprising a set of gates G of which a subset M are MUL gates, along with a set of wires W with subsets of input and output wires I and O, respectively. $\mathcal{P}$ is the sole recipient of a witness. Both parties also receive constants R and N (the latter of which we equate with the set $\{1, \ldots, N\}$ by abuse of notation). The prover $\mathcal{P}$ and verifier $\mathcal{V}$ run R independent executions of the following protocol in parallel.

Function-dependent preprocessing: $\mathcal{P}$ pseudorandomly derives shares $[\lambda_w]$ for each wire $w \in W$ and a Beaver triple for each multiplication gate as follows.

1. Generate a random master seed σ^*. Pseudorandomly derive a binary tree with root σ^* until there are as many leaves as parties. Assign the pth leaf as party key σ_p.
2. For each input wire $w \in I$ and party $p \in N$, pseudorandomly derive share $[\lambda_w]$ from key σ_p.
3. Go through C layer by layer, starting at the input layer. For every $g \in G$, do the following on gate C_g with input wires x, y and output wire z.
   - If C_g is an ADD gate: assign $[\lambda_z] := [\lambda_x] + [\lambda_y]$.
   - If C_g is a MUL gate:
     • Derive $[\lambda_z]$, $[\hat{\lambda}_{y,g}]$, and $[\hat{\lambda}_z]$ for every $p \in N$ from σ_p. (Note that y can be an input to many MUL gates, hence the two indices in $[\hat{\lambda}_{y,g}]$.)
     • Set $\hat{e}_z := \lambda_x \cdot \hat{\lambda}_{y,g} + \hat{\lambda}_z$, which creates a Beaver triple $\langle \lambda_x, \hat{\lambda}_{y,g}, \hat{e}_z - \hat{\lambda}_z \rangle$.

Interactive phase: Once $\mathcal{P}$ receives the witness, the parties interact as follows.

1. $(\mathcal{P} \to \mathcal{V})$ $\mathcal{P}$ executes the circuit to determine the value v_w of each wire $w \in W$, and assigns the offset $e_w := v_w + \lambda_w$ for each wire $w \in W$. It sends to $\mathcal{V}$:
   - Offsets e_w for input wires $w \in I$, and offsets e_z and $\hat{e}_z$ for the outputs of MUL gates. (The remaining offsets can then be computed.)
   - A commitment to all shares $[\lambda_w]$ for all output wires $w \in O$.
   - A commitment to the seeds σ_p for all parties $p \in N$.
2. $(\mathcal{V} \to \mathcal{P})$ $\mathcal{V}$ randomly selects two elements $\varepsilon_m, \hat{\varepsilon}_m \leftarrow \mathbb{F}$ for every MUL gate $m \in M$.

[There are two ways to complete this protocol, shown in Figures 2 and 4.]

Fig. 1. Beginning of an interactive zero knowledge protocol between prover $\mathcal{P}$ and honest verifier $\mathcal{V}$, given a relation represented as an arithmetic circuit with ADD and MUL gates over a field $\mathbb{F}$. All verifier messages are public coins, so the protocol can be made non-interactive using the Fiat-Shamir transform. There are two different endings to this protocol, given in Figs. 2 and 4.

To save space, we set the parties' shares $[\lambda_w]$ on each wire pseudorandomly, taking advantage of the external value e as an offset: the value on wire w is defined as simply $v_w = e_w - \lambda_w$.

$\mathcal{P}$ will generate all λ_w values for all wires in the circuit the same as in original Turbospeedz, but by generating each party's share pseudorandomly using a party key. Additionally, for each MUL gate m, the prover will generate additional pseudorandom shares $[\hat{\lambda}_{y,m}]$ and $[\hat{\lambda}_z]$. $\mathcal{P}$ computes $\hat{e}_z = \lambda_x \hat{\lambda}_{y,m} + \hat{\lambda}_z$, forming a correlated Beaver triple $\langle \lambda_x, \hat{\lambda}_{y,m}, \hat{e}_z - \hat{\lambda}_z \rangle$ that will be sacrificed. The double index on $[\hat{\lambda}_{y,m}]$ is due to the fact that wire y may be reused in several different mult gates m, each of which must define their own Beaver triple for the prover's

---

Interactive phase, continued from Fig. 1:

3. $(\mathcal{P} \to \mathcal{V})$ $\mathcal{P}$ sends all α_m values and commits to $\mathcal{P}$ commits to all $[\alpha_m]$ and $[Z]$ shares. These variables are computed as follows.
   - For every MUL gate $m \in M$, assign $[\alpha_m] := \varepsilon_m[\lambda_y] + \hat{\varepsilon}_m[\hat{\lambda}_{y,m}]$.
   - For every party $p \in N$, assign $[Z] := \sum_{m \in M}[\zeta_m]$, which is the sum of all
     $[\zeta_m] := \varepsilon_m e_z - \varepsilon_m e_x e_y + \hat{\varepsilon}_m \hat{e}_z + (\varepsilon_m e_y - \alpha_m)[\lambda_x] + \varepsilon_m e_x[\lambda_y] - \varepsilon_m[\lambda_z] - \hat{\varepsilon}_m[\hat{\lambda}_z]$.

4. $(\mathcal{V} \to \mathcal{P})$ $\mathcal{V}$ randomly selects a set $T = N \setminus \{i^*\}$ of $N-1$ parties to corrupt.

5. $(\mathcal{P} \to \mathcal{V})$ $\mathcal{P}$ reveals the $\log(N)$ seeds from preprocessing step 1 that suffice for $\mathcal{V}$ to recompute σ_p for all corrupted parties $p \in T$, but not the remaining seed σ_{i^*}.

Verification. $\mathcal{V}$ accepts only if all of the following are true:

- The output values (v_w for $w \in O$) provided by $\mathcal{P}$ correspond to logical true.
- The commitments in rounds 1 and 3 are consistent with the opened keys σ_p for corrupted parties, and with the shares of $[Z]$, $[\alpha_m]$, and $[\lambda_w]$ for output wires for *all* parties. $\mathcal{V}$ can compute $N-1$ shares of these from its seeds, and the remaining shares from the revealed α_m values and the known values for Z and output wires.

Fig. 2. End of the interactive zero knowledge protocol $\Pi_{\text{TurboIKOS}}$ between prover $\mathcal{P}$ and honest verifier $\mathcal{V}$, given a relation represented as an arithmetic circuit with ADD and MUL gates over a field $\mathbb{F}$. See Fig. 1 for the beginning of this protocol.

privacy. (For legibility, we sometimes omit this double-subscript when the gate under consideration is clear from context.)

Creating a Test for Consistency of all Gates. The largest change is in how ζ_m is calculated for each MUL gate m. To save space, we check the consistency of all of these values with one random linear combination of Eq. (1) for all MUL gates. We begin similarly to the Baum-Nof challenge: $\mathcal{V}$ will send random challenges $\varepsilon_m, \hat{\varepsilon}_m \leftarrow \mathbb{F}$. Our α_m values are defined slightly differently, for a reason we will explain shortly. The prover will send $\alpha_m = \varepsilon_m \lambda_y + \hat{\varepsilon}_m \hat{\lambda}_y$. Then, the parties compute:

$$[\zeta_m] = \varepsilon_m e_z - \varepsilon_m e_x e_y + \hat{\varepsilon}_m \hat{e}_z + (\varepsilon_m e_y - \alpha_m)[\lambda_x] + \varepsilon_m e_x[\lambda_y] - \varepsilon_m[\lambda_z] - \hat{\varepsilon}_m[\hat{\lambda}_z].$$

First, we wish to show that this ζ_m serves a similar purpose to Baum-Nof's, assuming (for the moment) that the prover $\mathcal{P}$ honestly computes all α_m values from the parties' shares. For each MUL gate $m \in M$, define:

$$\Delta_{z,m} = (e_z - \lambda_z) - (e_x - \lambda_x)(e_y - \lambda_y) \text{ and } \hat{\Delta}_{z,m} = (\hat{e}_z - \hat{\lambda}_z) - \lambda_x \hat{\lambda}_y.$$

Observe that if $\mathcal{P}$ is honest, then $\langle e_x - \lambda_x, e_y - \lambda_y, e_z - \lambda_z \rangle$ and $\langle \lambda_x, \hat{\lambda}_y, \hat{e}_z - \hat{\lambda}_z \rangle$ are both valid Beaver triples and therefore $\Delta_{z,m} = \hat{\Delta}_{z,m} = 0$.

Lemma 1. *Fix a MUL gate $m \in M$. If ε_m and $\hat{\varepsilon}_m$ are chosen uniformly randomly from $\mathbb{F}$, and if either $\Delta_{z,m} \neq 0$ or $\hat{\Delta}_{z,m} \neq 0$ (or both), then $\zeta_m \neq 0$ with probability at least $1 - 1/|\mathbb{F}|$.*

Proof. Observe that

$$
\begin{aligned}
\zeta_m &= \varepsilon_m e_z - \varepsilon_m e_x e_y + \hat{\varepsilon}_m \hat{e}_z + (\varepsilon_m e_y - \alpha_m)\lambda_x + \varepsilon_m e_x \lambda_y - \varepsilon_m \lambda_z - \hat{\varepsilon}_m \hat{\lambda}_z \\
&= \varepsilon_m e_z - \varepsilon_m e_x e_y + \hat{\varepsilon}_m (\lambda_x \hat{\lambda}_y + \hat{\Delta}_{z,m}) + (\varepsilon_m e_y - \alpha_m)\lambda_x + \varepsilon_m e_x \lambda_y - \varepsilon_m \lambda_z \\
&= \varepsilon_m e_z - \varepsilon_m e_x e_y + \hat{\varepsilon}_m \hat{\Delta}_{z,m} + (\varepsilon_m e_y - \varepsilon_m \lambda_y)\lambda_x + \varepsilon_m e_x \lambda_y - \varepsilon_m \lambda_z \\
&= \varepsilon_m e_z - \varepsilon_m \lambda_z - \varepsilon_m e_x e_y + \varepsilon_m e_x \lambda_y + \varepsilon_m e_y \lambda_x - \varepsilon_m \lambda_y \lambda_x + \hat{\varepsilon}_m \hat{\Delta}_{z,m} \\
&= \varepsilon_m((e_z - \lambda_z) - (e_x - \lambda_x)(e_y - \lambda_y)) + \hat{\varepsilon}_m \hat{\Delta}_{z,m} \\
&= \varepsilon_m \Delta_{z,m} + \hat{\varepsilon}_m \hat{\Delta}_{z,m}.
\end{aligned}
$$

Now, consider the probability that $\zeta_m = 0$ over the uniform choice of ε_m and $\hat{\varepsilon}_m$ from $\mathbb{F}$. The only way for this to occur is if $\varepsilon_m \Delta_{z,m} = -\hat{\varepsilon}_m \hat{\Delta}_{z,m}$. If $\Delta_{z,m} = 0$, this happens if and only if $\hat{\varepsilon}_m = 0$, which occurs with probability $1/|\mathbb{F}|$. If $\Delta_{z,m} \neq 0$, then for any choice of $\hat{\varepsilon}_m$ there exists a single option for $\varepsilon_m = -\hat{\varepsilon}_m \hat{\Delta}_{z,m} \Delta_{z,m}^{-1}$ that makes $\zeta_m = 0$, so again we arrive at a probability of $1/|\mathbb{F}|$. These two cases are mutually exclusive, which yields the desired bound.

Similar to Baum-Nof, we can combine these in a linear combination Z to test all multiplication gates at once. However, because we defined ζ_m to already include two different random coefficients on the different Δ values, these coefficients already suffice to serve as challenge coefficients for this linear combination. As we show in Lemma 2, the upshot is that we can test all gates in the circuit with a soundness error of only $1/|\mathbb{F}|$ by merely revealing $[Z] = \sum_{m \in M}[\zeta_m]$.

Lemma 2. *If ε_m and $\hat{\varepsilon}_m$ are chosen uniformly randomly from $\mathbb{F}$ for all multiplication gates in the circuit, and if there exists at least one MUL gate $\bar{m} \in M$ such that $\Delta_{z,m} \neq 0$ or $\hat{\Delta}_{z,m} \neq 0$, then $Z \neq 0$ with probability at least $1 - 1/|\mathbb{F}|$.*

Proof. Consider $Z = \sum_{m \in M} \zeta_m = (\varepsilon_{\bar{m}} \Delta_{z,\bar{m}} + \hat{\varepsilon}_{\bar{m}} \hat{\Delta}_{z,\bar{m}}) + Z'$, where Z' is the sum of all other terms in the formula and $\bar{m} \in M$ is the gate where the sum is guaranteed to be nonzero; without loss of generality, suppose that $\Delta_{z,\bar{m}} \neq 0$. Then, $Z = 0$ if and only if $\varepsilon_{\bar{m}} = \Delta_{z,\bar{m}}^{-1} \cdot (-Z' - \hat{\varepsilon}_{\bar{m}} \hat{\Delta}_{z,\bar{m}})$, which occurs with probability $1/|\mathbb{F}|$.

Completing the Consistency Test. Rounds 3–5 of the protocol provide a method for the verifier to check whether $Z = 0$, up to $1/N$ soundness error. We will describe two ways to perform this task: a base protocol $\Pi_{\text{TurboIKOS}}$ described in this section (shown also in Fig. 2) and an improved protocol $\tilde{\Pi}_{\text{TurboIKOS}}$ in Sect. 3.4. Both techniques involve providing some 'advice' in the form of the non-privacy-sensitive α_m value for each MUL gate that assists the verifier in its computation of Z.

In round 3 of the base protocol $\Pi_{\text{TurboIKOS}}$ in this section, the prover provides for each MUL gate $m \in M$. Importantly, the prover also commits to all shares $[\alpha_m] = \varepsilon_m[\lambda_y] + \hat{\varepsilon}_m[\hat{\lambda}_y]$, and analogously for all $[Z]$ shares. There are three claims that the verifier must check:

- The committed $[\alpha_m]$ and $[Z]$ are consistent with the parties' individual views, at least for the $N-1$ emulated parties that the verifier can open.
- The committed $[\alpha_m]$ shares in round 3 collectively sum to the provided α_m value. That is, the prover provided the public α_m 'advice' value correctly.
- Assuming the advice is correct, then the $[Z]$ shares committed in round 3 sum to $Z = 0$. That is, the prover passes the test posed in Lemma 2.

After the prover reveals seeds for $N-1$ parties in round 5, the verifier can check these claims as follows. First, $\mathcal{V}$ can compute the remaining party's $[\alpha_m]$ by subtracting the known shares from the public α_m value, and then check whether these shares together constitute a valid opening of the commitment in round 3. This checks (most of) the first two claims simultaneously. The final claim is verified similarly; the key observation here is that if the prover is honest, then the value $Z = 0$ is publicly known. So, the $\mathcal{V}$ computes $N-1$ shares of Z, calculates what the remaining party's share must be in order for the overall value $Z = 0$ as required, and then checks whether these shares together constitute a valid opening of the commitment.

Putting it all Together. Our protocol is described in detail in Fig. 1. The prover $\mathcal{P}$ and verifier $\mathcal{V}$ interact in a 5-round protocol, and if all consistency checks pass then the verifier believes that the output wire labels derived from the circuit evaluation is correct.

Completeness is a straightforward consequence of the fact that the honest prover computes the desired circuit (many times, in fact). We prove the privacy and knowledge soundness of our ZK argument of knowledge in Sect. 4.

Compared to Baum-Nof [6], we reduce communication per multiplication gate from 4 to 3 field elements. Concretely, for each multiplication gate, Baum-Nof must send the f and g values described in Sect. 3.1. Their protocol must also send a Beaver triple offset (analogous to $\hat{e}_z$) as well as the offset for the output wire of the MUL gate (similar to e_z). By using the Turbospeedz approach, we reduce communication to only 3 field elements: e_z, $\hat{e}_z$, and α_m.

Algorithmic Optimizations. There are a few optimizations that we can apply to the base protocol $\Pi_{\text{TurboIKOS}}$ to save space even further. Some of these optimizations are deliberately omitted from Figs. 1 and 2 for brevity; they are simple to add, and they are built into our implementation in Sect. 5.

Our first optimization saves on the cost of commitments. Recall that we need to commit to values in each of the prover steps (rounds 1, 3, and 5), and also that the entire procedure from Figs. 1–2 is repeated R times. It suffices to build a single commitment per round across all repetitions: that is, just 2 commitments in total for the entire proof.

Second, we described the SPDZ-style MPC protocol by considering pseudorandom values for each party plus a public offset. Following prior works, we save space by integrating the offset into a single party's value (say, party 1). While this party no longer has pseudorandom value, the upshot is that we only need to reveal the $\hat{e}_z$ values within party 1's view, or in other words we don't need to reveal these values for the $1/N$ fraction of repetitions in which party 1 is the unopened party. (Note that we still need to publish the e_z and α_m values on all repetitions because $\mathcal{V}$ needs this information to perform its consistency check.)

Third, if the circuit has a single known value that represents 'logical true' (say, the value 0), then we can save on the cost of opening the output wire shares $[\lambda_w]$ for all parties (i.e., including the unopened party). Instead, we can follow a similar trick as we described above for $[\alpha_m]$ and $[Z]$. In round 1 of the protocol, the prover $\mathcal{P}$ commits to all output wire shares. Once the verifier $\mathcal{V}$ learns the seeds to reconstruct $N - 1$ of these shares for itself, it assumes that the output wires collectively reconstruct to logical true and calculates the remaining share accordingly. Finally, $\mathcal{V}$ checks that all shares match $\mathcal{P}$'s commitment.

3.4   Constructing Smaller Consistency Tests

In this section, we describe an improved protocol $\tilde{\Pi}_{\text{TurboIKOS}}$ that reduces the cost per multiplication gate from 3 field elements down to 2. Specifically, we show a new method to check the consistency of Z in rounds 3–5 without revealing an α_m element for each MUL gate. The motivation for this change is twofold. The first reason is obvious: reducing the number of field gates required per MUL gate shrinks the proof size. The second and more subtle reason is to improve the performance of TurboIKOS on smaller fields, such as the field GF(256) used in AES, without blowing up the size of the protocol with additional zero-checks.

We will explain this second motivation at a high level here; for more detail see the soundness analysis (Theorems 2 and 3) in Sect. 4. A cheating prover must have a sufficiently low chance of getting a set of coefficients $\varepsilon_m, \hat{\varepsilon}_m$ where $Z = 0$ even though at least one MUL constraint is violated. For small fields, a malicious prover has a decently-high probability of passing a single zero-test Z by pure chance. While one could overcome this issue by increasing the number of repetitions R, there is an alternative solution: run multiple Z values with fresh random ε_m and $\hat{\varepsilon}_m$ coefficients for each, but the same wire shares λ_z and offsets e_z and $\hat{e}_z$.

This alternative method doesn't fare well in the original protocol $\Pi_{\text{TurboIKOS}}$ because our method requires revealing an α_m value per MUL gate for each test, so each additional Z value used to improve the soundness error would reveal an additional field element per MUL gate, making the proof size much larger. Thus, our goal in this section is to show how to consistency-check multiple zero-tests $Z_1, \ldots, Z_U$ without transmitting additional information proportional to the number of MUL gates beyond the two field elements e_z and $\hat{e}_z$ we already transmitted in round 1.

Recall that for a single MUL gate m,

$$[\zeta_m] = \varepsilon_m e_z - \varepsilon_m e_y e_y + \hat{\varepsilon}_m \hat{e}_z + \varepsilon_m e_y [\lambda_x] - \alpha_m [\lambda_x] + \varepsilon_m e_x [\lambda_y] - \varepsilon_m [\lambda_z] - \hat{\varepsilon}_m [\hat{\lambda}_z]$$

is a sharing of $\zeta_m = \varepsilon_m \Delta_{z,m} + \hat{\varepsilon}_m \hat{\Delta}_{z,m} = 0$ for an honest prover. Observe that each party can calculate most of the terms in this sum even without receiving α_m. Specifically, for each MUL gate, define $\phi_m =: \zeta_m + \alpha_m \lambda_x$. Each party has the information to compute its own share $[\phi_m]$ using information already available: the public ε_m and $\hat{\varepsilon}_m$ values, the known offsets e, and the corrupted shares $[\lambda]$.

Also, recall from the original protocol that the parties never test each $[\zeta_m]$ directly, but rather they only test that the sum $Z = \sum_{m \in M} \zeta_m$ equals zero. We can rewrite the shares of this test in the following way. (We add a subscript m to the wire values to make it unambiguous which gate each wire belongs to.)

$$[Z] = \sum_{m \in M} [\zeta_m] = \sum_{m \in M} [\phi_m] - \sum_{m \in M} \alpha_m [\lambda_{m,x}].$$

The corrupted parties can compute their shares for the left sum. However, the sharing of the remaining term, which we will name

$$\beta = \sum_{m \in M} \alpha_m \lambda_{m,x} \qquad (2)$$

is problematic because it seems to require each α_m to be known in the clear to calculate the sum. This is where the original protocol $\Pi_{\text{TurboIKOS}}$ revealed all α_m, so that each party could compute their share of β as $\sum_{m \in M} \alpha_m [\lambda_{m,x}]$.

We proceed to show a different way that the prover can commit to and provide the shares for $[\beta]$, which we also describe pictorially in Fig. 3. Let $[x]_i$ denote the ith share of x. The crucial observation is that all shares $[\alpha_m]$ can be revealed without a loss in privacy; our only objective here is a performance improvement to avoid sending these shares, even though we could safely do so. Furthermore, observe that:

$$\beta = \sum_{m=1}^{M} \alpha_m \lambda_{m,x} = \sum_{m=1}^{M} \left(\sum_{i=1}^{N} [\alpha_m]_i \right) \left(\sum_{j=1}^{N} [\lambda_{m,x}]_j \right) = \sum_{m=1}^{M} \sum_{i=1}^{N} \sum_{j=1}^{N} [\alpha_m]_i [\lambda_{m,x}]_j$$

$$= \sum_{j=1}^{N} \sum_{i=1}^{N} \beta_{i,j}, \text{ where } \beta_{i,j} = \sum_{m=1}^{M} [\alpha_m]_i [\lambda_{m,x}]_j \qquad (3)$$

We will take advantage of the MPC-in-the-head structure of our proof to create a sharing where each party essentially holds a "column" of these values: that is, party j's share of β is $\sum_{i=1}^{N} \beta_{i,j}$. In a normal MPC protocol, each pair of parties i and j could collaborate to compute $\beta_{i,j}$. In MPC-in-the-head this is mostly unnecessary, because $\mathcal{V}$ has corrupted $N - 1$ of the parties, it has $N - 1$ of these $[\alpha_m]_i$ shares and therefore can compute $\beta_{i,j}$ for all corrupted parties $i, j \in T$. It is missing only $\beta_{i^*,j}$, where i^* is the remaining, uncorrupted party.

In Fig. 3, the parties' shares of β are the sum of the elements in each column. $\mathcal{V}$ has $N - 1$ elements (the unshaded regions in each column) out of the N elements needed to compute the full share (column sum), but needs to be sent the remaining (shaded) element to sum the column and compute the share.

For soundness, we require that all $\beta_{i,j}$ be committed to in advance. To do this, we concatenate all elements in each column and commit to them; call these commitments $h_1, \ldots, h_N$. Each commitment h_j must be randomized since the field elements might be small enough not to provide the required min-entropy

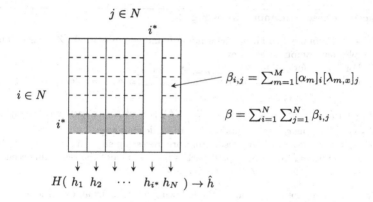

Fig. 3. Creating a more efficient sharing of β (Eq. 2). Each cell holds a single $\beta_{i,j}$ value (Eq. 3). A single commitment $\hat{h}$ binds the entire matrix. To open $N-1$ of the columns, $\mathcal{P}$ gives $\mathcal{V}$ the field elements in the shaded region along with h_{i^*}.

on their own, but this can be done "for free" by using party j's seed to generate this random value. We then commit to the concatenation of those commitments and give the result $\hat{h}$ to $\mathcal{V}$ in round 3, before the corrupted parties are chosen.

To check the commitments, $\mathcal{V}$ checks two properties: First, the commitment to the $\beta_{i,j}$ values must be consistent with the party views, and second, the shares of Z must sum to 0. To show the first property, $\mathcal{V}$ first recreates all $(N-1)^2$ elements it can from the parties it corrupted. It then receives $(N-1)$ missing elements (the shaded region in Fig. 3) from $\mathcal{P}$, which lets it compute the shares $[\beta]_j$ for the parties it corrupted and also the commitment h_j to the concatenation of the elements in each column. $\mathcal{V}$ does not get the missing share $[\beta]_{i^*}$; instead, it is given h_{i^*}, the missing commitment. Using all these, it can check $\hat{h}$ to ensure the corrupted party views are consistent with the commitment to the $\beta_{i,j}$.

Second, as in the other version of this protocol, the shares to Z are also committed to, but where the β component of Z is shared using this method. $\mathcal{V}$ checks that $Z = 0$ by recomputing the $N-1$ shares it corrupted, and then computes the last share by subtracting those shares from 0. The recomputed shares are checked against the commitment to the $[Z]$ shares from round 3.

This portion of the proof sends $(N-1)$ field elements (the shaded elements) and one commitment (h_{i^*}) per repetition; the additional commitments to the shares of Z and the $\hat{h}$ need only use one commitment for the entire proof, across all repetitions. It bears repeating that this method was able to check the consistency of all multiplication gates without revealing an additional α_m value per MUL gate. This allows us to add additional fresh zero-tests independently of the number of MUL gates as well. If there are U of these tests, our communication per repetition becomes about $(2M + UN)$ field elements, which can outperform Katz et al. [55] when the number of parties N is small. The description of this version of the protocol is given in Fig. 4.

Interactive phase, continued from Fig. 1:

3. $(\mathcal{P} \rightarrow \mathcal{V})$ $\mathcal{P}$ commits to all $\beta_{i,j}$ by sending $\hat{h}$ and commits to all $[Z]$ shares. These variables are computed as follows.
   - For $i \in N$, for $j \in N$, $\beta_{i,j} = \sum_{m=1}^{M} [\alpha_m]_i [\lambda_{m,x}]_j$.
   - For every party $j \in N$, assign $[Z]_j = \sum_{m \in M} \left(\varepsilon_m e_{m,z} - \varepsilon_m e_{m,y} e_{m,y} + \hat{\varepsilon}_m \hat{e}_z + \varepsilon_m e_y [\lambda_{m,x}] + \varepsilon_m e_{m,x} [\lambda_{m,y}] - \varepsilon_m [\lambda_{m,z}] - \hat{\varepsilon}_m [\hat{\lambda}_{m,z}] \right) - \sum_{i \in N} \beta_{i,j}$.

4. $(\mathcal{V} \rightarrow \mathcal{P})$ As before, $\mathcal{V}$ samples a set $T = N \setminus \{i^*\}$ of $N-1$ parties to corrupt.

5. $(\mathcal{P} \rightarrow \mathcal{V})$ $\mathcal{P}$ opens commitments to $\mathcal{V}$ in the following way:
   - As before, reveal $\log(N)$ seeds from preprocessing step 1 that suffice for $\mathcal{V}$ to recompute σ_p for all corrupted parties $p \in T$, but not the remaining seed σ_{i^*}.
   - Reveal $\beta_{i^*,j}$ for all $j \neq i^*$ and reveal h_{i^*}.

Verification. $\mathcal{V}$ accepts only if all of the following are true for all executions:

- The output values (v_w for $w \in O$) provided by $\mathcal{P}$ correspond to logical true.
- The commitments in rounds 1 and 3 are consistent with the opened keys σ_p for corrupted parties, with the $\beta_{i,j}$ opened, and with the shares of $[Z]$ and $[\lambda_w]$ for output wires for *all* parties. $\mathcal{V}$ computes these using the party seeds, the remaining $\beta_{i^*,j}$ values it is given, and the known Z and output values.

Fig. 4. Ending of the improved zero knowledge protocol $\tilde{\Pi}_{\text{TurboIKOS}}$ between prover $\mathcal{P}$ and honest verifier $\mathcal{V}$, given a relation represented as an arithmetic circuit with ADD and MUL gates over a field $\mathbb{F}$. See Fig. 1 for the beginning of this protocol. Compared to Fig. 2, step 3 is new, and this change affects the opening and checking of commitments in step 5 and verification; the remainder of the protocol is unchanged from before. If multiple zero tests are desired, then steps 2, 3, and 5 are repeated with independent ε_m and $\hat{\varepsilon}_m$, Z, and $\beta_{i,j}$ values.

4   Security Analysis

In this section we prove the honest-verifier zero-knowledge and knowledge soundness properties of the two protocols constructed in Sect. 3. For each property, we first analyze the base protocol $\Pi_{\text{TurboIKOS}}$, and then we describe how the analysis changes for the improved protocol $\tilde{\Pi}_{\text{TurboIKOS}}$.

Theorem 1. *When instantiated with a pseudorandom function PRF and a computationally hiding commitment scheme Com, both the base protocol $\Pi_{TurboIKOS}$ and improved protocol $\tilde{\Pi}_{TurboIKOS}$ run with N parties and R repetitions is honest-verifier computational zero knowledge with distinguishing bound at most $R \cdot (Adv_{Com} + Adv_{PRF})$.*

Proof. We focus here on the privacy argument for the base protocol $\Pi_{\text{TurboIKOS}}$. The privacy of the improved protocol $\tilde{\Pi}_{\text{TurboIKOS}}$ then follows immediately from the fact that it provides strictly less information to the verifier than the base protocol $\Pi_{\text{TurboIKOS}}$ does. Additionally, we prove the statement for a single repetition of the base protocol $\Pi_{\text{TurboIKOS}}$, from which the theorem follows by a union bound over the independent repetitions.

Let I and M' represent the set of input wires and MUL-gate-output wires respectively. Consider a simulator that follows the following steps during the interactive protocol.

1. The simulator samples all verifier challenges uniformly at random: all $\varepsilon_m, \hat{\varepsilon}_m$ in round 2, and a party $i^* \in N$ in round 4 to be the "uncorrupted party" whose key will not be revealed to $\mathcal{V}$.
2. Choose keys σ_p for all parties $p \in N$ uniformly at random, honestly following step 1 of preprocessing.
3. For all corrupted parties, derive all shares $[\lambda_w]$ for all wires w from the keys honestly, as in step 3 of the preprocessing.
4. For the output wires $w \in O$, choose the e_w values uniformly at random, and set party i^*'s share of λ_w such that $v_w = e_w - \lambda_w$ represents logical true.
5. Now, work backward through the circuit in reverse topological order.
   (a) For ADD gates, choose a random setting of the e_x and e_y values on the input wires to the ADD gate, conditioned on meeting the linear constraints induced by all ADD gates at this layer.
   (b) For a MUL gate with input wires x and y and output wire z, the values of e_x, e_y, and the corrupted shares of $\hat{\lambda}_y, \hat{\lambda}_z$, and $\hat{e}_z$ must all be simulated. Note that e_x, e_y, or both may already be set by an existing constraint (e.g. if the wire was reused in a later layer or used in multiple gates).
      i. Generate $\hat{\lambda}_y$ and initialize the $\hat{\lambda}_z$ shares honestly for the corrupted parties from the party keys (leaving it unspecified for party i^*).
      ii. Generate $\hat{e}_z$ uniformly (and also e_x or e_y, if they are unspecified).
      iii. Let Δ_z be the difference between the value on the output wire z and the product of the value on the input wires xy. That is, $\Delta_z = v_z - v_x v_y = e_z - e_x e_y - \lambda_z + e_x \lambda_y + e_y \lambda_x - \lambda_x \lambda_y$. Let $\hat{\Delta}_z$ be the difference between $(\hat{e}_z - \hat{\lambda}_z)$ and $\lambda_x \hat{\lambda}_y$; that is, $\hat{\Delta}_z = \hat{e}_z - \hat{\lambda}_z - \lambda_x \hat{\lambda}_y$. For an honest prover, $\Delta_z = \hat{\Delta}_z = 0$, but the simulator is not honest so these values are likely to be non-zero. Using the foreknowledge of ε_m and $\hat{\varepsilon}_m$, alter party i^*'s share of $\hat{\lambda}_z$ so that $\zeta = \varepsilon_m \Delta_z + \hat{\varepsilon}_m \hat{\Delta}_z$ equals 0 (or alter λ_z if $\hat{\Delta}_z = 0$ but $\Delta_z \neq 0$).
6. In round 1, commit honestly to all parties' keys σ_p and all parties' shares $[\lambda_z]$ for all output wires $z \in O$. Also, send the offsets e_z for all $z \in I \cup M'$.
7. In round 3, commit to all shares $[\alpha_m]$ and $[Z]$, where $[Z]$ is computed correctly from the already-manipulated ζ shares from above.
8. In round 5, honestly open the key commitments for all parties except i^*. Also, honestly reveal party i^*'s shares $[Z]$, $[\alpha_m]$, and $[\lambda_w]$ for output wires.

It is straightforward to confirm that the simulated proof passes all verification checks. It remains to show that the simulated proof is computationally indistinguishable from a real one. As a stepping stone, we consider a hybrid proof H that is constructed like the real one, except using an ideal commitment scheme Com (where it is impossible to recover an un-opened key) and a truly random function in place of PRF. The distinguishing probability between the real game and H is at most $\mathsf{Adv}_{\mathsf{Com}} + \mathsf{Adv}_{\mathsf{PRF}}$.

In the hybrid world, we claim that all of the information provided by $\mathcal{P}$ to $\mathcal{V}$ throughout the proof is meaningless. The commitment to σ_{i^*} is now useless, values like the output wires or Z are publicly known to $\mathcal{V}$ beforehand, and the remaining information (e_w for all wires $w \in W$, $\hat{e}_z$ and α_m values for all MUL gates, and the shares $[Z]$) contains masks that hide the real values from $\mathcal{V}$.

- On each wire w, the revealed $e_w = v_w + \lambda_w$ does not reveal anything about the value on the wire v_w because it is masked by party i^*'s share of λ_w.
- For each MUL gate $m \in M$, information in α_m is masked by i^*'s share of $\hat{\lambda}_y$.
- For each MUL gate, $\hat{e}_z$ hides info about $\lambda_x \hat{\lambda}_y$ by masking it with party i^*'s share of $\hat{\lambda}_z$.
- Party i^*'s share of Z reveals no information because it can be computed as $-\sum_{p \in T}[Z]$ (leveraging the fact that $Z = 0$ is public knowledge), and the corrupted parties' shares of Z are only a function of their own data.

All of these masks are truly random in the hybrid world. Observe that e_w, $\hat{e}_z$ and α_m all have the uniform distribution in the simulated world as well. Therefore, the distance between the hybrid and simulated games is 0, which completes the proof for the base protocol $\Pi_{\text{TurboIKOS}}$.

Next, we examine the soundness of the base protocol $\Pi_{\text{TurboIKOS}}$. We focus on its security for the non-interactive version of the MPC-in-the-head construction using the Fiat-Shamir transform using a random oracle H with 2κ bits of output, so that finding a collision has 2^κ cost. (The interactive version of the protocol has even better soundness because the prover cannot rewind the verifier.)

Theorem 2. *Consider the non-interactive version of the base protocol $\Pi_{\text{TurboIKOS}}$ over a large field $|\mathbb{F}| = 2^\kappa$ and instantiated with a random oracle H with 2κ output length. Then, Protocol $\Pi_{\text{TurboIKOS}}$ with $R = \frac{\kappa}{\log_2(N)} + 1$ repetitions provides knowledge soundness with error at most $1/2^\kappa$.*

Proof. We focus here on proving the traditional soundness property. The stronger knowledge soundness claim immediately follows by applying the analysis from Katz et al. [55, §3.1] in order to build an extractor that recovers a witness by observing the inputs to the random oracle-based commitment scheme on a single execution. The reduction is tight because the extractor never needs to rewind.

To prove soundness, consider a malicious prover $\mathcal{P}^*$ that is attempting to prove a false statement. Since an honest execution of the circuit would return logical false, the prover must deviate from the protocol on each repetition. There are effectively four different places where the malicious prover $\mathcal{P}^*$ can deviate from the protocol in order to gain an advantage:

1. In round 1 of the protocol, $\mathcal{P}^*$ can change the offsets for one or more MUL gates, so that the Δ_z or $\hat{\Delta}_z$ values on these gate(s) are non-zero. (We presume it is simple for the prover to determine a sufficient set of gates to tamper in order to cause the circuit to return logical true.) $\mathcal{P}^*$ will learn in round 2 whether $\mathcal{V}$ catches this deviation or whether $\mathcal{P}^*$ has successfully evaded detection. By Lemma 2, the prover is successful with probability $1/|\mathbb{F}|$.

2. In round 3, $\mathcal{P}^*$ can change one party's $[\alpha_m]$ and $[Z]$ shares so that the verifier reconstructs a Z value of 0. The success of this attack is revealed in round 4, and $\mathcal{P}^*$ evades detection with probability $1/N$.
3. In rounds 1 or 3, $\mathcal{P}^*$ can attempt to break the binding property of the commitment scheme and open it later to different values.
4. In round 1, $\mathcal{P}^*$ can change one party's share of the final output so the result becomes logical true. $\mathcal{P}^*$ will learn in round 4 whether $\mathcal{V}$ catches this deviation or whether $\mathcal{P}^*$ has successfully evaded detection (this occurs with probability $1/N$).

(Observe that the pseudorandom function has no impact on soundness. It only exists to 'compress' each party's share of each wire label $[\lambda_w]$, and any tampering of these wire labels is equivalent to tampering the corresponding offset e_w.)

The key observation in this proof is that item 1. is strictly better for $\mathcal{P}^*$ than item 3. and that item 2. is strictly better than item 4.. The first part of this claim follows from the observation that items 1. and 3. both require the prover to deviate in round 1 and the first has better probability of success since the commitment scheme has soundness κ. The second part of this claim is true because the attacks in items 4. and 2. both give the same probability of success and are both revealed in round 4, yet the alteration of $[\alpha_m]$ and $[Z]$ occurs later. Delaying the start of the attack is strictly better for $\mathcal{P}^*$ because it can wait to see if the attack on wire offsets in round 1 was successful, and only attempt this attack if necessary.

Concretely, we use the same proof technique as several recent analyses of non-interactive zero knowledge proofs that apply the Fiat-Shamir transform to protocols with more than three rounds [7,16,54]. We consider all *attacker strategies* (r_1, r_2) in which the prover $\mathcal{P}^*$ changes wire offsets in round 1 until r_1 repetitions happen to have $Z = 0$ anyway, and then $\mathcal{P}^*$ attacks the remaining $r_2 = R - r_1$ repetitions in round 3 by altering α_m and Z. In general, the cost of any multi-round attack strategy is given by $C = 1/p_1 + 1/p_2$, where p_1 and p_2 denote the probability that the first and second parts of the attack succeed, respectively. To achieve κ soundness, we must choose a sufficiently large number of repetitions R so that any attacker strategy $(r_1, R - r_1)$ has a total cost $C \geq 2^\kappa$.

In this case, one attacker strategy dominates the rest: $r_1 = 1$ and $r_2 = R - 1$. In more detail, the malicious prover $\mathcal{P}^*$ changes the wire offsets for all repetitions in round 1, and rewinds until finding an input that evades detection from the verifier's round 2 challenge on $r_1 = 1$ instance. Because each instance evades detection only with probability $1/|\mathbb{F}| = 1/2^\kappa$, the malicious prover $\mathcal{P}^*$ can only expect to evade detection on $r_1 = 1$ instance in time less than 2^κ. Even succeeding on 2 instances is exceedingly unlikely in the adversary's runtime, and the $\mathcal{P}^*$ gains no benefit by foregoing an attack on round 1 altogether. Thereafter, $\mathcal{P}^*$ must complete the attack on the remaining $r_2 = R - 1$ repetitions by altering $[\alpha_m]$ and $[Z]$. This change is undetected by the verifier with probability $1/N$ independently for each repetition. Hence, the overall probability of success for the second repetition is $(1/N)^{r_2}$, and thus its cost exceeds 2^κ when $R = \frac{\kappa}{\log_2(N)} + 1$.

Theorem 3. *Consider the improved protocol $\tilde{\Pi}_{TurboIKOS}$ that is instantiated with a random oracle H with 2κ output length and executed over the field $\mathbb{F}$ with N parties, R repetitions, and U tests per repetition. Then, the protocol satisfies knowledge soundness with security parameter κ if:*

$$\max_{0 \le r_1 \le R} \left\{ \left[p_1 = \sum_{i=r_1}^{R} \binom{R}{i} \cdot \left[\frac{1}{|\mathbb{F}|} \right]^{Ui} \cdot \left[1 - \frac{1}{|\mathbb{F}|} \right]^{U(R-i)} \right]^{-1} + N^{(R-r_1)} \right\} > 2^\kappa. \tag{4}$$

Proof. Once again, we focus on proving traditional soundness, after which we can build an extractor for knowledge soundness using the same technique as before. Additionally, the analysis from Theorem 2 about the options for a malicious prover $\mathcal{P}^*$ to deviate from the protocol holds here too. The prover's dominant strategy remains to change the offsets for one or more MUL gates in a way that causes the remainder of the circuit (computed honestly) to return logical true; note that this will also cause the corresponding Δ_z or $\hat{\Delta}_z$ values to be nonzero. For each repetition independently, there are two ways for the malicious prover $\mathcal{P}^*$ to evade detection by the verifier:

1. Based on the verifier's U independent random choices of ε_m and $\hat{\varepsilon}_m$ in round 2, there is a $(1/|\mathbb{F}|)^U$ probability that all of the Z tests happen to equal 0 (by Lemma 2).
2. If even a single Z value is non-zero, then $\mathcal{P}^*$ can commit to erroneous $\beta_{i,j}$ values to 'fix' this error. Note that $\mathcal{P}^*$ can only inject erroneous data in one row of the table in Fig. 3 because the verifier can check the remaining $N-1$ rows directly. This attack evades detection only if the verifier chooses in round 4 to leave this row as the uncorrupted party, which happens with probability $1/N$.

As before, we can analyze the malicious prover $\mathcal{P}^*$'s probability of success by analyzing all attacker strategies (r_1, r_2) that operate as follows. First, the prover $\mathcal{P}^*$ rewinds round 1 until at least r_1 repetitions have the property that the verifier's choice of ε_m and $\hat{\varepsilon}_m$ are such that *all* of the Z tests within these repetitions equal 0. Second, $\mathcal{P}^*$ rewinds round 3 until the remaining $r_2 = R - r_1$ have been tampered in the locations chosen by the verifier in round 4.

To achieve κ soundness, we must select enough repetitions R so that any attacker strategy $(r_1, R - r_1)$ has a total cost $C \ge 2^\kappa$. Here, the *cost* of this multi-round attack strategy is given by $C = 1/p_1 + 1/p_2$, and p_1 and p_2 denote the probability that the first and second parts of the attack succeed, respectively.

Because we consider an arbitrary field size in this theorem, the cost analysis here is more complicated than in Theorem 2. Our argument is very similar to that of Banquet [7]. The first probability boils down to the chance that the attacker has r_1 successes out of R trials, where each trial succeeds with probability $(1/|\mathbb{F}|)^U$. This is the right tail of a binomial distribution:

$$p_1 = \sum_{i=r_1}^{R} \binom{R}{i} \cdot (1/|\mathbb{F}|)^{Ui} \cdot (1 - 1/|\mathbb{F}|)^{U(R-i)}. \qquad (5)$$

The second probability is simply $p_2 = (1/N)^{r_2}$ because the malicious prover must succeed on all remaining repetitions of the protocol. Combining the costs of both parts of the attack results in Eq. (4), completing the proof of the theorem.

The goal here is to find the "minimum" choices of N, R, and U that yield a desired soundness parameter κ for a circuit with a given field size $|\mathbb{F}|$. While it is challenging to write a closed-form version of Eq. 4 that connects the five parameters, it is easy to find satisfying tuples empirically. In Table 2, we show several such choices for the field $\mathbb{F}_{2^8}$. We include a computer program that calculates valid parameter settings within our open source repository [49].

Table 2. Valid parameter settings for $\mathbb{F}_{2^8}$. The body of the table shows the number of repetitions R based on the soundness parameter κ, number of parties N, and number of tests per repetition U.

κ	N	U				
		1	2	4	6	9
128	8	66	53	47	45	44
	16	54	41	36	34	33
	31	47	35	30	28	27
192	8	99	79	70	68	66
	16	81	62	54	52	50
	31	71	53	45	43	41
256	8	132	106	95	91	89
	16	108	83	73	69	67
	31	95	71	61	57	55

5   Performance and Prototype Implementation

In this section, we compare our $\tilde{\Pi}_{\text{TurboIKOS}}$ system's performance against other MPC-in-the-head based systems, and we describe our prototype Python implementation of $\Pi_{\text{TurboIKOS}}$.

5.1   Performance Analysis

To evaluate our performance, we measure our signature size when computing a variant of the Picnic signature scheme [61]. Picnic uses MPC-in-the-head (specifically, a variant of the Katz et al. protocol [55]) and LowMC [2], a block cipher with few multiplications that is designed to be efficient in secure computation. Picnic is currently an "alternate candidate" in round 3 of the NIST post-quantum crypto competition [1]. BBQ [34] introduced the idea of using AES in Picnic-like signatures and showed that the signature sizes could be competitive with those using LowMC. To achieve this, rather than evaluating the binary circuit for AES, they used an arithmetic MPC-in-the-head system over $\mathbb{F}_{2^8}$; this facilitates proving constraints about inverses in $\mathbb{F}_{2^8}$, the non-linear component of the AES S-box. They also show how each field inversion can be reduced to a single multiplication gate (without testing for the case in which the input and output are both equal to 0) with very small reduction in the soundness of the resulting system (less than 3 bits of security). We follow their approach in this section.

Table 3 shows the proof sizes of $\tilde{\Pi}_{\text{TurboIKOS}}$ when computing signatures using AES at different security levels. We compare against the following systems:

- BBQ [34]: The figures are taken directly from their paper, except the number of parties is not listed. We make an educated guess that they use approximately $N = 64$ parties; for lower N their proof size will be larger.
- Katz et al. [55]: We calculate the proof size using the formula in [55], assuming that a field inversion constraint can be verified with two field elements per MUL gate like in this work; we believe this should be true but did not check. Also, our calculations use 32 parties rather than 31; this result should be a conservative smaller estimate of the actual proof size when $N = 31$.
- Baum-Nof [6]: We calculate a conservative underestimate of the proof size using the formula in [6], assuming that only a single zero-check is needed per repetition. However, this is unlikely to be the case in $\mathbb{F}_{2^8}$ for the same reason as in our work.
- Banquet [7]: The figures are taken directly from their paper.

Banquet [7] is independent recent work that reduce the size of AES-based Picnic signatures using very different techniques based on polynomial interpolation in extension fields of $\mathbb{F}_{2^8}$ [20,31]. They achieve a smaller proof size than all competitors, including us. However, this advantage comes with two downsides relative to our scheme and prior ones. First, performing polynomial arithmetic in extension fields would be costly on embedded devices whose CPU architectures typically have a small word size. Second, the polynomials are proportional to the entire circuit size, making their system more memory-costly than traditional MPC-in-the-head based methods like ours where the memory is only proportional to the circuit width (i.e., the memory required to compute the circuit).

Table 3. Signature size comparison for the Picnic signature scheme at different security levels for different systems. All signature sizes are shown in kilobytes (KB). AES-128 has $(M, I) = (200, 128)$, AES-192 $\times$ 2 has $(M, I) = (416, 192)$, and AES-256 $\times$ 2 has $(M, I) = (500, 256)$.

Scheme	N	Protocol *(all sizes in KB)*				
		BBQ [34]	Katz et al. [55]	Baum-Nof [6]	$\tilde{\Pi}_{\text{TurboIKOS}}$	Banquet [7]
AES-128 (L1)	8	|	26.7	37.3	23.8	–
	16	31.6	22.4	29.4	20.6	19.8
	31	|	19.8	24.8	19.8	17.5
AES-192x2 (L3)	8	|	76.3	110.8	66.7	–
	16	86.9	63.1	87.4	56.3	51.2
	31	|	54.9	73.4	52.2	45.1
AES-256x2 (L5)	8	|	122.6	179.9	109.3	–
	16	133.7	101.9	140.7	90.4	83.5
	31	|	89.1	118.0	82.8	73.9

5.2 Prototype Implementation

We created a prototype implementation for $\Pi_{\text{TurboIKOS}}$ in Python. We did not optimize the runtime or memory usage of our code, thus, we will likely not win on prover runtime with other MPC-in-the-head approaches written in C or C++, e.g. [6,55]. That having been said, our protocol is amenable to all of the optimizations made by the recent Reverie software [69] implementing the protocol of Katz et al. Our code currently achieves runtimes about twice as long as Reverie for the same size circuit. In this section we briefly describe our implementation.

Our Python implementation [49] supports both Bristol circuit formats and Prover Worksheet (PWS) formats as input. The circuit is parsed into a list of Gate objects, found in gate.py, and initializes a Wire data structure, found in wire.py, that takes in a list of dictionaries containing the values on each wire.

Dictionaries are used extensively to manage information. Circuit information such as the number of various types of gates are stored in a dictionary. Values on each wire such as e and λ are also stored in a dictionary. Each wire has a dictionary of values, resulting in a list of dictionaries with length of the number of wires. This list of dictionaries is later used as the input to the Wire object, found in wire.py, which defines functions to access values on the wire.

On the Prover side, $\mathcal{P}$ calculates all the parties as she parses through the circuit, so $\mathcal{P}$ uses the Wire objects to access a party's value. On the Verifier side, $\mathcal{V}$ picks one party to leave unopened and reconstructs the other $N-1$ views from the seeds given by $\mathcal{P}$. We generate the shares λ, $\hat{\lambda}_y$, and $\hat{\lambda}_z$ pseudorandomly using

AES as a PRF with the party's seed as the key and the concatenation of the
(fixed-length) wire index and type of value as the message.

The prover is required to send a commitment in Round 1 and Round 3. As
discussed in Sect. 2, when committing to values with sufficient min-entropy, we
simply use $\mathsf{Com}(m) := H(m)$, thus decommitments are "free" aside from the
cost of m itself. This remains computationally hiding as long as m has sufficient
min-entropy and H is a random oracle. We use SHA2 from `hashlib` for our
instantiation of H. To achieve non-interactivity via the Fiat-Shamir Transform
[36], the random messages sent by the Verifier in Round 2 and Round 4 are
replaced by a call to H on the info sent by $\mathcal{P}$ in all previous rounds.

Acknowledgments. This material is supported by a Google PhD Fellowship, the
DARPA SIEVE program under Agreement No. HR00112020021, and the National
Science Foundation under Grants No. 1414119, 1718135, 1739000, 1801564, 1915763,
and 1931714.

References

1. Alagic, G., et al.: Status report on the second round of the NIST post-quantum
   cryptography standardization process (2020). https://csrc.nist.gov/publications/
   detail/nistir/8309/final
2. Albrecht, M.R., Rechberger, C., Schneider, T., Tiessen, T., Zohner, M.: Ciphers
   for MPC and FHE. In: Oswald, E., Fischlin, M. (eds.) EUROCRYPT 2015, Part
   I. LNCS, vol. 9056, pp. 430–454. Springer, Heidelberg (2015). https://doi.org/10.
   1007/978-3-662-46800-5_17
3. Ames, S., Hazay, C., Ishai, Y., Venkitasubramaniam, M.: Ligero: lightweight sublinear arguments without a trusted setup. In: Thuraisingham, B.M., Evans, D.,
   Malkin, T., Xu, D. (eds.) ACM CCS 2017, pp. 2087–2104. ACM Press, Octo-
   ber/November 2017
4. Araki, T., Furukawa, J., Lindell, Y., Nof, A., Ohara, K.: High-throughput semi-
   honest secure three-party computation with an honest majority. In: Weippl, E.R.,
   Katzenbeisser, S., Kruegel, C., Myers, A.C., Halevi, S. (eds.) ACM CCS 2016, pp.
   805–817. ACM Press, October 2016
5. Baum, C., Malozemoff, A.J., Rosen, M., Scholl, P.: Mac'n'cheese: zero-knowledge
   proofs for arithmetic circuits with nested disjunctions. Cryptology ePrint Archive,
   Report 2020/1410 (2020). https://eprint.iacr.org/2020/1410
6. Baum, C., Nof, A.: Concretely-efficient zero-knowledge arguments for arithmetic
   circuits and their application to lattice-based cryptography. In: Kiayias, A.,
   Kohlweiss, M., Wallden, P., Zikas, V. (eds.) PKC 2020, Part I. LNCS, vol. 12110,
   pp. 495–526. Springer, Cham (2020). https://doi.org/10.1007/978-3-030-45374-
   9_17
7. Baum, C., de Saint Guilhem, C.D., Kales, D., Orsini, E., Scholl, P., Zaverucha, G.:
   Banquet: short and Fast Signatures from AES. In: Garay, J.A. (ed.) PKC 2021.
   LNCS, vol. 12710, pp. 266–297. Springer, Cham (2021). https://doi.org/10.1007/
   978-3-030-75245-3_11
8. Bellare, M., Goldwasser, S.: New paradigms for digital signatures and message
   authentication based on non-interactive zero knowledge proofs. In: Brassard, G.
   (ed.) CRYPTO 1989. LNCS, vol. 435, pp. 194–211. Springer, New York (1990).
   https://doi.org/10.1007/0-387-34805-0_19

9. Ben-Efraim, A., Nielsen, M., Omri, E.: Turbospeedz: double your online SPDZ! Improving SPDZ using function dependent preprocessing. In: Deng, R.H., Gauthier-Umaña, V., Ochoa, M., Yung, M. (eds.) ACNS 2019. LNCS, vol. 11464, pp. 530–549. Springer, Cham (2019). https://doi.org/10.1007/978-3-030-21568-2_26

10. Ben-Sasson, E., et al.: Zerocash: decentralized anonymous payments from bitcoin. In: 2014 IEEE Symposium on Security and Privacy, pp. 459–474. IEEE Computer Society Press, May 2014

11. Ben-Sasson, E., Chiesa, A., Genkin, D., Tromer, E., Virza, M.: SNARKs for C: verifying program executions succinctly and in zero knowledge. In: Canetti, R., Garay, J.A. (eds.) CRYPTO 2013, Part II. LNCS, vol. 8043, pp. 90–108. Springer, Heidelberg (2013). https://doi.org/10.1007/978-3-642-40084-1_6

12. Ben-Sasson, E., Chiesa, A., Riabzev, M., Spooner, N., Virza, M., Ward, N.P.: Aurora: transparent succinct arguments for R1CS. In: Ishai, Y., Rijmen, V. (eds.) EUROCRYPT 2019, Part I. LNCS, vol. 11476, pp. 103–128. Springer, Cham (2019). https://doi.org/10.1007/978-3-030-17653-2_4

13. Ben-Sasson, E., Chiesa, A., Spooner, N.: Interactive oracle proofs. In: Hirt, M., Smith, A. (eds.) TCC 2016, Part II. LNCS, vol. 9986, pp. 31–60. Springer, Heidelberg (2016). https://doi.org/10.1007/978-3-662-53644-5_2

14. Ben-Sasson, E., Chiesa, A., Tromer, E., Virza, M.: Succinct non-interactive zero knowledge for a von neumann architecture. In: Fu, K., Jung, J. (eds.) USENIX Security 2014, pp. 781–796. USENIX Association, August 2014

15. Bendlin, R., Damgård, I., Orlandi, C., Zakarias, S.: Semi-homomorphic encryption and multiparty computation. In: Paterson, K.G. (ed.) EUROCRYPT 2011. LNCS, vol. 6632, pp. 169–188. Springer, Heidelberg (2011). https://doi.org/10.1007/978-3-642-20465-4_11

16. Beullens, W., Delpech de Saint Guilhem, C.: LegRoast: efficient post-quantum signatures from the legendre PRF. In: Ding, J., Tillich, J.-P. (eds.) PQCrypto 2020. LNCS, vol. 12100, pp. 130–150. Springer, Cham (2020). https://doi.org/10.1007/978-3-030-44223-1_8

17. Bhadauria, R., Fang, Z., Hazay, C., Venkitasubramaniam, M., Xie, T., Zhang, Y.: Ligero++: a new optimized sublinear IOP. In: Ligatti, J., Ou, X., Katz, J., Vigna, G. (eds.) ACM CCS 2020, pp. 2025–2038. ACM Press, November 2020

18. Bitansky, N., Chiesa, A., Ishai, Y., Paneth, O., Ostrovsky, R.: Succinct non-interactive arguments via linear interactive proofs. In: Sahai, A. (ed.) TCC 2013. LNCS, vol. 7785, pp. 315–333. Springer, Heidelberg (2013). https://doi.org/10.1007/978-3-642-36594-2_18

19. Blum, M., Feldman, P., Micali, S.: Non-interactive zero-knowledge and its applications (extended abstract). In: 20th ACM STOC, pp. 103–112. ACM Press, May 1988

20. Boneh, D., Boyle, E., Corrigan-Gibbs, H., Gilboa, N., Ishai, Y.: Zero-knowledge proofs on secret-shared data via fully linear PCPs. In: Boldyreva, A., Micciancio, D. (eds.) CRYPTO 2019, Part III. LNCS, vol. 11694, pp. 67–97. Springer, Cham (2019). https://doi.org/10.1007/978-3-030-26954-8_3

21. Bootle, J., Cerulli, A., Chaidos, P., Groth, J., Petit, C.: Efficient zero-knowledge arguments for arithmetic circuits in the discrete log setting. In: Fischlin, M., Coron, J.-S. (eds.) EUROCRYPT 2016, Part II. LNCS, vol. 9666, pp. 327–357. Springer, Heidelberg (2016). https://doi.org/10.1007/978-3-662-49896-5_12

22. Bootle, J., Cerulli, A., Ghadafi, E., Groth, J., Hajiabadi, M., Jakobsen, S.K.: Linear-time zero-knowledge proofs for arithmetic circuit satisfiability. In: Takagi, T., Peyrin, T. (eds.) ASIACRYPT 2017, Part III. LNCS, vol. 10626, pp. 336–365. Springer, Cham (2017). https://doi.org/10.1007/978-3-319-70700-6_12

23. Boyle, E., Couteau, G., Gilboa, N., Ishai, Y.: Compressing vector OLE. In: Lie, D., Mannan, M., Backes, M., Wang, X. (eds.) ACM CCS 2018, pp. 896–912. ACM Press, October 2018

24. Boyle, E., Couteau, G., Gilboa, N., Ishai, Y., Kohl, L., Scholl, P.: Efficient pseudorandom correlation generators: silent OT extension and more. In: Boldyreva, A., Micciancio, D. (eds.) CRYPTO 2019, Part III. LNCS, vol. 11694, pp. 489–518. Springer, Cham (2019). https://doi.org/10.1007/978-3-030-26954-8_16

25. Bünz, B., Bootle, J., Boneh, D., Poelstra, A., Wuille, P., Maxwell, G.: Bulletproofs: short proofs for confidential transactions and more. In: 2018 IEEE Symposium on Security and Privacy, pp. 315–334. IEEE Computer Society Press, May 2018

26. Bünz, B., Fisch, B., Szepieniec, A.: Transparent SNARKs from DARK compilers. In: Canteaut, A., Ishai, Y. (eds.) EUROCRYPT 2020, Part I. LNCS, vol. 12105, pp. 677–706. Springer, Cham (2020). https://doi.org/10.1007/978-3-030-45721-1_24

27. Camenisch, J., Lysyanskaya, A.: An efficient system for non-transferable anonymous credentials with optional anonymity revocation. In: Pfitzmann, B. (ed.) EUROCRYPT 2001. LNCS, vol. 2045, pp. 93–118. Springer, Heidelberg (2001). https://doi.org/10.1007/3-540-44987-6_7

28. Chase, M., et al.: Post-quantum zero-knowledge and signatures from symmetric-key primitives. In: Thuraisingham, B.M., Evans, D., Malkin, T., Xu, D. (eds.) ACM CCS 2017, pp. 1825–1842. ACM Press, October/November 2017

29. Chiesa, A., Forbes, M.A., Spooner, N.: A zero knowledge sumcheck and its applications. Cryptology ePrint Archive, Report 2017/305 (2017). http://eprint.iacr.org/2017/305

30. Chiesa, A., Hu, Y., Maller, M., Mishra, P., Vesely, N., Ward, N.: Marlin: preprocessing zkSNARKs with universal and updatable SRS. In: Canteaut, A., Ishai, Y. (eds.) EUROCRYPT 2020, Part I. LNCS, vol. 12105, pp. 738–768. Springer, Cham (2020). https://doi.org/10.1007/978-3-030-45721-1_26

31. Corrigan-Gibbs, H., Boneh, D.: Prio: private, robust, and scalable computation of aggregate statistics. In: NSDI, pp. 259–282. USENIX Association (2017)

32. Costello, C., et al.: Geppetto: versatile verifiable computation. In: 2015 IEEE Symposium on Security and Privacy, pp. 253–270. IEEE Computer Society Press, May 2015

33. Damgård, I., Pastro, V., Smart, N., Zakarias, S.: Multiparty computation from somewhat homomorphic encryption. In: Safavi-Naini, R., Canetti, R. (eds.) CRYPTO 2012. LNCS, vol. 7417, pp. 643–662. Springer, Heidelberg (2012). https://doi.org/10.1007/978-3-642-32009-5_38

34. de Saint Guilhem, C.D., De Meyer, L., Orsini, E., Smart, N.P.: BBQ: using AES in picnic signatures. In: Paterson, K.G., Stebila, D. (eds.) SAC 2019. LNCS, vol. 11959, pp. 669–692. Springer, Cham (2020). https://doi.org/10.1007/978-3-030-38471-5_27

35. De Santis, A., Persiano, G.: Zero-knowledge proofs of knowledge without interaction (extended abstract). In: 33rd FOCS, pp. 427–436. IEEE Computer Society Press, October 1992

36. Fiat, A., Shamir, A.: How to prove yourself: practical solutions to identification and signature problems. In: Odlyzko, A.M. (ed.) CRYPTO 1986. LNCS, vol. 263, pp. 186–194. Springer, Heidelberg (1987). https://doi.org/10.1007/3-540-47721-7_12

37. Frederiksen, T.K., Nielsen, J.B., Orlandi, C.: Privacy-free garbled circuits with applications to efficient zero-knowledge. In: Oswald, E., Fischlin, M. (eds.) EURO-CRYPT 2015, Part II. LNCS, vol. 9057, pp. 191–219. Springer, Heidelberg (2015). https://doi.org/10.1007/978-3-662-46803-6_7

38. Gabizon, A.: AuroraLight: improved prover efficiency and SRS size in a sonic-like system. Cryptology ePrint Archive, Report 2019/601 (2019). https://eprint.iacr.org/2019/601

39. Gabizon, A., Williamson, Z.J., Ciobotaru, O.: PLONK: permutations over lagrange-bases for oecumenical noninteractive arguments of knowledge. Cryptology ePrint Archive, Report 2019/953 (2019). https://eprint.iacr.org/2019/953

40. Ganesh, C., Kondi, Y., Patra, A., Sarkar, P.: Efficient adaptively secure zero-knowledge from garbled circuits. In: Abdalla, M., Dahab, R. (eds.) PKC 2018, Part II. LNCS, vol. 10770, pp. 499–529. Springer, Cham (2018). https://doi.org/10.1007/978-3-319-76581-5_17

41. Gennaro, R., Gentry, C., Parno, B., Raykova, M.: Quadratic span programs and succinct NIZKs without PCPs. In: Johansson, T., Nguyen, P.Q. (eds.) EURO-CRYPT 2013. LNCS, vol. 7881, pp. 626–645. Springer, Heidelberg (2013). https://doi.org/10.1007/978-3-642-38348-9_37

42. Giacomelli, I., Madsen, J., Orlandi, C.: ZKBoo: faster zero-knowledge for Boolean circuits. In: Holz, T., Savage, S. (eds.) USENIX Security 2016, pp. 1069–1083. USENIX Association, August 2016

43. Goldreich, O., Micali, S., Wigderson, A.: How to play any mental game or a completeness theorem for protocols with honest majority. In: Aho, A. (ed.) 19th ACM STOC, pp. 218–229. ACM Press, May 1987

44. Goldreich, O., Micali, S., Wigderson, A.: Proofs that yield nothing but their validity or all languages in NP have zero-knowledge proof systems. J. ACM 38(3), 691–729 (1991)

45. Goldwasser, S., Micali, S., Rackoff, C.: The knowledge complexity of interactive proof systems. SIAM J. Comput. 18(1), 186–208 (1989)

46. Groth, J.: Short pairing-based non-interactive zero-knowledge arguments. In: Abe, M. (ed.) ASIACRYPT 2010. LNCS, vol. 6477, pp. 321–340. Springer, Heidelberg (2010). https://doi.org/10.1007/978-3-642-17373-8_19

47. Groth, J.: On the size of pairing-based non-interactive arguments. In: Fischlin, M., Coron, J.-S. (eds.) EUROCRYPT 2016, Part II. LNCS, vol. 9666, pp. 305–326. Springer, Heidelberg (2016). https://doi.org/10.1007/978-3-662-49896-5_11

48. Groth, J., Kohlweiss, M., Maller, M., Meiklejohn, S., Miers, I.: Updatable and universal common reference strings with applications to zk-SNARKs. In: Shacham, H., Boldyreva, A. (eds.) CRYPTO 2018, Part III. LNCS, vol. 10993, pp. 698–728. Springer, Cham (2018). https://doi.org/10.1007/978-3-319-96878-0_24

49. Gvili, Y., Ha, J., Varia, S.S.M., Yang, Z., Zhang, X.: TurboIKOS (2021). https://github.com/sarahscheffler/TurboIKOS

50. Heath, D., Kolesnikov, V.: Stacked garbling for disjunctive zero-knowledge proofs. In: Canteaut, A., Ishai, Y. (eds.) EUROCRYPT 2020, Part III. LNCS, vol. 12107, pp. 569–598. Springer, Cham (2020). https://doi.org/10.1007/978-3-030-45727-3_19

51. Ishai, Y., Kushilevitz, E., Ostrovsky, R., Sahai, A.: Zero-knowledge from secure multiparty computation. In: Johnson, D.S., Feige, U. (eds.) 39th ACM STOC, pp. 21–30. ACM Press, June 2007

52. Ishai, Y., Kushilevitz, E., Ostrovsky, R., Sahai, A.: Cryptography with constant computational overhead. In: Ladner, R.E., Dwork, C. (eds.) 40th ACM STOC, pp. 433–442. ACM Press, May 2008

53. Jawurek, M., Kerschbaum, F., Orlandi, C.: Zero-knowledge using garbled circuits: how to prove non-algebraic statements efficiently. In: Sadeghi, A.R., Gligor, V.D., Yung, M. (eds.) ACM CCS 2013, pp. 955–966. ACM Press, November 2013

54. Kales, D., Zaverucha, G.: An attack on some signature schemes constructed from five-pass identification schemes. In: Krenn, S., Shulman, H., Vaudenay, S. (eds.) CANS 2020. LNCS, vol. 12579, pp. 3–22. Springer, Cham (2020). https://doi.org/10.1007/978-3-030-65411-5_1

55. Katz, J., Kolesnikov, V., Wang, X.: Improved non-interactive zero knowledge with applications to post-quantum signatures. In: Lie, D., Mannan, M., Backes, M., Wang, X. (eds.) ACM CCS 2018, pp. 525–537. ACM Press, October 2018

56. Keller, M., Pastro, V., Rotaru, D.: Overdrive: making SPDZ great again. In: Nielsen, J.B., Rijmen, V. (eds.) EUROCRYPT 2018, Part III. LNCS, vol. 10822, pp. 158–189. Springer, Cham (2018). https://doi.org/10.1007/978-3-319-78372-7_6

57. Kilian, J.: A note on efficient zero-knowledge proofs and arguments (extended abstract). In: 24th ACM STOC, pp. 723–732. ACM Press, May 1992

58. Lindell, Y., Pinkas, B.: An efficient protocol for secure two-party computation in the presence of malicious adversaries. In: Naor, M. (ed.) EUROCRYPT 2007. LNCS, vol. 4515, pp. 52–78. Springer, Heidelberg (2007). https://doi.org/10.1007/978-3-540-72540-4_4

59. Lund, C., Fortnow, L., Karloff, H.J., Nisan, N.: Algebraic methods for interactive proof systems. In: 31st FOCS, pp. 2–10. IEEE Computer Society Press, October 1990

60. Maller, M., Bowe, S., Kohlweiss, M., Meiklejohn, S.: Sonic: zero-knowledge SNARKs from linear-size universal and updatable structured reference strings. In: Cavallaro, L., Kinder, J., Wang, X., Katz, J. (eds.) ACM CCS 2019, pp. 2111–2128. ACM Press, November 2019

61. Microsoft Corporation: Picnic. https://microsoft.github.io/Picnic/

62. Miers, I., Garman, C., Green, M., Rubin, A.D.: Zerocoin: anonymous distributed E-cash from Bitcoin. In: 2013 IEEE Symposium on Security and Privacy, pp. 397–411. IEEE Computer Society Press, May 2013

63. Naor, M., Pinkas, B.: Oblivious transfer and polynomial evaluation. In: 31st ACM STOC, pp. 245–254. ACM Press, May 1999

64. Nielsen, J.B., Nordholt, P.S., Orlandi, C., Burra, S.S.: A new approach to practical active-secure two-party computation. In: Safavi-Naini, R., Canetti, R. (eds.) CRYPTO 2012. LNCS, vol. 7417, pp. 681–700. Springer, Heidelberg (2012). https://doi.org/10.1007/978-3-642-32009-5_40

65. Parno, B., Howell, J., Gentry, C., Raykova, M.: Pinocchio: nearly practical verifiable computation. In: 2013 IEEE Symposium on Security and Privacy, pp. 238–252. IEEE Computer Society Press, May 2013

66. Reingold, O., Rothblum, G.N., Rothblum, R.D.: Constant-round interactive proofs for delegating computation. In: Wichs, D., Mansour, Y. (eds.) 48th ACM STOC, pp. 49–62. ACM Press, June 2016

67. Setty, S.: Spartan: efficient and general-purpose zkSNARKs without trusted setup. In: Micciancio, D., Ristenpart, T. (eds.) CRYPTO 2020, Part III. LNCS, vol. 12172, pp. 704–737. Springer, Cham (2020). https://doi.org/10.1007/978-3-030-56877-1_25

68. Setty, S., Lee, J.: Quarks: quadruple-efficient transparent zkSNARKs. Cryptology ePrint Archive, Report 2020/1275 (2020). https://eprint.iacr.org/2020/1275

69. Trail of Bits: Reverie (2021). https://github.com/trailofbits/reverie

70. Wahby, R.S., Tzialla, I., shelat, A., Thaler, J., Walfish, M.: Doubly-efficient zkSNARKs without trusted setup. In: 2018 IEEE Symposium on Security and Privacy, pp. 926–943. IEEE Computer Society Press, May 2018
71. Weng, C., Yang, K., Katz, J., Wang, X.: Wolverine: fast, scalable, and communication-efficient zero-knowledge proofs for boolean and arithmetic circuits. Cryptology ePrint Archive (2020)
72. Xie, T., Zhang, J., Zhang, Y., Papamanthou, C., Song, D.: Libra: succinct zero-knowledge proofs with optimal prover computation. In: Boldyreva, A., Micciancio, D. (eds.) CRYPTO 2019, Part III. LNCS, vol. 11694, pp. 733–764. Springer, Cham (2019). https://doi.org/10.1007/978-3-030-26954-8_24
73. Zahur, S., Rosulek, M., Evans, D.: Two halves make a whole - reducing data transfer in garbled circuits using half gates. In: Oswald, E., Fischlin, M. (eds.) EUROCRYPT 2015, Part II. LNCS, vol. 9057, pp. 220–250. Springer, Heidelberg (2015). https://doi.org/10.1007/978-3-662-46803-6_8
74. Zhang, J., Xie, T., Zhang, Y., Song, D.: Transparent polynomial delegation and its applications to zero knowledge proof. In: 2020 IEEE Symposium on Security and Privacy, pp. 859–876. IEEE Computer Society Press, May 2020

Cryptanalysis of the Binary Permuted Kernel Problem

Thales Bandiera Paiva[(✉)][iD] and Routo Terada[iD]

Universidade de São Paulo, São Paulo, Brazil
{tpaiva,rt}@ime.usp.br

Abstract. In 1989, Shamir presented an efficient identification scheme (IDS) based on the permuted kernel problem (PKP). After 21 years, PKP was generalized by Lampe and Patarin, who were able to build an IDS similar to Shamir's one, but using the binary field. This binary variant presented some interesting advantages over Shamir's original IDS, such as reduced number of operations and inherently resistance against side-channel attacks. In the security analysis, considering the best attacks against the original PKP, the authors concluded that none of these existing attacks appeared to have a significant advantage when attacking the binary variant. In this paper, we propose the first attack that targets the binary PKP. The attack is analyzed in detail, and its practical performance is compared with our theoretical models. For the proposed parameters originally targeting 79 and 98 bits of security, our attack can recover about 100% of all keys using less than 2^{63} and 2^{77} operations, respectively.

Keywords: Permuted kernel problem · Cryptanalysis · Post-quantum cryptography

1 Introduction

With the engineering progress on building larger quantum computers, the main cryptographic schemes used today become more and more vulnerable. Since 2016, the National Institute of Standards and Technology (NIST), is running a standardization process for post-quantum cryptography [4]. A similar initiative is conducted by the Chinese Association for Cryptographic Research (CACR).

One of the candidate for CACR's competition is PKP-DSS [3], a digital signature scheme based on the hardness of the permuted kernel problem (PKP). This signature scheme is obtained by applying the Fiat-Shamir [6] transform on Shamir's PKP-based identification scheme [20], which dates back from 1989. Given a matrix $\mathbf{A}$ and a vector $\mathbf{v}$ with elements in a finite field, PKP asks to find a permutation of the entries of $\mathbf{v}$ that is in the kernel of $\mathbf{A}$. PKP is NP-hard

T. B. Paiva is supported by CAPES. R. Terada is supported by CNPq grant number 442014/2014-7.

K. Sako and N. O. Tippenhauer (Eds.): ACNS 2021, LNCS 12727, pp. 396–423, 2021.
https://doi.org/10.1007/978-3-030-78375-4_16

and there is no known quantum algorithm which have a significant advantage over classical algorithms when solving the problem.

In 2010, Lampe and Patarin proposed a generalized version of PKP, in which vector $\mathbf{v}$ is substituted by a matrix $\mathbf{V}$. This enabled them to instantiate PKP in the binary field, without an apparent security loss. At the time, this binary variant presented some interesting advantages such as a reduction in the number of operations and an inherently resistance to side-channel attacks. To estimate the security of binary PKP, the authors considered the best attacks against the original PKP, with minor adjustments to make they work against the binary variant. They noted that none of the available attacks was significantly faster against binary PKP.

However, the use of binary coefficients for matrix $\mathbf{A}$ comes with a security risk. We observed that low weight binary words occur with non-negligible probability in two public spaces: one is generated by the matrix $\mathbf{A}$ while the other is generated by the kernel of $\mathbf{V}$. It is then possible to devise an attack against binary PKP by matching these low weight codewords using subgraph isomorphism algorithms, and recovering the secret permutation from these matchings.

Contribution. In this paper, we present the first attack that specifically targets the binary PKP. Unlike previous attacks, which need a very large amount of memory to run efficiently, our attack uses only a negligible amount of memory. This allows us to provide a concrete implementation of the attack. We provide a detailed analysis of the attack, and then compare these results with the attack's performance in practice. As an example of the power of the attack: for binary PKP parameters originally targeting 80 bits of security, it uses about 2^{63} CPU cycles to fully recover the key, while the best previously known attack [12] needs about 2^{76} matrix-vector multiplications and 2^{50} bytes of memory.

Paper Organization. In Sect. 2, we introduce our notation and review basic concepts of Coding Theory. Then, PKP and its binary variant are presented in Sect. 3, where we also review previous attacks against PKP. The attack is described in Sect. 4 and its performance is analyzed in Sect. 5. The asymptotic analysis of the attack is given in Sect. 6. In Sect. 7 we briefly describe how to choose secure parameters for binary PKP. In Sect. 8 we conclude and provide directions for future work.

2   Background

This section introduces the notation and reviews important concepts in Coding Theory.

Notation. Vectors and matrices are denoted by lower and upper case bold letters, respectively. In general, vectors are rows, except when explicitly mentioning specific columns of matrices. If ϕ is a permutation of n elements and $\mathbf{M}$ is an $n \times n$ matrix, then $\mathbf{M}_\phi$ and $\phi(\mathbf{M})$ correspond to the action of permutation ϕ

over rows and columns of $\mathbf{M}$, respectively. For any matrix $\mathbf{X}$, we denote its i-th column as $(\mathbf{X})^i$. We denote the finite field of q elements as $\mathbb{F}_q$.

We abuse the factorial notation to avoid overloading expressions in the analysis of the attack. For any $x \in [0, +\infty)$, we let

$$
x! = \begin{cases} \Gamma(x+1), & \text{if } x \geq 1, \text{ and} \\ 1, & \text{otherwise.} \end{cases}
$$

Clearly it does not affect the definition of factorials of integers. Furthermore, it allows us to evaluate upper bounds of products of factorials of real numbers without having to worry about the interval $x \in (0,1)$, where $\Gamma(x+1) < 1$, which could make the product vanish rapidly. Using this notation, we can then write $\binom{x}{y} = x!/((x-y)!y!)$, for $x, y \in [0, +\infty)$ with $x > y$. These will make for a more clear description of our approximations in Sect. 5.

Coding Theory. A binary $[n, k]$-linear code is a k-dimensional linear subspace of $\mathbb{F}_2^n$, where $\mathbb{F}_2$ denotes the binary field. Let $\mathcal{C}$ be a binary $[n, k]$-linear code. If $\mathcal{C}$ is the linear subspace spanned by the rows of a matrix $\mathbf{G}$ in $\mathbb{F}_2^{k \times n}$, we say that $\mathbf{G}$ is a generator matrix of $\mathcal{C}$. The Hamming weight of a vector $\mathbf{v}$, denoted by $\mathrm{w}(\mathbf{v})$, is the number of its non-null entries. The support of a vector $\mathbf{v}$, denoted by $\mathrm{supp}(\mathbf{v})$, is the set of indexes of its non-null entries.

3   The Permuted Kernel Problem

Let us begin by formally defining the permuted kernel problem. Let $\mathbf{A}$ be an $m \times n$ matrix and $\mathbf{v}$ be a vector of n entries whose coordinates are taken from a finite field $\mathbb{F}_p$. Then, the permuted kernel problem asks to find some permutation π of the coordinates of $\mathbf{v}$ such that $\mathbf{A}\mathbf{v}_\pi^\top = \mathbf{0}$.

PKP is well-known to be NP-hard [8], and it is conjectured to be hard on the average case. The naive approach to solve this problem would be to test all permutations of the entries of $\mathbf{v}$. Intuitively, there are two components which make the problem hard. The first is the large number of possible permutations, which is close to $n!$, when $\mathbf{v}$ does not have a large number of equal entries. The second is the small number of permutations of $\mathbf{v}$ which are in the kernel of $\mathbf{A}$.

In 2011, Lampe and Patarin [13] considered a PKP variant with $p = 2$. The authors pointed a few problems when transitioning to the binary setting that need to be taken into account. One is that the number of different permutations is significantly reduced, since every two binary vectors of the same weight are equal, up to some permutation. Furthermore, for a fixed matrix $\mathbf{A}$, there are effectively only n possibilities for $\mathbf{v}$, corresponding to one for each possible value of $\mathrm{w}(\mathbf{v})$. To avoid these problems, they proposed the use of an $n \times \ell$ matrix $\mathbf{V}$ instead of the vector $\mathbf{v}$, obtaining the following PKP variant.

Definition 1 (Binary PKP [13]). *Let $\mathbf{A}$ be an $m \times n$ binary matrix and $\mathbf{V}$ be an $n \times \ell$ binary matrix. Then, the permuted kernel problem asks to find some permutation π of the rows of $\mathbf{V}$ such that $\mathbf{A}\mathbf{V}_\pi = \mathbf{0}$.*

Notice that the original PKP can be seen as an instance of this generalized variant, by taking p instead of 2, and $\ell = 1$.

Even though the main interest on PKP is for the construction of signature schemes, we will not review details of Shamir's protocol [20] or PKP-DSS [3] this construction because they are not relevant for our attack.

3.1 Previous Attacks on PKP

After Shamir introduced the PKP-based IDS [20], there has been some effort to find efficient algorithms to solve the problem. In 1990, Georgiades [9] discussed how one can use symmetric equations, such as the sum of the entries of $\mathbf{v}$ or the sum of their squares, can help in lowering the number of permutations one needs to test. This, combined with the linear relations among the coordinates of kernel elements, can reduce the number of permutations to test in a brute force attack from $n!$ to $n!/(m+2)!$ permutations.

Soon after, in 1992, Baritaud et al. [1] proposed a time-memory tradeoff, where one first precompute a large table of partial solutions, which is then used to speed up a bruteforce search. In particular, for attack parameters (k, k'), their algorithm searches for solutions of a set of $k \leq m$ equations, after precomputing partial values of the equations when some set of k' variables are fixed by some arrangement of the entries in $\mathbf{v}$.

In 1993, Patarin and Chauvaud [17] showed a significant improvement on the cryptanalysis of PKP, which is also based on a time-memory tradeoff. Their idea was to partition the variables of the linear equation $\mathbf{A}\mathbf{v}_{\pi}^{\top} = \mathbf{0}$ into two sets. For one set, all the possible values for their linear combination is computed and stored in a file. Then, a brute-force search, which is sped-up by the precomputed values, is used to find the values of the other set of variables. Furthermore, in 1997, Poupard [18] provided a careful and realistic extension on the analysis of Patarin and Chauvaud's algorithm by considering the impact of reasonable memory limitations on the time-memory trade-off.

In 2001, Jaulmes and Joux [10] proposed a new attack against PKP, which is also based on a time-memory tradeoff, but used a very different strategy. Their attack consists in adapting an algorithm for counting points in an elliptic curve [11] to solve a new problem, called 4SET, to which PKP can be reduced. Interestingly, this approach resulted in an algorithm somewhat similar to the one by Patarin and Chavaud [17], but, for years after the attack was published, it appeared to be more efficient.

More recently, in 2019, Koussa, Macario-Rat and Patarin [12] presented two important contributions on the hardness of PKP. Their first contribution is to provide a detailed analysis of the attack proposed by Jaulmes and Joux [10], which was considered to be the most efficient attack against PKP. They concluded that Jaulmes and Joux's attack may not be as efficient as previously thought for the current PKP security parameters. Koussa, Macario-Rat and Patarin's second contribution is a combination of the ideas of Patarin and Chauvaud [17] with the ones by Poupard [18] to obtain a new algorithm to solve PKP, together with a detailed analysis on their time and space complexity.

The main drawback of Koussa's et al. attack is that they use a significant amount of memory, and their implementation may not be efficient in practice. Moreover, all of the published attacks against PKP target the original version of the problem. And even though they all can be adapted to attack the binary PKP, as done by Lampe and Patarin [13] for their analysis, it appears that none of the attacks are significantly more efficient in the binary case.

3.2 Instantiation

We now present the parameter sets for PKP, in which the security level is estimated based on the best attacks available by Koussa et al. [12]. Table 1 shows these parameter sets for different security levels. The focus of this work is in the parameter sets given in the first two rows, corresponding to the binary PKP. It is important to notice that what we now consider to be the parameter sets BPKP–76 and BPKP–89, originally targeted security levels 79 and 98, respectively. However, these had to be revised after Koussa et al.'s [12] attack.

Table 1. Parameter sets for different security levels. The security level is estimated based on the attack by Koussa et al. [12].

Parameter set	Security level	Targeted security level when proposed	p	n	m	ℓ
BPKP–76 [13]	76	79	2	38	15	10
BPKP–89 [13]	89	98	2	42	15	11
PKP–128 [3]	128	128	251	69	41	1
PKP–192 [3]	192	192	509	94	54	1
PKP-256 [3]	256	256	4093	106	47	1

4 A Novel Attack Against Binary PKP

We are given the public matrices $\mathbf{A}$ and $\mathbf{V}$ and we want to find the secret permutation π such that $\mathbf{A}\mathbf{V}_\pi = \mathbf{0}$. Let $\mathcal{C}_\mathbf{A}$ and $\mathcal{C}_\mathbf{K}$ be the binary codes generated by $\mathbf{A}$ and $\mathbf{K}$, respectively, where $\mathbf{K}$ is the left kernel matrix of $\mathbf{V}$. Fix an integer w small enough so that we can build the sets $\mathcal{L}_\mathbf{A}^w$ and $\mathcal{L}_\mathbf{K}^w$ consisting of all the codewords of weight w in $\mathcal{C}_\mathbf{A}$ and $\mathcal{C}_\mathbf{K}$, correspondingly. Notice that, since $\mathbf{A}\mathbf{V}_\pi = \mathbf{0}$, then $\mathcal{L}_\mathbf{A}^w \subset \mathcal{L}_{\pi(\mathbf{K})}^w = \{\mathbf{u}_\pi : \mathbf{u} \in \mathcal{L}_\mathbf{K}^w\}$.

This idea gives the following simple algorithm to find the secret permutation π. First find a subset S of $\mathcal{L}_\mathbf{K}^w$, such that, for some permutation τ, $\mathcal{L}_\mathbf{A}^w = \{\mathbf{u}_\tau : \mathbf{u} \in S\}$. Then, test if the corresponding column permutation τ is valid, that is, if $\mathbf{A}\mathbf{V}_\tau = \mathbf{0}$. If τ is valid, return it as π. Otherwise, restart the search. Figure 1 can be useful for visualizing the relationship between the two sets of codewords, which is the core of the attack.

Secret permutation π

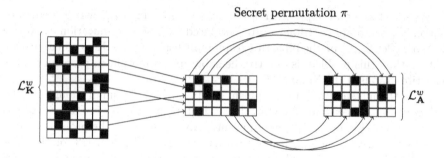

Fig. 1. Illustration of the relationship between $\mathcal{L}_A^w$ and $\mathcal{L}_K^w$ with respect to the secret column permutation π for codewords of weight $w = 2$. White and black squares represent null and non-null entries, respectively.

Even though it has a rather simple description, we need to carefully deal with the following two problems. The first one is that matching vectors in $\mathcal{L}_A^w$ and a subset of $\mathcal{L}_K^w$ is closely related to the subgraph isomorphism problem, which is NP-hard [8]. The second problem is that, since we are dealing with sparse codewords, there may be a large number of repeated columns in $\mathcal{L}_A^w$. This could potentially make it infeasible to find the secret permutation π because of the combinatorial explosion on the number of possible permutations between columns.

In the following sections, we formally describe the algorithms for the attack against the binary PKP. Then, after this initial exposition, each component of the algorithm is analyzed in Sect. 5.

4.1 Searching for Codewords of Small Weight

The problem of finding codewords of small weight is hard in general, with the security of some well known cryptographic schemes, such as McEliece's one [15], depend on this problem's hardness. However, in the binary PKP setting, the length n of the codes in question, namely C_A and C_K, is typically very small, which makes it even possible to use brute force. Using brute force, one has to test exactly if $\binom{n}{w}$ words are elements of each of the codes.

A better approach would be to use specialized algorithms from Coding Theory such as Stern's algorithm [22], which we used in our attack implementation, or its improved variants [2,7]. All of these are well-known probabilistic algorithms that can be used to find low weight codewords in binary codes.

4.2 Searching for Matchings

Aiming to simplify the description of the attack, we identify sets $\mathcal{L}_A^w$ and $\mathcal{L}_K^w$ as matrices where each row is one vector in the corresponding set. This is arguably a natural identification when we consider a real implementation of the algorithm in a programming language such as C.

We now focus on the problem of finding a submatrix of $\mathcal{L}_{\mathbf{K}}^{w}$ which is equal to matrix $\mathcal{L}_{\mathbf{A}}^{w}$ when its coordinates are permuted by some permutation τ. Notice that, if we let $\mathcal{G}(\mathbf{X})$ be the bipartite graph built using matrix $\mathbf{X}$ as a biadjacency matrix, then this problem is exactly the subgraph isomorphism problem for the bipartite graphs $\mathcal{G}(\mathcal{L}_{\mathbf{A}}^{w})$ and $\mathcal{G}(\mathcal{L}_{\mathbf{K}}^{w})$.

Even though subgraph isomorphism is NP-hard [8], for small enough inputs, the problem has been widely studied because of its importance in Pattern Recognition. It is well-known that, for sufficiently small instances, the problem can be solved efficiently using algorithms such as the one by Ullman [23] or the ones from the VF family [5, 19]. The main problem with these widely used algorithms is that they use heuristics that make it hard to perform a sound average case complexity analysis for our case. Since such analysis is critical for estimating the concrete security of the scheme, we propose a different algorithm with two remarkable advantages. The first one is that it runs faster than other generic subgraph isomorphism algorithms for our specific case of bipartite graphs. The second is that it is simpler to analyze and give realistic estimates on its performance.

The algorithm we propose is based on a simple depth-first search strategy. In each level α of the search, a node represents a matrix built using a set of α rows of $\mathcal{L}_{\mathbf{K}}^{w}$ which is equal to the first α rows of $\mathcal{L}_{\mathbf{A}}^{w}$, when its columns are permuted by some permutation. Whenever a matching is found, the searching algorithm calls a procedure that tries to extract the secret permutation from the matching. In the following sections, we describe each component of the algorithm in more detail.

Signature of a Matrix. It is crucial for the subgraph isomorphism algorithms to efficiently determine whether a matrix $\mathbf{S}$ is equal to a submatrix of $\mathcal{L}_{\mathbf{A}}^{w}$ up to some column permutation. For this task, we can use a function σ such that, if $\sigma(\mathbf{S}_1) = \sigma(\mathbf{S}_2)$, then with high probability $\mathbf{S}_1 = \tau(\mathbf{S}_2)$ for some permutation τ, for any two matrices $\mathbf{S}_1$ and $\mathbf{S}_2$ with equal dimensions.

One easy way to build such a function is to sort the columns of $\mathbf{S}$ using a lexicographical ordering obtaining $\mathbf{S}^{\text{Sorted}}$. Then, the signature of $\mathbf{S}$ is simply $\sigma(\mathbf{S}) = h(\mathbf{S}^{\text{Sorted}})$, for some cryptographic hash function h. It is clear, by this construction, that σ is invariant with respect to column permutations.

The problem with sorting is that, since this function will be executed a very large number of times, it can become expensive. One alternative is to use the following approximation $\sigma(\mathbf{S}) = \sum_{\mathbf{c} \text{ column of } \mathbf{S}} h(\mathbf{c})$, for some hash function h.

Precomputation of Signatures. This step consists in building the $|\mathcal{L}_{\mathbf{A}}^{w}| \times |\mathcal{L}_{\mathbf{A}}^{w}|$ matrix $\mathbf{H}$ containing signatures of submatrices of $\mathcal{L}_{\mathbf{A}}^{w}$ that are used for pruning the possible child nodes in each level of the search. Let $\mathbf{a}_1, \ldots, \mathbf{a}_{|\mathcal{L}_{\mathbf{A}}^{w}|}$ be the vectors in $\mathcal{L}_{\mathbf{A}}^w$, and let $\mathbf{L}_j$ denote the matrix formed by the first j rows of $\mathcal{L}_{\mathbf{A}}^w$. Then, we let

$$
\mathbf{H}_{i,j} = \left\{ \begin{array}{ll} \sigma\left(\begin{bmatrix} \mathbf{L}_j \\ \hline \mathbf{a}_i \end{bmatrix}\right) & \text{if } i > j, \text{ and} \\[3ex] 0 & \text{otherwise.} \end{array} \right. \tag{1}
$$

Key Recovery Algorithm. In this step, the algorithm effectively tries to build a submatrix $\mathbf{S}$ of $\mathcal{L}_{\mathbf{K}}^w$ such that $\tau(\mathbf{S}) = \mathcal{L}_{\mathbf{A}}^w$, for some column permutation τ. The algorithm is formally described as Algorithm 1 but we give a brief description next.

Algorithm 1: KEYSEARCH: Key search algorithm using depth-first search

---

Data: $\mathbf{A}$ and $\mathbf{V}$: the PKP public parameters
$\quad\quad\mathcal{L}_{\mathbf{A}}^w$: a set of codewords in $\mathcal{C}_{\mathbf{A}}$ of weight w
$\quad\quad\mathcal{L}_{\mathbf{K}}^w$: the set of all codewords in $\mathcal{C}_{\mathbf{K}}$ of weight w
$\quad\quad\mathbf{H}$: the precomputed matrix of signatures
$\quad\quad\alpha$: the level in the search tree (initially, $\alpha = 0$)
$\quad\quad\mathbf{S}$: an $\alpha \times n$ matrix (initially, $\mathbf{S}$ is the empty $0 \times n$ matrix)
$\quad\quad\mathcal{P} = \left(P_1, \ldots, P_{|\mathcal{L}_{\mathbf{A}}^w|}\right)$: the sets of children (initially, each $P_i = \mathcal{L}_{\mathbf{K}}^w$)
Result: π: a permutation such that $\mathbf{A}\mathbf{V}_\pi = \mathbf{0}$ or $\perp$ if none exists

1 **begin**
2 $\quad$ **if** $\alpha = |\mathcal{L}_{\mathbf{A}}^w|$ **then**
3 $\quad\quad$ **return** EXTRACTPERMUTATIONFROMMATCHING$(\mathbf{A}, \mathbf{V}, \mathbf{S})$
$\quad$ /* Updates the possible children for each level not yet defined: */
4 $\quad$ **for** $i = \alpha + 1$ *to* $|\mathcal{L}_{\mathbf{A}}^w|$ **do**
5 $\quad\quad$ $\hat{P}_i \leftarrow \left\{ \mathbf{p} \in P_i : \sigma\left(\begin{bmatrix} \mathbf{S} \\ \hline \mathbf{p} \end{bmatrix}\right) = \mathbf{H}_{i,\alpha} \right\}$
6 $\quad$ $\mathcal{P} \leftarrow \left(P_1, \ldots, P_\alpha, \hat{P}_{\alpha+1}, \ldots, \hat{P}_{|\mathcal{L}_{\mathbf{A}}^w|}\right)$
7 $\quad$ **for** *each* $\mathbf{p}$ *in* $\hat{P}_{\alpha+1}$ **do**
8 $\quad\quad$ Update $\mathbf{S}$ by inserting $\mathbf{p}$ as its last row
$\quad\quad$ /* Recursive call: */
9 $\quad\quad$ $\pi \leftarrow$ KEYSEARCH$(\mathbf{A}, \mathbf{V}, \mathcal{L}_{\mathbf{A}}^w, \mathcal{L}_{\mathbf{K}}^w, \mathbf{H}, \alpha + 1, \mathbf{S}, \mathcal{P})$
10 $\quad\quad$ **if** $\pi \neq \perp$ **then**
11 $\quad\quad\quad$ **return** π
12 $\quad\quad$ Update $\mathbf{S}$ by removing its last row $\mathbf{p}$
13 $\quad$ **return** $\perp$

The search starts at level $\alpha = 0$, with $\mathbf{S}$ being a $0 \times n$ empty matrix. At each level α in the search tree, the algorithm runs a pruning procedure, that updates the lists of possible vectors for each level greater than α using the precomputed matrix of signatures $\mathbf{H}$. This ensures that the main invariant of the recursive algorithm is that, at level α, the algorithm holds an $\alpha \times n$ submatrix $\mathbf{S}$ of $\mathcal{L}_{\mathbf{K}}^w$ which is equal to the matrix formed by the first α rows of $\mathcal{L}_{\mathbf{A}}^w$, up to some column permutation. The search proceeds by selecting a vector from set $P_{\alpha+1} \subset \mathcal{L}_{\mathbf{K}}^w$ of vectors which can be safely added to the next level without breaking the invariant. Each time the algorithm successfully gets to a leaf, that is, it adds a vector to level $\alpha = |\mathcal{L}_\mathbf{A}^w|$, then a full matching $\mathbf{S}$ is found and the procedure that tries to extract the permutation π from matching $\mathbf{S}$ is executed. If the permutation π is successfully extracted, then π is returned. Otherwise, the depth-first search proceeds.

The procedure for extracting the secret permutation from the matching, if possible, is described in the next section.

4.3   Extracting Permutations from Matchings

After each each matching found in the previous step, we are given a matrix $\mathbf{S}$ such that $\tau(\mathbf{S}) = \mathcal{L}_\mathbf{A}^w$ for at least one permutation of columns τ. In this section we describe how to efficiently extract the secret permutation π from this matching, if possible.

We first consider the brute force solution. Let T be the set of permutations that match equal columns in $\mathbf{S}$ and $\mathcal{L}_\mathbf{A}^w$. Then, we can just test, for each permutation τ in T, if $\mathbf{AV}_\tau = \mathbf{0}$. If one such τ is found, then the algorithm returns $\pi \leftarrow \tau$. Suppose that there are β unique columns $\mathbf{c}_1, \ldots, \mathbf{c}_\beta$ of matrix $\mathcal{L}_\mathbf{A}^w$, and let c_i denote the number of times column $\mathbf{c}_i$ appears in $\mathcal{L}_\mathbf{A}^w$. This implies that the number of candidate permutations is given by $|T| = \prod_{i=1}^{\beta} (c_i!)$. The brute force approach may be efficient when $\mathbf{S}$ has a large number of unique columns. However, due to the combinatorial nature of this problem, even a small increase in the number of equal columns can make the algorithm very inefficient.

To reduce the number of permutations to test we can use the fact that $\dim(\ker \mathbf{A}) = n - m$. Therefore, there are $n - m$ rows of $\mathbf{V}_\pi$ which, together with the m equations defined by $\mathbf{A}$, completely determine the other m rows of $\mathbf{V}_\pi$. Intuitively, this means we can focus on partial permutations in T corresponding to these $n - m$ indexes.

More formally, let I_1 and I_2 be a partition of the set of possible n indexes such that $|I_1| = m$ and the $m \times m$ matrix $\mathbf{A}_1$ built using the columns from $\mathbf{A}$ whose indexes are in I_1 is invertible. Similarly, let $\mathbf{A}_2$ be the $m \times (n - m)$ matrix whose columns are taken from $\mathbf{A}$, but with indexes in I_2. Let ϕ be the permutation of n elements such that $\phi(\mathbf{A}) = [\mathbf{A}_1 | \mathbf{A}_2]$, and define as $\mathbf{U}_1$ and $\mathbf{U}_2$ the matrices such that $\phi\left((\mathbf{V}_\pi)^\top\right) = (\mathbf{V}_{\pi\phi})^\top = [\mathbf{U}_1^\top | \mathbf{U}_2^\top]$. Then, we have

$$\mathbf{AV}_\pi = \phi(\mathbf{A})\mathbf{V}_{\pi\phi} = [\mathbf{A}_1 | \mathbf{A}_2] \begin{bmatrix} \mathbf{U}_1 \\ \mathbf{U}_2 \end{bmatrix} = \mathbf{A}_1\mathbf{U}_1 + \mathbf{A}_2\mathbf{U}_2 = \mathbf{0},$$

which implies that $\mathbf{U}_1 = \left(\mathbf{A}_1^{-1}\mathbf{A}_2\right)\mathbf{U}_2$.

Therefore, one can reduce the number of permutations in T to test by using the following procedure. Let I be a sequence of n column indexes sorted, in decreasing order, by the number of times in which the corresponding column of matrix $\mathcal{L}_\mathbf{A}^w$ occurs in this same matrix.[1] Now let I_1 to be composed by the first

---

[1] The reason why it is interesting to sort the indexes in this way is explained in the last paragraph of this section.

m indexes in I whose corresponding columns of $\mathbf{A}$ are linearly independent, and let $I_2 = I - I_1 = \{i_1, \ldots, i_{n-m}\}$. Consider the set

$$\mathcal{J} = \left\{ (j_1, \ldots, j_{n-m}) : (\mathbf{S})^{j_k} = (\mathcal{L}_{\mathbf{A}}^w)^{i_k} \text{ for all } k = 1, \ldots, n - m \right\},$$

where $(\mathbf{X})^y$ denotes the y-th column of matrix $\mathbf{X}$. Intuitively, set $\mathcal{J}$ captures the parts of the permutations in T corresponding only to the $n - m$ indexes in I_2, and therefore $|\mathcal{J}|$ may be much smaller than $|T|$. For each sequence J of $\mathcal{J}$, we let $\mathbf{U}_2$ be the $(n-r) \times \ell$ matrix built from rows of $\mathbf{V}$ whose indexes are in J. For each of these possible values of $\mathbf{U}_2$, we compute the matrix $\mathbf{U}_1 = \left(\mathbf{A}_1^{-1} \mathbf{A}_2 \right) \mathbf{U}_2$, and test if $\begin{bmatrix} \mathbf{U}_1 \\ \mathbf{U}_2 \end{bmatrix}$ corresponds to a permutation of the rows of $\mathbf{V}$. If this is indeed the case, then the secret matrix $\mathbf{V}_\pi$ is simply $\mathbf{V}_\pi = \begin{bmatrix} \mathbf{U}_1 \\ \mathbf{U}_2 \end{bmatrix}_{\phi^{-1}}$.

It is important to notice that, since we want to make $|\mathcal{J}|$ as low as possible, we sorted the set of indexes I so that, when defining I_1 and I_2, the columns of $\mathcal{L}_{\mathbf{A}}^w$ whose indexes are in I_2 tend to appear a lower number of times. In Sect. 5.3, we show how to estimate the size of $\mathcal{J}$.

5   Concrete Analysis of the Attack

In this section we estimate the attack complexity. We begin by analyzing, in the first three subsections, the work factor of the three components of the attack algorithm: building sets $\mathcal{L}_{\mathbf{A}}^w$ and $\mathcal{L}_{\mathbf{K}}^w$, matching the low weight vectors in these sets, and extracting the secret permutation from matchings. Then, we put these components together to give the complexity of the attack in Sect. 5.4. Finally, in Sect. 5.5, we show the performance of the attack in practice.

The work factor of attacks against PKP is typically stated in number of matrix-vector products, as it is the basic operation to test if a vector is in the kernel of a matrix. Even though binary PKP uses two matrices, we can see the rows of $\mathbf{V}$ as elements of $\mathbb{F}_{2^\ell}$ and, since ℓ is typically small, then the product $\mathbf{AV}$ can be seen as a matrix-vector multiplication where sum is replaced by a XOR.

5.1   Searching for Codewords of Small Weight

Let us analyze the first step of the attack: the construction of sets $\mathcal{L}_{\mathbf{A}}^w$ and $\mathcal{L}_{\mathbf{K}}^w$. Each of these sets can be computed by searching exhaustively the whole set of $\binom{n}{w}$ possible vectors of n bits of weight w, and testing if they belong to $\mathcal{C}_{\mathbf{A}}$ and $\mathcal{C}_{\mathbf{K}}$. However, as we pointed in Sect. 4.1, we can do a lot better by using Stern's [22] algorithm. Consider a random $[n, k]$–linear code generated by matrix $\mathbf{G}$. Given parameters (p, q), Stern's algorithm first permutes the columns of $\mathbf{G}$ hoping to obtain a matrix $\hat{\mathbf{G}} = \phi(\mathbf{G})$, called a good permutation, for which there is a linear combination of its rows that has the form $\mathbf{c} = [\mathbf{c}_1 | \mathbf{c}_2 | \mathbf{c}_3 | \mathbf{c}_4]$, such that

$\mathrm{w}\,(\mathbf{c}_1) = \mathrm{w}\,(\mathbf{c}_2) = p$, component $\mathbf{c}_3$ is the zero vector of length q, and $\mathbf{c}_4$ has weight $\mathrm{w}\,(\mathbf{c}_4) = w - 2p$.

When such conditions are met, Stern's algorithm finds a vector $\mathbf{c}$ with such properties, which can then be permuted to give a vector $\mathbf{c}_{\phi-1}$ of weight w in the code generated by $\mathbf{G}$. To compute the work factor of Stern's algorithm then, we have to take into account the average number of iterations until it chooses a good permutation $\hat{\mathbf{G}}$ and the average number of operations performed by the algorithm each time. Considering Finiasz and Sendrier's [7] approximation, which takes parameter $q \approx \log\binom{k/2}{p}$, the work factor of Stern's algorithm, considering the number of binary operations, until it gives us a random codeword of weight w in a random $[n,k]$–linear code is

$$\mathbf{BinOpsWF}_{\mathrm{Stern}}^{(n,k,w)} \approx \min_{p} \frac{2q\binom{n}{w}}{\binom{n-k-q}{w-2p}\binom{k/2}{p}}.$$

Each time Stern's algorithm runs successfully, it finds a random codeword of weight w. Therefore we can model the expected number of iterations until all codewords are found as an instance of the coupon collector problem. Let us consider the time to build $\mathcal{L}_{\mathbf{A}}^{w}$. Each low weight vectors is modeled as a coupon, and we need to collect all $\ell_{\mathbf{A}}$ of them. Let C be the random variable that counts the number of low weight vectors we need to find before obtaining $\ell_{\mathbf{A}}$ different vectors. Then, it is well known that $\mathbb{E}\,(C) = \Theta\,(\ell_{\mathbf{A}} \log \ell_{\mathbf{A}})$. Furthermore, the upper tail estimate for the coupon collector problem ensures that

$$\Pr\,(C \le \gamma_{\mathbf{A}} \ell_{\mathbf{A}} \log \ell_{\mathbf{A}}) \le \ell_{\mathbf{A}}^{-\gamma_{\mathbf{A}}+1}.$$

Let $\mathbf{WF}_{\mathcal{L}_{\mathbf{A}}^{w}}$ be the work factor of building the set $\mathcal{L}_{\mathbf{A}}^{w}$, counted in number of binary matrix-vector multiplications. Since $\dim \mathbf{A} = m$, we can get an upper bound on $\mathbf{WF}_{\mathcal{L}_{\mathbf{A}}^{w}}$ as

$$\mathbf{WF}_{\mathcal{L}_{\mathbf{A}}^{w}}^{(n,m,w,\ell_{\mathbf{A}})} \le \mathbf{BinOpsWF}_{\mathcal{L}_{\mathbf{A}}^{w}}^{(n,m,w,\ell_{\mathbf{A}})} = \gamma_{\mathbf{A}}\,(\ell_{\mathbf{A}} \log \ell_{\mathbf{A}})\,\mathbf{BinOpsWF}_{\mathrm{STERN}}^{(n,m,w)},$$

where $\gamma_{\mathbf{A}} > 1$ is chosen so that $\ell_{\mathbf{A}}^{-\gamma_{\mathbf{A}}+1}$ gives a small error probability.

Now we want do the same thing for the construction of $\mathcal{L}_{\mathbf{K}}^{w}$. Let $\ell_{\mathbf{K}} = |\mathcal{L}_{\mathbf{K}}^{w}|$. and let us estimate $\ell_{\mathbf{K}}$. As usual in coding theory, to count elements of a given weight, we approximate the number of elements of weight w in a random code as a binomial distribution. Thus, out of the $\binom{n}{w}$ possible vectors of weight w, we expect that a fraction of $2^{\dim \mathbf{K}}/2^n$ belong to $\mathcal{C}_{\mathbf{K}}$. Since $\mathbf{K}$ is the left kernel matrix of $\mathbf{V}$, then $\dim \mathbf{K} = (n - \dim \mathbf{V}) = (n - \ell)$, and we can approximate the expected value of $\ell_{\mathbf{K}}$ as

$$\hat{\ell}_{\mathbf{K}} = \mathbb{E}\,(\ell_{\mathbf{K}}) \approx \frac{2^{n-l}}{2^n}\binom{n}{w} = 2^{-l}\binom{n}{w}. \tag{2}$$

Therefore, for some factor $\gamma_{\mathbf{K}} > 1$ we can define an upper bound on the work factor of building $\mathcal{L}_{\mathbf{K}}^{w}$ as

$$\mathbf{WF}_{\mathcal{L}_{\mathbf{K}}^{w}}^{(n,\ell,w,\ell_{\mathbf{A}})} \le \gamma_{\mathbf{K}}\left(\hat{\ell}_{\mathbf{K}} \log \hat{\ell}_{\mathbf{K}}\right)\mathbf{BinOpsWF}_{\mathrm{STERN}}^{(n,n-\ell,w)}.$$

Notice that if $\mathcal{L}_{\mathbf{K}}^w$ does not contain the permutations of all vectors of $\mathcal{L}_{\mathbf{A}}^w$, then the search will fail. Thus, factor $\gamma_{\mathbf{K}}$ must be chosen conservatively, but since $\ell_{\mathbf{K}}$ is typically very large, the probability $\ell_{\mathbf{K}}^{(1-\gamma_{\mathbf{K}})}$ of not collecting all vectors can be made negligible even for relatively small $\gamma_{\mathbf{K}}$.

5.2   Searching for Matchings

In this section, we evaluate the number of paths that will be tested by the subgraph isomorphism algorithm. For this evaluation, we need to estimate the number of possible child nodes in each level.

Consider the case when the search is holding matrix $\mathbf{S}$ at level α. We want to estimate the size of set $\hat{P}_{\alpha+1}$ of possible rows to add to $\mathbf{S}$ in the next level of the search. In other words, we want to compute the number of vectors that survive the filter imposed by the line 5 of Algorithm 1. The first thing to notice is that the result of the filtering is exactly the same if we filter from $\mathbf{p} \in \mathcal{L}_{\mathbf{K}}^w$ instead of $\mathbf{p} \in P_i$, that is

$$\hat{P}_i = \left\{ \mathbf{p} \in P_i : \sigma\left(\left[\frac{\mathbf{S}}{\mathbf{p}}\right]\right) = \mathbf{H}_{i,\alpha} \right\} = \left\{ \mathbf{p} \in \mathcal{L}_{\mathbf{K}}^w : \sigma\left(\left[\frac{\mathbf{S}}{\mathbf{p}}\right]\right) = \mathbf{H}_{i,\alpha} \right\}.$$

The reason why the algorithm keeps updating the list $\mathcal{P} = \left(P_1, \ldots, P_{|\mathcal{L}_{\mathbf{A}}^w|}\right)$ of possible vectors in all levels, is solely for efficiency. Without it, the filtering would be very inefficient for nodes in lower levels down the search because it would have to run, every time, through set $\mathcal{L}_{\mathbf{K}}^w$, which may be very large.

Let $\mathbf{L}_\alpha$ be the matrix formed by the first α rows of $\mathcal{L}_{\mathbf{A}}^w$, and let $\mathbf{r}$ be the $(\alpha + 1)$–th row of $\mathcal{L}_{\mathbf{A}}^w$. Now, using the definition of $\mathbf{H}_{i,\alpha}$, we want to estimate how many vectors $\mathbf{p}$ in $\mathcal{L}_{\mathbf{K}}^w$ satisfy $\sigma\left(\left[\frac{\mathbf{S}}{\mathbf{p}}\right]\right) = \sigma\left(\left[\frac{\mathbf{L}_\alpha}{\mathbf{r}}\right]\right).$

One problem that makes estimating the number of child nodes difficult is that, since vectors in $\mathcal{L}_{\mathbf{K}}^w$ are low-weight codewords of a fixed linear code, the vectors in $\mathcal{L}_{\mathbf{K}}^w$ are not independently distributed. This is a common problem when analyzing bounds on weight distribution in coding theory, and as usual in the field, we overcome this problem by assuming that the set $\mathcal{L}_{\mathbf{K}}^w$ consists of vectors chosen uniformly at random over the vectors of length n and weight w.

Now, under our model, let us fix $\mathbf{L}_\alpha$ and estimate the probability $q_{\alpha+1}(\mathbf{L}_\alpha)$ that vector $\hat{\mathbf{p}}$ of $\mathcal{L}_{\mathbf{K}}^w$ is a possible child node in $\hat{P}_{\alpha+1}$. Because of the way that the algorithm builds $\mathbf{S}$, its columns are the same as the ones of $\mathbf{L}_\alpha$, up to some permutation, and therefore

$$q_{\alpha+1}(\mathbf{L}_\alpha) = \mathrm{Pr}\left(\sigma\left(\left[\frac{\mathbf{S}}{\hat{\mathbf{p}}}\right]\right) = \sigma\left(\left[\frac{\mathbf{L}_\alpha}{\mathbf{r}}\right]\right) \right)$$

$$= \mathrm{Pr}\left(\sigma\left(\left[\frac{\mathbf{L}_\alpha}{\mathbf{p}}\right]\right) = \sigma\left(\left[\frac{\mathbf{L}_\alpha}{\mathbf{r}}\right]\right) \right),$$

where $\mathbf{p}$ is a random n–bit vector of weight w.

The signatures of the two matrices will be the same if the columns above the non-null entries of $\mathbf{p}$ and $\mathbf{r}$ are equal, up to some permutation. Therefore, $q_{\alpha+1}(\mathbf{L}_\alpha)$ is simply the probability that two subsets of w columns drawn from $\mathbf{L}_\alpha$ are the same, up to some permutation. In the simple case when all columns of $\mathbf{L}_\alpha$ are unique, then $q_{\alpha+1}(\mathbf{L}_\alpha) = 1/\binom{n}{w}$. However, in general, $\mathbf{L}_\alpha$ may have non-unique columns, which occur with high probability for small values of α, since $\mathbf{L}_\alpha$ is sparse.

Let $\mathbf{R}$ be the $\alpha \times w$ matrix built by taking columns of $\mathbf{L}_\alpha$ whose indexes are in supp $(\mathbf{r})$. Define two counting functions N and $N_{\mathbf{R}}$ that, given a column $\mathbf{c}$, output the number of times column $\mathbf{c}$ appears in matrices $\mathbf{L}_\alpha$ and $\mathbf{R}$, respectively. For each column $\mathbf{c}$, which should appear $N_{\mathbf{R}}(\mathbf{c})$ times in the columns above the non-null entries of $\mathbf{p}$, there are $\binom{N(\mathbf{c})}{N_{\mathbf{R}}(\mathbf{c})}$ ways in which different column indexes of $\mathbf{R}$ can be chosen. Therefore

$$q_{\alpha+1}(\mathbf{L}_\alpha) = \frac{1}{\binom{n}{w}} \prod_{\mathbf{c}\in\mathbb{F}_2^\alpha} \binom{N(\mathbf{c})}{N_{\mathbf{R}}(\mathbf{c})}.$$

To estimate the average attack performance, we want to compute the expected value $\bar{q}_{\alpha+1} = \mathbb{E}(q_{\alpha+1}(\mathbf{L}_\alpha))$ when $\mathbf{L}_\alpha$ is obtained from a randomly generated key. This value can be easily estimated using simulations by sampling $\mathbf{L}_\alpha$ from the set of $\alpha \times n$ matrices in which each row has weight w. However, to give an analytic approximation, we face the problem of computing the expected value of the binomial coefficients over the random variables $N(\mathbf{c})$ and $N_{\mathbf{R}}(\mathbf{c})$ for each possible column $\mathbf{c}$. To deal with this problem, we use of the following rough approximation

$$\bar{q}_{\alpha+1} \approx \frac{1}{\binom{n}{w}} \prod_{\mathbf{c}\in\mathbb{F}_2^\alpha} \binom{\mathbb{E}(N(\mathbf{c}))}{\mathbb{E}(N_{\mathbf{R}}(\mathbf{c}))}.$$

To compute the expected values $\mathbb{E}(N(\mathbf{c}))$ and $\mathbb{E}(N_{\mathbf{R}}(\mathbf{c}))$, we consider $\mathbf{L}_\alpha$ as a random sparse matrix of density w/n as an approximation of the real case where each of its rows have a fixed weight w. Under this model, the probability that a random column of $\mathbf{L}_\alpha$ is equal to $\mathbf{c}$ depends only on its the weight $k = \mathrm{w}(\mathbf{c})$ and the number α of rows in $\mathbf{L}_\alpha$. This probability is given by

$$p(k,\alpha) = \left(\frac{w}{n}\right)^k \left(1 - \frac{w}{n}\right)^{\alpha-k}. \tag{3}$$

Thus both $N(\mathbf{c})$ and $N_{\mathbf{R}}(\mathbf{c})$ follow binomial distributions with parameters $(n, p(\mathrm{w}(\mathbf{c}), \alpha))$ and $(w, p(\mathrm{w}(\mathbf{c}), \alpha))$, respectively. Therefore[2]

$$\bar{q}_{\alpha+1} \approx \frac{1}{\binom{n}{w}} \prod_{\mathbf{c} \in \mathbb{F}_2^\alpha} \binom{np(\mathrm{w}(\mathbf{c}), \alpha)}{wp(\mathrm{w}(\mathbf{c}), \alpha)}$$

$$\approx \frac{1}{\binom{n}{w}} \prod_{k=0}^{\alpha} \binom{np(k, \alpha)}{wp(k, \alpha)}^{\binom{\alpha}{k}}.$$

One can then use this analytic approximation or simulations for $\bar{q}_\alpha$ to obtain the number of possible nodes in each level as $\left|\hat{P}_\alpha\right| = \bar{q}_\alpha \hat{\ell}_{\mathbf{K}}$, where $\hat{\ell}_{\mathbf{K}} = \mathbb{E}\left(|\mathcal{L}_{\mathbf{K}}^w|\right)$ is given approximately by Eq. 2. Figure 2 shows how the analytic approximation and the value obtained by simulations compare with what is observed during a real attack. We can see that simulations can accurately be used to estimate $\bar{q}_\alpha$ and that the analytic estimate tends to overestimate the number of possible nodes in each level.

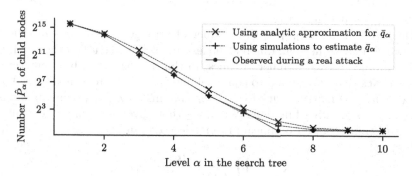

Fig. 2. Comparison of estimates on the average number of possible vectors to add in each level of the search. The attack parameters ($w = 8, \ell_{\mathbf{A}} = 10$) were used against the BPKP–76 parameter set.

The work factor of the search procedure, denoted by $\mathbf{WF}_{\mathrm{SEARCH}}$, consists of the expected number of possible paths, which is given by

$$\mathbf{WF}_{\mathrm{SEARCH}}^{(n,w,\ell_{\mathbf{A}})} = \prod_{\alpha=1}^{\ell_{\mathbf{A}}} \left|\hat{P}_\alpha\right| \approx \left(\hat{\ell}_{\mathbf{K}}\right)^{\ell_{\mathbf{A}}} \prod_{\alpha=1}^{\ell_{\mathbf{A}}} \bar{q}_\alpha.$$

---

[2] Recall, from Sect. 2, that binomials are defined over non-negative real numbers to allow our approximations.

5.3   Extracting Permutations from Matchings

We now analyze the complexity of the procedure that tries to extract the secret permutation after a matching is found. The main quantity we need to estimate is the number of permutations that the procedure needs to test each time it is called. Formally, we need to estimate the average size of set $\mathcal{J}$ for each parameter set (n, m, ℓ) when the scheme is attacked with attack parameters $(w, \ell_{\mathbf{A}})$.

Let I_1 and $I_2 = \{i_1, \ldots, i_{n-m}\}$ be the sets constructed from $\mathcal{L}_{\mathbf{A}}^w$ and $\mathbf{A}$ as described in Sect. 4.3. The first thing to notice is that $|\mathcal{J}|$ can be computed directly from matrix $\mathcal{L}_{\mathbf{A}}^w$, that is, it does not depend on a each $\mathbf{S}$. This is a consequence of the fact that, by construction, $\mathbf{S} = \tau(\mathcal{L}_{\mathbf{A}}^w)$, for some column permutation τ. Formally, what we mean is that, since[3]

$$\mathcal{J} = \left\{ (j_1, \ldots, j_{n-m}) : (\tau(\mathcal{L}_{\mathbf{A}}^w))^{j_k} = (\mathcal{L}_{\mathbf{A}}^w)^{i_k} \text{ for all } k = 1, \ldots, n-m \right\}$$

$$= \left\{ (j_1, \ldots, j_{n-m})_\tau : (\mathcal{L}_{\mathbf{A}}^w)^{j_k} = (\mathcal{L}_{\mathbf{A}}^w)^{i_k} \text{ for all } k = 1, \ldots, n-m \right\},$$

then $|\mathcal{J}| = \left| \left\{ (j_1, \ldots, j_{n-m}) : (\mathcal{L}_{\mathbf{A}}^w)^{j_k} = (\mathcal{L}_{\mathbf{A}}^w)^{i_k} \text{ for all } k = 1, \ldots, n-m \right\} \right|,$

which does not depend on τ.

Thus we can model $|\mathcal{J}|$ as the number of arrangements of $n-m$ different balls, which may come from different boxes, under the restriction that each box will be sampled a fixed number of times. In this analogy, each box represents a set of indexes that correspond to equal columns in $\mathcal{L}_{\mathbf{A}}^w$. More formally, let $\mathbf{L}_2$ be the $\ell_{\mathbf{A}} \times (n-m)$ matrix formed by taking columns of $\mathcal{L}_{\mathbf{A}}^w$ whose indexes are in I_2. Define two counting functions N and N_2 that, given a column $\mathbf{c}$, output the number of times column $\mathbf{c}$ appears in matrices $\mathcal{L}_{\mathbf{A}}^w$ and $\mathbf{L}_2$, respectively. Then, we have

$$|\mathcal{J}| = \prod_{\mathbf{c} \in \mathcal{C}_2} \frac{N(\mathbf{c})!}{(N(\mathbf{c}) - N_2(\mathbf{c}))!}.$$

Now, let us consider the expected value of $\mathcal{J}$ when $\mathbf{A}$ is a random matrix such that $\mathcal{L}_{\mathbf{A}}^w$ contains $\ell_{\mathbf{A}}$ vectors of weight w. This number can easily be estimated by simulations, which perfectly correspond to what is observed in a real attack since, up to this point no simplification has been made. Furthermore, we can also give an analytic estimate using the very same ideas from the previous section. First we approximate this case by modeling $\mathcal{L}_{\mathbf{A}}^w$ as a random $\ell_{\mathbf{A}} \times n$ sparse matrix with density w/n, and let $p(k, \ell_{\mathbf{A}})$ denote the probability that a given column of $\mathcal{L}_{\mathbf{A}}^w$ is equal to a fixed column of weight k and height $\ell_{\mathbf{A}}$, as defined by Eq. 3. Then, the rough approximation on $\mathbb{E}(|\mathcal{J}|)$ is given by

---

[3] Recall that $(\mathbf{X})^i$ denotes the i–th column of matrix $\mathbf{X}$.

$$\mathbb{E}\left(|\mathcal{J}|\right) \approx \prod_{\mathbf{c} \in \mathbb{F}_2^{\ell_\mathbf{A}}} \frac{\mathbb{E}\left(N(\mathbf{c})\right)!}{\left(\mathbb{E}\left(N(\mathbf{c})\right) - \mathbb{E}\left(N_2(\mathbf{c})\right)\right)!}$$

$$= \prod_{k=0}^{\ell_\mathbf{A}} \left(\frac{(np\left(k,\ell_\mathbf{A}\right))!}{(np\left(k,\ell_\mathbf{A}\right) - (n-m)p\left(k,\ell_\mathbf{A}\right))!} \right)^{\binom{\ell_\mathbf{A}}{k}}$$

$$= \prod_{k=0}^{\ell_\mathbf{A}} \left(\frac{(np\left(k,\ell_\mathbf{A}\right))!}{(mp\left(k,\ell_\mathbf{A}\right))!} \right)^{\binom{\ell_\mathbf{A}}{k}}.$$

Figure 3 shows how $|\mathcal{J}|$ rapidly decreases as larger values of $\ell_\mathbf{A}$ are used. It also provides a comparison between our analytic estimate on $\mathbb{E}\left(|\mathcal{J}|\right)$ and the observed values in our simulations. Notice that, for small values of $\ell_\mathbf{A}$, the analytic estimate tends to overestimate the real values of $|\mathcal{J}|$, but for sufficiently large $\ell_\mathbf{A}$, the estimate converges to the observed values. Now, since each sequence $\mathbb{E}\left(|J|\right)$ needs one matrix multiplication to be tested, we define the work factor of the permutation extraction procedure, as $\mathbf{WF}_{\mathrm{PERMS}}^{(n,m,w,\ell_\mathbf{A})} = \mathbb{E}\left(|J|\right)$.

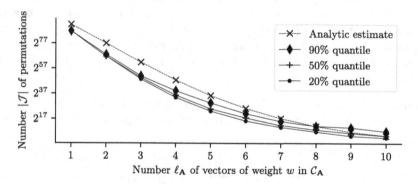

Fig. 3. The number of permutations to test after each matching considering the BPKP–76 parameter set. The attack parameter $w = 8$ was fixed, and the simulations were run for increasing values of parameter $\ell_\mathbf{A}$.

5.4 Attack Complexity

This section builds upon the three previous sections to explicitly state the attack complexity and the fraction of keys that can be attacked for different attack parameters $(w, \ell_\mathbf{A})$.

The full complexity of the attack is given by the following lemma.

Lemma 1. *Let* (n, m, ℓ) *be a binary PKP parameter set. Then, the work factor of the attack with parameters* $(w, \ell_\mathbf{A})$ *is given as*

$$\mathbf{WF}_{\mathrm{ATTACK}}^{(n,m,\ell,w,\ell_\mathbf{A})} = \mathbf{WF}_{\mathrm{LOWWEIGHTSETS}}^{(n,m,\ell,w,\ell_\mathbf{A})} + \left(\mathbf{WF}_{\mathrm{SEARCH}}^{(n,w,\ell_\mathbf{A})}\right)\left(\mathbf{WF}_{\mathrm{PERMS}}^{(n,m,w,\ell_\mathbf{A})}\right).$$

Proof. The complexity of the attack is given by summing the costs of building the sets of vectors of small weight $\mathcal{L}_{\mathbf{A}}^w$ and $\mathcal{L}_{\mathbf{K}}^w$, and the complexity of the key recovery algorithm. The cost of the key recovery algorithm is computed as follows. Remember that, for each path, from the root to one leaf, the number of permutations we have to test is given as $\mathbf{WF}_{\mathrm{PERMS}}^{(n,m,w,\ell_{\mathbf{A}})}$. Since the average number of paths is $\mathbf{WF}_{\mathrm{SEARCH}}^{(n,w,\ell_{\mathbf{A}})}$, the complexity of the key recovery algorithm is simply the product $\left(\mathbf{WF}_{\mathrm{SEARCH}}^{(n,w,\ell_{\mathbf{A}})}\right)\left(\mathbf{WF}_{\mathrm{PERMS}}^{(n,m,w,\ell_{\mathbf{A}})}\right)$. □

Figure 4 shows how $\mathbf{WF}_{\mathrm{ATTACK}}^{(n,m,\ell,w,\ell_{\mathbf{A}})}$ varies with respect to the attack parameters used, when attacking BPKP–76 parameter set. To estimate the work factor of the attack, we used simulations[4] for $\mathbf{WF}_{\mathrm{SEARCH}}^{(n,w,\ell_{\mathbf{A}})}$ and analytic estimation for $\mathbf{WF}_{\mathrm{PERMS}}^{(n,m,w,\ell_{\mathbf{A}})}$. Notice how, as $\ell_{\mathbf{A}}$ gets larger, the work factor stabilizes. This happens because the number of permutations to test gets closer to 1. Furthermore, it is clear that when w is smaller, the attack is more efficient, which happens because, in this case, $|\mathcal{L}_{\mathbf{K}}^w|$ is smaller, which makes the search much faster. The problem however, is that the attack parameters for which the attack is most efficient occur with lower probability, as we elaborate next.

Lemma 1 does not say anything about the fraction of keys that one can attack using parameters $(w, \ell_{\mathbf{A}})$. To compute this fraction, we have to take into account the probability that a public matrix $\mathbf{A}$, selected at random, generates a code with at least $\ell_{\mathbf{A}}$ codewords of weight w. This is considered in the following lemma.

Lemma 2. *Let (n, m, ℓ) be a binary PKP parameter set. Then, the fraction of keys against which the attack is effective when using parameters $(w, \ell_{\mathbf{A}})$ is given as*

$$\mathbf{KF}_{\mathrm{ATTACK}}^{n,m,\ell,w,\ell_{\mathbf{A}}} \approx 1 - e^{-\lambda}\sum_{k=0}^{\ell_{\mathbf{A}}-1}\frac{\lambda^k}{k!}, \tag{4}$$

where $\lambda = \binom{n}{w}2^{m-n}$.

Proof. Take a random matrix $\mathbf{A}$, generated with parameters (n, m, ℓ). Let L_w be the random variable that represents the number of vectors of weight w in the code generated by matrix $\mathbf{A}$. Since the code generated by $\mathbf{A}$ is a random code, we can approximate L_w by a binomial distribution which samples $\binom{n}{w}$ vectors and each one of them is in the code with probability 2^{m-n}.

The probability that $L_w \geq \ell_{\mathbf{A}}$ would be then simply $\left(1 - \sum_{k=0}^{\ell_{\mathbf{A}}-1}\Pr(L_w = k)\right)$. However, the probability mass function of the binomial can be costly to compute for some values of k, since N may be very large, and $N - k$ appears as an exponent. But, for large N and small probability 2^{m-n}, the binomial may

---

[4] Even though the analytic approach is useful to estimate the number of nodes in each level, the errors would accumulate exponentially in the product necessary to compute the work factor of the search.

be approximated as a Poisson distribution with parameter $\lambda = \binom{n}{w}2^{m-n}$. Then, the approximation given as Eq. 4 is easily achieved by considering the cumulative distribution function of the Poisson distribution, instead of the binomial.   □

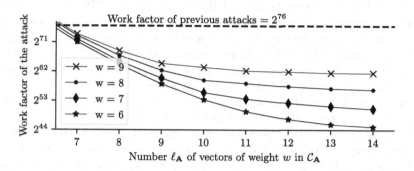

Fig. 4. Work factor of the attack against BPKP–76 parameter set using different attack parameters $(w, \ell_{\mathbf{A}})$.

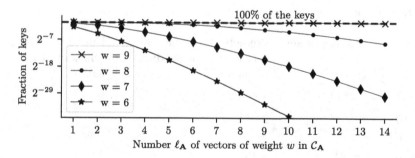

Fig. 5. Fraction of the keys generated with BPKP–76 parameter set against which the attack is successful using different attack parameters $(w, \ell_{\mathbf{A}})$.

Figure 5 shows the effect of parameters $(w, \ell_{\mathbf{A}})$ in the fraction of keys that we can attack. The first thing to notice is that large $\ell_{\mathbf{A}}$ and small w tend to occur with smaller probability. Now we can combine both Figs. 4 and 5 to understand the power of the attack. For example, considering parameters $(w = 7, \ell_{\mathbf{A}} = 10)$, we can attack about 1 in each 150.000 keys of BPKP–76 with less than 2^{55} operations, and about 100% of all keys can be recovered using 2^{62} operations.

5.5 Experimental Results

To validate our proposed attack, we implemented it in SageMath and in C language, using M4RI [14] library for efficient binary linear algebra computations. The source code is publicly available at www.ime.usp.br/~tpaiva.

Table 2 shows the performance of the attack against BPKP-76. To obtain empirical estimates on its performance, we considered the average number of clock cycles for the smallest level $\hat{\alpha}$ in the search for which we can get a significant number of samples. Then, the empirical estimate is given by the product between this average number of clock cycles and the average number of total nodes in level $\hat{\alpha}$. Thus smallest values of α give more accurate results. The values of $\ell_{\mathbf{A}}$ are chosen as to guarantee that the number of permutations to test is within reasonable computational limits and so that $\hat{\alpha} \leq 3$.

Notice how, in general, the estimates on the work factor of the attack tend to overestimate the real complexity of the attack. The main explanation for this fact seems to be that, for sufficiently large $\ell_{\mathbf{A}}$, the algorithm rarely enters in a leaf node, which is where most of the matrix product operations occur. This is exemplified by the decay, shown in Fig. 2, of the curve representing the observed number of nodes in each level during a real attack, where, after level $\alpha = 7$, a node rarely has more than one child.

Table 2. Estimates on the number of clock cycles necessary for a successful attack.

w	$\ell_{\mathbf{A}}$	$\hat{\alpha}$	Fraction of keys	Predicted work factor (matrix-vector products)	Empirical estimate (clock cycles)
5	14	1	0	$2^{39.46}$	$2^{34.39}$
6	11	2	$2^{-43.32}$	$2^{49.75}$	$2^{47.58}$
7	10	2	$2^{-17.86}$	$2^{55.84}$	$2^{48.62}$
8	9	3	$2^{-2.88}$	$2^{62.28}$	$2^{60.54}$
9	9	3	$2^{-0.00}$	$2^{64.16}$	$2^{62.31}$

6 Asymptotic Analysis

In the previous section, a detailed analysis of the attack is presented. However, the concrete analysis fails to provide a general idea of how the complexity grows, as the complexity of the components are not easy to simplify and must be computed using iterative procedures for products of binomial coefficients. Therefore we aim, in this section, to give simpler and closed expressions for the asymptotic attack complexity, but without compromising the reliability of the analysis.

6.1   Asymptotic Growth of the Attack Parameters

First let us recall the growth of parameters m and ℓ with respect to n. To ensure that the binary PKP instances are difficult to solve on average, we need that, out of the $n!$ possible permutations of the rows of $\mathbf{V}$, about only one of them is in the kernel of $\mathbf{A}$. The dimension of $\mathbf{A}$ is m, which means the probability that a random vector belongs to the kernel is $2^{(n-m)}/2^n = 2^{-m}$. Therefore, since the binary PKP is solved only when all ℓ column vectors of $\mathbf{V}_\pi$ are in the kernel of $\mathbf{A}$, then $n! 2^{-m\ell} \approx 1$. As suggested by Lampe and Patarin [13], we consider that m and l should be roughly the same size

$$m \approx l \approx \sqrt{\log n!} = O(\sqrt{n \log n}). \tag{5}$$

From Eq. 5, we see that the dimension m of the code generated by $\mathbf{A}$ grows much slower than its size n. Intuitively then, as n gets larger, it gets harder to obtain codewords of weight much smaller than $n/2$, because of the small dimension. Since we need to deal with values of w close to $n/2$, we are interested in using the following lemma that gives approximations on binomial coefficients $\binom{n}{w}$ under this regime.

Lemma 3 (Eq. 5.41 [21]). *Let n and w be positive integers such that $|n/2 - w| = o(n^{2/3})$. Then*

$$\binom{n}{w} \sim 2^n \sqrt{\frac{2}{n\pi}} e^{\frac{-(n-2w)^2}{2n}}.$$

$\square$

We are now ready to show, in the following lemma, how to carefully choose values of w such that Lemma 3 ensures us that $\mathcal{L}_\mathbf{A}^w$ has a reasonable number of vectors.

Lemma 4. *Take the attack parameter w as*

$$w = \left\lfloor \frac{n}{2} - \sqrt{\frac{mn^{4/5}}{2 \log e}} \right\rceil. \tag{6}$$

Then, on average, the attack can effectively use parameters $(w, \ell_\mathbf{A})$ when $\ell_\mathbf{A}$ is smaller than

$$\ell_\mathbf{A} \leq \left(\sqrt{\frac{2}{\pi}}\right) 2^{\left(m\left(1-n^{(-1/5)}\right)-(\log n)/2\right)}.$$

Proof. Let $\mathbf{A}$ be an $m \times n$ random binary PKP public matrix. The attack parameters $(w, \ell_\mathbf{A})$ are effective when $\ell_\mathbf{A}$ is smaller than or equal to the number of vectors of weight w in the code generated by $\mathbf{A}$. Therefore, on average, the attack works when

$$\ell_\mathbf{A} \leq 2^{m-n} \binom{n}{w}.$$

Now take w as defined by Eq. 6, and notice that, since $m = O\left(\sqrt{n \log n}\right)$, then

$$|n/2 - w| = \sqrt{\frac{mn^{4/5}}{2 \log e}} = O\left(\sqrt{n^{4/5}\sqrt{n \log n}}\right)$$
$$= O\left(n^{13/20} (\log n)^{1/4}\right) = o\left(n^{13/20+\epsilon}\right)$$
$$= o\left(n^{2/3}\right).$$

Therefore we can use Lemma 3 to obtain the approximation

$$2^{m-n}\binom{n}{w} \approx 2^{m-n}\left(2^n\sqrt{\frac{2}{n\pi}}e^{\frac{-(n-2w)^2}{2n}}\right) = 2^m\left(\sqrt{\frac{2}{n\pi}}e^{\frac{-(n-2w)^2}{2n}}\right).$$

But notice that

$$e^{\frac{-(n-2w)^2}{2n}} = e^{\frac{-(n/2-w)^2}{n/2}} = \exp\left(-\frac{1}{n/2}\sqrt{\frac{mn^{4/5}}{2\log e}}^2\right) = \exp\left(-\frac{mn^{-1/5}}{\log e}\right).$$

That is

$$e^{\frac{-(n-2w)^2}{2n}} = 2^{-mn^{-1/5}}. \tag{7}$$

Therefore the attack is effective for

$$\ell_{\mathbf{A}} \le 2^m\left(\sqrt{\frac{2}{n\pi}}2^{-mn^{-1/5}}\right) = \left(\sqrt{\frac{2}{\pi}}\right)2^{(m(1-n^{(-1/5)})-(\log n)/2)}.$$

$\square$

Notice that when w is chosen according to the lemma above, then w/n approaches $1/2$ when n gets larger. This motivates the following corollary, which has an important role in simplifying the analysis.

Corollary 1. *As n gets larger and w is taken as in Lemma 4, the values of $p(k, \alpha)$ stop depending on k, and we have*

$$p(k,\alpha) = \left(\frac{1}{2}\right)^k\left(1-\frac{1}{2}\right)^{\alpha-k} = 2^{-\alpha}.$$

$\square$

As a first application of Corollary 1, we show that, for sufficiently large n, we do not need $\ell_{\mathbf{A}}$ to be very large. With roughly $\ell_{\mathbf{A}} \approx \log n$, the number $\mathbf{WF}_{\mathrm{PERMS}}$ of permutations to test after each matching is very close to 1.

Lemma 5. *Consider binary PKP parameters (n, m, ℓ). Take attack parameters w as in Lemma 4 and $\ell_\mathbf{A} \geq \lceil \log n \rceil$. Then, for sufficiently large values of n, the average number of permutations to test after each matching is*

$$\mathbf{WF}_{\text{PERMS}} = 1.$$

Proof. From our concrete analysis, we know that

$$\mathbf{WF}_{\text{PERMS}} = \prod_{k=0}^{\ell_\mathbf{A}} \left(\frac{(np(k, \ell_\mathbf{A}))!}{(mp(k, \ell_\mathbf{A}))!} \right)^{\binom{\ell_\mathbf{A}}{k}}.$$

But Corollary 1 tells us that $p(k, \ell_\mathbf{A}) \approx 2^{-\ell_\mathbf{A}}$ when n is large. Therefore,

$$\mathbf{WF}_{\text{PERMS}} = \prod_{k=0}^{\ell_\mathbf{A}} \left(\frac{(n2^{-\ell_\mathbf{A}})!}{(m2^{-\ell_\mathbf{A}})!} \right)^{\binom{\ell_\mathbf{A}}{k}} = \prod_{k=0}^{\ell_\mathbf{A}} \left(\frac{(n2^{-\lceil \log n \rceil})!}{(m2^{-\lceil \log n \rceil})!} \right)^{\binom{\lceil \log n \rceil}{k}} = 1.$$

$\square$

It is important to understand that the lemma above needs a relatively large n, because it uses Corollary 1. Therefore, to lower the number of permutations to test after each matching when attacking small values of n, we typically want to use $\ell_\mathbf{A}$ near the maximum provided by Lemma 4. Notice that even for relatively small values of n, there are usually more than $\log n$ vectors of weight w in the code generated by $\mathbf{A}$. For example, when $n = 38$ we have

$$\log(n) \approx 5.25 < 5.99 \approx \sqrt{\frac{2}{\pi}} 2^{m(1 - n^{-1/5}) - (\log n)/2}.$$

We are now ready to derive the asymptotic complexity of $\mathbf{WF}_{\text{SEARCH}}$, which is the most critical step of the attack.

6.2 Searching for Matchings

Let us begin by deriving an asymptotic bound on the number of child nodes in each level of the search tree.

Lemma 6. *Take the attack parameter w as in Lemma 4. Then, for sufficiently large values of n, the number of child nodes in each level α of the search is given as*

$$\left| \hat{P}_{\alpha+1} \right| = \begin{cases} 2^{n - l - mn^{-1/5}} \left(2^\alpha 2^\alpha / 2 \right) \sqrt{\frac{2}{n\pi}}^{2^\alpha} & \text{if } \alpha \leq (\lceil \log n \rceil - 2); \\ 1 & \text{otherwise.} \end{cases}$$

Proof. By our concrete analysis, we know that $\left| \hat{P}_{\alpha+1} \right|$ is given as

$$\left| \hat{P}_{\alpha+1} \right| = \ell_\mathbf{K} \bar{q}_{\alpha+1} = \left(2^{-l} \binom{n}{k} \right) \frac{1}{\binom{n}{w}} \prod_{k=0}^{\alpha} \binom{np(k, \alpha)}{wp(k, \alpha)}^{\binom{\alpha}{k}}$$

$$= 2^{-l} \prod_{k=0}^{\alpha} \binom{np(k, \alpha)}{wp(k, \alpha)}^{\binom{\alpha}{k}}.$$

Using Corollary 1, we can simplify the above expression as

$$\left|\hat{P}_{\alpha+1}\right| = 2^{-l} \prod_{k=0}^{\alpha} \binom{n2^{-\alpha}}{w2^{-\alpha}}^{\binom{\alpha}{k}} = 2^{-l} \binom{n2^{-\alpha}}{w2^{-\alpha}}^{\left(\sum_{k=0}^{\alpha} \binom{\alpha}{k}\right)}$$

$$= 2^{-l} \binom{n2^{-\alpha}}{w2^{-\alpha}}^{2^{\alpha}}.$$

Now, if $\alpha \geq (\lceil \log n \rceil - 1)$, then $w2^{-\alpha} < 1$, and

$$\binom{n2^{-\alpha}}{w2^{-\alpha}}^{2^{\alpha}} \leq \binom{n2^{-\alpha}}{\frac{n}{2}2^{-\alpha}}^{2^{\alpha}} \approx 1.$$

Therefore, we can focus on approximating the case when $\alpha \leq (\lceil \log n \rceil - 2)$. Remember that w is close to $n/2$, thus we can use Lemma 3 to get the approximation

$$\binom{n2^{-\alpha}}{w2^{-\alpha}} \approx 2^{n2^{-\alpha}} \sqrt{\frac{2}{n2^{-\alpha}\pi}} e^{\frac{-(n2^{-\alpha}-2w2^{-\alpha})^2}{2n2^{-\alpha}}}$$

$$= 2^{n2^{-\alpha}} 2^{\alpha/2} \sqrt{\frac{2}{n\pi}} e^{\frac{-(n-w)^2}{2n}2^{-\alpha}}.$$

Recall Eq. 7, which lets us further simplify the expression above as

$$\binom{n2^{-\alpha}}{w2^{-\alpha}} = 2^{n2^{-\alpha}} 2^{\alpha/2} \sqrt{\frac{2}{n\pi}} \left(2^{-mn^{-1/5}}\right)^{2^{-\alpha}}.$$

Now, getting back to $\left|\hat{P}_{\alpha+1}\right|$, we have

$$\left|\hat{P}_{\alpha+1}\right| = 2^{-l} \binom{n2^{-\alpha}}{w2^{-\alpha}}^{2^{\alpha}}$$

$$= 2^{-l} \left(2^{n2^{-\alpha}} 2^{\alpha/2} \sqrt{\frac{2}{n\pi}} \left(2^{-mn^{-1/5}}\right)^{2^{-\alpha}}\right)^{2^{\alpha}}$$

$$= 2^{n-l-mn^{-1/5}} \left(2^{\alpha 2^{\alpha}/2}\right) \sqrt{\frac{2}{n\pi}}^{2^{\alpha}}.$$

$\square$

Now that we have bounded the number of nodes in each level, we are ready to give the asymptotic bound on the search procedure.

Lemma 7. *Take attack parameters w and $\ell_{\mathbf{A}} \geq \lceil \log n \rceil$ as in Lemma 4. Then, the asymptotic work factor of the search is given as*

$$\mathbf{WF}_{\text{SEARCH}} \approx 2^{\left(n-l-mn^{-1/5}\right)\left(\lceil \log n \rceil - 1\right) - 0.91n + \frac{1}{2} \log n + 1.33}.$$

Proof. From our concrete analysis, we know that the complexity of the search is the product of the number of nodes in each level of the search. Furthermore, Lemma 6 says that we only need to compute these values for $\alpha \leq \lceil \log n \rceil - 2$, because after this point, typically there is at most one possible child node. Therefore, the complexity of the search is given as

$$
\mathbf{WF}_{\text{SEARCH}} = \prod_{\alpha=0}^{\ell_{\mathbf{A}}-1} \left| \hat{P}_{\alpha+1} \right| = \prod_{\alpha=0}^{\lceil \log n \rceil - 2} \left| \hat{P}_{\alpha+1} \right|
$$

$$
= \prod_{\alpha=0}^{\lceil \log n \rceil - 2} \left(2^{n-l-mn^{-1/5}} \left(2^{\alpha 2^{\alpha}/2} \right) \sqrt{\frac{2}{n\pi}}^{2^{\alpha}} \right)
$$

$$
= 2^{\left(n-l-mn^{-1/5}\right)\left(\lceil \log n \rceil - 1\right)} 2^{\left(\sum_{\alpha=0}^{\lceil \log n \rceil - 2} \alpha 2^{\alpha}/2\right)} \left(\frac{2}{n\pi} \right)^{\left(\sum_{\alpha=0}^{\lceil \log n \rceil - 2} 2^{\alpha}/2\right)}
$$

$$
= 2^{\left(n-l-mn^{-1/5}\right)\left(\lceil \log n \rceil - 1\right)} 2^{\left(1+\frac{n}{4}\left(\lceil \log n \rceil - 3\right)\right)} 2^{\left(\log \frac{2}{n\pi}\right)(n/4 - 1/2)}
$$

$$
\approx 2^{\left(n-l-mn^{-1/5}\right)\left(\lceil \log n \rceil - 1\right) - 0.91n + \frac{1}{2}\log n + 1.33}.
$$

$\square$

6.3   Asymptotic Complexity of the Attack

We are almost ready to complete the asymptotic analysis of the attack. The only missing component to consider is $\mathbf{WF}_{\text{LowWeightSets}}$. Using the bruteforce algorithm, one needs to test, for all $\binom{n}{w} = O(2^n)$ possible vectors of weight w, if they are in the space generated by $\mathbf{A}$ or in the left kernel of $\mathbf{V}$. Therefore, the complexity of building sets $\mathcal{L}_{\mathbf{A}}^w$ and $\mathcal{L}_{\mathbf{K}}^w$ is

$$
\mathbf{WF}_{\text{LowWeightSets}} = O(2^n).
$$

We can then combine the result above with Lemmas 5 and 7 to obtain the complexity of the attack, as given next.

Theorem 1. *Take attack parameters w and $\ell_{\mathbf{A}} \geq \lceil \log n \rceil$ as in Lemma 4. Then, the asymptotic work factor of the attack is given as*

$$
\mathbf{WF}_{\text{ATTACK}} = \mathbf{WF}_{\text{LowWeightSets}} + \left(\mathbf{WF}_{\text{SEARCH}}\right)\left(\mathbf{WF}_{\text{PERMS}}\right)
$$

$$
= O\left(2^{\left(n-l-mn^{-1/5}\right)\left(\lceil \log n \rceil - 1\right) - 0.91n + \frac{1}{2}\log n} \right).
$$

$\square$

Figure 6 shows how the asymptotic complexity presented above compares with the simulations based on the concrete analysis. We can see that the asymptotic estimate appears to be realistic, even though the ceiling operation used for $\lceil \log n \rceil$ makes the function rapidly increase when $n - 1$ is a power of 2, and then decrease until the next power of 2 is found.

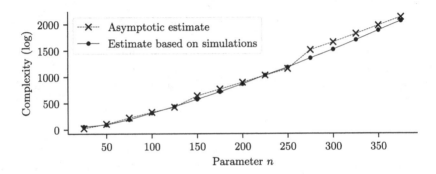

Fig. 6. Asymptotic complexity of the attack.

Figure 7 shows an asymptotic comparison between our algorithm and the one by Koussa et al. [12]. Even though their algorithm is currently the best generic algorithm for solving PKP in every field, we can see that our algorithm has a considerable advantage in the binary case. To help us visualize the asymptotic growth of our attack, we consider a smooth version of the estimate that consists in using $\log n$ instead of $\lceil \log n \rceil$ in the expression provided in Theorem 1.

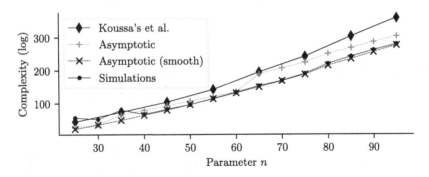

Fig. 7. Comparison between our attack and the one by Koussa et al. [12].

7   On Secure Parameters for Binary PKP

A conservative approach to select parameters for binary PKP, considering security level λ, would be to choose them in such a way that no class of keys that occurs with probability greater than $2^{-\lambda}$ should be attacked with less 2^{λ} operations. Furthermore, the choice of parameters should consider the use of binary PKP when building a signature scheme, and, as such, should aim to minimize not only the key sizes, but also signature sizes and the computational cost to sign and verify each signature.

The safest possible choice of parameters would be the ones that make it difficult to even build sets $\mathcal{L}_A^w$ and $\mathcal{L}_K^w$. If we take schemes that rely on the difficulty of finding small weight codewords such as MDPC [16], this would result in a very large matrix $\mathbf{A}$. This, however, would have a very negative impact on performance, key sizes and signature length.

A less conservative approach is to scale parameters (n, m, ℓ) and compute $\mathbf{WF}_{\text{ATTACK}}^{(n,m,\ell,w,\ell_\mathbf{A})}$ and $\mathbf{KF}_{\text{ATTACK}}^{(n,m,\ell,w,\ell_\mathbf{A})}$ for different attack parameters $(w, \ell_\mathbf{A})$. The search is efficient and can be done with the code that we provide. However, it is important to notice that it seems to be early to state sets of parameters for BPKP, as there may be some opportunities to improve this attack, which could thwart the security of parameters suggested without careful consideration. Our recommendation therefore is to avoid the Binary PKP, and more generally, the PKP using small fields for matrix $\mathbf{A}$, for which the search for low weight codewords can be done efficiently.

8 Conclusion and Future Work

In this paper, we present the first attack that targets binary PKP and provide a detailed analysis on the attack's components. The attack is practical and we provide an implementation of the attack in SageMath and C. Furthermore, the attack shows an inherently weakness of PKP using small fields, and we recommend that binary PKP be avoided while its security is not well understood against this new type of attack.

For future work, we plan to extend this attack to the original PKP, hoping to better understand what is the minimum finite field size p that can used securely. Furthermore, we believe that there are some opportunities to improve this attack. For example, it may be possible to increase the fraction of keys that one can attack by considering different parameters w simultaneously, or one can try to reduce the complexity of matching by introducing heuristics.

Acknowledgments. The authors would like to thank Augusto C. Ferrari for his helpful comments on earlier drafts of this paper. This study was financed in part by the Coordenação de Aperfeiçoamento de Pessoal de Nível Superior - Brasil (CAPES) - Finance Code 001. This research is part of the INCT of the Future Internet for Smart Cities funded by CNPq proc. 465446/2014-0, Coordenação de Aperfeiçoamento de Pessoal de Nível Superior – Brasil (CAPES) – Finance Code 001, FAPESP proc. 14/50937-1, and FAPESP proc. 15/24485-9.

References

1. Baritaud, T., Campana, M., Chauvaud, P., Gilbert, H.: On the security of the permuted kernel identification scheme. In: Brickell, E.F. (ed.) CRYPTO 1992. LNCS, vol. 740, pp. 305–311. Springer, Heidelberg (1993). https://doi.org/10.1007/3-540-48071-4_21
2. Bernstein, D.J., Lange, T., Peters, C.: Smaller decoding exponents: ball-collision decoding. In: Rogaway, P. (ed.) CRYPTO 2011. LNCS, vol. 6841, pp. 743–760. Springer, Heidelberg (2011). https://doi.org/10.1007/978-3-642-22792-9_42

3. Beullens, W., Faugère, J.-C., Koussa, E., Macario-Rat, G., Patarin, J., Perret, L.: PKP-based signature scheme. In: Hao, F., Ruj, S., Sen Gupta, S. (eds.) INDOCRYPT 2019. LNCS, vol. 11898, pp. 3–22. Springer, Cham (2019). https://doi.org/10.1007/978-3-030-35423-7_1
4. Chen, L., et al.: Report on post-quantum cryptography. US Department of Commerce, National Institute of Standards and Technology (2016)
5. Cordella, L.P., Foggia, P., Sansone, C., Vento, M.: A (sub)graph isomorphism algorithm for matching large graphs. IEEE Trans. Pattern Anal. Mach. Intell. **26**(10), 1367–1372 (2004)
6. Fiat, A., Shamir, A.: How to prove yourself: practical solutions to identification and signature problems. In: Odlyzko, A.M. (ed.) CRYPTO 1986. LNCS, vol. 263, pp. 186–194. Springer, Heidelberg (1987). https://doi.org/10.1007/3-540-47721-7_12
7. Finiasz, M., Sendrier, N.: Security bounds for the design of code-based cryptosystems. In: Matsui, M. (ed.) ASIACRYPT 2009. LNCS, vol. 5912, pp. 88–105. Springer, Heidelberg (2009). https://doi.org/10.1007/978-3-642-10366-7_6
8. Garey, M.R., Johnson, D.S.: Computers and Intractability: A Guide to the Theory of NP-Completeness. W. H. Freeman and Company, New York (1979)
9. Georgiades, J.: Some remarks on the security of the identification scheme based on permuted kernels. J. Cryptol. **5**(2), 133–137 (1992). https://doi.org/10.1007/BF00193565
10. Jaulmes, É., Joux, A.: Cryptanalysis of PKP: a new approach. In: Kim, K. (ed.) PKC 2001. LNCS, vol. 1992, pp. 165–172. Springer, Heidelberg (2001). https://doi.org/10.1007/3-540-44586-2_12
11. Joux, A., Lercier, R.: "Chinese & Match", an alternative to Atkin's "Match and Sort" method used in the SEA algorithm. Math. Comput. **70**(234), 827–836 (2001)
12. Koussa, E., Macario-Rat, G., Patarin, J.: On the complexity of the Permuted Kernel Problem. IACR Cryptology ePrint Archive 2019, 412 (2019)
13. Lampe., R., Patarin., J.: Analysis of some natural variants of the PKP algorithm. In: Proceedings of the International Conference on Security and Cryptography - Volume 1: SECRYPT, (ICETE 2012), pp. 209–214. INSTICC, SciTePress (2012). https://doi.org/10.5220/0004012202090214
14. Albrecht, M., Bard, G.: The M4RI Library - Version 20121224. The M4RI Team (2012)
15. McEliece, R.J.: A public-key cryptosystem based on algebraic coding theory. Deep Space Network Progress Report 44, pp. 114–116 (1978)
16. Misoczki, R., Tillich, J.P., Sendrier, N., Barreto, P.S.: MDPC-McEliece: New McEliece variants from moderate density parity-check codes. In: 2013 IEEE International Symposium on Information Theory Proceedings (ISIT), pp. 2069–2073. IEEE (2013)
17. Patarin, J., Chauvaud, P.: Improved algorithms for the permuted kernel problem. In: Stinson, D.R. (ed.) CRYPTO 1993. LNCS, vol. 773, pp. 391–402. Springer, Heidelberg (1994). https://doi.org/10.1007/3-540-48329-2_33
18. Poupard, G.: A realistic security analysis of identification schemes based on combinatorial problems. Eur. Trans. Telecommun. **8**(5), 471–480 (1997)
19. Sansone, P.F.C., Vento, M.: An improved algorithm for matching large graphs. In: Proceedings of the 3rd IAPR-TC-15 International Workshop on Graph-Based Representations (2001)
20. Shamir, A.: An efficient identification scheme based on permuted kernels (extended abstract). In: Brassard, G. (ed.) CRYPTO 1989. LNCS, vol. 435, pp. 606–609. Springer, New York (1990). https://doi.org/10.1007/0-387-34805-0_54

21. Spencer, J.: Asymptopia, vol. 71. American Mathematical Society, Providence (2014)
22. Stern, J.: A method for finding codewords of small weight. In: Cohen, G., Wolfmann, J. (eds.) Coding Theory 1988. LNCS, vol. 388, pp. 106–113. Springer, Heidelberg (1989). https://doi.org/10.1007/BFb0019850
23. Ullmann, J.R.: An algorithm for subgraph isomorphism. J. ACM (JACM) 23(1), 31–42 (1976)

Security Comparisons and Performance Analyses of Post-quantum Signature Algorithms

Manohar Raavi[1]([✉]), Simeon Wuthier[1]([✉]), Pranav Chandramouli[1],
Yaroslav Balytskyi[2], Xiaobo Zhou[1], and Sang-Yoon Chang[1]([✉])

[1] Department of Computer Science, University of Colorado, Colorado Springs, USA
{mraavi,swuthier,pchandra,xzhou,schang2}@uccs.edu
[2] Department of Physics and Energy Science, University of Colorado,
Colorado Springs, USA
ybalytsk@uccs.edu

Abstract. Quantum computing challenges the computational hardness assumptions anchoring the security of public-key ciphers, such as the prime factorization and the discrete logarithm problem. To prepare for the quantum era and withstand the attacks equipped with quantum computing, the security and cryptography communities are designing new quantum-resistant public-key ciphers. National Institute of Standards and Technology (NIST) is collecting and standardizing the post-quantum ciphers, similarly to its past involvements in establishing DES and AES as symmetric cipher standards. The NIST finalist algorithms for public-key signatures are *Dilithium*, *Falcon*, and *Rainbow*. Finding common ground to compare these algorithms can be difficult because of their design, the underlying computational hardness assumptions (lattice based vs. multivariate based), and the different metrics used for security strength analyses in the previous research (qubits vs. quantum gates). We overcome such challenges and compare the security and the performances of the finalist post-quantum ciphers of *Dilithium*, *Falcon*, and *Rainbow*. For security comparison analyses, we advance the prior literature by using the depth-width cost for quantum circuits (DW cost) to measure the security strengths and by analyzing the security in Universal Quantum Gate Model and with Quantum Annealing. For performance analyses, we compare the algorithms' computational loads in the execution time as well as the communication costs and implementation overheads when integrated with Transport Layer Security (TLS) and Transmission Control Protocol (TCP)/Internet Protocol (IP). Our work presents a security comparison and performance analysis as well as the trade-off analysis to inform the post-quantum cipher design and standardization to protect computing and networking in the post-quantum era.

Keywords: Quantum-resistant cryptography · Post-quantum cryptography · Quantum computing · Public-key cipher · Digital signature algorithms · Security analysis · Performance analysis

© Springer Nature Switzerland AG 2021
K. Sako and N. O. Tippenhauer (Eds.): ACNS 2021, LNCS 12727, pp. 424–447, 2021.
https://doi.org/10.1007/978-3-030-78375-4_17

1 Introduction

Public-key digital signatures provide authentication and integrity protection and are critical in securing digital systems. The security of the most used present-day digital signature standards like Rivest-Shamir-Adleman (RSA) [44] and Elliptic Curve Digital Signature Algorithm (ECDSA) [14] are based on the computational hardness problems such as prime factorization and discrete logarithm problem. Shor's polynomial-time algorithm effectively solve these problems when equipped with a powerful quantum computer [45]. Securing digital communication against attackers that have access to the quantum computing resources [39] requires new public-key cryptographic algorithms which can withstand such quantum attackers.

Recent advancements in quantum computing and quantum computers (Sect. 2) yields a need for transitioning to post-quantum cryptography (quantum-resistant cryptography). This involves identifying the relevant hardness problems and designing and constructing the quantum-resistant algorithms for securing digital communications.

National Institute of Science and Technology (NIST) launched the Post-Quantum Cryptography (PQC) standardization project to establish and standardize quantum-resistant algorithms. NIST has a track record of preparing for the impending cryptanalysis and breaks on cryptographic ciphers and is preparing for the post-quantum era before the emergence of the practical quantum computer implementations capable of breaking the current systems. NIST's involvement in cryptography has global and lasting impacts on digital systems, as demonstrated by their involvement in standardizing DES in the 1970's and AES in the late 1990's. The standardization process starts with an open public call that lists the requirements of the algorithms. All the submission algorithms are openly published and subjected to analyses and, after the analyses, an algorithm is selected for standardization. PQC standardization project follows the same process and requested the interested parties to provide submissions for quantum-resistant cryptographic candidates.

In this paper, we study the security and performances of the third round digital signature candidate algorithms from NIST's PQC standardization project. The digital signature algorithms include three finalist candidates: *Crystals-Dilith- ium (Dilithium)*, *Falcon*, and *Rainbow*, design principles and hardness problems underlying these digital signature algorithms come from Lattice-based and multivariate-based cryptography (Sect. 3). The researchers designed and developed these cipher schemes and algorithms separately, including the security analyses, which makes the cross-cipher comparison analyses challenging. Our work addresses such a gap and provides a comparison analyses between the different cipher families/schemes and the algorithms within the families to inform the security communities at this time of selecting the PQC cipher standard[1].

---

[1] Our work has been shared with NIST.

Contributions. We compare the PQC digital signature cipher schemes in both security and performances. Our security analyses include two contributions. First, we adopt a model for visual representations to compare the size-security trade-offs of digital signature algorithms (Sect. 4). These include the security offered by the digital signature algorithms with respect to public key length and signature length. Second, we analyze the security of digital signature candidates based on DW cost and with and without quantum annealing (Sect. 5). We also make the following two contributions in performance analyses. First, we analyze the implementation overheads in the execution time and its scalability in message sizes of the individual signature algorithms for key-pair generation, signature generation, and signature verification (Sect. 6). Second, we analyze the communication/handshake overheads on TLS 1.3 and TCP/IPv4 connection when integrating the signature algorithms (Sect. 7).

Methodologies and Approaches. We use both theory and empirical measurements in our paper. We take a theoretical approach to analyze the security against quantum cryptanalysis, since practical quantum computers supporting a sufficient number of quantum bits (qubits) to implement the theoretical cryptanalysis attacks are currently unavailable and under active research and development. In Sect. 4, we build on the previous analyses on the NIST finalist PQC schemes and adopt the visualization model proposed by Bernstein [12] to show the size-security trade-offs of the digital signature algorithms. In Sect. 5, we build on the quantum physics theory to compare and analyze the PQC schemes, which previously have been analyzed separately using different metrics of qubits and quantum gates, challenging the inter-scheme comparison. We adopt the quantum circuit DW cost combining qubits and quantum gate costs [34] to compare the security of the algorithms in the Universal Quantum Gate Model and the model with Quantum Annealing.

For the performance analyses of the PQC schemes, we implement prototypes and empirically measure performances between the schemes. While the post-quantum era prepares for adversaries equipped with quantum computing, the PQC cipher schemes are designed to be implemented on classical computers to defend the common user. We build on the algorithm implementations from *liboqs* by *Open Quantum Safe* [47] and deployed it on a virtual machine with 6 processing cores and 6 *GB* of RAM on a computer equipped with a 16-core 32-thread AMD Ryzen 9 3950X processor with 3.5 GHz processor frequency, and 32 *GB* RAM. While the absolute performance costs vary depending on the computer platform and its hardware specifications, we focus on the comparison results in this paper so that our results and insights are applicable to classical non-quantum computers beyond our platform. We compare the performance costs of the algorithms by themselves in Sect. 6 and when integrated with TLS 1.3 and TCP/IP in Sect. 7.

Fig. 1. PQC history and the events leading up to NIST's standardization. Highlighted in blue are the events specifically involving NIST.

2 Background: PQC History and NIST

We describe the PQC history and the NIST involvement to motivate our work in this section, and Fig. 1 shows the timeline of events regarding cryptography and quantum computing. Cryptography provides the backbone to secure the digital systems in our society. While the practical quantum computers currently only support a small number of qubits and at the proof-of-concept stages, the theoretical algorithms building on quantum computing emerged to expedite the solving of the computational hardness problems anchoring the security of the current public-key ciphers. Shor's algorithm [45], invented in 1994, provides a polynomial-time algorithm in quantum computing for solving the prime factorization and discrete log problem, threatening the security of the public-key ciphers such as RSA and Diffie-Hellman Key Exchange. Grover's algorithm [31] in 1996 expedites the brute-force search of the general problems, such as the original database search problem and hash collision finding. The first successful implementation of quantum searching was performed, in 1998, on a two-qubit Nuclear Magnetic Resonance (NMR) quantum computer. It used Grover's algorithm to search for a system that has four states [19]. Followed by Grover's implementation, in 2001, a seven qubit NMR quantum computer [48] used Shor's algorithm to find prime factors for the number 15.

Inspired by the extraordinary opportunities in quantum computing, major tech giants started research into quantum computers. The first of such kind was D-Wave Systems, whose quantum computing capabilities are based on quantum annealing. In 2019, D-Wave unveiled a 5000 qubit processor [49]. On the other hand, International Business Machines (IBM) and Google follow the universal quantum gate model. IBM showed significant progress from 5 qubit processor [9] and reached a 53 qubit processor. IBM's quantum experience provides access to up to 32 qubit processor quantum computers for registered users at free of cost [16]. Google announced a 72 qubit quantum processor [35]. With steady growth in practical quantum computers and raising concerns in cryptography, NIST initiated PQC standardization project. NIST requested nominations in Dec 2016 for public-key post-quantum cryptographic algorithms [4]. NIST's PQC standardization project aims to replace the present recommended digital signature standard of RSA, and ECDSA [27] with post-quantum algorithms. Instead of measuring the security in bits, all these post-quantum algorithms are referenced with security categories defined by NIST (Table 1). Each of these categories sets the minimum required computational resources to break well known symmetric block cipher or hash functions. Breaking a symmetric block cipher indicates a successful brute-force key search attack, and breaking a hash function means a successful brute-force collision attack. Computational resources can be restricted by a new parameter, defined by NIST, called MAXDEPTH. It can be used to limit the quantum attacks to fixed running time or circuit depth. PQC standardization is a multi-year process and involves multiple rounds of analyses and scrutiny for the maturity of cipher design before the standardization.

Table 1. NIST security categories, where X is the MAXDEPTH

Security Category	Reference Algorithm	Classical Bit Cost	Qubit Security	Circuit Size to Break the Algorithm [4]
1	AES 128	128 (key search)	64 (Grover [31])	$2^{170}/X$ quantum gates or 2^{143} classical gates
2	SHA3-256	128 (collision)	85 (Brassard [13])	2^{146} classical gates
3	AES 192	192 (key search)	96 (Grover [31])	$2^{233}/X$ quantum gates or 2^{207} classical gates
4	SHA3-384	192 (collision)	128 (Brassard [13])	2^{210} classical gates
5	AES 256	256 (key search)	128 (Grover [31])	$2^{298}/X$ quantum gates or 2^{272} classical gates
6	SHA3-512	256 (collision)	170 (Brassard [13])	2^{274} classical gates

In response to the open public call for the PQC standardization proposal [4], NIST received 82 submissions, and only 69 of the submissions satisfied the minimum required conditions. The first-round of the PQC standardization project started in Dec 2017, selected 26 candidate algorithms. With fewer algorithms to analyze, the second-round of the PQC standardization project started in Jan 2019 and selected 15 algorithms for third-round [5]. These 15 algorithms are categorized as seven finalist candidates and eight alternate candidates (Sect. 3). Seven finalists candidate algorithms include four public-key encryption/KEM mechanisms and three digital signature schemes. Eight alternate candidate algorithms include five public-key encryption/KEM mechanisms and three digital signature schemes. At-most one of the finalist candidate algorithms in each of the public-key encryption/KEM and digital signature standard schemes are expected to be standards at the end of the PQC standardization project. Started in July 2020, the PQC standardization project aims to complete the analysis by early 2022 and confirm the candidates for standardization.

We focus on the digital signatures in this paper, while NIST solicits and plans to standardize both key exchange ciphers/key encapsulation mechanisms and digital signature ciphers. The current Round 3 includes three finalists and three alternate schemes for the digital signatures. At most one of the finalist schemes is expected to be standardized in Round 3, which is planned to occur in 2022. Our work focuses on the NIST finalist candidates for PQC signature schemes/algorithms in: *Dilithium*, *Falcon*, and *Rainbow*.

3 PQC Signature Schemes

The current third-round PQC standardization is planned to undergo public and researchers scrutiny/analyses until 2022 and includes three digital signatures schemes for its finalists: *Dilithium*, *Falcon*, and *Rainbow*. These families of algorithms can be categorized into two different schemes, listed in Table 2, based on the hardness problems on which they rely. These include Lattice-based signature schemes (for *Dilithium* and *Falcon*) in Sect. 3.1 and Multivariate-based signature schemes (for *Rainbow*) in Sect. 3.2. We also include the description for *GeMSS* (the only other Multivariate-based signature scheme which got selected as an alternate scheme by NIST) in order to compare it with the security of *Rainbow* in Sect. 4.

Table 2. Signature algorithms descriptions (the last column indicates the color code used in our paper)

Algorithm	Scheme	NIST Status	Security Level	Reference	Color
Dilithium	Lattice-based	Finalist	1 (AES128) 2 (SHA256) 3 (AES192)	[23]	Blue
Falcon	Lattice-based	Finalist	1 (AES128) 5 (AES256)	[28]	Red
Rainbow	Multivariate	Finalist	1 (AES128) 3 (AES192) 5 (AES256)	[22]	Green
GeMSS	Multivariate	Alternate	1 (AES128) 3 (AES192) 5 (AES256)	[15]	Magenta

Within each algorithm families (*Dilithium*, *Falcon*, and *Rainbow*), there are multiple algorithms depending on the parameter choices for the security level control. The parameters affect the public key length and the private key length as well as the signature length for the PQC signature algorithms, and the security strengths increase as the length increase (using greater number/options to yield greater entropy), as we study in Sect. 4. The public key and the signature lengths for the different algorithms are also listed in the horizontal axis in Fig. 2. For example, *Dilithium 2* has a public key length of 897 Bytes, *Dilithium 3* with 1472 Bytes, and *Dilithium 4* with 1760 Bytes. Thus, *Dilithium 4* is designed to have greater security strength than *Dilithium 3*, and *Dilithium 3* greater than *Dilithium 2*. This section describes the overview of the PQC schemes without the scheme-specific details, such as the actual parameters/variables to control for the different algorithms within the family; we refer the interested readers for the scheme-specific design details to the design documents for *Dilithium* [23], *Falcon* [28], and *Rainbow* [22].

3.1   Lattice-Based Signature Schemes

Lattice-based signature schemes are based on a set of points in n-dimensional space with periodic structure [42]. The security of lattice-based cryptography comes from the use of NP-hard problems such as i) Short Vector Problems (SVP) which involves finding the shortest non-zero vector, ii) Closed Vector Problems (CVP) which involves finding the shortest vector, iii) Learning With Errors (LWE) which is computationally intensive as it requires a linear function over a finite ring of given samples, iv) Short Integer Solutions (SIS) which is based on Ajtai's theorem where if polynomial-time algorithm A solves the SIS problem, then there exists an Algorithm B that can solve the Short Vector Integer Problem (SVIP), v) Learning With Rounding (LWR) is the non-rounding variant of LWE. LWR is more efficient than LWE as it removes LWE's complex randomization elements [40]. *Dilithium* and *Falcon* are the two finalist lattice-based signatures schemes in the NIST third-round standardization process. Both are categorized as finalist candidate algorithms, and one of the two is expected to be a digital signature standard at the end of the PQC standardization process in 2022–2024 [3].

Dilithium. *Dilithium* is one of the two lattice-based signature algorithms in the third round. *Dilithium* relies on Fiat-Shamir and Aborts framework and SVP's for its security [23]. *Dilithium* introduces three algorithms in *Dilithium 2*, *Dilithium 3*, and *Dilithium 4* correspond 1, 2, and 3 of NIST's post-quantum security categories respectively.

Falcon. *Falcon* is Fast Fourier lattice-based compact signatures over N-th Degree Truncated Polynomial Ring (NTRU) [28], and one of the two lattice-based signature algorithms of the third round. *Falcon* relies on the NTRU for key generation, encryption and decryption data, Short Integer Problems (SIS), Floating-Point arithmetic, and gaussian sampling floating-point arithmetic for its security. *Falcon 512* and *Falcon 1024* algorithms correspond to 1 and 5 of NIST's post-quantum security strengths respectively.

3.2   Multivariate-Based Signature Schemes

Multivariate-based signature schemes are known as an unbalanced Oil-Vinegar (UOV) system which is the process of hiding quadratic equations in n unknowns or Oil and $v = n$ unknowns called "vinegar" in a finite field k [36], and it is based on solving quadratic equations over finite fields, making it an NP-hard problem. The security of the signature scheme is based on the number of variables and the field size, which leads to large key sizes. *Rainbow* is the only finalist from multivariate-based signature schemes.

Rainbow. *Rainbow*, a Multivariate signature scheme, is the only finalist Multivariate candidate of the third round. *Rainbow* relies on binary field L over

Unbalanced Oil and Vinegar (LUOV) and raises it to a bigger field K for its security [24]. The *Rainbow* family includes the following algorithms: *Rainbow Ia, Rainbow IIIc,* and *Rainbow Vc* where *I, III,* and *V* correspond to 1, 3, and 5 of NIST's post-quantum security strength, respectively. *Rainbow* has variants of cyclic and compressed algorithms.

GeMSS. A Great Multivariate Short Signature (*GeMSS*) is one of the alternate candidates in the third round. *GeMSS* relies on Hidden Field Equations cryptosystem (HFE) to achieve its level of security and efficiency. *GeMSS* algorithm variants are *GeMSS 128, GeMSS 192, GeMSS 256* where 128, 192 and 256 correspond to 1, 3, and 5 of NIST's post-quantum security strengths respectively. *GeMSS* has variants of *BlueGeMSS* and *RedGeMSS*.

4 Security Analysis Using Visualization Model

In this section, we analyze the size-security trade-offs of NIST finalist algorithms. We build our analyses on the visualization model developed to compare cipher designs [12] and the individual analyses of the NIST finalist cipher designs, including the individual cipher developer's security analyses and the threats/attack discoveries and research targeting the individual cipher schemes.

Lattice-based algorithms analyze the cipher security strength against quantum attackers (the attacker's cost in breaking the ciphers) in qubit cost, and multivariate-based algorithms analyze the security strength in quantum gates cost. For multivariate-based algorithms, we include the comparison with *GeMSS* for *Rainbow*; *GeMSS* is the only other multivariate-based family selected by NIST to advance in the third round but it is selected as an Alternate as opposed to Finalist. The metrics of qubit and quantum gate to measure the security strength are relatively new and depend on the quantum computer physics and hardware architecture, which are in active research and development.

In this section, we separately analyze the size-security trade-offs of the lattice-based schemes using the attacker's security cost in qubits and the size-security trade-offs of the multivariate schemes using the attacker's cost in quantum gates. However, in Sect. 5, unlike the previous research approach analyzing the PQC ciphers individually, we compare them together by using the quantum circuit's depth-width cost (*DW* cost) which incorporates both qubit and quantum gate.

4.1 Metrics: Qubits and Quantum Gates

In classical computing, the state of a particular bit is always known. In the quantum case, before the measurement is done, the state of a qubit is unknown. Although qubit resembles a classical bit *after the measurement,* it takes two possible values and additionally can exploit the interference effects; *before the measurement,* a qubit can be in a *superposition* of these two states described by the wave function. The classical brute force attacker searches blindly and cannot distinguish if some particular value is closer or further from the key being searched and while checking if the key is found may get only the binary result of "true" or "false". In the quantum case, a brute force attacker always has an overlap of the wave function of the current state of qubits and the key, and this overlap is bigger if some particular state of qubits is closer to the key being searched. Even if the cipher's structure is unknown for the attacker, interference helps to move in the direction towards the key enabling a faster search.

Qubit Cost. A qubit cost indicates the number of qubits the attacker needs to break the cipher assuming a sufficient number of gates. For *Dilithium*, qubit cost represents the cost of solving SVP which is exponential to Block-Korkine-Zolotarev (BKZ) algorithm's block-size (b) [23] For *Falcon*, core SVP hardness indicates the cost for one call to SVP oracle in dimension b [8,28].

Quantum Gate Cost. Quantum gate cost indicates the minimum number of logical quantum gates required to perform a successful attack assuming a sufficient number of qubits. For Rainbow, quantum gate cost indicates the minimum number of logical gates required to perform key recovery attacks including Min-Rank, HighRank, UOV, and RBS attacks [22]. Against Rainbow, the number of quantum gates (#Gates) can be measured as follows where q is the Galois Field's Order: #Gates = #Field Multiplications $\cdot(2 \cdot \log_2(q)^2 + \log_2(q))$.

4.2 Lattice-Based Signature Schemes Security and Length Trade-Off

Figure 2 shows the classical and quantum security cost trade-offs with respect to the public key length and the signature length of lattice-based signature algorithms. Public key length and signature length are important parameters controlling the trade-off between security strength and communication overhead in digital communications. For example, when Alice sends a signed message to Bob, Bob uses Alice's public key and signature to verify the message. Public key and signature are the overheads in the communication. Many real-world applications use the same private/public key-pair to sign/verify multiple messages than using One Time Pad/Ephemeral Keys resulting in the transfer of signatures more often than public-keys. Low signature size and public key lengths help in reducing communication costs. In Fig. 2, an ideal algorithm will have a small communication cost (left in the plot) and provide strong security (top).

Dilithium and *Falcon*, the two lattice-based NIST finalists schemes, display the security vs. overhead/length trade-off, and the security costs measured in (classical) bits or qubits increase as the public key length or the signature length increase. Figure 2a analyzes the classical security cost to the public key length trade-offs. For additional 33 Bytes of public key length from *Dilithium* at 1760 Bytes, *Falcon* offers 89 bits more security cost. Figure 2b analyzes the classical security cost to the signature length trade-offs. For less than half the signature size of the *Dilithium* at 2044 Bytes, the classical security cost of the *Falcon* at 690 Bytes is 14 bits more. *Falcon* signature size at its highest security cost is 714

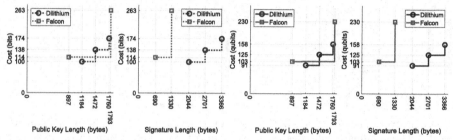

(a) Security in bits (b) Security in bits (c) Security in qubits (d) Security cost vs. vs. public key length vs. signature length vs. public key length signature length

Fig. 2. Security costs for lattice-based signature candidates. The dotted line shows the classical bit security level (the left two figures), whereas the solid line shows the quantum bit security level (the right two figures). The vertical scales are consistent across the figures.

Bytes less to *Dilithium* at its lowest security. Figure 2c analyzes the quantum security cost to the public key length trade-offs. For an additional 33 Bytes of public key length from *Dilithium* at 1760 Bytes, *Falcon* offers 72 qubits more quantum security cost. Figure 2d analyzes the quantum security cost to the signature length. For less than half the signature size of the *Dilithium* at 2044 Bytes, the quantum security cost of the *Falcon* at 690 Bytes is 12 qubits more. *Falcon* is close to ideal reference position of top-left corner compared to *Dilithium*.

For applications targeting security levels 2 and 3, *Falcon* doesn't have parameter sets and yet it is advantageous to use *Falcon 1024* security level 5 parameter set as it provides better security for less overhead compared to *Dilithium* parameter sets.

4.3   Multivariate-Based Signatures Security and Length Trade-Off

Figure 3 shows the classical and quantum security trade-offs with respect to the public key length and the signature length of multivariate-based signature algorithms. *Rainbow* and *GeMSS* security costs are measured in both classical gates and quantum gates, and the security costs increase as the public key length and signature length increases. Multivariate-based signature algorithms generate larger public keys and small signatures compared to the lattice-based schemes in Sect. 4.2.

Figure 3a analyzes the classical gate cost to the public key length trade-offs. Horizontal axis of the plot has Bytes of order 10^6 for huge public key lengths. For less than half the public key length of *GeMSS* at 0.3522×10^6 Bytes, *Rainbow* at 0.1490×10^6 Bytes requires 2^{17} more classical gates. Figure 3b analyzes the classical gate cost to the signature length trade-offs. *Rainbow* generates signature length of two to three times than that of *GeMSS* signature size for respective security categories. Figure 3c analyzes the quantum gate cost to the public key length trade-offs. For less than half the public key length of *GeMSS* at

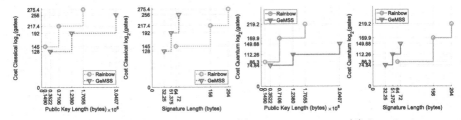

(a) Security in clas- (b) Security in clas- (c) Security in quan- (d) Security in quan-
sical gates vs. public sical gates vs. signa- tum gates vs. public tum gates vs. signa-
key length   ture length   key length   ture length

Fig. 3. Security costs for multivariate-based signature candidates. The dotted line shows the classical gate security level (the left two figures), whereas the solid line shows the quantum gate security level (the right two figures). The vertical scales are in $\log_2(\#\text{Gates})$ and are consistent across the figures.

0.3522×10^6 Bytes, *Rainbow* at 0.1490×10^6 Bytes requires 2^{12} more quantum gates. Figure 3d analyzes the quantum gate cost to the signature length trade-offs. Overall, *Rainbow* has smaller key lengths and greater security costs compared to *GeMSS*. Our analysis shows that with the current cryptanalysis research and knowledge, *Rainbow* provides a greater length- or bit-efficient scheme over *GeMSS*.

5   Security Analysis Between Dilithium, Falcon, and Rainbow

In this section, we present a security analysis of PQC algorithms with respect to qubit, quantum gate, and DW cost metrics working in the framework of the universal quantum gate model and quantum annealing against a cryptanalyst using Grover's algorithm (discussed in Sect. 2). Even though the computational hardness problems differ between the lattice-based (*Dilithium* and *Falcon*) vs. multivariate-based (*Rainbow*), Grover's algorithm-based attacker enables us to compare the security costs for its generality which expedites the search/brute-force process.

5.1   Universal Quantum Gate and Quantum Annealing

We provide a brief overview in this section about the universal quantum gate model, Clifford+T gates, and quantum annealing to provide the background of our inter-scheme security comparison analysis. While the universal quantum gate model is applicable to all schemes, including the three NIST finalist schemes we compare, quantum annealing is only applicable to the lattice-based schemes of *Dilithium* and *Falcon*.

The *universal quantum gate model* consists of gates connected by wires [21]. Quantum gates are the basic building blocks that perform operations on a small number of qubits. Clifford+T gates are used as the universal underlying fault-tolerant logical quantum gate set [30]. Wires represent the motion of a carrier which encodes information both logically and physically. External inputs and outputs are provided by sources and sinks respectively. The structure of the ciphers implies the methods which can be used to break them. The security of *Dilithium* and *Falcon* is based on the hardness of finding the shortest vectors on the lattice, while the security of *Rainbow* is based on the hardness of solving multivariate polynomials over a finite field. Finding shortest vectors can be reformulated as a problem of finding a minimum, which can potentially be solved by *quantum annealing* [26,32] which is designed to find a minimum of the cost function while being less demanding in terms of quantum error correction. Of course, finding a minimum is also possible by the universal quantum gate model [25]. However, in addition to qubits, its implementation would be complicated by the need for a large number of gates.

Quantum annealing works in the following way: the system is initialized in the ground state of the Hamiltonian H_{init} which we assume to be simple to implement. The minimum which we are looking for corresponds to the ground state of another Hamiltonian, H_{key}. Over the time τ, we change the Hamiltonian such that $H_{init} \rightarrow H_{key}$. Adiabatic theorem [10,18,38,43] guarantees that if the time τ is sufficiently large and the change is sufficiently slow (adiabatical), then the system will end up in the ground state of the Hamiltonian H_{key} which corresponds to the key being searched. As we show in Sect. 5.4, the combination of *quantum annealing* and *universal gate model* provides significant advantages for the attacker.

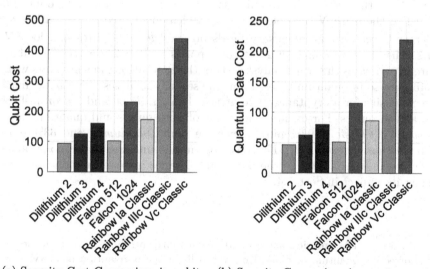

(a) Security Cost Comparison in qubits   (b) Security Comparison in quantum gates

Fig. 4. Security cost comparison across signature candidates

5.2   Metric for All Ciphers: DW Cost to Combine Qubits and Quantum Gates

The security analyses of the PQC schemes in Sect. 4 and in the prior research literature are separate in the security strength metrics used, which makes them difficult to compare. The security costs (the attacker effort/requirement to break the ciphers) of *Dilithium* and *Falcon* are given in qubits, while the security of *Rainbow* is measured in terms of quantum gates, as discussed in Sect. 4. In this section, we introduce and apply the depth-width cost (DW cost) to our post-quantum cipher analyses to enable the inter-scheme comparison, in contrast to the previous research. The number of RAM operations needed to execute a quantum circuit is proportional to the DW cost metric which incorporates both the cryptanalyst cost factors in qubits and quantum gates and assumes an active error correction [34][2].

Definition 1. *A logical Clifford+T quantum circuit having D gates in-depth, W qubits in width, and consisting of an arbitrary number of gates is assigned a DW cost of $\theta(DW)$ RAM operations.*

From Definition 1, DW cost incorporates both qubits and quantum gates and thus enables the comparison between the NIST digital signature finalists.

5.3   Security Analysis in Universal Quantum Gate Model

We provide estimates assuming an adversary executing Grover's search algorithm [31] for the key search in a universal quantum circuit model, introduced in Sect. 4.1. If there are N key options among which one is used by the authorized sender and receiver, the adversary needs on average $\frac{\pi\sqrt{N}}{4}$ gates and $\log_2(N)$ cubits. Therefore, G quantum gates corresponds to $W = 2 \times \log_2(\frac{4}{\pi}G)$ qubits. Figure 4a compares the cryptanalyst costs of the PQC algorithms in qubits while Fig. 4b does so in quantum gates. From the security analyses, *Rainbow* is much more expensive for a cryptanalyst to attack than *Dilithium* and *Falcon* in both gates and in qubits. For example, in terms of both qubits and quantum gates, *Rainbow Vc Classic* is 93% more expensive than *Dilithium 4* and 63% more expensive than *Falcon 1024*. The DW cost in the universal gate model alone is provided in Fig. 5a. Due to the practical relevance of quantum annealing, we consider its impact in Sect. 5.4.

---

[2] In addition to DW metrics, Jaques and Schanck [34] introduce G cost metrics for self-correcting quantum memory. However, self-correcting quantum memory is not available even theoretically. The two dimensional toric code [37], is not thermally stable [6]. Even though in a non-physical case of four spatial dimensions, it is thermally stable [7], it remains an open question if it is possible to implement it in three dimensions in which we live. Therefore, for our purposes, we use conservative DW cost metrics.

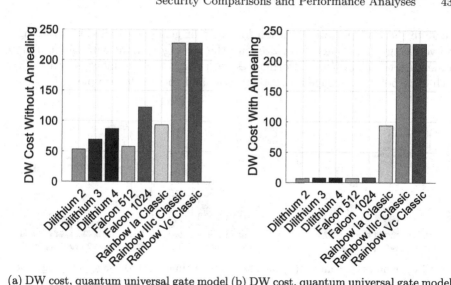

(a) DW cost, quantum universal gate model (b) DW cost, quantum universal gate model
without annealing   with annealing

Fig. 5. Security cost comparison across signature candidates in DW cost without annealing and DW cost with annealing.

5.4 Security Analysis with Quantum Annealing

Quantum annealing is much more restricted than the universal quantum gate model; for example, it cannot execute Shor's algorithm. However, since it relies on adiabatic Hamiltonian evolution rather than on the gates, it's much cheaper in terms of the DW metrics. Figure 5b shows our analysis results. If quantum annealing is used to break *Dilithium* and *Falcon* by finding the minimum of the length of the vector on a lattice (quantum annealing is not applicable to *Rainbow*), it can significantly expedite the cryptanalysis effort for those lattice-based ciphers, and the gap in the security cost between *Rainbow* and the others grow even further. Even without quantum annealing, as seen in Sect. 5.3, *Rainbow Vc Classics* costs more for the adversary to break than *Dilithium* and *Falcon*. In DW cost, *Rainbow Vc Classic* is 188% more expensive than *Dilithium 4* and 187% more expensive than *Falcon 1024*. Our analyses based on a cryptanalyst using Grover's algorithm shows that *Rainbow* has the greatest security cost (the most computational effort for the adversary) with or without quantum annealing (applicable to the lattice-based schemes of *Dilithium* and *Falcon*).

6 Performance Analysis of Cipher Algorithms

In this section, we analyze the execution times of each finalist algorithm for key-pair generation, signature generation (signing), and signature verification (verifying). We use the *liboqs* library to analyze the performance of the algorithms. Using our benchmark software, each of the algorithms is sampled to calculate the average time duration for key-pair generation, signing a message, and verifying the messages. We also vary the message lengths with random data to measure the algorithm performances with respect to the message scalability. Each data point is averaged over 1000 runs, and the results are plotted.

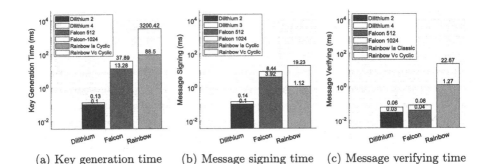

(a) Key generation time   (b) Message signing time   (c) Message verifying time

Fig. 6. Performance analysis of the fastest (colored bar) and slowest (outlined bar) signature candidates from each family across the three signature phases, with a message length of 100 Bytes.

Algorithm Performances. Figure 6 shows the computing costs for every algorithm of each family. While we experiment with all algorithms, our presentation/plot focuses on the slowest from each algorithm family (outlined bar) and the fastest from each algorithm family to show the performance span across $Dilithium(D)$, $Falcon(F)$, and $Rainbow(R)$.

We analyze the performances within each PQC family of algorithms in order to compare the performances between the algorithms once the scheme/family is selected, for example, an application chooses a PQC family or NIST selects the standard PQC signature. We introduce the *intra-family performance ratio*, R_i where i specifies the algorithm family, i.e., $i \in \{D, F, R\}$. For example, R_D is the ratio between the execution time for the slowest $Dilithium$ algorithm and the time for the quickest $Dilithium$ algorithm. By definition, $R_i > 1, \forall i$. By dividing the slowest algorithm's duration with the fastest for each family of algorithms, the key generation data (Fig. 6a) shows that $R_D = 1.3$, $R_F = 2.85$, and $R_R = 36.16$. For the message signing phase (Fig. 6b), $R_D = 1.4$, $R_F = 2.15$, and $R_R = 17.17$. For message verification (Fig. 6c), $R_D = 2$, $R_F = 2$, and $R_R = 17.85$. This makes it clear that $Dilithium$, when compared to $Falcon$ and $Rainbow$, shows optimal behavior with regards to the time taken to run the algorithms from each family.

While the intra-family comparison analysis helps in understanding how each algorithm in a family performs independently, an inter-family comparison analysis gives additional insights when compared with algorithms from other families. For key generation, our data shows that $Dilithium$ is between 102.15 and 32004.2

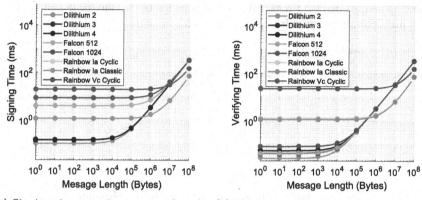

(a) Signing time, varying message lengths (b) Verifying time, varying message lengths

Fig. 7. Performance analysis for the fastest and slowest candidates from each family. The horizontal axis is in logarithmic scale. The dots show the discrete experimental data, and the solid lines are our LoBF estimates.

times faster than the other finalist algorithms. For message signing, *Dilithium* is between 8 and 192.3 times faster than the other family of finalist algorithms. For message verification, *Dilithium* is up to 755.67 times faster than the other algorithms, but only 0.01 milliseconds faster than *Falcon*. From our intra-family and inter-family comparisons, we conclude that *Dilithium* is the fastest algorithm across all algorithms. We extend the analysis to algorithm scalability by using variable message lengths, to compare how the performance changes when the input size increases.

Message Scalability Performances. We measure the signing and verifying performance of the PQC algorithms when the message length varies from 1 Byte to 100 MB in order to analyze the message scalability. Figure 7 shows the fastest and slowest algorithms in each family so that the algorithms within a cipher family have performances between the two algorithms. Using our results in Fig. 7, we estimate the line of best fit (LoBF) based on minimizing the mean squared error to enable the analyses with greater precision. Table 3 includes the LoBF estimations. Our results from Fig. 7a show that *Dilithium 2* is the optimal algorithm for signing, until the message length reaches the intersection with *Rainbow Ia Cyclic*, at 387578 Bytes. Therefore if the message length exceeds 387578 Bytes, *Rainbow Ia Cyclic* becomes the fastest signing algorithm instead of *Dilithium 2*. For verifying (Fig. 7b), *Dilithium 2* is the fastest algorithm until a message length reaches 461478 Bytes, and for messages of greater length, *Rainbow Ia Classic* has the best verifying time.

Application Dependency. The choice of the PQC cipher algorithm depends on its application since the cipher application determines the usage frequencies of

Table 3. The Line of Best Fit (LoBF) estimations for the signing time and verifying time in milliseconds, where x is the message length in Bytes

Algorithm	LoBF (signing time)	LoBF (verifying time)
Dilithium 2	$1.845 \times 10^{-15}x^2 + 3.215 \times 10^{-6}x + 0.09799$	$1.865 \times 10^{-15}x^2 + 3.213 \times 10^{-6}x + 0.02525$
Dilithium 3	$1.767 \times 10^{-15}x^2 + 3.225 \times 10^{-6}x + 0.1398$	$1.815 \times 10^{-15}x^2 + 3.221 \times 10^{-6}x + 0.04121$
Dilithium 4	$1.865 \times 10^{-15}x^2 + 3.216 \times 10^{-6}x + 0.1384$	$1.902 \times 10^{-15}x^2 + 3.211 \times 10^{-6}x + 0.05348$
Falcon 512	$1.783 \times 10^{-15}x^2 + 3.233 \times 10^{-6}x + 3.923$	$1.848 \times 10^{-15}x^2 + 3.225 \times 10^{-6}x + 0.03987$
Falcon 1024	$1.859 \times 10^{-15}x^2 + 3.216 \times 10^{-6}x + 8.4$	$1.867 \times 10^{-15}x^2 + 3.215 \times 10^{-6}x + 0.08054$
Rainbow Ia Cyclic	$1.802 \times 10^{-15}x^2 + 5.265 \times 10^{-7}x + 1.14$	$1.915 \times 10^{-15}x^2 + 5.135 \times 10^{-7}x + 1.271$
Rainbow Ia Classic	$1.792 \times 10^{-15}x^2 + 5.311 \times 10^{-7}x + 1.146$	$1.939 \times 10^{-15}x^2 + 5.143 \times 10^{-7}x + 1.129$
Rainbow Vc Cyclic	$1.463 \times 10^{-15}x^2 + 1.181 \times 10^{-6}x + 19.23$	$1.915 \times 10^{-15}x^2 + 1.135 \times 10^{-6}x + 22.67$

the signing vs. verifying and the message payload size. The frequency discrepancy of signing to verifying a message varies significantly according to the cipher applications For example, in cryptocurrency applications, once a transaction is created, it gets signed a single time. In contrast, as the transaction propagates across the network, every node verifies that the message is genuine [29], thus the signing-to-verifying ratio is close to zero in this case. We aim to prioritize the algorithm with fast message verification. In addition, the message payload size provided by the application requirement affects the performance prioritization and the cipher selection. Our results show that *Dilithium 2* is the most execution-time-efficient if the application message length is short and *Rainbow Ia Classic* for verifying if the message length is large.

7 Performance Analysis with Integration with TCP/IP and TLS

In this section, we analyze the communication/handshake overhead of the PQC algorithms at packet level when integrated with TLS 1.3 and TCP/IPv4. The handshake connection involves multiple transmissions between the client and the server, where the client initiates the connection by sending a *client hello* packet to the server and the server responds with *server hello* carrying the certificate signed by the Certificate Authority (CA), which contains the public key (post-quantum) of the server and the signature (post-quantum). The client then verifies the signature and sends a finished message to the server indicating the end of the handshake. After a successful handshake, application data is securely transferred. Our analysis focuses on packet-level overhead as opposed to the broader networking overhead between the two hosts. We use local virtual machines loaded with *OQS-OpenSSL_1_1_1* [47] acting as a client and server to establish a TLS 1.3 connection using post-quantum digital signature algorithms. We use *tcpdump* [33] to capture the TLS & TCP/IP handshake packets and *Wireshark* [2] to collect the packet data. More details about the experimental setup are provided below. We establish the TLS 1.3 connection 1000 times for the experimental samples and run and compare the performances with the RSA (not quantum-resistant) to provide a reference.

Table 4 shows the algorithms, time, CPU usage, Certificate Size (CS), total TCP Segment Size (TSS), number of Server Hello Packets (SHP), Server Hello Size (SHS), and number of Handshake Packets (HP). Time refers to the average handshake time elapsed for a connection, CPU usage represents the highest percentage logged while connection establishment, CS provides the size of the certificate generated using the algorithms listed. We observed that Server Hello with large certificates uses TCP segmentation. SHP represents the number of packets used to transfer the Server Hello message. TSS provides the total data transferred by TCP segments. SHS represents the total Server Hello size in bytes that contains the certificate and TLS extensions. HP represents the total number of packets used to establish the connection (counted to client finished message).

The implementation of *Rainbow* into TLS 1.3 fails due to excessively large certificate sizes, logged using *tcpdump*, that are responsible for overflowing the TCP window and thus causing errors. By default, the X.509 certificate size in TLS 1.3 has a limit of $2^{24} - 1$ Bytes [46]. *Rainbow*'s certificate size exceeds the X.509 limit and therefore causes the TLS 1.3 connection to fail.

Table 4. TLS performance with different digital signature algorithms. The CPU samples have a confidence interval to 95%. The *Rainbow* algorithms were unable to complete the TLS connection due size limitations, and are therefore marked with asterisks (*).

Algorithm	Time(ms)	CPU ± CI	CS(B)	TSS(B)	SHP	SHS(B)	HP	CS/SHS	SHP/HP
Dilithium 2	3.12	23.90% ± 2.25%	4700	5875	2	5743	10	0.818	0.2
Dilithium 3	3.13	27.33% ± 2.17%	5900	7477	2	7345	10	0.803	0.2
Dilithium 4	3.21	31.29% ± 0.51%	7200	9161	3	8963	12	0.803	0.25
Falcon 512	6.91	29.84% ± 0.47%	2400	2726	1	2660	8	0.902	0.125
Falcon 1024	11.49	31.43% ± 0.61%	4400	4923	2	4791	10	0.918	0.2
Rainbow Ia Cyclic*	7.53	26.04% ± 1.39%	204700						
Rainbow Ia Classic*	6.51	31.78% ± 0.82%	204700						
Rainbow Vc Cyclic*	75.52	32.45% ± 0.73%	2300000						
RSA 2048	3.46	17.16% ± 0.58%	1000	1319	1	1253	8	0.798	0.115

Packet-Level Handshake Analysis: Time Overhead. This section analyzes the handshake overheads in the unit of average connection time, and processing (CPU utilization). Our results in Table 4 show that *Dilithium 2* outperforms the other quantum-resistant algorithms in average handshake time. The average handshake time for *Falcon 512* is 2.21 times more than *Dilithium 2*. *Dilithium 2* is the most efficient in CPU usage, it is 30.92% more efficient than *Dilithium 4*, and 24.85% more efficient than *Falcon 512*. *Falcon 1024*'s CPU usage is 5.33% more than *Falcon 512*.

Packet-Level Handshake Analysis: Certificate Size and Server Hello. This section analyzes the overhead caused by the CS and SHS on the connection handshake. *Falcon 512*'s CS (2400 B) is 0.51 times smaller than *Dilithium 2* (4700 B). *Falcon 512* is the only post-quantum algorithm that transfers its Server Hello message in a single packet and is suitable for devices capable of handling only small certificate sizes due to small buffer sizes. We compute the fraction that the CS takes up inside the Server Hello with $\frac{CS}{SHS}$. This provides the additional extension overhead that each algorithm enforces on the TLS connection. *Falcon 1024* has $\frac{CS}{SHS}$ percentage of 92%, causing only 8% overhead. Except for *Falcon 512*, all other post-quantum algorithms use TCP segmentation for their Server Hello message, indicating the additional overhead within the handshake. Fraction $\frac{SHP}{HP}$ implicates the effect of post-quantum certificate carrying Server Hello on the handshake. A handshake using *Falcon 512* is composed of 12.5% Server Hello, while the other post-quantum algorithms have a percentage of 20% or more.

PQC Algorithm Choices with TLS Integration. From our analysis, *Dilithium 2* has the fastest connection time among the PQC cipher algorithms, and even outperforms RSA in some ways. *Falcon 512* is a better alternative to the *Dilithium* family for its low CS and similar packet overheads to RSA. Multivariate-based algorithms are not suitable for TLS implementations since the large CS's are bigger than the CS limit for TLS 1.3.

8   Takeaways and Discussions

We analyze the PQC ciphers in security and performances in this paper and summarize our choices and recommendations based on the analyses in this section. In security costs, *Falcon 512/1024* incurs the most computational effort against a quantum-equipped cryptanalyst among the lattice-based algorithms in qubits (Sect. 4.2). The multivariate-based schemes are also compared but in quantum gates. Comparing the finalist scheme of *Rainbow* with the alternate scheme of *GeMSS* according to the security categories defined by NIST, *Rainbow Ia* incurs 2^{12} greater security costs in quantum gates than *GeMSS* 128; *Rainbow IIIc* incurs 2^{67} greater quantum gates than *GeMSS* 192; and *Rainbow Vc* 2^{70} greater security costs than *GeMSS* 256 (Section 4.3). In our inter-scheme comparisons, *Rainbow Vc* has 188% and 187% greater security costs in DW cost against an adversary compared to *Dilithium 4* and *Falcon 1024*, respectively, when quantum annealing is enabled in the universal quantum gate model (Sect. 5). Our performance analyses focusing on the algorithms only (Sect. 6) yield that *Dilithium 2* is the quickest for signing for messages shorter than 390 kB and *Rainbow Ia Cyclic* is the quickest for signing messages longer than 390 kB; *Dilithium 2* is the quickest for verifying messages shorter than 460 kB and *Rainbow Ia Classic* for verifying messages longer than 460 kB. When the PQC algorithm is integrated with TLS and TCP/IP (Sect. 7), *Dilithium 2* is the best both in connection handshake time and in CPU processing, while *Falcon 512* has the shortest certificate size affecting the payload and memory size.

The choice of the PQC digital signature algorithm depends on both the PQC application requirements and the R&D in quantum computing and crypt-analysis. Our PQC recommendations are based on standard practices in net-working security. For example, the key exchange occurs more sporadically than the message communication frequency[3], and therefore we prioritize the recom-mendations based on the signature length as opposed to the public key length in Sect. 4.2. Other choices depend on the application domains and properties, including the application-layer message size affecting the efficiency performance comparison in the PQC ciphers in Sect. 6 and the signing frequency vs. verifying frequency providing different prioritization between the efficiency performances of signing vs. verifying in Sect. 6. For example, the cryptocurrency blockchain utilizing digital signatures for the transaction integrity would prioritize the ver-ifying efficiency (since, for every signing to generate a transaction, numerous miners would verify the signature/transaction) and has a message input size less than 460 kB (e.g., Bitcoin has the transaction sizes in the order of hundreds to thousands of Bytes), so the performance-focused PQC cipher choice would be *Dilithium 2*. For networking-constrained applications, the algorithm can also be chosen in order to minimize the number of transmitted packets, which depends on the algorithm's certificate size and the networking protocol's packet specifi-cation including the field length. For example, if the PQC cipher is used for TLS and TCP/IP, then *Falcon 512* would be the choice as studied in Sect. 7

Our security analyses depend on the state-of-the-art R&D in quantum com-puting, including quantum physics (quantum annealing), quantum computing model (universal quantum gate model), and quantum cryptanalysis (the crypt-analysis on lattice-based and multivariate-based schemes as well as Grover's' algorithm). These fields are dynamically evolving in research. In fact, the NIST's finalist selection in advance of standardization is designed to facilitate cryptanal-ysis on *Dilithium*, *Falcon*, and *Rainbow*. While this paper focuses on the current state of the art, the R&D advancement will affect our future analyses and the PQC algorithm recommendations.

9   Related Work in PQC Analyses

Section 3 describes the background to our research including the post-quantum digital signature algorithms, and Sect. 2 explains the history of the post-quantum cryptography and NIST's involvement. In this section, we discuss more related work to our research, including the post-quantum algorithm performance studies, cryptanalysis, and security studies.

Post-quantum Signature Algorithms. Over the past few years, the inter-ests in post-quantum cryptography have significantly increased, and various standardization authorities initiated projects to develop new quantum-resistant

---

[3] If they are comparable, using one-time pad can be an option for information-theoretic security resistant against (quantum-)computationally capable adversaries.

cryptography [1,17]. Numerous submissions and candidate designs underwent extensive analyses. Previous research to that end analyzed the security of the PQC digital signature algorithms by themselves, e.g., *Dilithium* [23], *Falcon* [28], and *Rainbow* [22]. We discuss this in greater detail as we introduce the post-quantum algorithms in Sect. 3. Our work provides inter-scheme comparison analyses by incorporating the DW cost (combining qubits and quantum gates) and by introducing a cryptanalyst attacker using Grover's algorithm. Our security analyses also incorporates the state of the art in quantum computing and, more specifically, universal quantum gate and quantum annealing.

Performance Analysis in TLS and TCP/IP. The authors in [46] provided a performance study on the post-quantum digital signature algorithm candidates of NIST's PQC standardization project. The few selected parameters of seven out of the nine algorithms in the second-round were integrated with TLS 1.3 and analyzed for networking latency for respective algorithms. The Authors proposed a scheme to use different post-quantum algorithms at Certificate Authority (CA) and Intermediate Certificate Authority (ICA) to improve the overall handshake speed and throughput. Our work is comparable to theirs in that it includes the performance analyses when the PQC algorithms are integrated with TLS. However, our work provides the performance analyses with finer granularity at the packet level, enabling richer analyses (e.g., analyzing the required number of packet transmissions to capture the relationship between the certificate size and the protocol's segmentation). Furthermore, we limit our analyses on the NIST finalist schemes for sharper focus and include the security analyses.

Basu et al. conducted a hardware evaluation study on the signature candidates, including Dilithium, in [11]. Out of the three signature algorithms they analyzed, only *Dilithium* advanced to the third-round of NIST's PQC standardization project. Based on implementations on Field Programmable Gate Arrays (FPGA) and Application-Specific Integrated Circuit (ASIC), their analysis recommends the use of *Dilithium* in server implementations with low latency.

Cryptanalysis and Security Analyses. Lattice-based cryptanalysis is provided in [20] and [41]. Authors in [20] provided a software toolkit named Sage 9.0, to perform side-channel attacks on lattice-based cryptography. They also proposed a cryptanalysis framework that can take advantage of side information or hints to perform lattice reduction attacks. Their analysis shows a significant cost reduction in performing cryptanalysis that utilizes the hints. In [41], the authors performed cryptanalysis based on skip-addition fault attacks. They made use of the determinism in the signature algorithm and inject a single fault targeting the signing operation. A portion of the secret key was extracted and used by the proposed forgery algorithm to generate signatures. Their analyses included the skip-addition attacks on *Dilithium* and zero-cost mitigation solutions.

10   Conclusion

This paper presents security comparisons and performance analyses of NIST finalist post-quantum digital signature candidate ciphers. In our security comparison, we use a visualization model to analyze the trade-off between the key/signature size vs. security. We also analyze and compare the security strengths across different schemes (based on lattice-based vs. multivariate-based cipher designs) by building our analyses on the state of the art research (including DW cost, Grover's algorithm, universal quantum gate model, and quantum annealing). Moreover, we analyze the performances of the NIST finalist PQC digital signature schemes for key generation, signing, and verifying signatures. To measure the PQC implementation costs and the overheads in the communication, time, and processing, we also integrate the PQC algorithms with TLS and TCP/IP. Our paper includes discussions and recommendations and intends to facilitate further research in the PQC ciphers/cryptanalysis and aid the standardization in order to better secure the digital systems in the emerging era of quantum computing.

Acknowledgment. This material is based upon work supported by the National Science Foundation under Grant No. 1922410. This research is also supported in part by Colorado State Bill 18-086.

References

1. ETSI-Standards. https://www.etsi.org. Accessed 1 Sept 2020
2. Wireshark tool. https://www.wireshark.org. Accessed 1 Sept 2020
3. Workshops   and   timeline.   https://csrc.nist.gov/projects/post-quantum-cryptography/workshops-and-timeline. Accessed 1 Sept 2020
4. Alagic, G., et al.: Status report on the first round of the NIST post-quantum cryptography standardization process. US Department of Commerce, National Institute of Standards and Technology (2019)
5. Alagic, G., et al.: Status report on the second round of the NIST post-quantum cryptography standardization process, NIST, Technical report, July 2020
6. Alicki, R., Fannes, M., Horodecki, M.: On thermalization in Kitaev's 2D model. J. Phys. A: Math. Theoret. **42**(6), 065303 (2009)
7. Alicki, R., Horodecki, M., Horodecki, P., Horodecki, R.: On thermal stability of topological qubit in Kitaev's 4D model. Open Syst. Inf. Dyn. **17**(01), 1–20 (2010)
8. Alkim, E., Ducas, L., Pöppelmann, T., Schwabe, P.: Post-quantum key exchange-a new hope. In: 25th USENIX Security Symposium (USENIX Security 16), pp. 327–343 (2016)
9. Alsina, D., Latorre, J.I.: Experimental test of Mermin inequalities on a five-qubit quantum computer. Phys. Rev. A **94**(1), 012314 (2016)
10. Amin, M.H.: Consistency of the adiabatic theorem. Phys. Rev. Lett. **102**(22), 220401 (2009)
11. Basu, K., Soni, D., Nabeel, M., Karri, R.: NIST post-quantum cryptography-A hardware evaluation study. IACR Cryptology ePrint Archives, p. 47 (2019)
12. Bernstein, D.J.: Visualizing size-security tradeoffs for lattice-based encryption. IACR Cryptology ePrint Archives, p. 655 (2019)

13. Brassard, G., Høyer, P., Tapp, A.: Quantum cryptanalysis of hash and claw-free functions. ACM SIGACT News **28**(2), 14–19 (1997)
14. Caelli, W.J., Dawson, E.P., Rea, S.A.: PKI, elliptic curve cryptography, and digital signatures. Comput. Secur. **18**(1), 47–66 (1999)
15. Casanova, A., Faugere, J.C., Macario-Rat, G., Patarin, J., Perret, L., Ryckeghem, J.: GeMSS: a great multivariate short signature. Submission to NIST (2017)
16. Castelvecchi, D.: IBM's quantum cloud computer goes commercial. Nat. News **543**(7644), 159 (2017)
17. Chen, L., et al.: Report on post-quantum cryptography, vol. 12. US Department of Commerce, National Institute of Standards and Technology (2016)
18. Cheung, D., Høyer, P., Wiebe, N.: Improved error bounds for the adiabatic approximation. J. Phys. A: Math. Theoret. **44**(41), 415302 (2011)
19. Chuang, I.L., Gershenfeld, N., Kubinec, M.: Experimental implementation of fast quantum searching. Phys. Rev. Lett. **80**(15), 3408 (1998)
20. Dachman-Soled, D., Ducas, L., Gong, H., Rossi, M.: LWE with side information: attacks and concrete security estimation. IACR Cryptology ePrint Archives 2020, 292 (2020)
21. Deutsch, D.E.: Quantum computational networks. Proc. R. Soc. Lond. A Math. Phys. Sci. **425**(1868), 73–90 (1989)
22. Ding, J., Schmidt, D.: Rainbow, a new multivariable polynomial signature scheme. In: Ioannidis, J., Keromytis, A., Yung, M. (eds.) ACNS 2005. LNCS, vol. 3531, pp. 164–175. Springer, Heidelberg (2005). https://doi.org/10.1007/11496137_12
23. Ducas, L., et al.: Crystals-dilithium: a lattice-based digital signature scheme. IACR Trans. Cryptogr. Hardw. Embed. Syst. **2018**, 238–268 (2018)
24. Duong, D.H., Tran, H.T.N., et al.: Choosing subfields for LUOV and lifting fields for rainbow. IET Inf. Secur. **14**(2), 196–201 (2020)
25. Durr, C., Hoyer, P.: A quantum algorithm for finding the minimum. arXiv preprint quant-ph/9607014 (1996)
26. Finnila, A.B., Gomez, M., Sebenik, C., Stenson, C., Doll, J.D.: Quantum annealing: a new method for minimizing multidimensional functions. Chem. Phys. Lett. **219**(5–6), 343–348 (1994)
27. FIPS, P.: 186–4: Federal information processing standards publication. Digital Signature Standard (DSS). Information Technology Laboratory, National Institute of Standards and Technology (NIST), Gaithersburg, MD, pp. 20899–8900 (2013)
28. Fouque, P.A., et al.: Falcon: fast-Fourier lattice-based compact signatures over NTRU. Submission to the NIST's post-quantum cryptography standardization process (2018)
29. Gao, Y.L., Chen, X.B., Chen, Y.L., Sun, Y., Niu, X.X., Yang, Y.X.: A secure cryptocurrency scheme based on post-quantum blockchain. IEEE Access **6**, 27205–27213 (2018)
30. Gottesman, D.: Theory of fault-tolerant quantum computation. Phys. Rev. A **57**(1), 127 (1998)
31. Grover, L.K.: A fast quantum mechanical algorithm for database search. In: Proceedings of the Twenty-Eighth Annual ACM Symposium on Theory of Computing, pp. 212–219 (1996)
32. Hauke, P., Katzgraber, H.G., Lechner, W., Nishimori, H., Oliver, W.D.: Perspectives of quantum annealing: methods and implementations. Rep. Prog. Phys. **83**(5), 054401 (2020)
33. Jacobson, V., Leres, C., McCanne, S.: TCPDUMP public repository (2003). http://www.tcpdump.org

34. Jaques, S., Schanck, J.M.: Quantum cryptanalysis in the RAM model: claw-finding attacks on SIKE. In: Boldyreva, A., Micciancio, D. (eds.) CRYPTO 2019. LNCS, vol. 11692, pp. 32–61. Springer, Cham (2019). https://doi.org/10.1007/978-3-030-26948-7_2
35. Kelly, J.: A preview of Bristlecone, Google's new quantum processor. Google Research Blog 5 (2018)
36. Kipnis, A., Patarin, J., Goubin, L.: Unbalanced oil and vinegar signature schemes. In: Stern, J. (ed.) EUROCRYPT 1999. LNCS, vol. 1592, pp. 206–222. Springer, Heidelberg (1999). https://doi.org/10.1007/3-540-48910-X_15
37. Kitaev, A.Y.: Fault-tolerant quantum computation by anyons. Ann. Phys. 303(1), 2–30 (2003)
38. Messiah, A.: Quantum Mechanics: Translated [from the French] by J. Potter. North-Holland (1962)
39. Moses, T.: Quantum computing and cryptography. Entrust Inc., January 2009
40. Nejatollahi, H., Dutt, N., Ray, S., Regazzoni, F., Banerjee, I., Cammarota, R.: Post-quantum lattice-based cryptography implementations: A survey. ACM Comput. Surv. (CSUR) 51(6), 1–41 (2019)
41. Ravi, P., Jhanwar, M.P., Howe, J., Chattopadhyay, A., Bhasin, S.: Exploiting determinism in lattice-based signatures: practical fault attacks on pqm4 implementations of NIST candidates. In: Proceedings of the 2019 ACM Asia Conference on Computer and Communications Security, pp. 427–440 (2019)
42. Regev, O.: Lattice-based cryptography. In: Dwork, C. (ed.) CRYPTO 2006. LNCS, vol. 4117, pp. 131–141. Springer, Heidelberg (2006). https://doi.org/10.1007/11818175_8
43. Rezakhani, A., Kuo, W.J., Hamma, A., Lidar, D., Zanardi, P.: Quantum adiabatic brachistochrone. Phys. Rev. Lett. 103(8), 080502 (2009)
44. Rivest, R.L., Shamir, A., Adleman, L.: A method for obtaining digital signatures and public-key cryptosystems. Commun. ACM 21(2), 120–126 (1978)
45. Shor, P.W.: Polynomial-time algorithms for prime factorization and discrete logarithms on a quantum computer. SIAM Rev. 41(2), 303–332 (1999)
46. Sikeridis, D., Kampanakis, P., Devetsikiotis, M.: Post-quantum authentication in TLS 1.3: a performance study. IACR Cryptology ePrint Archives, p. 71 (2020)
47. Stebila, D., Mosca, M.: Post-quantum key exchange for the internet and the open quantum safe project. In: Avanzi, R., Heys, H. (eds.) SAC 2016. LNCS, vol. 10532, pp. 14–37. Springer, Cham (2017). https://doi.org/10.1007/978-3-319-69453-5_2
48. Vandersypen, L.M., Steffen, M., Breyta, G., Yannoni, C.S., Sherwood, M.H., Chuang, I.L.: Experimental realization of Shor's quantum factoring algorithm using nuclear magnetic resonance. Nature 414(6866), 883–887 (2001)
49. Wheatley, M.: D-Wave debuts new 5,000-qubit quantum computer, September 2019. https://siliconangle.com/2019/09/24/d-wave-debuts-new-5000-qubit-quantum-computer

Tighter Proofs for the SIGMA and TLS 1.3 Key Exchange Protocols

Hannah Davis[1($\boxtimes$)] and Felix Günther[2($\boxtimes$)]

[1] Department of Computer Science and Engineering, UC San Diego, La Jolla, USA
`h3davis@eng.ucsd.edu`
[2] Department of Computer Science, ETH Zürich, Zürich, Switzerland
`mail@felixguenther.info`

Abstract. We give new, fully-quantitative and concrete bounds that justify the SIGMA and TLS 1.3 key exchange protocols not just in principle, but in practice. By this we mean that, for standardized elliptic curve group sizes, the overall protocol actually achieves the intended security level.

Prior work gave reductions of both protocols' security to the underlying building blocks that were loose (in the number of users and/or sessions), so loose that they gave no guarantees for practical parameters. Adapting techniques by Cohn-Gordon et al. (Crypto 2019), we give reductions for SIGMA and TLS 1.3 to the strong Diffie–Hellman problem which are tight, and prove that this problem is as hard as solving discrete logarithms in the generic group model. Leveraging our tighter bounds, we meet the protocols' targeted security levels when instantiated with standardized curves and improve over prior bounds by up to over 90 bits of security across a range of real-world parameters.

Keywords: Key exchange · SIGMA · TLS 1.3 · Security bounds · Tightness

1 Introduction

The Transport Layer Security (TLS) protocol [41] is responsible for securing billions of Internet connections every day. Usage statistics for Google Chrome and Mozilla Firefox report that 76–98% of all web page accesses are encrypted.[1] At the heart of TLS is an authenticated key exchange (AKE) protocol, the so-called handshake protocol, responsible for providing the parties (client and server) with a shared, symmetric key that is fresh, private and authenticated. The ensuing record layer secures data using this key. The AKE protocol of TLS is based on the SIGMA ("SIGn-and-MAc") design of Krawczyk [32] for the Internet Key Exchange (IKE) protocol [28] of IPsec [31], which generically augments an unauthenticated, ephemeral Diffie–Hellman (DH) key exchange with authenticating signatures and MACs.

---

[1] https://transparencyreport.google.com/, https://telemetry.mozilla.org/.

© Springer Nature Switzerland AG 2021
K. Sako and N. O. Tippenhauer (Eds.): ACNS 2021, LNCS 12727, pp. 448–479, 2021.
https://doi.org/10.1007/978-3-030-78375-4_18

Naturally, the SIGMA AKE protocol and its incarnation in TLS have been the recipients of proofs of security. We contend that these largely justify the AKE protocols in principle, but not in practice, meaning not for the parameters in actual use and at the desired or expected level of security. Our work takes steps towards filling this gap.

Qualitative and Quantitative Bounds. Let us expand on this. The protocols KE we consider are built from a cyclic group $\mathbb{G}$ in which some DH problem P is assumed to be hard, a pseudorandom function PRF and unforgeable signature and MAC schemes S and M. The target for KE is session-key security with explicit authentication as originating from [10,12,16]. A proof of security has both a qualitative and quantitative dimension. Qualitatively, a proof of security for the AKE protocol KE says that KE meets its target definition assuming the building blocks meet theirs, where, in either case, meeting the definition means any poly-time adversary has negligible advantage in violating it.

The quantitative dimension associates to each adversary in the security game of KE a set of resources r, representing its runtime and attack surface (e.g., the number of users and executed protocol sessions the adversary has access to). It then relates the maximum advantage of any r-resource adversary in breaking KE's security to likewise advantage functions for the building blocks through an equation of the (simplified) form

$$\mathsf{Adv}_{\mathsf{KE}}(r) \le f_{\mathbb{G}} \cdot \mathsf{Adv}_{\mathbb{G}}^{\mathsf{P}}(r_{\mathbb{G}}) + f_{\mathsf{S}} \cdot \mathsf{Adv}_{\mathsf{S}}^{\mathsf{EUF\text{-}CMA}}(r_{\mathsf{S}}) + \dots,$$

deriving quantitative factors f_{X} and resources r_{X} for the advantage of each building block X.

Speaking asymptotically again, when f_{X} and r_{X} are polynomial functions in r, then $\mathsf{Adv}_{\mathsf{KE}}(r)$ is negligible whenever all building blocks' advantages are. Due to the complexity of key exchange models and the challenging task of combining the right components in a secure manner, key exchange analyses (including prior work on SIGMA [17] and TLS 1.3 [22,24,26,35]) indeed often remain abstract and consider only qualitative, asymptotic security bounds.

Standardized protocols like TLS in contrast have to define concrete choices for each cryptographic building block. This involves considering reasonable estimates for adversarial resources (like runtime t and number of key-exchange model queries q) and specific instances and parameters for the underlying components X. One would hope that key exchange proofs can provide guidance in making sound choices that result in the desired overall security level. Unfortunately, AKE security bounds regularly are highly non-tight, meaning that f_{X} and/or r_{X} for some components X are so large that reasonable stand-alone parameters for X yield vacuous key exchange advantages for practical parameters. While the asymptotic bound tells us that scaling up the parameters for X (say, the DDH problem [14]) will at some point result in a secure overall advantage, this causes efficiency concerns (e.g., doubling elliptic curve DH security parameters means quadrupling the cost for group operations) and hence does not happen in practice.

Table 1. Exemplary concrete advantages of a key exchange adversary with given resources t (running time), $\#U$ (number of users), $\#S$ (number of sessions), in breaking the security of the SIGMA and TLS 1.3 protocols when instantiated with curve `secp256r1`, `secp384r1`, or `x25519`, based on the prior bounds by Canetti-Krawczyk [17] resp. Dowling et al. [24], and the bounds we establish (Theorem 4 and 5). Target indicates the maximal advantage $t/2^b$ tolerable when aiming for the respective curve's security level ($b = 128$ resp. 192 bits); entries in red-shaded cells miss that target. See Sect. 7 for full details and curves `secp521r1` and `x448`.

Adv. resources					SIGMA		TLS 1.3	
t	$\#U$	$\#S$	Curve	Target	CK [17]	Us (Theorem 4)	DFGS [24]	Us (Theorem 5)
2^{60}	2^{20}	2^{35}	secp256r1	2^{-68}	$\approx 2^{-61}$	$\approx 2^{-116}$	$\approx 2^{-64}$	$\approx 2^{-116}$
2^{60}	2^{30}	2^{55}	secp256r1	2^{-68}	$\approx 2^{-21}$	$\approx 2^{-106}$	$\approx 2^{-24}$	$\approx 2^{-106}$
2^{60}	2^{20}	2^{35}	x25519	2^{-68}	$\approx 2^{-57}$	$\approx 2^{-112}$	$\approx 2^{-60}$	$\approx 2^{-112}$
2^{60}	2^{30}	2^{55}	x25519	2^{-68}	$\approx 2^{-17}$	$\approx 2^{-102}$	$\approx 2^{-20}$	$\approx 2^{-102}$
2^{80}	2^{20}	2^{35}	secp256r1	2^{-48}	$\approx 2^{-21}$	$\approx 2^{-76}$	$\approx 2^{-24}$	$\approx 2^{-76}$
2^{80}	2^{30}	2^{55}	secp256r1	2^{-48}	1	$\approx 2^{-66}$	1	$\approx 2^{-66}$
2^{80}	2^{20}	2^{35}	x25519	2^{-48}	$\approx 2^{-17}$	$\approx 2^{-72}$	$\approx 2^{-20}$	$\approx 2^{-72}$
2^{80}	2^{30}	2^{55}	x25519	2^{-48}	1	$\approx 2^{-62}$	1	$\approx 2^{-62}$
2^{80}	2^{20}	2^{35}	secp384r1	2^{-112}	$\approx 2^{-149}$	$\approx 2^{-204}$	$\approx 2^{-152}$	$\approx 2^{-204}$
2^{80}	2^{30}	2^{55}	secp384r1	2^{-112}	$\approx 2^{-109}$	$\approx 2^{-194}$	$\approx 2^{-112}$	$\approx 2^{-194}$

We illustrate in Table 1 the effects of the non-tight bounds for SIGMA and TLS 1.3 when instantiating the protocols with NIST curves `secp256r1`, `secp384r1` [39], or curve `x25519` [37] and idealizing the protocols' other components (see Sect. 7 for full details). Following the curves' security, we aim at a security level of 128 bits, resp. 192 bits, meaning the ratio of an adversary's runtime to its advantage should be bounded by 2^{-128}, resp. 2^{-192}. When considering the advantage of key exchange adversaries running in time t, interacting in the security game with $\#U$ users and $\#S$ sessions, we can see that previous security bounds fail to meet the targeted security level for real-world–scale parameters ($\#U$ ranging in 2^{20}–2^{30} based on 2^{27} active certificates on the Internet, $\#S$ ranging in 2^{35}–2^{55} based on 2^{32} Internet users and 2^{33} daily Google searches[2]). In the security analysis by Canetti and Krawczyk [17] (CK) for SIGMA, the factor associated to the decisional Diffie–Hellman problem is $f_{\mathsf{DDH}}(t, \#U, \#S) = \#U \cdot \#S$, where $\#U$ and $\#S$ again are the number of users, resp. sessions, accessible by the adversary. The analysis by Dowling et al. [24] (DFGS) for TLS 1.3 reduces to the strong Diffie–Hellman problem [1]—via the PRF-ODH assumption [15,29]—with factor $f_{\mathsf{stDH}}(t, \#U, \#S) = (\#S)^2$. In contrast, we reduce to the strong Diffie–Hellman problem with a constant factor for both SIGMA and TLS 1.3.

Let us discuss three data points from Table 1:

---

[2] https://letsencrypt.org/stats/, https://www.internetlivestats.com/.

1. Already with medium-sized resources, investing time $t = 2^{60}$ and interacting with a million users ($\#U = 2^{20}$) and a few billion sessions ($\#S = 2^{35}$), the CK [17] and DFGS [24] advantage bounds for SIGMA and TLS 1.3 with curves secp256r1 and x25519 fall 6–11 bits below the target of 2^{-68} for 128-bit security.

2. When considering a more powerful, global-scale adversary ($t = 2^{80}$, $\#U = 2^{30}$, $\#S = 2^{55}$), both CK and DFGS bounds for secp256r1/x25519 become fully vacuous; the upper bound on the probability of the adversary breaking the protocol is 1. We stress that secp256r1 is the mandatory-to-implement curve for TLS 1.3; secp256r1 and x25519 together make up for 90% of the TLS 1.3 ECDHE handshakes reported through Firefox Telemetry.

3. Finally, and notably, even switching to the higher-security curve secp384r1 helps only marginally in the latter case: the resulting advantage against SIGMA falls 3 bits short of the 192-bit security target of 2^{-112}, and the TLS advantage bound only barely meets that target.

For all curves and choices of parameters, our bounds do better.

Contributions. Most prior results in tightly secure key exchange (e.g., [4,27]) apply only to bespoke protocols, carefully designed to allow for tighter proof techniques, at the cost of requiring more complex primitives which, in the end, eat up the gained practical efficiency. Our work in contrast establishes tight security for standardized AKE protocols. We give tight reductions for the security of SIGMA and TLS 1.3 to the strong Diffie–Hellman problem [1], which in addition we prove is as hard as the discrete logarithm problem in the generic group model (GGM) [38,42]. Instantiating our bounds shows that, with standardized real-world parameters, we achieve the intended security levels even when considering powerful, globally-scaled attackers.

Tighter Security Proof of SIGMA(-I). We establish fully quantitative security bounds for SIGMA and its identity-protecting variant SIGMA-I [32] in Sects. 3 and 4. Our result is for BR-like [12] key exchange security and gives a tight reduction to the strong Diffie–Hellman problem [1] in the used DH group, and to the multi-user (mu) security of the employed pseudorandom function (PRF), signature scheme, and MAC scheme, adapting the techniques by Cohn-Gordon et al. [19] in the random oracle model [11]. The latter mu-security bounds are essentially equivalent to the corresponding bounds by CK [17]. Our improvement comes from shaving off a factor of $\#U \cdot \#S$ (number of users times number of sessions) on the DH problem advantage compared to CK. While we move to the interactive strong Diffie–Hellman problem (compared to DDH [14] used in [17]), we prove (in Appendix C) that the strong DH problem, like DDH, is as hard as solving discrete logarithms in the generic group model [38,42].

Tighter Security Proof for the TLS 1.3 DH Handshake. We likewise establish fully quantitative security bounds for the key exchange of the recently standardized newest version of the Transport Layer Security protocol, TLS 1.3 [41], in

Sects. 5 and 6. The main quantitative improvement in our reduction is again a tight reduction to the strong DH problem, whereas prior bounds by DFGS [24] incurred a quadratic loss to the PRF-ODH assumption [15,29], a loss which translates directly to strong DH [15]. While TLS 1.3 roughly follows the SIGMA-I design, its cascading key schedule impedes the precise technique of Cohn-Gordon et al. [19] and a direct application of our results on SIGMA-I, as no single function (to be modeled as a random oracle) binds the Diffie–Hellman values to the session context. We therefore have to carefully adapt the proof to accommodate the more complex key schedule and other core variations in TLS 1.3's key exchange, achieving conceptually similar tightness results as for SIGMA-I.

Evaluation. In Sect. 7, we evaluate the concrete security implications of our improved bounds for SIGMA and TLS 1.3 for a wide range of real-world resource parameters and all five elliptic curves standardized for use in TLS 1.3 [41], a summary of which is displayed in Table 1. We report that our tighter proofs indeed materialize for a wide range of real-world resource parameters. The resulting attacker advantages meet the targeted security levels of all five curves. In comparison to the prior CK [17] SIGMA and DFGS [24] TLS 1.3 bounds, our results improve the obtained security across these real-world parameters by up to 85 bits for SIGMA and 92 bits for TLS 1.3, respectively.

Concurrent Work. In concurrent and independent work, Diemert and Jager (DJ) [21] studied the tight security of the main TLS 1.3 handshake. Their work also tightly reduces the security of TLS 1.3 to the strong Diffie–Hellman problem by extending the technique of Cohn-Gordon et al. [19], and their bounds and ours are similarly tight. When instantiated with real-world parameters, both bounds are dominated by the same terms, as we will demonstrate in Sect. 7. Our proof differs from theirs in two key ways: We use an incomparable security model that is weaker in some ways and stronger in others, and we approximate the TLS 1.3 key schedule with fewer random oracles. We also contextualize our results quite differently than the DJ work, with a detailed numerical analysis that is enabled by our fully parameterized, concrete bounds. Uniquely to this work, we treat the more generic SIGMA-I protocol and justify our use of the strong DH problem with new bounds in the generic group model. Diemert and Jager [21] in turn study tight composition with the TLS record protocol.

The DJ analysis is carried out in the multi-stage key exchange model [25], proving security not only of the final session key, but also of intermediate handshake encryption keys and further secrets. While our proof does show security of these intermediate keys, we do not treat them as first-class keys accessible to the adversary through dedicated queries in the security model. Unlike either the DJ or Cohn-Gordon et al. works, our model addresses explicit authentication, which we prove via HMAC's unforgeability.

To tackle the challenge that TLS 1.3's key schedule does not bind DH values and session context in one function, DJ model the full cascading derivation of each intermediate key monolithically as an independent, programmable random oracle (cf. [21, Theorem 6]). We instead model the key schedule's inner

HKDF [34] extraction and expansion functions as two individual random oracles, carefully connected via efficient look-up tables, yielding a slightly less extensive use of random oracles and compensating for the existence of shared computations in the derivation of multiple keys. This approach produces more compact bounds and allows our analysis to stay closer to the use of HKDF in TLS 1.3, where the output of one extraction call is used to derive multiple keys.

2 AKE Security Model and Multi-user Building Blocks

We provide our results in a game-based key exchange model formalized in Fig. 1, at its core following the seminal work by Bellare and Rogaway [12] considering an active network adversary that controls all communication (initiating sessions and determining their next inputs through SEND queries) and is able to corrupt long-term secrets (REVLONGTERMKEY) as well as session keys (REVSESSIONKEY). The adversary's goal is then to (a) distinguish the established shared *session key* in a "fresh" (not trivially compromised, captured through a Fresh predicate) session from a uniformly random key obtained through TEST queries (breaking *key secrecy*), or (b) make a session accept without matching communication partner (breaking *explicit authentication*).

Following Cohn-Gordon et al. [19], we formalize our model in a real-or-random version (following Abdalla, Fouque, and Pointcheval [3] with added forward secrecy [2]) with *many* TEST queries which all answer with a real or uniformly random session key based on the *same* random bit b. We focus on the security of the *main* session key established. While our proofs (for both SIGMA and TLS 1.3) establish security of the intermediate encryption and MAC keys, too, we do not treat them as first-class keys available to the adversary through TEST and REVSESSIONKEY queries. We expect that our results extend to a multi-stage key exchange (MSKE [25]) treatment and refer to the concurrent work by Diemert and Jager [21] for tight results for TLS 1.3 in a MSKE model.

In contrast to the work by Cohn-Gordon et al. [19] and Diemert and Jager [21], our model additionally captures explicit authentication through the ExplicitAuth predicate in Fig. 1, ensuring sessions with non-corrupted peer accept with an honest partner session. We and [21] further treat protocols where the communication partner's identity of a session may be unknown at the outset and only learned during the protocol execution; this setting of "post-specified peers" [17] particularly applies to the SIGMA protocol family [32] as well as TLS 1.3 [41].

Key Exchange Protocols. We begin by formalizing the syntax of key exchange protocols. A key exchange protocol KE consists of three algorithms (KGen, Activate, Run) and an associated key space KE.KS (where most commonly KE.KS $= \{0,1\}^n$ for some $n \in \mathbb{N}$). The key generation algorithm KGen() $\xrightarrow{\$} (pk, sk)$ generates new long-term public/secret key pairs. In the security model, we will associate key pairs to distinct *users* (or *parties*) with some identity $u \in \mathbb{N}$ running the protocol, and log the public long-term keys associated with each user identity in a list *peerpk*. (The adversary will be in control of initializing new users, identified by an increasing counter, and we assume it only references existing user identities.) The activation algorithm Activate(id, sk, $peerid$, $peerpk$, $role$) $\xrightarrow{\$}$ (st', m') initiates a new session for a given user identity id (and associated long-term secret key sk) acting in a given role $role \in \{$initiator, responder$\}$ and aiming to communicate with some peer user identity *peerid*. Activate also takes as input the list *peerpk* of all users' public keys; protocols may use this list to look up their own and their peers' public keys. We provide the entire list instead of just the user's and peers' public keys to accommodate protocols with post-specified peer. These protocols may leave *peerid* unspecified at the time of session activation; when the peer identity is set at some later point, the list can be used to find the corresponding long-term key. Activation outputs a session state and (if $role = $ initiator) first protocol message m', and will be invoked in the security model to create a new session π_u^i at a user u (where the label i distinguishes different sessions of the same user). Finally, Run(id, sk, st, $peerpk$, m) $\xrightarrow{\$}$ (st', m') delivers the next incoming key exchange message m to the session of user id with secret key sk and state st, resulting in an updated state st' and a response message m'. Like Activate, it relies on the list *peerpk* to look up its own and its peer's long-term keys.

The state of each session in a key exchange protocol contains at least the following variables, beyond possibly further, protocol-specific information:

peerid $\in \mathbb{N}$. Reflects the (intended) partner identity of the session; if post-specified, this is learned and set (once) during protocol execution.
role $\in \{$initiator, responder$\}$. The session's role, determined upon activation.
status $\in \{$running, accepted, rejected$\}$. The session's status; initially *status* $=$ running, a session accepts when it switches to *status* $=$ accepted (once).
skey $\in$ KE.KS. The derived session key (in KE.KS), set upon acceptance.
sid. The session identifier used to define partnered session in the security model; initially unset, *sid* is determined (once) during protocol execution.

Key Exchange Security. We formalize our key exchange security game $G_{\text{KE},\mathcal{A}}^{\text{KE-SEC}}$ in Fig. 1, based on the concepts introduced above in Fig. 1 and following the framework for code-based game playing by Bellare and Rogaway [13]. After initializing the game, the adversary $\mathcal{A}$ is given access to queries NEWUSER (generating a new user's public/secret key pair), SEND (controlling activation and message processing of sessions), REVSESSIONKEY (revealing session keys), REVLONGTERMKEY (corrupting user's long-term secrets), and TEST (providing challenge real-or-random session keys), as well as a FINALIZE query to which it will submit its guess b' for the challenge bit b, ending the game.

The game $G_{\text{KE},\mathcal{A}}^{\text{KE-SEC}}$ then (in FINALIZE) determines whether $\mathcal{A}$ was successful through the following three predicates, formalized in pseudocode in Fig. 1: Sound ensures session identifiers are set in a sound manner (non-colliding, ensuring agreement on session keys). ExplicitAuth encodes explicit authentication, requiring that accepted sessions agree on the intended peer (if non-corrupted). Finally,

$G_{\mathsf{KE},\mathcal{A}}^{\mathsf{KE-SEC}}$

<u>INITIALIZE:</u>

1 time ← 0; users ← 0
2 $b \xleftarrow{\$} \{0,1\}$

<u>NEWUSER:</u>

3 users ← users + 1
4 $(pk_{\mathsf{users}}, sk_{\mathsf{users}}) \xleftarrow{\$} \mathsf{KGen}()$
5 revltk_{\mathsf{users}} ← ∞
6 $peerpk[\mathsf{users}] \leftarrow pk_{\mathsf{users}}$
7 return pk_{users}

<u>SEND(u, i, m):</u>

8 if $\pi_u^i = \bot$ then
9    $(peerid, role) \leftarrow m$
10   $(\pi_u^i, m') \xleftarrow{\$} \mathsf{Activate}(u, sk_u, peerid,$
     $peerpk, role)$
11   $\pi_u^i.t_{\mathsf{acc}} \leftarrow 0$
12 else
13   $(\pi_u^i, m') \xleftarrow{\$} \mathsf{Run}(u, sk_u, \pi_u^i, peerpk, m)$
14 if $\pi_u^i.status = \mathsf{accepted}$ then
15   time ← time + 1
16   $\pi_u^i.t_{\mathsf{acc}} \leftarrow$ time
17 return m'

<u>REVSESSIONKEY(u, i):</u>

18 if $\pi_u^i = \bot$ or $\pi_u^i.status \neq \mathsf{accepted}$ then
19   return $\bot$
20 $\pi_u^i.\mathsf{revealed} \leftarrow \mathsf{true}$
21 return $\pi_u^i.skey$

<u>REVLONGTERMKEY(u):</u>

22 time ← time + 1
23 revltk$_u$ ← time
24 return sk_u

<u>TEST(u, i):</u>

25 if $\pi_u^i = \bot$ or $\pi_u^i.status \neq \mathsf{accepted}$ or
   $\pi_u^i.\mathsf{tested}$ then
26   return $\bot$
27 $\pi_u^i.\mathsf{tested} \leftarrow \mathsf{true}$
28 $T \leftarrow T \cup \{\pi_u^i\}$
29 $k_0 \leftarrow \pi_u^i.skey$
30 $k_1 \xleftarrow{\$} \mathsf{KE.KS}$
31 return k_b

<u>FINALIZE(b'):</u>

32 if ¬Sound then return 1
33 if ¬ExplicitAuth then return 1
34 if ¬Fresh then $b' \leftarrow 0$
35 return $[[b = b']]$

<u>Sound:</u>

1 if $\exists$ distinct π_u^i, π_v^j, π_w^k with $\pi_u^i.sid =$
   $\pi_v^j.sid = \pi_w^k.sid$ then // no triple sid match
2   return false
3 if $\exists \pi_u^i, \pi_v^j$ with
     $\pi_u^i.status = \pi_v^j.status = \mathsf{accepted}$
     and $\pi_u^i.sid = \pi_v^j.sid$
     and $\pi_u^i.peerid = v$ and $\pi_v^j.peerid = u$
     and $\pi_u^i.role \neq \pi_v^j.role$, but $\pi_u^i.skey \neq$
     $\pi_v^j.skey$ then // partnering implies same key
4   return false
5 return true

ExplicitAuth:

1 return
   $\forall \pi_u^i : \pi_u^i.status = \mathsf{accepted}$
        and $\pi_u^i.t_{\mathsf{acc}} < \mathsf{revltk}_{\pi_u^i.peerid}$
   // all sessions accepting with a non-corrupted
   peer ...
       $\Longrightarrow \exists \pi_v^j : \pi_u^i.peerid = v$
          and $\pi_u^i.sid = \pi_v^j.sid$
          and $\pi_u^i.role \neq \pi_v^j.role$
   // ... have a partnered session ...
          and $(\pi_v^j.status = \mathsf{accepted} \Longrightarrow$
   $\pi_v^j.peerid = u)$ // ... agreeing on the peerid
   (upon acceptance)

<u>Fresh:</u>

1 for each $\pi_u^i \in T$
2   if $\pi_u^i.\mathsf{revealed}$ then
3   return false // tested session may not
   be revealed
4   if $\exists \pi_v^j \neq \pi_u^i : \pi_v^j.sid = \pi_u^i.sid$
       and $(\pi_v^j.\mathsf{tested}$ or $\pi_v^j.\mathsf{revealed})$ then
5   return false // tested session's part-
   nered session may not be tested or revealed
6   if $\mathsf{revltk}_{\pi_u^i.peerid} < \pi_u^i.t_{\mathsf{acc}}$ then
7   return false // tested session's peer may
   not be corrupted prior to acceptance
8 return true

Fig. 1. Key exchange security game.

to capture key secrecy, we have to restrict the adversary to testing only *fresh*
(i.e., not trivially compromised) sessions in order to exclude trivial attacks; this
is ensured through Fresh.

We call two distinct sessions π_u^i and π_v^j *partnered* if $\pi_u^i.sid = \pi_v^j.sid$. We refer
to sessions generated by Activate (i.e., controlled by the game) as *honest* sessions
to reflect that their behavior is determined honestly by the game and not the
adversary. The long-term key of an honest session may still be corrupted, or its
session key may be revealed without affecting this notion of "honesty".

Definition 1 (Key exchange security). *Let* KE *be a key exchange protocol
and* $G_{KE,\mathcal{A}}^{KE\text{-}SEC}$ *be the key exchange security game defined in Fig. 1. We define*

$$\mathsf{Adv}_{KE}^{KE\text{-}SEC}(t, q_N, q_S, q_{RS}, q_{RL}, q_T) := 2 \cdot \max_{\mathcal{A}} \Pr\left[G_{KE,\mathcal{A}}^{KE\text{-}SEC} \Rightarrow 1\right] - 1,$$

where the maximum is taken over all adversaries, denoted $(t, q_N, q_S, q_{RS}, q_{RL}, q_T)$-
KE-SEC-*adversaries, running in time at most* t *and making at most* q_N, q_S,
q_{RS}, q_{RL}, *resp.* q_T *queries to their oracles* NewUser, Send, RevSessionKey,
RevLongTermKey, *resp.* Test.

Security Properties. We capture regular *key secrecy* of the main session key
through Test queries, incorporating *explicit authentication* as well as ("perfect") *forward secrecy* by allowing corruption as long as each tested sessions
accepted prior to corrupting its intended peer. This strengthens our model compared to that of Cohn-Gordon et al. [19] which only captures implicit authentication and weak forward secrecy; while Diemert and Jager [21] additionally treat
the security of intermediate and further keys beyond the main session key in
a multi-stage approach [25], but without capturing explicit authentication. Like
[19,21], our model captures *key-compromise impersonation*, but not *session-state
or randomness reveals* [16,36] or *post-compromise security* [18].

Multi-user Security Advantages. Before we continue to our technical results,
let us briefly introduce notation and discuss the multi-user security of the
involved building blocks: PRFs, digital signatures, MAC schemes, and hash functions. We defer full definitions to Appendix B and only explain how to read the
advantage bounds here.

PRF: $\mathsf{Adv}_{PRF}^{mu\text{-}PRF}(t, q_{Nw}, q_{FN}, q_{FN/U})$. The maximal advantage in distinguishing
PRF from a random function of any adversary running in time t with access
to at most q_{Nw} users, making at most q_{FN} function queries overall and $q_{FN/U}$
function queries per user.

Signature: $\mathsf{Adv}_S^{mu\text{-}EUF\text{-}CMA}(t, q_{Nw}, q_{SG}, q_{SG/U}, q_C)$. The maximal advantage for
an existential signature forgery for S of any adversary running in time t
with access to at most q_{Nw} users, making at most $q_{SG}/q_{SG/U}$ signing queries
total/per user, allowed to adaptively corrupt at most q_C users.

MAC: $\mathsf{Adv}_M^{\text{mu-EUF-CMA}}(t, q_{\text{Nw}}, q_{\text{TG}}, q_{\text{TG/U}}, q_{\text{VF}}, q_{\text{VF/U}}, q_C)$. The maximal advantage for an existential MAC forgery for M of any adversary running in time t with access to at most q_{Nw} users, making at most $q_{\text{TG}}/q_{\text{TG/U}}$ and $q_{\text{VF}}/q_{\text{VF/U}}$ tagging resp. verification queries total/per user, allowed to adaptively corrupt at most q_C users.

Hash: $\mathsf{Adv}_H^{\text{CR}}(t)$. The advantage of a given adversary running in time t in outputting a hash collision under H.

Strong Diffie–Hellman GGM Bound. The strong Diffie–Hellman (strong DH) assumption, a weakening of the gap DH assumption [40], states that solving the computational DH problem given a restricted decisional DH [14] oracle is hard.

Definition 2 (Strong Diffie–Hellman problem [40]). *Let* $\mathbb{G} = \langle g \rangle$ *be a cyclic group of prime order* q. *Let* $\mathsf{DDH}(X, Y, Z) := [[X^{\log_g(Y)} = Z]]$ *be a decisional Diffie–Hellman oracle. We define*

$$\mathsf{Adv}_{\mathbb{G}}^{\text{stDH}}(t, q_{\text{sDH}}) := \max_{\mathcal{A}} \Pr\left[\mathcal{A}^{\mathsf{DDH}(g^x, \cdot, \cdot)}(\mathbb{G}, g, g^x, g^y) = g^{xy} \mid x, y \xleftarrow{\$} \mathbb{Z}_q\right],$$

where the maximum is taken over all adversaries, denoted (t, q_{sDH})-stDH-*adversaries, running in time at most* t *and making at most* q_{sDH} *queries to their* DDH *oracle.*

The strong (or gap) DH assumption has been deployed in numerous works to analyze practical key exchange designs, directly or through the PRF-ODH assumption [15,29] it supports, including [22–26,29,35] as well as in the closely related works on practical tightness by Cohn-Gordon et al. [19] and Diemert and Jager [21]. To argue that it is reasonable to rely on the strong DH assumption, we turn to the generic group model [38,42]. Although some known algorithms for solving discrete logarithms in finite fields like index calculus fall outside the generic group model, the best known algorithms for elliptic curve groups are generic. Shoup [42] proved that, in the generic group model, any adversary computing at most t group operations in a group of prime order p has advantage at most $\mathcal{O}(t^2/p)$ in solving the discrete logarithm, CDH, or DDH problem. We claim, and prove in Appendix C, that any adversary in the generic group model making at most t group operations and DDH oracle queries, also has advantage at most $\mathcal{O}(t^2/p)$ in solving the strong Diffie–Hellman problem.

Theorem 3. *Let* $\mathbb{G}$ *be a group with prime order* p. *In the generic group model,* $\mathsf{Adv}_{\mathbb{G}}^{\text{stDH}}(t, q) \leq 4t^2/p$.

3 The SIGMA Protocol

The SIGMA family of key exchange protocols introduced by Krawczyk [32,33] describes several variants for building authenticated Diffie–Hellman key

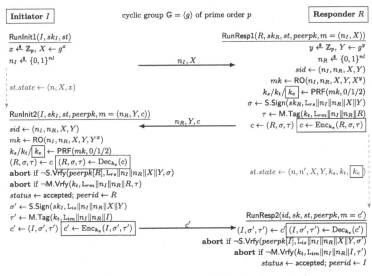

Fig. 2. The SIGMA/SIGMA-I protocol flow diagram. $\boxed{\text{Boxed}}$ code is only performed in the SIGMA-I variant. Values L_x indicate label strings (distinct per x).

exchange using the "SIGn-and-MAc" approach. Its design has been adopted in several Internet security protocols, including, e.g., the Internet Key Exchange protocol [28,30] as part of the IPsec Internet security protocol [31] and the newest version 1.3 of the Transport Layer Security (TLS) protocol [41].

Beyond the basic SIGMA design, we are particularly interested in the SIGMA-I variant which forms the basis of the TLS 1.3 key exchange and aims at hiding the protocol participants' identities as additional feature. We here present an augmented version of the basic SIGMA/SIGMA-I protocols which includes explicit exchange of session-identifying random numbers (nonces) to be closer to SIGMA(-like) protocols in practice, somewhat following the "full-fledged" SIGMA variant [33, Appendix B]. We illustrate these protocol flows in Fig. 2.

The SIGMA and SIGMA-I protocols make use of a signature scheme $S = (KGen, Sign, Vrfy)$, a MAC scheme $M = (KGen, Tag, Vrfy)$, a pseudorandom function PRF, and a function RO which we model as a random oracle. The parties' long-term secret keys consist of one signing key, i.e., $KE.KGen = S.KGen$. The protocols consists of three messages exchanged and accordingly two steps performed by both initiator and responder, which we describe in more detail now.

Initiator Step 1. The initiator picks a Diffie–Hellman exponent $x \xleftarrow{\$} \mathbb{Z}_p$ and a random nonce n_I of length nl and sends n_I and g^x.

Responder Step 1. The responder also picks a random DH exponent y and a random nonce n_R. It then derives a master key as $mk \leftarrow RO(n_I, n_R, X, Y, X^y)$ from nonces, DH shares, and the joint DH secret $g^{xy} = (g^x)^y$. From mk, keys are derived via PRF with distinct labels: the session key k_s, the MAC key k_t, and (only in SIGMA-I) the encryption key k_e.

The responder computes a signature σ with sk_R over nonces and DH shares (and a unique label L_{rs}) and a MAC value τ under key k_t over the nonces and its identity R (and unique label L_{rm}). It sends n_I, g^y, as well as R, σ, and τ to the initiator. In SIGMA-I the last three elements are encrypted using k_e to conceal the responder's identity against passive adversaries.

Initiator Step 2. The initiator also computes mk and keys k_s, k_t, and (in SIGMA-I, used to decrypt the second message part) k_e. It ensures both the received signature σ and MAC τ verify, and aborts otherwise.

It computes its own signature σ' under sk_I on nonces and DH shares (with a different label L_{is}) and a MAC τ' under k_t over the nonces and its identity I (with yet another label L_{im}). It sends I, σ', and τ' to the responder (in SIGMA-I encrypted under k_e) and accepts with session key k_s using the nonces and DH shares (n_I, n_R, X, Y) as session identifier.

Responder Step 2. The responder finally checks the initiator's signature σ' and MAC τ' (aborting if either fails) and then accepts with session key $skey = k_s$ and session identifier $sid = (n_I, n_R, X, Y)$.

4   Tighter Security Proof for SIGMA-I

We now come to our first main result, a tighter security proof for the SIGMA-I protocol. Note that by omitting message encryption our proof similarly applies to the basic SIGMA protocol.

Theorem 4. *Let the SIGMA-I protocol be as specified in Fig. 2 based on a group $\mathbb{G}$ of prime order p, a PRF PRF, a signature scheme S, and a MAC M, and let RO in the protocol be modeled as a random oracle. For any $(t, q_N, q_S, q_{RS}, q_{RL}, q_T)$-KE-SEC-adversary against SIGMA-I making at most q_{RO} queries to RO, we give algorithms $\mathcal{B}_1$, $\mathcal{B}_2$, $\mathcal{B}_3$, and $\mathcal{B}_4$ in the proof, with running times $t_{\mathcal{B}_1} \approx t + 2q_{RO}\log_2 p$ and $t_{\mathcal{B}_i} \approx t$ (for $i = 2, \ldots, 4$) close to that of $\mathcal{A}$, such that*

$$\mathsf{Adv}^{\mathsf{KE\text{-}SEC}}_{\mathsf{SIGMA\text{-}I}}(t, q_N, q_S, q_{RS}, q_{RL}, q_T)$$

$$\leq \frac{3q_S^2}{2^{nl+1} \cdot p} + \mathsf{Adv}^{\mathsf{stDH}}_{\mathbb{G}}(t_{\mathcal{B}_1}, q_{RO}) + \mathsf{Adv}^{\mathsf{mu\text{-}PRF}}_{\mathsf{PRF}}(t_{\mathcal{B}_2}, q_S, 3q_S, 3)$$

$$+ \mathsf{Adv}^{\mathsf{mu\text{-}EUF\text{-}CMA}}_{\mathsf{S}}(t_{\mathcal{B}_3}, q_N, q_S, q_S, q_{RL}) + \mathsf{Adv}^{\mathsf{mu\text{-}EUF\text{-}CMA}}_{\mathsf{M}}(t_{\mathcal{B}_4}, q_S, q_S, 1, q_S, 1, 0).$$

Here, nl is the nonce length in SIGMA-I and $\mathbb{G}$ is the used Diffie–Hellman group of prime order p.

In terms of multi-user security for the employed primitives, multi-user PRF and MAC security can be obtained tightly, e.g., via the efficient AMAC construction [6], and multi-user signature security can be generically reduced to single-user security of any signature scheme with a loss in the number of users, here parties (not sessions) in the key exchange game.

Proof Outline. We defer the detailed game-based description of the proof to the full version [20] and only outline its core and novel technical steps here. We give a more detailed proof for our TLS 1.3 bound in Sect. 6 which requires careful handling of the more complex key schedule, but is still structurally close.

The heart of the proof is the reduction to the strong DH problem. In prior analyses of SIGMA and TLS 1.3, this reduction embeds a DH challenge into a single tested session. This technique incurs a loss in the number of sessions because the reduction must guess in advance which session will be tested. Translating techniques from Cohn-Gordon et al. [19], we instead use the random self-reducibility of DH to embed a single challenge into every session which could possibly accept and be tested without violating the Fresh predicate.

We can divide all sessions into two categories: (A) those who receive nonces or DH shares that have been tampered with by an adversary and (B) those who receive unaltered nonces and DH shares from an honest peer. Embedding a DH challenge into each of these types of sessions must be addressed differently.

If an adversary controls the DH share received by an honest session (category (A)), it can compute that session's DH secret, from which are derived master key, session key, and MAC key. If such a session has an embedded challenge, the simulator cannot honestly produce the proper master key. Instead, it uses the strong DH oracle to detect if the adversary ever makes an RO query containing the session's nonces, DH shares, and the corresponding DH secret, and it programs the response to this query to maintain consistency. The reduction also cannot produce the proper master key for sessions in category (B); however, it can again use the strong DH oracle to detect RO queries containing a valid DH secret that would output the proper master key. This secret can be used to extract the challenge secret and hence win the strong DH game. One particular nuance here is that checking each RO query for every session's DH secret would lead to a quadratic loss in the number of strong DH oracle queries. We maintain tightness by instead using the nonces and group elements in the RO query to identify the relevant sessions and efficiently program responses.

For sessions in category (B), the master key is now chosen uniformly at random. Invoking PRF security allows the session, traffic encryption, and MAC keys to be selected at random as well. Each accepting session must receive a valid signature and MAC tag on its nonces and group elements. Excluding the small probability that nonces and group elements collide between honest sessions, the adversary can only produce these by corrupting a long-term key or by forgery. The former approach violates the Fresh predicate; the latter violates the EUF-CMA security of either the signature or MAC scheme. Therefore, these sessions will accept only if they complete an entire protocol execution without tampering with an honest peer holding the same master key and thus same session key.

For sessions in category (A), the master key may be known to the adversary. However, these sessions still must receive a valid signature to accept. Since the nonces and group elements were tampered with, no honest session will produce this signature. Again, the adversary must resort to either corruption or forgery, hence violating either freshness or signature EUF-CMA security.   □

5 The TLS 1.3 Handshake Protocol

The Transport Layer Security (TLS) protocol in version 1.3 [41] bases its key exchange design (the so-called handshake protocol) on a variant of SIGMA-I. Following the core SIGMA design, the TLS 1.3 main handshake is an ephemeral Diffie–Hellman key exchange, authenticated through a combination of signing and MAC-ing the (full, hashed) communication transcript.[3] Additionally, and similar to SIGMA-I, beyond establishing the main (application traffic) session key, handshake traffic keys are derived and used to encrypt part of the handshake.

Beyond additional protocol features like negotiating the cryptographic algorithms to be used, communicating further information in extensions, etc.—which we do not capture here—, TLS 1.3 however deviates in two core cryptographic aspects from the more simplistic and abstract SIGMA(-I) design: it hashes the communication transcript when deriving keys and computing signatures and MACs, and it uses a significantly more complicated key schedule. In this section we revisit the TLS 1.3 handshake and discuss the careful technical changes and additional assumptions needed to translate our tight security results for SIGMA-I to TLS 1.3's main key exchange mode.

Protocol Description. We focus on a slightly simplified version of the handshake encompassing all essential cryptographic aspects for our tightness results. In particular, we only consider mutual authentication and security of the main application traffic keys and accordingly leave out some computations and additional messages. We illustrate the handshake protocol and its accompanying key schedule in Fig. 3, the latter deriving keys in the extract-then-expand paradigm of the HKDF key derivation function [34].[4]

In the TLS 1.3 handshake, the client acts as initiator and the server as responder. Within Hello messages, both send nonce values n_C resp. n_S together with ephemeral Diffie–Hellman shares g^x resp. g^y. Based on these values, both parties extract a handshake secret HS from the shared DH value $DHE = g^{xy}$ using HKDF.Extract with a constant salt input. In a second step, client and server derive their respective handshake traffic keys tk_{chs}, tk_{shs} and MAC keys fk_C, fk_S through two levels of HKDF.Expand steps from the handshake secret HS, including in the first level distinct labels and the hashed communication transcript $H(CH\|SH)$ so far as context information.

The handshake traffic keys are then used to encrypt the remaining handshake messages. First the server, then the client send their certificate (carrying their identity and public key), a signature over the hashed transcript up to including their certificate, as well as a MAC over the (hashed) transcript up to incl. their signatures. Note the similarity to SIGMA-I here: each party signs both nonces

---

[3] TLS 1.3 also specifies an abbreviated resumption-style handshake based on pre-shared keys; we focus on the main DH-based handshake in this work.

[4] HKDF.Extract(XTS, SKM) on input salt XTS and source key material SKM outputs a pseudorandom key PRK. HKDF.Expand($PRK, CTXinfo$) on input a pseudorandom key PRK and context information $CTXinfo$ outputs pseudorandom key material KM.

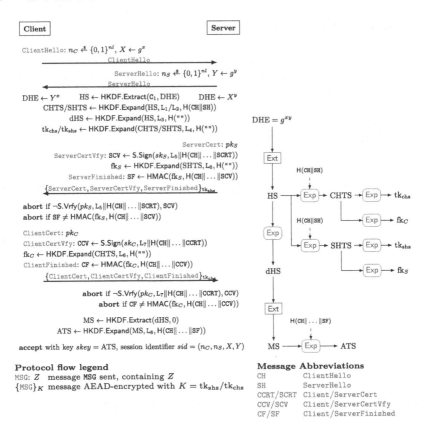

Fig. 3. The simplified TLS 1.3 main Diffie–Hellman handshake protocol (left) and key schedule (right). Values L_i and C_i indicate bitstring labels, resp. constant values, (distinct per i). Boxes Ext and Exp denote HKDF extraction resp. expansion, dashed inputs to Exp indicating context information (see protocol figure for detailed computations).

and DH values (within CH∥SH, modulo transcript hashing) together with a unique label, and then MACs both nonces and their own identity (the latter being part of their certificate). The application traffic secret ATS—which we treat as the session key $skey$, unifying secrets of both client and server—is then derived from the master secret MS through HKDF.Expand with handshake context up to the ServerFinished message. The master secret in turn is derived through (context-less) Expand and Extract from the handshake secret HS.

Handling the TLS 1.3 Key Schedule. What crucially differentiates the TLS 1.3 handshake from the basic SIGMA-I design is the way keys are derived. While SIGMA-I derives its master key through a random oracle with input *both* the shared DH secret *and* the session identifying nonces and DH shares, TLS 1.3 separates them in its HKDF-based extract-then-expand key schedule: The core HS and MS secrets are derived *without* further context purely from the shared DH secret DHE $= g^{xy}$. Only when deriving the specific-purpose secrets—handshake traffic keys, MAC keys, and the session key ATS—are the nonces and DH shares add as session-identifying context. To complicate matters even further, this context is hashed and the final session key ATS depends on more messages than just the session-identifying ones. Recall that the original techniques by Cohn-Gordon et al. [19] heavily relies on (exactly) the session identifiers being input together with DH secrets to a random oracle when programming the latter, impeding a more direct application like for SIGMA-I. In their concurrent work, Diemert and Jager [21] satisfy this requirement by modeling the full derivation of each stage key in their multi-stage treatment as a separate random oracle. This directly connects inputs to keys, but results in a monolithic random oracle treatment of the key schedule which loses the independence of the intermediate HKDF.Extract and HKDF.Expand steps in translation. As we will show next, we overcome the technical obstacle of this linking while directly modeling HKDF.Extract and HKDF.Expand as individual random oracles, carefully orchestrating the programming of intermediate secrets and session keys and connecting them through constant-time look-ups. This leads to a slightly less excessive use of the random oracle technique and allows us to stay much closer to the structure of TLS 1.3's key schedule.

6   Tighter Security Proof for the TLS 1.3 Handshake

We now give our second main result, the tighter-security bound for TLS 1.3.

Theorem 5. *Let $\mathcal{A}$ be a key exchange security adversary against the TLS 1.3 handshake protocol as specified in Fig. 3 based on a hash function H, a signature scheme S, and a group $\mathbb{G}$ of prime order p, and let the HKDF functions Extract and Expand in the protocol be modeled as (independent) random oracles RO_1, resp. RO_2. For any $(t, q_N, q_S, q_{RS}, q_{RL}, q_T)$-KE-SEC-adversary against SIGMA-I making at most q_{RO} queries to the random oracle, we give algorithms $\mathcal{B}_1$, $\mathcal{B}_2$, $\mathcal{B}_3$, and $\mathcal{B}_4$ in the proof, with running times $t_{\mathcal{B}_i} \approx t$ (for $i = 1, 3, 4$) and $t_{\mathcal{B}_2} \approx t + 2q_{RO}\log_2 p$ close to that of $\mathcal{A}$, such that*

$$\mathsf{Adv}_{TLS\,1.3}^{KE\text{-}SEC}(t, q_N, q_S, q_{RS}, q_{RL}, q_T) \leq \frac{3q_S^2}{2^{nl+1} \cdot p} + \mathsf{Adv}_H^{CR}(t_{\mathcal{B}_1})$$

$$+\, 2 \cdot \mathsf{Adv}_{\mathbb{G}}^{stDH}(t_{\mathcal{B}_2}, q_{RO}) + \frac{q_{RO} \cdot q_S}{2^{kl-1}} + \mathsf{Adv}_S^{mu\text{-}EUF\text{-}CMA}(t_{\mathcal{B}_3}, q_N, q_S, q_S, q_{RL})$$

$$+\, \mathsf{Adv}_{HMAC}^{mu\text{-}EUF\text{-}CMA}(t_{\mathcal{B}_4}, q_S, q_S, 1, q_S, 1, 0).$$

Here, $nl = 256$ is the nonce length in TLS 1.3, kl is the output length of $RO_2 =$ HKDF.Expand, $\mathbb{G}$ is the used Diffie–Hellman group of prime order p, and $q_S \cdot q_{RO} \leq 2^{kl-3}$.[5]

---

[5] We simplify the factor on $\mathsf{Adv}_{\mathbb{G}}^{stDH}$ to 2 by assuming $q_S \cdot q_{RO} \leq 2^{kl-3}$, which is true for any reasonable real-world parameters. See the proof for the exact bound.

Proof Idea. Let us first outline the core and novel technical steps, before we give some more proof details below; for space reasons we defer the full proof to the full version [20]. We note that as all keys in the SIGMA exchange are derived from the master key mk, which is itself derived from the shared Diffie–Hellman secret, all intermediate keys in TLS 1.3 are derived from the handshake secret HS, which is derived directly from the shared Diffie–Hellman secret DHE. Embedding a DH challenge into all sessions robs the reduction of the ability to compute HS; as in the SIGMA proof, we will need to use the strong DH oracle to detect and program queries that would output an inconsistent value of HS. Since HS is derived without context, a naive method would have to check every input to HKDF.Extract against the DH shares received by each session, which would however result in a non-tight, quadratic runtime loss.

We instead leverage that the handshake secret HS is an internal value, not exposed by any oracle. The adversary hence cannot detect an inconsistent HS value until it makes the entire chain of queries leading to one of the keys tk_{shs}, tk_{chs}, fk_C, fk_S, or ATS used in SEND, REVSESSIONKEY, and TEST responses. Our reduction prudently sets up a separate bidirectional lookup table for each "link" in that chain. The adversary can make the RO queries in the chain in any order; we need only program the last one for consistency, at which time we have seen the session's DH secret, nonces, and group elements as query inputs. Linking the output of one key-derivation step to the input of the next this way, the reduction can identify the relevant sessions using only constant time and linear space. Together with a careful argument that the attacker is unlikely to guess an intermediate chain value, this allows us to treat HKDF.Extract and HKDF.Expand as two individual random oracles. Thereby, we stay close to how HKDF is used in TLS 1.3 and obtain two compact strong-DH bounds.

Now we give a more precise view of the structure of our proof, with a particular focus on nonstandard techniques and the critical random oracle programming in the reduction step to the strong Diffie–Hellman problem, handling the complexity of TLS 1.3's key schedule.

Proof. We develop the bound via a series of code-based game hops.

Game 0. The first game G_0 is the key exchange security game (cf. Fig. 1) for the TLS 1.3 handshake protocol (Fig. 3). So, $\Pr[G_0 \Rightarrow 1] = \Pr[G_{\mathsf{TLS},\mathcal{A}}^{\mathsf{KE\text{-}SEC}} \Rightarrow 1]$.

Games 1–4. Over the next four games we ensure the uniqueness of each session's protocol transcript by aborting if an honest session chooses a nonce and DH share that have already been sent or received by another honest session, or if a collision occurs in the hash function H. We limit the probability of nonce and DH share collisions using a union bound, and give a simple reduction $\mathcal{B}_1$ to the collision resistance of the hash function H. We also lazily sample the random oracles RO_1 and RO_2 using internal tables H_1 and H_2. Excluding collisions, we obtain the bound $\Pr[G_0 \Rightarrow 1] - \Pr[G_4 \Rightarrow 1] \leq \frac{3q_s^2}{2^{nl+1} \cdot p} + \mathsf{Adv}_{\mathsf{H}}^{\mathsf{CR}}(t_1)$.

Games 5–6. Following the technique of [19], we let initiator sessions in category (A) copy session, MAC, and traffic encryption keys from their partners via a table indexed by session IDs. In TLS 1.3, there are two encryption keys $\mathrm{tk_{shs}}$ and $\mathrm{tk_{chs}}$, and two MAC keys fk_S and fk_C to copy. One significant difference from both [19] and our SIGMA-I proof is that the session key ATS now depends on the messages SCRT, SCV, and SF. We have not yet ensured that partnered sessions agree on these values. Therefore honest initiators will only copy ATS from their partners if they received the exact same (SCRT, SCV, SF) sent by their partner, which they check via an internal look-up table. Otherwise, ATS is still computed as in previous games. Since keys are only copied when partners agree on all of the information entering the key derivation function, this change is unobservable to $\mathcal{A}$, hence $\Pr[G_6 \Rightarrow 1] = \Pr[G_4 \Rightarrow 1]$.

Games 7–8. These two games contain both the most critical step and the one that diverges the most from the SIGMA-I proof. We let all category (A) sessions that are not already copying their keys pick the handshake traffic keys SHTS and CHTS, and the session key ATS uniformly at random, checking for consistency with the random oracle $\mathrm{RO_2}$ and retroactively programming it when necessary. (Category (A) initiator sessions who do not copy ATS due to tampering sample only ATS.) Then, we eliminate the consistency check and let these sessions' handshake traffic keys and session key be uniformly random and inconsistent with the adversary's queries to $\mathrm{RO_2}$. We argue that the adversary can only detect this inconsistency if it queries $\mathrm{RO_2}$ on the correct input to derive one of SHTS, CHTS, or ATS for a category (A) session, an event we refer to as event F.

We give a reduction $\mathcal{B}_2$ to the strong DH assumption in group $\mathbb{G}$ which wins with high probability if event F occurs. Given a challenge C, D, algorithm $\mathcal{B}_2$ simulates Game 7. It embeds C in the DH shares of all initiators and D in the DH shares of all category (A) responders. Because $\mathcal{B}_2$ cannot compute the DH secret for embedded sessions, it uses its stDH oracle to catch and program all queries to $\mathrm{RO_2}$ which are dependent on this secret. When event F occurs, $\mathcal{B}_2$ uses its own randomness to extract the challenge DH secret from the DH secret contained in the query that triggered event F. In addition to the details covered in Sect. 6, the reduction has a few nuances:

1. If for some category (A) session, $\mathcal{A}$ can guess without making the corresponding query any of the intermediate values $\mathrm{HS} = \mathrm{RO_1(C_1, DHE)}$, $\mathrm{dHS} = \mathrm{RO_2(HS, L_3, H(""))}$, or $\mathrm{MS} = \mathrm{RO_1(dHS, 0)}$, where DHE is the DH secret associated to some pair of embedded shares (X, Y) chosen by honest sessions, then it can trigger event F without ever submitting DHE to an oracle. Without knowing DHE, $\mathcal{B}_2$ cannot detect this query, so it does not program $\mathrm{RO_2}$ appropriately and the simulation fails. $\mathcal{B}_2$ does not itself compute HS, dHS, or MS for category (A) sessions, so if $\mathcal{A}$ does not make the appropriate queries than all three values are uniformly random and each can be guessed with probability at most $\frac{q_{\mathrm{RO}} \cdot q_{\mathrm{S}}}{2^{kl}}$.

2. In TLS 1.3, the context string including the Diffie–Hellman shares is hashed with H before it enters the key derivation, so $\mathcal{B}_2$ cannot directly associate an $\mathrm{RO_2}$ query with an honest *sid*. We address this by logging hash computations of honest sessions in a reverse look-up table R. Then in the $\mathrm{RO_2}$ oracle, $\mathcal{B}_2$ can use R to efficiently find the context associated with a particular query.

When $q_{RO} \cdot q_S \leq 2^{kl-3}$, we obtain the bound $\Pr[G_6 \Rightarrow 1] - \Pr[G_8 \Rightarrow 1] \leq 2 \cdot \mathsf{Adv}_{\mathbb{G}}^{\mathsf{stDH}}(t_{\mathcal{B}_2}, q_{RO}) + \frac{q_{RO} \cdot q_S}{2^{kl}}$.

The reduction $\mathcal{B}_2$ queries the stDH oracle at most once for each query to RO_2 query and once more when event F occurs. Computing the input to each stDH query requires 1 multiplication and one exponentiation in the base group, which can be done using $1 + 2\log_2 p$ total group operations. In our runtime analysis, we count each group operation as 1 step, so $t_{\mathcal{B}_2} \approx t + 2q_{RO}\log_2 p$.

Game 9. In game G_9, category (A) sessions sample all encryption and MAC keys uniformly at random. This is distinguishable only if the adversary can query RO on a string containing one of the random values SHTS or CHTS, so by the birthday bound $\Pr[G_8 \Rightarrow 1] - \Pr[G_9 \Rightarrow 1] \leq \frac{q_{RO} \cdot q_S}{2^{kl}}$.

Games 10–13. In the remaining games, we eliminate signature and MAC forgeries via straightforward reductions $\mathcal{B}_3$ and $\mathcal{B}_4$ to the multi-user EUF-CMA security of S and M. This gives the bound $\Pr[G_9 \Rightarrow 1] - \Pr[G_{13} \Rightarrow 1] \leq \mathsf{Adv}_S^{\mathsf{mu\text{-}EUF\text{-}CMA}}(t_{\mathcal{B}_3}, q_{Nw}, q_S, q_S, q_{RL}) + \mathsf{Adv}_M^{\mathsf{mu\text{-}EUF\text{-}CMA}}(t_{\mathcal{B}_4}, q_S, q_S, 1, q_S, 1, 0)$.

Finally, we argue that $\mathcal{A}$ has advantage 0 in game G_{13}, using logic similar to that in our SIGMA-I proof, with two slight differences: 1. Partnered sessions no longer use labels to distinguish their MAC tags; instead we note that messages tagged by initiator sessions are strictly longer than messages tagged by responder sessions. 2. We cannot immediately conclude that partnered sessions agree on the same session key because the session key ATS relies on values that are not contained in the session identifier. However, since we have excluded MAC forgeries, all the information entering the derivation of ATS is authenticated by the responder session's MAC tag.   □

7 Evaluation

Tighter security results in terms of loss factors are practically meaningful only if they materialize in better concrete advantage bounds when taking the underlying assumptions into account. In our case, this amounts to the question: How does the overall concrete security of the SIGMA/SIGMA-I and the TLS 1.3 key exchange protocols improve based on our tighter security proofs?

Parameter Selection. In order to evaluate our and prior bounds practically, we need to make concrete choices for each of the parameters entering the bounds. Let us explain the choices we made in our evaluation:

Runtime $t \in \{2^{40}, 2^{60}, 2^{80}\}$. We parameterize the adversary's runtime between well within computational reach (2^{40}) and large-scale attackers (2^{80}).

Number of users $\#U = q_N \in \{2^{20}, 2^{30}\}$. We consider the number of users a global-scale adversary may interact with to be in the order of active public-key certificates on the Internet, reported at 130–150 million[6] ($\approx 2^{27}$).

---

[6] https://letsencrypt.org/stats/,   https://trends.builtwith.com/ssl/traffic/Entire-Internet.

Number of sessions $\#S \approx q_S \in \{2^{35}, 2^{45}, 2^{55}\}$. Chrome and Firefox report that 76–98% of all web page accesses through these browsers are encrypted, with an active daily base of about 2 billion ($\approx 2^{30}$) users.[7] We consider adversaries may easily see 2^{35} sessions and a global-scale attacker may have access to 2^{55} sessions over an extended timespan. Note that the number of send queries essentially corresponds to the number of sessions.

Number of RO queries $\#RO = q_{\mathrm{RO}} = \frac{t}{2^{10}}$. We fix this bound at a 2^{10}-fraction of the overall runtime accounting for all adversarial steps.

Diffie–Hellman groups and group order p. We consider all five elliptic curves standardized for TLS 1.3 (bit-security b, order p in parentheses): secp256r1 ($b = 128$, $p \approx 2^{256}$), secp384r1 ($b = 192$, $p \approx 2^{384}$), secp521r1 ($b = 256$, $p \approx 2^{521}$), x25519 ($b = 128$, $p \approx 2^{252}$), and x448 ($b = 224$, $p \approx 2^{446}$). We focus on elliptic curve groups, as they provide high efficiency and the best known algorithms for solving discrete-log and DH problems are generic, allowing us to apply GGM bounds for DDH and strong DH.

Signature schemes. In order to unify the underlying hardness assumptions, we consider the ECDSA/EdDSA signature schemes standardized for use with TLS 1.3, based on the five elliptic curves above, treating their single-user unforgeability as equally hard as the corresponding discrete logarithm.

Symmetric schemes and key/output/nonce lengths kl, ol, nl. Since our focus is mostly on evaluating ECDH parameters, we idealize the symmetric primitives (PRF, MAC, and hash function) in the random oracle model. Applying lengths standardized for TLS 1.3, we set the key and output length to $kl = ol = 256$ bits for 128-bit security curves and 384 bits for higher-security curves, corresponding to ciphersuites using SHA-256 or SHA-384. The nonce length is fixed to $nl = 256$ bits, again as in TLS 1.3.

Reveal and Test queries q_{RS}, q_{RL}, q_{T}. Using a generic reduction to single-user signature unforgeability, the number of REVLONGTERMKEY, REVSESSIONKEY, and TEST queries do not affect the bounds; we hence do not place any constraints on them.

Fully-Quantitative CK/DFGS Bounds for SIGMA/TLS 1.3. For our evaluation, we need to reconstruct fully-quantitative security bounds from the more abstract prior security proofs for SIGMA by Canetti-Krawczyk [17] and for TLS 1.3 by Dowling et al. [24]. We report them in Appendix A for reference. In terms of their reduction to underlying DH problems, the CK SIGMA bound reduces to the DDH problem with a loss of $\#U \cdot \#S$, whereas the DFGS TLS 1.3 bound reduces to the strong DH problem with a loss of $(\#S)^2$.

Numerical Advantage Bounds. We report the numerical advantage bounds for SIGMA and TLS 1.3 based on prior (CK [17], DFGS [24]) and our bounds when ranging over the full parameter space detailed above in Table 2. Table 1 summarizes the key data points for 128-bit and 192-bit security levels.

---

[7] https://transparencyreport.google.com/, https://telemetry.mozilla.org/.

Table 2. Advantages of a key exchange adversary with given resources in breaking the security of the SIGMA and TLS 1.3 protocols. See Section 7 for further details.

	Adv. resources					SIGMA		TLS 1.3	
t	$\#U$	$\#S$	$\#RO$	Curve (bit sec. b, order p)	Target $t/2^b$	CK [17]	Us (Theorem 4)	DFGS [24]	Us (Theorem 5)
2^{40}	2^{20}	2^{35}	2^{30}	secp256r1 ($b=128, p\approx 2^{256}$)	2^{-88}	$\approx 2^{-101}$	$\approx 2^{-156}$	$\approx 2^{-104}$	$\approx 2^{-156}$
2^{40}	2^{20}	2^{45}	2^{30}	secp256r1 ($b=128, p\approx 2^{256}$)	2^{-88}	$\approx 2^{-91}$	$\approx 2^{-156}$	$\approx 2^{-84}$	$\approx 2^{-156}$
2^{40}	2^{20}	2^{55}	2^{30}	secp256r1 ($b=128, p\approx 2^{256}$)	2^{-88}	$\approx 2^{-81}$	$\approx 2^{-156}$	$\approx 2^{-64}$	$\approx 2^{-156}$
2^{40}	2^{30}	2^{35}	2^{30}	secp256r1 ($b=128, p\approx 2^{256}$)	2^{-88}	$\approx 2^{-81}$	$\approx 2^{-146}$	$\approx 2^{-104}$	$\approx 2^{-146}$
2^{40}	2^{30}	2^{45}	2^{30}	secp256r1 ($b=128, p\approx 2^{256}$)	2^{-88}	$\approx 2^{-71}$	$\approx 2^{-146}$	$\approx 2^{-84}$	$\approx 2^{-146}$
2^{40}	2^{30}	2^{55}	2^{30}	secp256r1 ($b=128, p\approx 2^{256}$)	2^{-88}	$\approx 2^{-61}$	$\approx 2^{-146}$	$\approx 2^{-64}$	$\approx 2^{-146}$
2^{40}	2^{20}	2^{35}	2^{30}	secp384r1 ($b=192, p\approx 2^{384}$)	2^{-152}	$\approx 2^{-229}$	$\approx 2^{-284}$	$\approx 2^{-232}$	$\approx 2^{-284}$
2^{40}	2^{20}	2^{45}	2^{30}	secp384r1 ($b=192, p\approx 2^{384}$)	2^{-152}	$\approx 2^{-219}$	$\approx 2^{-284}$	$\approx 2^{-212}$	$\approx 2^{-284}$
2^{40}	2^{20}	2^{55}	2^{30}	secp384r1 ($b=192, p\approx 2^{384}$)	2^{-152}	$\approx 2^{-209}$	$\approx 2^{-284}$	$\approx 2^{-192}$	$\approx 2^{-284}$
2^{40}	2^{30}	2^{35}	2^{30}	secp384r1 ($b=192, p\approx 2^{384}$)	2^{-152}	$\approx 2^{-209}$	$\approx 2^{-274}$	$\approx 2^{-232}$	$\approx 2^{-274}$
2^{40}	2^{30}	2^{45}	2^{30}	secp384r1 ($b=192, p\approx 2^{384}$)	2^{-152}	$\approx 2^{-199}$	$\approx 2^{-274}$	$\approx 2^{-212}$	$\approx 2^{-274}$
2^{40}	2^{30}	2^{55}	2^{30}	secp384r1 ($b=192, p\approx 2^{384}$)	2^{-152}	$\approx 2^{-189}$	$\approx 2^{-274}$	$\approx 2^{-192}$	$\approx 2^{-274}$
2^{40}	2^{20}	2^{35}	2^{30}	secp521r1 ($b=256, p\approx 2^{521}$)	2^{-216}	$\approx 2^{-298}$	$\approx 2^{-318}$	$\approx 2^{-282}$	$\approx 2^{-317}$
2^{40}	2^{20}	2^{45}	2^{30}	secp521r1 ($b=256, p\approx 2^{521}$)	2^{-216}	$\approx 2^{-288}$	$\approx 2^{-308}$	$\approx 2^{-262}$	$\approx 2^{-307}$
2^{40}	2^{20}	2^{55}	2^{30}	secp521r1 ($b=256, p\approx 2^{521}$)	2^{-216}	$\approx 2^{-278}$	$\approx 2^{-298}$	$\approx 2^{-242}$	$\approx 2^{-297}$
2^{40}	2^{30}	2^{35}	2^{30}	secp521r1 ($b=256, p\approx 2^{521}$)	2^{-216}	$\approx 2^{-288}$	$\approx 2^{-318}$	$\approx 2^{-282}$	$\approx 2^{-317}$
2^{40}	2^{30}	2^{45}	2^{30}	secp521r1 ($b=256, p\approx 2^{521}$)	2^{-216}	$\approx 2^{-278}$	$\approx 2^{-308}$	$\approx 2^{-262}$	$\approx 2^{-307}$
2^{40}	2^{30}	2^{55}	2^{30}	secp521r1 ($b=256, p\approx 2^{521}$)	2^{-216}	$\approx 2^{-268}$	$\approx 2^{-298}$	$\approx 2^{-242}$	$\approx 2^{-297}$
2^{40}	2^{20}	2^{35}	2^{30}	x25519 ($b=128, p\approx 2^{252}$)	2^{-88}	$\approx 2^{-97}$	$\approx 2^{-152}$	$\approx 2^{-100}$	$\approx 2^{-152}$
2^{40}	2^{20}	2^{45}	2^{30}	x25519 ($b=128, p\approx 2^{252}$)	2^{-88}	$\approx 2^{-87}$	$\approx 2^{-152}$	$\approx 2^{-80}$	$\approx 2^{-152}$
2^{40}	2^{20}	2^{55}	2^{30}	x25519 ($b=128, p\approx 2^{252}$)	2^{-88}	$\approx 2^{-77}$	$\approx 2^{-152}$	$\approx 2^{-60}$	$\approx 2^{-152}$
2^{40}	2^{30}	2^{35}	2^{30}	x25519 ($b=128, p\approx 2^{252}$)	2^{-88}	$\approx 2^{-77}$	$\approx 2^{-142}$	$\approx 2^{-100}$	$\approx 2^{-142}$
2^{40}	2^{30}	2^{45}	2^{30}	x25519 ($b=128, p\approx 2^{252}$)	2^{-88}	$\approx 2^{-67}$	$\approx 2^{-142}$	$\approx 2^{-80}$	$\approx 2^{-142}$
2^{40}	2^{30}	2^{55}	2^{30}	x25519 ($b=128, p\approx 2^{252}$)	2^{-88}	$\approx 2^{-57}$	$\approx 2^{-142}$	$\approx 2^{-60}$	$\approx 2^{-142}$
2^{40}	2^{20}	2^{35}	2^{30}	x448 ($b=224, p\approx 2^{446}$)	2^{-184}	$\approx 2^{-291}$	$\approx 2^{-318}$	$\approx 2^{-282}$	$\approx 2^{-317}$
2^{40}	2^{20}	2^{45}	2^{30}	x448 ($b=224, p\approx 2^{446}$)	2^{-184}	$\approx 2^{-281}$	$\approx 2^{-308}$	$\approx 2^{-262}$	$\approx 2^{-307}$
2^{40}	2^{20}	2^{55}	2^{30}	x448 ($b=224, p\approx 2^{446}$)	2^{-184}	$\approx 2^{-271}$	$\approx 2^{-298}$	$\approx 2^{-242}$	$\approx 2^{-297}$
2^{40}	2^{30}	2^{35}	2^{30}	x448 ($b=224, p\approx 2^{446}$)	2^{-184}	$\approx 2^{-271}$	$\approx 2^{-318}$	$\approx 2^{-282}$	$\approx 2^{-317}$
2^{40}	2^{30}	2^{45}	2^{30}	x448 ($b=224, p\approx 2^{446}$)	2^{-184}	$\approx 2^{-261}$	$\approx 2^{-308}$	$\approx 2^{-262}$	$\approx 2^{-307}$
2^{40}	2^{30}	2^{55}	2^{30}	x448 ($b=224, p\approx 2^{446}$)	2^{-184}	$\approx 2^{-251}$	$\approx 2^{-298}$	$\approx 2^{-242}$	$\approx 2^{-297}$
2^{60}	2^{20}	2^{35}	2^{50}	secp256r1 ($b=128, p\approx 2^{256}$)	2^{-68}	$\approx 2^{-61}$	$\approx 2^{-116}$	$\approx 2^{-64}$	$\approx 2^{-116}$
2^{60}	2^{20}	2^{45}	2^{50}	secp256r1 ($b=128, p\approx 2^{256}$)	2^{-68}	$\approx 2^{-51}$	$\approx 2^{-116}$	$\approx 2^{-44}$	$\approx 2^{-116}$
2^{60}	2^{20}	2^{55}	2^{50}	secp256r1 ($b=128, p\approx 2^{256}$)	2^{-68}	$\approx 2^{-41}$	$\approx 2^{-116}$	$\approx 2^{-24}$	$\approx 2^{-116}$
2^{60}	2^{30}	2^{35}	2^{50}	secp256r1 ($b=128, p\approx 2^{256}$)	2^{-68}	$\approx 2^{-41}$	$\approx 2^{-106}$	$\approx 2^{-64}$	$\approx 2^{-106}$
2^{60}	2^{30}	2^{45}	2^{50}	secp256r1 ($b=128, p\approx 2^{256}$)	2^{-68}	$\approx 2^{-31}$	$\approx 2^{-106}$	$\approx 2^{-44}$	$\approx 2^{-106}$
2^{60}	2^{30}	2^{55}	2^{50}	secp256r1 ($b=128, p\approx 2^{256}$)	2^{-68}	$\approx 2^{-21}$	$\approx 2^{-106}$	$\approx 2^{-24}$	$\approx 2^{-106}$
2^{60}	2^{20}	2^{35}	2^{50}	secp384r1 ($b=192, p\approx 2^{384}$)	2^{-132}	$\approx 2^{-189}$	$\approx 2^{-244}$	$\approx 2^{-192}$	$\approx 2^{-244}$
2^{60}	2^{20}	2^{45}	2^{50}	secp384r1 ($b=192, p\approx 2^{384}$)	2^{-132}	$\approx 2^{-179}$	$\approx 2^{-244}$	$\approx 2^{-172}$	$\approx 2^{-244}$
2^{60}	2^{20}	2^{55}	2^{50}	secp384r1 ($b=192, p\approx 2^{384}$)	2^{-132}	$\approx 2^{-169}$	$\approx 2^{-244}$	$\approx 2^{-152}$	$\approx 2^{-244}$
2^{60}	2^{30}	2^{35}	2^{50}	secp384r1 ($b=192, p\approx 2^{384}$)	2^{-132}	$\approx 2^{-169}$	$\approx 2^{-234}$	$\approx 2^{-192}$	$\approx 2^{-234}$
2^{60}	2^{30}	2^{45}	2^{50}	secp384r1 ($b=192, p\approx 2^{384}$)	2^{-132}	$\approx 2^{-159}$	$\approx 2^{-234}$	$\approx 2^{-172}$	$\approx 2^{-234}$
2^{60}	2^{30}	2^{55}	2^{50}	secp384r1 ($b=192, p\approx 2^{384}$)	2^{-132}	$\approx 2^{-149}$	$\approx 2^{-234}$	$\approx 2^{-152}$	$\approx 2^{-234}$
2^{60}	2^{20}	2^{35}	2^{50}	secp521r1 ($b=256, p\approx 2^{521}$)	2^{-196}	$\approx 2^{-278}$	$\approx 2^{-298}$	$\approx 2^{-250}$	$\approx 2^{-285}$
2^{60}	2^{20}	2^{45}	2^{50}	secp521r1 ($b=256, p\approx 2^{521}$)	2^{-196}	$\approx 2^{-268}$	$\approx 2^{-288}$	$\approx 2^{-240}$	$\approx 2^{-285}$
2^{60}	2^{20}	2^{55}	2^{50}	secp521r1 ($b=256, p\approx 2^{521}$)	2^{-196}	$\approx 2^{-258}$	$\approx 2^{-278}$	$\approx 2^{-222}$	$\approx 2^{-277}$
2^{60}	2^{30}	2^{35}	2^{50}	secp521r1 ($b=256, p\approx 2^{521}$)	2^{-196}	$\approx 2^{-268}$	$\approx 2^{-298}$	$\approx 2^{-250}$	$\approx 2^{-285}$
2^{60}	2^{30}	2^{45}	2^{50}	secp521r1 ($b=256, p\approx 2^{521}$)	2^{-196}	$\approx 2^{-258}$	$\approx 2^{-288}$	$\approx 2^{-240}$	$\approx 2^{-285}$
2^{60}	2^{30}	2^{55}	2^{50}	secp521r1 ($b=256, p\approx 2^{521}$)	2^{-196}	$\approx 2^{-248}$	$\approx 2^{-278}$	$\approx 2^{-222}$	$\approx 2^{-277}$

(*continued*)

Table 2. (*continued*)

t	#U	#S	#RO	Curve (bit sec. b, order p)	Target $t/2^b$	SIGMA CK[17]	SIGMA Us (Theorem 4)	TLS 1.3 DFGS[24]	TLS 1.3 Us (Theorem 5)
2^{60}	2^{20}	2^{35}	2^{50}	x25519 ($b{=}128, p{\approx}2^{252}$)	2^{-68}	$\approx 2^{-57}$	$\approx 2^{-112}$	$\approx 2^{-60}$	$\approx 2^{-112}$
2^{60}	2^{20}	2^{45}	2^{50}	x25519 ($b{=}128, p{\approx}2^{252}$)	2^{-68}	$\approx 2^{-47}$	$\approx 2^{-112}$	$\approx 2^{-40}$	$\approx 2^{-112}$
2^{60}	2^{20}	2^{55}	2^{50}	x25519 ($b{=}128, p{\approx}2^{252}$)	2^{-68}	$\approx 2^{-37}$	$\approx 2^{-112}$	$\approx 2^{-20}$	$\approx 2^{-112}$
2^{60}	2^{30}	2^{35}	2^{50}	x25519 ($b{=}128, p{\approx}2^{252}$)	2^{-68}	$\approx 2^{-37}$	$\approx 2^{-102}$	$\approx 2^{-60}$	$\approx 2^{-102}$
2^{60}	2^{30}	2^{45}	2^{50}	x25519 ($b{=}128, p{\approx}2^{252}$)	2^{-68}	$\approx 2^{-27}$	$\approx 2^{-102}$	$\approx 2^{-40}$	$\approx 2^{-102}$
2^{60}	2^{30}	2^{55}	2^{50}	x25519 ($b{=}128, p{\approx}2^{252}$)	2^{-68}	$\approx 2^{-17}$	$\approx 2^{-102}$	$\approx 2^{-20}$	$\approx 2^{-102}$
2^{60}	2^{20}	2^{35}	2^{50}	x448 ($b{=}224, p{\approx}2^{446}$)	2^{-164}	$\approx 2^{-251}$	$\approx 2^{-298}$	$\approx 2^{-250}$	$\approx 2^{-285}$
2^{60}	2^{20}	2^{45}	2^{50}	x448 ($b{=}224, p{\approx}2^{446}$)	2^{-164}	$\approx 2^{-241}$	$\approx 2^{-288}$	$\approx 2^{-234}$	$\approx 2^{-285}$
2^{60}	2^{20}	2^{55}	2^{50}	x448 ($b{=}224, p{\approx}2^{446}$)	2^{-164}	$\approx 2^{-231}$	$\approx 2^{-278}$	$\approx 2^{-214}$	$\approx 2^{-277}$
2^{60}	2^{30}	2^{35}	2^{50}	x448 ($b{=}224, p{\approx}2^{446}$)	2^{-164}	$\approx 2^{-231}$	$\approx 2^{-296}$	$\approx 2^{-250}$	$\approx 2^{-285}$
2^{60}	2^{30}	2^{45}	2^{50}	x448 ($b{=}224, p{\approx}2^{446}$)	2^{-164}	$\approx 2^{-221}$	$\approx 2^{-288}$	$\approx 2^{-234}$	$\approx 2^{-285}$
2^{60}	2^{30}	2^{55}	2^{50}	x448 ($b{=}224, p{\approx}2^{446}$)	2^{-164}	$\approx 2^{-211}$	$\approx 2^{-278}$	$\approx 2^{-214}$	$\approx 2^{-277}$
2^{80}	2^{20}	2^{35}	2^{70}	secp256r1 ($b{=}128, p{\approx}2^{256}$)	2^{-48}	$\approx 2^{-21}$	$\approx 2^{-76}$	$\approx 2^{-24}$	$\approx 2^{-76}$
2^{80}	2^{20}	2^{45}	2^{70}	secp256r1 ($b{=}128, p{\approx}2^{256}$)	2^{-48}	$\approx 2^{-11}$	$\approx 2^{-76}$	$\approx 2^{-4}$	$\approx 2^{-76}$
2^{80}	2^{20}	2^{55}	2^{70}	secp256r1 ($b{=}128, p{\approx}2^{256}$)	2^{-48}	$\approx 2^{-1}$	$\approx 2^{-76}$	1	$\approx 2^{-76}$
2^{80}	2^{30}	2^{35}	2^{70}	secp256r1 ($b{=}128, p{\approx}2^{256}$)	2^{-48}	$\approx 2^{-1}$	$\approx 2^{-66}$	$\approx 2^{-24}$	$\approx 2^{-66}$
2^{80}	2^{30}	2^{45}	2^{70}	secp256r1 ($b{=}128, p{\approx}2^{256}$)	2^{-48}	1	$\approx 2^{-66}$	$\approx 2^{-4}$	$\approx 2^{-66}$
2^{80}	2^{30}	2^{55}	2^{70}	secp256r1 ($b{=}128, p{\approx}2^{256}$)	2^{-48}	1	$\approx 2^{-66}$	1	$\approx 2^{-66}$
2^{80}	2^{20}	2^{35}	2^{70}	secp384r1 ($b{=}192, p{\approx}2^{384}$)	2^{-112}	$\approx 2^{-149}$	$\approx 2^{-204}$	$\approx 2^{-152}$	$\approx 2^{-204}$
2^{80}	2^{20}	2^{45}	2^{70}	secp384r1 ($b{=}192, p{\approx}2^{384}$)	2^{-112}	$\approx 2^{-139}$	$\approx 2^{-204}$	$\approx 2^{-132}$	$\approx 2^{-204}$
2^{80}	2^{20}	2^{55}	2^{70}	secp384r1 ($b{=}192, p{\approx}2^{384}$)	2^{-112}	$\approx 2^{-129}$	$\approx 2^{-204}$	$\approx 2^{-112}$	$\approx 2^{-204}$
2^{80}	2^{30}	2^{35}	2^{70}	secp384r1 ($b{=}192, p{\approx}2^{384}$)	2^{-112}	$\approx 2^{-129}$	$\approx 2^{-194}$	$\approx 2^{-152}$	$\approx 2^{-194}$
2^{80}	2^{30}	2^{45}	2^{70}	secp384r1 ($b{=}192, p{\approx}2^{384}$)	2^{-112}	$\approx 2^{-119}$	$\approx 2^{-194}$	$\approx 2^{-132}$	$\approx 2^{-194}$
2^{80}	2^{30}	2^{55}	2^{70}	secp384r1 ($b{=}192, p{\approx}2^{384}$)	2^{-112}	$\approx 2^{-109}$	$\approx 2^{-194}$	$\approx 2^{-112}$	$\approx 2^{-194}$
2^{80}	2^{20}	2^{35}	2^{70}	secp521r1 ($b{=}256, p{\approx}2^{521}$)	2^{-176}	$\approx 2^{-258}$	$\approx 2^{-278}$	$\approx 2^{-210}$	$\approx 2^{-245}$
2^{80}	2^{20}	2^{45}	2^{70}	secp521r1 ($b{=}256, p{\approx}2^{521}$)	2^{-176}	$\approx 2^{-248}$	$\approx 2^{-268}$	$\approx 2^{-200}$	$\approx 2^{-245}$
2^{80}	2^{20}	2^{55}	2^{70}	secp521r1 ($b{=}256, p{\approx}2^{521}$)	2^{-176}	$\approx 2^{-238}$	$\approx 2^{-258}$	$\approx 2^{-190}$	$\approx 2^{-245}$
2^{80}	2^{30}	2^{35}	2^{70}	secp521r1 ($b{=}256, p{\approx}2^{521}$)	2^{-176}	$\approx 2^{-248}$	$\approx 2^{-278}$	$\approx 2^{-210}$	$\approx 2^{-245}$
2^{80}	2^{30}	2^{45}	2^{70}	secp521r1 ($b{=}256, p{\approx}2^{521}$)	2^{-176}	$\approx 2^{-238}$	$\approx 2^{-268}$	$\approx 2^{-200}$	$\approx 2^{-245}$
2^{80}	2^{30}	2^{55}	2^{70}	secp521r1 ($b{=}256, p{\approx}2^{521}$)	2^{-176}	$\approx 2^{-228}$	$\approx 2^{-258}$	$\approx 2^{-190}$	$\approx 2^{-245}$
2^{80}	2^{20}	2^{35}	2^{70}	x25519 ($b{=}128, p{\approx}2^{252}$)	2^{-48}	$\approx 2^{-17}$	$\approx 2^{-72}$	$\approx 2^{-20}$	$\approx 2^{-72}$
2^{80}	2^{20}	2^{45}	2^{70}	x25519 ($b{=}128, p{\approx}2^{252}$)	2^{-48}	$\approx 2^{-7}$	$\approx 2^{-72}$	1	$\approx 2^{-72}$
2^{80}	2^{20}	2^{55}	2^{70}	x25519 ($b{=}128, p{\approx}2^{252}$)	2^{-48}	1	$\approx 2^{-72}$	1	$\approx 2^{-72}$
2^{80}	2^{30}	2^{35}	2^{70}	x25519 ($b{=}128, p{\approx}2^{252}$)	2^{-48}	1	$\approx 2^{-62}$	$\approx 2^{-20}$	$\approx 2^{-62}$
2^{80}	2^{30}	2^{45}	2^{70}	x25519 ($b{=}128, p{\approx}2^{252}$)	2^{-48}	1	$\approx 2^{-62}$	1	$\approx 2^{-62}$
2^{80}	2^{30}	2^{55}	2^{70}	x25519 ($b{=}128, p{\approx}2^{252}$)	2^{-48}	1	$\approx 2^{-62}$	1	$\approx 2^{-62}$
2^{80}	2^{20}	2^{35}	2^{70}	x448 ($b{=}224, p{\approx}2^{446}$)	2^{-144}	$\approx 2^{-211}$	$\approx 2^{-266}$	$\approx 2^{-210}$	$\approx 2^{-245}$
2^{80}	2^{20}	2^{45}	2^{70}	x448 ($b{=}224, p{\approx}2^{446}$)	2^{-144}	$\approx 2^{-201}$	$\approx 2^{-266}$	$\approx 2^{-194}$	$\approx 2^{-245}$
2^{80}	2^{20}	2^{55}	2^{70}	x448 ($b{=}224, p{\approx}2^{446}$)	2^{-144}	$\approx 2^{-191}$	$\approx 2^{-258}$	$\approx 2^{-174}$	$\approx 2^{-245}$
2^{80}	2^{30}	2^{35}	2^{70}	x448 ($b{=}224, p{\approx}2^{446}$)	2^{-144}	$\approx 2^{-191}$	$\approx 2^{-256}$	$\approx 2^{-210}$	$\approx 2^{-245}$
2^{80}	2^{30}	2^{45}	2^{70}	x448 ($b{=}224, p{\approx}2^{446}$)	2^{-144}	$\approx 2^{-181}$	$\approx 2^{-256}$	$\approx 2^{-194}$	$\approx 2^{-245}$
2^{80}	2^{30}	2^{55}	2^{70}	x448 ($b{=}224, p{\approx}2^{446}$)	2^{-144}	$\approx 2^{-171}$	$\approx 2^{-256}$	$\approx 2^{-174}$	$\approx 2^{-245}$

Throughout Table 2, we assume that an adversary with running time t makes no more than $t \cdot 2^{-10}$ queries to its random oracles. We target the bit-security of whatever curve we use; this means that for b bits of security we want an advantage of $t/2^b$. If a bound does not achieve this goal, we color it red. We consider runtimes between 2^{40} and 2^{80}, a total number of users between to vary between 2^{20} and 2^{30}, and a total number of sessions between 2^{35} and 2^{55} (see above for the discussion of these parameter choices). We evaluate these parameters in relation to all of the elliptic curve groups standardized for use with TLS 1.3. We idealize symmetric primitives, assuming the use of 256-bit keys in conjunction with 128-bit security curves and 384-bit keys in conjunction

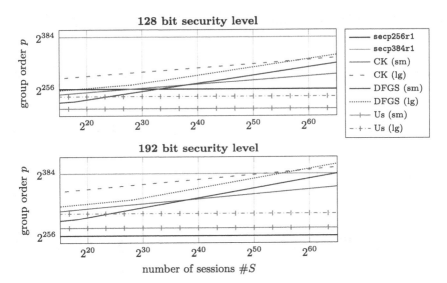

Fig. 4. Elliptic curve group order (y axis) required to achieve 128-bit (top) and 192-bit (bottom) AKE security for SIGMA and TLS 1.3 based on the CK [17] SIGMA, DFGS [24] TLS 1.3, and our bounds (ours giving the same result for SIGMA and TLS 1.3), for a varying number of sessions $\#S$ (x axis). Both axes are in log-scale. For each security and bound, we plot a smaller-resource "(sm)" setting with runtime $t = 2^{60}$, number of users $\#U = 2^{20}$, and number of random oracle queries $\#RO = 2^{50}$ and a larger-resource "(lg)" setting with $t = 2^{80}$, $\#U = 2^{30}$, and $\#RO = 2^{70}$. We let symmetric key/output lengths be 256 bits for 128-bit security and 384-bits for 192-bit security; nonce length is 256 bits. The group orders of NIST elliptic curves secp256r1 ($p \approx 2^{256}$) and secp384r1 ($p \approx 2^{384}$) are shown as horizontal lines for context.

with higher-security curves, this corresponds to the available SHA-256 and SHA-384 functions in TLS 1.3. The nonce length is fixed to 256 bits (as in TLS 1.3).

Our bounds do better than the CK [17] and DFGS [24] bounds across all considered parameters and always meet the security targets, which these prior bounds fail to meet for secp256r1 and x25519 for almost all parameters, but notably also for the 192-bit security level of curve secp384r1 for large-scale parameters. We improve over prior bounds by at least 20 and up to 85 bits of security for SIGMA, and by at least 35 and up to 92 bits of security for TLS 1.3.

In comparison, the TLS 1.3 bounds from the concurrent work by Diemert and Jager [21] yield bit security levels similar to ours for TLS 1.3: While some sub-terms in their bound are slightly worse (esp. for strong DH), the dominating sub-terms are the same.

Group Size Requirements. Finally, let us take a slightly different perspective on what the prior and our bounds tell us: Fig. 4 illustrates the group size required to achieve 128-bit resp. 192-bit AKE security for SIGMA and TLS 1.3 based on the different bounds, dependent on a varying number of sessions $\#S$.

The CK SIGMA and our SIGMA and TLS 1.3 bounds are dominated by the signature scheme advantage (with a $\#S \cdot (\#U)^2$ loss for CK and a $\#U$ loss for our bound); the DFGS TLS 1.3 bound instead is mostly dominated by the $(\#S)^2$–loss reduction to strong DH. The CK and DFGS bounds require the use of larger, less efficient curves to achieve 128-bit security even for 2^{35} sessions. For large-scale attackers, they similarly require a larger curve than `secp384r1` above about 2^{55} sessions. We highlight that, in contrast, with our bounds a curve with 128-bit, resp. 192-bit, security is sufficient to guarantee the same security level for SIGMA and TLS 1.3, for both small- and large-scale adversaries and for very conservative bounds on the number of sessions.

Acknowledgments. We thank Mihir Bellare for insightful discussions and helpful comments, and Denis Diemert and Tibor Jager for their kind handling of our concurrent work. We thank the anonymous reviewers for valuable comments. Both authors were supported in part by National Science Foundation (NSF) grant CNS-1717640. Felix Günther has been supported in part by Research Fellowship grant GU 1859/1-1 of the German Research Foundation (DFG).

A   Evaluation Details

Fully-Quantitative CK SIGMA Bound. Comparing our SIGMA bound from Theorem 4 to the original security proof by Canetti and Krawczyk [17] (CK) faces two complications. First, we must reconstruct a concrete security bound from the CK proof, which merely refers to the decisional Diffie–Hellman and "standard security notions" for digital signatures, MACs, and PRFs (i.e., single-user EUF-CMA and PRF security). Second, the CK result is given in a stronger security model for key exchange [16] which allows state-reveal attacks. Further, the CK proof assumes out-of-band unique session identifiers, whereas protocols in practice have to establish those from, e.g., nonces (introducing a corresponding collision bound as in our analysis). We are therefore inherently constrained to compare qualitatively different security properties here.

Let us informally consider a game-based definition of the CK model [16] in the same style as our AKE model (cf. Definition 1), capturing the same oracles plus an additional state-reveal oracle, with q_{RST} denoting the number of queries to this oracle, and session identifiers that, like ours, consist of the session and peers' nonces and DH shares. Translating the SIGMA-I security proof from [17, Theorem 6 in the full version], we obtained the following concrete security bound:

$$\mathsf{Adv}^{CK}_{SIGMA\text{-}I}(t, q_N, q_S, q_{RS}, q_{RL}, q_{RST}, q_T)$$

$$\leq \frac{2q_S^2}{2^{nl}\cdot p} + \mathsf{Adv}^{mu\text{-}EUF\text{-}CMA}_S(t_{\mathcal{B}_1}, q_N, q_S, q_S, q_{RL}) \quad /\!/ \text{ sid collision \& property P1}$$

$$+ q_N \cdot q_S \cdot \left(\mathsf{Adv}^{DDH}_G(t_{\mathcal{B}_2}) + \mathsf{Adv}^{mu\text{-}PRF}_{PRF}(t_{\mathcal{B}_5}, 1, 3)\right) \quad /\!/ \text{ property P2} \dots$$

$$+ (q_N + 1) \cdot \mathsf{Adv}^{mu\text{-}EUF\text{-}CMA}_S(t_{\mathcal{B}_3}, 1, q_S, q_S, 0) + \mathsf{Adv}^{mu\text{-}EUF\text{-}CMA}_M(t_{\mathcal{B}_4}, 1, 2, 2, 2, 2, 0)\Big),$$

where nl is the nonce length, $\mathbb{G}$ the used Diffie–Hellman group of prime order p, the number of test queries is restricted to $q_T = 1$, and $\mathcal{B}_i$ (for $i = 1, \ldots, 5$) are the described reductions in [17, Theorem 6 in the full version] all running in time $t_{\mathcal{B}_i} \approx t$. For simplicity, we present the above bound in terms of "multi-user" PRF, signature, and MAC advantages for a single user $q_{Nw} = 1$, which are equivalent to the corresponding single-user advantages (cf. Appendix B).

Fully-Quantitative DFGS TLS 1.3 Bound. We compare our security bound for TLS 1.3 from Theorem 5 with the bound of Dowling et al. [24] (DFGS). Note that this bound is established in a multi-stage key exchange model [25], here we focus only on the main application key derivation, as in our proof. The DFGS bound needs instantiation through the random oracle only in one step (the PRF-ODH assumption on HKDF.Extract) while other PRF steps remain in the standard model. Our proof instead models both HKDF.Extract and HKDF.Expand as random oracles. Translating the bound from [24, Theorems 5.1, 5.2] yields:

$$
\begin{aligned}
\mathsf{Adv}&_{\mathsf{TLS\,1.3}}^{\mathsf{DFGS}}(t, q_N, q_S, q_{RS}, q_{RL}, q_T) \\
&\leq \frac{q_S^2}{2^{nl} \cdot p} + q_S \cdot \left(\mathsf{Adv}_H^{\mathsf{CR}}(t_{\mathcal{B}_1}) + q_N \cdot \mathsf{Adv}_S^{\mathsf{mu\text{-}EUF\text{-}CMA}}(t_{\mathcal{B}_2}, 1, q_S, q_S, 0) \right. \\
&\quad + q_S \cdot \left(\mathsf{Adv}_{\mathsf{HKDF.Extract},\mathbb{G}}^{\mathsf{dual\text{-}snPRF\text{-}ODH}}(t_{\mathcal{B}_3}) + \mathsf{Adv}_{\mathsf{HKDF.Expand}}^{\mathsf{mu\text{-}PRF}}(t_{\mathcal{B}_4}, 1, 3, 3, 0) \right. \\
&\quad + 2 \cdot \mathsf{Adv}_{\mathsf{HKDF.Expand}}^{\mathsf{mu\text{-}PRF}}(t_{\mathcal{B}_5}, 1, 2, 2, 0) + \mathsf{Adv}_{\mathsf{HKDF.Extract}}^{\mathsf{mu\text{-}PRF}}(t_{\mathcal{B}_6}, 1, 1, 1, 0) \\
&\quad \left. \left. + \mathsf{Adv}_{\mathsf{HKDF.Expand}}^{\mathsf{mu\text{-}PRF}}(t_{\mathcal{B}_7}, 1, 1, 1, 0) \right) \right).
\end{aligned}
$$

Let us further unpack the PRF-ODH term. Following Brendel et al. [15], it can be reduced to the strong Diffie–Hellman assumption modeling HKDF.Extract as a random oracle.[8] In this reduction, the single DH oracle query is checked against each random oracle query via the strong-DH oracle, hence establishing the following bound: $\mathsf{Adv}_{\mathsf{RO},\mathbb{G}}^{\mathsf{dual\text{-}snPRF\text{-}ODH}}(t_{\mathcal{B}_3}, q_{RO}) \leq \mathsf{Adv}_{\mathbb{G}}^{\mathsf{stDH}}(t_{\mathcal{B}_3}, q_{RO})$

B   Assumptions, Building Blocks, Multi-user Security

Definition 6 (Multi-user PRF security). *Let* $\mathsf{PRF} \colon \{0,1\}^k \times \{0,1\}^m \to \{0,1\}^n$ *be a function (for* $k, n \in \mathbb{N}$ *and* $m \in \mathbb{N} \cup \{*\}$*) and* $\mathsf{G}_{\mathsf{PRF}}^{\mathsf{mu\text{-}PRF}}$ *be the multi-user PRF security game defined as in Fig. 5. We define* $\mathsf{Adv}_{\mathsf{PRF}}^{\mathsf{mu\text{-}PRF}}(t, q_{Nw}, q_{FN}, q_{FN/U}) := 2 \cdot \max_{\mathcal{A}} \Pr\left[\mathsf{G}_{\mathsf{PRF},\mathcal{A}}^{\mathsf{mu\text{-}PRF}} \Rightarrow 1 \right] - 1$, *where the maximum is taken over all adversaries, denoted* $(t, q_{Nw}, q_{FN}, q_{FN/U})$-mu-PRF-*adversaries, running in time at most* t *and making at most* q_{Nw} *queries to their* New *oracle, at most* q_{FN} *total queries to their* Fn *oracle, and at most* $q_{FN/U}$ *queries* $\mathrm{Fn}(i, \cdot)$ *for any user* i.

---

[8] The same paper suggests that a standard-model instantiation of the PRF-ODH assumption via an algebraic black-box reduction to common cryptographic problems is implausible.

Generically, the multi-user security of PRFs reduces to single-user security (formally, $G_{\mathsf{PRF},\mathcal{A}}^{\mathsf{mu\text{-}PRF}}$ with $\mathcal{A}$ restricted to $q_{\mathrm{Nw}} = 1$ queries to NEW) with a factor in the number of users via a hybrid argument [7], i.e., $\mathsf{Adv}_{\mathsf{PRF}}^{\mathsf{mu\text{-}PRF}}(t, q_{\mathrm{Nw}}, q_{\mathrm{FN}}, q_{\mathrm{FN/U}}) \le q_{\mathrm{Nw}} \cdot \mathsf{Adv}_{\mathsf{PRF}}^{\mathsf{mu\text{-}PRF}}(t', 1, q_{\mathrm{FN/U}}, q_{\mathrm{FN/U}})$, where $t \approx t'$. (Note that the total number q_{FN} of queries to the FN oracle across all users does not affect the reduction.) There exist simple and efficient constructions, like AMAC [6], that however achieve multi-user security tightly. If we use a random oracle RO as a PRF with key length kl, then $\mathsf{Adv}_{\mathsf{RO}}^{\mathsf{mu\text{-}PRF}}(t, q_{\mathrm{Nw}}, q_{\mathrm{FN}}, q_{\mathrm{FN/U}}, q_{\mathrm{RO}}) \le \frac{q_{\mathrm{Nw}} \cdot q_{\mathrm{RO}}}{2^{kl}}$.

$G_{\mathsf{PRF},\mathcal{A}}^{\mathsf{mu\text{-}PRF}}$	NEW:	FN(i, x):
INITIALIZE:	3 $u \leftarrow u + 1$	7 return $f_i(x)$
	4 if $b = 1$ then	
1 $b \xleftarrow{\$} \{0,1\}$	5 $K_u \xleftarrow{\$} \{0,1\}^k$; $f_u := \mathsf{PRF}(K_u, \cdot)$	FINALIZE(b^*):
2 $u \leftarrow 0$	6 else $f_u \xleftarrow{\$} \mathsf{FUNC}$	8 return $[\![b = b^*]\!]$

Fig. 5. Multi-user PRF security of a pseudorandom function $\mathsf{PRF} \colon \{0,1\}^k \times \{0,1\}^m \to \{0,1\}^n$. FUNC is the space of all functions $\{0,1\}^m \to \{0,1\}^n$.

Definition 7 (Signature mu-EUF-CMA security [4]). *Let S be a signature scheme and $G_{\mathsf{S},\mathcal{A}}^{\mathsf{mu\text{-}EUF\text{-}CMA}}$ be the game for signature multi-user existential unforgeability under chosen-message attacks with adaptive corruptions (see the full version [20] for the formal definition). We define* $\mathsf{Adv}_{\mathsf{S}}^{\mathsf{mu\text{-}EUF\text{-}CMA}}(t, q_{\mathrm{Nw}}, q_{\mathrm{SG}}, q_{\mathrm{SG/U}},$ $q_{\mathrm{C}}) := \max_{\mathcal{A}} \Pr\left[G_{\mathsf{S},\mathcal{A}}^{\mathsf{mu\text{-}EUF\text{-}CMA}} \Rightarrow 1\right]$, *where the maximum is taken over all adversaries, denoted* $(t, q_{\mathrm{Nw}}, q_{\mathrm{SG}}, q_{\mathrm{SG/U}}, q_{\mathrm{C}})$-mu-EUF-CMA-*adversaries, running in time at most t and making at most $q_{\mathrm{Nw}}, q_{\mathrm{SG}}$, resp. q_{C} total queries to their* NEW, SIGN, *resp.* CORRUPT *oracle, and making at most $q_{\mathrm{SG/U}}$ queries* SIGN$(i, \cdot)$ *for any user i.*

Multi-user EUF-CMA security of signature schemes (with adaptive corruptions) can be reduced to classical, single-user EUF-CMA security (formally, $G_{\mathsf{S},\mathcal{A}}^{\mathsf{mu\text{-}EUF\text{-}CMA}}$ with $\mathcal{A}$ restricted to $q_{\mathrm{Nw}} = 1$ queries to NEW) by a standard hybrid argument, losing a factor of number of users. Formally, this yields $\mathsf{Adv}_{\mathsf{S}}^{\mathsf{mu\text{-}EUF\text{-}CMA}}(t, q_{\mathrm{Nw}}, q_{\mathrm{SG}}, q_{\mathrm{SG/U}}, q_{\mathrm{C}}) \le q_{\mathrm{Nw}} \cdot \mathsf{Adv}_{\mathsf{S}}^{\mathsf{mu\text{-}EUF\text{-}CMA}}(t', 1, q_{\mathrm{SG/U}}, q_{\mathrm{SG/U}}, 0)$, where $t \approx t'$. (Note that the reduction is not affected by the total number of signature queries q_{SG} across all users.) In many cases, such loss is indeed unavoidable [5].

Definition 8 (MAC mu-EUF-CMA security). *Let M be a MAC scheme and $G_{\mathsf{M},\mathcal{A}}^{\mathsf{mu\text{-}EUF\text{-}CMA}}$ be the game for MAC multi-user existential unforgeability under chosen-message attacks with adaptive corruptions (see the full version [20] for the formal definition). We define* $\mathsf{Adv}_{\mathsf{M}}^{\mathsf{mu\text{-}EUF\text{-}CMA}}(t, q_{\mathrm{Nw}}, q_{\mathrm{TG}}, q_{\mathrm{TG/U}}, q_{\mathrm{VF}}, q_{\mathrm{VF/U}}, q_{\mathrm{C}}) :=$ $\max_{\mathcal{A}} \Pr\left[G_{\mathsf{M},\mathcal{A}}^{\mathsf{mu\text{-}EUF\text{-}CMA}} \Rightarrow 1\right]$, *where the maximum is taken over all adversaries,* denoted $(t, q_{\mathrm{Nw}}, q_{\mathrm{TG}}, q_{\mathrm{TG/U}}, q_{\mathrm{VF}}, q_{\mathrm{VF/U}}, q_{\mathrm{C}})$-mu-EUF-CMA-adversaries, *running in time at most t and making at most q_{Nw}, q_{TG}, q_{VF}, resp. q_{C} queries to their* NEW, SIGN, VRFY, *resp.* CORRUPT *oracle, and making at most $q_{\mathrm{TG/U}}$ queries* TAG$(i, \cdot)$, *resp. $q_{\mathrm{VF/U}}$ queries* VRFY$(i, \cdot)$ *for any user i.*

As for signature schemes, multi-user EUF-CMA security of MACs reduces to the single-user case ($q_{\mathrm{Nw}} = 1$) by a standard hybrid argument: $\mathsf{Adv}_{\mathsf{M}}^{\mathsf{mu\text{-}EUF\text{-}CMA}}(t, q_{\mathrm{Nw}}, q_{\mathrm{TG}}, q_{\mathrm{TG/U}}, q_{\mathrm{VF}}, q_{\mathrm{VF/U}}, q_{\mathrm{C}}) \leq q_{\mathrm{Nw}} \cdot \mathsf{Adv}_{\mathsf{M}}^{\mathsf{mu\text{-}EUF\text{-}CMA}}(t, 1, q_{\mathrm{TG/U}}, q_{\mathrm{TG/U}}, q_{\mathrm{VF/U}}, q_{\mathrm{VF/U}}, 0)$, where $t \approx t'$. (Note that the reduction is not affected by the total number of tagging and verification queries q_{TG} resp. q_{VF} across all users.)

Our multi-user definition of MACs provides a verification oracle, which is non-standard (and in general not equivalent to a definition with a single forgery attempts, as Bellare, Goldreich and Mityiagin [9] showed). For PRF-based MACs (which in particular includes HMAC used in TLS 1.3), it however is equivalent and the reduction from multi-query to single-query verification is tight [9].

In our key exchange reductions, we actually do not need to corrupt MAC keys, i.e., we achieve $q_{\mathrm{C}} = 0$. This in particular allows specific constructions like AMAC [6] achieving tight multi-user security (without corruptions).

If we use a random oracle RO as PRF-like MAC with key length kl and output length ol, then $\mathsf{Adv}_{\mathsf{RO}}^{\mathsf{mu\text{-}EUF\text{-}CMA}}(t, q_{\mathrm{Nw}}, q_{\mathrm{TG}}, q_{\mathrm{TG/U}}, q_{\mathrm{VF}}, q_{\mathrm{VF/U}}, q_{\mathrm{C}}, q_{\mathrm{RO}}) \leq \frac{q_{\mathrm{VF}}}{2^{ol}} + \frac{(q_{\mathrm{Nw}} - q_{\mathrm{C}}) \cdot q_{\mathrm{RO}}}{2^{kl}}$.

Definition 9 (Hash function collision resistance). *Let* $\mathsf{H}: \{0,1\}^* \to \{0,1\}^{ol}$ *for $ol \in \mathbb{N}$ be a function. For a given adversary $\mathcal{A}$ running in time at most t, we can consider* $\mathsf{Adv}_{\mathsf{H}}^{\mathsf{CR}}(t) := \Pr\left[(m, m') \overset{\$}{\leftarrow} \mathcal{A} : m \neq m' \text{ and } \mathsf{H}(m) = \mathsf{H}(m')\right]$.

If we use a random oracle RO as hash function, then $\mathsf{Adv}_{\mathsf{RO}}^{\mathsf{CR}}(t, q_{\mathrm{RO}}) \leq \frac{q_{\mathrm{RO}}^2}{2^{ol+1}} + \frac{1}{2^{ol}}$

C   Proof of the Strong Diffie–Hellman GGM Bound

We establish the bound of Theorem 3 through a sequence of incrementally changing code-based games; see the full version [20] for complete details.

Game 0. We formalize the strong Diffie–Hellman problem in the GGM using the setting and notation of Bellare and Dai [8]. Briefly, we represent a group a group of prime order p using an arbitrary set $\mathbb{G}$ of label strings and a randomly chosen bijection $E : \mathbb{Z}_p \to \mathbb{G}$, called the encoding function. For any two strings $A, B \in \mathbb{G}$, we define the operation $A \, \mathsf{OP}_E \, B = E(E^{-1}(A) + E^{-1}(B) \mod p)$. The adversary is given the identity element $\mathbb{1} = E(0)$, a generator $g = E(1)$, challenges X and Y, and oracle access to OP_E through an oracle OP. Note that for any integer $a \in \mathbb{Z}_p$, we can compute $g^a = E(a)$. On an input A, B, the stDH oracle uses this property to find the discrete logarithm a of A in order to check whether $E(xa) = X^a = B$. Throughout, we track the set GL of group element labels the adversary has seen, and return $\perp$ in response to all oracle queries containing other labels. By definition, $\mathsf{Adv}_{\mathbb{G}}^{\mathsf{stDH}}(t, q_{\mathrm{sDH}}) = \Pr[\mathsf{G}_0 \Rightarrow 1]$.

$\underline{G_1}$

INITIALIZE():

  1   $p \leftarrow |\mathbb{G}|;\ E \xleftarrow{\$} \text{Bijections}(\mathbb{Z}_p, \mathbb{G})$

  2   $\mathbb{1} \leftarrow \text{VE}(\vec{0});\ g \leftarrow \text{VE}(\vec{e_1})$

  3   $x, y \xleftarrow{\$} \mathbb{Z}_p^*;\ \vec{x} \leftarrow 1, x, y$

  4   $X \leftarrow \text{VE}(\vec{e_2});\ Y \leftarrow \text{VE}(\vec{e_3})$

  5   return $(\mathbb{1}, g, x, y)$

$\underline{\text{OP}(A, B, \text{sgn }):}$

  6   $\vec{c} \leftarrow TI(A) \text{ sgn } TI(B) \mod p$

  7   $C \leftarrow \text{VE}(\vec{c});$ return C

$\underline{\text{VE}(\vec{t}):}$

  1   if $TV[\vec{t}] \neq \bot$ then return $TV[\vec{t}]$

  2   $v \leftarrow \langle \vec{t}, \vec{x} \rangle;\ TV[\vec{t}] \leftarrow E(v);$

  3   $GL \leftarrow GL \cup \{TV[\vec{t}]\};\ TI[TV[\vec{t}]] \leftarrow \vec{t}$

  4   return $TV[\vec{t}]$

$\underline{\text{stDH}(A, B):}$

  8   $\vec{a} \leftarrow TI(A);\ \vec{b} \leftarrow TI(B)$

  9   return $[[\text{VE}(x\vec{a}) = B]]$

$\underline{\text{FINALIZE}(Z):}$

  10   return $[[\text{VE}(x\vec{e_3}) = Z]]$

Fig. 6. Game G_1 of the stDH proof.

Game 1. Although the notation of G_0 is simpler and more intuitive, it is more useful for the proof game to internally represent elements of $\mathbb{G}$ with vectors over $\mathbb{Z}_p^3$ instead of integers in $\mathbb{Z}_p$, as we do in Fig. 6. We map elements $\vec{t} \in \mathbb{Z}_p^3$ back to $\mathbb{Z}_p$ by taking the inner product of $\vec{t}$ with the vector $(1, x, y)$. (Effectively, we take $\vec{t}$ to be the coefficients of a linear combination of 1, x, and y, which are represented respectively by the basis vectors $\vec{e_1}$, $\vec{e_2}$, and $\vec{e_3}$.)

Composing this map with the encoding function E induces a transformation from $\mathbb{Z}_p^3$ to $\mathbb{G}$, which we implement via an internal oracle VE. We cache the transformation in table TV and its inverse in table TI. Each element of $\mathbb{G}$ now has multiple vector representations, but the bilinearity of the inner product ensures that the view of the adversary is not changed, and $\Pr[G_1] = \Pr[G_0]$.

Games 2–3. In Game G_3, we make two undetectable changes: we lazily sample the bijection E, and in the stDH oracle, we replace the condition $\text{VE}(x\vec{a}) = B = \text{VE}(\vec{b})$ with the equivalent condition $\langle x\vec{a} - \vec{b}, \vec{x} \rangle = 0$.

We continue in the next game by sampling the entries of TV directly instead of through calls to E. Distinct vectors $\vec{t}$ and $\vec{t'}$ no longer map to the same group element when $\langle \vec{t}, \vec{x} \rangle = \langle \vec{t'}, \vec{x} \rangle$. The adversary cannot notice this change unless two such t, t' are queried to VE; we call this event F_1 and let FINALIZE return true when it occurs. This only increases the success probability of the adversary, so $\Pr[G_1] \leq \Pr[G_3]$. At this point, function E is unused and becomes redundant.

Game 4. The adversary can trivially get a true response from the stDH oracle by computing $A = g^a$ for any integer a and $B = X^a$. We now return false in all other cases. Let F_2 be the event where the adversary makes a nontrivial query (A, B) to stDH that should return true, i.e., one where $\langle xTI(A) - TI(B), \vec{x} \rangle = 0$. Unless F_2 occurs, the output of stDH does not change, so $\Pr[G_3] \leq \Pr[G_4 \text{ and } \overline{F_2}] + \Pr[F_2]$.

Game 5. This game is identical to G_4, except FINALIZE returns true whenever event F_2 could have occurred. It follows that $\Pr[G_3] \leq \Pr[G_5]$. At this point, variables x, y, and $\vec{x}$ are not used by any oracle except FINALIZE, so we delay their initialization until the end of the game without detection by the adversary.

Collecting bounds reveals that $\mathsf{Adv}_{\mathbb{G}}^{\mathsf{stDH}}(t, q_{\mathrm{sDH}}) \leq \Pr[\mathrm{G}_5*]$. A t-query adversary playing G_5* wins only if events F_1 or F_2 occur, or if $[\mathrm{VE}(x\vec{e_3}) = Z]$. Event F_1 occurs when table TI contains distinct $\vec{t_i}, \vec{t_j}$ such that $\langle \vec{t_i} - \vec{t_j}, (1, x, y) \rangle$. This means (x, y) is a root of the bivariate linear polynomial $(\vec{t_i} - \vec{t_j})[0] + (\vec{t_i} - \vec{t_j})[1] \cdot x + (\vec{t_i} - \vec{t_j})[2] \cdot y$. Since x and y are sampled independently by the FINALIZE oracle, this occurs with probability at most $1/p$ for each polynomial by Lemma 1 of [42]. Event F_2 occurs when $\langle x\vec{t_i} - \vec{t_j}, \vec{x} \rangle = 0$ for some t_i, t_j in TI. Similarly, this means that (x, y) must be a root of the quadratic $(x\vec{t_i} - \vec{t_j})[0] + (x\vec{t_i} - \vec{t_j})[1] \cdot x + (x\vec{t_i} - \vec{t_j})[2] \cdot y$. By Lemma 1, this occurs with probability at most $2/p$ for each $(\vec{t_i}, \vec{t_j})$ pair. Finally, $[\mathrm{VE}(x\vec{e_3}) = Z]$ holds with probability at most $1/p$ because $\mathrm{VE}(x\vec{e_3})$ is uniformly random.

Taking a union bound over the $(t + 4)^2$ possible pairs $(\vec{t_i}, \vec{t_j})$, we obtain $\Pr[\mathrm{G}_5*] \leq (3(t + 4)^2 + 1)/p$. The theorem statement follows for all $t > 25$.   □

References

1. Abdalla, M., Bellare, M., Rogaway, P.: The oracle Diffie-Hellman assumptions and an analysis of DHIES. In: Naccache, D. (ed.) CT-RSA 2001. LNCS, vol. 2020, pp. 143–158. Springer, Heidelberg (2001). https://doi.org/10.1007/3-540-45353-9_12
2. Abdalla, M., Benhamouda, F., MacKenzie, P.: Security of the J-PAKE password-authenticated key exchange protocol. In: 2015 IEEE Symposium on Security and Privacy, pp. 571–587. IEEE Computer Society Press, May 2015
3. Abdalla, M., Fouque, P.-A., Pointcheval, D.: Password-based authenticated key exchange in the three-party setting. In: Vaudenay, S. (ed.) PKC 2005. LNCS, vol. 3386, pp. 65–84. Springer, Heidelberg (2005). https://doi.org/10.1007/978-3-540-30580-4_6
4. Bader, C., Hofheinz, D., Jager, T., Kiltz, E., Li, Y.: Tightly-secure authenticated key exchange. In: Dodis, Y., Nielsen, J.B. (eds.) TCC 2015, Part I. LNCS, vol. 9014, pp. 629–658. Springer, Heidelberg (2015). https://doi.org/10.1007/978-3-662-46494-6_26
5. Bader, C., Jager, T., Li, Y., Schäge, S.: On the impossibility of tight cryptographic reductions. In: Fischlin, M., Coron, J.-S. (eds.) EUROCRYPT 2016, Part II. LNCS, vol. 9666, pp. 273–304. Springer, Heidelberg (2016). https://doi.org/10.1007/978-3-662-49896-5_10
6. Bellare, M., Bernstein, D.J., Tessaro, S.: Hash-function based PRFs: AMAC and its multi-user security. In: Fischlin, M., Coron, J.-S. (eds.) EUROCRYPT 2016, Part I. LNCS, vol. 9665, pp. 566–595. Springer, Heidelberg (2016). https://doi.org/10.1007/978-3-662-49890-3_22
7. Bellare, M., Canetti, R., Krawczyk, H.: Pseudorandom functions revisited: the cascade construction and its concrete security. In: 37th FOCS, pp. 514–523. IEEE Computer Society Press, October 1996
8. Bellare, M., Dai, W.: The multi-base discrete logarithm problem: non-rewinding proofs and improved reduction tightness for identification and signatures. In: INDOCRYPT 2020 (2020). https://eprint.iacr.org/2020/416
9. Bellare, M., Goldreich, O., Mityagin, A.: The power of verification queries in message authentication and authenticated encryption. Cryptology ePrint Archive, Report 2004/309 (2004). http://eprint.iacr.org/2004/309

10. Bellare, M., Pointcheval, D., Rogaway, P.: Authenticated key exchange secure against dictionary attacks. In: Preneel, B. (ed.) EUROCRYPT 2000. LNCS, vol. 1807, pp. 139–155. Springer, Heidelberg (2000). https://doi.org/10.1007/3-540-45539-6_11

11. Bellare, M., Rogaway, P.: Random oracles are practical: a paradigm for designing efficient protocols. In: Denning, D.E., Pyle, R., Ganesan, R., Sandhu, R.S., Ashby, V. (eds.) ACM CCS 1993, pp. 62–73. ACM Press, November 1993

12. Bellare, M., Rogaway, P.: Entity authentication and key distribution. In: Stinson, D.R. (ed.) CRYPTO 1993. LNCS, vol. 773, pp. 232–249. Springer, Heidelberg (1994). https://doi.org/10.1007/3-540-48329-2_21

13. Bellare, M., Rogaway, P.: The security of triple encryption and a framework for code-based game-playing proofs. In: Vaudenay, S. (ed.) EUROCRYPT 2006. LNCS, vol. 4004, pp. 409–426. Springer, Heidelberg (2006). https://doi.org/10.1007/11761679_25

14. Buhler, J.P. (ed.): ANTS 1998. LNCS, vol. 1423. Springer, Heidelberg (1998). https://doi.org/10.1007/BFb0054849

15. Brendel, J., Fischlin, M., Günther, F., Janson, C.: PRF-ODH: relations, instantiations, and impossibility results. In: Katz, J., Shacham, H. (eds.) CRYPTO 2017, Part III. LNCS, vol. 10403, pp. 651–681. Springer, Cham (2017). https://doi.org/10.1007/978-3-319-63697-9_22

16. Canetti, R., Krawczyk, H.: Analysis of key-exchange protocols and their use for building secure channels. In: Pfitzmann, B. (ed.) EUROCRYPT 2001. LNCS, vol. 2045, pp. 453–474. Springer, Heidelberg (2001). https://doi.org/10.1007/3-540-44987-6_28

17. Canetti, R., Krawczyk, H.: Security analysis of IKE's signature-based key-exchange protocol. In: Yung, M. (ed.) CRYPTO 2002. LNCS, vol. 2442, pp. 143–161. Springer, Heidelberg (2002). https://doi.org/10.1007/3-540-45708-9_10. http://eprint.iacr.org/2002/120/

18. Cohn-Gordon, K., Cremers, C., Garratt, L.: On post-compromise security. In: 2016 Computer Security Foundations Symposium, pp. 164–178. IEEE (2016)

19. Cohn-Gordon, K., Cremers, C., Gjøsteen, K., Jacobsen, H., Jager, T.: Highly efficient key exchange protocols with optimal tightness. In: Boldyreva, A., Micciancio, D. (eds.) CRYPTO 2019, Part III. LNCS, vol. 11694, pp. 767–797. Springer, Cham (2019). https://doi.org/10.1007/978-3-030-26954-8_25

20. Davis, H., Günther, F.: Tighter proofs for the SIGMA and TLS 1.3 key exchange protocols. Cryptology ePrint Archive, Report 2020/1029 (2020). https://eprint.iacr.org/2020/1029

21. Diemert, D., Jager, T.: On the tight security of TLS 1.3: theoretically-sound cryptographic parameters for real-world deployments. J. Cryptol. (2020, to appear). Available as Cryptology ePrint Archive, Report 2020/726. https://eprint.iacr.org/2020/726

22. Dowling, B., Fischlin, M., Günther, F., Stebila, D.: A cryptographic analysis of the TLS 1.3 handshake protocol candidates. In: Ray, I., Li, N., Kruegel, C. (eds.) ACM CCS 2015, pp. 1197–1210. ACM Press, October 2015

23. Dowling, B., Fischlin, M., Günther, F., Stebila, D.: A cryptographic analysis of the TLS 1.3 draft-10 full and pre-shared key handshake protocol. Cryptology ePrint Archive, Report 2016/081 (2016). http://eprint.iacr.org/2016/081

24. Dowling, B., Fischlin, M., Günther, F., Stebila, D.: A cryptographic analysis of the TLS 1.3 handshake protocol. J. Cryptol. (2021, to appear). Available as Cryptology ePrint Archive, Report 2020/1044. https://eprint.iacr.org/2020/1044

25. Fischlin, M., Günther, F.: Multi-stage key exchange and the case of Google's QUIC protocol. In: Ahn, G.J., Yung, M., Li, N. (eds.) ACM CCS 2014, pp. 1193–1204. ACM Press, November 2014

26. Fischlin, M., Günther, F.: Replay attacks on zero round-trip time: the case of the TLS 1.3 handshake candidates. In: 2017 IEEE European Symposium on Security and Privacy, EuroS&P 2017, pp. 60–75. IEEE, April 2017

27. Gjøsteen, K., Jager, T.: Practical and tightly-secure digital signatures and authenticated key exchange. In: Shacham, H., Boldyreva, A. (eds.) CRYPTO 2018, Part II. LNCS, vol. 10992, pp. 95–125. Springer, Cham (2018). https://doi.org/10.1007/978-3-319-96881-0_4

28. Harkins, D., Carrel, D.: The Internet Key Exchange (IKE). IETF RFC 2409 (Proposed Standard) (1998)

29. Jager, T., Kohlar, F., Schäge, S., Schwenk, J.: On the security of TLS-DHE in the standard model. In: Safavi-Naini, R., Canetti, R. (eds.) CRYPTO 2012. LNCS, vol. 7417, pp. 273–293. Springer, Heidelberg (2012). https://doi.org/10.1007/978-3-642-32009-5_17

30. Kaufman, C. (ed.): Internet Key Exchange (IKEv2) Protocol. RFC 4306 (Proposed Standard), December 2005. https://www.rfc-editor.org/rfc/rfc4306.txt. Obsoleted by RFC 5996, updated by RFC 5282

31. Kent, S., Atkinson, R.: Security Architecture for the Internet Protocol. RFC 2401 (Proposed Standard), November 1998. https://www.rfc-editor.org/rfc/rfc2401.txt. Obsoleted by RFC 4301, updated by RFC 3168

32. Krawczyk, H.: SIGMA: the 'SIGn-and-MAc' approach to authenticated Diffie-Hellman and its use in the IKE protocols. In: Boneh, D. (ed.) CRYPTO 2003. LNCS, vol. 2729, pp. 400–425. Springer, Heidelberg (2003). https://doi.org/10.1007/978-3-540-45146-4_24

33. Krawczyk, H.: SIGMA: the 'SIGn-and-MAc' approach to authenticated Diffie-Hellman and its use in the IKE protocols (2003). https://webee.technion.ac.il/~hugo/sigma-pdf.pdf

34. Krawczyk, H.: Cryptographic extraction and key derivation: the HKDF scheme. In: Rabin, T. (ed.) CRYPTO 2010. LNCS, vol. 6223, pp. 631–648. Springer, Heidelberg (2010). https://doi.org/10.1007/978-3-642-14623-7_34

35. Krawczyk, H., Wee, H.: The OPTLS protocol and TLS 1.3. In: 2016 IEEE European Symposium on Security and Privacy, pp. 81–96. IEEE, March 2016

36. LaMacchia, B., Lauter, K., Mityagin, A.: Stronger security of authenticated key exchange. In: Susilo, W., Liu, J.K., Mu, Y. (eds.) ProvSec 2007. LNCS, vol. 4784, pp. 1–16. Springer, Heidelberg (2007). https://doi.org/10.1007/978-3-540-75670-5_1

37. Langley, A., Hamburg, M., Turner, S.: Elliptic Curves for Security. RFC 7748 (Informational), January 2016. https://www.rfc-editor.org/rfc/rfc7748.txt

38. Maurer, U.: Abstract models of computation in cryptography. In: Smart, N.P. (ed.) Cryptography and Coding 2005. LNCS, vol. 3796, pp. 1–12. Springer, Heidelberg (2005). https://doi.org/10.1007/11586821_1

39. National Institute of Standards and Technology: FIPS PUB 186-4: Digital Signature Standard (DSS) (2013)

40. Okamoto, T., Pointcheval, D.: The gap-problems: a new class of problems for the security of cryptographic schemes. In: Kim, K. (ed.) PKC 2001. LNCS, vol. 1992, pp. 104–118. Springer, Heidelberg (2001). https://doi.org/10.1007/3-540-44586-2_8

41. Rescorla, E.: The Transport Layer Security (TLS) Protocol Version 1.3. RFC 8446 (Proposed Standard), August 2018. https://www.rfc-editor.org/rfc/rfc8446.txt

42. Shoup, V.: Lower bounds for discrete logarithms and related problems. In: Fumy, W. (ed.) EUROCRYPT 1997. LNCS, vol. 1233, pp. 256–266. Springer, Heidelberg (1997). https://doi.org/10.1007/3-540-69053-0_18

Improved Structured Encryption for SQL Databases via Hybrid Indexing

David Cash[1], Ruth Ng[2(✉)], and Adam Rivkin[1]

[1] University of Chicago, Chicago, USA
{davidcash,amrivkin}@uchicago.edu
[2] University of California, San Diego, USA
ring@eng.ucsd.edu

Abstract. We introduce a new technique for indexing joins in encrypted SQL databases called *partially precomputed joins* which achieves lower leakage and bandwidth than those used in prior constructions. These techniques are incorporated into state-of-the-art structured encryption schemes for SQL data, yielding a *hybrid indexing* scheme with both partially and fully precomputed join indexes. We then introduce the idea of *leakage-aware query planning* by giving a heuristic that helps the client decide, at query time, which index to use so as to minimize leakage and stay below a given bandwidth budget. We conclude by simulating our constructions on real datasets, showing that our heuristic is accurate and that partially-precomputed joins perform well in practice.

1 Introduction

SQL applications are often deterred from using cloud storage solutions because they do not wish to grant a third party access to their sensitive data. Yet, in-house solutions often are less convenient than these large-scale ones and are vulnerable to compromise as well. This calls for a cryptographic solution which allows data on the cloud to be end-to-end encrypted so that the server never "sees" the sensitive data. This in turn poses a challenge when the server is called upon to perform SQL operations on the data.

Most current offerings of this technology depend heavily on property-revealing encryption (PRE), making them vulnerable to leakage abuse attacks (LAAs). For example, Always Encrypted either deterministically encrypts columns or stores them with an ordered index [4]. These techniques have been shown to offer little-to-no privacy in certain practical scenarios [26,37].

A more promising approach is structured encryption (StE) which uses auxiliary encrypted data structures (e.g. encrypted multimaps) to support a subset of SQL queries [15]. This is done by translating the SQL query into tokens which can be passed to the server to query the auxiliary structures. The outputs of this are compiled, decrypted and processed to retrieve the SQL query result. Security is measured by *leakage profiles*, which characterize what information a curious server can learn. In particular, StE-based constructions leak equal or less than PRE-based constructions and resist most known LAAs [8,9,20,25–27,37].

K. Sako and N. O. Tippenhauer (Eds.): ACNS 2021, LNCS 12727, pp. 480–510, 2021.
https://doi.org/10.1007/978-3-030-78375-4_19

<u>OUR CONTRIBUTIONS.</u> Our work can be grouped into three main contributions:

1. **Partially precomputed joins:** We introduce a new way to index (equi)joins which stems from the simple observation that when the server fully precomputes (FP) joins, the client has to download and decrypt a quadratic number of rows and the server learns the equality pattern of said rows. In our approach, the server partially precomputes (PP) joins: instead of indexing exactly which rows from the input table should be concatenated and returned, it just stores the set of rows from each input table that appears anywhere in the join output. At query time, the client downloads these sets and computes the join. When this is used to support SQL queries of the form "**select** * **from** id_1 **join** id_2 **on** $at_1 = at_2$", PP outperforms FP in both leakage and bandwidth at the cost of a logarithmic factor of client computation (in the worst case).

2. **Hybrid indexing:** When we incorporate PP joins into state-of-the-art StE schemes, we discover that some queries (e.g. those with a selection subquery) cannot be computed in the same way because the server does not know the equality pattern on the join columns (i.e. how the rows "match up"). So while PP joins are still the more secure choice, they sometimes incur more bandwidth than FP. To address this, we develop a hybrid StE scheme with both forms of indexing. The client chooses which to use at query time. We provide the first heuristic (that we are aware of) to enable this type of *leakage-aware client-side query planning*, helping the client decide how to minimize leakage without exceeding a given bandwidth budget.

3. **Simulations on real data:** We quantify the effect of using FP and PP join indexing on bandwidth incurred by simulating our constructions on data from the City of Chicago's Data Portal and MySQL's sample Sakila database [2,3]. On simple (non-recursive) join queries, PP's bandwidth is on average 231 times less than FP's but more complex (recursive) queries are split down the middle as to which option used less bandwidth. We also demonstrate the accuracy of our heuristic under different client storage constraints. Assuming client storage comparable to that which is used in SQL Server, our heuristic chose a query plan with the maximal number of PP joins 79% of the time, and the optimal query plan 68% of the time.

<u>RELATED WORK.</u> Encrypted databases have been treated from a variety of perspectives. Structured encryption (StE) was defined by Chase and Kamara (CK) and is a special case of SSE, which was first defined by SWP [41].

We see our work as a direct extension and improvement upon SPX and OPX, two schemes which applied StE to the problem of indexing SQL databases [15,32,34]. Both our scheme and OPX address a similar query class to the one introduced in SPX, but lower leakage by using the hashset technique from OXT and primitives inspired by CJJJKRS [12,13]. In particular, our FpSj scheme in Sect. 4.2 bears many similarities to OPX with minor leakage improvements from using a single indexing data structure. Our PpSj and HybStl schemes (in Sect. 4.2 and Sect. 5 respectively) introduce a new technique which further lowers leakage and server storage. For non-recursive queries, there are also substantial bandwidth savings.

PRE-based solutions achieves higher query support at the cost of higher leakage [1,21,24,39,43], and are particularly susceptible to leakage abuse attacks [8,9,20,25–27,37].

Finally, encrypted search has also been attempted using alternate models and architectures including the database-provider model [28], MPC [6,16], ORAM [23] and trusted execution environments [5,11,35].

Other works have also partially delegated computation to the client, to reduce leakage or increase query support, though none have applied it to joins [17,19,42].

2   Preliminaries

We denote the empty string with ϵ. Given positive integer n, let $[n] = \{1, 2, \ldots, n\}$. Given tuples $\mathbf{t}_1 = (x_1, \ldots, x_n)$ and $\mathbf{t}_2 = (y_1, \ldots, y_m)$ we write $\mathbf{t}_1 \| \mathbf{t}_2$ as a shorthand for $(x_1, \ldots, x_n, y_1, \ldots, y_m)$. We extend set operations $\cap, \cup \in, \subseteq$ from sets to tuples by interpreting the tuples as sets.

Our algorithms often make use of dictionaries $\mathbf{D}$ which map labels $\ell \in \{0, 1\}^*$ to values $\mathbf{D}[\ell] \in \{0, 1\}^* \cup \{\bot\}$. We also adopt the shorthand $\mathbf{D}.\mathsf{Lbls} = \{\ell \in \{0, 1\}^* : \mathbf{D}[\ell] \neq \bot\}$. A multimap $\mathbf{M}$ is an dictionary where $\mathbf{M}[\ell]$ is either a set of strings or $\bot$.

PSEUDOCODE. In pseudocode, we will assume that all integers , strings and sets are initialized to 0 , ϵ and $\emptyset$ respectively. For dictionaries and multimaps, they are initialized with all labels mapping to $\bot$. If S is a set or dictionary value, we write $S \xleftarrow{\cup} x$ in pseudocode as a shorthand for $S \leftarrow S \cup \{x\}$, initializing it first to $\emptyset$ if necessary. If $\mathbf{t}$ is a tuple, we similarly mean $\mathbf{t} \leftarrow \mathbf{t} \| (x)$ by writing $\mathbf{t} \leftarrow \mathbf{t} \xleftarrow{\cup} x$. Finally, we will write "Define X : $pred$" to set X (a function or constant) in such a way that the predicate $pred$ is true. If there are undefined variables in $pred$ we treat it as a random variable and expect that X is defined such that $pred$ will always be true.

GAMES. Our work uses the code-based game-playing framework of BR [7]. Let G be a game and A an adversary. Then, we write $\Pr[\mathsf{G}(A)]$ to denote the probability that A plays G and the latter returns true. G may provide oracles to A, and if so we write $A^{O_1, \ldots, O_n}$ to denote that A is run with access to oracles $O_1, \ldots, O_n$.

Game $\mathsf{G}_{\mathsf{SE}}^{\mathrm{ind}\$}(A)$	Game $\mathsf{G}_{\mathsf{F}}^{\mathrm{prf}}(A)$
$b \leftarrow_{\$} \{0, 1\}$; $K_e \leftarrow_{\$} \mathsf{SE.KS}$	$b \leftarrow_{\$} \{0, 1\}$; $K_f \leftarrow_{\$} \mathsf{F.KS}$
$b' \leftarrow_{\$} A^{\mathrm{ENC}}$; Return $b = b'$	$b' \leftarrow_{\$} A^{\mathrm{FN}}$; Return $b = b'$
Alg $\mathrm{ENC}(m)$	**Alg** $\mathrm{FN}(X)$
$c_1 \leftarrow_{\$} \mathsf{SE.Enc}(K_e, m)$	If $\mathbf{C}[X] = \bot$ then $\mathbf{C}[X] \leftarrow_{\$} \{0, 1\}^{\mathsf{F.ol}}$
$c_0 \leftarrow_{\$} \{0, 1\}^{|c_1|}$; Return c_b	$c_1 \leftarrow_{\$} \mathsf{F.Ev}(K_f, X)$; $c_0 \leftarrow \mathbf{C}[X]$; Return c_b

Fig. 1. Games used in defining IND$ security of SE scheme SE (right) and PRF security of function family F (left)

SYMMETRIC ENCRYPTION, IND$-SECURITY. Symmetric Encryption (SE) scheme SE defines key set SE.KS, encryption algorithm SE.Enc and decryption algorithm SE.Dec. Encryption is randomized, taking a key $K_e \in$ SE.KS and a message $M \in \{0,1\}^*$ and returns a ciphertext $C \in \{0,1\}^*$. Decryption is deterministic and takes a key and ciphertext, returning a message. SE also defines a ciphertext length function SE.cl. We require that if $C \leftarrow_s$ SE.Enc(K_e, M) then $|C| =$ SE.cl$(|M|)$ and $\Pr[$SE.Dec$(K_e, C) = M] = 1$. We want our SE schemes to protect the privacy of M, so ciphertexts should be indistinguishable from a random string of length SE.cl$(|M|)$. We capture this with the game $G_{SE}^{ind\$}$ in Fig. 1 and say that a scheme is IND$-secure if $\mathbf{Adv}_{SE}^{ind\$}(A) = 2[\Pr[G_{SE}^{ind\$}(A)] - 1$ is small for all adversaries A.

FUNCTION FAMILIES, PRF-SECURITY. A function family F defines a key set F.KS and an output length F.ol. It defines a deterministic evaluation algorithm F.Ev: F.KS $\times \{0,1\}^* \to \{0,1\}^{F.ol}$. We define PRF security for function family F via the game G_F^{prf} depicted in Fig. 1. We say that F is a PRF if $\mathbf{Adv}_F^{prf}(A) = 2\Pr[G_F^{prf}(A)] - 1$ is small for all A.

3   Structured Indexing for SQL Data Types

We now generalize CK's definition of structured encryption and provide a new framework for modeling encrypted SQL systems [15].

ABSTRACT DATA TYPES. An *abstract data type* ADT defines a domain set ADT.Dom, a query set ADT.QS, and a deterministic specification function ADT.Spec : ADT.Dom $\times$ ADT.QS $\to \{0,1\}^*$.

An example is the dictionary ADT DyAdt. DyAdt.Dom, DyAdt.QS contain all possible dictionaries $\mathbf{D}$ and labels respectively (as defined in Sect. 2). Then, DyAdt.Spec$(\mathbf{D}, \ell) = \mathbf{D}[\ell]$. Multimap ADT MmAdt is defined analogously.

STRUCTURED INDEXING. We generalize Structured Encryption (StE) schemes (as defined by CK [15]) to *structured indexing* (StI) schemes. These are StE schemes without a decryption algorithm. The intuition here is that the handling of outsourced data often indexes the data in addition to encrypting it and we would like these encrypted indexes, whatever form they take, to achieve semantic security as well. Later, we show how this primitive allows us to modularize StE schemes. A StI scheme StI for ADT defines a set of keys StI.KS and the following algorithms:

- Randomized encryption algorithm StI.Enc which takes a key $K' \in$ StI.KS and an element of ADT.Dom and returns an updated key K and index IX $\in \{0,1\}^*$. This syntax generalizes that of CK by allowing key generation to occur within or outside StI.Enc.
- Possibly randomized token generation algorithm StI.Tok which takes a key and a query from ADT.QS, and returns fixed length token tk $\in \{0,1\}^{StI.tl}$.
- Deterministic evaluation algorithm StI.Eval which takes a token and index, and returns a ciphertext string $C \in \{0,1\}^*$.

– Finalization algorithm Stl.Fin which takes K, q and an input string, and returns an output string.

Intuitively, the client indexes his data then encrypts this index with Stl.Enc, storing IX on the server. At query time, the client uses Stl.Tok to generate a token and sends it to the server who runs Stl.Eval, returning C to the client. Stl.Fin can be used for client-side post-processing of the data. Note that the output of Stl.Eval need not be the input to Stl.Fin. In our indexing schemes the server will use the output of Stl.Eval as "pointers" to retrieve rows of SQL data stored in a different data structure which in turn form the input to Stl.Fin.

STRUCTURED ENCRYPTION. We can now define StE as a special cases of StI. Intuitively, an StE scheme is an StI scheme where the data structure is also used to store query responses (as opposed to just indexing them). The output of evaluation can be fed into finalization for decryption and should return the query result. To highlight this, StE schemes have a *decryption algorithm* StE.Dec in place of a finalization algorithm which takes as input K, q, C and returns the query result. We define correctness via game G_{StE}^{cor} in Fig. 2 and say that StE is correct if the advantage of all adversaries A, defined $\mathbf{Adv}_{StE}^{cor}(A) = \Pr[G_{StE}^{cor}(A)]$, is low. The correctness of our schemes will depend on the collision resistance of their function family primitives. Since we assume these are PRFs to prove security, we will also assume that their key-lengths are sufficient to ensure correctness.

We subdivide StE schemes into two types. We say that a scheme StE_{rr} is *response revealing* (RR) if evaluation itself returns the query result. In other words, decryption must be such that $StE_{rr}.Dec(K, q, C) = C$ for all K, q, C. An StE scheme that is not RR is *response hiding* (RH).

We refer to StE for the multimap and dictionary data types as multimap and dictionary encryption (MME/DYE) respectively. Our constructions make use of a specific dictionary encryption scheme adapted from CJJ+'s SSE scheme $\prod_{bas}$ (2Lev in the Clusion library) [12,36]. In this scheme, the encrypted data structure is itself a dictionary $\mathbf{D}'$. We start by padding all values in the input dictionary to the same length, then for each label-value pair $\ell, \mathbf{D}[\ell]$, we do $\mathbf{D}'[\mathsf{F.Ev}(K_f, \ell)] \leftarrow \mathsf{SE.Enc}(K_e, \mathbf{D}[\ell])$ where F is a pseudorandom function family and SE is a symmetric encryption scheme. For completeness, we include the pseudocode of this dictionary encryption scheme (which we call Dye_π) in Appendix A. Our constructions also make use of a generic RR multimap encryption scheme. We adapt Dye_π to Mme_π^{rr} (using a counter and label-dependent K_e) as an example of such a scheme in Appendix A.

SEMANTIC SECURITY. We define semantic security for Stl using game $G_{Stl,\mathcal{L},\mathcal{S}}^{ss}$ depicted in Fig. 2, where Stl is a StI scheme for ADT and $\mathcal{L}, \mathcal{S}$ are algorithms we refer to as the leakage algorithm and simulator respectively. The adversary runs in a setup and guessing phase, as indicated by the first argument to it. Its advantage is $\mathbf{Adv}_{Stl,\mathcal{L},\mathcal{S}}^{ss}(A) = 2\Pr[G_{Stl,\mathcal{L},\mathcal{S}}^{ss}(A) = 1] - 1$. Note that when Stl is an StE scheme we recover CK's non-adaptive security notion.

Game $G_{StE}^{cor}(A)$	Game $G_{Stl,\mathcal{L},\mathcal{S}}^{ss}(A)$
$(DS, st) \leftarrow_\$ A(\mathbf{s})$; $K' \leftarrow_\$ StE.KS$	$(DS, (q_1, \ldots, q_n), st) \leftarrow_\$ A(\mathbf{s})$
If $DS \notin ADT.Dom$ then return false	$b \leftarrow_\$ \{0, 1\}$; $K' \leftarrow_\$ Stl.KS$
$(K, EDS) \leftarrow_\$ StE.Enc(K', DS)$	If $DS \notin ADT.Dom$ or $\{q_i\}_{i=1}^n \not\subseteq ADT.QS$ then
$A^{TOK}(\mathbf{g}, EDS, st)$; Return win	Return false
	If $b = 1$ then
Oracle $TOK(q)$	$\quad (K, IX) \leftarrow_\$ Stl.Enc(K', DS)$
If $q \notin ADT.QS$ then win $\leftarrow$ false	$\quad$ For $i \in [n]$ do $tk_i \leftarrow_\$ Stl.Tok(K, q_i)$
$tk \leftarrow_\$ StE.Tok(K, q)$	Else
$M \leftarrow StE.Dec(K, StE.Eval(tk, EDS))$	$\quad (IX, (tk_1, \ldots, tk_n)) \leftarrow_\$ \mathcal{S}(\mathcal{L}(DS, (q_1, \ldots, q_n)))$
If $ADT.Spec(DS, q) \neq M$ then	$b' \leftarrow_\$ A(\mathbf{g}, IX, (tk_1, \ldots, tk_n), st)$
$\quad$ win $\leftarrow$ false	Return $(b = b')$
Return tk	

Fig. 2. Games used in defining correctness for StE (structured encryption scheme for ADT) and semantic security for Stl (structured indexing scheme for ADT) with respect to leakage algorithm $\mathcal{L}$ and simulator $\mathcal{S}$.

3.1 SQL Data Types

We now describe our notation for SQL data, queries and operations. We then define a class of ADTs we call *SQL data types* to construct StE schemes for.

SQL RELATIONS, DATABASES, SCHEMAS. SQL relation R defines a tuple of distinct attributes $R.Ats = (at_1, \ldots, at_n)$. Each attribute is a bitstring $at \in \{0, 1\}^*$ and represents a "column" in the relation. R also defines a table R.T consisting of n-tuples of bitstrings representing the "rows" in the relation. Given a row $(x_1, \ldots, x_n) = \mathbf{r} \in R.T$, we refer to the i-th entry of the row with $\mathbf{r}[at_i] = x_i$. We can initialize a relation with $NewRltn((at_1, \ldots, at_n))$ which returns R with the desired attribute set and no rows.

We define a *database* to be a set of relations with disjoint attributes and their (distinct) identifiers, i.e. a set of the form $DB = \{(id_1, R_1), \ldots, (id_N, R_N)\}$ where $i \neq j$ implies $id_i \neq id_j$ and $R_i.Ats \cap R_j.Ats = \emptyset$. We denote the identifier set of such a database as $DB.IDs = \{id_i\}_{i \in [N]}$ and retrieve relations by identifier using $DB[id_i] = R_i$. Since database attributes are non-repeating, we allow the retrieval of a table by any of its attributes using getID (i.e. if $getID(at, DB) = id$ then $at \in DB[id].Ats$). Similarly, if $\mathbf{t} \subseteq DB[id].Ats$, then $getID(\mathbf{t}, DB) = id$.

We require that each $(id, R) \in DB$ has a *unique key attribute* $uk(id) \in R.Ats$. This functions as a "row number" which is not secret and uniquely identifies each row. In other words, for all distinct $\mathbf{r}, \mathbf{r}' \in R.T$, we have $\mathbf{r}[uk(id)] \neq \mathbf{r}'[uk(id)]$. Given some $\mathbf{r} \in DB[id]$ we refer to the tuple $(id, \mathbf{r}[uk(id)])$ as its *coordinates* and note that it uniquely identifies that row within the database. Additionally, we refer to the values in a "column" with $rng(at, DB) = \{\mathbf{r}[at] : \mathbf{r} \in DB[getID(at, DB)]\}$.

A database's schema communicates all information about DB except the tables: $Schema(DB) = \{(id, R.Ats) : (id, R) \in DB\}$. As shorthand, if $scma =$

$R_1.T$	
uk(id_1)	at_1
aa	Alice
bb	Alice
cc	Bob
dd	Charlie
ee	David

$R_2.T$		
uk(id_2)	at_2	at_3
11	Alice	Math
22	Alice	Chem
33	Bob	CS
44	Eve	CS
55	Eve	Bio

$(R_1 \bowtie_{at_1,at_2} R_2).T$				
uk(id_1)	at_1	uk(id_2)	at_2	at_3
aa	Alice	11	Alice	Math
aa	Alice	22	Alice	Chem
bb	Alice	11	Alice	Math
bb	Alice	22	Alice	Chem
cc	Bob	33	Bob	CS

$(\sigma_{at_2,\text{Eve}}(R_2)).T$		
uk(id_2)	at_2	at_3
44	Eve	CS
55	Eve	Bio

$(\sigma_{at_3,\text{cs}}(R_1 \bowtie_{at_1,at_2} R_2)).T$				
uk(id_1)	at_1	uk(id_2)	at_2	at_3
cc	Bob	33	Bob	CS

Fig. 3. Examples of SQL relations R_1, R_2 and the output of joins/ selects on them.

Schema(DB) then $\text{scma}[id] = \text{DB}[id].\text{Ats}$ and $\text{getID}(at, \text{scma}) = \text{getID}(at, \text{DB})$. In our schemes, the client stores Schema(DB) as part of the key in order to appropriately format data returned by the server. This is a result of our explicit handling of schemas, coordinates and attributes, something which was left implicit in prior work.

SQL OPERATIONS. In our work, we address the secure computation of SQL (equi)joins and (equality) selections. These operations work as follows.

The selection operation is parametrized by a pair of bitstrings (at, x), takes a relation R_1 with $at \in R.\text{Ats}$ as input, and returns $R = \sigma_{(at,x)}(R_1)$ where:

$$R.\text{Ats} = R_1.\text{Ats} \text{ and } R.T = \{\mathbf{r} \in R_1.T : \mathbf{r}[at] = x\}.$$

In Fig. 3, we provide an example of such a selection on a relation in a database.

The join infix operation is a function parametrized by two equal-length tuples of attributes $\mathbf{t}_1, \mathbf{t}_2$. It takes two relations R_1, R_2 with disjoint attribute sets where $(at_1^i, \ldots, at_n^i) = \mathbf{t}_i \subseteq R_i.\text{Ats}$. It returns $R = R_1 \bowtie_{\mathbf{t}_1, \mathbf{t}_2} R_2$ where:

$$R.\text{Ats} = R_1.\text{Ats} \| R_2.\text{Ats} \text{ and} \tag{1}$$

$$R.T = \{\mathbf{r}_1 \| \mathbf{r}_2 : \mathbf{r}_1 \in R_1.T, \ \mathbf{r}_2 \in R_2.T, \forall i \in [n], \mathbf{r}_1[at_i^1] = \mathbf{r}_2[at_i^2]\}. \tag{2}$$

In the case of a join on singleton tuples, we abbreviate $\bowtie_{(at),(at')}$ as $\bowtie_{at,at'}$. In Fig. 3, we provide an example such a join. Attribute tuples can be empty in which case it returns the Cartesian product of the input rows. This is also known as the "cross" operation $\times$.

ADT FOR SQL DATABASES. We say that an ADT SqlDT is a *SQL data types* if its domain elements DB $\in$ SqlDT are *SQL databases* which take the form $\mathbf{DB} = (\text{DB}, \alpha)$ where DB is as defined in Sect. 3.1 and $\alpha \in \{0, 1\}^*$ is the auxiliary data. The purpose of α is to allow annotations on DB consistent with real world applications. In this work, we use α to indicate the allowed joins, and SqlDT.Spec always returns either a relation or $\perp$.

3.2 Constructing StE for SQL Data Types Using Encrypted Indexes

Our end goal is structurally encrypted databases supporting response-hiding SQL queries. We build these by constructing StI schemes for classes of SQL queries, then converting these into StE schemes for SQL data types via a generic transform. We now describe this conversion, then dedicate the remainder of this work to the above mentioned StI schemes.

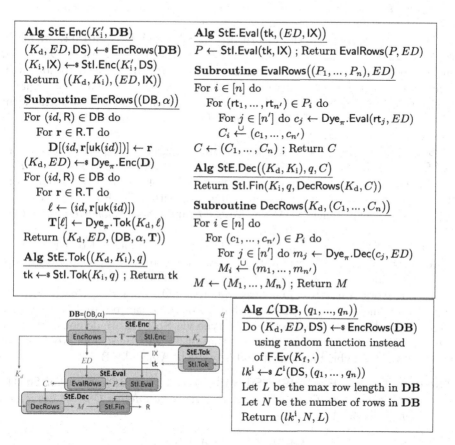

Alg StE.Enc(K_i', **DB)**
$(K_d, ED, DS) \leftarrow_\$ \text{EncRows}(\textbf{DB})$
$(K_i, \text{IX}) \leftarrow_\$ \text{StI.Enc}(K_i', DS)$
Return $((K_d, K_i), (ED, \text{IX}))$

Subroutine EncRows($(\textbf{DB}, \alpha)$)
For $(id, R) \in \textbf{DB}$ do
　For $\mathbf{r} \in R.T$ do
　　$\mathbf{D}[(id, \mathbf{r}[\text{uk}(id)])] \leftarrow \mathbf{r}$
$(K_d, ED) \leftarrow_\$ \text{Dye}_\pi.\text{Enc}(\mathbf{D})$
For $(id, R) \in \textbf{DB}$ do
　For $\mathbf{r} \in R.T$ do
　　$\ell \leftarrow (id, \mathbf{r}[\text{uk}(id)])$
　　$\mathbf{T}[\ell] \leftarrow \text{Dye}_\pi.\text{Tok}(K_d, \ell)$
Return $(K_d, ED, (\textbf{DB}, \alpha, \mathbf{T}))$

Alg StE.Tok($(K_d, K_i), q$)
$tk \leftarrow_\$ \text{StI.Tok}(K_i, q)$; Return tk

Alg StE.Eval$(tk, (ED, \text{IX}))$
$P \leftarrow \text{StI.Eval}(tk, \text{IX})$; Return $\text{EvalRows}(P, ED)$

Subroutine EvalRows$((P_1, \ldots, P_n), ED)$
For $i \in [n]$ do
　For $(rt_1, \ldots, rt_{n'}) \in P_i$ do
　　For $j \in [n']$ do $c_j \leftarrow \text{Dye}_\pi.\text{Eval}(rt_j, ED)$
　　$C_i \overset{\cup}{\leftarrow} (c_1, \ldots, c_{n'})$
$C \leftarrow (C_1, \ldots, C_n)$; Return C

Alg StE.Dec$((K_d, K_i), q, C)$
Return $\text{StI.Fin}(K_i, q, \text{DecRows}(K_d, C))$

Subroutine DecRows$(K_d, (C_1, \ldots, C_n))$
For $i \in [n]$ do
　For $(c_1, \ldots, c_{n'}) \in P_i$ do
　　For $j \in [n']$ do $m_j \leftarrow \text{Dye}_\pi.\text{Dec}(c_j, ED)$
　　$M_i \overset{\cup}{\leftarrow} (m_1, \ldots, m_{n'})$
$M \leftarrow (M_1, \ldots, M_n)$; Return M

Alg $\mathcal{L}(\textbf{DB}, (q_1, \ldots, q_n))$
Do $(K_d, ED, DS) \leftarrow_\$ \text{EncRows}(\textbf{DB})$
　using random function instead
　of $\text{F.Ev}(K_f, \cdot)$
$lk^i \leftarrow_\$ \mathcal{L}^i(DS, (q_1, \ldots, q_n))$
Let L be the max row length in **DB**
Let N be the number of rows in **DB**
Return (lk^i, N, L)

Fig. 4. Algorithms and for structured encryption scheme StE = **SqlStE[StI, SE, F]** expressed both in pseudocode (top) and diagrammatically (bottom left), and leakage algorithm for StE (bottom right). Here, Dye_π is the RH dictionary encryption scheme Dye_π in Appendix A (which uses SE, F as primitives) and $\mathcal{L}^i$ is StI's leakage profile.

STE, STI FOR SqlDT. Intuitively, our StE schemes handle the indexing and storage of SQL data separately. We do the former with an StI scheme and the latter with an RH dictionary encryption scheme. This modularization simplifies pseudocode and reduces the problem of designing secure StE schemes to that of StI schemes.

More formally, we construct an StE scheme for SQL data type SqlDT using the transform **SqlStE** which which takes uses an StI scheme for SqlDT_1 (described below), symmetric encryption scheme SE and function family F. We capture the syntax and pseudocode of StE's algorithms in Fig. 4. Note that StE.KS = StI.KS and Dye_π is the RH dictionary encryption scheme given in Appendix A which uses SE, F as primitives. It is used in EncRows, EvalRows, DecRows, which encrypt, retrieve and decrypt the rows of database DB. We used a specific RH dictionary encryption scheme because pathological alternatives may introduce circular security issues, preventing a more general approach.

We now describe how the algorithms in StI and StE = **SqlStE**[StI, SE, F] work. During StE.Enc, algorithm EncRows will store the rows of DB in an encrypted dictionary ED using Dye_π.Enc. It also prepares a token dictionary **T** which maps each row coordinate to a token for Dye_π. SQL data type SqlDT_1 is the same as SqlDT except that its domain elements now take the form $\mathsf{DS} = (\mathsf{DB}, \alpha, \mathbf{T})$ where $(\mathsf{DB}, \alpha) \in \mathsf{SqlDT.Dom}$. The output of StE.Enc is ED and the index returned by StI.Enc(DS).

StE's tokens are those generated by StI. As such, the server's first step in StE.Eval is to run StI.Eval. We require that StI.Eval returns a *pointer tuple* $P = (P_1, \ldots, P_n)$ which is a tuple of sets of tokens. The tokens in each P_i come from **T** and point to rows from the same table. Algorithm EvalRows replaces each token with relevant (encrypted) row from ED and returns *ciphertext tuple* $C = (C_1, \ldots, C_n)$, the output of StE.Eval.

During StE.Dec, algorithm DecRows decrypts each ciphertext to get *plaintext tuple* $M = (M_1, \ldots, M_n)$. StI.Fin takes these decrypted rows and performs any final client-side post-processing, returning the final output relation R.

In this work, we will define three different SQL data types, each with its own StI scheme(s). To demonstrate that all of these can be used to construct secure RH StE for their respective data type via **SqlStE**, we demonstrate that the semantic security of StE reduces to that of its primitives. The proof follows from a standard hybrid argument and is given in Appendix B.

Theorem 1. *Let* StE = **SqlStE**[StI, SE, F] *be a correct StE scheme for* SqlDT. *Then given algorithms* $\mathcal{L}^i, \mathcal{S}^i$ *and adversary A we can define $\mathcal{L}$ as in Fig. 4 and construct* $\mathcal{S}, A_s, A_f, A_i$ *such that:*

$$\mathbf{Adv}^{\mathrm{ss}}_{\mathsf{StE}, \mathcal{L}, \mathcal{S}}(A) \leq \mathbf{Adv}^{\mathrm{ind\$}}_{\mathsf{SE}}(A_s) + \mathbf{Adv}^{\mathrm{prf}}_{\mathsf{F}}(A_f) + \mathbf{Adv}^{\mathrm{ss}}_{\mathsf{StI}, \mathcal{L}^i, \mathcal{S}^i}(A_i).$$

4 Partially Precomputed Joins

We demonstrate our framework from Sect. 3 in action with two SQL data types: JnDT and SjDT. The former only supports non-recursive join queries and is presented for the purpose of introducing partially precomputed (PP) join indexing. The latter allows recursive queries, cluster joins and equality selections, and demonstrates how OPX's techniques can be modified to use PP joins.

Algs	FpJn.Enc$\left(K'_m, (DB, \alpha, \mathbf{T})\right)$,	PpJn.Enc$\left(K'_m, (DB, \alpha, \mathbf{T})\right)$

For $(at_1, at_2) \in \alpha$ do
   For $\mathbf{r} \in (DB[getID(at_i, DB)] \bowtie_{at_1, at_2} DB[getID(at_i, DB)]).\mathbf{T}$ do
      $rt_1 \leftarrow \mathbf{T}[(id_1, \mathbf{r}[uk(id_1)])]$; $rt_2 \leftarrow \mathbf{T}[(id_2, \mathbf{r}[uk(id_2)])]$
      $\boxed{\mathbf{M}[(at_1, at_2)] \xleftarrow{\cup} (rt_1, rt_2)}$; For $i \in \{1, 2\}$ do $\mathbf{M}[(at_1, at_2, i)] \xleftarrow{\cup} rt_i$
$(K_m, \mathsf{IX}) \leftarrow_\$ \mathsf{Mme.Enc}(K'_m, \mathbf{M})$; Return $\left((K_m, \mathsf{Schema}(DB)), \mathsf{IX}\right)$

Alg FpJn.Tok$\left((K_m, scma), q\right)$	**Alg** PpJn.Tok$\left((K_m, scma), (at_1, at_2)\right)$
Return Mme.Tok$\left(K_m, q\right)$	$mt_1 \leftarrow_\$ \mathsf{Mme.Tok}\left(K_m, (at_1, at_2, 1)\right)$
Alg FpJn.Eval(tk, IX)	$mt_2 \leftarrow_\$ \mathsf{Mme.Tok}\left(K_m, (at_1, at_2, 2)\right)$
Return (Mme.Eval(tk, IX))	Return (mt_1, mt_2)
Alg FpJn.Fin$\left((K_m, scma), q, (M)\right)$	**Alg** PpJn.Eval$\left((tk_1, tk_2), \mathsf{IX}\right)$
$at_1 \leftarrow scma[getID(at_1, scma)]$	Return (Mme.Eval(tk$_1$, IX), Mme.Eval(tk$_2$, IX))
$at_2 \leftarrow scma[getID(at_2, scma)]$	**Alg** PpJn.Fin$\left((K_m, scma), (at_1, at_2), (M_1, M_2)\right)$
$R \leftarrow \mathsf{NewRltn}(at_1 \| at_2)$	For $i = 1, 2$ do
$R.\mathbf{T} \leftarrow \{\mathbf{r}_1 \| \mathbf{r}_2 : (\mathbf{r}_1, \mathbf{r}_2) \in M\}$	$R_i \leftarrow \mathsf{NewRltn}(scma[getID(at_i, scma)])$
Return R	$R_i.\mathbf{T} \leftarrow \{\mathbf{r} : (\mathbf{r}) \in M_i\}$
	Return $R_1 \bowtie_{at_1, at_2} R_2$

Alg $\mathcal{L}^f(DS, (q_1, \dots, q_n))$	**Alg** $\mathcal{L}^P\left(DS, ((at_1, at'_1), \dots, (at_n, at'_n))\right)$
Construct $\mathbf{M}$ as in FpJn.Enc$(\cdot, DS)$	Construct $\mathbf{M}$ as in PpJn.Enc$(\cdot, DS)$
Return $\mathcal{L}^m(\mathbf{M}, (q_1, \dots, q_n))$	For $i \in [n]$ do
	$q_{2i-1} \leftarrow (at_i, at'_i, 1)$; $q_{2i} \leftarrow (at_i, at'_i, 2)$
	Return $\mathcal{L}^m(\mathbf{M}, (q_1, \dots, q_{2n}))$

Fig. 5. Algorithms of StI schemes FpJn, PpJn (top) and their leakage algorithms (bottom) where Mme is a RR multimap encryption scheme. Note that in the encryption algorithm, boxed code belongs only to the respective algorithm.

4.1 Indexing of Non-recursive Joins

JOIN DATA TYPE JnDT. We define JnDT.Dom to contain (DB, α) such that DB is a database and α is the set of join queries supported (i.e. if A is the set of attributes in DB that are not unique key attributes, then $\alpha \subseteq \{(at_1, at_2) \in A \times A : getID(at_1, DB) \neq getID(at_2, DB)\}$. Our goal here is to capture SQL queries of the form "id_1 **join** id_2 **on** $at_1 = at_2$" where $id_1, id_2 \in DB.\mathsf{IDs}$ and $at_i \in DB[id_i].\mathsf{Ats}$.

We allow queries to be any pair of attributes (i.e. JnDT.QS $= \{(at_1, at_2) : at_i \in \{0, 1\}^*\}$), but JnDT.Spec only computes the join if $(at_1, at_2) \in \alpha$:

$$\mathsf{JnDT.Spec}\left((at_1, at_2), (DB, \alpha)\right) = DB[getID(at_1, DB)] \bowtie_{at_1, at_2} DB[getID(at_2, DB)]$$

and returns $\perp$ otherwise. From here on we assume that all queries made are "non-trivial" meaning they return relations with at least one row.

FP INDEXING. FpJn is an StI scheme that "fully precomputes" joins and is modeled after SPX's handling of "type-2 selections" and OPX's handling of "leaf joins" [32,34]. The intuition here is that the output relation for each possible join query is precomputed and pointers to the rows therein are stored as an entry in a RR encrypted multimap. FpJn's detailed algorithms and leakage profile are given in Fig. 5. Note that FpJn.KS = Mme.KS and that each row in the output of a particular join is indexed as a pair of pointers to rows in DB.

Since join queries are handled directly by Mme the leakage and efficiency of FpJn depends entirely on Mme. For the rest of this discussion, we will assume Mme is one of the mainstream multimap encryption schemes (e.g. [12,15,18]) with the "standard" leakage profile consisting the label space size $|\mathbf{M}.\mathsf{Lbls}|$, mul-timap size $\sum_{\ell \in \mathbf{M}.\mathsf{Lbls}} |\mathbf{M}[\ell]|$, query pattern (equality pattern of queries $\ell_1, \dots, \ell_n$) and query responses $\mathbf{M}[\ell_1], \dots, \mathbf{M}[\ell_n]$.

Notice that when a query (at_1, at_2) is made in FpJn, the query responses reveal the equality pattern of columns at_1, at_2 for rows that appear in the join output. To illustrate, if the query is made on DB = $\{(id_1, \mathsf{R}_1), (id_2, \mathsf{R}_2)\}$ where $\mathsf{R}_1, \mathsf{R}_2$ are as depicted in Fig. 3, the server learns that the first two rows of each R_i all have the same value in their at_1, at_2 columns, but won't reveal anything about the last two rows of each R_i apart from the fact that they are not returned in the join. Note that in the worst case, the join returns all rows from both relations and the search pattern leakage reveals the entire equality pattern of both columns. This leakage is comparable to PRE-based techniques like deterministic encryption or adjustable joins (an observation also made by DPPS [20]). This is significant because, as discussed in Sect. 1, LAAs are highly effective against PRE and can be applied in this case. Beyond the worst case, FP indexing leaks strictly less than PRE-based solutions but this does not make them immune to LAAs. In particular, we believe that attacks (such as those using ℓ_p-optimization or graph matching [8,37]) can be extended to make use of partial equality patterns and cross column correlations, and be effective against FpJn's leakage.

We also note that FpJn achieves lower leakage than the analogous indexing in SPX or OPX because it uses a single multimap. The latter schemes had one encrypted multimap for each attribute (i.e. $\mathbf{M}_{at_1}$ indexes all joins $(at_1, at_2) \in \alpha$) this leaks additional metadata and tells the adversary when two queries join on the same at_1.

PP INDEXING. We introduce a new StI scheme PpJn which performs "partially precomputed" indexing, whose algorithms are also depicted in Fig. 5. PpJn.Enc proceeds in the same way as FpJn.Enc but we store the rows from each input relation separately. In other words, if $\mathbf{M}_f, \mathbf{M}_p$ are the multimaps constructed in the respective setup algorithms, then $\mathbf{M}_p[(at_1, at_2, i)] = \{\mathsf{rt}_i : (\mathsf{rt}_1, \mathsf{rt}_2) \in \mathbf{M}_f[(at_1, at_2)]\}$ for $i = 1, 2$ and $(at_1, at_2) \in \alpha$. Notice that this means the client needs to reassemble the output relation from the two sets of rows in Stl.Fin. We recommend that the client do so by sorting then joining the columns, avoiding the quadratic time nested loop join where rows are compared pairwise.

This small change in indexing technique has substantial impact on bandwidth and security. In the worst case, the number of rows sent with FP is quadratic while PP's is linear. This bandwidth reduction occurs because two sets of rows are sent instead of their cross product. Notice that modulo some metadata information (i.e. the multimap sizes), the PP leakage can be derived from the FP leakage meaning that PP indexing is no worse than FP indexing. In fact, if more than one row is returned to any query PP leakage is strictly lower. To illustrate, when join query (at_1, at_2) is made to the aforementioned database in Fig. 3, the adversary sees that the first three rows of both tables were returned and can infer that each row has at least one matching value in the other column – nothing specific about their equality patterns.

In summary, PpJn is the superior indexing choice for JnDT because its leakage is strictly lower, bandwidth is no worse and efficiency is comparable.

Semantic security. The security of FpJn, PpJn reduce to that of Mme. The proof follows directly from the definition of Mme's semantic security and is deferred to the full paper.

Theorem 2. *Let $\mathcal{L}, \mathcal{S}$ be the leakage algorithm and simulator for* Mme. *Let $\mathcal{L}^f, \mathcal{L}^p$ be the leakage algorithms given in Fig. 5. Then, given adversary A these exists adversary A_m and simulator $\mathcal{S}^p$ such that:*

$$\mathbf{Adv}^{ss}_{\mathsf{FpJn}, \mathcal{L}^f, \mathcal{S}}(A) \leq \mathbf{Adv}^{ss}_{\mathsf{Mme}, \mathcal{L}, \mathcal{S}}(A) \text{ and } \mathbf{Adv}^{ss}_{\mathsf{PpJn}, \mathcal{L}^p, \mathcal{S}^p}(A) \leq \mathbf{Adv}^{ss}_{\mathsf{Mme}, \mathcal{L}, \mathcal{S}}(A_m).$$

4.2 PP Indexing for Recursive Queries

SjDT. We expand the query support of JnDT to include equality selections, cluster joins (joins on more than one attribute) and recursively defined queries. The resultant query class is similar to the SPJ algebra defined by CM [14] except for the omission of the projection operation which we note can be handled as a post-processing step requiring no cryptographic techniques.

We capture this via the SQL data type SjDT. Its domain is unchanged from JnDT.Dom except that α allows tuple pairs in addition to attribute pairs. Below we describe the forms, evaluation and SQL equivalent of $q \in$ SjDT.QS. (Note that the r, s, j flags are included in SjDT queries for domain separation.) These are defined recursively so $q_i, \mathbf{q}_i$ are themselves queries of the respective type.

Query Type	SjDT query q	SjDT.Spec$(q, \mathbf{DB})$	SQL query $\mathbf{q}$
Relation retrieval	$(\mathbf{r}, id)$	DB$[id]$ where $\mathbf{DB} = (\mathrm{DB}, \alpha)$	select * from id
(Equality) selections	$(\mathbf{s}, at, x, q_1)$	$\sigma_{(at,x)}(\mathsf{SjDT.Spec}(q_1, \mathbf{DB}))$	select * from $\mathbf{q}_1$ where $at = c$
(Equi)joins	$(\mathbf{j}, \mathbf{t}_1, \mathbf{t}_2, q_1, q_2)$ where $(\mathbf{t}_1, \mathbf{t}_2) \in \alpha$	$(\mathsf{SjDT.Spec}(q_1, \mathbf{DB})) \bowtie_{\mathbf{t}_1, \mathbf{t}_2} (\mathsf{SjDT.Spec}(q_2, \mathbf{DB}))$	select * from $\mathbf{q}_1$ join $\mathbf{q}_2$ on $\mathbf{t}_1 = \mathbf{t}_2$

We say that queries of the form $(\mathbf{r}, id)$, $(\mathbf{s}, at, x, (\mathbf{r}, id))$ or $(\mathbf{j}, \mathbf{t}_1, \mathbf{t}_2, (\mathbf{r}, id_1), (\mathbf{r}, id_2))$ are *non-recursive* and all others are *recursive*. We require that all attributes in each $\mathbf{t}_i$ come from the same relation in DB (i.e. $\mathbf{t}_i \subseteq$ DB$[id]$.Ats for some $id \in$ DB.IDs). While allowing cluster joins may lead to an exponential-size index, a judicious database administrator would not allow this – cluster joins are rarely used and usually known in advance.

HASHSET FILTERING. To minimize the leakage of recursive queries in our StI schemes we employ the filtering hashset technique introduced in OXT [13]. We now review this technique and establish some notation for it.

This filtering hashset is a set denoted HS containing outputs of a function family F where $\mathsf{F.KS} = \{0,1\}^{\mathsf{F.ol}}$. In our algorithms, the hashset will be used to associate predicate bitstrings with a row tokens (from $\mathbf{T}$). Later, given a predicate p's key $K = \mathsf{F.Ev}(K_\mathsf{f}, p)$ we can filter a set of row tokens, retaining only those which satisfy the predicate. We formalize this via the following algorithms:

Alg $\mathsf{HsEnc}(K_\mathsf{f}, \mathsf{SET})$	**Alg** $\mathsf{HsFilter}(K, (P_1, \dots, P_n), \mathsf{HS})$
For $(p, \mathsf{rt}) \in \mathsf{SET}$ do	For $i \in [n]$ do
$\quad \mathsf{HS} \overset{\cup}{\leftarrow} \mathsf{F.Ev}\big(\mathsf{F.Ev}(K_\mathsf{f}, p), \mathsf{rt}\big)$	$\quad$ For $\mathsf{rt} \in \mathbf{rt} \in P_i$ if $\mathsf{F.Ev}(K, \mathsf{rt}) \in \mathsf{HS}$ then $S \overset{\cup}{\leftarrow} \mathbf{rt}$
Return HS	$\quad$ If $S \neq \emptyset$ then $P_i \leftarrow S$
	Return $(P_1, \dots, P_n)$

For notational convenience in our pseudocodes, HsFilter takes as input a tuple set $P = (P_1, \dots, P_n)$. It then attempts to filter each P_i and retain only the tuples where at least one rt satisfies the predicate. However, if no such tuple exists, it does not perform the filtering at all.

PP INDEXING FOR SjDT. We are now ready to extend the PP indexing technique introduced in Sect. 4 to construct StI for SjDT. On a high level, we do so by using an inverted index (similar to those used for SSE) to handle selections and a filtering hashset to handle recursively defined queries. The result is StI scheme PpSj whose algorithms are depicted in Fig. 6.

Now we provide some intuition for PpSj's algorithms. The scheme has two server-side data structures: an encrypted multimap and a hashset. The multimap is used to index non-recursive queries my mapping a query-derived label to the relevant rows in the database. For example, the label for relation retrieval query $(\mathbf{r}, id)$ is the query itself and its values are row tokens associated to rows in $\mathsf{DB}[id]$ (i.e. $\{(\mathbf{T}[(id, \mathbf{r}[\mathsf{uk}(id)])]) : \mathbf{r} \in \mathsf{DB}[id].\mathsf{T}\}$). Note that the latter are singleton tuples because we required that pointer tuples be made out of tuples of tokens. The hashset is used to filter the sets in a pointer tuple during a recursive query. For example, when processing the query $(\mathbf{j}, \mathbf{t}_1, \mathbf{t}_2, (\mathbf{s}, at, x, (\mathbf{r}, id_1)), (\mathbf{r}, id_2))$ (a select followed by a join), the server would use the multimap to retrieve row tokens for each of the non-recursive subqueries (i.e. $(\mathbf{s}, at, x, (\mathbf{r}, id_1))$ and $(\mathbf{r}, id_2)$). The token would also include two keys which can be used with HsFilter which tests if the rows being pointed to (in id_1 or id_2) are in $\mathsf{DB}[id_1] \bowtie_{\mathbf{t}_1, \mathbf{t}_2} \mathsf{DB}[id_2]$.

Alg PpSj.Enc$\big(K'_{\mathsf{m}}, (\mathsf{DB}, \alpha, \mathbf{T})\big)$

For all $(id, \mathsf{R}) \in \mathsf{DB}$ and $\mathbf{r} \in \mathsf{R.T}$ do
  $\mathsf{rt} \leftarrow \mathbf{T}[(id, \mathbf{r}[\mathsf{uk}(id)])]$; $\mathbf{M}[(\mathbf{r}, id)] \overset{\cup}{\leftarrow} (\mathsf{rt})$
  For $at \in \mathsf{R.Ats}$ where $at \neq \mathsf{uk}(id)$ do
    $\mathbf{M}[(\mathbf{s}, at, \mathbf{r}[at])] \overset{\cup}{\leftarrow} (\mathsf{rt})$
    $\mathsf{SET} \overset{\cup}{\leftarrow} ((\mathbf{s}, at, \mathbf{r}[at]), \mathsf{rt})$
For $(\mathbf{t}_1, \mathbf{t}_2) \in \alpha$ do
  $id_1 \leftarrow \mathsf{getID}(\mathbf{t}_1)$; $id_2 \leftarrow \mathsf{getID}(\mathbf{t}_2)$
  For $\mathbf{r} \in (\mathsf{DB}[id_1] \bowtie_{\mathbf{t}_1, \mathbf{t}_2} \mathsf{DB}[id_2]).\mathsf{T}$ do
    For $i = 1, 2$ do
      $\mathsf{rt} \leftarrow \mathbf{T}[(id_i, \mathbf{r}[\mathsf{uk}(id_i)]]$
      $\mathbf{M}[(\mathbf{j}, \mathbf{t}_1, \mathbf{t}_2, i)] \overset{\cup}{\leftarrow} (\mathsf{rt})$
      $\mathsf{SET} \overset{\cup}{\leftarrow} ((\mathbf{j}, \mathbf{t}_1, \mathbf{t}_2, i), \mathsf{rt})$
$(K_{\mathsf{m}}, \mathsf{EM}) \leftarrow_\$ \mathsf{Mme.Enc}(K'_{\mathsf{m}}, \mathbf{M})$
$K_{\mathsf{f}} \leftarrow_\$ \mathsf{F.KS}$; $\mathsf{HS} \leftarrow \mathsf{HsEnc}(K_{\mathsf{f}}, \mathsf{SET})$
Return $\big((\mathsf{Schema}(\mathsf{DB}), K_{\mathsf{m}}, K_{\mathsf{f}}), (\mathsf{EM}, \mathsf{HS})\big)$

Alg PpSj.Tok$\big((\mathsf{scma}, K_{\mathsf{m}}, K_{\mathsf{f}}), q\big)$

If $q = (\mathbf{r}, id)$ then
  Return $(\mathbf{r}, \mathsf{Mme.Tok}(K_{\mathsf{m}}, (\mathbf{r}, id)))$
Else if $q = (\mathbf{s}, at, x, (\mathbf{r}, id))$ then
  Return $(\mathbf{r}, \mathsf{Mme.Tok}(K_{\mathsf{m}}, (\mathbf{s}, at, x)))$
Else if $q = (\mathbf{s}, at, x, q_1)$ then
  $\mathsf{tk}_1 \leftarrow_\$ \mathsf{PpSj.Tok}((\mathsf{scma}, K_{\mathsf{m}}, K_{\mathsf{f}}), q_1)$
  Return $(\mathbf{s}, \mathsf{F.Ev}(K_{\mathsf{f}}, (\mathbf{s}, at, x)), \mathsf{tk}_1)$
Else if $q = (\mathbf{j}, \mathbf{t}_1, \mathbf{t}_2, q_1, q_2)$ then
  For $i = 1, 2$ do
    If $q_i = (\mathbf{r}, id_i)$ then
      $\mathsf{tk}_i \leftarrow_\$ (\mathbf{r}, \mathsf{Mme.Tok}(K_{\mathsf{m}}, (\mathbf{j}, \mathbf{t}_1, \mathbf{t}_2, i)))$
    Else
      $\mathsf{tk}' \leftarrow_\$ \mathsf{PpSj.Tok}((\mathsf{scma}, K_{\mathsf{m}}, K_{\mathsf{f}}), q_i)$
      $\mathsf{tk}_i \leftarrow (\mathbf{j}, \mathsf{F.Ev}(K_{\mathsf{f}}, (\mathbf{j}, \mathbf{t}_1, \mathbf{t}_2, i), \mathsf{tk}'))$
  Return $(\mathbf{j}, \mathsf{tk}_1, \mathsf{tk}_2)$

Alg PpSj.Eval(tk, IX)

$(\mathsf{EM}, \mathsf{HS}) \leftarrow \mathsf{IX}$
If $\mathsf{tk} = (\mathbf{r}, \mathsf{tk}_1)$ then
  Return $(\mathsf{Mme.Eval}(\mathsf{tk}, \mathsf{IX}))$
Else If $\mathsf{tk} = (\mathbf{s}, K, \mathsf{tk}_1)$ then
  $P \leftarrow \mathsf{PpSj.Eval}(\mathsf{tk}_1, \mathsf{IX})$
  Return $\mathsf{HsFilter}(K, P, \mathsf{HS})$
Else if $\mathsf{tk} = (\mathbf{j}, \mathsf{tk}_1, \mathsf{tk}_2)$ then
  For $i = 1, 2$ do
    If $\mathsf{tk}_i = (\mathbf{j}, K, \mathsf{tk}')$ then
      $P^i \leftarrow \mathsf{PpSj.Eval}(\mathsf{tk}', \mathsf{IX})$
      $P^i \leftarrow \mathsf{HsFilter}(K, P^i, \mathsf{HS})$
    Else If $\mathsf{tk}_i = (\mathbf{r}, \mathsf{tk}')$ then
      $P^i \leftarrow (\mathsf{Mme.Eval}(\mathsf{tk}', \mathsf{IX}))$
  Return $P^1 \| P^2$

Alg PpSj.Fin(K_{i}, q, M)

$(\mathsf{scma}, K_{\mathsf{m}}, K_{\mathsf{f}}) \leftarrow K_{\mathsf{i}}$
If $q = (\mathbf{r}, id)$ then
  $(M_1) \leftarrow M$
  $\mathsf{R} \leftarrow \mathsf{NewRltn}(\mathsf{scma}[id])$
  $\mathsf{R.T} \leftarrow M_1$; Return R
Else if $q = (\mathbf{s}, at, x, q_1)$ then
  Return $\mathsf{PpSj.Fin}(K_{\mathsf{i}}, q_1, M)$
Else if $q = (\mathbf{j}, \mathbf{t}_1, \mathbf{t}_2, q_1, q_2)$ then
  Define $M^1, M^2 : M^1 \| M^2 = M$,
    M^1 has as many M_i as
    q_i has $(\mathbf{r}, id)$ subqueries
  For $i = 1, 2$ do
    $R_i \leftarrow \mathsf{PpSj.Fin}(K_{\mathsf{i}}, q_i, M^i)$
  Return $R_1 \bowtie_{\mathbf{t}_1, \mathbf{t}_2} R_2$

Fig. 6. Algorithms for PpSj the StI scheme for SjDT using PP indexing.

FP INDEXING FOR SjDT. We analogously extend FpJn introduced in Sect. 4 to construct FpSj, an StI for SjDT. Just like with PpSj, non-recursive queries will be added to the encrypted multimap that is used to index the non-recursive joins while all recursive queries are filtered using the hashset. The only subtlety in this extension is the handling of "internal joins" which are queries of the form $q = (\mathbf{j}, \mathbf{t}_1, \mathbf{t}_2, (\mathbf{r}, id), q_1)$ (or $q = (\mathbf{j}, \mathbf{t}_1, \mathbf{t}_2, q_1, (\mathbf{r}, id))$) because we want to limit the row tokens leaked from id to those who join with some row returned by q_1. Similar to OPX, we construct an index where each row token returned in the subquery will "point to" the tokens of the rows joined to in $\mathsf{DB}[id]$. As alluded to in Sect. 3.2, this self-referential indexing (where Mme tokens are stored in $\mathbf{M}$) may introduce circular security issues if pathological Mme primitives are used. We avoid this by indexing internal joins with a specific, non-pathological primitive (as was done in OPX). To avoid the increased leakage and complexity of an additional data structure, we will assume that Mme is the $\mathsf{Mme}_\pi^{\mathrm{rr}}$ scheme recounted in Appendix A and co-locate this index with the one used for non-recursive queries. Notice that this subtlety does not come up in PpSj because we do not reveal join equality patterns so all recursive joins can be handled similarly.

The StE scheme $\mathsf{StE} = \mathbf{SqlStE}[\mathsf{FpSj}, \mathsf{SE}, \mathsf{F}]$ is essentially the same as OPX with minor improvements in leakage (analogous to those described in our discussion of FpJn in Sect. 4) and a slightly revised approach to "internal joins". For this reason, we defer a complete description of FpSj to the full version of this work.

PpSj LEAKAGE PROFILE. While a pseudocode description of PpSj's leakage profile may seem convoluted, we believe the intuition behind it enables helpful comparisons with FpSj and OPX [34]. As such, we aim to give some intuition by describing the components of PpSj's leakage profile via a running example, deferring a full description of PpSj's leakage algorithm and the associated security proof to Appendix C. Below, we assume that MME primitives have the "standard" leakage profile (as described in Appendix A).

Our example database contains $\mathsf{R}_1, \mathsf{R}_2$ from Fig. 3. If no queries are made, the server-side data structures reveal only *metadata leakage*. This includes the number of values in the multimap, the maximum-length of a value in the multimap and the number of F outputs in the hashset. The leakage of FpSj is comparable but on OPX it is higher because different data structures are used to index different SQL operations.

We will refer to all other forms of leakage as "query dependent leakage". This is where PP indexing has substantial savings over FP and OPX.

Now lets assume the client makes the following queries: $q_1 = (\mathsf{s}, at_3, \mathsf{CS}, (\mathsf{r}, id_2))$, $q_2 = (\mathsf{s}, at_2, \mathsf{Eve}, (\mathsf{r}, id_2))$, $q_3 = (\mathsf{r}, id_1)$ and $q_4 = (\mathsf{j}, at_1, at_2, (\mathsf{r}, id_1), (\mathsf{s}, at_3, \mathsf{CS}, (\mathsf{r}, id_2)))$. The server will receive four tokens, where $\mathsf{tk}_1, \mathsf{tk}_2, \mathsf{tk}_3$ are such that $\mathsf{tk}_i = (\mathsf{r}, \mathsf{mt}_i)$ and $\mathsf{tk}_4 = (\mathsf{j}, (\mathsf{r}, \mathsf{mt}_4), (\mathsf{j}, K, \mathsf{mt}_5))$. Here, each mt_i is a token for Mme while K is a hashset key. Just from inspecting these, the adversary learns the *recursion structure* of the queries. Specifically, he learns that the first three queries were non-recursive while q_4 was a join followed by a select. This leakage is slightly lower in FpSj, PpSj compared to OPX because the adversary cannot differentiate between non-recursive selections and relation retrievals.

The Mme tokens leak *the multimap query pattern* and *multimap responses*. The former reveals whenever the associated query or subquery is repeated. In our case, the adversary learns that $\mathsf{mt}_1, \mathsf{mt}_5$ are associated to the same query. Note that this does not extend to $\mathsf{mt}_3, \mathsf{mt}_4$ because the latter is in a join. From the multimap query responses he "sees" the row tokens that are returned by each Mme.Eval(mt_i, EM). This reveals the equality pattern of the rows returned by each associated query/subquery. For example, this reveals that q_1, q_2 both return two rows, one of which is shared. On join queries, we enjoy similar leakage savings as described in the non-recursive case. For example, tk_4 will reveal that three rows are returned from the left relation (i.e. id_1) but doesn't say anything about whether they are in the final output relation or how they "match up" with rows from the right relation. In FpSj and OPX, both of the above are revealed.

Finally, the hashset keys reveal the *hashset key query pattern* and *hashset filtering results*. The former reveals when the exact same predicate is repeated and is detectable because the keys would be the same. The latter is because the adversary is free to apply hashset keys (in the tokens) to filter all the row tokens he can retrieve from EM thereby learning the *hashset filtering results*. This means that using K he can learn that one row returned by q_2 satisfies the predicate associated to K even though it is not in the output of q_4. Similarly, he learns that two rows returned by q_1 satisfies the predicate but only one is returned by q_4. Using FpSj the adversary would additionally learn which row returned in q_3 is "paired up" with this row in the q_4 output.

LEAKAGE COMPARISON. From the above discussion, one might expect decreasing query-dependent leakage from PpSj to FpSj to OPX. While the leakage for FpSj can always be derived from OPX, the comparison of PpSj to FpSj is not as straightforward because they sometimes do not return the same rows when recursive queries are made (which we discuss in more detail below).

However, when restricted to non-recursive queries, PpSj's query-dependent leakage is strictly superior for the same reasons that PpJn was superior in Sect. 4. Extending this, we can upper bound the leakage lk_p of PpSj on queries $q_1, \dots, q_n$ with its leakage lk'_p on the minimal set of non-recursive queries $q'_1, \dots, q'_m$ with which the server can still deduce the pointer tuples it should return on $q_1, \dots, q_n$. Doing the same for FpSj, we have $lk_f \leq lk'_f$ as well. Then, via the above observation about non-recursive queries we have $lk'_p \leq lk'_f$, with the inequality being strict if at least one join query with at least two rows is made. Our being able to *bound* PpSj*'s query-dependent leakage lower than* FpSj*'s* gives credence to the intuition that PpSj is the more secure variant in practice.

EFFICIENCY DRAWBACK OF PpSj. Comparing the bandwidth of PpSj, FpSj is also not clear cut: On non-recursive queries, PpSj will perform equal or better than FpSj but on recursive queries the converse is sometimes true.

Consider the query $q = (\mathtt{s}, at_3, \mathtt{CS}, (\mathtt{j}, at_1, at_2, (\mathtt{r}, id_1), (\mathtt{r}, id_2)))$ in our toy example. With FpSj, the server returns pointers to the two rows that feature in the output relation (i.e. those with coordinates $(id_1, \mathtt{cc}), (id_2, \mathtt{33})$) but PpSj returns four (i.e. with coordinates $(id_1, \mathtt{aa}), (id_1, \mathtt{bb}), (id_1, \mathtt{cc}), (id_2, \mathtt{33})$) because without the equality pattern over the join columns and it cannot filter out the first and second rows of R_1.

More generally, this overhead may occur anytime that a recursive query (involving at least one join) is made and grows with query complexity. Depending on the data and query workload, this overhead ranges from negligible to quite substantial, something we explore further in Sect. 6.

5 Hybrid Indexing

We showed that the choice between FP and PP indexing depends heavily on query load. This motivates our hybrid StI scheme that postpones this decision till query time. We first cover the technical details of supporting both indexing techniques, then give a heuristic for the client to choose between them.

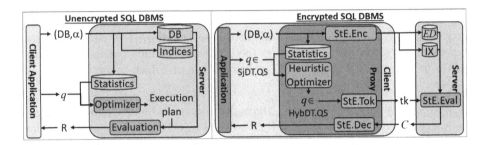

Fig. 7. Data/ query processing in unencrypted SQL databases (left) and the analogous processes using **SqlStE** with hybrid indexing (right).

HYBRID DATA PROCESSING. We give a new ADT where each join in a query is annotated with the desired indexing technique, HybDT. This ADT is equivalent to SjDT except that its join queries take the form (op, t_1, t_2, q_1, q_2) where $op \in \{fp, pp\}$. When evaluating HybDT.Spec, these are both functionally equivalent to the analogous SjDT join query's (j, t_1, t_2, q_1, q_2).

The hybrid system we envision makes the same assumption as in (unencrypted) SQL DBMSes – that client queries are unoptimized and have no canonical form – and therefore mirrors its data flow as depicted in Fig. 7. It also borrows its architecture (i.e. use of a client-side proxy) from existing encrypted SQL solutions [39,42]. The client's SjDT query is annotated using a heuristic optimizer to get a HybDT query. This latter query is then tokenized, evaluated and decrypted using hybrid indexing scheme HybStI in StE = **SqlStE**[HybStI, SE, F].

As best we know, no existing work has looked into query optimization in StE schemes. We believe this area to be of independent interest because unlike encrypted systems where optimization runs on the server (with full access to the data) and is solely interested in maximizing efficiency, optimization in encrypted SQL DBMSes should be done (at least partially) by the proxy with only precomputed statistics about the data and may additionally seek to minimize leakage. We initiate this study with our heuristic below.

HybStI DETAILS. This StI merges FpSj, PpSj by essentially storing both kinds of indexes on the server. More specifically, HybStI.Enc will merge the multimaps and hashsets generated by PpSj, FpSj (avoiding repetition where possible) so that it can take join tokens of either form. When a HybDT join query is made, the client indicates which index to use in its query with op.

We believe the intuition for how HybStl works is straightforward, so we defer a full pseudocode, leakage algorithm and proof of security to the full version of this paper. The only subtlety comes when a query contains both FP and PP joins. Notice that pointer tuples in this case will contain more than one P_i (unlike FpSj) and the tuples in at least one P_i will contain more than one rt (unlike PpSj). As such, after the client performs the PP joins in HybStl.Fin some column reordering may be necessary.

HybStl LEAKAGE. We will describe HybStl's leakage profile in comparison to that of PpSj and FpSj. The metadata leakage is comparable, with each size (multimap or hashset) being the sum of respective FpSj and PpSj sizes. The recursion structure leakage is technically higher but only because we leak the join annotations that weren't present in the other two schemes.

For the same reason that PpSj and FpSj's query-dependent leakages were not directly comparable, they also cannot be compared with that of HybStl. However, like we did in Sect. 4.2, we can upper bound HybStl's query-dependent leakage on $q_1, \dots, q_n \in$ HybDT.QS with that of $q_1', \dots, q_m'$, the minimal set of non-recursive queries in HybDT.QS (with consistent join annotation) with which the server can still compute its output on $q_1, \dots, q_n$. This leakage is no better than the analogous bound in PpSj and no worse than that of FpSj, this confirms the intuition that hybrid indexing achieves an *intermediate level of query-dependent leakage* compared to solely using FP or PP indexing.

LEAKAGE-AWARE QUERY PLANNING. The join annotation selected by our query planning heuristic will minimize leakage without exceeding a predetermined bandwidth limit. More specifically, suppose the user supplies a query $q \in$ SjDT with J joins and a bandwidth limit L indicating the maximum number of rows from ED that can be returned in the ciphertext tuple. We estimate the bandwidth of all possible HybDT queries, then select an annotation by:

1. Eliminating options which exceed L rows. If none remain, return $\perp$.
2. Maximize number of PP joins
3. If multiple choices remain, minimize bandwidth.

We argue that our setup is realistic because (1) we expect the J joins made in a query to be modest enough for the client to evaluate all 2^J HybDT queries, (2) bandwidth measurement can be reduced to the number of rows from ED sent as they are padded to the same length, and (3) is it common for SQL applications to limit bandwidth to prevent the client from maxing out its memory.

To complete this setup, we need a way for the client to estimate the bandwidth of a query with only partial information about **DB** computed during setup.

Alg EvalBW(q)	**Schema** scma
If $q = (\mathbf{r}, id)$ then $\mathbf{B}[(id)] \leftarrow \mathcal{N}(id)$	Return Schema(DB)
Else if $q = (\mathbf{s}, at, x, q_1)$ then	**Table size** $\mathcal{N}(id)$
$\quad \mathbf{B} \leftarrow$ EvalBW(q_1) ; $id \leftarrow$ getID(at, scma)	Return $|\mathsf{DB}[id].\mathsf{T}|$
$\quad \mathbf{B}[(id)] \leftarrow \mathbf{B}[(id)] \cdot \mathcal{H}_{at}(x)$	**Freq. histogram** $\mathcal{H}_{at}(x)$
Else if $q = (op, \mathbf{t}_1, \mathbf{t}_2, q_1, q_2)$ then	$R \leftarrow \sigma_{(at,x)}(\mathsf{DB}[\mathsf{getID}(at, \mathsf{scma})])$
$\quad \mathbf{B} \leftarrow$ EvalBW(q_1) $\cup$ EvalBW(q_2)	Return $\frac{|R.\mathsf{T}|}{\mathcal{N}(id)}$
$\quad$ For $i = 1, 2$	**FP join size** $\mathcal{F}(\mathbf{t}_1, \mathbf{t}_2)$
$\quad\quad$ let $\mathbf{i}_i \in \mathbf{B}.$Lbls be s.t. getID($\mathbf{t}_i$, scma) $\in \mathbf{i}_i$	For $i = 1, 2$ do $id_i \leftarrow$ getID($\mathbf{t}_i$, scma)
$\quad$ If $op =$ fp then	$R \leftarrow \mathsf{DB}[id_1] \bowtie_{\mathbf{t}_1, \mathbf{t}_2} \mathsf{DB}[id_2]$
$\quad\quad N \leftarrow \frac{\mathcal{F}(\mathbf{t}_1, \mathbf{t}_2) \cdot \mathbf{B}[\mathbf{i}_1] \cdot \mathbf{B}[\mathbf{i}_2]}{\mathcal{N}(\mathsf{getID}(\mathbf{t}_1, \mathsf{scma})) \cdot \mathcal{N}(\mathsf{getID}(\mathbf{t}_2, \mathsf{scma}))}$	Return $|R.\mathsf{T}|$
$\quad\quad \mathbf{B}[\mathbf{i}_1 \| \mathbf{i}_2] \leftarrow 2 \cdot N$	**PP join sizes** $\mathcal{P}_j(\mathbf{t}_1, \mathbf{t}_2)$
$\quad\quad \mathbf{B}[\mathbf{i}_1] \leftarrow \bot$; $\mathbf{B}[\mathbf{i}_2] \leftarrow \bot$	For $i = 1, 2$ do $id_i \leftarrow$ getID($\mathbf{t}_j$, scma)
$\quad$ Else if $op =$ pp then	$R \leftarrow \mathsf{DB}[id_1] \bowtie_{\mathbf{t}_1, \mathbf{t}_2} \mathsf{DB}[id_2]$
$\quad\quad$ For $i = 1, 2$ do	Return $|\{\mathbf{r}[\mathsf{uk}(id_j)] : \mathbf{r} \in R.\mathsf{T}\}|$
$\quad\quad\quad \mathbf{B}[\mathbf{i}_i] \leftarrow \mathcal{P}_i(\mathbf{t}_1, \mathbf{t}_2) \cdot \frac{\mathbf{B}[\mathbf{i}_i]}{\mathcal{N}(\mathsf{getID}(\mathbf{t}_i, \mathsf{scma}))}$	
Return $\mathbf{B}$	

Fig. 8. EvalBW algorithm (left) defined in terms of precomputed statistics (right) stored on the client. Our heuristic assumes that q incurs bandwidth $\sum_{i \in \mathbf{B}.\mathsf{Lbls}} \mathbf{B}[i]$ where $\mathbf{B} = $ EvalBW(q).

These precomputed statistics are listed on the right of Fig. 8 and the bandwidth estimation algorithm is EvalBW. Intuitively, EvalBW will populate a dictionary $\mathbf{B}$ with entries $\mathbf{B}[i]$ representing the bandwidth for the ciphertext set containing rows from all $\mathsf{DB}[id]$ where $id \in i$. We estimate that a query $q \in$ HybDT.QS incurs bandwidth $\sum_{i \in \mathbf{B}.\mathsf{Lbls}} \mathbf{B}[i]$ where $\mathbf{B} = $ EvalBW(q). We will next explore the tradeoffs involved in storing these statistics.

MEMORY TRADEOFFS. Notice that the client storage required for the precomputed statistics (as given in Fig. 8) increases with number of joins (i.e. $|\alpha|$) and size of histograms (i.e. $|\mathsf{rng}(at, \mathsf{DB})|$ for each at). In practice, data may be too complex or client devices may be too memory strapped (e.g. mobile devices) to store this in full. We describe two tradeoffs application designers can explore to better fit their system requirements.

When it is unfeasible to store full frequency histograms for some at, the client can partition $\mathsf{rng}(at, \mathsf{DB})$ into ranges and store this bucketed frequency histogram. EvalBW will approximate $\mathcal{H}_{at}(x)$ by assuming that values within a bucket are uniformly distributed. This approach is used in SQL server and the literature recommends 200 equiDepth (as opposed to equiWidth) buckets [10, 40]. In the extreme case, the client uses a single bucket and needs only store $|\mathsf{rng}(at, \mathsf{DB})|$ and uses $\mathcal{H}_{at}(x) \approx \frac{1}{|\mathsf{rng}(at, \mathsf{DB})|}$. Note that this only works when the elements of $\mathsf{rng}(at, \mathsf{DB})$ can be closely approximated and ordered. For example, this may not work with a "name" column because the names in $\mathsf{rng}(at, \mathsf{DB})$ are not dense in any easily enumerated set. In general, bucketing sacrifices the

Query Type	Indexed Data	Chicago data set					Sakila data set				
		JnDT		SjDT		HybDT	JnDT		SjDT		HybDT
		FpJn	PpJn	FpSj	PpSj	HybStl	FpJn	PpJn	FpSj	PpSj	HybStl
Non-Rec. join	MM lbls	1249	2498	1249	2498	3747	631	1262	631	1262	1893
	MM vals	1.495e10	2.796e7	1.495e10	2.796e7	1.498e10	5.103e8	2.201e6	5.103e8	2.201e6	5.125e8
Rec. join	MM lbls	–	–	2.796e7	–	2.796e7	–	–	2.202e6	–	2.202e6
	MM vals	–	–	1.496e10	–	1.496e10	–	–	5.107e8	–	5.107e8
	HS vals	–	–	7.477e9	2.796e7	7.505e9	–	–	2.552e8	2.201e6	2.574e8
Relation retrieval	MM lbls	–	–	15	15	15	–	–	15	15	15
	MM vals	–	–	4.010e5	4.010e5	4.010e5	–	–	4.409e4	4.409e4	4.409e4
Select	MM lbls	–	–	1.082e6	1.082e6	1.082e6	–	–	1.190e5	1.190e5	1.190e5
	MM vals	–	–	5.749e6	5.749e6	5.749e6	–	–	2.945e5	2.945e5	2.945e5
	HS vals	–	–	5.749e6	5.749e6	5.749e6	–	–	2.945e5	2.945e5	2.945e5
Total	MM lbls	1249	2498	2.905e7	1.085e6	2.905e7	631	1262	2.321e6	1.203e5	2.322e6
	MM vals	1.495e10	2.796e7	2.991e10	3.412e7	2.994e10	5.103e8	2.201e6	1.021e9	2.540e6	1.023e9
	HS vals	–	–	7.483e9	3.371e7	7.511e9	–	–	2.555e8	2.496e6	2.577e8

Fig. 9. Simulated server storage for each data set using each of our schemes in terms of multimap (MM) labels/values and hashset (HS) values broken down by the query type being indexed (i.e. relation retrievals, non-recursive/ recursive joins, or selections).

accuracy of EvalBW to reduce client memory. We study this tradeoff more in Sect. 6.

Above, we assumed the client would pre-compute and store the join sizes. When this is infeasible due to memory constraints, the client can alternatively compute join sizes using table sizes and the $\mathcal{H}_{at}(x)$ during EvalBW whenever $\mathsf{rng}(at)$ is enumerable. Notice that we can express each co-occurrence frequency as a function of the relevant occurrence frequencies. With a single attribute join, let $X = \mathsf{rng}(at_1, \mathsf{DB}) \cap \mathsf{rng}(at_2, \mathsf{DB})$, $N_i = \mathcal{N}(\mathsf{getID}(at_i, \mathsf{scma}))$ then

$$\mathcal{F}(at_1, at_2) = N_1 \cdot N_2 \cdot \sum_{x \in X} \mathcal{H}_{at_1}(x) \cdot \mathcal{H}_{at_2}(x) \quad \text{and} \quad \mathcal{P}_j(at_1, at_2) = N_j \cdot \sum_{x \in X} \mathcal{H}_{at_j}(x).$$

We can extend this to a cluster join $(\mathbf{t}_1, \mathbf{t}_2)$ where $\mathbf{t}_j = (at_1^j, \ldots, at_n^j)$. We substitute the above histogram values for $\mathcal{H}_{\mathbf{t}_j}(x_1, \ldots, x_n)$ and take the sum over all $(x_1, \ldots, x_n)$ where $x_i \in \mathsf{rng}(at_i^1, \mathsf{DB}) \cap \mathsf{rng}(at_i^2, \mathsf{DB})$. These frequencies are approximated by assuming that columns are independently distributed: $\mathcal{H}_{\mathbf{t}_i}(x_1, \ldots, x_n) \approx \prod_{i \in [n]} \mathcal{H}_{at_i^j}(x_i)$. Note also that accuracy issues are compounded if frequency histograms are themselves estimated using bucketing. In general, approximating join sizes trades efficiency (of EvalBW) and accuracy (for cluster joins) to reduce memory.

6 Simulations on Real-World Datasets

To get some indication of how our schemes would fare in practice we simulate the storage and bandwidth they would incur in a real-world context. We show that in practice, PP indexing is likely to be more storage efficient than FP. We also confirm three claims made in this work: (1) PP indexing has equal or better bandwidth than FP on non-recursive joins (i.e. JnDT queries), (2) On recursive selects and joins (i.e. SjDT queries), the analogous choice is data and query dependent, and (3) our heuristic is accurate in finding optimal hybrid query execution plans.

500   D. Cash et al.

Join category	# joins	Ratio of FpJnto PpJn BW		
		Min	Ave	Max
One-one	237	1.0	1.0	1.0
One-many	711	1.0	1.8	2.0
Many-many	932	1.5	465	8000

Fig. 10. Breakdown of all possible non-recursive join queries which returns at least one row by join types. For each type, we simulated the number of rows that would be sent using FP and PP indexing, and report the minimum, average and maximum overhead incurred.

We note that our goal here is not to make broad statements about all SQL data nor to perform a full system evaluation. We see our simulations more as a sanity check which might motivate large-scale implementations of our schemes. Additionally, we are not aware of any benchmarks with just join and select queries so we generate our own as described below.

SIMULATION SETUP. Our simulation dataset uses all relations from the MySQL Sakila benchmark[1] and the following fifteen frequently accessed relations from Chicago's Open Data Portal: Bike_Racks, Census_Data, Crimes_2019, Employee_Debt, Fire_Stations, Grafitti, Housing, IUCR_Codes, Land_Inventory, Libraries, Lobbyists, Police_Stations, Reloc_Vehicles, Street_Names, Towed_Vehicles. In total, our setup involved 30 relations, 175 attributes and 219,992 rows.

We include in α all single-attribute joins that return at least one row. This helps to filter out meaningless join queries (e.g. joining on "language" and "actor"). We consider joins within the Sakila relations and joins within the Chicago relations, but we do not attempt joins between the two independent sources. We generate recursive queries with J joins and S selections by selecting uniformly at random J distinct joins from α as well as S attributes and elements of their domains, discarding queries that return no rows. When $J \geq 2$ we only use input tables with less than 1000 rows to avoid very large output relations.

SERVER STORAGE. With the above setup we can get an idea of how much server-side storage would be required by each of our indexing schemes. Recall that our schemes make use of a RR multimap primitive and/or a hashset filtering primitive. Therefore, in Fig. 9 we report the number of multimap[2] labels and values as well as the values in hashset HS for each of our StI schemes. We present our simulation results for the two datasets separately since the Chicago data set contains many more rows and would dominate the Sakila statistics. Additionally, we also show a breakdown of these statistics in terms of the queries they index to better understand the cost of each type of query support.

A number of observations can be made from this data. In our simulation we see that even though there are more selections to index (as evidenced by the number of labels), the multimap size (i.e. number of values) is dominated by

---

[1] We excluded the film_text relation since it is a subset of the film relation.
[2] Note that in the case of FpSj, HybStl, this includes the multimap for internal joins.

join indexes. We expect this cost to be lower in a real system because a judicious database administrator can reduce the set of supported joins (α) to a smaller number than we did. Our simulation also brings forth another advantage of PP join indexing – it is more storage efficient by several orders of magnitude. This is because each row token is stored at most once per join (the same thing which causes PP to have better bandwidth) and, in the case of SjDT, there is no need for the "internal join" indexing which essentially doubles the multimap's labels and values. Finally, for the above reason, the storage overhead of hybrid indexing over FP indexing is very small so systems which currently use indexing schemes like FP (e.g. OPX or SPX) can upgrade its security at low cost.

JOIN CATEGORIES. We partition joins into three classes which behave quite differently: *one-one*, *one-many* and *many-many*. We say that a join $R \leftarrow R_1 \bowtie_{at_1, at_2} R_2$ is one-one if each row in R_1, R_2 occurs at most once in R. It is one-many if the above is true for one relation but not for the other. It is many-many if there exists rows in both R_1, R_2 which occur more than once in R. We record the breakdown of these classes in our datasets in Fig. 10.

STI FOR JnDT. In Sect. 4 we showed that PP indexing has superior bandwidth on non-recursive join queries. We demonstrate that these savings by computing all 1880 possible joins in α and report our findings in Fig. 10. As one would expect, PP indexing always performs equal or better to FP – they perform equally for one-one joins but there are moderate and significant savings for one-many and many-many joins respectively.

Query type	Ratio of BW to ideal					
	FpSj			PpSj		
	Min	Ave	Max	Min	Ave	Max
$1 \bowtie, 0\,\sigma$	1.0	9.6	37	1.0	1.0	1.0
$1 \bowtie, 1\,\sigma$	1.0	1.6	4.0	1.0	60	302
$1 \bowtie, 2\,\sigma$	1.0	1.3	2.0	1.0	90	500
$2 \bowtie, 0\,\sigma$	1.0	3.3	57	1.3	13	54
$2 \bowtie, 1\,\sigma$	1.0	15	201	1.0	41	201
$2 \bowtie, 2\,\sigma$	1.0	14	121	1.0	93	535
$3 \bowtie, 0\,\sigma$	1.0	7.2	48	2.4	9.1	17
$3 \bowtie, 1\,\sigma$	1.0	6.5	63	2.6	23	60
$3 \bowtie, 2\,\sigma$	1.0	5.0	61	2.3	30	84

Fig. 11. On randomly generated queries involving the indicated number of joins ($\bowtie$) and selects (σ), we report the minimum, average and maximum ratios of rows sent using each indexing technique compared to the theoretical minimum possible.

STI FOR SjDT. In Sect. 4.2 we noted that neither PP nor FP joins are strictly superior when it comes to recursive SjDT queries. We demonstrate this using our datasets. For each combination of 1 to 3 joins and 0 to 2 selects, we randomly sampled 25 queries and report the results in Fig. 11. As can be seen, neither scheme can reliably achieve the optimal bandwidth. While FpSj performed better on average, its maximum overhead exceeds that of PpSj in about half the cases.

Query type	Bucketed $B = 1$ Correct	Wrong R1	R2	R3	Bucketed $B = 200$ Correct	Wrong R1	R2	R3	Full histograms Correct	Wrong R1	R2	R3
$1 \bowtie, 0\,\sigma$	14	11	0	0	25	0	0	0	25	0	0	0
$1 \bowtie, 1\,\sigma$	6	17	0	6	12	0	12	1	16	0	8	1
$1 \bowtie, 2\,\sigma$	5	0	0	20	14	0	1	10	15	0	0	10
$2 \bowtie, 0\,\sigma$	5	0	0	20	21	3	0	1	25	0	0	0
$2 \bowtie, 1\,\sigma$	15	0	1	9	18	6	1	0	24	0	1	0
$2 \bowtie, 2\,\sigma$	17	8	0	0	20	0	1	4	23	0	0	2
$3 \bowtie, 0\,\sigma$	5	20	0	0	8	10	7	0	21	2	2	0
$3 \bowtie, 1\,\sigma$	2	23	0	0	19	1	5	0	25	0	0	0
$3 \bowtie, 2\,\sigma$	7	18	0	0	16	4	5	0	24	0	1	0

Fig. 12. On randomly generated queries involving the indicated number of joins ($\bowtie$) and selects (σ), we report the accuracy of our heuristic under three different client storage settings. When a suboptimal query execution plan is returned, we report the point at which our heuristic fails (with R3 being the closest to success).

HYBRID STI. In Sect. 5 we provided a heuristic for client-side leakage-aware query planning. We demonstrate its efficacy when frequency histograms are estimated via three bucketing options: $B = |\mathsf{rng}(at, \mathsf{DB})|$ (full histograms), $B = 200$ and $B = 1$. We use the same 225 queries as the SjDT simulations and set the bandwidth limit L for each $q \in$ SjDT to be the mean incurred by all 2^J possible HybDT queries to ensure that the optimization is non-trivial. Additionally, join sizes $\mathcal{F}, \mathcal{P}_1, \mathcal{P}_2$ are estimated using the histogram. Therefore, our simulation is conservative and we expect our heuristic to perform better in applications with a fixed L and precomputed join sizes.

In Fig. 12 we show how our heuristic performed for each query type and histogram estimation technique. When the optimal join annotation is not returned we note which "level" the heuristic failed at, where the levels are defined in relation to our definition of "optimality" given in Sect. 5. In particular, an R1 failure means the returned q' exceeds bandwidth limit L when StE.Eval is run, an R2 failure means q' used more FP joins than was necessary to reduce bandwidth below L and an R3 failure means q' was not the smallest bandwidth option which uses the minimal number of FP joins while meeting L.

Unsurprisingly, there is a direct tradeoff between client memory and the heuristic's accuracy: across all 225 queries, the heuristic returned the optimal q' on 198 with full histograms but only 143 and 76 when $B = 200$ and $B = 1$ respectively. More interestingly, our heuristic seems to improve when the search space increases: when there is one join the heuristic performed slightly better averaged across all three B values than guessing (58.7% vs 50%) but when there are three it performs significantly better (56.4% vs 12.5%). This demonstrates that our heuristic works when it is most needful since we expect the bandwidth overhead from an incorrect choice to increase with query complexity.

7   Conclusion

Our work introduces partially precomputed join indexing and incorporates it into a hybrid StE scheme. While we did not explore it in this work, we believe that our schemes can be extended to support dynamic queries and adaptive security via multimap primitives of the same kind. We believe the former can be achieved in a similar way to KM's extension of SPX to SPX$^+$. To achieve the latter, our schemes can be reframed in JN's model for adaptive compromise [30]. Future work can also extend our query support, possibly by incorporating cryptographic techniques for range queries or aggregations [22,29]. Higher query support would also enable more rigorous testing using real-world applications and query benchmarks. Stronger security can be achieved using lower-leakage indexing primitives [31,33,38].

We also introduce leakage-aware query planning which we believe to be of independent interest as it incorporates structured indexing into DBMS architecture, which may help StE become a part of commercial DBMSes. Future work could improve our heuristic's efficiency and accuracy, or develop analogous hybrid schemes for other query classes.

Acknowledgements. We would like to thank the anonymous reviewers for their comments on our work. We are also grateful to Mihir Bellare and Francesca Falzon for discussion and insights. Cash was supported in part by NSF CNS 1703953. Ng was supported by DSO National Laboratories. Rivkin was supported by the Liew Family College Research Fellows Fund.

A   CJJ+'s Multimap/Dictionary Encryption Schemes

CJJ+'s RH DICTIONARY ENCRYPTION SCHEME. In our StE scheme constructed using **SqlStE** (in Sect. 3) we use a specific RH dictionary encryption scheme to store the rows in DB. We formalize this as Dye_π whose algorithms are in Fig. 13. The primitives (given as input to **SqlStE**) used in Dye_π are symmetric encryption scheme SE and function family F. Note that $\mathsf{Dye}_\pi.\mathsf{KS} = \mathsf{F.KS} \times \mathsf{SE.KS}$.

EXAMPLE RR MULTIMAP ENCRYPTION SCHEME. In our StI schemes such as $\mathsf{PpJn}, \mathsf{PpSj}, \mathsf{HybStI}$ we use a RR multimap Mme as a primitive. We give an example of such a scheme $\mathsf{Mme}_\pi^{\mathsf{rr}}$ which is also based on Π_{bas}. Its algorithms are in algorithms are in Fig. 13. The primitives are as in Dye_π but we require that $\mathsf{SE.KS} = \{0,1\}^{\mathsf{F.ol}}$. Note that $\mathsf{Mme}_\pi^{\mathsf{rr}}.\mathsf{KS} = \mathsf{F.KS}$.

B   Proof of Theorem 1

Theorem 1. *Let* $\mathsf{StE} = \mathsf{SqlStE}[\mathsf{StI}, \mathsf{SE}, \mathsf{F}]$ *be a correct StE scheme for* SqlDT. *Then given algorithms* $\mathcal{L}^i, \mathcal{S}^i$ *and adversary A we can define* $\mathcal{L}$ *as in Sect. 3.2 and construct* $\mathcal{S}, A_s, A_f, A_i$ *such that:*

$$\mathbf{Adv}^{\mathsf{ss}}_{\mathsf{StE},\mathcal{L},\mathcal{S}}(A) \leq \mathbf{Adv}^{\mathsf{ind\$}}_{\mathsf{SE}}(A_s) + \mathbf{Adv}^{\mathsf{prf}}_{\mathsf{F}}(A_f) + \mathbf{Adv}^{\mathsf{ss}}_{\mathsf{StI},\mathcal{L}^i,\mathcal{S}^i}(()A_i).$$

Alg $\mathsf{Dye}_\pi.\mathsf{Enc}\big((K_{\mathsf{f}}, K_{\mathsf{e}}), \mathbf{D}\big)$	**Alg** $\mathsf{Dye}_\pi.\mathsf{Tok}\big((K_{\mathsf{f}}, K_{\mathsf{e}}), \ell\big)$
Pad all values in $\mathbf{D}$ to the same length	$\mathsf{tk} \leftarrow \mathsf{F}.\mathsf{Ev}(K_{\mathsf{f}}, \ell)$; Return tk
For $\ell \in \mathbf{D}.\mathsf{Lbls}$ do	**Alg** $\mathsf{Dye}_\pi.\mathsf{Eval}(\mathsf{tk}, \mathbf{D}')$
$\quad \mathbf{D}'[\mathsf{F}.\mathsf{Ev}(K_{\mathsf{f}}, \ell)] \leftarrow_{\$} \mathsf{SE}.\mathsf{Enc}(K_{\mathsf{e}}, \mathbf{D}[\ell])$	Return $\mathbf{D}'[\mathsf{tk}]$
Return $\big((K_{\mathsf{f}}, K_{\mathsf{e}}), \mathbf{D}'\big)$	**Alg** $\mathsf{Dye}_\pi.\mathsf{Dec}\big((K_{\mathsf{f}}, K_{\mathsf{e}}), C\big)$
	Unpad and return $\mathsf{SE}.\mathsf{Dec}(K_{\mathsf{e}}, C)$

Alg $\mathsf{Mme}_\pi^{\mathsf{rr}}.\mathsf{Enc}(K_{\mathsf{f}}, \mathbf{M})$	**Alg** $\mathsf{Mme}_\pi^{\mathsf{rr}}.\mathsf{Tok}(K_{\mathsf{f}}, \ell)$
Pad all values in $\mathbf{M}$ to the same length	Return $\big(\mathsf{F}.\mathsf{Ev}(K_{\mathsf{f}}, \ell\|0), \mathsf{F}.\mathsf{Ev}(K_{\mathsf{f}}, \ell\|1)\big)$
For $\ell \in \mathbf{M}.\mathsf{Lbls}$ do	**Alg** $\mathsf{Mme}_\pi^{\mathsf{rr}}.\mathsf{Eval}\big((K_{\mathsf{e}}, K), \mathbf{D}\big)$
$\quad K_{\mathsf{e}} \leftarrow \mathsf{F}.\mathsf{Ev}(K_{\mathsf{f}}, \ell\|0)$; $K \leftarrow \mathsf{F}.\mathsf{Ev}(K_{\mathsf{f}}, \ell\|1)$	While $\mathbf{D}[\mathsf{F}.\mathsf{Ev}(K, \mathsf{ctr})] \neq \bot$ do
$\quad$ For $v \in \mathbf{M}[\ell]$ do	$\quad x \leftarrow \mathsf{SE}.\mathsf{Dec}(K_{\mathsf{e}}, \mathbf{D}[\mathsf{F}.\mathsf{Ev}(K, \mathsf{ctr})])$
$\qquad \mathbf{D}[\mathsf{F}.\mathsf{Ev}(K, \mathsf{ctr})] \leftarrow_{\$} \mathsf{SE}.\mathsf{Enc}(K_{\mathsf{e}}, v)$	$\quad \mathsf{ctr} \leftarrow \mathsf{ctr} + 1$
$\qquad \mathsf{ctr} \leftarrow \mathsf{ctr} + 1$	$\quad$ Unpad x then $S \overset{\cup}{\leftarrow} x$
Return $(K_{\mathsf{f}}, \mathbf{D})$	Return S

Fig. 13. Algorithms for RH dictionary encryption scheme Dye_π and RR multimap encryption scheme $\mathsf{Mme}_\pi^{\mathsf{rr}}$.

Proof. The adversaries, simulator and games G_0, G_1, G_2, G_3 are given in Fig. 14. Notice that the EncRows algorithm used in the adversaries and games is given at the top, and uses two oracles ENC, FN which the algorithms define. Let b be the challenge bit selected in $G_{\mathsf{StE}, \mathcal{L}, \mathcal{S}}^{\mathsf{ss}}(A)$.

Notice that we can express $\mathbf{Adv}_{\mathsf{StE}, \mathcal{L}, \mathcal{S}}^{\mathsf{ss}}(A) = \Pr[G_{\mathsf{StE}, \mathcal{L}, \mathcal{S}}^{\mathsf{ss}}(A)|b = 1] - \Pr[G_{\mathsf{StE}, \mathcal{L}, \mathcal{S}}^{\mathsf{ss}}(A)|b = 0] = \Pr[G_3] - \Pr[G_0]$. In $b = 1$ case, this follows directly from the definition of A_{i}. In the $b = 0$ case, this follows from the definition of $\mathcal{L}^{\mathsf{i}}, \mathcal{S}^{\mathsf{i}}$.

The only difference between G_0 and G_1 is whether $\mathsf{IX}, \mathsf{tk}_1, \ldots, \mathsf{tk}_n$ are generated using Stl's algorithms or $\mathcal{S}$. In both cases, $\mathbf{D}'$'s values are encrypted using SE.Enc. This is the same differentiation going on in the semantic security game so $G_{\mathsf{Stl}, \mathcal{L}^{\mathsf{i}}, \mathcal{S}^{\mathsf{i}}}^{\mathsf{ss}}(A_{\mathsf{i}}) = \Pr[G_1] - \Pr[G_0]$. Similarly the difference between G_1 and G_2 is whether the values in $\mathbf{D}'$ are the output of SE.Enc or random strings which is what is going on in the IND\$-security game $G_{\mathsf{SE}}^{\mathsf{ind\$}}(A_{\mathsf{s}})$, so $\mathbf{Adv}_{\mathsf{SE}}^{\mathsf{ind\$}}(A_{\mathsf{s}}) = \Pr[G_2] - \Pr[G_1]$. Once again, the difference between G_2 and G_3 is whether the labels in $\mathbf{D}'$ (i.e. the tokens in $\mathsf{Dye}_\pi.\mathsf{Enc}$) are generated using F.Ev or a random function which is what is going on in the PRF-security game $G_{\mathsf{F}}^{\mathsf{prf}}(A_{\mathsf{f}})$, so $\mathbf{Adv}_{\mathsf{F}}^{\mathsf{prf}}(A_{\mathsf{f}}) = \Pr[G_3] - \Pr[G_2]$.

Combining all the above equations gives the desired bound on $\mathbf{Adv}_{\mathsf{StE}, \mathcal{L}, \mathcal{S}}^{\mathsf{ss}}(A)$.

Alg $\mathcal{S}(lk^{i}, N, L)$	**Subroutine** $\text{EncRows}^{\text{ENC,FN}}((DB, \alpha))$
$(IX, (tk_1, \ldots, tk_n)) \leftarrow \mathcal{S}^{i}(lk^{i})$	For $(id, R) \in DB$ do
$P \leftarrow \bigcup_{i \in [n]} \text{Stl.Eval}(tk_i, IX)$	For $r \in R.T$ do $\mathbf{D}[(id, r[uk(id)])] \leftarrow \mathbf{r}$
For $rt \in \bigcup_{rt \in P} rt$ do $\mathbf{D}'[rt] \leftarrow^{\$} \{0,1\}^{\text{SE.cl}(L)}$	Pad all values in $\mathbf{D}$ to the same length
While $\|\mathbf{D}'.\text{Lbls}\| < N$ do	For $\ell \in \mathbf{D}.\text{Lbls}$ do
$\quad rt \leftarrow^{\$} \{0,1\}^{\text{F.ol}}$; $\mathbf{D}'[rt] \leftarrow^{\$} \{0,1\}^{\text{SE.cl}(L)}$	$\quad T[\ell] \leftarrow^{\$} \text{FN}(\ell)$
Return $((IX, \mathbf{D}'), (tk_1, \ldots, tk_n))$	$\quad \mathbf{D}'[T[\ell]] \leftarrow \text{ENC}(\mathbf{D}[\ell])$
	Return $(\mathbf{D}', \alpha, T)$

Adversary $A_i(\mathbf{s})$	**Adversaries** $\boxed{A_s^{\text{ENC}}}, \boxed{A_f^{\text{FN}}}$
$(DB, q, st) \leftarrow^{\$} A(\mathbf{s})$	$(DB, q, st) \leftarrow^{\$} A(\mathbf{s})$; $K_f \leftarrow^{\$} \text{F.KS}$
$K_e \leftarrow^{\$} \text{SE.KS}$; $K_f \leftarrow^{\$} \text{F.KS}$	$\boxed{\text{Define } \text{FN} : \text{FN}(x) = \text{F.Ev}(K_f, \cdot)}$
Define $\text{ENC} : \text{ENC}(x) = \text{SE.Enc}(K_e, \cdot)$	$\text{Define } \text{ENC} : \text{ENC}(\cdot) \text{ is a random function}$
Define $\text{FN} : \text{FN}(x) = \text{F.Ev}(K_f, \cdot)$	$\quad \text{from } \{0,1\}^{L} \text{ to } \{0,1\}^{\text{SE.cl}(L)}$
$(\mathbf{D}', \alpha, T) \leftarrow^{\$} \text{EncRows}^{\text{ENC,FN}}(DB)$	$(\mathbf{D}', \alpha, T) \leftarrow^{\$} \text{EncRows}^{\text{ENC,FN}}(DB)$
Return $((\mathbf{D}', \alpha, T), q, (\mathbf{D}', st))$	$lk^{i} \leftarrow^{\$} \mathcal{L}^{i}(DS, q)$
Adversary $A_i(g, IX, tk, (\mathbf{D}', st))$	$(IX, (tk_1, \ldots, tk_n)) \leftarrow \mathcal{S}^{i}(lk^{i})$
$b' \leftarrow^{\$} A(g, (IX, \mathbf{D}'), tk, st)$	$b' \leftarrow^{\$} A(g, (IX, \mathbf{D}'), (tk_1, \ldots, tk_n), st)$
Return b'	Return b'

Games $\boxed{G_0(A)}, \boxed{G_1(A)}$	**Games** $\boxed{G_2(A)}, \boxed{G_3(A)}$
$(DB, q, st) \leftarrow^{\$} A(\mathbf{s})$	$(DB, q, st) \leftarrow^{\$} A(\mathbf{s})$; $K_f \leftarrow^{\$} \text{F.KS}$
$K_e \leftarrow^{\$} \text{SE.KS}$; $K_f \leftarrow^{\$} \text{F.KS}$	Define $\text{ENC} : \text{ENC}(\cdot)$ is a random function
Define $\text{ENC} : \text{ENC}(x) = \text{SE.Enc}(K_e, \cdot)$	$\quad \text{from } \{0,1\}^{L} \text{ to } \{0,1\}^{\text{SE.cl}(L)}$
Define $\text{FN} : \text{FN}(x) = \text{F.Ev}(K_f, \cdot)$	$\boxed{\text{Define } \text{FN} : \text{FN}(x) = \text{F.Ev}(K_f, \cdot)}$
$(\mathbf{D}', \alpha, T) \leftarrow^{\$} \text{EncRows}^{\text{ENC,FN}}(DB)$	$\text{Define } \text{FN} : \text{FN}(\cdot) \text{ is a random function}$
$K_i' \leftarrow^{\$} \text{Stl.KS}$	$\quad \text{from } \{0,1\}^{*} \text{ to } \{0,1\}^{\text{F.ol}}$
$(K_i, IX) \leftarrow \text{Stl.Enc}(K_i', DS)$	$(\mathbf{D}', \alpha, T) \leftarrow^{\$} \text{EncRows}^{\text{ENC,FN}}(DB)$
For $i \in [n]$ do $tk_i \leftarrow^{\$} \text{Stl.Tok}(K_i, q_i)$	$lk^{i} \leftarrow^{\$} \mathcal{L}^{i}(DS, (q_1, \ldots, q_n))$
$lk^{i} \leftarrow^{\$} \mathcal{L}^{i}(DS, (q_1, \ldots, q_n))$	$(IX, (tk_1, \ldots, tk_n)) \leftarrow \mathcal{S}^{i}(lk^{i})$
$(IX, (tk_1, \ldots, tk_n)) \leftarrow \mathcal{S}^{i}(lk^{i})$	$b' \leftarrow^{\$} A(g, (IX, \mathbf{D}'), (tk_1, \ldots, tk_n), st)$
$b' \leftarrow^{\$} A(g, (IX, \mathbf{D}'), (tk_1, \ldots, tk_n), st)$	Return $b' = 1$
Return $b' = 1$	

Fig. 14. Simulator, adversaries and games used in the proof of Theorem 1.

C Leakage Profile and Security Proof for PpSj

Theorem 3. *Let* $\mathcal{L}, \mathcal{S}$ *be the leakage algorithm and simulator for* Mme *respectively. Let* $\mathcal{L}^{p}, \mathcal{S}^{p}$ *be as defined in Fig. 15 and let* F *be the function family used. Then for all adversaries* A *there exists adversaries* A_m, A_f *such that:*

$$\mathbf{Adv}^{\text{ss}}_{\text{PpSj}, \mathcal{L}^{p}, \mathcal{S}^{p}}(A) \leq \mathbf{Adv}^{\text{ss}}_{\text{Mme}, \mathcal{L}, \mathcal{S}}(A_m) + (p+1) \cdot \mathbf{Adv}^{\text{prf}}_{\text{F}}(A_f).$$

Here, p *is the number of distinct predicates used in constructing* HS.

Alg $\mathcal{L}^{\mathrm{p}}(\mathrm{DS}, (q_1, \ldots, q_n))$

Construct $\mathbf{M}, \mathrm{SET}$ as
 in PpSj.Enc$(\cdot, \mathrm{DS})$
For $i = 1, \ldots, n$ do
 $(r_i, \mathbf{q}, \mathbf{p}, c_\mathsf{q}, c_\mathsf{p}) \leftarrow \mathrm{RS}(q_i, \mathbf{q}, \mathbf{p}, c_\mathsf{q}, c_\mathsf{p})$
$\mathbf{r} \leftarrow (r_1, \ldots, r_n)$; $lk \xleftarrow{\$} \mathcal{L}(\mathbf{M}, \mathbf{q})$
$\mathrm{SET}' \leftarrow \mathrm{HF}(\mathbf{p}, \bigcup_{q \in \mathbf{q}} \mathbf{M}[q], \mathrm{SET})$
Return $(\mathbf{r}, lk, \mathrm{SET}', \mathrm{HQ}(\mathbf{p}), c_\mathsf{p}, |\mathrm{SET}'|)$

Subroutine $\mathrm{HF}((p_1, \ldots, p_n), S, \mathrm{SET})$

For all $i \in [n]$ and $\mathsf{rt} \in S$ do
 If $(p_i, \mathsf{rt}) \in \mathrm{SET}$ then $\mathrm{SET}' \xleftarrow{\cup} (i, \mathsf{rt})$
Return SET'

Subroutine $\mathrm{HQ}((p_1, \ldots, p_n))$

For all $i, j \in [n]$ if $p_i = p_j$ then
 $\mathbf{P}[i, j] \leftarrow 1$ else $\mathbf{P}[i, j] \leftarrow 0$
Return $\mathbf{P}$

Subroutine $\mathrm{RS}(q, \mathbf{q}, \mathbf{p}, c_\mathsf{q}, c_\mathsf{p})$

If $q = (\mathbf{r}, id)$ then
 $\mathbf{q} \xleftarrow{\cup} (\mathbf{r}, id)$; $r \leftarrow (\mathsf{m}, c_\mathsf{q})$; $c_\mathsf{q} \leftarrow c_\mathsf{q} + 1$
Else if $q = (\mathbf{s}, at, x, (\mathbf{r}, id))$ then
 $\mathbf{q} \xleftarrow{\cup} (\mathbf{s}, at, x)$; $r \leftarrow (\mathsf{m}, c_\mathsf{q})$; $c_\mathsf{q} \leftarrow c_\mathsf{q} + 1$
Else if $q = (\mathbf{s}, at, x, q_1)$ then
 $(r_1, \mathbf{q}, \mathbf{p}, c_\mathsf{q}, c_\mathsf{p}) \leftarrow \mathrm{RS}(q_1, \mathbf{q}, \mathbf{p}, c_\mathsf{q}, c_\mathsf{p})$
 $\mathbf{p} \xleftarrow{\cup} (\mathbf{s}, at, x)$; $r \leftarrow (\mathbf{p}, c_\mathsf{p}, r_1)$; $c_\mathsf{p} \leftarrow c_\mathsf{p} + 1$
Else if $q = (\mathbf{t}_1, \mathbf{t}_2, q_1, q_2)$ then
 For $i = 1, 2$ do
  If $q_i = (\mathbf{r}, id)$ then
   $\mathbf{q} \xleftarrow{\cup} (\mathsf{j}, \mathbf{t}_1, \mathbf{t}_2, i)$
   $r_i \leftarrow (\mathsf{m}, c_\mathsf{q})$; $c_\mathsf{q} \leftarrow c_\mathsf{q} + 1$
  Else
   $(r_i', \mathbf{q}, \mathbf{p}, c_\mathsf{q}, c_\mathsf{p}) \leftarrow \mathrm{RS}(q_i, \mathbf{q}, \mathbf{p}, c_\mathsf{q}, c_\mathsf{p})$
   $\mathbf{p} \xleftarrow{\cup} (\mathsf{j}, \mathbf{t}_1, \mathbf{t}_2, i)$
   $r_i \leftarrow (\mathbf{p}, c_\mathsf{p}, r_i')$; $c_\mathsf{p} \leftarrow c_\mathsf{p} + 1$
 $r \leftarrow (\mathsf{j}, r_1, r_2)$
Return $(r, \mathbf{q}, \mathbf{p}, c_\mathsf{q}, c_\mathsf{p})$

Alg $\mathcal{S}^{\mathrm{p}}((r_1, \ldots, r_n), lk, \mathrm{SET}', \mathbf{P}, c_\mathsf{p}, N)$

$(EM, \mathbf{mt}) \xleftarrow{\$} \mathcal{S}(lk)$
For $i = 1, \ldots, c_\mathsf{p}$ do
 If $\exists c \in [i]$ where $\mathbf{P}[c, i] = 1$ then
  $K_i \leftarrow K_c$
 Else $K_i \xleftarrow{\$} \mathrm{F.KS}$
For $(i, \mathsf{rt}) \in \mathrm{SET}'$ do $\mathrm{HS} \xleftarrow{\cup} \mathrm{F.Ev}(K_i, \mathsf{rt})$
While $|\mathrm{HS}| < N$ do
 $x \xleftarrow{\$} \{0, 1\}^{\mathrm{F.ol}}$; $\mathrm{HS} \xleftarrow{\cup} x$
For $i = 1, \ldots, n$ do
 $\mathsf{tk}_i \leftarrow \mathrm{QuerySim}(r_i, \mathbf{mt}, (K_1, \ldots, K_{c_\mathsf{p}}))$
Return $((EM, \mathrm{HS}), (\mathsf{tk}_1, \ldots, \mathsf{tk}_n))$

Subroutine $\mathrm{QuerySim}(r, \mathbf{mt}, \mathbf{k})$

$(\mathsf{mt}_1, \ldots, \mathsf{mt}_{c_\mathsf{q}}) \leftarrow \mathbf{mt}$; $(K_1, \ldots, K_{c_\mathsf{p}}) \leftarrow \mathbf{k}$
If $r = (\mathsf{m}, i)$ then return $(\mathbf{r}, \mathsf{mt}_i)$
Else if $r = (\mathbf{p}, i, r_1)$ then
 Return $(\mathbf{s}, K_i, \mathrm{QuerySim}(r_1, \mathbf{mt}, \mathbf{k}))$
Else if $r = (\mathsf{j}, r_1, r_2)$
 For $i = 1, 2$ do
  If $r_i = (\mathsf{m}, i)$ then $\mathsf{tk}_i \leftarrow (\mathbf{r}, \mathsf{mt}_i)$
  Else if $r_i = (\mathbf{p}, j, r')$ then
   $\mathsf{tk}' \leftarrow \mathrm{QuerySim}(r', \mathbf{mt}, \mathbf{k})$
   $\mathsf{tk}_i \leftarrow (\mathsf{j}, \mathsf{tk}', K_j)$
 Return $(\mathsf{j}, \mathsf{tk}_1, \mathsf{tk}_2)$

Fig. 15. Leakage profile (top) and simulator (bottom) for PpSj. In $\mathcal{L}^{\mathrm{p}}$, RS, $\mathcal{L}$, HF, HQ compute the recursion structure leakage, Mme's leakage profile, hashset filtering results and hashset query pattern respectively, as discussed in Sect. 4.2. In $\mathcal{S}^{\mathrm{p}}$, $\mathcal{S}$ is a simulator for Mme.

Proof. Adversary A_m is given in Fig. 16. In the same diagram, we see A_1, A_2 which are both PRF adversaries playing $\mathrm{G}_\mathsf{F}^{\mathrm{prf}}$. We define A_f to randomly pick one at run time and use it.

Now we can proceed via a standard hybrid argument. Let $b_\mathsf{p}, b_\mathsf{f}, b_\mathsf{m}$ be the challenge bits in $\mathrm{G}_{\mathsf{PpSj}, \mathcal{L}^{\mathrm{p}}, \mathcal{S}^{\mathrm{p}}}^{\mathrm{ss}}$, $\mathrm{G}_\mathsf{F}^{\mathrm{prf}}$ and $\mathrm{G}_{\mathsf{Mme}, \mathcal{L}, \mathcal{S}}^{\mathrm{ss}}$ respectively.

From the various advantage definitions, we have that $\mathbf{Adv}_{\mathsf{PpSj}, \mathcal{L}^{\mathrm{p}}, \mathcal{S}^{\mathrm{p}}}^{\mathrm{ss}}(A)$
$= \Pr[\mathrm{G}_{\mathsf{PpSj}, \mathcal{L}^{\mathrm{p}}, \mathcal{S}^{\mathrm{p}}}^{\mathrm{ss}}(A) | b_\mathsf{p} = 1] - \Pr[\mathrm{G}_{\mathsf{PpSj}, \mathcal{L}^{\mathrm{p}}, \mathcal{S}^{\mathrm{p}}}^{\mathrm{ss}}(A) | b_\mathsf{p} = 0]$, $\mathbf{Adv}_{\mathsf{Mme}, \mathcal{L}, \mathcal{S}}^{\mathrm{ss}}(A_\mathsf{m})$

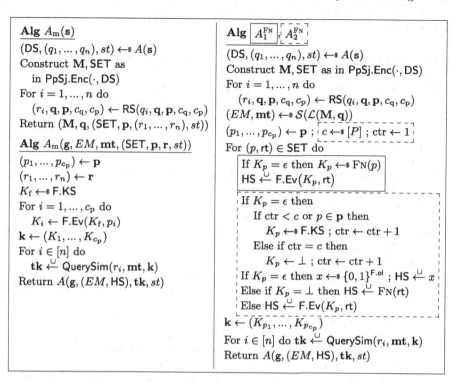

Fig. 16. Adversaries used in proof of Theorem 3. Note that when A_f is run it randomly selects one of A_1, A_2 and runs it.

$$= \Pr[G^{ss}_{\mathsf{Mme},\mathcal{L},\mathcal{S}}(A_m)|b_m = 1] - \Pr[G^{ss}_{\mathsf{Mme},\mathcal{L},\mathcal{S}}(A_m)|b_m = 0],$$ and $\mathbf{Adv}^{prf}_F(A_1)$
$= \Pr[G^{prf}_F(A_1)|b_f = 1] - \Pr[G^{prf}_F(A_1)|b_f = 0]$. Notice also that $\Pr[G^{prf}_F(A_2)|b_f = 0, c = i] = \Pr[G^{prf}_F(A_2)|b_f = 1, c = i + 1]$ for $i \in [p-1]$ and $\Pr[G^{prf}_F(A_2)|b_f = 1, c = j] - \Pr[G^{prf}_F(A_2)|b_f = 1, c = j] \leq \mathbf{Adv}^{prf}_F(A_2)$ for $j \in [p]$. This means that

$$p \cdot \mathbf{Adv}^{prf}_F(A_2) \geq \Pr[G^{prf}_F(A_2)|b_f = 1, c = p] - \Pr[G^{prf}_F(A_1)|b_f = 0, c = 1].$$

Notice that A_m in $G^{ss}_{\mathsf{Mme},\mathcal{L},\mathcal{S}}$ uses the game to simulate multimap encryption and performs the rest itself as it happens in the "real world" of $G^{ss}_{\mathsf{PpSj},\mathcal{L}^P,\mathcal{S}^P}(A)$. This gives $\Pr[G^{ss}_{\mathsf{PpSj},\mathcal{L}^P,\mathcal{S}^P}(A)|b_p = 1] = \Pr[G^{ss}_{\mathsf{Mme},\mathcal{L},\mathcal{S}}(A_m)|b_m = 1]$. Similarly, A_1 simulates multimap encryption as in the "ideal world" of $G^{ss}_{\mathsf{Mme},\mathcal{L},\mathcal{S}}$ and defers the filtering key production to FN which gives us $\Pr[G^{ss}_{\mathsf{Mme},\mathcal{L},\mathcal{S}}(A_m)|b_m = 0] = \Pr[G^{prf}_F(A_1)|b_f = 1]$. When A_2 plays $G^{prf}_F(A_2)$, if $c = p$ then all the K_i will be randomly selected. This means $\Pr[G^{prf}_F(A_1)|b_f = 0] = \Pr[G^{prf}_F(A_2)|b_f = 1, c = p]$. Over p hybrids, we get to the version where all the $F.\mathsf{Ev}(K_i, \cdot)$ (where K_i is not revealed to the adversary) are simulated with random functions, giving us $\Pr[G^{prf}_F(A_1)|b_f = 0, c = 1] = \Pr[G^{ss}_{\mathsf{PpSj},\mathcal{L}^P,\mathcal{S}^P}(A)|b_p = 0]$ because this selects all of HS elements as $\mathcal{S}^P$ does.

References

1. encrypted-bigquery-client (2015). https://github.com/google/encrypted-bigquery-client
2. City of Chicago data portal (2021). https://data.cityofchicago.org/
3. Sakila sample database (2021). https://dev.mysql.com/doc/sakila/en/
4. Antonopoulos, P., et al.: Azure SQL database always encrypted. In: Proceedings of the 2020 ACM SIGMOD International Conference on Management of Data, pp. 1511–1525 (2020)
5. Bajaj, S., Sion, R.: TrustedDB: a trusted hardware-based database with privacy and data confidentiality. IEEE Trans. Knowl. Data Eng. **26**(3), 752–765 (2013)
6. Bater, J., Elliott, G., Eggen, C., Goel, S., Kho, A., Rogers, J.: SMCQL: secure querying for federated databases. Proc. VLDB Endow. **10**(6), 673–684 (2017)
7. Bellare, M., Rogaway, P.: The security of triple encryption and a framework for code-based game-playing proofs. In: Vaudenay, S. (ed.) EUROCRYPT 2006. LNCS, vol. 4004, pp. 409–426. Springer, Heidelberg (2006). https://doi.org/10.1007/11761679_25
8. Bindschaedler, V., Grubbs, P., Cash, D., Ristenpart, T., Shmatikov, V.: The TAO of inference in privacy-protected databases. Proc. VLDB Endow. **11**(11), 1715–1728 (2018)
9. Blackstone, L., Kamara, S., Moataz, T.: Revisiting leakage abuse attacks. Cryptology ePrint Archive, Report 2019/1175 (2019). https://eprint.iacr.org/2019/1175
10. Bruno, N., Gravano, L.: Statistics on query expressions in relational database management systems. Ph.D. thesis, Columbia University (2003)
11. Cao, Y., Fan, W., Wang, Y., Yi, K.: Querying shared data with security heterogeneity. In Proceedings of the 2020 ACM SIGMOD International Conference on Management of Data, pp. 575–585 (2020)
12. Cash, D., et al.: Dynamic searchable encryption in very-large databases: data structures and implementation. In: NDSS, vol. 14, pp. 23–26. Citeseer (2014)
13. Cash, D., Jarecki, S., Jutla, C., Krawczyk, H., Roşu, M.-C., Steiner, M.: Highly-scalable searchable symmetric encryption with support for Boolean queries. In: Canetti, R., Garay, J.A. (eds.) CRYPTO 2013. LNCS, vol. 8042, pp. 353–373. Springer, Heidelberg (2013). https://doi.org/10.1007/978-3-642-40041-4_20
14. Chandra, A.K., Merlin, P.M.: Optimal implementation of conjunctive queries in relational data bases. In: Proceedings of the Ninth Annual ACM Symposium on Theory of Computing, pp. 77–90 (1977)
15. Chase, M., Kamara, S.: Structured encryption and controlled disclosure. In: Abe, M. (ed.) ASIACRYPT 2010. LNCS, vol. 6477, pp. 577–594. Springer, Heidelberg (2010). https://doi.org/10.1007/978-3-642-17373-8_33
16. Chow, S.S., Lee, J.-H., Subramanian, L.: Two-party computation model for privacy-preserving queries over distributed databases. In: NDSS. Citeseer (2009)
17. Ciriani, V., De Capitani di Vimercati, S., Foresti, S., Jajodia, S., Paraboschi, S., Samarati, P.: Keep a few: outsourcing data while maintaining confidentiality. In: Backes, M., Ning, P. (eds.) ESORICS 2009. LNCS, vol. 5789, pp. 440–455. Springer, Heidelberg (2009). https://doi.org/10.1007/978-3-642-04444-1_27
18. Curtmola, R., Garay, J., Kamara, S., Ostrovsky, R.: Searchable symmetric encryption: improved definitions and efficient constructions. Cryptology ePrint Archive, Report 2006/210 (2006). https://eprint.iacr.org/2006/210

19. Damiani, E., Vimercati, S.D.C., Jajodia, S., Paraboschi, S., Samarati, P.: Balancing confidentiality and efficiency in untrusted relational DBMSs. In: Proceedings of the 10th ACM Conference on Computer and Communications Security, pp. 93–102 (2003)
20. Demertzis, I., Papadopoulos, D., Papamanthou, C., Shintre, S.: Seal: attack mitigation for encrypted databases via adjustable leakage. In: 29th USENIX Security Symposium (USENIX Security 2020) (2020)
21. Evdokimov, S., Günther, O.: Encryption techniques for secure database outsourcing. In: Biskup, J., López, J. (eds.) ESORICS 2007. LNCS, vol. 4734, pp. 327–342. Springer, Heidelberg (2007). https://doi.org/10.1007/978-3-540-74835-9_22
22. Faber, S., Jarecki, S., Krawczyk, H., Nguyen, Q., Rosu, M., Steiner, M.: Rich queries on encrypted data: beyond exact matches. Cryptology ePrint Archive, Report 2015/927 (2015). https://eprint.iacr.org/2015/927
23. Garg, S., Mohassel, P., Papamanthou, C.: TWORAM: efficient oblivious RAM in two rounds with applications to searchable encryption. In: Robshaw, M., Katz, J. (eds.) CRYPTO 2016. LNCS, vol. 9816, pp. 563–592. Springer, Heidelberg (2016). https://doi.org/10.1007/978-3-662-53015-3_20
24. Grofig, P., et al.: Privacy by encrypted databases. In: Preneel, B., Ikonomou, D. (eds.) APF 2014. LNCS, vol. 8450, pp. 56–69. Springer, Cham (2014). https://doi.org/10.1007/978-3-319-06749-0_4
25. Grubbs, P., Lacharité, M.-S., Minaud, B., Paterson, K.G.: Pump up the volume: practical database reconstruction from volume leakage on range queries. In: Proceedings of the 2018 ACM SIGSAC Conference on Computer and Communications Security, pp. 315–331 (2018)
26. Grubbs, P., Sekniqi, K., Bindschaedler, V., Naveed, M., Ristenpart, T.: Leakage-abuse attacks against order-revealing encryption. In: 2017 IEEE Symposium on Security and Privacy (SP), pp. 655–672. IEEE (2017)
27. Gui, Z., Johnson, O., Warinschi, B.: Encrypted databases: new volume attacks against range queries. In: Proceedings of the 2019 ACM SIGSAC Conference on Computer and Communications Security, pp. 361–378 (2019)
28. Hacigümüş, H., Iyer, B., Li, C., Mehrotra, S.: Executing SQL over encrypted data in the database-service-provider model. In: Proceedings of the 2002 ACM Sigmod International Conference on Management of Data, pp. 216–227 (2002)
29. Hackenjos, T., Hahn, F., Kerschbaum, F.: SAGMA: secure aggregation grouped by multiple attributes. ACM SIGMOD Record (2020)
30. Jaeger, J., Tyagi, N.: Handling adaptive compromise for practical encryption schemes. In: Micciancio, D., Ristenpart, T. (eds.) CRYPTO 2020. LNCS, vol. 12170, pp. 3–32. Springer, Cham (2020). https://doi.org/10.1007/978-3-030-56784-2_1
31. Kamara, S., Moataz, T.: Encrypted multi-maps with computationally-secure leakage. IACR Cryptology ePrint Archive 2018, 978 (2018)
32. Kamara, S., Moataz, T.: SQL on structurally-encrypted databases. In: Peyrin, T., Galbraith, S. (eds.) ASIACRYPT 2018. LNCS, vol. 11272, pp. 149–180. Springer, Cham (2018). https://doi.org/10.1007/978-3-030-03326-2_6
33. Kamara, S., Moataz, T., Ohrimenko, O.: Structured encryption and leakage suppression. In: Shacham, H., Boldyreva, A. (eds.) CRYPTO 2018. LNCS, vol. 10991, pp. 339–370. Springer, Cham (2018). https://doi.org/10.1007/978-3-319-96884-1_12
34. Kamara, S., Moataz, T., Zdonik, S., Zhao, Z.: An optimal relational database encryption scheme. Cryptology ePrint Archive, Report 2020/274 (2020). https://eprint.iacr.org/2020/274. Accessed 29 Feb 2020

35. Kantarcıoğlu, M., Clifton, C.: Security issues in querying encrypted data. In: Jajodia, S., Wijesekera, D. (eds.) DBSec 2005. LNCS, vol. 3654, pp. 325–337. Springer, Heidelberg (2005). https://doi.org/10.1007/11535706_24

36. E. S. Lab. The clusion library (2020). https://github.com/encryptedsystems/Clusion

37. Naveed, M., Kamara, S., Wright, C.V.: Inference attacks on property-preserving encrypted databases. In: Proceedings of the 22nd ACM SIGSAC Conference on Computer and Communications Security, pp. 644–655 (2015)

38. Patel, S., Persiano, G., Yeo, K., Yung, M.: Mitigating leakage in secure cloud-hosted data structures: Volume-hiding for multi-maps via hashing. In: Proceedings of the 2019 ACM SIGSAC Conference on Computer and Communications Security, pp. 79–93 (2019)

39. Popa, R.A., Redfield, C.M., Zeldovich, N., Balakrishnan, H.: CryptDB: protecting confidentiality with encrypted query processing. In: Proceedings of the Twenty-Third ACM Symposium on Operating Systems Principles, pp. 85–100 (2011)

40. Sack, J.: Optimizing your query plans with the SQL server 2014 cardinality estimator (2014)

41. Song, D.X., Wagner, D., Perrig, A.: Practical techniques for searches on encrypted data. In: Proceeding 2000 IEEE Symposium on Security and Privacy, S&P 2000, pp. 44–55. IEEE (2000)

42. Tu, S.L., Kaashoek, M.F., Madden, S.R., Zeldovich, N.: Processing analytical queries over encrypted data (2013)

43. Yang, Z., Zhong, S., Wright, R.N.: Privacy-preserving queries on encrypted data. In: Gollmann, D., Meier, J., Sabelfeld, A. (eds.) ESORICS 2006. LNCS, vol. 4189, pp. 479–495. Springer, Heidelberg (2006). https://doi.org/10.1007/11863908_29

Author Index

Printed in the United States
by Baker & Taylor Publisher Services